THE AGE
OF REAGAN

THE FALL OF THE
OLD LIBERAL ORDER,
1964–1980

—⤞•⤝—

STEVEN F. HAYWARD

FORUM
An Imprint of Prima Publishing

Published by Prima Publishing, Roseville, California. Member of the Crown Publishing Group, a division of Random House, Inc.

Random House, Inc. New York, Toronto, London, Sydney, Auckland

PRIMA PUBLISHING, FORUM, and colophons are trademarks of Random House, Inc., registered with the United States Patent and Trademark Office.

Library of Congress Cataloging-in-Publication Data
Hayward, Steven F.
The age of Reagan : the fall of the old liberal order, 1964–1980 /
Steven F. Hayward.
p.   cm.
Includes index.
ISBN 0-7615-1337-X
1. United States—Politics and government—1945–1989.
2. Conservatism—United States—History—20th century.
3. Liberalism—United States—History—20th century.
4. Reagan, Ronald—Influence. I. Title.
E839.5 .H39   2001
973.92—dc21
2001036714

01 02 03 04 05 HH 10 9 8 7 6 5 4 3 2 1
Printed in the United States of America

First Edition

Visit us online at www.primapublishing.com

To Mom,
who knew everything else. . . .

CONTENTS

Contents

AUTHOR'S NOTE

———⊰●⊱———

ONE OF MY TEACHERS in graduate school insisted that "a history must serve its readers with explanations that suit the horizons of their curiosity and with writing that entertains and stirs them." Heeding this admonition led me to the unusual style of this book, which requires an explanation.

This book is one part biography, one part narrative chronicle, and one part political analysis—an amalgam that does not easily fit into a recognized nonfiction genre. It attempts to explain how and, more importantly, *why* Ronald Reagan became president in 1980. A capacious narrative seemed the best style to convey this broad theme. Winston Churchill noted the necessity of capturing the wider context of a person in his four-volume account of his ancestor, the Duke of Marlborough: "In a portrait or impression the human figure is best shown by its true relation to the objects and scenes against which it is thrown, and by which it is defined."

The decade-and-a-half preceding Reagan's ascent to the White House was arguably the most politically tumultuous for the nation since the decade before the Civil War. The events shaping the political climate of the country seemed to be larger than the personalities who tried to master them. To the extent that Reagan came to express the soul of America, it is necessary to understand the trials of that soul. Reagan, to borrow a metaphor from his first career, was only occasionally at center stage during these years, which is why he enters and leaves this narrative like a supporting actor.

Frederick Maitland wrote that the essential matter of history is not what happened but what men and women thought and said about it. This narrative pays special attention to the contemporaneous perception and evaluation of events. This not only offers frequent moments of irony when seen from the perspective of today, but also foreshadows the shape of a number of controversies that are still very much alive now.

Two special notes. First, although this narrative is hard on liberals and liberalism, it is not intended that "liberal" be taken as a pejorative. The years covered here—1964 to 1980—begin with the apogee of liberalism and end with its nadir, so it cannot be a happy time for liberals to contemplate. Yet it is my hope that liberal-minded readers will engage this narrative in a spirit of self-criticism, and also with an eye toward correcting any errors of fact or interpretation that have led me to an unduly harsh or unfair judgment. There ought to be more thoughtful occasions for political argument between Left and Right than *Geraldo* and *Crossfire*. It is my hope that this book can provide such an occasion. There have been many narratives that cover one half or the other of this story, i.e., the trials of liberalism or the rise of conservatism. I have sought here to bring the entire spectrum together into an interactive whole.

Second, one of the omissions of this account is that it slights the place of Nancy Reagan, whose role and influence on her husband is widely perceived, even if many of the details still remain private. I hope to remedy this defect in a second volume of this work, which will be tightly focused on Reagan's White House years, when the center stage spotlight fell fully on him alone. Liberals take heart: the second volume will reflect on what the Reagan experience teaches about the limitations of conservatism, and how conservatives may be failing to learn from the mistakes of liberals before them.

—Rescue, California, June 2001

PROLOGUE:
THEME OF THE BOOK

SCENE 1: LOS ANGELES, CALIFORNIA, OCTOBER 1964. FADE IN . . .

THAT BARRY GOLDWATER was heading for a landslide defeat of historic proportions had been evident for months before the November election. Goldwater and his partisans also knew. Goldwater himself had fueled media hostility with his intransigent rhetoric, most notably his infamous phrase: "Extremism in the defense of liberty is no vice, moderation in the defense of justice is no virtue." Then, too, the nation's natural caution and desire for stability worked against him. President John F. Kennedy's assassination was still too fresh in mind. Lyndon Johnson had been president for less than a year, and having three presidents in 14 months, William F. Buckley Jr. observed at the time, is the kind of thing people go for in banana republics, not here.

One seemingly small scene was still to be played out in the closing days of the doomed campaign: a nationwide TV address by Ronald Reagan. In what would have been a great historical irony, the Goldwater campaign almost stopped Reagan from making what was to become known as "The Speech."

Reagan's latest movie, *The Killers,* co-starring Angie Dickinson, had opened earlier in the year to a poor box office and mixed reviews. Originally intended for TV, the movie was deemed too violent and was diverted to theatrical release. Reviewers thought Reagan's character, a tough-guy con man who is killed at the end, didn't fit the nice-guy persona he had portrayed in previous movies—a persona that was obvious type-casting. The most jarring moment in *The Killers* was the roundhouse punch he delivered to Dickinson, knocking her to the floor. But

Reagan had been getting fewer and fewer movie roles. In 1964 he was supposedly rejected for a lead role in *The Best Man* because, a United Artists executive said, "Reagan doesn't have that presidential look."[1] *The Killers* was his first movie role in nearly 10 years. It would also be his last.

It didn't matter. He had made a good living for several years as a spokesperson for General Electric, traveling the nation giving speeches with a conservative theme. GE dropped him in 1962, coincidentally the same year Reagan finally joined the Republican Party—after having been a lifelong Democrat who had voted for Franklin Roosevelt four times, and who had appeared on campaign platforms with Harry Truman in 1948. He had also campaigned for Helen Gahagan Douglas against Richard Nixon in the 1950 California Senate race, and throughout the 1950s he declined invitations from the Democratic Party to run for Congress.

Reagan's conversion from a New Deal liberal to a Goldwater conservative in the 1950s is an underappreciated phenomenon, chiefly because it is yet another sign that Reagan was ahead of his time. As of the end of the 1940s, Reagan could still describe himself as a "near hopeless hemophiliac liberal." What happened to Reagan ideologically in the 1950s would happen to countless liberal intellectuals in the 1970s. Reagan could be considered the first "neoconservative," which Irving Kristol, the ex-Trotskyite, famously defined as "a liberal mugged by reality." Reagan's detractors assumed that someone—his second wife Nancy, perhaps—had talked him out of his liberalism. Reagan himself explained it in 1976: "Eventually what happened to me was, because I did my own speeches and did the research for them, I just woke up to the realization one day that I had been going out and helping to elect the people who had been causing the things I had been criticizing. So it wasn't any case of some mentor coming in and talking me out of it. I did it in my own speeches."[2] This was much the same formula for the wave of conversions to conservatism in the 1970s and 1980s. But how did Reagan come to see all by himself so much earlier than anyone else that liberalism's lack of a limiting principle would be its undoing, especially since the most severe derelictions of liberalism lay in the future?

Reagan played a small role in the Goldwater campaign before the fall. He gave a speech at the Republican National Convention in July, and, as co-chairman of California Citizens for Goldwater, gave several fundraising speeches in California. A speech before a thousand Republicans at the Ambassador Hotel in Los Angeles attracted the attention of several prominent Republicans. These Republican leaders asked Reagan if he would speak on national television for Goldwater if they could raise the money to buy TV time. Reagan agreed.

Reagan taped "The Speech" before a live audience, and a half-hour of national airtime was booked on NBC for October 27, a week before the election. But then the Goldwater campaign got cold feet. Reagan criticized Social Security in the speech—one of the issues that had been an albatross around Goldwater's neck for the whole campaign. But Reagan's reference to Social Security was mild (Goldwater reportedly said, "What the hell's wrong with that?" after he heard a tape of the speech). More likely the opposition to Reagan's speech among Goldwater's campaign managers stemmed from the "not-invented-here" syndrome, along with annoyance over the commissions the campaign's ad agency wouldn't collect from this independent effort. Even though Goldwater himself had assented to the speech, his campaign manager, William Baroody, kept up the pressure to quash the speech until a few hours before its broadcast, backing down only in the face of firm pressure from Reagan's influential supporters.

Called "A Time for Choosing," its most memorable lines were borrowed from Franklin Roosevelt and Lincoln: "We have a rendezvous with destiny. We'll preserve for our children this, the last best hope of man on earth, or we'll sentence them to take the last step into a thousand years of darkness." He also invoked the words of John Winthrop about America being "A shining city on a hill." "The Speech" would echo in American politics for 30 years, with Reagan repeating the "rendezvous with destiny" and "shining city on a hill" themes countless times. Reagan repeated many of Goldwater's policy themes, but there was something strikingly different about Reagan's conservatism. Whereas Goldwater's conservatism seemed angry and pessimistic, and wanting to overturn the past, Reagan exuded a forward-looking optimism rooted in the latent greatness of America. This was not the non-ideological Chamber of Commerce kind of conservatism, the kind that led Richard Nixon to say in the 1960 campaign, "It's the millions of people that are buying new cars that have faith in America." That kind of conservatism won't stir anyone's soul. For Reagan, faith in America transcended its material accomplishments. Though it was not evident at the time, Reagan's stylistic conservatism promised to lead the Republican Party out of the post–New Deal–era wilderness.

The speech was a spectacular success, generating several million dollars in campaign contributions, mostly in small sums. *Time* magazine called the speech "the one bright spot in a dismal campaign," and David Broder wrote that the speech was "the most successful political debut since William Jennings Bryan." A star was born—except he was already a star. The starstruck immediately began to ponder whether Reagan could make the transition to public office. The day after the election, a group of conservatives in Owosso, Michigan, formed "Republicans for Ronald Reagan."[3] Henry Salvatori, an oil industry tycoon and leading California Republican, immediately began talking to his friends about the idea of recruiting Reagan to run for governor of California in 1966. From there, it was immediately though silently assumed, he could run for the White House. Salvatori, auto dealer Holmes Tuttle, Union Oil chief executive Sy Rubel, and several other prominent Republican businessmen would soon form the "Friends of Ronald Reagan" committee to promote his candidacy. Other California Republican leaders, still smarting from Richard Nixon's loss to Pat Brown two years before, were cool to the idea. After all, Reagan was just an actor.

SCENE 2: WASHINGTON, D.C., JANUARY 20, 1981. FADE IN . . .

"GOLDWATER," COLUMNIST GEORGE WILL wrote, "won the election of 1964. It just took sixteen years to count the votes." Sixteen years after Goldwater's humiliation at the polls, Ronald Reagan stood on the west front of the U.S. capitol building—the first inauguration to take place on the side of the capitol that faces toward the broad expanse of the nation—and took the oath of office to be the 40th President of the United States. Reagan's rise to the summit of American politics was the political equivalent of light speed. To those many who had been electrified by his debut speech in 1964, his ascension seemed inevitable; to everyone else it was nearly unthinkable. Perhaps more than any inauguration since Franklin Roosevelt's in 1933, the inauguration of Reagan occurred at the climax of a crisis. The immediate crisis of the day involved the 53 Americans held hostage for more than a year by the revolutionary government of Iran. Inauguration day represented the 444th day of captivity; the previous year had proven to be an excruciating trauma for America. Negotiations seemed futile, and a military rescue mission had been a costly and embarrassing fiasco. The helplessness and frustration of the world's most powerful nation was underscored on the *CBS Evening News,* which anchorman Walter Cronkite concluded each night by adding to his famous signoff a running total of the days in captivity ("And that's the way it is, on day 310 of the Iranian hostage crisis").

Now the release of the hostages was expected at any moment, perhaps during the inaugural ceremony itself, in which case, according to a prearranged plan, President Reagan would interrupt the ceremony—even if he was in the middle of his inaugural address—and invite now ex-President Carter to join him at the podium for a joint announcement of the hostages' freedom. Anxiety was high. Even though a deal was done, you couldn't be sure about the Iranians, who had shown complete contempt for international law and civilized behavior. As it was, the Iranians would delay the release until the inaugural ceremony was complete, a last slap at Jimmy Carter.

Beyond this immediate drama there simmered a number of deep problems that the new chief executive would face, chief among them the economy. In the 1960s, economists thought that government had at long last mastered the business cycle and solved the fundamental problems of inflation and unemployment. Policy could now "fine-tune" the economy, curbing inflation or unemployment whenever either one showed a blip. But by the late 1970s, none of the pillars of policy worked anymore. Inflation in 1980 was over 12 percent. Unemployment was over 7 percent, and real wages were stagnant or falling. In 1971, President Nixon had declared a national emergency and imposed wage and price controls when inflation reached only 6 percent. Since then, the dollar's slide continued unabated, losing more than half its purchasing power—"the longest and one of the worst sustained inflations in our history," the new president called it in his address.

A number of ancillary events accompanied the economic crisis. Twice during the decade Americans had endured long lines to purchase gasoline, even though world oil reserves were abundant. The price had tripled, and gasoline rationing coupons, not seen since World War II, had been printed and warehoused for imminent use. The stock market, having suffered in 1974 its worst slide since the Great Depression, was at about the same level in 1980 as it had been in 1970. More than a few financial sages had declared "the death of equities." The price of gold, always the leading barometer of economic confidence, soared to an unprecedented $800 an ounce. The new chairman of the Federal Reserve, Paul Volcker, warned that the American standard of living would have to decline. Then he jacked up interest rates.

The economic crisis seemed related, somehow or dimly, to the general crisis that had befallen American democracy most acutely since Watergate, and perhaps more generally since the assassination of John F. Kennedy in 1963. It had been one long downhill slide for America's elite institutions, both public and private, since those bright glittering days of "Camelot." By 1979, for the first time since public opinion surveys had been taken, the majority of Americans doubted that the future would be better than the past, or even equal to the present. In its wrap-up edition in 1979, *Newsweek* magazine observed that there was "a growing sense that the country's institutions and leaders were no longer up to managing problems that were simply too complex to grasp."

The most doubtful institution of all, according to the conventional wisdom, was the presidency. Presidents Johnson, Nixon, Ford, and now Carter were reckoned as failures to one degree or another, and the notion was gaining credence that the presidency was an inherently impossible office in our modern complex world. Some thought America had become "ungovernable." Many leading political scientists thought wholesale reform of the presidency was necessary—either a single, six-year term, or a change to some kind of parliamentary system that would provide the president more power to be "effective." Above all, elite opinion, that is, the professional pundits and academics who constitute America's "chattering class," held out little hope of success for the former actor who was about to assume the office. He was much too lightweight.

In short, it seemed that the "American Century" was over, that an era of American optimism and progress had come to a close. The concatenation of Vietnam, Watergate, the recurrent energy crisis, the swooning economy, the increasingly disorderly world scene, and the failed presidencies associated with these events robbed Americans of their native optimism. President Carter had not helped matters by decrying a "crisis of confidence" in a famous speech in 1979, though Nixon had said very nearly the same thing in a speech in 1971. The two presidential uses of "crisis of confidence" could serve as bookends for the decade. Columbia University's Amitai Etzioni said of the 1970s that "the trauma and scars had the same psychological impact on America that the loss of the empire had on Britain." Former Secretary of Defense James Schlesinger told *Newsweek* that he worried that the ebbing of American power and influence in the world might become a rout, and that "the '80s look to me like a period of bleakness and confrontation."

Ronald Reagan literally began his first moments in office flying in the face of this pervasive climate of American decay and decline. There was a clear thread between "The Speech" in 1964 and what he told the American people on this day. Though America had changed dramatically since 1964, Reagan had not. This would be his great strength in the eight years to come. "These United States," he said early in his address, "are confronted with an economic affliction of great proportions. . . . Idle industries have cast workers into unemployment, causing human misery and personal indignity." But he used these melancholy observations merely to set up his resounding rejection of the pessimism gripping the nation. "We are too great a nation," Reagan said, "to limit ourselves to small dreams. We are not, as some would have us believe, doomed to an inevitable decline." He specifically rejected the reformist theme that the presidency, or our democracy in general, was inadequate to the times. Sounding a Jeffersonian note, Reagan asserted:

> From time to time, we have been tempted to believe that society has become too complex to be managed by self-rule, that government by an elite group is superior to government for, by, and of the people. But if no one among us is capable of governing himself, then who among us has the capacity to govern someone else?

Reagan had so fully internalized the thought of so many of his political forebearers, such as Jefferson, Lincoln, and Roosevelt, that it is not clear whether he knew he was paraphrasing them. Reagan had said much the same thing about self-government in his first inaugural address as governor in 1967, and now again in 1981. Where he got it is no mystery. In his first inaugural address in 1801, Thomas Jefferson said: "Sometimes it is said that man can not be trusted with the government of himself. Can he, then, be trusted with the government of others? Or have we found angels in the forms of kings to govern him? Let history answer this question."

Reagan's inaugural address was a classic mixture of his simultaneous optimism and harshness toward what he always saw as the chief was perhaps subliminal envy at Reagan's dual success, and at some level Reagan understood this.

The denigration of Reagan's acting career formed the basis for much of the liberal underestimation he experienced. It was a huge blunder by his opponents, for his acting experience was central to his political success, as Reagan himself remarked upon shortly before he left the White House. "I don't know how you could do this job and *not* be an actor," Reagan told a network anchorman in 1988. The liberal columnist Murray Kempton, certainly no admirer of Reagan, succinctly observed that "he could suggest that fluoridation induces hair on the palms of the hands and maintain a tone pregnant with common sense."

Consider how Reagan used to mispronounce "government." Throughout his political career Reagan reduced government to a two-syllable word: "guv-mint." "Guv-mint spending," "big guv-mint," and other combinations sprinkled Reagan's speeches. See, his critics would say, this shows his simplemindedness. Few stopped to ponder that Reagan began his career as a professional broadcaster, and was highly expert in diction and pronunciation. His subtle twist of "government" into "guv-mint" could not have been a mindless accident; it was surely a deliberate artifice. "Guv-mint" conveyed contempt for government without having to sneer. It took Garry Wills, an insightful but unfriendly observer of Reagan, to notice that Reagan's inspiration probably came from Mark Twain, who has Huck Finn's father complain: "Call this a govment! Why just look at it and see what it's like." But it wasn't until 1987 that Wills figured this out.[4]

Other critics fastened upon Reagan's penchant for telling "whoppers"—wildly inaccurate statistics or supposedly true stories that were easily exposed as exaggerations or falsehoods—as evidence of the man's unfitness to be taken seriously. Reagan could bring audiences to tears with the story of the airman who went down with his injured wingman in a flaming bomber in World War II, including recounting the airman's words to comfort his comrade: "It's okay—we'll go down together." Aside from the implausibility that someone could have heard these words spoken, it turned out the story originated in a World War II–era movie (though not one of Reagan's). Another time Reagan spoke of a black cook who had taken up arms at Pearl Harbor as evidence of declining segregation in the armed forces—a seemingly apocryphal story that reporters thought was surely untrue. (Reagan was right about this one, it turned out.) The one that stuck most in the craw of liberals was Reagan's "welfare queen" in Chicago public housing who supposedly collected public assistance under more than 100 separate names. The news media looked high and low, but no such person could ever be found.

Nearly all politicians tell whoppers to one degree or another. Most politicians, such as Lyndon Johnson, Bill Clinton, or Al Gore, tell whoppers about *themselves,* in an act of obvious self-aggrandizement. Reagan's whoppers were never about himself, but always about the deeper meaning of America, both what was right with America and what was wrong with America. That's why the accuracy of his whoppers was always secondary to their teaching, which resonated deeply with Americans who had grown disaffected with the leadership of the nation. Even when Reagan didn't have his facts right, there was usually a kernel of truth about the American character, or its corruption under the sway of liberal dogma. His critics refused or were unable to admit this, and it has warped their ability to judge Reagan.

On the surface Reagan is the most unlikely president in American history, which is why so many of his critics dismiss him as a fluke. Nearly all modern American presidents are the products of Ivy League or comparable educations, and enjoy long careers inside "The Establishment" before ascending to the Oval Office. Even the unlikely presidents who don't fit this mold—Harry Truman and Lyndon Johnson—nonetheless rose through the ranks as political insiders (and owed their presidencies in the first instance to the accident of death instead of popular election). And even Richard Nixon did penance for his humble outsider origins, working as a New York lawyer during his eight-year interregnum between the vice presidency and the presidency. Reagan, by contrast, came from tiny Eureka College in Illinois, where the presidency of the local Rotary Club is the highest office most alumni reach. Reagan was also the only president who has ever served as the head of a labor union, having served as president of the Screen Actors Guild six times—an experience that is much underrated in explaining Reagan's outlook and success.

Reagan is the first and arguably the sole authentic "outsider" president of our century. Only Jimmy Carter (an Annapolis graduate) comes close as an outsider, and his election really was more of a one-time reaction to Watergate than the expression of changing political trends in America. Hollywood, though regarded today as an important cash cow and megaphone for political causes, is not really a fully respected member of The Establishment. And although most successful politicians have a touch of the thespian, the thought of a president, let alone a major state governor, coming from the ranks of Tinsel Town struck enlightened members of The Establishment as abhorrent. Reagan's popularity over two terms as governor of California did little to prepare The Establishment for his eventual accession to the White House. "Reagan's election," John P. Roche, a former head of the liberal Americans for Democratic Action, wrote in 1984, "was thus an 8-plus earthquake on the political Richter scale, and it sent a number of eminent statesmen—Republican and Democratic—into shock."[5]

To paraphrase Churchill's remark about the Soviet Union, Reagan presents his biographers and critics with a riddle wrapped inside an enigma shrouded by a mystery. While Reagan can be *described,* he is nearly impossible to *explain.* Even such an astute observer as Henry Kissinger described Reagan's performance in office as "astonishing" and "nearly incomprehensible." Reagan did not have the kind of obvious, all-consuming ambition for higher office that characterizes—and mars—so many conventional politicians, like Richard Nixon or Bill Clinton. He is said to have been without close intimate friends, yet the role of Reagan's friends—the self-styled "Kitchen Cabinet" for instance—was crucial to his ascent. Without the urging and support of his friends and associates, Reagan's rise would not have been possible.

The book on Reagan even to this day is that he was lazy and uninterested in the details of politics and policy. Yet he was a highly energetic and decisive person, which doesn't square with the "lazy and uninformed" caricature of the man. Above all, he was a serious man. Beneath the affable and easy-going exterior, the penchant for delegation and eschewing details, beat the heart of one of the most determined and stubborn figures in American political history. Reagan's method is an object lesson in successful statesmanship that eludes many of the brightest minds today. *Newsweek* put its finger on the heart of the matter way back in 1970 with the offhand observation that "He cares little for the details of governing, very much for the principles of governance—and those principles are as fixed and unyielding as scripture."[6] Lou Cannon, perhaps the first major journalist to take Reagan seriously and who saw early his potential to reach the White House, summarized him thus: "As a governor,

Reagan had revealed an executive's temperament: He had the ability to go to the heart of the matter."[7] For the presidency—where the details are beyond any person, no matter how large and bright the staff around him—this is a much more important attribute.

Reagan was the epitome of sincerity in an age when, as Lionel Trilling famously pointed out, the virtue of sincerity had lost its credibility with the intellectual class. Lionel Barrymore is attributed with the remark that the secret to acting is the ability to fake sincerity, and too many observers of Reagan missed the irony of this remark and made it into an axiom by which to decode Reagan. But Reagan cannot be refracted through such a crude prism. This is one reason why Reagan was so seemingly mysterious to the intellectual class (in which class one must include his befuddled official biographer Edmund Morris), who struggled to find the hidden "authentic" Reagan only to miss that the "sincere" public Reagan was the real thing. Observers pondering the Reagan mystery point to the seemingly ironic title of his 1965 autobiography, *Where's the Rest of Me?*, a line taken from his best movie performance in *King's Row.* "The rest of me," Reagan thought, was in plain sight in his subsequent political career, in his mixture of unlimited optimism and dedication to the cause of individual freedom. "Ronald Reagan doesn't change personalities when he turns from the TV cameras and enters his private office," wrote Charles Hobbs, one of his associates from his days in Sacramento, in 1975. "Peel off the layers of formality that he adds for his public appearances and you find only an increasingly informal version of the same person."[8]

The key to both his sincerity and his decisiveness was his utter self-confidence. His one-time campaign manager John Sears—a person who did not share Reagan's ideology—offered an apt summary of Reagan's secret in 1980, *before* Reagan's presidency commenced (but *after* Reagan had fired Sears): "Since the primary prerequisite for handling the presidency is to ignore the immensity of it, a president must find the confidence to do so in self-knowledge. . . . Reagan knows himself better than most presidents and has kept his identity separate from politics. Reagan knows who he is and therefore he possesses the first prerequisite for being a good president."[9]

The greatest shock about Reagan was that he meant what he said. His "simplicity" was his chief virtue, and the key to his success. No one in Establishment politics could quite believe Reagan when he repeatedly said in various forms, "I say there are simple answers to many of our problems—simple but hard." "It's the complicated answer that's easy," Reagan liked to say, "because it avoids facing the hard moral issues." No one wants to take such simplicity at face value, but with Reagan what you saw was what you got. Beneath his easy geniality was a tough center. In this regard Margot Asquith's description of the young Churchill applies equally to Reagan. "What is it that gives Winston his pre-eminence?" Asquith wrote in her diary at the time of Churchill's 40th birthday. "It is certainly not his mind. I have said long ago and with truth Winston has a very noisy mind. Certainly not his judgment—he is constantly very wrong indeed. . . . *It is of course his courage and color—his amazing mixture of industry and enterprise.*" It is often suggested that Reagan was a creature of his "handlers," but at many points Reagan was often a minority of one against the advice of his political strategists and policy advisers, showing an independence of mind to go along with his force of character.

If Reagan wasn't the most intelligent or intellectual politician of his time, he instinctively grasped not only the power of ideas, but also the crucial relationship of ideas to power. It is a great injustice to suggest that Reagan got his ideas secondhand or in a superficial way. Lee Edwards, author of an early biography of Reagan, recalls being once left alone in Reagan's study while then-Governor Reagan went to the kitchen to prepare cocktails. Edwards began browsing Reagan's bookshelves, and was astonished to find dense works of political economy by authors such as Ludwig von Mises and Friedrich Hayek heavily underlined and annotated in Reagan's handwriting. This seemingly unintellectual politician was endlessly clipping articles from opinion journals, and even selected several senior appointees in his administration based on articles he had read in *Commentary, Policy Review,* or *National Review.* While Reagan was uninterested in the details of policy, he was much more deeply interested in the ideas behind policy than the average politician. As the recent collection of Reagan's extensive handwritten drafts of his radio speeches demonstrates, he had an interest in and capacity for a broad range of public affairs that surpasses most presidents and active politicians. Isaiah Berlin popularized the obscure epigram from the classical poet Archilochus: "The fox knows many things, but the hedgehog knows one big thing." Most politicians are, or pretend to be, cunning foxes. Reagan was a hedgehog; he knew one big thing—government is a threat to liberty, both in its vicious forms such as communism or socialism, but also in its supposedly benign forms, such as bureaucracy. This central insight, combined with his acting background, enabled him to be more cunning than the craftiest political fox.

At the same time Reagan absorbed and championed the work of leading conservative idealogues, it should be recognized that he was an unorthodox conservative in many ways. Although he hearkened back to the "good old days" of black and white (in both senses of the phrase) Hollywood movies, his future-oriented optimism vitiated what otherwise could have been a stereotypical "turn-back-the-clock" outlook. Conservatives occasionally took notice and complained about these tergiversations. In 1985 George Will wrote, "[Reagan] is painfully fond of the least conservative sentiment conceivable, a statement from an anti-conservative, Thomas Paine: 'We have it on our power to begin the world over again.' Any time, any place, that is nonsense." Yet Reagan believed this at a visceral level, and it is a key to his optimism.

Of equal importance to Reagan's character and views were the times in which his political career was incubated. The argument of this narrative is that Reagan will never be fully appreciated or understood unless he is placed in a broad context, unless the swirling currents and trends he and his supporters engaged are explored and diagnosed. Reagan's rise depended more on circumstances that most other presidents.

Reagan would have been unsuccessful as a politician in the 1940s or 1950s. He acquired his salience, in other words, precisely on account of the ideological polarization, the breakdown of the American liberal consensus, of the 1960s. The propitious moment for Reagan required that this polarization deepen and ripen in its consequences by 1980. Compelling counterfactual scenarios can be played out that have Reagan failing miserably as president had he been elected in 1968, or perhaps even 1976. In a dramatic sense that perhaps only an actor like Reagan could understand, his drive to the White House was not the matter of one campaign season, but should be understood as a 16-year unfolding of events upon which the 1980 campaign was merely a capstone. On the eve of his election to the presidency in 1980, *National Review* observed: "Ronald Reagan is the most important political figure produced by the conservative movement in the 1960s. Historians will undoubtedly view him in retrospect as a political spearhead, a candidate whose emergence marked a permanent turning-point."[10] This judgment began to settle in even before his presidency was completed. The *Wall Street Journal*'s Vermont Royster observed in 1987: "Ronald Reagan, in short, did not create the 'Reagan revolution.' He rode it to success because the time had come. Had his instinct not been in tune with the times in 1980 he would have lost, as did Barry Goldwater in 1964 when the time had not yet come."[11]

Perceptive liberals recognize this as well. Thomas Byrne Edsall and Mary Edsall wrote in their 1991 book *Chain Reaction:*

> [W]hile Reagan's role was indisputably critical, he was more a prin-
> cipal agent within—rather than the prime mover of—a sea change
> involving forces substantially more profound and extensive than the
> fortunes of the two political parties or of their candidates. To see
> Ronald Reagan as the cause of an ascendant conservatism minimizes
> the significance and consequence of large-scale social and economic
> transformations—developments beyond the power of any single po-
> litical player to determine.[12]

These "large-scale transformations" are the elements of the story this book aims to tell. Others, such as official biographer Edmund Morris, plumb the inner recesses of Reagan's character and tell the "inside" story of major events. The "outside" story is just as important, and in telling the outside story of Reagan and his times it is best to begin at the beginning, when Reagan first seriously appeared on the national political scene in 1964.

THE GENERAL CONTEXT of Reagan and Reaganism can begin to be understood by contrasting two famous presidential utterances. In a spontaneous moment on the campaign trail in September 1964, President Lyndon Johnson stood up on the roof of his car in Providence, Rhode Island, and ad-libbed: "And I just want to tell you this: we're in favor of a lot of things and we're against mighty few"—as good a single sentence definition of Great Society liberalism as can be conceived. Thirty-two years later, one of his successors in the Oval Office stood before Congress on the eve of his re-election campaign and proclaimed, "The era of big government is over."

These two remarks can stand as bookends for the political history of the last third of the century in the United States. Between the first statement and the second statement, public confidence in the federal government, according to Gallup Polls, declined from over 70 percent to less than 20 percent. In between also came Reagan. His critics and even a few of his friends view him merely as an instrumental figure, a fortuitous beneficiary of circumstances. A great American wit (Woody Allen) has said that 95 percent of life is just showing up. Reagan, his detractors think, simply had the good luck to hit his marks when the footlights were turned up on his adopted ideology. Many in the liberal remnant continue to think Reagan prospered by default, or because of the incompetence of the Democratic Party. Historian George Nash wrote in 1981: "If one were Hegelian, one might say the 1964 election created a thesis, the Great Society, and an antithesis, Ronald Reagan, who now, as President, is attempting to curb the excesses which the Great Society has wrought."[13]

Certainly chance and circumstance go a long way toward determining historical events, but it is a misjudgment to attribute Reagan's rise and success merely to chance and circumstance. "Luck," the great baseball manager Branch Rickey once said, "is the residue of design," and there was a design behind Reagan's political career that, while widely praised and admired, is not fully appreciated, and hence not successfully emulated by his Republican would-be successors. In other words, in matching a man and his times, it is not enough simply to know the man. You need to see how the times beckon the man, and vice versa. Although Reagan may have been an *unlikely* president, he was not an *accidental* president.

Two things happened in the 1960s and 1970s that made Reagan both inevitable and necessary. The first was a significant change in the character of American democracy—both how it worked and what it did. Reagan's arrival on the national political scene coincided with the beginning of what might be called the "third wave" of the progressive administrative state. The idea of the "progressive administrative state" began with the Progressive Era, when a bipartisan movement enhanced the power and scope of the national government's administrative apparatus to cope with what it saw as the new and threatening problems of a rapidly industrializing economy and society. Some of the problems of the modern economy were misperceived and mistakenly dealt with, and the idea of the "administrative state," along with the ideologized version of "progress" that Woodrow Wilson and others promoted, did violence to America's constitutional understanding, leading directly to the contentiousness about jurisprudence that continues to rage right down to our day. But this is the subject for another book.

The stage was nonetheless set for the twentieth century. The second wave of the progressive administrative state was of course the New Deal, where the idea of the administrative prowess of the national government was married to the new and highly convenient economic doctrine of Keynesianism—the idea that employment and economic growth depended ultimately upon aggregate demand that could only come in adequate amounts from the government. ("We achieve full employment and rapid economic growth by ensuring a sufficient volume of demand in the economy" was John Kenneth Galbraith's simple formula.[14]) The ostensible success of the New Deal carried into the post-war years and was seemingly confirmed by the sluggish economic performance of the Eisenhower years. Liberals thought the three mild recessions of the 1950s were due mainly to Republican resistance to spending enough money. "The only difference in domestic policy," Galbraith wrote, "is that liberals sought to do by calculated action—by public expenditure, deliberate deficits, tax reduction—what conservatives hoped to accomplish by balanced budgets, incantation, regular prayer and, perhaps, the sense of national dedications instilled by speeches by Richard Nixon."[15]

With the resumption of liberal Democratic rule starting in 1960, the third wave of the progressive administrative state began. Between the end of the Second World War and the beginning of the Kennedy administration in 1961, a seemingly profound development had taken place; Daniel Patrick Moynihan called it "the professionalization of reform." Social science research had been a booming business in the late 1950s, and it seemed as though the time had come for this new knowledge to guide policy. "How do you find the Kennedy administration?" a popular joke of the time began. "Take a left at Harvard Yard." "Confidence in the therapeutic power of reform had never been higher," historian Allen Matusow wrote in *The Unraveling of America*. What this meant is that the prestige of intellectuals had never been higher. "Removed from his own discipline," Henry Fairlie wrote in 1965, "no one is more vain than the intellectual."[16] Sure, FDR had had his "Brains Trust" during the New

Deal, but the New Deal was mostly a big civil engineering project, while the new intellectuals of the 1950s and 1960s were ready to launch a huge *social* engineering project.

The premise of the administrative state is that our public problems are *complicated,* with "no easy answers," whose remedy requires sophisticated legislation and extensive bureaucratic management. Anyone who says otherwise (like Ronald Reagan) is a "simpleton." But the creed of the administrative state makes the idea of citizen self-government seem quaint or obsolete, and it causes our government to be remote and esoteric to average citizens. Having eroded the old-time simplicity of popular government, liberals would come to wonder why they were no longer popular with simple average citizens.

The new frontier of the administrative state that began in the 1960s manifested itself most significantly in three ways: the Vietnam War, the War on Poverty, and the rise of social (as opposed to merely economic) regulation. These enterprises drew upon the common taproot of the cult of expertise, and were closely related to one another. All three would erode public trust in government, and public esteem for the liberalism that spawned them.

The Vietnam War—America's Gallipoli—nearly dealt a deathblow to American confidence and resolve. The consensus view among liberal writers is that the war resulted from the narrow vision of leaders hewing unblinkingly to the Cold War doctrine of "containment," and the utter catastrophe of the war called into question both containment and broader Western aims in the Cold War. The antics of Joe McCarthy in the 1950s had brought anti-Communism into disgrace among many liberals, and Vietnam would provide the second strike against the anti-Communist cause. Vietnam was worse because it was begun by liberals. Liberals always thought that the Vietnam War could be compartmentalized into a box wholly separate from the domestic policy initiatives of the Kennedy and Johnson administrations, but this narrative will argue that there was a common intellectual root—a "fearful symmetry," to borrow William Blake's famous phrase—between the Great Society and the Vietnam War.

The kind of social regulation begun in the 1960s and 1970s was, as we shall see, of a wholly different kind from the regulation of the Progressive and New Deal eras, and in many ways is ill-suited for American law and politics. Regulation is arguably more significant than mere taxation and spending, because its cost is hidden and, moreover, regulation subtly changes the relationship between the citizen and his government. Rising American resentment toward government often owes more to resistance to regulation than it does to high taxes and wasteful spending. While the balanced budget and fiscal restraint have become a bipartisan principle—at least in speech if not in deed—the political parties, and the American people, remain sharply divided about the regulatory functions of government.

The disaster of Vietnam and the manifest failure of the War on Poverty led to a dramatic transformation of liberalism—it lost its optimism and confidence, and liberalism took on at times the patina of crabby anti-Americanism. Liberalism's loss of confidence and optimism in such a short period of time—it happened virtually within the span of 10 years—represents one of the most drastic transformations of a dominant idea in history. "Most liberals," Daniel Patrick Moynihan wrote in 1975, "had ended the 1960s rather ashamed of the beliefs they had held at the beginning of the decade."[17] Democratic Senator Henry Jackson observed at the same time that liberals had become "demoralized by these overwhelming social issues."[18] The confidence and optimism behind the Great Society prompted a mad dash toward a finish line that turned out to be a mirage. But while liberalism as an ideology may have lost its prestige, its legacy—the administrative state—had a momentum that promised to keep it in place and growing for a long time to come.

With the Great Society in ruins by 1968, it seemed that time had run out for post–New Deal liberalism, and conservatives placed great hope in the election of Richard Nixon. Nixon said all the right things and hated all the right people, and he entered office with the intent of rolling back the Great Society. Yet Nixon proved to be not just a disappointment to conservatives, but a failure, as both government spending and the scope of regulation galloped ahead during his tenure in the White House. On top of it all, the herald of the "emerging Republican majority," as a famous book of the time predicted, had no coattails; even in landslide victory, Nixon barely budged the Democratic—and mostly liberal—dominance of Congress. The task would require someone not only more personally appealing, but also even more ferocious in his attitude about liberal governance. Reagan was the only person who fit the bill.

Reagan was the first national political figure since Calvin Coolidge to make a frontal assault on the esoteric premises of the administrative state.

Reagan anticipated the public distrust of the federal government years before it became obvious, and he understood instinctively the reasons why it would happen. In 1968, Reagan observed in a speech in New York:

> At the moment there appears to be a panic fear afloat in the air, partly due to a feeling that government is now a separate force beyond the people's control, that their voices echo unheeded in the vast and multitudinous halls of government. I do not remember a time when so many Americans, regardless of their economic and social standing, have been so suspicious and apprehensive of the aims, the credibility, and the competence of the Federal establishment.

To Reagan it was "obvious" that "the sophisticated approach of seeking complicated answers by government to complicated problems isn't necessarily the best approach." Reagan saw the thread of administrative expertise running through foreign policy as well. The prosecution of the Vietnam War offered an important object lesson for Reagan: "The fetish of complexity, the trick of making hard decisions harder to make— the art, finally, of rationalizing the non-decision, have made a ruin of American foreign policy."

The other big thing that began in the 1960s was what might be called America's cultural revolution. The cultural upheaval of the 1960s was also a disaster for liberalism, one from which it has still not fully recovered. Part of this cultural revolution manifested itself in the rise of the so-called New Left. The New Left that sprang to life in the mid-1960s brought grief to President Johnson and the Democratic Party, but it would also eventually clash directly with Reagan, first when he was governor of California, but also later as president, after the New Left had grown up a bit, put on weight around the waistline, and taken its place among the institutional furnishings of American life.

But many degrees removed from the extreme of the New Left the cultural revolution manifested itself in profound changes in American manners and mores. Yet here we encounter a striking paradox that lies at the heart of the political dynamic of America today. Since 1964, America has increasingly embraced political conservatism and rejected political liberalism. Yet at the same time Americans have become more conservative politically, they have become more liberal socially and culturally. What has been called "lifestyle liberalism" has advanced in tandem with political conservatism. (The term "lifestyle," it is worth noting, did not make its debut in *Webster's International Dictionary* until 1961.) Or, as Tom Wolfe put it, what was rebellion 30 years ago is now ordinary high school life. The tolerance of, if not approval for, abortion, homosexuality, illegitimacy and single motherhood, casual sex, pornography, coarsening of language, degraded educational standards, and public disorderliness—to name a few—grew alongside public disapproval for big government, even though Reagan and the conservative movement crusaded against both phenomena. "Eight years of Ronald Reagan hardly slowed the advance of political correctness," Shelby Steele wrote. "He won the Cold War, but not the culture war."[19] Should we conclude, then, that there is little or no connection between politics and culture? Or is it possible that, like the relationship between the money supply and inflation, there is a lag time in how political ideas play out in cultural and social life? There are many signs that the latter might be the case.

Opinion polls today tell us that uppermost in the concerns of Americans is the problem of "values" or "moral decay," and "family values" are close to the center of political discourse. There are some encouraging signs that a reversal in the trends of moral and cultural decay may be under way. Teen pregnancy, to take one measure, is declining. Households headed by single mothers are now the object of elite disapprobation, where they had been previously the object of elite celebration. Approval of abortion is noticeably slipping; a *Los Angeles Times* poll in 2000 found that only 43 percent of the public approved of the *Roe v. Wade* decision legalizing abortion on demand, down from 56 percent in 1991. The public concern with "values" is thought to represent a new phase of our public life, but in fact it may represent merely a more acute phase of a long-running strain of public sentiment that our elites have assiduously sought to ignore.

Reagan brought the same kind of simplicity to cultural issues that he did to policy issues. In addition to the principles of anti-Communism and limited government, Reagan also called for the "rejection of moral permissiveness." While the liberal establishment talked of the "idealism" of youthful protesters in the 1960s, blunting any criticism of even their worst behavior, Reagan took the no-nonsense approach that became a slogan on the wall of his office in Sacramento when he became governor: "Obey the rules or get out." Again Reagan was ahead of the experts and the chattering classes in knowing what was on the minds of the people. In a 1967 article that sought to explain to the cosmopolitan readership of *Commentary* the inexplicable rise of Ronald Reagan, political scientist James Q. Wilson observed:

> Surveys I have taken, and others I have read, indicate that the single most widespread concern of middle-class Americans is over the "decline of values"—evidenced by "crime in the streets," juvenile delinquency, public lewdness, and the like, but going much beyond these manifestations to include everything that suggests that people no longer act in accordance with decent values and right reason.[20]

Wilson, of course, would later become a well-known "neoconservative," and a champion of the cause of moral virtue, which he argued in a substantial book entitled *The Moral Sense*. But in 1967, this Harvard professor expressed the conventional wisdom on the subject of the place of moral concern in politics:

> In many places, especially the Northeast, our political institutions (happily) do not allow such views to play much part in elections. Parties, led by professionals, instinctively shun such issues, feeling somehow that public debate over virtue is irrelevant (what can government do about it?) and dangerous (nobody can agree on what virtue is or that your party has more of it).

That same year, Pat Moynihan wrote that "Family is not a subject Americans tend to consider appropriate as an area of public policy."[21] By 1980, Wilson surveyed the Reagan phenomenon again, and recognized its salience: "Reaganism stands in opposition to those who believe in the unrestrained right of personal self-expression and the need for government to rationalize all other aspects of human affairs by rule and procedure."[22] (Wilson avowed in 1967 that not only did he not sympathize with Reagan, but that "even if I thought like that, which I don't, I would never write it down anywhere my colleagues at Harvard might read it." Wilson is today the Ronald Reagan Professor of Public Policy at Pepperdine University.)

The kind of liberalism Wilson and others espoused in the mid-1960s certainly did not comprehend how the growth of the welfare state and the expansion of the regulatory state might have an adverse effect on the cultural and moral life of the nation. Wilson's change of mind is emblematic of how much the nation has learned from the experience of the last 30 years; America's thinking about social and political life has changed more than perhaps any nation in such a short time. The central idea of modern liberalism was that the state must be the primary agent for expanding the scope of individual liberty; chiefly this was to be accomplished through economic growth, ever-expanding social insurance schemes, and a touch of redistributionism. Today liberalism is thought to have lost its confidence and coherence as social insurance programs head for ruinous insolvency while economic growth is thought to depend almost wholly on the private sector. What remains undecided at this point, however, is whether our change of mind will continue to carry forward into our moral and cultural life as well.

Reagan may be judged at the moment as having been less successful in challenging the premises of lifestyle liberalism than he was in challenging big government liberalism. But in the fullness of time Reagan may yet come to be seen either as the turning point, or as the last gasp of the old morality. The linkages between politics and culture are unclear these days. Machiavelli famously taught that there is no connection between politics and morality, or, somewhat more precisely, that those politicians who exercise a prudent disregard for traditional morals will be more successful and achieve greater heights than politicians who bow to conventional morality. It was the medieval version of the modern slogan, "Character doesn't matter." Yet the amorality of Machiavellian politics has never sat well in America. The political philosopher Leo Strauss wrote that "The United States of America may be said to be the only country in the world which was founded in explicit opposition to Machiavellian principles." America's political culture, spectacularly founded on the natural rights of man and therefore assuming the mantle of justice, has always exhibited a clear sense of shame on those many occasions when the practice of our political leaders and institutions has not lived up to our ideals.

A gradual coarsening of American political life has taken place in recent years, however. By the late 1990s America seemed to have made its peace with Machiavellian politics in the person and presidency of Bill Clinton. Whereas within living memory a divorce was considered a nearly insurmountable handicap to Adlai Stevenson and Nelson Rockefeller (but not, significantly, to Reagan), today a large majority of Americans apparently accepts the idea that marital infidelities on a gargantuan scale are purely private matters and unrelated to the performance of public duties. While the "era of big government" may be over, the era of lifestyle liberalism seems to be advancing unabated at the moment.

This change in moral sentiment did not happen overnight, and the crucial transitions and taboo-smashing incidents that prepared the way for this moment are a key part of this narrative. This narrative begins, like Arthur Schlesinger's *Age of Roosevelt,* with "the crisis of the old order," which in this case was the twin crises of the old order. The coming of the Great Society began the crisis of American liberalism, while the coming of Goldwater and Reagan represented a crisis for the Eastern Republican establishment. Above all, the long view offered here is designed to bring clarity to that fact that what is here and elsewhere referred to as "the crisis of liberalism" has not been resolved, in part because the crisis of liberalism is also the crisis of conservatism. It is also the crisis of conservatism because American conservatism shares the central premise of American liberalism, that is, the principle of individual liberty. For modern liberalism, the principle of individual liberty has metastasized into the principle of unlimited individual autonomy, which cuts the ground from under traditional codes of moral restraint. Conservatives, still struggling to consolidate their positions against Great Society liberalism, are struggling to articulate a retail position against the new redoubt of lifestyle liberalism. While the crisis of the old order may have been resolved in favor of political conservatism, the clash today over lifestyle liberalism might well be called "the crisis of the new order," and it promises to dominate our politics and culture for the next generation.

Time is a stream, Richard Neustadt reminds us. You have to jump into it while it flows by, without exploring all the tributaries that make it run full. This narrative jumps in the stream where Reagan did—in 1964, when the GOP was at its nadir. The conventional wisdom was that it could only recover by becoming a moderate "me, too" party, offering a slightly more responsible and frugal form of liberalism. There was thought to be little promise for someone of Reagan's views. But the Republicans' 30-year drive to dominance owed more to the ascendancy of Reagan rather than Rockefeller or Romney.

Telling this story with a tolerable degree of detail requires that we re-call many names and events, some familiar and others obscure or half-forgotten. When Reagan first arrived on the scene, the liberal Ripon Society was still a major force in the Republican Party, just as the liberal Americans for Democratic Action (to which Ronald Reagan was once a member) was a significant force in the Democratic Party. In the early 1960s conservatism was still strongly associated with the kooky extremes of the John Birch Society. Today all three organizations have faded from view, and their pre-eminence at the time has been largely forgotten. And though this narrative is partial to Reagan and his cause, it aims to be fair to both sides of the great argument in America over the scope and role of politics and government. In this the narrative seeks to follow the method Lord Charnwood followed in his great biography of Lincoln: "Nor should the writer shrink too timidly from the display of a partisanship which, on one side or the other, it would be insensate not to feel. The true obligation of impartiality is that he should conceal no fact which, in his own mind, tells against his views."[23]

In addition to including the reasonable criticism of Reagan, this nar-rative also aims to tell the liberal's side of the story with due respect and sympathy, and does so partly from the perspective of the one figure whose experience bridges the entire time-span in view: Daniel Patrick Moyni-han, the thinking man's liberal, whose advice, had it been followed, might have saved liberalism from running aground and the Democratic Party from its electoral ruin at the hands of Reagan. Moynihan might be re-garded as the Forrest Gump of American politics; he has been on the scene, if not right in the middle, of most of the prominent controversies in America from 1964 until his retirement from the Senate in 2000. Like Forrest Gump, his detractors on both the Left and the Right think he didn't always understand what was going on around him, which means that he didn't fit into the pre-cut categories by which most of our public discourse takes place.

Moynihan's biographer, Godfrey Hodgson, notes the similarities be-tween Moynihan and Reagan: "Both had family backgrounds in the Mid-dle West. . . . Both had fathers who were Irish Democrats and alcoholics. Both started out as active New Deal liberals; indeed both were on the board of Americans for Democratic Action, the liberal high command. Both were shocked by the revival of the Left in the 1960s, and by the cultural upheaval that accompanied and ultimately buried it. Both were especially angry with student radicalism."[24] Part of their different outlook might be ascribed to their geographical divergence in early adulthood: Moynihan settled among the intellectual culture of the northeast, while Reagan settled amidst the entrepreneurial culture of the southwest. Moynihan was personally fond of his fellow Irishman in politics, though he always held Reagan's political views in disdain, which he barely but politely concealed, perhaps out of recognition that Reagan effectively tapped into the popular disaffection with liberalism that Moynihan tried in vain to warn liberals against. "These goddamned elitist liberals almost succeeded in running the working man out of the Democratic Party," Moynihan loudly complained in the mid-1970s. [25] "And into the hands of Reagan," he might have added.

But unlike Reagan, Moynihan never abandoned the idea of activist government and the traditional liberal creed, and was dismayed with what he rightly saw as the abdication of realism among liberals. "Wishing so many things so," Moynihan wrote 30 years ago about the "fatal flaw" of liberals, "we all too readily come to think them not only possible, which they very likely are, but also near at hand, which is seldom the case. . . . There now remains no question in my mind that the calamities of the Democratic administration-of-all-talents in the early 1960s were owing to hubris."[26] "[B]y the end of the 1960s," Moynihan ruefully concluded in 1973, "the Democratic party was near to having exhausted its potential as an agent of social change."[27]

If any person can claim vindication for his record of criticism and prognostication, it is Moynihan. Like a biblical prophet, he is without honor is his own time (not to mention his own party). Yet he is the right person to confront the conflict between politics and culture outlined previously. In 1986 Moynihan wrote: "The central conservative truth is that it is culture, not politics, that determines the success of a society. The central liberal truth is that politics can change a culture and save it from itself." A succinct statement for the theme of this book, and the course of the next generation.

PART ONE

———⟫•⟪———

THE
SELF-DESTRUCTION
OF LIBERALISM

CHAPTER ONE

HINGE: THE APOGEE OF LIBERALISM IN 1964

⸺⸺✦⸺⸺

THE YEAR 1964 was the Year of Lyndon. Lyndon Johnson and his party won a smashing victory at the polls, with Johnson racking up a lopsided 61 percent of the vote, the most since Franklin Roosevelt's 1936 landslide. The Democratic Party picked up 37 seats in the House of Representatives (giving them 295 to the Republicans' 140), and 2 seats in the Senate, giving them 68. Democrats also picked up 530 seats in state legislatures. These were the biggest majorities the Democrats had enjoyed since the glory days of the New Deal. The election seemingly confirmed— as if any confirmation was needed—the presumptive right of moderate liberals to rule America. "Johnson's sweep," political scientist Samuel Lubell wrote in a once-famous book, *The Future of American Politics,* "re-established the [New Deal] majority, releasing a new push of revolutionizing political change."[1]

It was the kind of victory from which dreams, and ambitious legislative programs, are made.

It was a victory from which the Democratic Party has never recovered, even to this day.

It would not become evident for a long time that Goldwater's was the most consequential election loss in American history, or that 1964 would prove to be, in the words of Michael Barone, the "hinge year" in postwar American life.[2] This was the year that would set in motion the major controversies of the next generation, many of which are still unresolved

today. Even before the story of the Goldwater campaign and its significance can be told, it is necessary to understand how 1964 unfolded.

Lyndon Johnson was surely one of the most ironic—some say tragic—
figures in American politics. He was, Pat Moynihan was among the first to
point out, "the first President to have spent his entire adult life in Washington, D.C., the company town of the American Republic."[3] He was the
polar opposite of Ronald Reagan, and not just in ideology. While the
Democratic Party would never have nominated him to be its presidential
standard bearer had he not been a necessity to John Kennedy's 1960 campaign, in a parliamentary form of government he would likely have been
chosen to be prime minister. Nearly every description of Johnson employs
the adjective "earthy" to describe his crude countenance and his scatologi-
cal language—"he couldn't pour piss out of a boot if the instructions were
printed on the heel" was one of his milder epithets. Johnson outraged pet
lovers everywhere when he picked up his dog by the ears in the presence of
reporters on the White House lawn, and similarly offended sensibilities
when he lifted up his shirt to display a surgery scar on his stomach.
"Lucky for us," comedian Dick Gregory commented, "that he didn't have
hemorrhoid surgery." "To put it delicately," the British journalist Henry
Fairlie wrote, "he invites the severest aesthetic judgments."[4]

While Goldwater was infamous for his remark that "this country
would be better off if we could just saw off the Eastern Seaboard and let
it float out to sea," Johnson held much the same opinion. He thought
Eastern journalists especially condescended to him because he was a
Southerner and a Texan. "Bigotry is born in some of the *New York Times*
people," he once remarked.[5] When Johnson heard that rioters threatened
to burn down Washington D.C.'s elite Georgetown, he said gleefully,
"I've waited 35 years for this day."[6] This contempt was mutual; Johnson
had never been held in much esteem among liberals, and in fact he had
acted to water down the civil rights bills that passed Congress under President Eisenhower. William F. Buckley Jr. observed during the election
campaign that "if America's liberals had been informed in 1960 that the
race in 1964 would be between Lyndon Johnson and Barry Goldwater,
they would probably have marched out into the ocean and drowned
themselves." Johnson would no doubt have taken deep satisfaction from
the fact that it has been only southern Democrats who have succeeded in
winning the White House since his time.

This inferiority complex fed his deep insecurity, and aggravated his will to power and his ego, which are usually outsized already in politicians. In Johnson the combination created a voracious appetite for political achievement, and an unquenchable thirst for distinction and adulation. He liked to claim that an ancestor fought at the Alamo—an easily disproven claim—and he exaggerated his modest World War II record. On the campaign trail he was indomitable. He lost more than 40 pounds in a 40-day period in one early campaign. In another, he maintained a rigorous schedule of campaign appearances despite being in severe pain from a kidney stone. "Johnson's instinct for power," Theodore White wrote, "is as primordial as a salmon's going upstream to spawn." Another liberal journalist, Robert Sherrill, described Johnson as "treacherous, dishonest, manic-aggressive, petty, spoiled."[7]

Politics is one arena where the will to power compensates for or at least papers over insecurity. Johnson was masterful in the political arts of persuasion, arm-twisting, and horse-trading. Goldwater described two modes of the legendary "treatment"—the "Half-Johnson" (one arm around your shoulder) and the "Full-Johnson" (facing you squarely just a few inches from your face with both arms on your shoulders). He nearly always got his way. Alabama Governor George Wallace, summoned to a White House confrontation over civil rights (Wallace was captain of the rearguard trying to preserve segregation), emerged from his one-on-one meeting with LBJ saying, "If I hadn't left when I did, he'd have had me coming out *for* civil rights."[8] Despite his forcefulness and political success, Johnson still felt unloved. Why don't people like me?, a plaintive LBJ asked Dean Acheson. "Because you are not a very likeable man" was the former diplomat's undiplomatic answer.

It was the height of historical irony that this graduate of San Marcos State Teachers College in Texas should inherit the administration and the grand agenda designed and staffed by the "best and the brightest" from Harvard and other precincts of the Eastern elite that he so disdained. John F. Kennedy had been the shining hero for liberals (though Johnson, undoubtedly in another of his self-aggrandizing moods, had remarked the day after Kennedy's assassination that "to tell the truth, John F. Kennedy was a little too conservative to suit my taste").[9] JFK's "New Frontier" evoked the most excitement among intellectuals since the New Deal. The New Frontier was the chance for a new generation—the junior officers of World War II, as Moynihan described Kennedy's administration—to strut their stuff. But the liberal agenda made only slight headway during Kennedy's brief tenure, while Johnson, added to the ticket in 1960 under still-murky circumstances, was relegated to the traditional vice-presidential role of unseen understudy. Kennedy and his circle actually had little liking for Johnson; he had been added to the ticket out of electoral necessity. Now, riding on the sentiment generated by Kennedy's assassination, Johnson would advance the liberal agenda further than any Democratic president, FDR not excluded. Yet liberals would end up despising and rejecting him—a fury that spilled over into an open civil war within liberalism itself.

Despite the trauma of Kennedy's assassination, Johnson took command of an America that was in its most optimistic frame of mind since the 1920s. The "unraveling of America," as historian Allen Matusow labeled the 1960s, would unfold slowly over the next few years. Like the parable of the frog being slowly boiled, there would not be any single moment or event that signaled a decisive turn in America's fortunes. In 1964 America was enjoying the Indian summer of its postwar prosperity and contentment; it might well be thought of as the tail end of the tail fin era.

Since World War II the American economy had become a colossus. Gross Domestic Product (GDP) grew by 7 percent in 1964—it would grow even faster in 1965—while inflation was a tame 1.2 percent and unemployment a tolerable 5.2 percent. GDP for the year would stand at $576 billion, and the federal budget would be balanced at less than $100 billion. There was no Occupational Safety and Health Administration (OSHA), no Environmental Protection Agency (EPA), no Consumer Product Safety Commission (CPSC), and the Federal Register, which lists all government regulations, was less than 17,000 pages. Over the next 10 years, the Federal Register would balloon to more than 60,000 pages.

Personal income had more than doubled between 1945 and 1964. Per capita income was $2,592; the average manufacturing job paid $2.53 per hour. Twenty-nine percent of the workforce was unionized. The stock market was booming; the Dow Jones Industrial Average crossed above 800 for the first time on February 17. The number of Americans living in poverty had fallen by half. Many economists thought the business cycle had been mastered at last, that serious recession might never be seen again. Twenty-five million women—about half of adult women—were employed, accounting for a third of the adult workforce. Only a third of married women were in the workforce.

With such a benign economic climate, it is not surprising that less than 10 percent of Americans in opinion polls listed the economy as the most important problem facing the nation. Trust in American leaders and institutions ran high. Three-quarters of the members of Congress were veterans, and polls found that 70 percent of Americans had confidence that the government in Washington would do the right thing most of the time. (By 1995 this number was down to 18 percent.) This trust perhaps explains a paradox that shows up in polls from that year; while 51 percent in a Gallup Poll identified "international relations" as the most important problem facing the nation, 63 percent said they were paying little or no attention to events in Vietnam.

Nineteen sixty-four found Richard Nixon practicing law in New York, and traveling the world burnishing his political reputation while mulling another possible presidential run. Nixon shrewdly recognized early on that Johnson would likely prove unbeatable, and that his best course was to bide his time for 1968. Thirty-nine-year-old peanut farmer Jimmy Carter was midway through his first term in the Georgia legislature. William Jefferson Clinton was completing his senior year of high school in Hot Springs, Arkansas; he lost the election to be student body secretary (because of a peculiar school rule, he was ineligible to run for class president), but he would head off to Georgetown University in the fall. Captain Colin Powell had returned from his first tour of duty in Vietnam late the previous year—where, he concluded, "It'll take half a million men to succeed"—and was assigned to Fort Benning, Georgia. A native of New York, Powell was shocked at the segregated hotels and restaurants he experienced during his drive to his new post. Another northern-born transplant to the South, Newt Gingrich, was a graduate student in history at Tulane University.

The fruits of progress were abundant. IBM began using the first microchip circuits in new models of its popular mainframe computer, the IBM 360. Basic models started at more than a million dollars, and were less powerful that today's $1,000 desktop computers. The U.S. Post Office began using zip codes. First-class postage was five cents. Other new consumer marvels included Pop Tarts, freeze-dried coffee, and push-button telephones—but you still couldn't buy your phone; all phones were the property of the phone company. Hardback books sold for about $6. The first sperm bank in the United States opened in the unlikely location of Iowa City. Surgeon General Luther Terry, a smoker himself, released a report concluding that smoking "contributes substantially to mortality from certain specific diseases." Terry subsequently quit smoking. California passed New York as the nation's most populous state.

The median home price in 1964 was $18,750. A car buyer could snap up a new Oldsmobile for $3,495, while the budget buyer could get around in a Volkswagen beetle for a mere $1,695. The big car news of 1964 was the debut of the Ford Mustang. Ford had been losing money for years, though it had recovered from the Edsel debacle with the strong selling but bland Falcon model—a project pushed vigorously in the late 1950s by Ford's young finance director, Robert S. McNamara. The Mustang was a flashy, sporty design with a jump seat. Ford's financial wizards projected that it would sell 100,000 to 125,000 units in the first year. Even though the car got good advance reviews from the trade press, Ford's bean counters were unenthusiastic about the Mustang because they feared it would cannibalize sales from other Ford models. The Mustang sold 418,812 units in the first year, earning Ford more than $1 billion in profits.

The smash success of the Mustang established the reputation of the Ford marketing man who had pushed the project against the company's apathy: Lee Iacocca. Overall the auto industry produced 7.6 million cars in 1964, breaking its previous record of 7.4 million cars set in 1955. It was a sign of the nation's advancing productivity that the auto industry achieved this new record with 14 percent fewer workers than in 1955, a trend that was a source of acute worry to liberals, who feared "automation" would lead to rising unemployment and inequality.

In sports, Arnold Palmer won the Masters tournament for the fourth time, but Jack Nicklaus was the top money winner for the year on the pro golf circuit, with total winnings of $113,284. Cassius Clay defeated Sonny Liston for the heavyweight boxing championship, and then changed his name to Muhammad Ali. More shocking than his boxing style or even his upset of the heavily favored Liston was his loud-mouthed self-promotion, which would become a new model for athletes. In the upstart American Football League, an aging quarterback named Jack Kemp led the Buffalo Bills to the AFL championship over his former team, the

San Diego Chargers, throwing for 188 yards on 10 completions. His teammates later recalled why they always thought their gregarious signal caller was a bit odd: He read obscure magazines in the locker room that didn't have any pictures, like *National Review.*

America in 1964 was a culturally conservative nation. A Gallup Poll found that 63 percent of Americans said they pray regularly, and a Lou Harris Poll found 88 percent favored prayer in public schools, which the Supreme Court had banned in 1962. The kids wore mostly short hair, with quite a few still sporting crew cuts. In a 1965 Gallup Poll, 80 percent of Americans said schools should require boys to keep their hair cut short. But the first signs of a generational split began to appear. At a public high school in Westbrook, Connecticut, Edward Kores Jr. was suspended when he showed up for the first day of school in September with a Beatles hairstyle. The school superintendent eventually compromised, readmitting Kores on the condition that he comb his bangs back.

Traditional mores on sex still held sway. Though the birth control pill had been available for a couple of years, the sexual revolution was not yet under way. Out-of-wedlock births were only about 5 percent of total births, though among blacks the number was creeping up above 25 percent and was beginning to attract the attention of worried social scientists. Less than 10 percent of households were headed by a single or divorced mother, about the same proportion it had been for the previous 25 years; over the next 20 years the proportion of families headed by single or divorced mothers would double. The divorce rate was 25 percent, not much higher than it had been in the 1940s. (It was nearly twice as high in California, however.) Divorce, though slowly on the rise, still carried a social stigma. The nation's first no-fault divorce law, which would be signed by Governor Ronald Reagan (a divorcé) in California, was still six years away. It was Nelson Rockefeller's divorce and remarriage to another divorceé, more than his liberalism, that proved the biggest handicap to his presidential ambitions in 1964. (Connecticut Senator Prescott Bush, father of George and a longtime friend of the Rockefeller family, attacked Rockefeller as a destroyer of American homes.) "With news of the remarriage," Theodore White wrote in *The Making of the President,* "the Rockefeller operation staggered."

Homosexuality remained a taboo. Although there was growing sentiment in New York state and elsewhere to decriminalize homosexuality

between consenting adults, in general homosexuality was nonetheless regarded as an unhealthy and immoral deviancy. In 1963 a *New York
Times* front page headline expressed the mood of the time: "Growth of
Homosexuality in City Provokes Wide Concern." In May 1964 the Committee on Public Health of the New York Academy of Medicine expressed
some surprise in finding that homosexuals were "proud" of their "deviancy." The *New York Times* noted that "The study takes strong issue
with the contention of spokesmen for homosexuals that their aberration
makes them merely 'a different kind of people leading an acceptable way
of life.'" "Homosexuality is indeed an illness," the Academy of Medicine
report concluded, adding that "The homosexual is an emotionally disturbed individual."[10]

The first signs in what would be come known as the "culture war"
were beginning to show up, though it was hard to see at the time. Most
popular culture was oriented thoroughly to the suburban middle class. The
Hollywood Hays Office, which served as the official censor for television
and movie productions, was still open and functioning; it would not close
down until 1966. Nineteen sixty-four was also the beginning of the slippery slope for the crime rate, educational test scores, and drug use. LSD
was still legal. Sandoz, the Swiss pharmaceutical manufacturer, would continue to distribute LSD until April 1966, at about the same time Congress
finally outlawed it. By that time a million Americans were estimated to
have tried it. The crime rate had been edging up in the early 1960s and
was about to explode, increasing by 54 percent over the next five years.
FBI Director J. Edgar Hoover ruffled civic pride in New York City when
he declared in July that Central Park was unsafe. He criticized judges for
"mollycoddling" criminals. The *New York Times* editorial page suggested
it was time for Hoover to retire, but also reported in its news pages that a
recent survey showed that a large majority of Upper West Side residents
had become afraid to go outside at night. But the most shocking sign of
things to come was the widely publicized murder of Kitty Genovese in
New York, where neighbors ignored her screams and cries for help as she
was being murdered. Liberals were looking fixedly the other way; the Ford
Foundation announced a $266,000 grant to the Judicial Administration
Institute to promote greater "pretrial liberty," that is, releasing prisoners
without bail while they were awaiting trial.

Even with these harbingers of trouble to come, it was not surprising that Americans had high esteem for the government. Within the recent memory of most living Americans, the U.S. government had successfully engaged in the largest war in history and had gone on to build the interstate highway system that accelerated the unfolding of the new suburbs in the postwar years. The GI Bill had sent a generation of veterans to college who would not otherwise have done so. It had taken the first thrilling steps to putting a man on the moon. And if we can put a man on the moon, a popular cliché went, surely we can end poverty in our cities. Why should social science be more difficult than rocket science?

Liberalism was about to cross a divide from its older "public works" and social insurance mentality of the New Deal to a more aggressive social engineering mentality. Social scientists had started flooding into government in huge numbers, starting with the creation of the cabinet-level Department of Health, Education, and Welfare under President Eisenhower. A later generation of liberals would come to understand the hubris and presumption of Great Society liberalism and the extravagance it led to, but in 1964 an expansion of liberal policy seemed plausible if not obvious to all but a handful of conservative ideologues. While a sense of practical realism was certainly absent from the intellectual content of the Great Society, as a political matter it was essentially an extension of the confidence and optimism built on the prior success of the liberal creed. "In the early 1960s in Washington," Daniel Patrick Moynihan reflected, "we thought we could do anything. . . . the central psychological proposition of liberalism . . . is that for every problem there is a solution."[11] "These, without doubt, are the years of the liberal," wrote a confident John Kenneth Galbraith. "Almost everyone now so describes himself."[12] No one among the growing ranks of preening social scientists newly entrusted to guide policy could imagine that they were about to make social problems dramatically worse.

HAVING INHERITED THE White House prematurely and under tragic circumstances, but with the next presidential election less than a year away, President Johnson faced a delicate balancing act. "I feel a moral obligation to finish the things that JFK proposed," Johnson said to a group of friends a week after JFK's death. But he also needed to begin to make his own mark in order to build a record for the election. Johnson's natural solution was to seek Texas-sized versions of Kennedy's already large ambitions. Kennedy had been moving cautiously with civil rights legislation and with plans for reducing poverty. Political constraints, especially the opposition of Southern Democrats, dictated the slow pace of these initiatives under Kennedy. Now Johnson would press the political gas pedal to the floor, exploiting the bereavement of the nation to overcome resistance.

He wasted no time. Just 48 hours after Kennedy's assassination, Johnson met with Walter Heller, the chairman of the Council of Economic Advisers, who briefed Johnson on the antipoverty plans they had been carefully developing. "That's my kind of program," Johnson told Heller. "It will help people. I want you to move full speed ahead on it."

The antipoverty planners of the Kennedy administration had actually been developing a modest "demonstration project" aimed chiefly at juvenile delinquency. Kennedy's people had targeted juvenile delinquency because, they admitted, they didn't know enough about poverty to launch a full-scale attack confidently. A series of task forces were formed, with the aim of studying the problems of poverty, trying modest pilot projects to test ideas, and developing a national policy over a period of years. The key figure in the evolving policy was David Hackett, prep school friend of Robert Kennedy's (and the model supposedly for the Phineas character in John Knowles' novel *A Separate Peace*), who had been driving the work of the President's Committee on Juvenile Delinquency and Crime.

The Committee had become intrigued with a "community action" program of the Ford Foundation that emphasized the involvement of poor people themselves in the design and action of local antipoverty programs. This program had helped inspire the "Mobilization for Youth" pilot project in New York City. Though how community action as a federal program would work in practice was a bit vague, Kennedy's antipoverty planners seized on this method as the model for approaching the general problems of poverty. A demonstration project for 10 cities starting in 1964 was mapped out. It would be called the Community Action Program. It was a decision that changed the character of American politics.

This would not do for Johnson. "Full speed ahead" for him meant something like the New Deal, with grand, sweeping programs of national scope. When presented with the details of the demonstration project for community action at Christmas, Johnson's impatience boiled over. "I was certain we could not start small," Johnson wrote in his memoirs. "It had to be big and bold and hit the whole nation with real impact. . . . I didn't want to paste together a lot of existing approaches. I wanted original, inspiring ideas."[13] Johnson initially wanted to scrap community action entirely, but his advisers persuaded him that it could be the cornerstone for a more ambitious program. Overnight the cautious, incremental approach of the demonstration project was swept aside in favor of a mad dash to an immediate national program.

Two weeks later, in his State of the Union speech, Johnson escalated the rhetoric to match the upgraded policy. Grandiloquent pronouncements are an occupational hazard of the presidency, especially for liberal presidents. Kennedy had etched several in the American mind, starting with "Ask not what your country can do for you, but what you can do for your country," as well as the more significant promise that "we shall pay any price, bear any burden, meet any hardship, support any friend, oppose any foe, in order to assure the survival and the success of liberty." Now Johnson would top these, declaring in his State of the Union speech on January 8: "This administration today, here and now, declares unconditional war on poverty in America." Kennedy's people had cautiously described their emerging antipoverty effort the year before as an "attack" on poverty. "All the living principals agree today," Nicholas Lemann has written, "that one thing Kennedy would not have done is publicly declare war on poverty."[14] Several of Kennedy's people, especially David Hackett, hated the new phrase. "I would never recommend to Robert Kennedy or the president of the United States that you could get up and announce to anybody that we're going to solve poverty," Hackett later recalled.[15] Notre Dame University President Father Theodore Hesburgh told Johnson that "it's just a terrible title."[16] But Johnson and his inner circle concluded that any lesser phrase did not match the ambition of their policy. Total war it had to be.

Behind the scenes, however, the effort to design the nuts and bolts of the War on Poverty was in chaos. The deliberations over a new policy quickly devolved into the typical dynamic of bureaucratic turf fighting, as each department scrambled to claim a share of the new money that would be spent. But the real problem was that the premises of policy were confused and contradictory from the start. On the one hand, the social scientists and economists who propounded the antipoverty crusade believed that further reductions in poverty were not susceptible to economic growth alone. Johnson himself had endorsed this view, saying "we cannot leave the further wearing away of poverty solely to the general progress of the economy."[17]

But on the other hand, neither Johnson nor congressional leaders would support any scheme that had the smallest hint of income redistribution, new taxes, or even a New Deal–style jobs program (which was favored by Johnson's Department of Labor, especially by Assistant Labor Secretary Moynihan). Robert Lampman, the economist who came up with the idea of defining a level of income that would be the official "poverty line" (no official statistical measure of poverty existed before the mid-1960s), wrote in a memo that "a politically acceptable program must avoid completely any use of the term 'inequality' or the term '*redistribution* of income or wealth.'"[18] Even as Johnson fueled expectations with his extravagant rhetoric about "unconditional war," he was imposing strict conditions indeed, and thus setting up the domestic equivalent of the Vietnam War. He told Lester Thurow, then a young White House aide, to monitor the writing of the antipoverty legislation and remove any feature that could be construed as an income subsidy. To his senior aide Bill Moyers, Johnson reiterated the point: "No doles." Johnson's visceral dislike of welfarism boiled to the surface in late January when he found that money for "illegitimate kids" had been left in the budget proposal after he had demanded that it be taken out. To Elmer Staats, the deputy budget director, Johnson exploded with language that could have come straight from the Goldwater campaign on a bad day: "I told you to cut the damn thing out. . . . They want to just stay up there and breed and won't work and we have to feed them. . . . I told you we don't want to take care of all these illegitimate kids and we want to make 'em get out there and go to work. . . . I don't want to be taking taxpayers' money and paying it to people just to breed."[19]

In other words, the poverty-fighting effort was going to embrace a "services" strategy rather than an "income" strategy. Rather that write checks, the poverty warriors would write social action plans to motivate and train individual poor people to think and behave like middle-class citizens, to embrace "opportunity." To sort out the confusion in the development of the program, Johnson in early February appointed a reluctant

Sargent Shriver, President Kennedy's brother-in-law, to head the War on Poverty program. Shriver had received good reviews for his leadership of the Peace Corps, one of Kennedy's marquee programs. Since the new antipoverty program would probably include a "Job Corps" training project, who better to head the effort? Shriver knew the nascent program was in a shambles, and immediately cranked up the efforts of a 137-person task force with personnel from several government agencies to iron out a plan in time to be introduced in Congress by mid-March. One participant described the frantic pace of the task force as "beautiful hysteria."[20]

"For the next six weeks," *The New Republic* reported, "inter-agency squabbling raged unchecked."[21] The more radical members of the task force, led by the socialist Michael Harrington, pressed for a large-scale employment program as the only effective means of reducing poverty. Shriver had some sympathy with this view, and in a meeting with Johnson on February 18 he proposed that the antipoverty program include a $1.25-billion jobs program for adults, to be funded with a five-cent-a-pack cigarette tax. Johnson was appalled. A Shriver aide present at the meeting later recalled: "I have never seen a colder reception from the president. He just—absolute blank stare—implied without opening his mouth that Shriver should move on to the next proposal. We weren't even going to discuss that one."[22] Pat Moynihan saw this decision as the key turning point in national poverty policy. "Had Shriver's employment proposal succeeded, the character of the antipoverty program would have changed. In the first place, it would have dwarfed the other items, but more importantly, it would have given an unavoidably 'conservative' cast to the entire undertaking" by putting people to work.[23]

But having eschewed an income transfer or even a public jobs program (that is, "workfare"), the antipoverty crusaders had set out to try something even worse. They would try to cure the "root causes" of poverty. And the "root cause" of poverty, as the task force on juvenile delinquency thought, was the "lack of opportunity." (It would be more than 10 years before pop psychologists and social scientists would seize upon "self-esteem" as a more fundamental root cause.) Young adults headed into antisocial channels because they lacked jobs skills and pathways to upward mobility. And one way to channel the energy of poor people into the paths of opportunity would be to bypass the existing "power structure" of local government and involve the poor directly in the design and implementation of local antipoverty programs. This was the vague theory of "community action."

At some early point in the crafting of the program, the phrase "maximum feasible participation" of the poor was born; the phrase originated with another Kennedy aide, Richard Boone. "This phrase," Moynihan recalled, "was taken to sanction a specific theory of social change. . . . It represented the direct transmission of social science theory into governmental policy."[24] By the time legislation was ready to present to Congress on March 16, the initial $500-million proposal for community action (a figure picked out of thin air the year before) had grown to nearly a billion dollars. The predictable result of an interagency task force approach, as Moynihan would later write, was "not choice among policies so much as a collection of them."[25] Community action remained the heart of the program, but a job-training program for youth known as the Job Corps was added, along with educational and rural assistance features. Legislation went to Congress on March 16 as the Economic Opportunity Act.

The irony is that Johnson thought he was being conservative with an approach to the problem that on the surface seemed entirely harmonious with the traditional American principles of individual opportunity and local control. No one seemed to take seriously the contradiction at the center of the premises of their program. The poverty fighters understood that the most severe pockets of poverty persisted because of a cycle of dependency that would be hard to break, but they nonetheless had the utmost confidence in the ability of social science to break through the pathologies of poverty. But if it were that easy, poverty might be expected to decline merely with economic growth. No one seemed to have the slightest idea that their supposedly more "conservative" approach that would harness social science to cure "root causes" would turn out to be more radical than an old-fashioned redistributionist jobs program. It was one thing for the extravagant Johnson to get carried away with the promises of social science; it was quite another for supposedly more sober policy planners to do so.

Nonetheless, as the Economic Opportunity Act unfolded before Congress, the planners got carried away too. Shriver would predict in 1966 that poverty could be wiped out in 10 years. An assistant secretary of defense said that "the new knowledge can literally solve any problem."[26]

Adam Yarmolinsky, another defense official turned antipoverty planner, thought that their efforts would lead the way to "the rebuilding of cities, not only in the United States but throughout the world."[27] The secretary of the Department of Health, Education, and Welfare predicted that "welfare costs can go down if our theories are right."[28] At the time only Robert Kennedy seemed to have reservations. "In my opinion," Kennedy wrote to Johnson early in the policy-planning process, "the antipoverty program could actually retard the solution of these problems."[29] But Johnson had political as well as temperamental reasons for disregarding Bobby Kennedy.

It would only become apparent later that, as Moynihan put it, *"The government did not know what it was doing. It had a theory. Or rather, a set of theories. Nothing more."*[30] The basic problem was that despite the intense interest of the social scientists, knowledge about poverty at that time was comparatively murky.

For starters, very few of the people classified as "poor" were destitute in the way the term "poverty" usually calls to mind. In fact, nearly half of the people classified as "poor" in the 1960 Census received their income in the form of dividends, interest, rents, royalties, veterans' payments, Social Security, and pensions of various kinds.[31] Most of the people in this category were elderly, often widows or widowers, living modest but adequate lives. Except for a few isolated pockets in Appalachia and the rural South (which the urban-oriented War on Poverty was not going to reach anyway), there were very few "poor" living at near-subsistence levels. Most people classified as poor lived in housing equipped with basic appliances; most had televisions; many owned automobiles. As the poverty-fighting industry grew, it would come to emphasize the idea of "relative" poverty as a way of keeping the initiative for expanding the welfare state.

The early efforts of the War on Poverty were rightly focused on reaching those segments of the poor that seemed trapped in a "culture of poverty" that embraced self-destructive behavior and blocked upward mobility. But actual knowledge of how the so-called "culture of poverty" worked was very scarce. Moynihan commented dryly that "literary productivity on the subject of poverty will appear in inverse ratio to the incidence of poverty in the 'group' to which the social scientists happen to 'belong.'" Poverty, Moynihan emphasized, was not just a lack of money; it was constituted also "by internal systems of values and preferences and interim personal relationships that have a validity and life of their own."[32]

One reason for confidence in the ability of social science to micromanage the transformation of the culture of poverty was the apparent success of the government's macromanagement of the economy. This, like the confidence that social science could end poverty, would prove to be a chimera, though it seemed plausible at the time. Underlying Johnson's ebullient boast that "We're the richest country in the world. . . . We can do it all" was a near-consensus among economists that they had at last unlocked the secret of perpetual prosperity. (John Maynard Keynes, the patron saint of government management of the economy, would appear on the cover of *Time* magazine in 1965, with the headline "We Are All Keynesians Now.") The Democratic platform of 1960 had called for achieving a 5 percent economic growth rate, and the economy of the first half of the 1960s obliged, handily exceeding this ambitious target while experiencing very low inflation. "We can't prevent every little wiggle in the economic cycle," Johnson's budget director Charles Schultze said, "but we now can prevent a major slide."[33] And central to the next stage of macroeconomic management would be a move that would later become a staple of conservative Republican politics—an income tax cut.

Here another great irony of the War on Poverty emerges—the role of what has been called the "New Economics" or "growth liberalism." For the first time in human history, the growth liberals thought, the main problem was not scarcity but abundance. In fact, as time went on growth liberals expected growing budget *surpluses* rather than deficits. "There is likely to be," Moynihan wrote, "$4–5 billion in additional, unobligated revenue coming in each year. *But this increment will only continue to come on condition that it is disposed of.* Therefore one of the important tasks to which an administration must address itself is that of devising new and responsible programs for expending public funds in the public interest."[34] (Emphasis added.)

The prospect of continuous growth made possible a measure of redistributionist policy without the need for the confiscation of existing wealth, which remained a taboo in American politics. An entire theory of political economy sprang up to justify this nascent redistributionism. The premise of growth liberalism was the view that the government should appropriate a larger share of the new wealth that growth was generating. Liberals felt some entitlement to the wealth that they presumed to have brought into being. John Kenneth Galbraith's influential book, *The Affluent Society*, argued that unless the government actively directed a larger and larger share of America's growing abundance, society would literally choke on its own affluence. We would buy too many cars and consumer goods, and invest our surplus less and less productively. The government, it was thought, could invest surplus capital more effectively than the private sector. Walter Heller had remarked that "A billion or two extra invested in better training, education, and housing—especially for the poor and the Negro—will give America a far bigger payoff than if we add that billion or two to already-swollen private consumption and investment."[35]

And yet President Kennedy had proposed a large income tax cut to stimulate economic growth even further, justified with the now-famous slogan, "A rising tide lifts all boats." The purpose of stimulating the economy was not to add to private wealth, but, as Kennedy and Johnson's economic adviser Walter Heller put it, to generate "a better economic setting for financing a more generous program of federal expenditures."[36] Yale University economist (and later Nobel Prize winner) James Tobin even endorsed what might be called the public sector equivalent of "trickle-down" economics: "Moreover, one effect of federal tax reduction is to increase the politically feasible tax base of states and localities, which can be counted on to spend new tax receipts for education and other urgent social needs." In other words, tax cuts would also lift the ship of state along with other small boats. Any concern for a budget deficit, meanwhile, could be dismissed. "Now at long last," wrote Tobin, "a planned deficit is accepted to gain economic strength."[37]

The Swedish economist Gunnar Myrdal went further, saying that "the analogy that a nation must handle its purse strings with the same prudence as an individual is false." The idea of budget balancing "has no support in economic theory," Myrdal insisted, "and is not commonly held in other advanced countries."[38] So Johnson went ahead with Kennedy's tax cut, which was enacted in February, a few weeks before the antipoverty program was submitted to Congress. (Goldwater voted against the tax cut in the Senate, fearing it would increase the federal budget deficit. In *Conscience of a Conservative*, Goldwater had expressed the orthodox conservative view: "I believe that as practical matter spending cuts must come before tax cuts. If we reduce taxes before firm, principled decisions are made about expenditures, we will court deficit spending and the inflationary effects that follow.")

Marginal income tax rates were reduced from a bottom rate of 20 percent and a top rate of 91 percent to a new bottom rate of 14 percent and a new top rate of 70 percent. Only a small handful of liberals, such as the *New Republic*'s "TRB" (aka Richard Strout), complained that the tax cuts would chiefly benefit the rich. Most liberals were on board the growth liberalism bandwagon, tax cuts and all. Johnson had wanted to go even further; he sought to establish presidential authority to cut taxes at the first sign of recession, a power that would have obvious election-year attractions. Congress was not amused.

Liberals were immediately restive, however, over the antipoverty program. While Moynihan correctly judged that Johnson's supposedly conservative approach would turn out to be quite radical in practice, most other liberals thought it was too conservative and were disappointed that it did not go further. Christopher Jencks complained that Johnson's program was "fundamentally conservative," consisting of "old programs aimed at traditional objectives." Richard Strout wrote that the program was fine "as a start," but added that there is "no alternative to really large-scale, ameliorative federal social welfare action and payments . . . something in the order of, say, $10 billion a year."[39]

The *New York Times* was similarly unimpressed, editorializing that "The dimensions of this crusade are still absurdly inadequate—in both money and comprehensiveness of plan."[40] Embracing the premise of economic abundance, critics even further to the left thought the time had come to decouple work and consumption completely. The Ad Hoc Committee on the Triple Revolution (the triple revolution being automation, civil rights, and nuclear weapons), a group of 32 leftist intellectuals led by Michael Harrington, thought the nation should provide "every individual and every family with an adequate income as a matter of right." The Committee thought the United States was "all too confused and frightened by a bogey we call the 'welfare state,' [a] term of pride in most parts of the world."[41]

Still other leftist critics understood that the poverty plan would mostly line the pockets of bureaucrats and consultants rather than deliver money directly to poor people (a view shared by Moynihan, who wrote that "A more cynical person might describe the strategy as one of feeding the sparrows by feeding the horses"). At root, these leftists thought, the poverty plan was a middle-class plot to keep poor people down. "Of all the devices that have been invented to keep the status-poor in their place," Adam Walinsky wrote in *The New Republic,* "putting them on a dole is by far the most effective."[42]

As for keeping expectations modest for his moderate program, Johnson was his own worst enemy. Johnson's gargantuan political appetite was not sated with a mere war on poverty; soon it metastasized into something even bigger. In an April speech, the phrase "the great society" appeared for the first time. (A 29-year-old aide named Bill Moyers wrote the speech, though it was another Johnson aide, Richard Goodwin, who first employed the phrase, which traces its etymology back to the turn-of-the-century Fabian socialists.) Johnson repeated the phrase 16 times over the next month before the media began to take notice. Then, in a speech in Ann Arbor, Michigan, on May 22, the "Great Society" was put in capital letters for the first time. "The Great Society," Johnson said, "rests upon abundance and liberty for all. It demands an end to poverty and racial injustice—to which we are totally committed in our time, but that is just the beginning. The Great Society is a place where every child can find knowledge to enrich his mind and enlarge his talents. It is a place where leisure is a welcome chance to build and reflect. . . .

"We are going to assemble the best thought and broadest knowledge from all over the world to find those answers. I intend to establish working groups to prepare a series of conferences and meetings—on cities, on natural beauty, on the quality of education, and on other emerging challenges. From these studies, we will begin to set our course toward the Great Society."

A child of the politically triumphant New Deal, Johnson had found his own signature theme. In the clash between Johnson's practical political sense and his extravagant ego, the extravagant part won. Conservatives naturally found Great Society language utopian and unrealistic, while liberals thought Johnson's policies were nowhere near utopian enough to justify the rhetoric. The public was skeptical from the start; in a Gallup Poll in 1965, an astonishingly high 83 percent doubted that the war on poverty could be won.[43] Johnson was beginning to store up a large fund of contempt among liberals, who were never wild about him in the first place. But what were they going to do—vote for Goldwater?

IF SOME LIBERALS were disappointed with Johnson's war on poverty, they had another cause on the ledger to offset this disappointment. Johnson was about to deliver the long sought-for civil rights law.

The cause of civil rights should have been, and to a great extent was, a victory for America's founding principles of equal rights that unite the nation in common citizenship. The civil rights legislation of the 1960s can be viewed as the last act of the Civil War, the culmination of the interrupted process of Reconstruction, and the too-long delayed delivery of Lincoln's great promise of "a new birth of freedom." Rightly understood, this is still what the civil rights movement should be about. But rather than effacing once and for all the last vestiges of the contradiction of slavery in a republic of freedom, the civil rights movement quickly spun out in a manner that has led not to the uniting of America but to the balkanization of America and the rise of a separatist "multiculturalism" at war with the idea of common citizenship and equality. The seeds of the contemporary controversy were sewn with the passage of the Civil Rights Act of 1964, though it was not clear at the time what those seeds would produce.

The complete story of the 1964 Civil Rights Act is too rich and complex to be told in full detail here. For the purpose of understanding its place in American life since then, it is necessary to understand the decisive watershed the Act has turned out to be. The Civil Rights Act effectively broke the back of the century-long Southern chokehold on the Democratic Party, though in doing so it released the pent-up energies of an immoderate liberalism that would soon crumble the foundations of the Democratic Party's majority coalition. And though the practical workings of the Act were extensively debated during its torturous course through Congress, it nonetheless introduced a legal and constitutional ambiguity that has become the plague bacillus of American politics.

Public support for the expansion of civil rights law had been welling up for two decades as the monstrosity of Jim Crow segregation in the South had become too obvious and inharmonious with the principles of American liberty to ignore. But the Democratic Party owed too much of its national power base to Southern Democrats. Without the "solid South," the party's prospects for capturing the White House, and maintaining its dominance of Congress, would be in doubt. Such progress as there was in the 1950s came mostly from Republicans, especially President Dwight Eisenhower, who pushed two civil rights bills through Congress in the teeth of Democratic opposition. Johnson, then the Senate majority leader, worked to water down Eisenhower's civil rights bills, ostensibly so they could get past implacable southern opposition. But Johnson wrote to constituents in 1957 and again in 1960 that "I am firmly opposed to forced integration and I firmly believe that the doctrine of states' rights should be maintained." (Back in 1948, Congressman Johnson had criticized proposed civil rights laws in terms that made Barry Goldwater look mild by comparison: "This civil rights program about which you have heard so much about is a farce and a sham—an effort to set up a police state in the guise of liberty. I am opposed to that program.")[44] And Democrats were also quick to criticize Eisenhower when he sent federal troops to Arkansas in 1957 to enforce public school desegregation.

President Kennedy had declared civil rights to be a top political priority for his first term in office. He had famously phoned Martin Luther King, jailed in Atlanta, days before the election in 1960, and had then quietly advertised the deed among black voters in the North (250,000 leaflets in Chicago alone)—a stratagem some analysts think clinched the close election. (Martin Luther King's father, Martin Luther King Sr., had supported Nixon up until this point, partly because, like other southern Baptists, he feared a Catholic in the White House. Upon hearing of this, Kennedy said, "Imagine Martin Luther King having a bigot for a father.")

But Kennedy proceeded slowly with civil rights. He appointed Thurgood Marshall to the federal judiciary, but also several southern segregationists. His order to desegregate federal housing was issued without fanfare. He did not propose a civil rights bill to Congress until June of 1963, and it left out an employment non-discrimination clause, a key demand of the civil rights movement. Attorney General Robert F. Kennedy knew about, but did not stop, the FBI's wiretaps of Martin Luther King, and his strategy on civil rights was mostly reactive to events. "I did not lie awake worrying about the problems of Negroes," he later admitted.[45] Later in 1963 the Kennedy brothers attempted to prevent the March on Washington—where Martin Luther King gave his "I have a dream" speech—and, having failed to stop the march, then worked closely with civil rights leaders to stage-manage the event.

Meanwhile, the strategy of the civil rights movement was beginning to pay off, not for the first time moving public opinion far ahead of the political leaders of the country. Following the successful model of the Montgomery bus boycott in 1955 (when Rosa Parks refused to give up her seat at the back of the bus), the civil rights movement's carefully planned marches, sit-ins, "Freedom Rides," and voter registration drives in Southern states generated large amounts of sympathetic media coverage, at a time when TV network news coverage was expanding rapidly. CBS, for example, lengthened Walter Cronkite's nightly broadcast from 15 to 30 minutes in the fall of 1963.

The other networks soon followed, and NBC broadcast a highly sympathetic three-hour special report on civil rights on September 2, 1963—the first three-hour show on a single subject ever done on TV. It helped that Southern authorities could be predictably counted upon to overreact to civil rights marchers, calling out attack dogs, and encouraging armed mobs of civilians to assault marches. (In the one case where authorities met non-violent resistance with benign neglect—in Athens, Georgia, in 1962—the march fizzled.) The civil rights marchers paid a high price for their strategy—hundreds were beaten and dozens were killed—but the scenes of fire hoses, attack dogs, police beatings, and shootings appalled America when they were seen on TV and on the front pages. It was clear that Southern segregation was not just an anachronism but an affront to decent democratic life.

By the beginning of the legislative struggle for the Civil Rights Act in February 1964, 61 percent of Americans declared themselves in favor of the proposed civil rights act; outside the South, support was more than 70 percent. This represented the culmination of a sea change in American attitudes about race. The proportion of American who thought that public schools should be integrated rose from 30 percent in 1942 to 62 percent in 1963, and the proportion supporting integrated neighborhoods had risen from 35 percent in 1942 to 64 percent in 1963.[46] Even in the South public opinion on race was beginning to moderate. Between the 1940s and the 1960s, public support in the South for school integration had risen from 3 percent to 31 percent; for integrated transportation, from 4 percent to 52 percent; and for housing, from 12 percent to 51 percent. "The white supremacist South of old was rapidly dying by the 1950s," Stephan and Abigail Thernstrom have written, "even though figures of reaction like George Wallace and Orval Faubus were still riding high."[47] One sign of this trend could be seen in the white voters of Birmingham, who voted out most of the municipal officials there in April 1963, though not in time to prevent Public Safety Commissioner Eugene "Bull" Connor from turning fire hoses on civil rights marchers when he ran out of jail space because he had arrested more marchers than the jails could hold.

These changes in public opinion about race were not yet fully evident to the political class in Washington. At the time of Kennedy's assassination, the civil rights bill was stalled out and unlikely to pass. It is doubtful that Kennedy would have pressed the issue in the upcoming election year. Joseph Rauh, a leading figure in the civil rights movement, said, "When Kennedy was killed, the bill was absolutely bogged down." Like the anti-poverty plan, Johnson was quick to seize upon the emotion of Kennedy's death, declaring that passage of the bill would be a fitting way to vindicate the late president's memory. Thus the stage was set for the greatest legislative battle of the twentieth century.

The Civil Rights Act easily passed the House in February, where simple majorities rule. The Senate, with its privileges that allow a determined minority to slow debate through procedure and filibuster, would be a different story. The votes were there to pass the act, but whether there were 67 votes to end a filibuster was more doubtful. Senate leaders decided to skip the usual committee mark-up process, and brought the bill straight to the Senate floor on March 9.

In what would prove to be the death spasm of the Old South, Southern Democratic senators immediately began what would become the longest filibuster in history. The filibuster went on for 736 hours over 83 days, easily eclipsing the old filibuster record of 37 days. The debate filled nearly 3,000 pages in the *Congressional Record*. During this time no other Senate business could be conducted. In addition to the full arsenal of parliamentary delaying tactics, the southern senators attempted to rally Southern sentimentalism. Virginia Sen. Willis Robertson (Pat Robertson's father) waved a small confederate flag as he spoke on the Senate floor. (Sen. Hubert Humphrey politely praised the stars and bars flag as a symbol of "bravery and courage and conviction." Thirty years later such senatorial courtesy evaporated when the Senate refused to renew a patent on the flag for the Daughters of the Confederacy.) Georgia Sen. Richard Russell, the leader of the southern forces, proposed at one point that America's black population be evenly relocated across the United States at federal expense. Liberal Democrats relished the opportunity to strike a death blow against the Southern wing of their party, whom they disliked even more than Republicans in many cases. "They have to be destroyed," Humphrey said at one point.

Amidst the political theater, a serious issue was being debated: whether and how the Civil Rights Act could be made to protect against

employment discrimination. A provision outlawing employment discrimination was a key goal of the civil rights movement, but the civil rights bill
Kennedy proposed in 1963 omitted an employment discrimination section.
(Kennedy's bill focused on public accommodations and other aspects of
segregation.) The employment discrimination clause that became Title VII
was added by the House Judiciary Committee in early 1964. Robert
Kennedy thought the House had killed the bill's chances. Those "sons of
bitches," Kennedy said, were "in love with death."[48] But as the bill moved
through the Senate, public support increased in the polls.

Title VII declared simply that it would henceforth be unlawful for
any employer to discriminate in hiring on the basis of race, religion, or
national origin. Southern opponents of the bill offered an amendment
adding "sex" to the protected categories, thinking it would kill the bill.
Instead, liberals embraced this "killer amendment," making it an early
victory for feminism. Southern senators immediately seized upon the
vague and general language of Title VII to suggest that it might lead to
hiring quotas. "If it means what I think it means," Sen. Robertson said,
"it means that a man could be required to have a quota or he would be
discriminating." Sen. George Smathers concurred, explaining how quotas
might become necessary simply as a defensive practice:

> It is not written in the bill that there must be a quota system, but the
> net effect of the adoption of the proposed law would be that employ-
> ers, in order to keep themselves from being charged with having dis-
> criminated, would, in time, have certain people working for them to
> meet the color qualifications, the religious qualifications, the creed
> qualifications, and so on.

Sen. Humphrey responded:

> If the Senator can find in Title VII . . . any language which provided
> that an employer will have to hire on the basis of percentage or
> quota related to color, race, religion, or national origin, I will start
> eating the pages one after another, because it is not there.[49]

Humphrey seemed sincere in this view, having earlier decried the
color-conscious group-rights mentality that was the basis for quotas: "Do
you want a society that is nothing but an endless power struggle among
organized groups? Do you want a society where there is no place for the

individual? I don't."[50] And President Kennedy had said, "We ought not to begin with a quota system" (though he did make the first use of the phrase "affirmative action" in connection with minority hiring).

Most civil rights leaders thought the same way. Frederick Douglass had opposed quotas as far back as 1871, writing that "equality of numbers has nothing to do with equality of attainment." Jack Greenberg of the NAACP said in the 1950s that "The chief problem with quotas is that they introduce a potentially retrogressive concept into the cherished notion of individual equality." And of course Martin Luther King held up a regime in which people were judged not by the color of their skin but by the content of their character. But the concern over the ambiguity of Title VII was thought sufficiently cogent to warrant adding a clause that became Section 703 (j) of the Civil Rights Act, which said that "nothing in this subchapter shall be interpreted to require any employer . . . to grant preferential treatment to any individual or group because of the race, color, religion, sex, or national origin of such individual or group on account of an imbalance that may exist with respect to the total number or percentage of persons of any race, color, religion, sex, or national origin employed by any employer . . . in comparison with the total number or percentage of persons . . . in the available workforce . . ." This language was explicitly directed against what would later become known as "disparate impact," that is, the proposition that if 10 percent of a local workforce is black, then any employer who has less than 10 percent black employees is *ipso facto* guilty of discrimination. Section 703 (j) would prove almost completely unavailing, despite the clarity and intent of the language.

The argument over prospective quotas took place amidst the last lingering doubt about the constitutionality of the federal government ordering private employers and private accommodations such as hotels and restaurants not to discriminate. The Civil Rights Act of 1875 had attempted to institute non-discrimination in "public accommodations," but the Supreme Court ruled in the 1880s that the law only applied to government-owned accommodations, not private parties. Yet ever since the New Deal the Supreme Court had broadened federal power to regulate commerce. The famous case brought after the Civil Rights Act passed involved Ollie's Barbeque, a tiny restaurant in Georgia that was ruled to be engaged in "interstate commerce" (and therefore subject to federal regulation) because it had bought its meat from a supplier in South Carolina.[51] By this imaginative device, no one could claim exemption from federal regulation under the old understanding of the Commerce Clause. The cases which came after the Civil Rights Act effectively completed the job of removing any effective limits on federal power that had been begun by the New Deal Supreme Court.

Nonetheless, this, rather than the prospect of quotas, would be the principled ground of Barry Goldwater's objections to the Civil Rights Act. Because he was to be the Republican nominee for president, he was excoriated in the media and by civil rights leaders for his "no" vote on the Civil Rights Act, though it was undeserved. His record on civil rights was better than nearly all of the Democrats who voted "no." He had been a member of the Arizona chapter of the NAACP (he was also a member of the Sierra Club), and as a Phoenix city councilman had voted to end segregation there. The department stores his family owned practiced non-discriminatory hiring. He had voted in favor of the Civil Rights Acts of 1957 and 1960. Early in the Senate debate he had remarked that "I am half-Jewish, and I know something about discrimination." He said he wanted to support the Civil Rights Act of 1964, but that he found "no constitutional basis for the exercise of federal authority" in the area of public accommodations or employment. If Americans wanted the federal government to wield this power, Goldwater argued, then we should go about this honestly by amending the Constitution. (He had been advised about the constitutional issues of the bill by Yale University law professor Robert Bork and a young Arizona lawyer named William Rehnquist.) Thus, he said in the closing debate, he must vote against the bill "reluctantly."

> I am unalterably opposed to discrimination of any sort and I believe that though the problem is fundamentally one of the heart, some law can help—but not law that embodies features like these, provisions which fly in the face of the Constitution and which require for their effective execution the creation of a police state. . . . With the exception of Titles II and VII, I could wholeheartedly support this bill . . .
>
> If my vote be misconstrued, let it be, and let me suffer the consequences. Just let me be judged in this by the real concern I have voiced here and not by words that others may speak or by what others may say about what I think.[52]

It was to no avail. Goldwater would be the first victim of race-baiting against anyone with principled reservations about civil rights law. Black civil rights activist A. Philip Randolph said the election of Goldwater "would be the greatest disaster to befall Negroes since slavery."[53] A labor union leader called Goldwater "a rallying point for all the racists in America," echoing the comments of columnist Walter Lippmann that Goldwater had become "the rallying point of the white resistance."[54] This was merely a mild preview of the invective he would face in the presidential campaign in the fall.

All the while the Southern filibuster was underway, public opinion in favor of the bill grew. A Harris Poll in late April found 70 percent in favor of the bill, and 63 percent in favor of stopping the filibuster. Republican Senate Leader Everett Dirksen, who had been supporting the bill behind the scenes while ineffectively trying to strike deals with Johnson to make some changes, finally went public and said he was ready to move to end the filibuster.

The Southern filibuster was finally broken in mid-June. With the filibuster broken and the Southern block worn down from the effort, the Civil Rights Act passed the Senate with a comfortable 73–27 margin on June 19. The Senate amendments to the Act were quickly adopted by the House in a similarly lopsided vote of 289–126 on July 2. It is significant to note, in light of the abuse Senator Goldwater received then and the Republican Party has received ever since on the issue of civil rights, that Republicans proportionately voted more heavily for the Act than Democrats. Four out of five Republican Senators voted in favor, while only two-thirds of Democratic Senators did; in the House, four-fifths of Republican members voted in favor, while only three-fifths of Democratic members did. Notable legislators who voted against the Civil Rights Act included Arkansas Sen. William Fulbright, Tennessee Senator Albert Gore Sr., and North Carolina Senator Sam Ervin. In Texas, Republican senate candidate George Bush declared himself against the Civil Rights Act. On election day in November, Bush lost by 300,000 votes to incumbent Senator Ralph Yarborough. Bush, who had been a Goldwater supporter, was especially chagrined that sixteen House Democrats from Texas who had voted against the Civil Rights Act were nonetheless reelected with over 95 percent of the black vote. Still, by flying in the face of one of the Democratic Party's most reliable voting blocks, Johnson feared that, as he said to a younger aide on the day he signed the Civil Rights Act, "I think we just delivered the South to the Republican Party for your lifetime."

The civil rights issue was to prove troublesome to Johnson and the cause of liberalism, but the trouble came from unpredictable sources—urban unrest in the North instead of the South, and widening fissures in the civil rights movement itself. Little more than a fortnight after the signing of the Civil Rights Act, a New York police officer, Thomas Gilligan, shot and killed 15-year-old James Powell, who was black, in a neighborhood close to Harlem. Two nights later, a protest meeting in Harlem organized by the Congress on Racial Equality (CORE) quickly turned into a riot. Much of the crowd directed its anger at the police, throwing rocks, bottles, and other objects, but another faction began looting and firebombing in Harlem's nearby business district.

The trouble in Harlem provides fodder for the contentious theory that revolutionary turmoil is often fueled more by rising expectations than repressive conditions. Harlem's per capita income in 1964 would have ranked it among the five richest nations in the world, yet there had been resentment festering in Harlem for a long time, rooted in the city's neglect of the borough and the lack of any meaningful local control. Like most northern big-city police forces at the time, the patrolmen in the area were mostly white, though it was the absence of police rather than their race that was more of a problem. (As a Ford Foundation researcher told a Senate committee later: "You can find 200 or 300 policemen around the Hilton Hotel protecting the Beatles, but in parts of Harlem you can't find them at any time of day or night."[55]) "They've been playing Russian roulette with us for years," said black psychologist Kenneth Clark. The disturbing aspect of the Harlem riot was not that it happened, but the radical impulse that boiled to the surface. Prominent leaders of the civil rights movement pleaded for calm. "The promise of the Civil Rights Act of 1964," said the NAACP's Roy Wilkins, "could well be diminished or nullified . . . I don't care how angry Negroes are . . . We can't leave [our cause] to the bottle droppers and rock throwers." (Wilkins said afterward that the riot had "brought shame upon the civil rights movement of a whole people."[56]) Wilkins and others were not only ignored, but shouted down. Bayard Rustin, one of the organizers of the March on Washington the year before, got on a loudspeaker urging people to go home. The crowd jeered back: "Uncle Tom! Uncle Tom! We want Malcolm X! We want Malcolm X!" At a church rally, Rustin's message of moderation was outdone by neighborhood activist Jesse Gray, who shouted that what was needed was "guerrilla warfare" led by "100 black revolutionaries who are ready to die!"[57] The dissention within the civil rights movement between the more dominant group who favored Martin Luther King's strategy of non-violent protest and resistance and a smaller group of radical blacks who favored more active measures was breaking out into the open. Although it was not yet obvious, the civil rights movement, flush with the success of the Civil Rights Act, was cracking up.

A few nights later another riot erupted across the East River in the Bedford-Stuyvesant section of Brooklyn. Again, a CORE rally had gotten out of hand. This time the looting was worse; about 400 stores, including those that had put out signs reading "This is a black store," were smashed and looted. Before the rioting was over in Harlem and in Brooklyn, there would be one dead, 141 seriously injured (48 of them police), and 519 arrests. But the unrest was not over. A few days later rioting erupted in Rochester, 250 miles to the north, after police arrested a 17-year-old black for public drunkenness. The riot raged for two nights. Governor Rockefeller had to dispatch 200 state troopers to quell the riot. Riots in Philadelphia (248 injured) and Chicago soon followed.

These riots were merely a modest preview of what was in store for northern cities over the next five years. That rioting should begin in the North was baffling on the surface for many Americans. The civil rights movement had effectively dramatized how the worst racial violence and most appalling conditions for blacks existed in the South, and it was this region for which the Civil Rights Act was designed. Yet here were riots in the North, while Southern cities were quiet.

Unrecognized at the time, however, was the fact that the North was nearly as segregated as the South, although the North didn't publicly codify this fact through separate drinking fountains, bathrooms, and other overt signs of the Jim Crow regime. Northerners were much too clever to segregate openly. Instead they resorted to subtle measures, such as Robert Moses deliberately designing bridge overpasses on the roads to Long Island beaches to be too low for buses to pass beneath. Since few blacks owned cars, the bridge design assured that Long Island beaches would be a playground mostly for whites. Buses that went to the beach by circuitous routes found additional obstacles. "Buses chartered by Negro groups found it very difficult to obtain [park] permits," writes Robert Caro in his biography of Robert Moses, "particularly to Moses' beloved Jones Beach; most were shunted to parks many miles further out on Long Island."[58] This pattern was repeated in various ways throughout the North. Chicago, for example, had segregated cemeteries. Several of Martin Luther King's marches in northern cities were met by hostile mobs of rock- and bottle-throwing whites, but these episodes have generally been forgotten in the narratives of the civil rights movements that dwell on Bull Connor. Although economic opportunity was much better for most blacks in the North, for those trapped in the worst slums there was much to be angry about.

"I think the Communists are in charge of it," was Johnson's private reaction to the riots. "Hell, these folks have got walkie-talkies. . . . Somebody's financing them big."[59] His immediate fear was that Goldwater would exploit the situation politically, and Goldwater was coming to the White House for a private meeting with Johnson in the middle of the riots. "He wants to encourage a backlash," Johnson said to Governor John Connally of Texas. "That's where his future is. It's not in peace and harmony." This was the only vulnerability Democrats feared as they looked to the fall campaign. Segregationist Alabama Governor George Wallace had shown the potential of courting the so-called "backlash vote" in the spring, with strong showings in several northern primaries. But Goldwater was not Wallace. Goldwater came to the White House bearing an extraordinary olive branch: He wanted to take civil rights and the Vietnam War off the table as campaign issues. It was a pledge that Goldwater honored. His refusal to exploit his opposition to the Civil Rights Act extended to declining to air a TV spot that showed blacks rioting that several political analysts judged the most effective TV spot they had ever seen.

Johnson was surely right about the role of provocateurs in fueling the Harlem riot (mimeographed instructions about how to make Molotov cocktails circulated widely after the rioting began), but it would also soon add fuel to the imagination of the poverty warriors. Johnson had already begun thinking about what would become his "model cities" program. The climate of social policy optimism was still high in the saddle, such that the growing discontent among some northern blacks was imperceptible. But while this storm was gathering at home, a more serious storm was gathering simultaneously halfway around the world.

SHORTLY AFTER 2 P.M. on Sunday, August 2, 1964, Commander James Stockdale took off for a routine training flight in his Crusader aircraft from the carrier *Ticonderoga,* then on patrol in the South China Sea not far from North Vietnam. Stockdale would become known to most Americans in 1992, as the seemingly hapless and reluctant running mate for Ross Perot's third-party presidential campaign. In 1964, the Annapolis graduate was the commander of Fighter Squadron Fifty-One on the *Ticonderoga.* A few minutes into the flight, Stockdale and the other three planes in his formation were ordered to fly toward the destroyer *Maddox,* on patrol 300 miles away in the Gulf of Tonkin. Enemy torpedo boats were menacing the *Maddox,* the *Ticonderoga*'s strike control informed Stockdale.

Stockdale tuned his radio to the *Maddox*'s frequency as he neared the scene. "It sounded like we had just tuned in to World War II," he recalled 20 years later.[60] Among the staccato radio chatter, Stockdale could make out the words, "Under attack by three PT boats . . . Torpedoes in the water . . . I am engaging the enemy with my main battery."

The PT boats were already in retreat from the *Maddox* by the time Stockdale and his three accompanying planes arrived. Stockdale's squadron swooped in to attack the PT boats with rockets and gunfire. His wingman, Lt. Dick Hastings, took hits on his wing from antiaircraft fire and had to withdraw from the battle, later landing safely at Danang airbase in South Vietnam. The remaining three planes continued to strafe the PT boats with gunfire, knocking out one and damaging the other two before the planes began to run short of fuel and had to retire back to the *Ticonderoga.* The only hit the *Maddox* took during the attack was a machine gun round that had punctured a gun pedestal.

Back in Washington, D.C., reaction to the attack was surprisingly muted, even though President Johnson's war planners had been seeking a pretext to ask Congress for wider powers to prosecute the counter-insurgency effort in Vietnam. One reason for this reticence is that the United States had been backing South Vietnamese covert operations against coastal targets in North Vietnam (known as OPLAN 34A), and Johnson thought the North Vietnamese attack was related to these raids, which had been taking place at the same moment as the *Maddox*'s patrol in the Gulf. The United States didn't want to have to acknowledge the OPLAN 34A raids. A Pentagon news release about the *Maddox* incident didn't even mention North Vietnam by name. Secretary of State Dean Rusk praised the "restraint" of the administration in a speech later that day in New York. In Saigon, Gen. Maxwell Taylor, the former chairman of the Joint Chiefs of Staff who had been at his new post as U.S. Ambassador to South Vietnam for less than a month, thought the U.S. response was too weak. The lack of retaliation would convey the impression that the United States "flinches from direct confrontation," Taylor cabled to Washington. McNamara and other war planners thought Taylor was overreacting, but the Pentagon nevertheless ordered the destroyer *Turner Joy* to join the *Maddox,* and the Gulf of Tonkin patrols resumed. Naval air patrols would also be stepped up. President Johnson sent a stiff note to North Vietnam protesting the "unprovoked attack," even though he knew about the covert attacks by South Vietnam.

On August 3, another OPLAN 34A raid by two South Vietnamese PT boats attacked a radar station and security post on the North Vietnamese coast. On August 4, the *Maddox* intercepted North Vietnamese radio traffic commenting on the location of the *Maddox* and the *Turner Joy.* This was not unusual on the face of it, however, since part of the purpose of the patrols was to "show the flag" in the Gulf, and the ships were visible from shore in daylight. Nevertheless, as heavy clouds and thunderstorm activity descended on the Gulf of Tonkin area in the evening, the *Maddox* and the *Turner Joy* thought they were about to be attacked again. Commander Stockdale immediately scrambled from the *Ticonderoga.* He approached the two destroyers shortly after 9 P.M. Vietnam time. It was 9 A.M. in Washington, D.C.

For the next hour and a half, Stockdale circled the two destroyers looking for signs in the darkness of the suspected North Vietnamese torpedo boats. "I had the best seat in the house from which to detect boats— if there were any," Stockdale later recalled. Radio traffic from the destroyers were full of talk about taking hits, about torpedoes in the water, and other signs of engagement. "Those destroyers are talkin' about hits," Stockdale thought, "but where are the metal-to-metal sparks? And the boat wakes—where are they? And boat gun flashes? The day before yesterday [the August 2 daylight attack], I saw all of those signs in broad daylight! Any of those telltale indicators would stand out like beacons in the black hole we're operating in." Stockdale began to suspect that thunderstorm activity or just raw nerves had misled the radar operators on the ships. "The *Joy* was firing at 'targets' the *Maddox* couldn't track on radar, and the *Maddox* was dodging 'torpedoes' the *Joy* couldn't hear on their sonar, and neither ship was detecting any electromagnetic emissions (enemy radio or sonar) in the area." Stockdale concluded after returning to the *Ticonderoga* that "It was all a Chinese fire drill!" (Indeed, Stockdale had nearly hit the *Turner Joy* with one of his own sidewinder missiles.)

Back in Washington D.C., even as Stockdale was still in the air while the "battle" raged, Defense Secretary Robert McNamara received the first urgent intelligence dispatch that another attack was under way. He immediately alerted President Johnson, who asked how quickly a reprisal air strike could be implemented. This time, Johnson told several congressmen visiting the White House for a weekly breakfast, the United States would have to retaliate. McNamara told Johnson that a reprisal raid could be ready to strike North Vietnam by 6 P.M. Washington time—less than nine hours later—even though the carrier-based fighter planes in the Gulf were not outfitted for bombing operations. Refitting the planes in time would be a difficult task. Johnson planned to go on national television as the attack was launched.

As the mood in the White House and the Pentagon reached fever pitch, in mid-afternoon a message from the Captain John Herrick, commander of the *Maddox*, came in: "A review of action makes many reported contacts and torpedoes fired appear doubtful. Freak weather effects on radar and overeager sonar men may have accounted for many reports. No actual visual sightings by *Maddox*. Suggest complete evaluation before any further action taken." McNamara immediately called the Pacific theater commander, Admiral Ulysses Sharp, in Hawaii. McNamara cast his question in the negative imperative:

"There isn't any possibility that there was no attack, is there?"

"Yes, I would say there is a slight possibility," Sharp answered. Sharp said he was seeking additional information, but that he thought the attack order should stand.

McNamara and the Joint Chiefs of Staff met at quarter to five in the afternoon to ponder the evidence. The Associated Press had made the affair public with a news bulletin earlier in the hour; the news was probably leaked to them by one of the congressmen who had visited the White House earlier that day. Under pressure, Captain Herrick said that he was sure that the original ambush was genuine. Admiral Sharp thought only that the "weight of evidence" supported that an attack had occurred. McNamara and the Chiefs drew solace from intelligence intercepts of North

Vietnamese claims that they had lost two PT boats and had shot at two American aircraft.

This was enough for Johnson; he told a group of visiting congressmen at the White House that "some of our boys are floating around in the water." Four years later, when McNamara testified about the Gulf of Tonkin affair before an increasingly skeptical Senate Foreign Relations Committee, these radio intercepts were represented as the evidence that the August 4 attack had in fact taken place. But a close examination of the facts detailed in these intercepts suggests that McNamara and the Pentagon confused intercepts of the August 2 attack with the August 4 events. For example, one intercept has the North Vietnamese PT boat crew claiming to have shot down an American jet. But no plane was shot on August 4; the intercept most likely is referring to the hit taken by Lt. Hastings' plane during the August 2 action. A bitter Stockdale commented: "to try to establish a connection between what the intercepts said and real-life happenings on the night of August 4, 1964, is ridiculous. And I find it difficult to believe that McNamara didn't know that." Indeed, a CIA analyst who examined the radio intercepts a few days after the August 4 "attack" concluded that they had been mixed up. The CIA's Ray Cline reported these discrepancies to the President's Foreign Intelligence Advisory Board. "I never heard any more about it from them," Cline later said, adding that he doubted President Johnson was told.[61] But eight months later, Johnson remarked to George Ball: "Hell, those dumb, stupid sailors were just shooting at whales out there!" (The Communist Chinese also smelled a rat. Two weeks after the affair, the *Peking Review* offered the observation that the six-hour chronology of the supposed attack made no sense for short-range torpedo boats.[62])

Stockdale's bitterness toward what was taking place began to take shape the morning after the second Tonkin incident, when he was assigned to fly in the reprisal strike. "We were about to launch a war under false pretenses, in the face of the on-scene military commander's advice to the contrary. This decision had to be driven from way up at the top. . . . I felt it a bad portent that we seemed to be under the control of a mindless Washington bureaucracy, vain enough to pick their own legitimacies regardless of evidence."

Sure enough, navy crews were having difficulty refitting jets for the bombing run, and the timetable for the raid was slipping. Johnson had to postpone his television address. Having already missed the 7 P.M. national news hour, he was now in danger of missing the 11 P.M. news and the deadline for the morning papers. He repeatedly phoned McNamara, asking for progress reports. At 9:15 P.M., LBJ said to McNamara, "I'd sure as hell hate to have some mother say, 'You announced it and my boy got killed.'"

"I don't think there's much danger of that, Mr. President," McNamara reassured him.[63]

At 11 P.M., an exasperated Johnson yelled at McNamara: "Bob, I'm exposed here. I've got to make my speech right now!" Johnson finally went on the air at 11:36 P.M., 90 minutes *before* the first U.S. warplanes reached their targets in North Vietnam. He emphasized once again that "We seek no wider war." Stockdale was just leaving the "ready room" on the *Ticonderoga* to board his jet when he heard that Johnson had announced the raid to the world. "That struck fear in my heart because surprise was so important," Stockdale wrote later. His was the first plane in the air.

The raid on oil storage facilities at Vinh and PT boat docks took only about 90 seconds, but the United States lost two planes—one pilot was killed and another was captured and held prisoner for the next nine years. A few days later, Jack Stempler, a special assistant to McNamara, traveled to the *Ticonderoga* to speak with Stockdale about the August 4 "attack" on the destroyers. "We were sent out here to find out one thing," Stempler told Stockdale. "Were there any f------ boats out there the other night or not?" (When McNamara asked North Vietnam's legendary General Vo Nguyen Giap in Hanoi in 1995 what really happened in the Tonkin Gulf on August 4, 1964, Giap answered: "Absolutely nothing.")

"That said it all," Stockdale wrote. "I could stand right there in the cabin and write the script of what was to come . . ." Thirteen months later, Stockdale was shot down over North Vietnam, and spent almost eight years as a POW in Hanoi.

Despite the well-founded doubts about the authenticity of the August 4 attack, the Johnson Administration went to Congress two days later asking for a congressional resolution granting authority to widen the war. This was to be Vietnam's Pearl Harbor. Many of Johnson's advisers had desired congressional authority for more active measures against North Vietnam, and drafts of a possible resolution had been floating around the White House since at least May. The resolution proposed on August 7 stated that "Congress approves and supports the determination of the

President and Commander in Chief, to take all necessary measures to repel any armed attack against the forces of the United States and to prevent further aggression." The resolution passed 88–2 in the Senate, and 416–0 in the House. Johnson now had his blank check to prosecute the war as he saw fit.

Not least of the benefits to Johnson was the political payoff. Johnson felt vulnerable on the issue of Vietnam. Even as he assured Americans during the presidential campaign that America sought "no wider war" and that "We are not going to send American boys away from home to do what Asian boys ought to be doing for themselves," he also privately resolved that "I am not going to lose Vietnam. I am not going to be the president who saw Southeast Asia go the way China went."[64] Goldwater had, as usual, spoken with clarity that the goal in Vietnam should be victory. On the eve of his nomination, Goldwater had said that the United States ought to adopt a "win policy," and "tell the military commanders it was their problem to solve and to get on with solving it." (The Joint Chiefs of Staff had told Johnson back in March that limited, covert operations would not work, and that the United States should "either get in or get out." Johnson had rejected their advice, citing political reasons.) A few days later in his infamous nomination acceptance speech, Goldwater castigated Johnson for "refus[ing] to say . . . whether or not the objective over there is victory. The secretary of defense continues to mislead and misinform the American people."

"We are at war in Vietnam," Goldwater forthrightly declared. "Don't try to sweep this under the rug."

The Tonkin Gulf affair allowed Johnson to be tough and restrained at the same time. Goldwater supported the Tonkin Gulf Resolution, stating that it seemed his suggestions for a tough policy of taking the war to the North Vietnamese were being adopted. (On August 3, in response to the first incident, Goldwater had cautiously asked: "I think the American people are entitled to ask some questions of their own in regard to this event: Does the presence of American destroyers in the area signify the possible landing of larger American ground forces? Does it mean medium bombers are going to be used to interdict supply lines? Does it mean a change is taking place in foreign policy at White House and State Department levels?") When Johnson reached a vacationing Goldwater at the Balboa Bay Club in Newport Beach, California, on the evening of August

4, all Goldwater could say was, "I think you've taken the right steps and I'm sure you'll find that everybody will be behind you."[65] Sure enough, Johnson's approval rating in opinion polls jumped 15 percent.

Although critical historians have emphasized the role of political opportunism in Johnson's decision to exploit the Gulf of Tonkin affair to defend against the potential Goldwater charge of weakness, it was in fact unnecessary. In Goldwater's aforementioned Oval Office meeting with Johnson before the Gulf of Tonkin affair, Goldwater told Johnson that "there was already too much division in the nation over the war" and that neither of them should make things worse "by making Vietnam an issue in the campaign." Johnson sighed in relief, Goldwater wrote in his autobiography. "I interpreted that to mean he agreed."[66] This was one of the great missed opportunities of the 1964 campaign, not so much for Goldwater as for the nation. A vigorous debate about Vietnam during the campaign might have forced Johnson to give clear commitments to the nation about what would and would not happen in Vietnam. Between Johnson's craftiness and opportunism, and Goldwater's fastidious patriotism, the nation was denied that debate.

The Gulf of Tonkin affair was not the beginning or even the decisive turning point of America's heavy involvement in Vietnam, but it was typical of how the United States approached the Vietnam War from the beginning. The subsequent controversies over the Gulf of Tonkin affair—whether the naval patrols were an intentional provocation, whether Johnson and McNamara deliberately lied about the matter to Congress—miss the deeper meaning of the episode entirely. Like the War on Poverty, the Vietnam War originated and grew amidst the attitude that American wealth, power, and expertise could engage in successful social engineering and "behavior modification." The Vietnamese Communists were not unlike America's poor in their minds: Apply the right carrots and sticks, and they'll swing around to what we want them to do. This attitude would turn out to be the most difficult and painful lesson in hubris in American history.

The story of America's involvement in Vietnam prior to the Gulf of Tonkin could go back four years or even 40 years before Tonkin, while the long saga of Vietnamese strife could easily go back 400 years. Even though Ho Chi Minh had been a Communist since the 1920s and had spent some of his exile in the Soviet Union, he received U.S. assistance during and immediately after World War II. U.S. intelligence operatives in the Office of Strategic Services (the precursor to the CIA) had trained Ho Chi Minh's guerrilla army in southern China during World War II, and Ho had invoked the famous second paragraph from the American Declaration of Independence ("All men are created equal . . .") in Vietnam's own Declaration of Independence in 1945. Even though the United States had some naive sympathy for Ho, it backed France's desire to reassert its colonial claims in Indochina after World War II ended.

The French threw in the towel less than 10 years later, after President Eisenhower decided against intervening on their behalf during the final siege of Dien Bien Phu. It was at this point that Vietnam was divided in half, a Communist North and a non-Communist South, with an unsigned treaty calling for elections to settle which side would preside over ultimate reunification. The elections never took place, and Soviet Union actually nominated *both* Vietnams for U.N. membership in 1957, suggesting that support for Vietnamese Communism was not a high priority for the Soviets at the time. But by 1960, North Vietnam's Communist leaders had resolved to take over South Vietnam first through guerrilla infiltration and later through regular army invasion.

The controversy over Vietnam has generally concentrated on geo-strategic issues connected with the Western strategy of "containment," along with furious argument over the probity of the "domino theory," that is, if Vietnam fell, the rest of Southeast Asia would quickly follow. Less clearly understood, except by a few strategists such as Harry Summers, is the more important role of the way American power was used and the conception of the nature of the war itself.

John F. Kennedy and the liberal intellectuals he brought along with him to Washington hoped to make a decisive break from the strategic doctrines of their predecessors. "To many of us liberals," wrote John P. Roche, president of the liberal group Americans for Democratic Action during the Kennedy years and later an adviser to Lyndon Johnson, "it seemed that American power under Eisenhower and Dulles was undergoing the death of a thousand cuts."[67] President Eisenhower's Secretary of State John Foster Dulles was famous for his supposed foreign policy of "brinksmanship," that is, threatening total war (meaning nuclear weapons) against America's enemies. But this policy, liberals thought, confined American leaders to the choice of total war or appeasement ("suicide or surrender"), which was especially unworthy of a great power in circumstances that did not amount to a full-blown crisis, such as Vietnam. (One of the most thorough outlines of this argument was produced by a young Harvard professor named Henry Kissinger.) Liberal internationalists thought the policy of brinksmanship amounted to *de facto* isolationism. "So," Roche wrote, "we assailed Dulles, called for an active foreign policy and beat the drums for flexible response."

"Flexible response" would be the ideal tool for the foreign policy domain of social engineering. Traditional ideas of warfare and victory, such as were found in Clausewitz or Sun-Tsu, were regarded as obsolete. President Kennedy told the graduates of West Point in 1962 that "we need a whole new kind of strategy, a wholly different kind of force, and a wholly different kind of training and commitment." Along with the flexible response correlates of limited war and graduated pressure, there emerged the doctrine of Mutual Assured Destruction (MAD) that liberals thought would make nuclear war impossible or obsolete. By 1964, the United States began dismantling an air and missile defense system consisting of more than 200 antimissile missiles and interceptors. At the same time, the United States began targeting its long-range ballistic missiles at Soviet population centers instead of military targets. All of these steps were meant to "communicate" to the Soviet Union that the United States had no intention of starting a nuclear war. The rapidly growing Soviet missile arsenal, however, remained targeted at U.S. military sites.

The Cuban Missile Crisis in 1962 became the archetype of flexible response rightly applied in the minds of Kennedy's circle. Instead of an ultimatum followed by air strikes and an invasion, the United States succeeded in its objective of removing the missiles from Cuba through "graduated pressure" starting with a partial blockade, and secret concessions negotiated through back-channels. Yet the "successful" outcome of the mishandled Cuban crisis reinforced all of the wrong lessons for McNamara, Kennedy, Johnson, and the other architects of flexible response. Kennedy and the "best and the brightest" architects of American security policy during this epoch thought great power relations were a matter of "calculation" rather than straightforward comparisons of strength and expressions of resolve. If, as Kennedy thought, wars start by "miscalculation" (one of Kennedy's favorite books was Barbara Tuchman's *The Guns of August*, which argued that World War I began because of "miscalculation"), then the task of leadership consists chiefly of sending the appropriate rational "signals" to affect the other side's calculations about the chances of war. During the heyday of this thinking, John P. Roche recalled, "Discussions of military security began to sound more and more like seminars in game theory. There was a kind of antiseptic quality permeating the atmosphere; one often had the feeling he was attending a chess match. . . . The atmosphere made those of us who come from the harsh training of poker decidedly uneasy."

This was precisely the problem with the settlement of the Cuban crisis and the lessons our leaders took from it: While Kennedy and his grandmasters were playing chess (and especially emphasizing their "restraint," thus reassuring the Soviets that the chance of an American attack was minimal), Khrushchev was playing poker. Khrushchev ironically "calculated" correctly that he could bluff the United States into giving a nonintervention guarantee for Cuba and a trade of Soviet missiles in Cuba for NATO missiles in Turkey. Kennedy and his grandmasters thought they had "won" because they had avoided war, even though the Soviet's were never prepared to engage in warfare at the time.[68]

While the Joint Chiefs of Staff, who had been excluded from the famous White House deliberations of the "ExComm" (short for "executive committee") that managed the crisis, despaired of the endgame ("We've been had!" protested the Navy's chief, Admiral George Anderson), McNamara emerged from the crisis with his reputation—and his arrogance—enhanced. (McNamara, military historian Jeffrey Record wrote, was "The most disastrous American public servant of the twentieth century," combining "a know-it-all arrogance with a capacity for monumental misjudgment and a dearth of moral courage worthy of Albert Speer."[69]) During the crisis McNamara virtually lived at the Pentagon, micromanaging the naval deployment for the Cuban blockade. McNamara and Kennedy even selected which ships approaching Cuba would be intercepted by the navy at sea. According to one account, when Admiral Anderson suggested to McNamara that he leave the details of the blockade to people who had a tradition of running blockades since John Paul Jones, McNamara said that the operation was "not a blockade but a means of communication between Kennedy and Khrushchev."[70]

American policy makers approached the contemporaneous problem in Vietnam in exactly the same spirit. Cyrus Vance, who was a McNamara deputy at the Pentagon in 1962 and who would later serve as

Jimmy Carter's Secretary of State, aptly summarizes their view: "We had seen the gradual application of force applied in the Cuban Missile Crisis and had seen a very successful result. We believed that, if this same gradual and restrained application of force were applied in South Vietnam, one could expect the same result."[71] Another State Department official from the Kennedy administration, Roger Hilsman, wrote that Kennedy "preferred to treat the problem in Vietnam as something other than a war." Johnson followed in the same path. It was the confidence in the ability to use carefully calibrated force to "communicate" with the enemy that led President Johnson to reject advice from the Joint Chiefs of Staff and Barry Goldwater alike in 1964 to either "get in or get out."

Because of the misapprehension of the nature of power and war combined with the confidence in the administrative capacity to engage in boundless social engineering, fundamental questions about Vietnam were never faced. Instead the United States began the lurch from one catastrophe to the next, never questioning the premises of policy. The real turning point was not the Gulf of Tonkin in 1964, but the assassination of South Vietnam's Premier Ngo Dinh Diem in 1963. This was America's social engineering conceit at its worst. Diem was unquestionably a repressive and corrupt autocrat who generated ill-will among the South Vietnamese people and grave doubts within the country's military leadership. Lyndon Johnson had famously called Diem "the Winston Churchill of Southeast Asia" during a visit there in 1961. Not satisfied with this encomium, Johnson added favorable comparisons to George Washington and Franklin Roosevelt as well. When reporter Stanley Karnow pressed him about the comment on the plane home, LBJ struck a more realistic tone: "Shit, Diem's the only boy we've got out there." But by 1963 American policy makers gradually came to the conclusion that the war effort could not succeed with Diem at the helm. He would need to be replaced. Many liberals who would later thump their chest protesting American intervention in the internal affairs of other nations led this crusade. The Americans for Democratic Action, for example, only narrowly defeated a resolution in the summer of 1963 calling for the United States to topple Diem.

The classical approach to this kind of problem was to ask, "If you kill the king, who takes his place?" The United States took a sanguine view of this problem. A CIA report concluded that "there is a reasonably large pool of under-utilized but experienced and trained manpower not only within the military and civilian sector of the present government but also, to some extent, outside. These elements, given continued support from the United States, could provide reasonably effective leadership for the government and the war effort."[72] This view was shared inside the Kennedy administration. Roger Hilsman, the Assistant Secretary of State for Far Eastern Affairs, wrote a memo to Secretary of State Dean Rusk in the late summer of 1963 suggesting that the United States should "encourage the [South Vietnamese] generals to move promptly with the coup," and that "We should make full use of any U.S. equipment available in Vietnam to assist the coup group. . . . If necessary," Hilsman added, "we should bring in U.S. combat forces to assist the coup group achieve victory."[73] (Hilsman resigned a year later, and went on to build a reputation as a critic of the war.)

Even though both the Joint Chiefs of Staff and Vice President Johnson opposed the Diem coup—the JCS said it would be the "Asian Bay of Pigs," while Johnson said it was "playing cowboys and Indians in Saigon"—the coup went forward with American approval on November 1, 1963. (One of the Vietnamese colonels who plotted the coup was discovered after the war to have been a Communist agent all along.) The Vietcong and their sympathizers were giddy at Diem's demise. The leftist British journalist Wilfred Burchett, who had traveled among the Vietcong, told the *Chicago Daily News* that the coup was "a wholly unexpected gift" and marked a turning point in the war. "Diem was a national leader, and you will never be able to replace him—never."[74]

Burchett was swiftly proven correct. Over the next year five different South Vietnamese governments formed and collapsed. Exasperated by this game of musical chairs, an angry President Johnson would later declare that he was "tired of this coup shit." Despite all of Diem's faults, American policy makers quickly came to miss him. Gen. Maxwell Taylor, sent to South Vietnam as American ambassador a few months after the Diem coup, wrote ruefully to Johnson: "I doubt that anyone appreciated the magnitude of the centrifugal political forces which had been kept under control by his iron rule. . . . There is no adequate replacement for Diem in sight."[75] Diem's murder also damaged American standing with other Asian nations. Pakistan's President Ayub Khan tartly told Richard Nixon, visiting Pakistan as a private citizen in 1964, that "Diem's murder meant three things to Asian leaders: that it is dangerous to be a friend of the United States; that it pays to be neutral; and that it sometimes helps to be an enemy!"[76]

Having backed the coup, the United States had effectively taken South Vietnam into receivership and assumed complete responsibility for the fate of the country. The calamitous outcome, however, prompted no doubts about the suitability of Vietnam as a laboratory for American social engineering and demonstrations of the doctrine of flexible response and graduated pressure. National Security Adviser McGeorge Bundy had even gone as far as to describe Vietnam as the key test of America's ability to move all nations toward what he called "a full-fledged *Pax Americana Technocratica.*"[77] Vietnam would get much more than just military advice and supplies; it would get the full welfare state treatment as well. Another Johnson adviser had even spoken in a memo of "a new deal in Vietnam," and the reference was not lost on Johnson, a prodigy of the New Deal. "Why can't we bring in more civilian governors and administrative advisers to help improve the civil problems," Johnson asked his advisers. "Why not get AID, Agriculture, and Peace Corps people in there to help their farming? Damnit, we need to exhibit more compassion for these Vietnamese plain people."[78] Johnson even spoke of establishing "a TVA [power project] on the Mekong Delta" and later of "an Asian Marshall Plan." And why not? If it was possible to speak of creating a new society, or the Great Society, in America, why should not a poor primitive nation be even more malleable to our expertise and wealth?

The confidence in American military and social know-how led to a schizophrenic policy from the earliest moments. Both Kennedy and Johnson emphasized that "it's their war," but did not engage in a serious effort to build up the war-fighting capacity of the South Vietnamese army (as was done in Korea), substituting increments of American power instead. ("Stop trying to set up New England town meetings in Vietnam," America's Ambassador to Thailand, Graham Martin, complained to Johnson's advisers, "and train the South Vietnamese army!") Both Kennedy and Johnson, despite private misgivings, repeatedly resolved that the United States would "win" in Vietnam, and do whatever was necessary to "win." Self-imposed constraints kept them from ever considering a serious war-fighting strategy. American strategists were understandably worried about the prospect of Chinese intervention if the United States took the war directly against the north. The fear of Chinese intervention (the Chinese exploded their first nuclear warhead in 1964), along with domestic political fears of an election year public backlash against a wider war, offered convenient reinforcements for the half-hearted essence of "graduated pressure" that characterized early Vietnam strategy.

The most revealing aspect of the Gulf of Tonkin affair, therefore, was not so much the alleged duplicity or opportunism of Johnson as it was the clear signal Johnson sent to North Vietnam that the United States did not regard the matter as a significant change in the nature of the war. In the meeting with congressional leaders on the afternoon of August 4, Johnson emphasized that the United States wished to "communicate" to North Vietnam that our objectives were narrowly defined, and that our response would be "limited." The word "limited" appeared three times in the draft of the public statement Johnson shared with Congressional leaders. Republican Senate Leader Everett Dirksen criticized this rhetorical restraint: "If I had to do it I would put the word 'limited' in deep freeze." Other legislators'in the meeting echoed Dirksen. Why not say "determined" instead of "limited," Sen. Leverett Saltonstall suggested. Johnson waved them off, saying "We are not going to take it lying down, *but we are not going to destroy their cities.*" (Emphasis added.) This is the same meeting where Johnson had said "some of our boys are floating in the water."[79]

"A great nation," Wellington wrote, "can have no such thing as a little war." The travail of Vietnam arose not so much from the thought that Vietnam was a little war as much as the confusion of the serious business of war and politics with an exercise in crisis management, to be solved through the matrices of game theory. The North Vietnamese leaders were not programmed according to the whiz kids' game theory. They fully intended to employ the same strategy against the United States that they had employed against the French: escalate the war to the point where it became politically unsustainable in the United States. North Vietnamese Premier Pham Van Dong had prophesied to journalist Bernard Fall in 1962 that "Americans do not like long inconclusive wars—and this is going to be a long inconclusive war."[80] America's military restraint and public declarations eschewing a wider war suggested that the United States meant what it said about being disinterested in victory, and reassured the North that they could patiently wait out America without having to face the classic choice between their war aims and the destruction of their country or the loss of their rule. Johnson and his civilian war planners were playing right into the North's hands, a fact that would not even begin to become dimly evident to them for another three years.

CHAPTER TWO

WEDGE: BREAKING UP
THE AMERICAN CONSENSUS

I N RETROSPECT IT IS CLEAR that 1964 witnessed the onset of liberalism's decay, though it was difficult to perceive. To appreciate how this unfolded, it is helpful before proceeding to review briefly two other large events of 1964, the significance of which was hard to judge at the time, but which represented the first glimmerings of the attack on liberalism's flanks that would occur simultaneously from the Right and the Left: the Goldwater campaign, and the Free Speech Movement. To the Goldwater movement, liberalism reacted with condescension; to the restiveness represented by the Free Speech Movement, liberalism responded with incomprehension. Both reactions would eventually prove fatal.

The three main elements of Johnson's presidency—the Civil Rights Act, the foundations of the Great Society, and the expansion of the Vietnam War—set the stage for the fall presidential campaign. Although the election was over before the campaign began, the 1964 campaign was still notable in several important ways that reverberate to this day. It is fashionable to speak nowadays of "wedge issues," which refers to the tactical use of "hot button" controversies in ways that fragment partisan political coalitions. The object is to drive a "wedge" between a candidate and his or her natural base of support. Most wedge issues exist because democratic political parties are always unstable coalitions of contradictory opinions and conflicting interests, never more so than the Democratic New Deal coalition, which united Southern segregationists and Northern

ethnics, intellectuals, and labor unions in the same party for three generations. In 1964 it seemed as though the Goldwater campaign worked two
wedges at once: a wedge splintering the Republican Party, and a wedge
driving the defection of Southern Democrats away from Johnson. Quite
unperceived at the time was the way in which liberalism was driving a
wedge into itself.

Barry Goldwater's wedge into the Republican Party left him with
deep self-inflicted wounds. The nomination contest between Goldwater
and New York Governor Nelson Rockefeller and Pennsylvania Governor
William Scranton had been especially bitter, culminating with the tumultuous convention in San Francisco. A last-ditch attempt by Gov. Scranton
to derail the Goldwater juggernaut backfired. Scranton released a vituper-
ative letter charging that "Goldwaterism has come to stand for a whole
crazy-quilt collection of absurd and dangerous positions." Though Scranton quickly repudiated the letter, which was supposedly written by a junior aide and released without Scranton's approval, the damage had been
done. It helped validate the charge that Goldwater was an "extremist."

So when Goldwater insisted on including his famous phrase, "Extremism in defense of liberty is no vice . . . moderation in the pursuit of justice
is no virtue," it did not matter that the statement's intellectual pedigree
stretched back to Aristotle and Cicero. In the context of 1964, critics
pounced to show that it meant Goldwater was himself an extremist.
Richard Nixon, watching from the convention gallery, said he felt "almost
physically sick" when the heard the famous aphorism. Even Pat Buchanan,
at the time an editorial writer for the *St. Louis Globe-Democrat,* thought
the "extremism" statement imprudent, for it "dealt the ace of trumps to a
Democratic campaign that already had a fistful of trumps to play."
Theodore White recorded the shock of a fellow reporter at Goldwater's
statement: "My God, he's going to run as Barry Goldwater."

The irony of the 1964 campaign is that although Goldwater was defined for all time by his "extremism" comment, the real extremism of the
campaign was mostly on the Democratic side. Negative campaigning and
ruthless personal invective have been staples of American politics since
the Founding, but the attack on Goldwater set some new lows in American political discourse and demonstrated a total loss of proportion. Goldwater's defense of "extremism" opened the floodgates for his foes and the
media to engage in the *reductio ad Hitlerum.* Samples include Martin

Luther King: "We see dangerous signs of Hitlerism in the Goldwater campaign"; Roy Wilkins: "Goldwater's election would bring a police state"; Senator J. William Fulbright: "Goldwater Republicanism is the closest thing in American politics to an equivalent of Russian Stalinism"; California Gov. Pat Brown: Goldwater's acceptance speech "had the stench of fascism. . . . All we needed to hear was 'Heil Hitler'"; Jackie Robinson: "I would say that I now believe I know how it felt to be a Jew in Hitler's Germany"; San Francisco Mayor John Shelley: The Republicans "had *Mein Kampf* as their political bible." Most of the media was happy to amplify this chorus. Columnist Drew Pearson, for example, wrote that "the smell of fascism has been in the air at this convention." The *Chicago Defender* ran the headline: "GOP Convention, 1964 Recalls Germany, 1933."[1] Even the London *Observer,* usually a sober publication, found "disquieting similarities" between Hitler and Goldwater. The media made much of a trumped up "poll" of 1,189 psychiatrists who thought Goldwater was "psychologically unfit" to be president. Goldwater later won a substantial libel suit against the magazine publisher behind this cheap stunt. Only a handful of newspapers endorsed Goldwater in November (one of them, however, was the *Los Angeles Times*).

Not until after the election did a few reporters sheepishly allow that the media had performed shamefully. The *Washington Post*'s David Broder admitted that reporters concealed Goldwater's "essential decency" and that they had presented a "fundamentally distorted picture of who Goldwater was." Even Goldwater remarked about himself that "If I had had to go by the media reports alone, I'd have voted against the sonofabitch, too." It is not much of a stretch to see Goldwater as the first victim of what would later become known as "political correctness."

With a huge lead in the polls and the media acting as a megaphone for every wild distortion made against Goldwater, the Johnson campaign would seem to have been afforded the luxury of taking the high road. But Johnson, thirsting for a record landslide, decided to pile on instead. The most notorious low blow was the famous "daisy" TV spot, where a little girl picking flower petals is drowned out by a countdown to a nuclear explosion. Although Goldwater was never mentioned in the ad, the implication was clear. The ad only ran once, but news broadcasts repeated the ad numerous times—an early example of clever manipulation of "free" media. Another ad showing two hands ripping up a Social Security card—a deliberate distortion of Goldwater's opinion that Social Security ought to be made voluntary some day—was a mainstay of the Johnson campaign. Johnson's campaign almost ran an ad linking Goldwater to the Ku Klux Klan; a Johnson aide admitted that "it strained the available evidence."[2] The Johnson campaign showed the future of political advertising. Kathleen Hall Jamieson estimates that in 1960 less than 15 percent of broadcast ads were negative ads; in 1964 fully half were. By the 1980s, nearly three-quarters of broadcast ads in presidential campaigns were negative.

Negative advertising was not the Johnson campaign's most egregious abuse. In a series of activities that make the Watergate burglary pale in comparison, Johnson used both the CIA and the FBI to gather intelligence on the Goldwater campaign. E. Howard Hunt, who would be a central figure in the Watergate affair eight years later, ran the CIA's intelligence operation within the Goldwater campaign. Johnson also ordered the FBI to bug Goldwater's campaign plane, and circumstantial evidence suggests that Goldwater's campaign office telephones were bugged too. The information generated from this effort enabled the Johnson campaign to anticipate and preempt Goldwater's campaign tactics. For Johnson, Goldwater biographer Lee Edwards ironically observed, "extremism in the pursuit of the presidency was no vice."

The real significance of the 1964 campaign, however, was not the new style of negative campaigning nor the abuse of government power by the president, but what it revealed about the state of American political culture, especially among the dominant liberals. The significance of the Goldwater campaign is that, as Lee Edwards wrote, "for the first time in thirty years, a presidential candidate was challenging the basic assumptions of the welfare state."[3] Liberals were used to dismissing conservatism as the lunatic conspiracy ravings of the John Birch Society (still very prominent in 1964), and simply wouldn't take Goldwater's substantive challenge seriously. The premises of the welfare state were so axiomatic among liberals as not to require any articulation or defense. Goldwater's themes were simply brushed aside with a wave. "Whether government should or should not tamper with the private economy," economist Robert Lekachman wrote, is an "obsolete question." Lekachman brusquely dismissed the economists advising Goldwater, including Milton Friedman and other members of the Chicago School, as an "ingenious sect" and "a minority position among economists."[4]

Instead of engaging Goldwater in a debate about the issues, Goldwater was treated with condescension. For liberals his ideas were so far beneath contempt as not to require serious discussion. Johnson refused to debate Goldwater, in contrast to President Kennedy, who had casually discussed with Goldwater the idea of a series of national debates. A few liberals recognized that this refusal to engage the enemy might have unfortunate consequences. Lekachman lamented after the election that "a realistic economic debate never occurred during the campaign. Never compelled to describe his program (if he has one) for the Great Society, the President remained the unchallenged master of the realm of generous platitude."[5]

For the most part, though, liberals discussed Goldwater and conservatism as though they were some kind of irrational pathology. The Republican Party was being patted on the head, as though it were an immature child, for having behaved irresponsibly. Liberal intellectuals wrote with the presumption that they had the right to determine what kind of conservatism was acceptable in American life, and who the Republican Party should be allowed to choose as its nominee. The tacit message was that the Republican Party could compete in national politics only insofar as it remained the "me too" party it had been in the aftermath of the New Deal, a loyal opposition or adjunct party to the natural majority Democrats. Hans Morgenthau, the dean of American strategic thought at the time (and in some ways the precursor to Henry Kissinger), wrote that Goldwater's philosophy amounted to "political romanticism . . . the historic recollection of a state once attained." This was a polite and sophisticated way of calling Goldwater a reactionary. "Goldwater has imposed an alien conservative philosophy upon an unwilling Republican party. . . . This kind of conservatism," Morgenthau concluded, "has no place in the American tradition of politics."[6] Richard Hofstadter wrote of Goldwater: "When, in all our history, has anyone with ideas so bizarre, so archaic, so self-confounding, so remote from the basic American consensus, ever got so far?"[7]

A related theme was that Goldwater represented the politics of "nostalgia." The theologian Reinhold Niebuhr wrote that Goldwaterism "could be more simply defined as an expression of national nostalgia, as a yearning for the good old days of uncomplicated domestic and foreign issues. . . . It is still one of the mysteries of the American political process that a man so far to the Right should have become the nominee of a major party." Political scientist Samuel Lubell wrote: "the Republicans remain what the Southern Democrats were after the Civil War—essentially a party of nostalgia. There is one instinctive Republican program, in whose favor all doubts are resolved—to turn the clock back to an earlier era."

Liberals saw the LBJ landslide as a vindication of their presumption that they needn't take Goldwater seriously. In the aftermath, liberals piled on even more gleefully. The American Jewish Committee's David Danzig wrote that "the Republican Party has been overwhelmingly repudiated for its secession from contemporary American society."[8] Lekachman gloated: "The Republican Party has been suitably punished for its self-indulgence in the politics of nostalgia." Richard Rovere wrote one of the most caustic and dismissive summaries: "One question posed—in my mind, anyway—by the repudiation of Goldwater was whether we could shake, once and for all, the notion that there was an important political dialogue taking place in this country between, on the one hand, the writers of the *National Review* school, and, on the other hand, just about everyone else. . . . Goldwaterism and Buckley conservatism simply do not contain any ideas that can be given institutional form. . . . From the rightist intellectuals we have had almost nothing but insults to the intelligence." But Rovere allowed, less than half-seriously, that "if Buckley and his men keep at it, Goldwaterism may triumph by 1996 or thereabouts."[9]

Liberals were not even slowed up by the fact that although Goldwater was buried, he still received 27 million votes, and 27 million voters in 1964 did not constitute an insignificant block. But liberals found easy rationalizations for this. Seymour Martin Lipset wrote that "the major factor determining how people voted was party allegiance."[10] Only about 5 or 6 million of the 27 million, it was said, were really Goldwater true-believers; the rest were just loyal Republicans. This overlooked the signs of enormous grassroots enthusiasm for Goldwater. Nixon's 1960 campaign had received about 40,000 individual donations; Goldwater had received more than 1 million donations, 400,000 of which were in amounts less than $10. (The Goldwater campaign, in the unsurprising fashion of fiscal conservatism, ended the campaign with a $1 million surplus.) The Goldwater campaign fielded 500,000 volunteers on election day. Against the charge that it was only habitual Republicans who voted for Goldwater, *National Review* remarked: "those 27,000,000 Goldwater voters knew precisely for whom and for what they were voting, and would have stuck their hands into a barrel of rattlesnakes to pull the Goldwater lever." There is something comical about the idea of middle-class American suburbanites who enthusiastically supported Goldwater being regarded as "extremists." It was the making of what would later be called "the silent majority." Only the true believers could see the possibilities arising from the Goldwater movement at the time. (One of them was a Kansas Congressman named Bob Dole, who told *Time* magazine: "Goldwater's victory anchors a party which has been adrift for some years. Now we can, in candor, go out and make speeches for spending cuts and sound conservative principles, certain that we won't be undercut by the leaders of our party."[11])

Liberals did themselves and the cause of liberalism a terrible disservice with this condescension, because, as Theodore White admitted, Goldwater arrived on the scene "at a time when the intellectual vitality had apparently run out of the generation-old liberal orthodoxy."[12] "[L]iberals had every reason to think of themselves as the governing class of the Nation," Pat Moynihan observed a decade later. But "this condition of unchallenged hegemony was in fact the primary challenge liberalism faced: a formula for decline. . . . The prolonged absence of a serious political and intellectual opposition was in the end deeply debilitating."[13]

The basic problem of American liberalism in the 1960s might best be explained this way. Whereas Goldwater's defensive slogan was "In your heart you know he's right," the liberal's tacit slogan, betrayed in countless ways, could have been: "In your heart you know Marx is right." While Goldwater was defensive about the acceptability of his ideas with the American people, sixties liberals were defensive about the acceptability of their own innermost ideals and aims, because of their great confusion and insecurity about democratic capitalism. Liberals (most of them anyway) did not regard themselves as socialists, but they were for government economic planning and regulation; they were against egalitarian redistributionism, but for vastly expanding the welfare state and eventually for instituting a guaranteed annual income. Liberals were not Marxists, but were besotted with class theory, and felt compelled at various turns to genuflect in Marx's direction. In the liberal mind Marx and Marxism was always the elephant in the room that everyone else pretended not to notice; the liberal intellectual journals of the day were filled with nods to Marx.

The root of liberal guilt was the view that the undemocratic socialist economies of the world were more fully committed than the United States to the liberal ideals of equality and justice, and perhaps even better able to deliver on those ideals, too. For example, Columbia University Professor Charles Frankel, whom President Johnson would appoint to be Assistant Secretary of State for Educational and Cultural Affairs, wrote in his book *The Case for Modern Man:* "Our fear of Marxism, one cannot help but suspect, reflects our interest in it, a nagging feeling that it is one step ahead of us in providing what we all need—some sense of where we are going and how we are to get there."[14] It was only the practical constraint of America's political moderation that kept liberals from fully embracing socialist policies. It was only a few years before that Soviet Premier Khrushchev had triumphantly promised that "History is on our side; we will bury you," and many western liberals (and, not insignificantly, the CIA) were prepared to believe that the Soviet economic model might well produce better results than democratic capitalism. For years successive editions of Paul Samuelson's leading college textbook on introductory economics said that "The Soviet economy is proof that . . . a socialist command economy can function and even thrive."[15] And even as late as 1984 John Kenneth Galbraith was still contending that "Communism succeeds because, unlike western industrial economies, it makes full use of its manpower."[16] To such thinking, any level of unemployment and poverty in western democracies was a mark of the West's moral inferiority and lack of social enlightenment.

This lack of confidence in the moral and economic superiority of democratic capitalism was not limited to liberal intellectuals. In an interview with the anchors of the three TV networks in March of 1964, President Johnson compared the United States and Soviet Union, noting that "they have more people and resources, but we have one thing they don't have, and that is our system of private enterprise." But then Johnson vitiated the high ground with his next sentence: "I may not be a great president, but as long as I am here, I am going to try my best to be a good president and do my level best *to see this system preserved.*"[17] (Emphasis added.) The New Left could sense liberalism's vulnerability in such equivocal and self-doubting rhetoric. Liberalism's defensiveness about the moral and economic superiority of the West would turn into a complete collapse in the face of the New Left's subsequent full frontal assault on the legitimacy of democratic capitalism. The Goldwater campaign represented an opportunity for mainstream liberalism to respond the challenge to justify itself and rearticulate its premises before a sympathetic electorate. Its refusal to do so would haunt them.

THE FIRST HARBINGER of the agony to come for liberalism started at the University of California at Berkeley in the fall of 1964, when five students were summoned to the Dean's office at the end of September for violating a new policy regarding political activity on university grounds. The students were facing suspension. By the time it was all over three months later, it was clear that university life would never be the same.

"The war began," Berkeley professor John Searle wrote later, "like many wars, over a boundary dispute." Activist groups enjoyed setting up tables outside the Bancroft Avenue entrance to the campus to hawk their literature and enlist new cadres to their cause. There was some ambiguity about whether the city of Berkeley or the university owned the sidewalk outside Sproul Gate—it was not until several years later that the question of title was determined in favor of the city. The university decided in mid-September to assert its ownership and enforce its rules restricting political activity on the sidewalk location. University rules had always prohibited "political activity" and political fundraising on campus, though this had not entailed any significant restriction on the range of opinion expressed. "Berkeley was one of the few places in the country," Nathan Glazer wrote, "where in 1964 one could hear a public debate between the supporters of Khrushchev and Mao on the Sino-Soviet dispute—there were organized student groups behind both positions."[18] But Berkeley's attempt to impose some reasonable restrictions related to the educational purpose of the campus was about to run headfirst into the kinetic energy of the student body. Students reacted to the new rules in predictable fashion: More groups immediately set up sidewalk tables in defiance of the ban. In the first of a series of miscalculations and blunders, the administration set about to enforce the new rules, citing unfounded concerns about how the sidewalk tables were "impeding traffic."

University administrators badly misjudged the temperament of student activists. Earnest protest and street theater were a revered collegiate tradition, and Berkeley students had always been politically active. Several students had been arrested in 1960 at a protest of hearings held in San Francisco by the House Committee on Un-American Activities. The 1964 Republican convention in San Francisco provided another convenient venue for student high jinks. In 1964 the political activism had taken a more serious turn. A number of Berkeley students had become active in the civil rights movement. There were campus chapters of the Congress on Racial Equality (CORE) and the Student Non-Violent Coordinating Committee (SNCC). (Both were chaired by white students at Berkeley.) Berkeley was not Mississippi, of course, though in the hothouse atmosphere of the civil rights movement any slight was taken as a pretext for alleging such an equivalence in the one-dimensional student mind. In addition to local protests and sit-ins against employers thought to discriminate against blacks in hiring, several students had traveled to Mississippi to participate in the civil rights movement's "Mississippi Freedom Summer." Like other civil rights activists from outside the South who were visiting there for the first time, it was a hardening experience. "A student who has been chased by the KKK in Mississippi," one Berkeley undergraduate laconically observed, "is not easily intimidated by academic bureaucrats."

So when the university administration attempted to enforce its rules against political activity, students newly acquainted with the civil rights tactics of nonviolent resistance saw an opportunity handed to them on a silver platter. Four hundred students appeared outside the Dean's office on the afternoon of September 30, declaring that they had been equally responsible for operating the sidewalk tables and demanding that they receive the same punishment as the five students originally cited. The administration ignored the assembled students, and announced at 11:45 P.M. (the student throng was still outside the Dean's office) that the five students, along with three others thought to be organizers of the sidewalk tables, were to be placed on "indefinite suspension," a punishment that was not a regular disciplinary measure. There would be no negotiation about the university's rules. "As soon as I heard the news," David Lance Goines, one of the suspended students, wrote, "I realized with a thrill that I was having the best time I'd ever had in my life. I was up to my ears in excitement. . . ."[19]

The thrill ride was just beginning. Subsequent legend held that the Free Speech Movement, as the Berkeley affair quickly became celebrated, involved radical leftists and libertines who wanted license to shout obscenities. With the passage of time the descent into the "Filthy Speech Movement" has become blurred; that episode actually occurred many months later. In fact the Free Speech Movement of 1964 encompassed students groups from across the entire political spectrum, including campus conservatives and religious groups. The Young Republicans and Cal Students for Goldwater joined the Free Speech Movement in opposing the university's arbitrary restrictions, though they did not join the sit-ins that were soon to come. (Indeed the far Left did not like the broad liberal scope of the protest; Seymour Martin Lipset reported later that a Communist trade union official from San Francisco quietly offered to the UC Regents to have the student protest ended if the University would expel the student leaders.[20]) As usually happens in politically volatile situations, the leftward most element, along with the merely rebellious element that can always be counted upon to magnify the difficulty of any situation, soon began driving events.

The day after the suspensions were announced, October 1, defiant students naturally set up tables outside Sproul Hall. A crowd of 2,000 soon assembled to take part in the rally. The police approached Jack Weinberg, an honors graduate in mathematics, and threatened him with arrest. The administration apparently singled out Weinberg for arrest because, as a non-student, he could be legitimately charged with trespassing. (Weinberg, the head of the Berkeley chapter of CORE, is credited with having promulgated the popular slogan, "Don't trust anyone over 30.") The police carried Weinberg away to a nearby police car, whereupon the theater began in earnest. Hundreds of students sat down around the police car, making it impossible for the police to remove Weinberg from the scene. Soon students began clambering atop the police car to make speeches. It was at this venue that Mario Savio emerged as the ironic leader of the Free Speech Movement—ironic because he had heretofore been known for his considerable stutter. When Savio was extremely angry, however, his stutter disappeared.

This tableau carried on through the night and into the next day, with a constant parade of speakers holding forth from the roof of the police car, offering Thoreau's meditations on civil disobedience as a refrain. The incident was front-page news throughout California, usually sensationalized with banner headlines such as the *San Francisco Examiner*'s "Reds on Campus." (The *Examiner* also ran a composite photograph prominently displaying a book on Marxism in the foreground.) As a large contingent of police moved in to surround the scene and fears of a riot grew, the president of the University of California, Clark Kerr, made his entrance, opening up negotiations with students leaders to end the situation.

A compromise was struck: The university would not press the trespassing charge against Weinberg, and would appoint a special committee to work out a new policy on political activity. The students and the police dispersed (the students later took up a collection to pay for damage to the police car), and Weinberg was released after a pro forma booking at the police station. By the time it was over, Weinberg had sat in the back seat of the police car for 37 hours, with only a single, carefully negotiated trip to the student union building to use the bathroom.

Kerr and the administration thought the commotion was over. During the next six weeks, an uneasy truce prevailed as the special committee of administrators and students deliberated about new rules. The administration agreed to relax rules on political activity on campus subject to one caveat—that advocacy of "illegal" activity be prohibited. The protestors aligned with the civil rights movement thought this proviso was directed against them, since they often rallied to recruit participants for sit-ins and other acts of civil disobedience. But many student activists were inclined to accept the terms of the compromise. The Free Speech Movement, by now a carefully organized body, called for a new protest sit-in outside Sproul Hall for November 23, but the sit-in only attracted about 300 people. The administration this time wisely did nothing, and the sit-in was called off after a few hours of boredom. The Free Speech Movement seemed to be fizzling out. Only a colossal blunder by the administration could revive its fortunes. And blunder is exactly what the administration proceeded to do.

During the negotiations after the police car incident, it was thought that some kind of amnesty would be given to the students involved in that incident, as well as perhaps the lifting of the suspensions of the original eight students disciplined on September 30. But over the Thanksgiving holiday weekend, the administration announced that it would expel several students involved in the October 1–2 events. The Free Speech Movement exploded back to life. On the following Wednesday a large crowd gathered outside Sproul Hall, where Mario Savio called for a student strike to bring the campus to a "grinding halt." Joan Baez appeared and sang "We Shall Overcome." Then 1,500 students marched into the building, led by the American flag at the head of the procession, and proceeded to sit down in the hallways. The sit-in was wholly peaceful; the students took care not to block doorways or otherwise seriously impede the operations of the university. As day gave way to night, no arrests had been made, and about half the students had left while the remainder bedded down for the night. "It appeared to me that at last the administration was getting clever," professor John Searle wrote. "I thought they would sit there harmlessly while the faculty came up with a solution."[21] Instead the administration made its second blunder of the week.

The publicity over the events at Berkeley was bringing pressure on Governor Pat Brown and the university regents, both of whom pressed Kerr to take a stronger stand against the student protesters. (Among local law enforcement officials who were concerned by reports, which proved to be erroneous, that students were vandalizing offices in Sproul Hall was Alameda County Assistant District Attorney Edwin Meese. Two years later Ronald Reagan would relentlessly attack Brown for not having demanded that "those damn kids ought to shut up and go back to class or get tossed out.") At 3 A.M., 600 police and state highway patrolmen entered Sproul Hall and began making arrests. In good civil rights fashion, the protesting students went limp and had to be carried out one at a time, a process that took over 12 hours. More than 800 students were arrested by the time the building was finally cleared.

By now the situation was spinning out of control. The student strike took hold as graduate teaching assistants and a large number of faculty cancelled classes. Rumors of a national guard occupation, mass expulsions of students and, most improbable of all, mass firings of faculty swept the campus over the weekend. The faculty, hitherto annoyed by the student protest, was beginning to swing over to the students' side. In the meantime President Kerr was working behind the scenes with senior faculty members to work out a new compromise settlement. The new settlement promised to desist from disciplinary proceedings against students involved in protests prior to December 3 (the students arrested in Sproul Hall would have to face the music, though), but did not resolve the issue of what restrictions the university would enforce on campus advocacy. "Any attempt to solve the crisis without meeting those issues was bound to fail," Professor Searle wrote. "Having ignited the fuel, one can't stop the fire by blowing on the match."[22]

President Kerr attempted to present the compromise as a *fait accompli* at an extraordinary campus meeting in the outdoor Greek theater on Monday, December 7—Pearl Harbor Day. Fifteen thousand students and faculty showed up. The meeting was a fiasco, culminating in yet another administration blunder. As the meeting adjourned, Mario Savio approached the microphone hoping to make some brief comments. Police intercepted Savio and carried him off the stage, one officer pulling him by his necktie. (In those days many students, including several Free Speech Movement leaders, routinely wore coats and ties on campus.) Faculty members were appalled. The students in the audience began to chant, "We want Mario! We want Mario!" Indignant faculty members besieged Kerr offstage, and amidst confusion Savio was released and allowed to give brief remarks. He announced simply that there would be a noon rally at Sproul Hall.

More than 10,000 students showed up for the Sproul Hall rally, where the crowd roared their disapproval for the new administration compromise. A telegram from Bertrand Russell arrived: "You have my full and earnest support. Warm greetings." (Russell had also telegrammed Gov. Brown demanding that he stop the "oppression" of Berkeley students). The leaders of the Free Speech Movement, sensing that events were moving in their favor, called off the strike. The next day the faculty senate delivered the *coup de grace* to the administration, voting, by a lopsided 824–115 margin, in favor of two resolutions that effectively called for the administration to capitulate to the students. This bold stroke made clear that the inmates were in charge of the asylum. Despite some rearguard attempts over the next few weeks by the administration and the university regents to reassert some control, the Free Speech Movement had won.

Exactly what this victory entailed was not immediately clear. Even critics of the Free Speech Movement admitted that many of their original grievances against arbitrary university restrictions of political activism were just, and faulted the administration for their ineptitude. Three months after the climax at Sproul Hall, Prof. Nathan Glazer, who had attempted to mediate between the students and the administration at various times during the crisis, wrote in *Commentary* that "one fears that the future of American higher education may be foreshadowed here. . . . A great wave of energy has been released." Norman Podhoretz saw it as a "warning shot across the bow." If liberal critics of the events at Berkeley seemed a bit vague in their unease, it was for two reasons: The Free Speech Movement had begun to expose and rub raw what would increasingly become the open sore of liberal hypocrisy, and liberal intellectuals could also recognize, somehow or dimly, the attenuation of their own ideas at work. If this was the opening act, what would the second and third acts bring?

Before the Free Speech Movement, the idea of a popular student movement on the Left seemed remote if not outlandish. Young people and students had shown little interest or enthusiasm for radical or avant-garde ideas. The veteran leftist writer I. F. Stone recalled that when he gave speeches at Harvard in the 1950s, most of his audience were older people; few students attended. Stone was not much impressed with the first wave of student radicals that did emerge, remarking that "I've seen snot-nosed Marxist-Leninists come and go."[23] Although the left-wing Students for a Democratic Society (SDS) had been founded with much fanfare in 1962, it had fewer than 2,000 members in 1964. Its famous *Port Huron Statement* calling for the founding of a new Left hadn't yet caught on. "Almost no students value activity as citizens," the *Port Huron Statement* lamented. "Passive in public, they are hardly more idealistic in arranging their private lives."

The biggest student political organization in the nation at the time was on the Right—the Young Americans for Freedom (YAF), which had nearly 28,000 members. Its founding document of principles, the *Sharon Statement*, adopted in 1960, would prove to be much more enduring, but much less celebrated, than the *Port Huron Statement*. The *Sharon Statement* was also a mere 370 words long, in contrast to the ponderous *Port Huron Statement* that meandered for 15 pages. While the SDS inaugural gathering at Port Huron in 1962 consisted of fewer than 60 people, YAF attracted 18,000 students to a Madison Square Garden rally the same year. In a 1962 book, *The Coming Campus Revolt,* conservative author M. Stanton Evans predicted that a wave of student activism was on the way—from the Right. Some liberals agreed. Murray Kempton wrote in the *New York Post* that "the conservative revival is *the* youth movement of the 60s and may even be as important to the epoch as the Young Communist League was to the 30s."[24] For several years establishment liberals had forecast that the radical threat existed on the Right, from the John Birch Society and other remnants of that favorite liberal bogeyman, "McCarthyism."

Yet the revolt against liberalism would end up being more ferocious from the Left than the Right. Most accounts explain the origins of the leftward direction of the 1960s ferment as a reaction to the "conformism" of the 1950s, and point to intellectual forebears such as Paul

Goodman's *Growing Up Absurd,* William White's *The Organization Man,* David Reisman's *The Lonely Crowd,* and especially the radical sociology of C. Wright Mills. The "counterculture" of the 1960s, according to the standard account, represented the mass retailing of this intellectual current along with the rebellious attitude and posturing of the Beat poets such as Allen Ginsberg and Jack Kerouac. When restless young people, surging onto college campuses in record numbers in the 1960s (the 1964 freshman class at Berkeley bulged by 37 percent over the year before), sought for the means to articulate their restlessness, they found a ready-made body of social criticism waiting for them.

It was natural that Berkeley students issued IBM punch cards at registration (with the infamous instruction, "Do not fold, spindle, or mutilate") would resist being regarded as cogs in the machine. Clark Kerr's ill-chosen description of the modern "multiversity" as "knowledge factories" for the industrial economy only fueled the fire of left-wing paranoia and resentment. "The employers will love this generation," Kerr said. "They aren't going to press many grievances. They are going to be easy to handle. There aren't going to be any riots."[25] Paul Goodman, for example, had written preposterously that "At the present time in the United States, students—middle class youths—are the major exploited class."[26]

Technocratic liberals like Kerr, whom historian William O'Neill aptly described as "the Robert McNamara of higher education," made easy and convenient targets. It was not surprising, therefore, that Mario Savio's most memorable refrain from the Free Speech Movement was "stop the machine!" At this early point Vietnam was not on anyone's mind. The SDS, in fact, was divided about whether to call for U.S. withdrawal. "The greatest problem of our nation," Savio said, was "depersonalized, unresponsive bureaucracy." This language, it is worth noting, was not far from what Barry Goldwater had told a YAF rally in 1961, where he praised the conservative student movement as "an intelligent and responsible revolt from the pigeon-holing effects of regimentation and centralization of power in the United States."[27]

Even Ronald Reagan would express sympathy with this critique of university life, acknowledging in the midst of a subsequent Berkeley controversy in 1969 the "resentment of an entire college generation that finds itself being fed into a knowledge factory with no regard to their individuality, aspirations or their dreams."[28] Clearly the liberal establishment was in for some long days ahead.

This standard interpretation of the origins of 1960s student radicalism is not wrong, but does not go deep enough. That the predominant attack on the liberal establishment found more strength on the Left than the Right should not have come as a surprise. If one takes a wide-angle view, it is possible to see that the 1960s began in the 1930s or earlier. All of the intellectual antecedents to the 1960s' radical critique of middle-class American life were present and spreading rapidly in the 1920s and 1930s, including the literature of "alienation" and, most importantly, the deep affinity for the Soviet Union among leftist intellectuals. The ideological Left has never been happy with the moderate liberal consensus that has characterized American politics practically since the Founding.

The Great Depression seemed momentarily to be an opportunity to shift America's political consensus to the Left, but one thing stopped the momentum of radical thought and prevented its wider acceptance: World War II and its aftermath. In addition to rallying the great mass of middle-class people to the cause of western democracy and inoculating them from the superficial charms of radicalism, at the same time a great number of the radical intellectuals of that earlier generation were severely disillusioned about Communism by the Soviet purge trails and the Hitler-Stalin pact that began the war. These jarring events caused thoughtful people on the Left to reevaluate their critique of democracy and the United States. Although remaining on the Left, many intellectuals surprised themselves with their newfound patriotism; Mary McCarthy remarked that she began to set aside her contempt for "bourgeois society" when she realized that she cared about the outcome of the war, and hoped the Allies would win.

But if there was a newfound moderation and realism among the Old Left (as it came to be known), their intellectual premises were still loose upon the land, waiting to be embraced and adapted by the next generation. Since the Enlightenment the essential premise of intellectual life has been that human nature is perfectible without limit, and that political power—to be wielded by intellectuals, of course—should be harnessed to achieve this improvement. It is not too great a vulgarization to stipulate that this premise is at the root of nearly every ideology and wave of idealism since the Enlightenment, and it seems to be the fate of the modern world to wrestle with this enthusiasm in a new form every generation. The 1960s would prove to be the Left's next big opportunity to challenge America's political consensus.

When the student movement turned increasingly radical as the decade wore on, old liberals were dismayed. The eminent literary critic Lionel Trilling, Norman Podhoretz observed, "ruefully reflected that the demonstrators he found himself opposing were in a profound sense his own students: where else had they learned the language of 'alienation' from American society but in his own classroom?"[29] The subsequent prominence of the Vietnam War as a focus of student protest obscures this, but the fact that the radical ferment of the later 1960s was a world-wide phenomenon, and not just limited to the campuses and Upper West Side salons of the United States, suggests that there was more at work than mere antiwar sentiment.

In retrospect it can be seen that the acceleration and extension of the critical tradition in the 1960s was a crucial step in the descent into the nihilistic anti-Americanism that characterized the student movement and campus radicalism in the latter half of the 1960s. Disillusionment would come to many of this generation of leftist intellectuals and activists, too, but not before they had achieved a vast impact on American culture and institutions. The Free Speech Movement led ironically to diminution of speech in the university, and to a new conformity vastly more stifling than anything Paul Goodman could have imagined at the time. Long after the fire of 1960s radicalism had burned itself out, its toxic residue remained to poison the intellectual life of most universities. That story is still being played out today.

CHAPTER THREE

RAZOR: THE GREAT SOCIETY AND ITS DISCONTENTS

———⋙⊸⊰———

Oскнам's Razor, as every college freshman learns, is the medieval axiom coined by William of Ockham that holds that the simplest explanation is usually the right one. Paul Potter, the new president of the SDS, may have had Ockham's Razor in mind on April 17, 1965, when he stepped to the microphone near the Washington Monument to address a crowd of 15,000 that had assembled in the first significant protest against the Vietnam War. "The incredible war in Vietnam," Potter said, "has provided the razor, the terrifying sharp cutting edge that has finally severed the last vestiges of illusion that morality and democracy are the guiding principles of American foreign policy." But the problem went far beyond mere hypocrisy, Potter thought. The war "has its roots deep in the institutions of American society." Underlying it all was "the system."

"We must name that system," Potter summed up. "We must name it, describe it, analyze it, understand it and change it." Although Carl Oglesby, Potter's successor as SDS president, tried to name the system "corporate liberalism," it was "The System" itself, in capital letters, that quickly became the rhetorical Holy Grail of the burgeoning protest movement, to which it was able to apply the equally amorphous "Movement" as the antidote. In so doing, a simple explanation decayed into a simplistic one; the razor morphed into a blunt instrument.

The rapidly escalating Vietnam War provided dry fuel for the fire of New Left radicalism that was otherwise in danger of flickering out. The New Left was losing interest in civil rights (especially now that the 1964 Act had passed), and needed a new focal point. The Old Left had had the labor movement as a rallying point; organizing the work force of major corporations was a large but coherent target. The New Left would have the Vietnam War as a convenient rallying point, and organizing the universities would serve as a substitute for organizing workers. The Free Speech Movement had shown the incendiary potential of the university to be, as the SDS's *Port Huron Statement* hoped, "a community of controversy." But the unspecific nature of the attack on "The System" belied an emptiness at the core of the New Left, even an anti-intellectualism that appalled older leftist intellectuals who hitherto regarded anti-intellectualism as the sole province of the Goldwater Right.

The *Port Huron Statement* (drafted chiefly by 22-year-old Tom Hayden) had attacked "the conventional moral terms of the age" such as "free world" and "people's democracy" as "ruling myths [rather] than . . . descriptive principles." Yet the New Left had little to offer in the way of concrete moral terms of its own, beyond watery appeals to "authenticity" and "participatory democracy," which seemed somehow to mean politics without acknowledged leaders and the raw pursuit of power for power's sake. Irving Howe was not alone in thinking that the energy of the New Left was mostly "a gesture of moral rectitude."[1] The legendary socialist Norman Thomas was similarly unimpressed, remarking about the *Port Huron Statement:* "I've seen a lot of manifestoes in my day, and this one's no worse, nor no better."[2] The New Left's sentimental slogans, noted Tom Kahn of the League for Industrial Democracy (an Old Left organization), appealed perfectly to the "romantic defeatism" of the free-floating anxiety that is typical among disaffected youth—how can we hope to prevail against a Leviathan-like "System"?[3] And Norman Podhoretz, who decided against publishing a condensed version of the *Port Huron Statement* in *Commentary,* was troubled by a premonition of "dogmatic authoritarianism" implied in the New Left's rhetoric.[4]

The war allowed the New Left to generate energy and acquire momentum without having to confront its intellectual weaknesses, and in the process it aimed a dagger at the heart of mainstream liberalism. The New Left set aside its last lingering reservations about opposing the war (as late as January 1965 Todd Gitlin could write that "there is dispute within SDS as to whether we should be for withdrawal") and began to prosper as a result. SDS membership grew from 2,000 at the end of 1964 to more than 10,000 by the following fall. Still, a 15,000-person Washington protest (which gradually fizzled as the day wore on), and "teach-ins" involving at best another 20,000 students (out of 5.5 million enrolled in colleges and universities at the time), amounted to no more than a blip on the radar screen of American public life.

"Don't pay any attention to what those little shits on the campuses do," President Johnson told George Ball. Johnson expected the political challenge to Vietnam to come from the Right. "The great beast is the reactionary elements in the country. Those are the people that we have to fear."[5] Mainstream liberal opinion held firm. Even as unease about the war began to grow, it did not appear likely that mainstream liberals, let alone the further reaches of the Old Left, would become unified or strongly vocal against the war. Arthur Schlesinger Jr., the liberal's liberal, advocated sending *more* troops to Vietnam in the Spring of 1965, and *Dissent* ("A Quarterly of Socialist Opinion" whose editorial board included such prominent leftists as Michael Harrington, Michael Walzer, and Paul Goodman) editorialized that U.S. withdrawal from Vietnam "would be an act of callousness" and "inhumane."[6] *New York Times* columnist James Reston deplored the first campus anti-war "teach-ins" in the spring of 1965 as "propaganda of the most vicious nature."[7]

Much has been made over the years of the New Left's supposed symbiotic relationship with the middle class it so ostentatiously rejected; most New Left activists were from middle-class households (quite a number from divorced middle-class households, Todd Gitlin observed), and the youth of the New Left depended upon the sentiment of middle-class negation for what little self-definition they had. More important as the months unfolded was the New Left's symbiotic relationship with the degeneracy of the Johnson administration, which seemed determined to squander the fund of support it had with liberals and the public.

The New Left leaders who had toyed with "corporate liberalism" as a name for "The System" were on to something, for corporate liberalism was simply another label for the ideology of the administrative state that had been developing since the Progressive Era. Indeed, Paul Potter had rightly noted in his April 17 speech that the Johnson administration regarded Vietnam as "a laboratory run by a new breed of gamesmen who approach war as a kind of rational exercise." Most narratives of the 1960s offer the view that the Vietnam War and the Great Society were in tension with one another, and it is certainly true on the surface that the war threatened to undermine the momentum for Johnson's beloved social programs. On a deeper level, though, the corporate liberal ideology at the heart of the Great Society was also central to the mishandling of the war, and is the common thread between them. At this early point the New Left still spoke in a critical and even generous spirit. Potter himself said that "I do not believe that the president or Mr. Rusk or Mr. McNamara or even McGeorge Bundy are particularly evil men. If asked to throw napalm on the back of a ten-year-old child they would shrink in horror." Within two years, of course, the war protests would be punctuated with chants of "Hey, hey LBJ, how many kids did you kill today?" It was not clear in 1965 that liberalism was entering a crisis phase, and would soon lose its virtue and cross the point of no return.

The basic premise of "corporate liberalism" or the "administrative state" is that the world's "complexity" requires active expert management, properly enlightened by social science. The corporate liberals of the 1960s brought this same attitude to its management of the Vietnam War. Air Force General Curtis LeMay thought that McNamara's "Whiz Kids" at the Pentagon were "the most egotistical people that I have ever seen in my whole life. They had no faith in the military at all. They felt that the Harvard Business School method of solving problems would solve any problem in the world."[8]

While the Joint Chiefs of Staff had told Johnson as early as March of 1964 that the United States should "either get in or get out," and that "half-measures won't win," the civilian war planners' supreme confidence in the ability of "graduated pressure" to mold the will of North Vietnam caused them to reject the military's counsel. A special Pentagon war games unit conducted its SIGMA I study in April 1964, and concluded with eerie prescience that graduated pressure starting with bombing would lead the United States inevitably to commit sizeable ground forces, to which the North Vietnamese would effectively respond by stepping up the tempo of guerrilla attacks in South Vietnam. McNamara and his aides were unimpressed. "This is a different kind of war," one of McNamara's aides lectured the Joint Chiefs.

"Every quantitative measure we have shows we're winning," McNamara had been saying since 1962. "North Vietnam will never beat us; they can't even make ice cubes," the former Ford man contemptuously remarked. He had dozens of wall charts tracking dozens of variables—body counts, weapons captured, aircraft sorties, river patrols, *ad nauseum, ad infinitum*—to prove it. If McNamara had been Moses, a joke ran, he would have come down from Mount Sinai with one stone tablet and three wall charts. It was at this time—March 1964—that McNamara famously said that "I don't object to it being called McNamara's war." His bureaucratic approach to the war led him to linguistic contortions to deny that conventional escalation was underway. When a reporter asked McNamara in 1966 whether a slight buildup in American troops signified an escalation, McNamara coolly replied, "Not at all. It is merely an incremental adjustment to meet a new stimulus level."[9]

The basic war strategy of 1964, dictated by Johnson's need to run as the "peace candidate," was simply to muddle through until after election day in November. For Johnson, graduated pressure had the added political virtue of being an intentionally ambiguous strategy, ostensibly leaving acres of wiggle room. The United States would only commit the minimum amount of force necessary to keep South Vietnam from losing, and generally keep quiet about what it was doing, hoping that North Vietnam would receive the correct "signals" from these restrained displays of force.

By the end of the year it was clear that North Vietnam was unimpressed with American displays of force to date. Far from shaking the resolve of the North Vietnamese, American restraint actually *reassured* them. In a seemingly calculated insult, Viet Cong sappers blew up 36 American bombers at the Ben Hoa airbase two days before the November election, killing four and wounding 72 American servicemen in the process. Pressure mounted to escalate reprisal bombing raids. McNamara authorized bombing raids a few weeks later: two attacks per week, consisting of four planes each.[10]

"The time has come for harder choices," National Security Adviser McGeorge Bundy wrote in a memo to Johnson in January. Johnson sent Bundy to Vietnam to gather a first-hand assessment. In another possibly calculated act of defiance, the Viet Cong bombed American barracks at Pleiku while Bundy was in South Vietnam, killing nine and wounding 107 Americans. Johnson ordered immediate retaliation, and then argued with his advisers about the wording with which to describe the reprisal. Johnson wanted to call the bombing "prompt and adequate and measured," but Bundy disagreed, saying "I think 'fitting' is a better word than 'prompt.' It may seem like semantics, but I think it is quite near the center of the problem of stating your desire precisely."[11] Johnson also reiterated that "we seek no wider war."

A few days later the Viet Cong struck again, bombing U.S. barracks at Qui Nhon, killing 23 soldiers and wounding 22—the largest single loss of life the United States had experienced so far. The Joint Chiefs of Staff wanted a heavy bombing raid against seven North Vietnamese military targets as a reprisal; McNamara wanted it limited to three targets; and Johnson eventually authorized only the two southernmost targets on the Joint Chiefs' list. Bad weather hampered the bombing. Over a three-day period, the United States launched 267 aircraft sorties against 491 buildings, but succeeded in destroying only 47 of them. North Vietnamese military operations were barely impeded. McNamara, though disappointed at the inefficiency of the operation, reassured himself that "our primary objective, of course, was to communicate our political resolve. This I believe we did."[12] Johnson expressed his agreement with McNamara's assessment with one of his typically earthy phrases: "I've got Ho's [Ho Chi Minh's] pecker in my pocket."

Even with the prospective escalation of bombing, Bundy returned from South Vietnam to tell Johnson that "The prospect in Vietnam is grim. . . . This situation is deteriorating, and without a new U.S. action defeat appears inevitable."[13] South Vietnamese soldiers, for example, were deserting at a rate of 350 a day. Johnson had now reached the "fork in the road," at which point further temporizing should not have been possible. The subsequent policy that unfolded, however, more closely resembled Yogi Berra's dissembling quip that "if you reach a fork in the road, take it" than it did a real choice. The momentum for stepping up bombing of North Vietnam had been building throughout the previous year. The war planners continued to believe that a "progressively intensifying bombing campaign" would change North Vietnam's "calculation of interests." But both the Pentagon, in its SIGMA II war simulation in the fall of 1964, and the CIA doubted that bombing would work. The Joint Chiefs of Staff supported what they called a "hard knock" campaign of heavy bombing against key military targets in Hanoi, Haiphong Harbor, and against the political leadership of North Vietnam.

McNamara refused to present this view to the president, favoring instead a bombing strategy his planners referred to as "progressive squeeze and talk," that is, gradually increased bombing that would supposedly bring pressure on the North Vietnamese to negotiate. Maxwell Taylor referred to this option as "strategic persuasion." William Bundy, Assistant Secretary of State for the Far East (and McGeorge's brother), wrote that it was to American advantage to attack "low-key targets not so much for the sake of damage as to show how hopeless the DRV [North Vietnam] is." This "undramatic 'water drip' technique," Bundy thought, would have a greater psychological effect than the "more dramatic attacks" the Joint Chiefs favored.[14]

Johnson was seeking his own Ockham's Razor to solve the war problem, and embraced the blunt instrument of escalated bombing. Operation "Rolling Thunder," as the bombing campaign was called, began officially on February 24 (though bad weather prevented serious missions from beginning until March 2). Most of the civilian war planners thought bombing would serve as a cheap substitute for the step they all dreaded—the introduction of significant numbers of U.S. ground troops. General William Westmoreland, the commander of U.S. forces in Vietnam, was skeptical, thinking the high hopes for the effectiveness of bombing was "pie in the sky." Undersecretary of State George Ball, a Vietnam skeptic from the beginning, was even more blunt, writing that "Dropping bombs was a pain-killing exercise that saved my colleagues from having to face the hard decision to withdraw."[15] In retrospect the launch of Rolling Thunder was the biggest mistake of the war, because it would mobilize critical opinion and swell the antiwar movement, but without achieving any significant military results.[16]

Yet the decision to intensify bombing also had the ironic effect of hastening the decision to send troops, because even before the launch of Rolling Thunder Gen. Westmoreland had requested two battalions of Marines to protect the Danang airfield from which the air raids would be launched. Gen. Maxwell Taylor, the U.S. Ambassador to South Vietnam, opposed Westmoreland's request, arguing that the deployment would make it "very difficult to hold the line on future deployments."[17] But it was hard to deny Westmoreland's reasonable request for base security— the Viet Cong had amply demonstrated their prowess at costly hit-and-run attacks on American bases—even if this entailed Marine patrols beyond the airbase to engage the enemy, as Westmoreland had in mind. Taylor relented, though at one point he recommended that troops should be deployed under the rubric of "flood relief." The first battalion of 3,500 Marines landed at Danang on March 8, and Johnson subsequently approved Westmoreland's request for two more battalions—another 15,000 to 20,000 troops—and a squadron of helicopters "as needed."

This latter decision, formalized during the first week of April in National Security Action Memorandum (NSAM) 328, represented the fatal turning point of the war. NSAM 328 authorized "a change in mission for all Marine battalions deployed in Vietnam to permit their more active use. . . ."[18] The decision to send troops into active combat was only the first part of a three-part mistake. Up to this point, it might have been possible, as George Ball forcefully argued at the time, for the United States to disengage from Vietnam while minimizing the blow to its international prestige. The fear of ending up with "another Korea," along with the echoes of warnings against fighting a land war in Asia from Douglas MacArthur and other military giants, were forefront in the minds of Johnson and his aides. But the fear of losing "credibility" with our allies weighed more heavily on their minds, and Ball's counsel was summarily dismissed.

The American troop commitment startled the North Vietnamese. They had been convinced that the United States was not going to intervene in a serious way to stave off the collapse of South Vietnam. "The leaders in Hanoi were dumbstruck by Washington's reaction," Army historian David Palmer wrote. "Consternation and disbelief were their initial reactions. Aspirations for early victory dimmed as U.S. units streamed ashore."[19] This surprise was eminently reasonable from Hanoi's point of view. Why would the United States, having done nothing to "save" China 15 years before, having given only fainthearted support for the Bay of Pigs operation in Cuba in their own backyard, and having agreed to the neutrality of Laos three years before, suddenly choose to make a stand for South Vietnam?

The American troop commitment set off a fierce debate on strategy among North Vietnam's senior military commanders, especially General Vo Nguyen Giap and General Nguyen Chi Thanh. Though Giap was the hero of the great victory at Dien Bien Phu, he had been eclipsed by Thanh in the early 1960s. Thanh had argued successfully in the early 1960s that North Vietnam should escalate its war in the South from guerrilla actions to regular army attacks aimed at speeding up their timetable for victory.

Until American troops arrived, Thanh's strategy was succeeding: Victory seemed within their grasp. Giap argued that North Vietnam should answer the arrival of American troops with a return to purely guerrilla warfare, which would mean reverting to a long struggle once again. Thanh's strategy won out; conventional war it would be. Thanh thought a quick victory could be gained if South Vietnam were cut in half by an offensive in the central highlands. Soon North Vietnamese troops and Viet Cong formations would be meeting U.S. forces in set-piece battles, where the U.S. firepower advantage inflicted savage casualties on the enemy.

At first the North Vietnamese decision to fight conventional action in the South played right into the hands of the United States. In August of 1965, U.S. forces had fought their first regimental-size action since the Korean War against 2,000 Viet Cong troops in the Van Tuong peninsula. After an amphibious landing and a week of hard fighting, U.S. Marines had killed a third of the VC force while suffering only 45 dead. Three months later the U.S. Army First Cavalry Division fought another pitched battle against regimental-sized formations of the North Vietnamese army in the Ia Drang Valley. Once again, U.S. troops prevailed, killing 1,200 Communist troops while suffering 200 deaths of their own. The "big unit" war had begun.

The North Vietnamese would soon realize, however, that although their timetable for victory might be slowed, their ultimate objective was not seriously threatened. While the concern for America's credibility was the most noble aspect of U.S. war planners' calculations, there was insufficient concern given to how a half-hearted and ineffectual war plan would affect American credibility. Above all, the American war effort lacked credibility with the one party to whom it mattered most: North Vietnam. Johnson's fear that China might intervene on the side of North Vietnam as it had in North Korea 15 years before caused Johnson and McNamara to limit the Rolling Thunder bombing campaign. At the outset of Rolling Thunder, McNamara told the Joint Chiefs of Staff that the limitations on the bombing campaign were designed to make sure the North Vietnamese did not get "the wrong signal and think we are launching an offensive."[20]

To ensure that neither North Vietnam nor China would misinterpret the "signals" the American military force was intended to convey, the United States sent a Canadian diplomat, Blair Seaborn, as an intermediary to reassure North Vietnam that the United States "had no designs on the territory of North Vietnam, nor any desire to destroy the D.R.V." (Johnson also had the American ambassador to Poland convey a letter to the China's envoy to Poland stating that the United States had no intention to destroy North Vietnam.) When the United States later sent Seaborn back to Hanoi to tell the North Vietnamese that the United States would increase bombing if the North Vietnamese did not restrain the Viet Cong in the South, North Vietnamese Premier Pham Van Dong refused to see Seaborn. Maxwell Taylor cabled Washington that Seaborn sensed "a mood of confidence" among the North Vietnamese; "Hanoi has the impression that our air strikes are a limited attempt to improve our bargaining position and hence are no great cause for immediate concern."[21]

Taylor had it exactly right. In 1967, North Vietnam's General Giap remarked that "They [the United States] must restrict their participation in order to avoid upsetting the political, economic, and social life of the United States."[22] Hanoi had not only judged Washington correctly, but had their judgment confirmed by the United States itself. The North Vietnamese knew they would not have to face the classical dilemma of having to choose between their war aims and the destruction of their country. Sure, the United States had the capability to turn North Vietnam into a parking lot, but would they? The answer was no. The limitations on the use of American power showed that we meant what we said about being disinterested in military victory in the traditional sense.

Nothing in the bombing campaign caused the North Vietnamese to change their assessment of U.S. weakness and reluctance. The tonnage of bombs dropped increased over the next two months, but Johnson and McNamara, who approved all targets ("They can't even bomb an outhouse without my permission," Johnson boasted), refused to attack key military installations, such as antiaircraft radar sites, Soviet-made planes, harbors, rail lines, and, above all, the political leadership in Hanoi. American pilots throughout the war were forbidden to attack surface-to-air missile sites that were under construction, for fear of killing a Soviet or Chinese technical adviser who might be supervising the project. Much of the bombing was ineffectual. The United States dropped 432 bombs on a single bridge in April, and though damaged the bridge was not put out of use.[23]

A navy pilot commented bitterly: "At times it seemed as if we were trying to see how much ordnance we could drop on North Vietnam without disturbing their way of life."[24] CIA Director John McCone warned

Johnson that "I think what we are doing is starting on a track which involves ground force operations which, in all probability, will have limited effectiveness against guerrillas." The obvious problem, McCone thought, was that the bombing campaign and small contingent of Marines "will not impose unacceptable damage on it, nor will they threaten the DRV's vital interests. Hence, they will not present them with a situation with which they cannot live. . . ."[25] By late June, the State Department concluded in an intelligence finding that the bombing campaign had actually *increased* morale in North Vietnam.[26] A RAND corporation analyst concurred: "In terms of its morale effects, the U.S. campaign may have presented the [North Vietnamese] regime with a near-ideal mix of intended restraint and accidental gore."[27]

The objective of protecting American "credibility" with a limited bombing campaign was already beginning to backfire with U.S. allies. British Prime Minister Harold Wilson sent a cable to President Johnson objecting to bombing North Vietnamese oil facilities, noting: "If you and the South Vietnamese Government were conducting a declared war on the conventional pattern . . . this operation would clearly be necessary and right. But since you have made it abundantly clear—and you know how much we have welcomed and supported this—that your purpose is to achieve a negotiated settlement, and that you are not striving for total military victory in the field, I remain convinced that the bombing of these targets, without producing decisive military advantage, may only increase the difficulty of reaching an eventual settlement. . . ."[28]

Within weeks of the launch of Rolling Thunder, it was becoming clear that the situation on the ground in South Vietnam was growing more precarious. A unilateral one-week bombing halt in mid-May, coupled with a U.S. call for negotiations that was summarily rejected by North Vietnam, further punctuated America's feckless display of strength and resolve. In early June Gen. Westmoreland warned that South Vietnam might collapse by mid-summer or fall, unless the United States put its "finger in the dike." He wanted 44 battalions—150,000 troops—sent right away. The CIA thought that "The arrival of U.S. forces in these numbers (150,000) would not change the Communists' basic calculation that their staying power is inherently superior to that of Saigon and Washington."[29] The Joint Chiefs of Staff, however, concurred with Westmoreland's recommendation, even though a JCS study had concluded five months previously that it would require 500,000 to 700,000 troops—and five years—to defeat the insurgency in the South. The same logic that had led to the bombing escalation—that disengagement would inflict unacceptable damage to American credibility—drove the troop deployment decision in the same inevitable direction. The United States was about to go over the precipice.

Hindsight has been very unkind to the decision-making process of Johnson and his advisers. Reviewing the war decisions of 1965 has always seemed like a slow-motion scene from a horror movie, where the innocent victim walks down the dark hallway toward a rendezvous with the ax-wielding fiend. Critics on all sides today talk as though they would have resisted the logic of escalation, but in fact *not* escalating would have been nearly impossible for Johnson or any other administration. While the strategy and tactics can be second-guessed, the basic commitment cannot. Public support for Vietnam was strong. A February 1965 poll found nearly 80 percent of Americans opposed to a complete withdrawal from Vietnam (a number that actually rose as the fighting escalated later in 1965); 75 percent supported the new bombing campaign. Johnson's approval rating on Vietnam hovered steady at about 60 percent.[30] Most importantly, 48 percent of Americans supported "sending a large number of American troops to help save Vietnam"—a latent support level that could easily have been driven higher with a presidential PR effort.

A strong presidential PR effort was exactly what the public would not get. Johnson would not give a serious public speech about the purpose of the war until September 1967, which was way too late. The most disastrous decision of the war was not its escalation but the decision to conceal the escalation from Congress and the public. "The President desires," read the National Security Action Memo that authorized offensive troop deployment in April, "that premature publicity be avoided by all possible precautions. The actions themselves . . . should minimize any appearance of sudden changes in policy. . . . The President's desire is that these movements and changes should be understood as being gradual and wholly consistent with existing policy."[31] Taylor had cabled from Saigon to Secretary of State Dean Rusk that "Under these circumstances we believe that the most useful approach to press problems is to make no, repeat, no special public announcement to the effect that U.S. ground troops are now engaged in offensive combat operations."[32]

But reporters smelled a rat, as Johnson's penchant for the tall tale began to turn around on him. It seemed a small event on May 23 when a copy editor at the *New York Herald-Tribune* coined the phrase "credibility gap" in a headline for an article on Johnson, but the phrase quickly caught on. *Washington Post* reporter Murray Marder wrote that there was "a growing doubt and cynicism concerning administration pronouncements. . . . The problem could be called a credibility gap."[33] Things got worse in early June, when a low-level State Department public affairs officer confirmed to an inquiring reporter that U.S. forces would be used in offensive combat operations. The *New York Times* editorialized that "the American people were told by a minor State Department official yesterday that, in effect, they were in a land war on the continent of Asia. . . . The nation is informed about it not by the president, not by a Cabinet member, not even by a sub-Cabinet official, but by a public relations officer." Even as the White House was in the midst of deliberations about deploying over 100,000 additional troops, press secretary George Reedy issued a quick and emphatic denial: "There has been no change of mission of U.S. ground combat units in Viet Nam in recent days or recent weeks."[34]

So the Johnson administration embarked on a course of action that was virtually guaranteed to result in the demoralization of American Cold War foreign policy. It nearly led to the complete undoing of the principal Cold War strategy of containment. Democracies need *reasons* for fighting wars, and these reasons must be proportionate to the means of the warfare being conducted. Distant conflicts require a strong articulation of the rationale behind them precisely because distant threats to national security are more ambiguous than nearby threats, the more so the earlier a distant threat is confronted. But in the case of Vietnam, the primary U.S. interest, according to Johnson and his advisers, was our "credibility," and not our security. This description lowered the stakes of the conflict, precisely at the time that the case for Vietnam as a national security matter was growing more and not less necessary. The logic of the Western alliance was taken for granted, but in the age of nuclear weapons the traditional strategic logic of alliances was beginning to dim in the popular mind. Why do we need to have troops in faraway lands when we have the massive power of nuclear weapons to guarantee our national security? Conventional warfare based on geopolitical considerations was beginning to seem a quaint relic of antiquity, as outmoded as coaling stations for the navy. The American people were never reminded, for example, that the erosion of the American position in Asia would mean that the defense of the United States would rest on Alaska and Hawaii; that Hawaii is closer to Beijing than it is to Washington, D.C.; that the western Aleutian Islands are closer to China than they are to Seattle.

Most importantly, the outcome of Vietnam would have a strong effect on the strength of the Western alliance. If the United States abandoned Vietnam, for example, the Japanese would have reason to question their alliance with the United States. They might well rethink their willingness to serve as hosts for major U.S. military bases, and an accommodation with China and the Soviet Union might become the sensible course for Japanese leaders. Without access to Japanese and other Pacific Rim bases such as the Philippines, the initiative in any new Pacific war would rest with the Asian powers and not the United States. This is the circumstance that the United States vowed never to face again after Pearl Harbor. The World War II generation of "liberal internationalists" understood this instinctively, but for the surging baby boom generation this was not so obvious. Secretary of State Dean Rusk finally made a strong statement of this case in late 1967, but it was too late; by then the tide of public opinion was ebbing. (It didn't help that these and other tough-minded explanations Rusk offered received scant press attention.)

The main strategic articulation offered was the "domino theory." If Vietnam fell, the domino theory held, the rest of Southeast Asia would quickly fall like a row of dominoes. The domino theory has been severely ridiculed in the years since the United States left Vietnam. When it was all over in the mid-1970s, none of the other dominoes (with the notable exception of Cambodia) had fallen. But this may be evidence that in fact the 10-year American intervention in Vietnam actually succeeded in slowing the momentum of Communist-inspired "wars of revolution." Thailand might not have been susceptible to the domino theory as was then thought, but an early American exit from the region would have brought Thailand and other nations in the region under destabilizing pressure.

Burma and even India (which was on the brink of a border war with China) would need to rethink their "nonaligned" position. Indonesia's dictator, Sukarno, was making confrontational noises, and seemed likely to throw in his lot with the Communist bloc if Vietnam fell. The integrity of the ANZUS (Australia–New Zealand–United States) alliance hung in the balance. The contemporary critics of the domino theory forget the very real regional anxieties of the time. "In 1964–65 the Australian government made Barry Goldwater sound like a pacifist," John P. Roche wrote in 1985. "Australia (population 11 million) was terrified of the hostile Indonesians (population 160 million) sitting one hundred miles across the Torres Strait. Aussies, Brits, Malays, and Gurkhas were fighting a very nasty jungle war in Borneo. It is bemusing for one who has seen the cables from Canberra to Washington in 1963–65 to recall their emphasis on ANZUS, which in 1985 is regarded as a slightly comic U.S. venture into the Antipodes."[35]

And if Johnson did not see the war effort in geopolitical terms, he might still have been able to convince Americans and our allies that it was the right war in the wrong place, and limited our engagement suitably. But despite Johnson's cowboy determination not to sacrifice American "credibility" in Vietnam, he had little imagination for or interest in foreign policy. "It wasn't the war he wanted," Lady Bird Johnson told LBJ biographer Robert Dallek; "The one he wanted was on poverty. . . ."[36] And Johnson knew that a full-fledged public discourse about Vietnam, and a call-up of the reserves (as had been urged by some military advisers and as had taken place during the Korean War) would derail Johnson's greater war—the War on Poverty—that was escalating as rapidly as Vietnam under the rubric of the Great Society. A larger escalation of the war, Cyrus Vance said to McNamara in a memo, would "kill [the] domestic legislative program."[37] But in a case of fearful symmetry, the Great Society was heading over the same precipice as the Vietnam War, and Johnson would be just as surprised and dismayed at its fateful turning. The Great Society was on its way to killing itself.

THE HUGE CONGRESSIONAL MAJORITIES Democrats enjoyed as a result of the 1964 election stimulated Johnson's political bloodlust. LBJ wanted to outdo FDR in social legislation, and the early indications suggested that he might succeed. Senate Majority Leader Mike Mansfield would shortly declare that "Johnson has outstripped Roosevelt, no doubt about that. He has done more than FDR ever did or ever thought of doing."[38] With the way clear for the passage of Medicare and federal aid for education in the early months of 1965, Johnson seemed well on his way to cementing his legacy as a liberal reformer worthy of the same adulation as FDR.

"This was the point of unparalleled opportunity for the liberal community," Daniel P. Moynihan was to write ruefully two years later, "and it was exactly the point where that community collapsed."[39] The liberal community collapsed because liberals began a bitter civil war amongst themselves. Viewed as an abstract continuum, reform liberalism and radical leftism (or what Moynihan called the "liberal Left") may seem mere shadings on the spectrum, but they are in fact quite different. Radical leftism had always been frustrated in America by the success of liberal reformism, but the new efforts of reform liberalism in the 1960s gave radical leftism its biggest opening since the Great Depression. Reform liberalism is a defensive creed; it sees middle-class American democracy as essentially sound, but in need of constant improvements to realize the promise of equal opportunity. Radical leftism rejects middle-class American democracy root and branch, and sees every incremental effort of reform liberalism as a tacit acknowledgement that American democracy is a fraud. Thus the reform liberal's nightmare paradox: The more bold and far-reaching the reform (such as the Civil Rights Act or the poverty-fighting measures of the Great Society), the more ferocious the indictment radical leftism made against it. Hence reform liberalism became the sworn enemy of radical leftism, and the Democratic Party, as the agent of reform liberalism, became the object of supreme contempt. "Liberals!" Todd Gitlin wrote. "The very word had become the New Left's curse."[40]

The first sign of trouble appeared in the beginning stages of the keystone of the War on Poverty—the Community Action Program (CAP). The CAP program, and its central principle—"maximum feasible participation"—was never very clearly thought through by the hurried antipoverty crusaders in the Johnson administration. The Office of Economic Opportunity (OEO), which was to oversee the program, was placed in the Executive Office of the President, that is, in the White House instead of in the Department of Health, Education, and Welfare. This way Johnson could maintain closer political control over the program, but it also exposed him to maximum political liability if things went wrong. (This is perhaps why he delayed the start of the program until after the 1964 election.) In general, the politicians thought that the CAPs would serve mainly as "coordinators" of the disparate federal, state, and local social service programs already in existence. The poor would "participate," to be sure, but mostly by advising the CAPs about their particular needs; yet this was mostly an afterthought. Some poor people might be formally included as members of advisory panels, or might be directly employed to help administer Job Corps projects, but no one had given it much thought. Robert Kennedy had told a congressional committee that maximum feasible participation involved "giving [the poor] a real voice in their institutions," but he hadn't really thought it through either.

But some of the administration's poverty warriors, along with local radical Left activists, had a different idea. For them, "maximum feasible participation," as Moynihan observed, "was taken to sanction a specific theory of social change."[41] Moynihan later reflected: "The apparent function of many of these programs as they actually came into being was to raise the level of perceived and validated discontent among poor persons with the social system about them, without improving the conditions of life of the poor in any comparable degree. Can it be that this had *nothing* to do with the onset of urban violence?"[42] Poverty activists saw "community action" as an opportunity to organize poor people to challenge and transform local political authority—the city "machines" that were the backbone of the Democratic Party in many urban areas. Sargent Shriver even described it at one point as "the business corporation of the new social revolution."[43]

Local activists, and many of the poor, despised the urban political machines (along with the police, housing authorities, and other bureaucracies), often with good reason. The antipoverty warriors structured the program so that money and projects could be established independent of state governors, local mayors, city councils, and bureaucracies. Federal grant money would go directly to local antipoverty programs, even if those programs were (as some turned out to be) voter-registration drives. What was designed to be a service program quickly morphed into an advocacy program. A *Community Action Workbook* was produced instructing low-income people how to use the program to assert political power, and even how to stage protest demonstrations. (Copies of the *Workbook* were eventually withdrawn from circulation and destroyed; recent researchers have been unable to locate a copy.) One local community action manual, ostensibly produced for a remedial reading program, said that "No ends are accomplished without the use of force. . . . Squeamishness about force is the mark not of idealistic, but moonstruck morals."[44] Even the NAACP thought such language was "geared to rioting."

The White House was rejecting grant requests from city agencies in Cleveland, New York, Los Angeles, and San Francisco, and instead federal community action grants were being given to people like Saul Alinsky (author of *Rules for Radicals*). Sanford Kravitz, the administrator in charge of dispensing the comically misnamed "demonstration grants," quickly became known as "Dr. Strangegrant." Sargent Shriver, whose main attention was focused on the Job Corps program, would often ask, "What have you nuts got cooked up for me now?" when presented with new grant proposals.

The most infamous flash point for the CAP was in Syracuse, New York, a town of 222,000 at the time, with a black population of just 16,000. The White House gave a $314,000 grant to Syracuse University to establish a "Community Action Training Center," whose organizers set about forming tenant unions in public housing, bailing out arrested protestors, and registering voters with the tacit purpose of ousting the city's Republican mayor. (The effort backfired; Mayor William Walsh was reelected handily in 1965 as Syracuse voters rallied to his defense in reaction to the CAP agitations.) Meanwhile, the efforts to start job-training projects—hitherto a main purpose of the CAP—floundered, and much of the money did not seem to get to the poor. Of the $8 million spent in Syracuse by mid-1967, Moynihan recalled, "about $7 million had gone for salaries for the various consultants and organizers running the programs." The record of the program was scarcely better in other cities.

Mayors were not amused. "Local governments didn't bargain for all this—being sued, being demonstrated against, having sit-ins in their offices," a White House official admitted.[45] The U.S. Conference of Mayors placed on their annual meeting agenda a resolution denouncing the Community Action Program for encouraging "class struggle." The resolution was blocked, but not before a group of mayors, led by Chicago's Richard Daley, roasted Vice President Hubert Humphrey in a private meeting. President Johnson was similarly agitated when word began filtering back to him of the program's troubles. "For God's sake," Johnson told Bill Moyers, "get on top of this and put a stop to it at once."[46] Johnson referred to the radical visionaries of community action as "kooks and sociologists."

Johnson and Congress moved quickly to rein in the Community Action Program by remaking it into a traditional federal grant-in-aid program, with money routed through local political structures and bureaucracies. Shriver pressed for huge increases in the budget for the program in successive years, but he didn't get them. Historian Allen Matusow concluded that "its radicalism was the exception that proved the rule of the Great Society," that is, that the Great Society's War on Poverty was conceived and implemented within the political framework of middle-class individualism.[47] But community action had let the genie out of the bottle, and Johnson would not be able to get it back in again. As with the Vietnam War, Johnson and other reform liberals were certain that opposition to the War on Poverty would come from conservative Republicans, but it was radical leftists who undermined the effort more.

The furor over the Community Action Program would prove to be a small foreshadowing of what was ahead for the Great Society. It soon faded to insignificance beside the storm that erupted over civil rights. In 1965 the civil rights movement commenced what seemed like a mop-up operation. Congress would be asked to fill in the major missing piece of the 1964 Civil Rights Act, a law that would break down the barriers to black voting such as poll taxes and literacy tests. Once again there would be stubborn Southern filibusters and complaints that the proposed Voting Rights Act violated the Constitution, but it was clear from the outset that the Act was going to pass without serious difficulty. Another burst of Southern violence against civil rights marchers in the spring of 1965, most famously at Selma, Alabama, assured the passage of the Voting Rights Act. This would essentially complete the ambitious agenda of the civil rights movement; a top aide to Martin Luther King remarked in August 1965 that "there is no more civil rights movement; President Johnson signed it out of existence when he signed the voting rights bill."[48]

But the expansive Lyndon Johnson wasn't through. In June he delivered an extraordinary speech at Washington D.C.'s Howard University that broke with the precedents of American social thought. It was, Pat Moynihan poignantly observed, Johnson's last peacetime speech. Entitled "To Fulfill These Rights," Johnson opened a new direction for civil rights. Now that the goal of establishing the legal basis of equal opportunity had been achieved through civil rights legislation (the principal goal of the civil rights movement), Johnson declared that "it is not enough just to open the gates of opportunity. . . . You do not take a person who for years has been hobbled in chains and liberate him, bring him up to the starting line of a race and then say, 'You are free to compete with all the others,' and still justly believe that you have been completely fair."

So far so good. This analogy was not insensible, though it was vulnerable to the charge that it implied, as Abigail and Stephan Thernstrom put it, "that blacks were too crippled to be judged on their individual merit."[49] The legacy of slavery, segregation, and the heroic actions of the civil rights movement had stored up a fund of goodwill among Americans such that a consensus for moderate ameliorative measures was within reach. But Johnson upped the stakes. "Equal opportunity," Johnson said, "was essential, but not enough." It was now necessary, he said "to move beyond opportunity to achievement. . . . This is the next and more profound stage of civil rights. We seek not just freedom but opportunity—not just legal equity but human ability"—and then came the key sentence—"not just equality as a right and a theory, but *equality as a fact and as a result.*" (Emphasis added.)

Declaring that equal result instead of equal opportunity should now be the basis of policy was a wholesale departure from traditional American political principles, and threatened to undermine the consensus for civil rights that had been so painfully forged over the previous decade. This speech represented the formal intersection of the War on Poverty and the civil rights movement, and the beginning of the undoing of both, though it was not instantly apparent. In fact, the "chattering class" of editorial writers and intellectuals strongly approved of the speech (which Martin Luther King and other civil rights leaders had vetted in advance), and Johnson, whose vanity led him to keep a running count of how many times he was applauded during a speech, sent out 4,500 copies of the Howard speech afterward. A few months later Johnson followed up with Executive Order 11246, which called on federal agencies to "take affirmative action to ensure that [black] applicants are employed." This was intended to mean aggressive recruitment—not quotas or preferences—though it opened the way for the corruption of discrimination law.

Johnson also proposed to follow up the speech with a major White House conference, also to be called "To Fulfill These Rights," in the fall. For what was most on his mind was not egalitarianism, but black poverty. "Negro poverty is not white poverty," he said in his speech. And the key to this problem was the state of the black family: "The family is the cornerstone of our society. . . . When the family collapses it is the children that are usually damaged. When it happens on a massive scale the community itself is crippled." Trends among poor black families were increasingly worrisome. "Only a minority—less than half—of all Negro children reach the age of eighteen having lived with both of their parents. At this moment a little less than two-thirds are living with both of their parents." Strengthening the black family would therefore be a key item on the agenda for the follow-up White House conference, the planning for which began within a week of the speech. Strengthening the family should have seemed like a pure derivative of the classic American triad of "mom, the flag, and apple pie." Instead, all hell broke loose.

Much of Johnson's Howard University speech had been inspired by Pat Moynihan's research. A month before the speech, Moynihan's boss, Secretary of Labor Willard Wirtz, had transmitted to the White House a confidential report about black families that Moynihan had written (though his name never appeared anywhere in the report), which served as the basis for the Howard University speech. (It is doubtful, however, that Johnson ever read the report.) It was intended as an internal document; less than 100 copies had been printed, "but with no expectation of using even that few," Moynihan wrote later. Secretary Wirtz emphasized that "there are no other copies in circulation."[50] The report argued that the economic legacy of slavery and segregation had taken its toll on the stability of black families, and that equality of opportunity would not be sufficient to meet the needs of poor black communities. "The principal challenge of the next phase of the Negro revolution is to make certain that equality of result will now follow," Moynihan wrote. "If we do not, there will be no social peace in the United States for generations." This view merely echoed what some influential leaders of the civil rights movement were already starting to say themselves. Bayard Rustin had written four months earlier that the civil rights movement "is now concerned not merely with removing the barriers to full *opportunity* but with achieving the fact of *equality*."[51]

This was not, however, the linchpin of the Moynihan report. The key to the report was its emphasis on the black family, and especially the alarming rise in the black illegitimacy rate. It had stood at 21 percent in

1960 (up from 18 percent in 1950), but new census estimates in 1965 found that it had risen sharply to 25 percent. Moynihan thought a European-style family allowance—a guaranteed minimum income—was the main remedy that should be considered. Present welfare programs, Moynihan observed, operated on the perverse basis of being available only to broken homes; "It was past time we came to our senses on the subject, and stopped penalizing families with a father in the home." To be sure, a family allowance would have cost $5 billion to $10 billion a year, Moynihan admitted, *"but we had the money."*

A major source of concern with the report's distribution was the fear that conservatives and segregationists might exploit some of the sensitive aspects of the report to oppose civil rights and welfare proposals. They should have been so lucky. The report, which had begun to leak out (perhaps by Moynihan himself, it has been speculated), drew the fire of bureaucrats within the Department of Health, Education, and Welfare and in Shriver's Office of Economic Opportunity, the command center for the War on Poverty. After all, this report came out of *Labor* Department, and what were *they* doing mucking around with poverty and welfare issues anyway? As Moynihan later characterized the reaction, "No one was going to talk about their poor people that way." A whispering campaign spread the word that Moynihan was a "subtle racist" on account of his bleak portrayal of the condition of the black family. The report had serious technical flaws, it was said. The mystery surrounding the supposedly confidential and still-unavailable report (it was in fact soon widely available) compounded the effect of the whispering campaign. Soon the attack was becoming more public, and was causing controversy within the civil rights movement.[52]

The controversy might have blown over. There was considerable support for Moynihan's position within key elements in the civil rights movement. The National Urban League had emphasized family stability as the key to any effective welfare plan to aid blacks. Roy Wilkins of the NAACP, Whitney Young Jr., and Martin Luther King had all spoken similarly about the condition of the black family (King had described it as a "social catastrophe"), and Wilkins publicly defended Moynihan. Then, in early August, only a week after Johnson had signed the Voting Rights Act, gasoline was poured on the fire.

In an anonymous interview in *National Review* in 1966, a Los Angeles policeman described the most delicate aspect of patrol work in low-income minority neighborhoods: "If you have to use your siren to pull someone over, by the time you get out of your car there are people around you that are spectators. If the situation isn't handled properly it can be an explosive situation."[53] This is exactly what happened in the early evening of August 11, 1965, in Watts, a community located about five miles from downtown Los Angeles.[54] Shortly after 7 P.M., California Highway Patrolman Lee Minikus turned on his motorcycle siren to get the attention of a gray 1955 Buick that he had observed driving erratically down Avalon Boulevard. He suspected the driver was drunk. (Minikus had initially been alerted to look for a potential reckless driver by a black motorist on 122nd Street.) The Buick finally pulled over four blocks later. The siren had attracted attention in the neighborhood, so within moments officer Minikus and the driver, 21-year-old Marquette Frye, were surrounded by a small crowd of about 25 or 30 people. The sobriety check went smoothly enough; Frye even joked with Minikus. Police backups started arriving, as did Frye's mother, who lived only two blocks away. She initially berated her son for his drinking.

As the crowd continued to grow to more than 250, suddenly events took a wrong turn. Frye turned hostile to the police and tried to run away into the crowd. Mrs. Frye jumped on an officer's back and tore his shirt. Another officer hit Marquette Frye with his nightstick while subduing him. Soon all three members of the Frye family (Marquette Frye's younger brother was a passenger in the Buick) were under arrest in the back seat of a squad car. As police units were beginning to withdraw from the tense scene, a new provocation occurred. A woman in the crowd spat on a policeman. She was promptly arrested. The woman, a hairdresser, was wearing a barber's smock, and because of her appearance the rumor spread that the police had arrested a pregnant woman. As the police completed their withdrawal, the still-growing crowd started throwing rocks.

Thus began four days of intense rioting that required nearly 14,000 National Guard troops making shoulder-to-shoulder, street-by-street sweeps to quell. By the time it was over, 34 were killed, more than 1,000 injured, and 3,952 arrested. (Only 14 of the rioters arrested, however, were given jail sentences of longer than seven months; only 730 received any jail sentence at all.[55]) Property damage from the more than 600 buildings that were set afire topped $40 million. The riot stunned America. President Johnson took it personally, to the point of being distraught. White House aides had trouble reaching Johnson on the phone; the usually prompt Johnson ignored repeated phone calls, and he refused to look at the cables from Los Angeles. "How is it possible, after all we've accomplished?" he asked, doubtless thinking of the Civil Rights and Voting Rights Acts.[56]

Most shocking was the credo the rioting crowd shouted during their rampage—"burn, baby, burn." The phrase apparently originated with "Magnificent Montague," the most popular black DJ on KGFJ radio in Los Angeles, who made "burn, baby, burn" his signature phrase to tout up-tempo tracks he cued up for listeners. He stopped using the phrase after the riots.[57] The pattern of looting looked purposeful; pawn shops were a special target for the firearms they held (more than 19,000 firearms were looted during the riots; fewer than 1,000 were recovered). The commission appointed by California Governor Pat Brown to investigate the riot (Los Angeles lawyer Warren Christopher was vice chairman of the commission) concluded that only about 2 percent of people in the Watts area participated in the riot (no more than 10,000), but social scientists who swarmed to Watts estimated the proportion much higher, perhaps as many as 10 to 15 percent, or well over 30,000.[58] While no one would suggest that conditions in Watts were good, the severity of the riot came as a surprise in the city that the National Urban League had rated as one of the best for blacks in America. A survey of more than 1,000 arrestees added to the seeming anomaly of the riot: 73 percent of this sample had full-time jobs; half earned between $200 and $400 a month—a near middle-class wage at that time.[59] And the *New York Times* reported a 1966 poll of blacks in Watts that found they were more concerned about "police protection" than "police brutality."[60]

More shocking and consequential than the riot itself was the reaction to the riot. Though riots have been a feature of urban life since the dawn of civilization and had not been rare in America's history, the Watts riot took on an unprecedented political character. Black voices began referring to the riot as a "rebellion," "insurrection," or even "manifesto." A poll of blacks in Watts found 27 percent held a favorable view of the riot, 38 percent thought it helped the Negro cause, and 58 percent expected a favorable outcome. The pollsters concluded that "a riot 'ideology' is developing in the Negro community, an ideology in which riots assume the position of a legitimate and justifiable form of protest."[61] "Riot ideology," urban affairs critic Fred Siegel later observed, became "a racial version of collective bargaining."[62] Burn your neighborhood; get a federal grant. (Indeed, the federal government rushed $18 million to Watts in the first six months after the riot; the Hispanic community in Los Angeles promptly complained that they weren't getting their fair share.) The *right* to riot was born. It would not be long after Watts that the civil rights movement endorsed a $100 billion "Marshall Plan" for American cities. Mainstream reform liberals failed to see how their own words had paved the way for the legitimization of the right to riot. Even President Kennedy had remarked in 1963 that "In too many parts of the country, wrongs are inflicted on Negro citizens for which there are no remedies at law. Unless the Congress acts, their only remedy is in the streets." Bobby Kennedy went further: "There is no point in telling Negroes to obey the law. To many Negroes the law is the enemy."[63]

As had been foreshadowed in the Harlem riot the year previously, the riot widened the fissure within the civil rights movement between moderate leaders such as Martin Luther King, who urged non-violent protest as a means of generating change through the democratic process, and more militant radicals who embraced a violent racial overlay to garden-variety class struggle ideology. Martin Luther King was very coolly received in Watts when he visited a few days after the riot ended. One meeting of more than 500 people jeered him. "All over America," King exhorted, "the Negroes must join hands." "And burn!" yelled a heckler. King's plea that the crowd treat Los Angeles Mayor Sam Yorty and Police Chief William Parker "with courtesy" brought a roar of laughter.[64] King and other civil rights leaders who flocked to the scene were stunned at the triumphalism that was evident among many rioters. "We won," a young unemployed black man told Bayard Rustin. How? Rustin asked. Homes and businesses have been destroyed, and people were killed. "We won because we made the whole world pay attention to us," the youth replied. (Two years later, a survey found that 92 percent of the small businesses burned during the riot had not reopened.[65])

At the same time that black opinion was facing the pressure of radicalization, liberal guilt among whites began to kick in. Thus began a polarization among white liberals that was nearly as severe as the polarization among blacks. Mayor Yorty, a Democrat, blamed the unrest on the Great Society rhetoric that he thought was unreasonably raising expectations. (Yorty had been one of the prime movers behind the U.S. Conference of Mayors draft resolution attacking Community Action as "class struggle."[66]) "It's politicians running around making promises to the people in the ghettoes they can't keep that have created an intolerable situation for the police," Yorty said a year later in a heated exchange with Bobby Kennedy. Even the official commission that investigated the riot suggested that a major contributing cause was the failure of the War on Poverty "to live up to press notices."

Police Chief Parker was more direct, blaming the violence on liberals who "keep telling people they are unfairly treated." President Johnson, who spoke cautiously in the days after the riot, let slip a few days later that more rioting might be expected anywhere "people feel they don't get a fair shake . . . that justice is not open to them."[67] It was just the first in a long line of expressions of liberal sympathy for rioters, the worst being Vice President Hubert Humphrey's incautious comment that if he had been born in a ghetto, he might riot too.

It didn't take long for intellectuals to pick up the cue and begin assigning metaphysical meaning to riots. The approval of the ideology of riot-as-legitimate-protest would eventually start to meld with the growing protest against the Vietnam War, and both were reducible to the razor of "The System." The "System" that made the Vietnam War possible was also the "System" responsible for poverty and racism. (The apotheosis of this sentiment was the infamous cover of the *New York Review of Books* in 1967 featuring a diagram of how to make a Molotov cocktail.)

In the near term, however, it was the Moynihan report that received the brunt of the fury Watts unleashed. The Watts riot occurred at the very moment that press coverage of the Moynihan report was reaching a crescendo. A *Newsweek* article about the report appeared the same week as Watts. A Roland Evans and Robert Novak column a week later hyped the story with sensational prose about the "much-suppressed, much-leaked" report that was becoming "a political atom bomb." The media spin on the Moynihan report was that it was the government's explanation of Watts. This infuriated the Left, which saw any attempt to shift the focus from society's injustice as "blaming the victim." *The Nation* magazine, in a widely reprinted article by William Ryan that grossly distorted the report, attacked the Moynihan report as a "smug document" filled with "irresponsible nonsense."

What might have been a manageable debate about a chicken-and-egg–style misunderstanding had spun out of control. Was black family instability the *cause* of poverty or the *effect* of poverty and racism? The Left emphatically thought the latter, and though Moynihan did not fundamentally disagree (the report had declared, "white America must accept responsibility; it [black poverty and family decay] flows from centuries of oppression and persecution of the Negro man"), the differing emphasis of the two sides in the volatile atmosphere after Watts made calm debate impossible. The irony of the reaction to the Moynihan report is that Moynihan was trying to discredit "color-blind" policy, and hoped to establish policy directed specifically to the problems of black Americans—exactly what his leftist critics would soon demand themselves. But the Left's moral fervor for the wholesale transformation of society ("justice now!") trumps calm discussion of real policies for real problems.

Yet it was not enough for the Left to charge that Moynihan was "blaming the victim." Soon critics began asking: What's wrong with single-parent families anyway? Andrew Young, whom Martin Luther King tapped as his representative to the White House conference on the issue, said that "there probably isn't anything wrong with the Negro family as it exists."[68] The concern with family stability, critics said in a now-familiar refrain, was an attempt to "impose middle class values" on the poor. In fact, it was asserted, the black female-headed household is "a cultural pattern superior in its vitality to middle-class mores." "College professors," Moynihan observed, "waxed lyrical on the subject of the female-headed household. . . . This is the scholarship of Che Guevara."[69]

The White House was now putting as much distance as it could between itself and Moynihan (who had left the government for an academic job in New York in the fall), and was distressed about the upcoming White House conference on black poverty that Johnson had announced at Howard University. The conference was postponed to the following spring, and a "planning session" held in November instead. At the opening of the planning session, White House conference director Beryl Bernhard attempted to soothe the critics by announcing that "I want you to know that I have been reliably informed that no such person as Daniel

Patrick Moynihan exists."[70] But the critics were not to be appeased. A planning panel reported out the sense of the delegates that "All families should have the right to evolve in directions of their own choosing . . . and should have the supports—economic and non-economic—to exercise that right."[71] The conference planners demanded that "the question of 'family stability' be stricken entirely from that agenda." The White House—and liberals—beat a hasty retreat; it would be 20 years before the subject of black family stability could be discussed again.

The short span of these few weeks in the summer of 1965 transformed the national debate about poverty and race, and doomed the Great Society. It was only a short step from the just-grievance mentality given fresh life by the riots to the view that government aid is a just entitlement for the oppressed. Henceforth, historian Gareth Davies has written, "references to self-help, equality of opportunity, and reciprocal obligation were conspicuous by their absence."[72] Only the government had any responsibility or obligation—to give money and power to the dispossessed.

Meanwhile, the escalation of rioting and the rhetoric of riot ideology delivered a grievous blow to the civil rights movement. "Until then," Moynihan noted, "theirs had been the aggrieved, the just, the righteous cause." The civil rights movement had prospered because they understood the rule that the first side to resort to violence lost. Every televised beating of a peaceful marcher by a Southern sheriff was good for another five points of public approval in the polls. Watts reversed this presumption. The civil rights movement, associated in the public mind, however unfairly, with rioting, began hemorrhaging public support. Martin Luther King and other civil rights moderates were compelled to begin equivocating their views about civil unrest in a desperate attempt to maintain their leadership position among blacks. It wouldn't work.

This "preposterous and fruitless controversy," as Moynihan called it, left him despondent about the prospect for meaningful social reform. Though the Johnson administration had disavowed him (when Moynihan was appointed a year later to a federal advisory committee, Johnson blew up, penning a note: "Ask who the hell appointed Moynihan and get him out now"), an administration official wrote him to say "I'm really sorry that the press and everyone else took after you the way they did. . . . Rather than being the hero, having stimulated the government into action, you became the villain."[73] Moynihan came to see that "the liberal

Left can be as rigid and destructive as any force in America." A window of opportunity had slammed shut: "The era of white initiatives on behalf of Negroes is over. . . . An era of bad manners is almost certainly begun." Sure enough, public opinion surveys showed that between 1964 and 1966, the number of people who thought that integration efforts were being pushed too fast rose from 28 percent to 52 percent; the numbers first started jumping right after the Watts riot.[74] Moynihan also wrote, with a prescience that would not be vindicated for more than a decade, that "The nation is turning conservative at a time when its serious internal problems may well be more amenable to conservative solutions than to liberal ones."[75]

Yet conservatives, let alone Republicans, were not yet ready to seize the initiative Moynihan saw open to them. Still prostrate and paralyzed from their beating at the polls in the 1964 election, Republicans did not offer much significant resistance to the advance of the Great Society, which makes all the more remarkable the severity of the self-inflicted wounds that liberals were suffering. Events in 1965 suggested that Republicans would follow the advice of the pundits and swing back to the center. Goldwater's handpicked chairman of the Republican National Committee, Dean Burch, was ousted in a coup led by the party moderates. In New York City, liberal Republican Congressman John Lindsay was elected mayor (despite the insurgent campaign of William F. Buckley Jr.), and was celebrated on the cover of news magazines as the brightest sign of Republican revival. In Congress, House Republicans booted their floor leader, Charlie Halleck, in favor of Michigan Representative Gerald Ford, who was thought to be more articulate and aggressive. President Johnson was unworried. "Don't worry about Gerald Ford," he told Sargent Shriver, "because he can't fart and chew gum at the same time."[76]

But Republican opposition to the Great Society continued to sputter without effect. A Republican alternative to Johnson's Medicare proposal—Republican proposals in those days were dismissed as the "conservative Republican alternative program," or CRAP—was simply absorbed by the Democrats, making the new Medicare program even bigger and costlier than the liberals had originally proposed. Polls found Michigan Governor George Romney, a moderate with close ties to Nelson Rockefeller (who might himself be a candidate again), to be the early frontrunner for the 1968 Republican presidential nomination. Richard

Nixon was quietly planning another run, however, and the chattering class expected that he would run from the center, as he had during his losing run for the California governorship in 1962 ("You won't have Dick Nixon to kick around any more"). An Evans and Novak column reported that "in a recent conversation with newspaper reporters, Nixon described the Buckleyites as a threat to the Republican Party even more menacing than the Birchers." *National Review* immediately demanded an explanation from Nixon, and received correspondence back from "someone named" (as *NR* put it) Patrick J. Buchanan, a young newspaper editorial writer Nixon had hired to be a campaign aide. Though Nixon was determined to avoid the errors of the Goldwater campaign, he would confide to Buckley in 1967 that the lesson he learned from his two losing races is that while you cannot win with only the right wing of the Republican Party, you can't win without it either. Nixon could see the potency of the Goldwater movement, and set out to harness it to his ambition. Conservatives were wary of this embrace.

So it was not clear that the conservative surge that had propelled Goldwater to the nomination would yet mature into the dominant force within the Republican Party. It was obvious that California would be a key battleground. Democratic Governor Pat Brown, dubbed "the giant killer" for his victories over Nixon in 1962 and Goodwin Knight in 1958, was expected to run for a third term. On the Republican side it was thought perhaps liberal Senator Thomas Kuchel might run. Kuchel earned the wrath of conservatives for publicly refusing to endorse or support Goldwater's candidacy, even after the Republican nominating convention. Ronald Reagan had Kuchel in mind when, a week after the election, he told Los Angeles County Young Republicans that "We don't intend to turn the Republican Party over to the traitors in the battle just ended. We will have no more of those candidates who are pledged to the same goals of our opposition and who seek our support. Turning the party over to the so-called moderates wouldn't make any sense at all." But would Reagan himself be the alternative?

There are competing accounts of when and how Reagan arrived at the decision to run for governor. One biographer (Anne Edwards) claims that right after the 1964 election Reagan actually contemplated running straightaway for president in 1968, and had to be persuaded that his chances for the brass ring would be better if he was elected governor first.[77] Most Reaganites discount this, and it seems out of character with Reagan's persistent modesty and realism. Biographer Lee Edwards (no relation to Anne Edwards) says that when Sy Rubel, the chairman of Union Oil Company, first asked Reagan to run for governor in February 1965, Reagan initially said no.[78] But he yielded to the entreaties of Rubel, Henry Salvatori, Holmes Tuttle, and others who would later compose his "kitchen cabinet" to keep an open mind. In April Reagan held the first of three decisive meetings with Stuart Spencer and Bill Roberts, whose political consulting firm, Spencer-Roberts, was regarded as the best Republican campaign firm in the west. Spencer-Roberts was the epitome of the political "hired gun." They had run campaigns for conservatives, but had also run Rockefeller's losing 1964 California primary campaign against Goldwater, and also Senator Thomas Kuchel's 1962 senatorial campaign. Evans and Novak described the first meeting: "The two political managers made clear that an 'ultraconservative' campaign would not win in California and that they were not interested in joining another Goldwater debacle. Neither was he, rejoined Reagan."[79]

Reagan's political instincts and shrewdness were evident in these early meetings, and belie the persistent claim that he was a political naïf. Reagan understood that with a Democratic voting edge of three-to-two in California, a Republican could only win by appealing to crossover voters. This required a united Republican Party more than a centrist campaign. A unified Republican Party would be his primary strategy as well as a condition of running. Rather than declaring his candidacy straightaway, Reagan decided to travel the state to showcase his strongest political asset—his speaking ability—as a means of building support.

Rather than give long set speeches, Reagan's chose to give short speeches followed by questions and answers from the audience. This helped dispel the view that he was "merely an actor" reciting lines. It worked. Journalist Jack Roberts reflected: "It was apparent to those of us who really had spent some time covering the guy on the campaign trail that he was not dumb. Really the thing that drove that home was the Q and A. He would throw back sensible answers—not just as press conferences, but to audiences."[80] Reagan not only got the jump on other potential Republican candidates; his early informal campaigning allowed him to concentrate on issues rather than having to attack party rivals. It also gave him an interval of time to begin learning about California state government, which, by his own admission, he knew little. During his years speaking for General Electric, Reagan explained, he had spent so much time researching "the overall philosophy, national and international policy, that I did not know anything about the organization of state government . . . I had just a citizen's resentment of certain things that had happened."

"At the end of that period [of the speaking tour]," Stuart Spencer recalled, "we realized this guy was for real."[81] It has been a constant refrain since his first campaign that Reagan is the creation of his handlers, and more that a few political operatives have sought to claim the mantle of being the "brains" behind Reagan. Spencer is notably not among them. "That kingmaker stuff is a lot of bull," Spencer said at the time. "In politics you don't change a guy's image and get anywhere. If you try to put words in his mouth, people see right through him."[82]

In September, by which time Reagan had traveled 10,000 miles (mostly by car because Reagan disliked flying) and delivered 150 speeches, he made the decision to enter the race. Reagan formally announced his candidacy in a statewide televised address on January 4, 1966. In his announcement speech and early press comments Reagan articulated several themes that became staples of his entire subsequent career. He explained his move to conservative Republicanism as a lament for the apostasy of the leadership of the Democratic Party: "I have often said that I think that there was as much the Democratic Party leaving me, or the leadership of the party leaving me, as my leaving the party."[83] In his campaign speeches he showed his skill at explaining the essence of complicated issues with user-friendly illustrations—Ockham's Razor applied to practical politics. The state budget of $4.6 billion was an incomprehensible figure to ordinary people, he noted. But think of it in terms of a stack of dollar bills; a four-inch stack of $1,000 bills would be a million dollars. A stack of $1,000 bills would reach 1,500 feet in the air to equal the state budget. Reagan also honed his skill at the telling epigram: "You have to live in California for five years to be governor, but you can get on welfare in 24 hours." He would also show the combination of his optimism with his penchant for offering a positive alternative to the liberalism he attacked with such zest. In place of the Great Society, Reagan would move us toward the "creative society" that harnesses the power of the people to solve problems themselves.

Reagan would not get the nomination without a contest, however. Sen. Kuchel decided shortly after Watts not to run (but in his non-candidacy announcement he attacked conservatives as a "fanatical, neo-fascist, political cult, overcome by a strange mixture of corrosive hatred and sickening fear"[84]), but two-term San Francisco Mayor George Christopher, a moderate, would. Christopher, a wealthy dairy farmer, was a bland character—David Broder and Stephen Hess wrote that Christopher "looked and sounded like a tired TV wrestler."[85] Early polls showed Reagan beating Christopher among Republicans, but that Christopher would run more strongly against Brown. "I had heard of Ronald Reagan, of course," Christopher later said, "but I believed what so many people were saying, that 'an actor' couldn't win the Republican primary over a businessman-politician."[86] Party moderates who had backed Rockefeller against Goldwater in 1964 spoke up in favor of Christopher (who had been the northern California campaign chairman for Rockefeller in 1964). One of them was a State Assemblyman named Caspar Weinberger, who told the *New York Times* that "Christopher will do much better than Rockefeller did. Reagan will get the great bulk of the Goldwater support but it does not represent much more than one-third of the party."[87] Striving to avoid the kind of divisiveness that helped to ruin Goldwater's candidacy, it was during this period that the chairman of the California Republican Party, Gaylord Parkinson, enunciated what became known as the 11th Commandment—"Thou shalt not speak ill of a fellow Republican," a phrase which later became attributed to Reagan. Reagan and Christopher held to this maxim to a remarkable extent in the primary campaign that followed.

As the June primary approached, Reagan's early lead over Christopher dwindled. Reagan's lead dropped from 17 points in the fall of 1965 to 13 percent in January, to 9 percent in March, and just 6 percent in May. At this point the Democrats blundered. The Brown campaign was ecstatic at the prospect of running against Reagan. They would simply dust off the trash-Goldwater playbook. "We thought the notion was absurd and rubbed our hands in gleeful anticipation of beating this politically inexperienced, right-wing extremist and aging actor," Governor Brown reminisced later. Brown's confidence in a run against Reagan led him to work surreptitiously to help Reagan win the Republican primary. Democrats leaked damaging information about Christopher to the media, and in mid-May a story by *Washington Post* columnist Drew Pearson about 20-year-old milk price-control violations by Christopher damaged his campaign. Reagan won the Republican primary by a landslide margin of 65 to 31 percent. Christopher was at first hesitant about endorsing Reagan for the fall campaign, but Reagan took an immediate step that he would repeat in his successful run for the White House in 1980: he hired several of Christopher's key campaign staff, sending the signal that he was serious about uniting the party, and that his party opponents would be welcome in his government.

While Reagan had to overcome intra-party opposition and prove that he could be a consistent campaigner, Brown was not without problems of his own. Los Angeles Mayor Sam Yorty, still angered by Brown's handling of the Watts riot the year before (another riot in Watts in March 1966, while Brown was again out of the country as he had been during the initial riot the previous summer, added fuel to Yorty's ire), entered the Democratic primary contest against Brown. (Yorty, incidentally, shared Brown's view of Reagan: "I always felt that Reagan was the only candidate Brown could possibly beat."[88] A decade later Yorty switched parties and became a Reagan supporter.) The fissures among Democrats over the Vietnam War were starting to widen, and began to take their toll on Brown, who as a loyal Democrat defended President Johnson's war policy. Assailed from both the Left and the Right, Brown fared poorly in the Democratic primary. Yorty captured nearly a million votes. Democrats knew they were in deep trouble. "It's going to be a long, hot summer," Brown remarked on primary election night.

Although early primary polls suggested the race would be close, Brown's efforts to tag Reagan as "the crown prince of the radical right" sputtered from the start and never achieved any traction, in part because Brown never did perceive how vastly different Reagan was from Goldwater. "Like Barry Goldwater," Brown would say after Reagan's June primary victory, "he is the spokesman for a harsh philosophy of doom and darkness." But Reagan's positive rhetoric and genial nature was in sharp contrast to Goldwater's angry and defiant visage. Even when Reagan attacked the same targets as Goldwater, he did so with a light and humorous touch. Reagan quipped, for example, that student radicals "act like Tarzan, look like Jane, and smell like Cheetah."[89] (Polls had shown that student turmoil on campus was highly unpopular with voters.) Keeping up with Brown's promises, Reagan joked, "is like trying to read *Playboy* magazine while your wife turns the pages."

Brown and the Democrats made several attempts to tie Reagan to the John Birch Society. The California Democratic Party produced a 13-page report entitled "Ronald Reagan Extremist Collaborator: An Expose." "Ronald Reagan is an extremist's candidate for Governor of California," the paper said. "He is the extremist's collaborator in California. He endorses their projects, promotes their policies, takes their money. He is their 'front man.' Meanwhile, he pretends to be a moderate, middle-of-the-roader. The record belies him. It shows that he has collaborated directly with a score of top leaders of the super-secret John Birch Society."[90]

Reagan regarded the leadership of the John Birch Society as kooky, and understood that the Society was a political liability with the moderate voters whose votes he had to attract. He had pointedly criticized some of the Society's frothier pronouncements (such as the allegation that President Eisenhower belonged to the Communist conspiracy). His campaign took care to keep out John Birch Society adherents whose presence in campaign posts could be exploited by the media and the Democrats. Yet Reagan didn't wish to alienate the block of voters who sympathized with the Bircher's fervent anti-Communism. This dilemma, which had plagued Nixon and other Republican politicians over the previous decade, became yet another opportunity for Reagan. Reagan began disclaiming "labels" of all kinds, and disavowed support from "any blocs or groups." About the John Birch Society specifically, Reagan said that he would welcome the support of their members, but that such support was evidence that he had "persuaded them to accept my philosophy, not me accepting theirs."

Reagan's sincerity made this demurral effective. Brown's attacks on Reagan began to backfire, especially a TV ad with Brown reminding schoolchildren that Reagan was an actor, and that it was an actor who had shot Lincoln. Reagan even began quoting Brown's statements in his own speeches. Brown had said that conservatives are "the shock troops of bigotry, echoes of Nazi Germany, echoes of another hate binge that began more than 30 years ago in a Munich beer hall." Reagan calmly parried: "Extreme phraseology from one who professes to deplore extremism."[91] To charges that he was an agent of "white backlash," Reagan replied: "I'm the agent of a *Brown* backlash." As Republicans united behind Reagan—Eisenhower and Nixon both made public appearances for him—Democrats squabbled. Two of Brown's top aides ended up in fisticuffs over a campaign disagreement. The New Left began saying openly that a Brown defeat would strengthen the Left. The *New York Times,* in a rare editorial endorsement for a California election, deplored Reagan and hoped that California voters would "understand where reality ends and fantasy begins." The *Los Angeles Times,* however, endorsed Reagan.

Reagan won the November election in a landslide, by a margin of nearly 1 million votes. He carried all but five of California's 58 counties. Not since Earl Warren in 1950 had a Republican run so strongly. A large number of the Democratic voters who had gone with Yorty in the primary had crossed over for Reagan, including as much as 30 percent of labor union members. He did especially well in several working-class communities with heavy Democratic registration, prefiguring how he would draw votes in his presidential runs in the 1980s. Reagan's big win was the crest of a nationwide Republican tidal wave. Republicans did well down the ticket as well, gaining five state Senate seats, five state Assembly seats, and three House seats in Congress. Nationally Republicans gained 47 House seats (Nixon, stumping for the GOP around the country, had predicted Republicans would gain 46 House seats), three Senate seats, eight governorships, and 677 state legislative seats. Among the GOP winners was George Bush, who won a congressional seat in Houston. It would be the Republicans' best showing until 1980. President Johnson, who ducked promised campaigning for Democrats as election day drew closer and party prospects sagged, thought there was a bright side. At least the new Republicans would be more likely to support his Vietnam policy.

Reagan was sworn in as governor of California at three minutes after midnight on January 3, 1967. His inaugural address, delivered the next day, contained the delicate mixture of the two halves of Reagan's political persona—hard foreboding and cheerful optimism—that gave him his broad appeal. "Freedom is a fragile thing and never more than one generation away from extinction," he began. "Knowing this," he continued a little later, "it is hard to explain those who question the people's capacity for self-rule. Will they answer this: if no one among us is capable of governing himself, then who among us has the capacity to govern someone else?" This in fact is vintage Lincoln, derived directly from Thomas Jefferson, making Reagan atypical; no one on the political scene talked this way anymore.

From this general, historical beginning, Reagan zeroed in on the specific defects of the moment, especially the welfare state and high taxes. "As presently constituted, welfare's great flaw and weakness is that it perpetuates poverty for the recipients of poverty, institutionalizes their poverty into a kind of permanent degradation. . . . There is no humanity or charity in destroying self-reliance, dignity, and self-respect—the very substance of moral fibre." Most fundamentally, Reagan utterly rejected the premise of the progressive administrative state that the progress of society and government depended upon specialized expertise. "For many years now, you and I have been shushed like children and told there are no simple answers to complex problems which are beyond our comprehension. Well, the truth is, there are simple answers—but there are no easy ones. The time has come for us to decide whether collectively we can afford everything and anything we think of just because we think of it." (In a subsequent speech in mid-1967, Reagan adumbrated the point even more directly: "I think we have had enough of nineteenth-century rule of the many by the few, even if the few are supposed to be some kind of intellectual elite, who are more gifted than the rest of us.") This theme, more than any of his views on specific issues, constituted the chief source of liberal contempt for Reagan.

Reagan seldom ended a speech on the sour notes of discontent, and this time was no different. He closed with his equally typical forward-looking optimism, this time with reference to his "Creative Society," which was clearly intended to be his alternative to the Great Society. "Some who are inclined to resent any dilutions of government's influence continue to charge that people like ourselves are turning back the clock. The Creative Society is not a retreat into the past. It is taking the dream that gave birth to this nation and updating it, making it practical for the 20th century. It is a good dream. It is a dream that is worthy of your generation."

There was a final touch to the speech that would become a Reagan signature: the tribute to an American hero. "If, in glancing aloft, some of you were puzzled by the small size of our state flag—there is an explanation. That flag was carried into battle in Vietnam by young men of California. Many will not be coming home. One did, Sergeant Robert Howell, grievously wounded. He brought that flag back. I thought we would be proud to have it fly over the Capitol today. It might even serve to put our problems in better perspective. It might remind us of the need to give our sons and daughters a cause to believe in and banners to follow."

The structure and substance of the speech came to be known as "vintage Reagan," and would be the model for his first Presidential Inaugural Address 14 years later. Not many citizens of California would have heard this address had he given it at his midnight swearing-in ceremony. Reagan ostensibly picked this odd hour to be sworn in to prevent Brown from appointing any more judges—Brown appointed nearly 80 during his lame duck period after the election—Reagan joked that "I am probably the only governor in the United States who can't fix a parking ticket"—or granting any more pardons, but it has long been reported that the time was picked at the insistence of Nancy Reagan, whose penchant for astrology would provoke controversy 20 years later. Regardless, it provided Reagan with yet another opportunity to display his light touch. After the swearing-in ceremony, Reagan turned to Senator George Murphy, like Reagan a former movie actor, and quipped: "Well, George, here we are on the late show again."

CHAPTER FOUR

CENTRIFUGE:
THE LOSS OF CONTROL

W ITH EVERY PASSING DAY in the middle years of the 1960s,
each of the main troubled currents in American public life—
Vietnam, civil rights and race relations, the welfare state, and the student
movement—gained momentum. What began as a mere fraying of the
edges was becoming a wholesale unraveling, as though threads from the
four sides of a square fabric were being pulled away all at once. For a society whose intellectual premise was that the increasing mastery of people
and events through managerial expertise was an uninterrupted and irreversible process, the loss of control over events began to gnaw away at
the confidence of America's elites. The years 1966 and 1967 saw the currents of discontent achieve an unstoppable momentum.

Though events were spinning out of control, none of the technocratic
savants of the Establishment thought to question the premises behind their
policies. Vietnam was the worst case. Fighting a "limited war" was turning
out to be more difficult than fighting a total war. The Vietnam problem was
turning by imperceptible degrees into an agony. The Kennedy-McNamara
premise of American power—the calibration of "graduated pressure"—was
clearly failing, but the illusion of control persisted. By 1966 the Vietnam
War was looking more and more like a real ground war. The first troops
had been sent in 1965 to "plug the hole in the dike," as General William
Westmoreland put it at the time, but the ruinous process of fully "Ameri-
canizing" the war proceeded apace. This slippery slope might have been

avoided. Even at this point it might have been possible to train South Vietnam's army to do the job, just as the United States had raised up an effective South Korean army. "Robert S. McNamara and his assorted 'games' experts decided that it was a waste of time and energy to train the South Vietnamese army," John P. Roche wrote. "After all, it took almost two years to train the first competent Republic of Korea divisions, and in that time we could win the war all by ourselves."[1] In the fall of 1966 the South Vietnamese army was broken up into company-sized units and dispersed to the provinces to be something like a National Guard. They would not even be equipped with M-16s until 1968, and so were regularly outgunned by Viet Cong troops with Soviet AK-47s.

The American troop level passed the 200,000 mark early in 1966, and U.S. troops were increasingly engaged in serious combat. The ratio of U.S. to Viet Cong deaths in the early engagements of the war encouraged General Westmoreland and other military strategists to think that the strategy of attrition would work—eventually. In late 1966 Westmoreland uttered the infamous phrase that "there was light at the end of the tunnel," but only if the United States was "geared for the long pull."[2]

"We'll just go on bleeding them until Hanoi wakes up to the fact that they have bled their country to the point of national disaster for generations," Westmoreland reiterated in 1967. "Then they will have to reassess their position."[3] A National Security Council analyst wrote that "the communists by now ought to be in really serious trouble. . . . I don't see how they can possibly hold out beyond the summer of 1969."[4] No one seems to have done the math to see how many of the enemy would need to be "attrited" for this optimistic scenario to work. North Vietnam enjoyed a high birth rate, with about 250,000 males coming of age for military service each year. Even if the Viet Cong and North Vietnamese suffered losses at their highest rate (which came in 1968), it would have taken the United States 13 years to exhaust the enemy's manpower pool.[5]

The other trouble with a strategy of attrition in a war without fixed fronts and without the objective of conventional defeat of the enemy on his own territory is that it ceded the initiative to the North Vietnamese. They could choose the time and place for battle, and could decide what level of casualties they would accept. The Viet Cong also enjoyed the advantage of being able to mass superior numbers at the point of attack.

The Viet Cong initiated 90 percent of all engagements with U.S. forces in 1965, 1966, and 1967; most of the attacks were well organized.[6]

The United States enjoyed superior firepower and mobility, but to maintain the conventional force ratio of 10-1, which is thought necessary to defeat guerilla insurgencies, required an increasingly large commitment of troops and material throughout Vietnam. U.S. casualties mounted sharply in 1966; by the end of 1966, the American death toll for the year topped 5,000. By April of 1967, Westmoreland was asking for 200,000 more troops above and beyond the 469,000 already authorized for deployment to Vietnam. LBJ authorized only 50,000.

The North Vietnamese strategy was transparent. They sought to draw American forces away from populated areas, and hoped to cut South Vietnam in half with a thrust through the central highlands to the coast. The United States willingly obliged, rejecting the option of adopting an "enclave strategy" whereby the United States would hold a purely defensive perimeter around major cities and selected regions and wait for the North Vietnamese to tire of fighting and agree to negotiate. Such a strategy was inharmonious with not only the logistical force structure of America's military, but also its manly spirit. In order to mitigate the North's freedom of initiative, U.S. forces adopted an aggressive "search-and-destroy" tactic: They would seek out the enemy and engage him wherever they could find him. By the end of 1966 the number of armed helicopter sorties had doubled from 14,000 per month to 29,000, and troop patrols had increased by 44 percent. Viet Cong and North Vietnamese troop losses, however, did not significantly change, and overall North Vietnamese troop strength was undiminished.

The futility of search-and-destroy tactics was evident early on. "If NVA and VC units do not wish to make contact with U.S. forces in an area," a senior commander observed in early 1967, "they will simply move aside and let the enemy [U.S. forces] move past their location. When the enemy has searched the area and moved out, the VC will move back into the area."[7] Assistant Secretary of Defense John McNaughton ruefully concluded that North Vietnam's "intention is a stalemate; he can get it at whatever level [of troops] we choose to deploy."[8] A 1968 CIA report estimated that U.S. troops were able to find and engage the enemy about once out of every hundred tries; nearly all of these engagements were with enemy companies that seldom exceeded 150 troops.[9]

An even more insidious aspect of the search-and-destroy cat-and-mouse game was the Viet Cong's practice of firing on American troops from within small villages and hamlets. Anxious American troops, Guenter Lewy observed, "usually fell for the bait and assaulted the hamlets utilizing artillery barrages, aerial rocketry and tactical air strikes."[10] The Viet Cong were essentially using American firepower to brutalize the South Vietnamese population. American commanders thought the collateral destruction of hamlets and villages was unavoidable, though John Paul Vann argued that "The overwhelming majority of hamlets thus destroyed failed to yield sufficient evidence of damage to the enemy to justify the destruction of the hamlet. Indeed, it has not been unusual to have a hamlet destroyed and find absolutely no evidence of damage to the enemy."[11]

Despite the best efforts of American forces to minimize civilian casualties (policy called for hamlets to be evacuated before being attacked or destroyed), the skirmishes in and around the hamlets generated thousands of civilian casualties and resentful refugees. U.S. forces attempted to mitigate this ill will through social work—the Great Society, Vietnam chapter. "We ought to be excited about this challenge," Vice President Hubert Humphrey said about U.S. social engineering efforts in Vietnam in 1966, "because here's where we can put to work some of the ideas about . . . nation building, of new concepts of education, development of local government, the improvement of health standards of people and really the achievement and fulfillment of full social justice."[12] In 1967, for example, U.S. forces provided to the South Vietnamese people: 572,121 cakes of soap; personal hygiene classes for 212,372 people; baths for 7,555 children; and 69,652 haircuts.[13] Many soldiers sympathized with the Marine commander who wrote in a report: "It is extremely difficult for a ground commander to reconcile his tactical mission and a people-to-people program."[14]

The wasting of hamlets also generated powerful propaganda for the North Vietnamese and the antiwar movement. One of the first skeptical TV accounts was Morley Safer's *CBS Evening News* report on August 5, 1965, showing U.S. Marines using their cigarette lighters to set fire to the village of Cam Ne. Safer reported that 120 to 150 houses were burned, without mentioning the casualties Marines had suffered fighting in the hamlet, or the VC trenches and tunnels Marines had uncovered. "There is little doubt that American fire power can win a military victory here," Safer said in his stand-up conclusion to the piece. "But to a Vietnamese peasant whose home means a lifetime of backbreaking labor, it will take more than presidential promises to convince him that we are on his side."[15] Safer's report infuriated President Johnson. "Are you trying to fuck me?" an irate LBJ yelled at CBS president Frank Stanton over the phone; "Your boys shat on the American flag." GIs in Vietnam began referring to CBS as the "Communist Broadcasting System."

America's attempt to minimize civilian exposure to the war only served to fuel perceptions among casual observers (that is, anyone who watched the evening news) that the war effort was violence without clear purpose. The "nation builders" in the State Department provided the rationale for U.S. troops to resettle large numbers of rural population and to impose "land reform," so that U.S. forces could use defoliants to create "free-fire zones" in which U.S. forces would have a free hand to use their firepower to the maximum extent. But with no front and no advance toward an enemy objective, it was hard to demonstrate progress convincingly through statistical measures alone. It is politically hazardous to claim progress and control in a war situation where the enemy has the initiative.

Meanwhile, the Rolling Thunder bombing campaign was showing no sign of breaking the will of North Vietnam. "There were men of eminence in the administration," John P. Roche recalled, "who were certain that the first time an American jet flew over Hanoi, Ho would come running out with a white flag."[16] The number of bombing missions nearly tripled in 1966, rising from 55,000 in 1965 to 148,000 in 1966; total bomb tonnage increased from 33,000 tons in 1965 to 128,000 tons in 1966. By the end of 1967, the U.S. bomb tonnage exceeded the tonnage dropped against Germany and Japan in World War II.[17] The United States lost 255 planes during Rolling Thunder in 1967; by the time Rolling Thunder ended in 1968, the United States would lose 938 planes. One of those lost in 1967 belonged to Captain John McCain, who was shot down over Hanoi on October 26, breaking his right knee and both arms when he ejected from his A-4E Skyhawk fighter plane. His North Vietnamese captors were going to let him die of his wounds until they realized that McCain's father was a prominent American Navy Admiral, thus making prisoner McCain a valuable commodity.

The cost of Rolling Thunder in 1966 topped $1 billion (not counting the cost of lost aircraft), yet a Pentagon bomb-damage assessment concluded that its economic cost to North Vietnam was less than $100 million.

One reason for this out-of-whack ratio of bombing costs to economic losses is that much of the bombing had been directed against the lines of communication—roads and railroads principally—by which North Vietnam supplied men and material to its forces in South Vietnam. But the North Vietnamese proved to be highly resourceful in overcoming bomb damage to its transportation network. They were able to organize a workforce of nearly 500,000 people for bomb-damage repairs. Their ability to repair roads and rail lines rapidly (many bridges were repaired within hours of being bombed), and to transport weapons and munitions by low-tech means, such as bicycles and mules, rendered the bombing a mere inconvenience.

"The tempo of American bombing in North Vietnam was so slow that it allowed the enemy to recover from each operation," Angelo Codevilla and Paul Seabury observed.[18] "There is no case in history of a war won through the piecemeal commitment of resources." Furthermore, "As of July 1966," the Pentagon assessment of Rolling Thunder found, "the U.S. bombing of North Vietnam had had no measurable direct effect on Hanoi's ability to mount and support military operations in the South at the current level."[19] Indeed, the level of infiltration into the South had accelerated over the previous year. Moreover, the assessment found, the bombing "clearly strengthened popular support for the regime." In the meantime, American pilots were still prohibited from attacking most anti-aircraft sites and North Vietnamese warplanes that were exacting a fearsome toll on American pilots.

North Vietnam's primitive agrarian economy also presented an inherent limit to the amount of damage bombing could inflict. There was little heavy industry to bomb. Retired Air Force Chief of Staff Curtis LeMay had famously said that the United States should "bomb North Vietnam back into the Stone Age." McGeorge Bundy quipped in response to LeMay, "Maybe they're already there." While U.S. forces could (and did) bomb many transportation targets over and over again, they were running out of new targets to hit within the limits under which they had been operating since February 1965. Both Hanoi and Haiphong harbor remained substantially off limits to Rolling Thunder, as did most power plants, dams, dikes, and oil storage facilities. The Joint Chiefs of Staff had chaffed under these political restrictions since the beginning, and finally persuaded President Johnson in May 1966 to lift the restrictions partially.

Johnson authorized the bombing of oil storage facilities, and limited bombing of selected targets at Haiphong harbor (though most of the targets the Joint Chiefs wanted to hit remained off limits). By July, the Defense Intelligence Agency estimated, 70 percent of North Vietnam's oil storage facilities had been destroyed, but there was no effect on the flow of men and material to the South. North Vietnam left most of the bombed storage facilities unrepaired, and shifted to small dispersed storage sites that were nearly impossible to bomb. North Vietnam's electricity requirements were so modest that the use of 2,000 portable generators compensated for the loss of central power stations in 1967.[20] The Pentagon bombing assessment glumly concluded: "there is currently no adequate basis for predicting the levels of U.S. military effort that would be required to achieve the stated objectives—indeed, there is no firm basis for determining if there is any feasible level of effort that would achieve these objectives."[21]

This conclusion came as a body blow to the Pentagon whiz kids who thought the ends and means of warfare could be precisely predicted and calibrated with the tools of quantitative systems analysis. McNamara, who the year before had thought that the limited bombing was "getting our point across," now began to suspect that nothing "short of destruction of the regime or occupation of North Vietnamese territory will with high confidence reduce the flow of men and material" to the South. The Joint Chiefs of Staff had something like this very much in mind: an intensified, gloves-off bombing campaign, and a partial invasion of North Vietnam. The specter of Korea haunted Johnson; he feared that intensified bombing, the mining of Haiphong harbor, or a partial invasion might provoke the Chinese. McNamara rejected the Chiefs views for more craven reasons. "There may be a limit beyond which many Americans and much of the world will not permit the United States to go," McNamara answered. "It [intensified bombing and an invasion] could conceivably produce a costly distortion in the American national consciousness and in the world image of the United States."[22]

Yet the distortion of the national conscience was limited chiefly to certain elite precincts such as McNamara's old neighborhood in Ann Arbor, Michigan. The radicalized mobs shouting "Hey, hey, LBJ, how many kids did you kill today?" did not have a significant effect on the mainstream of American public opinion, except to increase the unpopularity of the antiwar movement. The largest block of public opinion supported a *stronger* war policy. A Lou Harris Poll in May 1967 found that 45 percent of the public favored "total military victory," with Johnson receiving a 72 percent approval rating for his handling of the war.[23] The Harris Poll also revealed that 65 percent agreed with the statement that "the military has been handicapped by civilians who won't let them go all out."[24] A Gallup Poll taken the same week reported that 25 percent of the American public favored using nuclear weapons in Vietnam, while only 14 percent were for withdrawal.[25] Another Gallup Poll in the fall found that 53 percent favored increasing attacks. Most candidates who ran on an antiwar platform in 1966 were defeated, and in November 1967, San Francisco voters voted 63 to 37 percent against an advisory measure calling for U.S. withdrawal.[26] A popular bumper sticker expressed the common sense view of a great many Americans: WIN OR GET OUT.

The very restraint of the bombing campaign ironically fueled rather than alleviated the intensity of the criticism of the war. In addition to the sharp limits on bomb targets (intended in part to minimize civilian casualties), periodic halts in the bombing campaign designed to entice the North Vietnamese to negotiate only served to make the bombing seem a capricious display of American petulance rather than a military necessity. With each bombing halt, Roche recalled, "emissaries were practically shot out of cannons into the wide world to spread the tidings of American willingness to negotiate." (Johnson had publicly called for "unconditional negotiations" in April 1965.) The North Vietnamese continued to refuse all invitations to negotiate, while skillfully playing the negotiation game themselves to the maximum disadvantage of the United States. As Roche explained the game:

> The North Vietnamese political warfare experts had a marvelous time. Kites would be flown in the most unlikely places: a Hanoi actor performing in some African nation would pointedly tell the French (or British or Dutch . . .) second secretary at a cocktail party that . . . maybe there was some room for maneuver. First, of course, the bombing must stop, but then . . . ? This would lead to a spasm in the Harriman office, a small unit in the State Department charged with following up all chances for negotiations. Cables would flow off to Ft. Lamy, or wherever, and inevitably, when the smoke cleared,

there was nothing there. Except perhaps some headlines in the American press to the effect that we had thrown away another chance for peace by our rigidity.[27]

"We are no longer fighting a war in Vietnam," Roche told President Johnson in March 1967; "we are fighting a 'negotiation.'" As a good Leninist, Roche tried to make Johnson understand, Ho Chi Minh viewed negotiations as just another weapons system. Johnson kept asking, Roche recalls, "'What does Ho want?' as if Ho were a mayor of Chicago holding out for five new post offices."[28] Roche presciently predicted to Johnson in April 1967 that North Vietnam would agree to negotiate "at the worst possible time in terms of American internal unity"—right before the 1968 presidential election.

Johnson's incredulity over North Vietnam's refusal to negotiate was only one aspect of the confusion amidst the senior levels of the administration. Johnson's desire for consensus among his advisers meant that a fundamental rethinking of the course of the war would not take place. The Joint Chiefs of Staff and other hawkish civilian advisers (not to mention many members of Congress) wanted a stepped-up effort, and Johnson was inclined to agree much of the time. "In retrospect, we may have been too cautious for too long," Johnson said in the fall of 1967. "Eisenhower may be right. If gradualism doesn't pay off early, then the enemy must be regarded as the enemy and fought with all resources, with no sanctuary or quarter given."[29] He began to understand that his attempt to minimize the magnitude of the war on account of domestic political considerations was exacting a toll on his ability to wage war successfully. "We have no songs, no parades, no bond drives and we can't win the war otherwise," Johnson complained. Johnson and Westmoreland steadfastly denied that the United States was stuck in a stalemate (which, of course, had been the express goal of policy two years before), but the prestige press wasn't buying. On August 7, 1967, the *New York Times* ran the headline: "Vietnam, the Signs of Stalemate."

The principal architect of Vietnam policy, McNamara, was beginning to have growing doubts as 1966 gave way to 1967. He urged Johnson to halt the bombing starting in the fall of 1966. His substitute for bombing and for still more troops bordered on the bizarre. He suggested the United States construct an "infiltration barrier," a physical barrier running across the width of Vietnam near the demilitarized zone at the 17th parallel that would cut off South Vietnam. The barrier, which was first suggested by Harvard Law School professor Roger Fisher, would consist of a 10-mile-wide defoliated strip, with land mines (20 million a month would be required), "self-sterilizing gravel," barbed-wire fencing, acoustic and seismic sensors that could distinguish human from animal footfalls, chemical sensors, and round-the-clock air patrols. McNamara's study team estimated that it would cost $800 million a year to build and maintain the barrier. Pentagon skeptics recognized this as the military equivalent of trying to keep ants out of the kitchen, and tried to kill the idea in a study committee. But the idea went forward, and by the end of 1967 the Pentagon had ordered five million steel fence posts and enough barbed wire to circle the globe twice. The Joint Chiefs of Staff privately referred to the whiz kids' latest technocratic scheme as an "Alice in Wonderland solution to insurgency," while soldiers on the ground in Vietnam called the project "McNamara's Line"—a slighting reference to the Maginot Line (France's famous fixed fortification that Hitler simply went around in 1940).[30] Major Colin Powell thought the most absurd feature of the McNamara Line was the "people sniffer," which was "a device that could detect concentrations of urine on the ground from an airplane. . . . If the urine was detected in likely enemy territory, we now had an artillery target. But woe to any innocent peasants or water buffaloes that happened to relieve themselves in the wrong place."[31] Governor Reagan was similarly acerbic: "One wonders," Reagan said, "if that billion dollar electronic fence McNamara ordered built along the demilitarized zone to keep out the Communists shouldn't properly be considered part of the federal highway program—there is so much enemy traffic using it as a thoroughfare these days."[32] Like the Maginot Line in 1940, it was a simple matter for the North Vietnamese to flank the barrier through Laos.

McNamara's doubts continued to grow, and on June 17, 1967, he commissioned an in-depth "study" to explain how and why Vietnam policy had run aground—the study that would come to be known as the "Pentagon Papers" when they were leaked in 1971. He did not tell Johnson that he had ordered the study. It is not clear what McNamara hoped to learn from a "study" that would be nearly two-dozen volumes long at its completion.

It is a measure of McNamara's technocratic soullessness that he disdained to refer to the North Vietnamese as "the enemy." When McNamara testified to the Senate Armed Services Committee and contradicted previous testimony from top military officials about the effects of the bombing campaign, the Joint Chiefs of Staff reportedly considered resigning in mass to protest McNamara's malfeasance and ineptitude. But General Wheeler, the chairman of the JCS, got cold feet and changed his mind. "We can't do it," Wheeler is reported to have said. "It's mutiny. If we resign they'll just get someone else. And we'd be forgotten."[33] McNamara had also undermined his stature with the one person who counted most— President Johnson—and by the fall Johnson was ready to rid himself of McNamara. On November 28, Johnson named McNamara (who Johnson had esteemed so highly in 1964 that he seriously considered him to become his running mate) to head the World Bank.

While the once-confident McNamara was ready to throw in the towel, others retained their optimism. General Westmoreland continued to make the case that progress was being made, but, significantly, Westmoreland recalled in his memoirs that when he addressed Congress in 1967 "I specifically avoided using the word 'victory,' for the national goal was not to win a military victory over North Vietnam."[34] Though he was publicly upbeat, he was telling Johnson that the war might go on for another five years. In 1967 Johnson agreed to relax a few more of the restrictions on bombing, finally allowing the military to target power plants and some airfields. By the end of 1967 the American troop level in Vietnam was up to 469,000, and the Joint Chiefs argued again for calling up the reserves. Johnson's special assistant Bruce Komer returned from a 10-day trip to Vietnam early in 1967 "more optimistic than ever before. . . . indisputably, we are winning the war in the South. . . . Indeed, my broad feeling . . . is that our side now has in presently programmed levels all the men, money and other resources needed to achieve success."[35] After another trip to Vietnam four months later, Komer was even more ebullient: "The real question is not whether we need more U.S. troops to 'win' the war in the South, but rather how fast we want to win it."[36] The year 1968, Komer and other optimists thought, would see the turning point in favor of the United States.

History has not been kind to these optimists, but they may have been more correct than the fierce historiography of the Vietnam War admits. North Vietnam's strategy of cutting South Vietnam in half with offensive actions in the central highlands had been thwarted, at a cost of more than 40,000 troops killed in the last six months of 1967. Though the North

Vietnamese always enjoyed the tactical initiative, they had lost the strategic initiative. No North Vietnamese division or regiment had launched a successful attack in more than two years. Resupply of Communist troops was eroding. Viet Cong desertions were up sharply, and morale, according to captured North Vietnamese documents, was suffering. The population control figures generated by the U.S. "hamlet evaluation system," which *U.S. News and World Report* described as "run by sociologists and aided by computers," may be rightly regarded with skepticism, but the reported trend of decreased Viet Cong control of the population was generally correct. Moreover, General Nguyen Thanh, the architect of North Vietnam's war plans, had been killed in July.

The military situation, viewed on narrow objective grounds, justified the Johnson administration's public relations campaign presenting an optimistic view to the public. That this public optimism proved to be a major mistake was the result of persisting in the two fundamental errors of the whole war. The United States underestimated the will and the capacity of North Vietnam to carry on indefinitely, and Johnson continued to signal the underlying weakness of the U.S. commitment to the war. If, as the military situation suggested, the United States was gaining the upper hand, why continue to beg the North Vietnamese to negotiate? Although Johnson publicly stated, most forcefully in his "San Antonio Formula" speech in September 1967, that the United States would not give in to the North Vietnamese strategy of outlasting the patience of the United States, Johnson's increasingly plaintive calls for negotiation reassured the North Vietnamese that the United States didn't mean it. In the San Antonio Formula (in which the United States offered to halt the bombing of the North in exchange for negotiations and a pledge that the North wouldn't exploit the bombing halt—a ceasefire, in essence), Johnson said he would "send a trusted representative of America to any spot on this earth" to negotiate. Hanoi twitted Johnson by saying no thanks, but since Johnson had said "any spot on this earth," Phnom Penh in Cambodia would suit Hanoi just fine as a meeting place if the United States unilaterally halted bombing and included the Viet Cong as a negotiating party.

If the resolve of the North Vietnamese toward negotiations didn't cause the Johnson administration to pause before making a public relations campaign proclaiming progress, then fresh reports of enemy troop levels should have. In the late summer of 1967, a dispute broke out within the U.S. intelligence community over how to count enemy troop strength in South Vietnam. The CIA wanted to include 120,000 so-called Viet Cong "Self-Defense" and "Secret Self-Defense" forces in the official estimate of the enemy Order of Battle. These Viet Cong irregulars mostly engaged in defensive actions such as planting mines and booby-traps in close defense of their strongholds. Though most of these irregular forces were not well armed, the CIA argued that they were nonetheless available for military action against the United States in the event of a major offensive. Adding these 120,000 troops to the official Order of Battle estimate would swell the total enemy troop level to more than 430,000. Moreover, the CIA thought that reinforcements of North Vietnamese regular army troops were increasing, rather than decreasing—a view that would be proven correct in a few months.

The CIA's view clashed with military intelligence in Saigon, which excluded all self-defense forces in their total enemy troop estimate of 298,000, which was the number the United States had furnished to the media. Bureaucratic and political infighting occurred over which estimate would be accepted as the "official" figure for enemy troop strength. A higher official estimate, obviously, would vitiate claims of "progress" in the war, and present fresh political problems for the administration.

Ultimately the CIA relented, and the lower figure preferred by military intelligence in Saigon was sent on to President Johnson. This episode entered the lore of Vietnam demonology as yet another mendacious deception, culminating in famous *CBS News* special broadcast 15 years later, "The Uncounted Enemy: A Vietnam Deception," and a subsequent libel suit that Gen. Westmoreland brought against CBS. CBS followed the demonologists' line that Westmoreland and military intelligence had deceived Johnson with a low enemy troop estimate they knew to be false. This thesis seems superficially plausible in light of the surprise of the Tet Offensive a few months later, which involved many of the Viet Cong Self-Defense forces that military intelligence wanted left out of the official count. But it is highly unlikely that a deliberate deception took place. As Vietnam scholar Larry Berman argued, "Westmoreland would have needed literally hundreds of accomplices in the State Department, Defense Department, CIA, and the White House in order to suppress reports of North Vietnamese regular army infiltration."[37] Intelligence is only as good as the interpretation that is given to it, and in a war situation, where the opening strategy of seeking a stalemate needs to be sold to the public as "progress," intelligence gathering and interpretation will always be compromised. Johnson would soon pay dearly for his misconception of the war, but the war was not the only place where the nation's leaders were misleading themselves.

ON THE HOME FRONT, many in the Johnson administration in 1966 were optimistic that a turning point in the war on poverty was also in reach. In his State of the Union speech in January 1966, Johnson declared again his can-do attitude: "This Nation is mighty enough, its society is healthy enough, its people are strong enough, to pursue our goals in the rest of the world while still building a Great Society here at home." In other words, as many a critic has noted, it would be "guns and butter" for LBJ. Johnson proposed 113 separate legislative measures to expand the Great Society. Congress would end up enacting 97 of them. On the surface this would seem to be an indication of substantial momentum for the Great Society; in fact below the surface the War on Poverty was spinning out of control just as surely as the Vietnam War, and for much the same reasons: Resources were being wasted, and the ideological conflict over what should be done whipsawed policy makers. In 1966 Sargent Shriver was still proclaiming that poverty could be completely eliminated in 10 years. But by the middle of 1967, Lyndon Johnson, whose inflated rhetoric had done much to generate unrealistic expectations, was so discouraged at the loss of control over the Great Society agenda that he worried aloud that "we may never live to see an America without poverty."[38] What happened?

Since the end of World War II poverty in America had been steadily declining, from 30.2 percent in 1950 to 17.3 percent in 1965. Then, with the launching of the War on Poverty, this progress slowed and within a few years began to reverse. Coincidence? The question will be forever debated, but it is a matter of record that the number of people on welfare started soaring in the middle of the 1960s. During the sharp decline in poverty in the 1950s (which decade, remember, liberals had scorned for its slow economic growth and unimaginative policy under President Eisenhower), the welfare caseload grew by only 7 percent. From 1960 to 1965 it grew by 24 percent. Still, even with this 24 percent increase, at the beginning of the Great Society only about one-third of all poor people who were eligible to receive welfare were on the rolls. But between 1965 and 1970, the welfare caseload would grow by 125 percent, and by 1970, 90 percent of eligible poor people were on the welfare rolls.[39] (In raw terms, the number of welfare recipients increased from three million in 1960 to 9.6 million in 1970.)

Thoughtful liberals, who had seen how the Community Action Program was misfiring, were beginning to have second thoughts about the course of the Great Society. The early Great Society, as we have seen, emphasized opportunity rather than income equalization as its main theme. In the quest to treat the "lack of opportunity" as the "root cause" of poverty, the social scientists who designed the idea had shied away from confronting some basic conceptual problems. Moynihan posed the unexamined question: "In what way are the poor different from others?" Poverty, Moynihan and other social scientists were starting to see, was not simply a lack of money, but involved deep-seated cultural patterns that were not susceptible to easy remedy. Though Moynihan favored switching to an income strategy, he admitted to not knowing whether or how it might work. "We possess hardly two bits worth (or two bits of) reliable information as to how changes in income affect individual styles of life."[40] Moynihan and other social scientists hoped to find out, while the Johnson administration and many leading members of Congress were hoping to affect a mid-course correction that would impose some discipline on the rising welfare rolls.

The expansion of welfare and other poverty programs (the number of people receiving food stamps was rising rapidly during this period as well) represented a willy-nilly move toward an income strategy, though it suffered the defect of requiring, in the case of welfare, that fathers be absent from the home in order to be eligible for welfare. The great irony of the Community Action Program's emphasis on opportunity, as we have seen, was that this supposedly conservative program mostly succeeded in providing opportunity for radical-minded people to organize mischief among poor neighborhoods. The same dynamic would come into play with the effort to make sense of the soaring welfare rolls. While reform liberals, true to their tradition, sought to restrain the burgeoning welfare state and render it harmonious with democratic principles of social responsibility, the Marx-besotted Left saw a growing welfare state as a means of advancing their radical critique of American society. The poor were a convenient pawn. While conservatives attacked the welfare state for already having gone too far, the Left was starting to attack welfare for not going far enough. They wanted it vastly expanded. The attack from the Left would end up being much more harmful to the interests of the poor than the attack from the Right.

The skirmish line over the character of welfare programs first formed in the small New York town of Newburgh several years earlier. A town of about 30,000, Newburgh's city manager Joseph Mitchell attempted to impose some limits and conditions on welfare recipients after the city's welfare costs had risen higher than what the city spent for police protection. President Eisenhower's administration had given states and localities wide latitude in crafting their welfare systems, and Newburgh followed several states that had imposed residency requirements for eligibility. Mitchell wanted to go further, and adopt a work requirement for all recipients of aid, monthly reviews of each recipient's case, and, most dramatic of all, a complete cutoff for any mother who bore an illegitimate child. The New York State Board of Social Welfare came down hard on Newburgh, saying the proposals violated state and federal law. The State Board threatened to withhold funds. Governor Nelson Rockefeller concurred with the State Board, and threatened additional executive action against the town. The message was clear: Cities and states would not be allowed to impose responsible behavioral conditions on their welfare recipients. It was the beginning of the entitlement mentality.

The Newburgh incident occurred in 1961, just as the Kennedy administration's first attempts at "welfare reform" (which really meant "welfare expansion") were getting underway. By the mid-1960s the entitlement mentality was hardening, and welfare was starting to be described as an individual *right* every bit as fundamental as the individual political rights to free speech and free assembly. The distinction between political rights against government encroachment—negative liberties, they are often called—and "rights" which impose an obligation on others to fulfill, was beginning to be lost from liberal discourse.

The traditional social policy anchor of individual responsibility might have won out had welfare policy remained the province of the political branches of government. But in the mid-1960s welfare policy came to be driven by bureaucrats, pressure groups, and lawsuits. In 1966 a civil rights activist named George Wiley founded the National Welfare Rights

Organization (NWRO), which was intended to serve as something like a labor union for poor people. The NWRO immediately began to lobby for the expansion of welfare as a right, which found a willing ear among the growing ranks of professional social workers with a bureaucratic interest in finding more poverty.

"Getting rid of the stigma of welfare was a deliberate goal," Charles Murray observed.[41] In New York City, Mayor John Lindsay's commissioner of social services, Mitchell Ginsberg, announced a major shift in policy. The city's welfare department would no longer scrutinize the eligibility of welfare applicants. A "simplified" system of "self-declaration" would suffice. If you claimed to be poor, that was good enough to get a check. Ginsberg even discontinued the practice of home visits, wherein welfare caseworkers would verify eligibility as well as make assessments of the problems of a welfare household. Ginsberg was unconcerned with the soaring cost to the taxpayers: "I have always viewed the cost of welfare to be whatever it is."[42] Ginsberg encouraged welfare caseworkers to actively seek for more people to put on the welfare rolls (it was estimated that less than half of the people who were eligible to collect welfare in New York City were on the rolls), prompting the New York *Daily News* to dub him Mitchell "Come-And-Get-It" Ginsberg.

"It became something of a badge of honor," one welfare expert wrote, "for caseworkers to manipulate the regulations to build the largest possible grant for a client."[43] Mayor Lindsay went along with this strategy in part because he regarded it as "riot insurance," and in part because he thought he could pass the cost along to the federal government. Welfare costs were already second only to education in the city's budget. In 1966 Lindsay asked the federal government for $50 billion in aid for New York City over the next 10 years. He would get much of this aid, but the city would still go bankrupt. The statistics on the explosion of the welfare rolls in New York City are shocking: In 1960, one person in 30 had been on welfare. By 1970, the ratio had soared to one out of seven.

In addition to lobbying the bureaucracy to expand welfare, the NWRO and other welfare advocates realized that they could perhaps emulate the civil rights movement and get some of what they wanted through litigation. The Department of Health, Education, and Welfare issued new guidelines forbidding unannounced visits to welfare recipient's homes to check eligibility. The U.S. Supreme Court struck down the "man in the house" rule, which had allowed welfare agencies to deny benefits to any woman who lived with a man (even if the man was not her husband). Another court ruling struck down residency requirements. The expansion of government social aid was not limited to the old AFDC (Aid to Families with Dependent Children) welfare program; the number of people enrolling in disability programs and for Food Stamps was also skyrocketing. Between 1960 and 1970, two million people were added to disability relief, a 288 percent increase. (The total number of workers covered by disability had risen by only about 15 percent.)[44] The Food Stamp program had 424,000 recipients in 1965; by the time Johnson left office in 1969, 2.2 million were collecting Food Stamps, a 418 percent increase. Federal spending for social programs was growing at about a 20 percent annual rate.

To the argument that this rapid expansion in welfare spending would entail the fiscal ruin of state and local governments, the welfare lobby replied: precisely. A "welfare crisis" was the explicit goal of the pro-welfare lobby. Richard Cloward and Frances Fox Piven of Columbia University's department of social work (where Mitchell Ginsberg had been recruited from) explained the strategy in *The Nation* magazine:

> Widespread campaigns to register the eligible poor for welfare aid, and to help existing recipients obtain their full benefits, would produce bureaucratic disruption in welfare agencies and fiscal disruption in local and state governments. These disruptions would generate severe political strains. . . . If this strategy were implemented, a political crisis would result that could lead to legislation for a guaranteed annual income and thus an end to poverty. . . . By crisis, we mean a *publicly visible* disruption in some institutional sphere.[45]

"The ultimate aim of this strategy," Cloward and Piven admitted later in the article, "is a new program for direct income distribution." It was not simply that the existing welfare program was inadequate and imposed a variety of "demeaning" eligibility regulations, Cloward and Piven thought. Their main objection was philosophical; they rejected the individualist premise of the War on Poverty programs such as the Office of Economic Opportunity that sought to transform poor people into functioning members of middle class society through education and job training. Cloward, Piven, and the NWRO constituted a radical rejection of the

Great Society, as well as an embrace of Leninist tactics to attack the welfare state from the Left. They would use The System to undermine The System. And violence and rioting in the cities, when it came, would be viewed by the radicals as a sign of their *success*.

The radical campaign on behalf of direct income redistribution coincided with the growing support among moderate reform liberals such as Moynihan for a guaranteed annual income (GAI). But it was not only liberals and the extreme Left that flirted with the idea; the GAI also had some support on the Right. Milton Friedman endorsed a version of the GAI through what he called the "negative income tax," while the Ripon Society, which represented Republican "moderates," endorsed the GAI in 1967. Even Richard Nixon, then in the midst of his long march to the White House, was privately flirting with the idea.

Meanwhile, antipoverty warriors in the White House were coming to the view that the opportunity strategy would not work, and that the radicals were right: An income maintenance strategy might have to be adopted. And whereas Franklin Roosevelt had warned against a permanent dole as "a narcotic, a subtle destroyer of the human spirit," practically no one on any side of the question seemed to give much serious thought to the problem of welfare dependence, and whether a GAI would make that problem intractable. A major blow to the Great Society's opportunity strategy came with the famous Coleman Report in 1966, which concluded that educational spending had little effect on outcomes. Both the Left and the Right seized upon the Coleman Report—the Right to support the view that federal social engineering was misguided and should be ended, and the Left to support the view that income redistribution was the only answer. Johnson opened a crack in the door for a GAI when he commented that he would "examine any plan, however unconventional."

Support for the GAI was generally limited to the intellectual class, however; Congress was less than lukewarm about the idea. To the extent that liberal politicians seriously entertained the idea of a GAI, it was out of a desire to find a way to disassociate themselves from the growing unpopularity of Johnson's handling of the Vietnam War. Among the skeptics of a GAI at that time was South Dakota Senator George McGovern, who criticized "the handout approach to the problems of the poor." He endorsed the original Great Society emphasis on programs that "enable the poor and indolent to contribute to society rather than surviving as a drag on society."[46] The principles of individual responsibility and expanded opportunity still held sway among reform liberals.

So even as the nascent welfare lobby was succeeding in swelling the welfare rolls, the political momentum was already beginning to shift in the other direction. In 1967 the first attempt at "welfare reform," that is, rolling back the expansion of welfare, took place. Wilbur Mills, the powerful chairman of the House Ways and Means Committee, pushed through a series of reforms including a freeze on federal matching funds for welfare cases attributable to illegitimacy or the desertion of the father. Mills and other reformers hoped to push states to discourage illegitimacy and to track down "deadbeat dads." The reformers also sought to impose a work requirement on welfare recipients, though the provision was riddled with exemptions that made it wholly ineffective.

Most welfare advocates, and many Johnson Administration officials, thought that less than 1 percent of people on welfare were capable of work. (The program was called WIN, for "Work INcentive program," because the more direct acronym—WIP—was thought to convey an unfortunate connotation.) The funding freeze and strictures on illegitimacy and absentee fathers created an uproar among the welfare rights advocates and their allies within social service bureaucracies. After considerable hesitation, the Johnson Administration declined to enforce the funding freeze, and it was quietly repealed under the Nixon Administration in 1969. It would be 25 years before such serious reforms would be attempted again.

The uproar against imposing some modest conditions of individual responsibility on welfare recipients was a manifestation of the growing weakness of the liberal mind, if not an expression of liberal guilt itself. But if liberals were proving increasingly weak-minded about welfare, they had completely lost their minds about crime. Serious crime, which had been flat since 1950, had been growing by about 20 percent a year starting in 1964. As most crimes are committed by young males, some of this upswing could have been anticipated on demographic grounds alone. The liberal reaction to the sudden escalation in crime was a mixture of denial and excuse. Attorney General Ramsey Clark, who would later distinguish himself for embracing every anti-American enthusiasm that erupted anywhere in the world, worked the denial angle, saying in 1967 that "The level of crime has risen a little bit, but there is no wave of crime in the country." What about the statistics showing crime rising 20 percent a year? a reporter asked Clark. "We do ourselves a great disservice with statistics," Clark answered.[47] This flight in the face of the public's common sense about crime would prove to be perhaps liberalism's most damaging long-term mistake.

Like poverty, liberals talked of treating the "root causes" of crime, which practically invited the public to draw the connection between expanding welfare and rising crime (not to mention rioting). And it was not an accident in the public mind that the upswing in crime coincided with a series of Supreme Court cases, most famously the *Miranda* case in 1966, that broadened the legal protections for criminal suspects. Given that roughly one out of four criminal cases is solved through the voluntary confession of the suspect (courts routinely excluded involuntary or coerced confessions before *Miranda*), the *Miranda* decision had an immediate and dramatic effect on the "clearance" rate of crimes by the police. In New York City, the proportion of suspects who confessed dropped from 49 percent to 14 percent; in Pittsburgh, from 48 percent to 29 percent. Overall, the rate of violent crimes solved by police fell by one-third, and the rate of property crimes solved fell almost in half.[48] The ultimate irony of *Miranda* came to pass a decade later, when Ernesto Miranda, the plaintiff in the case, was stabbed to death in an Arizona bar. Police detained a suspect, who, having been apprised of his *Miranda* rights, refused questioning and was released. Miranda's murder was never solved.

The deterioration in criminal justice was not limited merely to catching criminals; punishment also began to slip. Even as crime was rising sharply, the number of criminals in prison was *falling*, and average time-served was declining. Punishment was out; "rehabilitation" was in. The public went along with this—for a while. In July 1966, a Gallup Poll found for the first time a larger number of Americans *opposed* the death penalty, by a 47 to 42 percent margin. This did not last long, however, and as crime rose, support for the death penalty soared back to 67 percent by 1976, peaking at 79 percent in September 1988.

In the face of this obvious deterioration in the criminal justice system, liberals decided to blame—society. Johnson had appointed a President's Commission on Law Enforcement and the Administration of Justice, which reported to the American people in February 1967 that neither law enforcement nor the administration of justice could do very much by themselves to stem rising crime. "The underlying problems are ones that the criminal justice system can do little about," the Commission said. "Unless society does take concerted action to change the general conditions and attitudes that are associated with crime, no improvement in law enforcement and administration of justice, the subjects this Commission was specifically asked to study, will be of much avail."

The Commission's report became a collateral endorsement for enlarging the Great Society: "Warring on poverty, inadequate housing and unemployment, is warring on crime. A civil rights law is a law against crime. Money for schools is money against crime. Medical, psychiatric, and family-counseling services are services against crime." The Commission endorsed, among other progressive measures, giving convicts furloughs to work in the community during daytime hours. The only measures the Commission didn't endorse were the ones the public most strongly desired: money for police protection and more prisons. To the contrary, the Commission endorsed lenience toward criminals: "Above all, the Commission's inquiries have convinced it that it is undesirable that offenders travel any further along the full course from arrest to charge to sentence to detention than is absolutely necessary for society's protection and the offenders' own welfare."[49]

Liberalism would be a generation recovering from this kind of thinking. Many poor urban neighborhoods have yet to recover, for it was precisely the poor, and largely black, populations of central cities who suffered most from this negligent criminology—the very constituency liberals thought they were advancing. Blacks were two and a half times more likely than whites to be victims of crime in 1966, and this gap would widen over the next decade as black victimization in the inner city soared. Charles Murray noted that "it was much more dangerous to be black in 1972 than it was in 1965, whereas it was not much more dangerous to be white." By 1970, social scientists at the Massachusetts Institute of Technology concluded, a person living in a central city faced a higher risk of being murdered than a World War II soldier did of dying in combat.[50] But when Richard Nixon and conservatives called for a return to "law and order," the phrase was attacked as "a code phrase for racism."

Even among many Democrats, the Great Society was losing its allure. Wilbur Mills, as we have seen, led the unsuccessful charge to restrain welfare. But the surest signal that the political tide was turning against the

War on Poverty came in the summer of 1967, when, just days after the Newark riot, Congress voted down Johnson's proposal for a $40 million federal rat extermination program for the cities. It was a typical expression of the view that social problems required a centralized federal solution. Moynihan noted that there was no serious data on the extent of the rat problem in American cities. "That wild rats should be controlled, no one would question," Moynihan wrote, "but it was not unreasonable to ask whether yet another Federal categorical aid program—a few million dollars to be spread over a continent—was the most sensible approach."[51]

Fifty-nine House Democrats joined with 148 Republicans to vote down the rat bill. It was the rhetoric, and not the comparatively modest sum involved, that made this a notable episode. Congressmen joked about LBJ's "civil rats" bill, with a "rat corps" to be presided over by "a high commissioner of rats." "Mr. Speaker," the typical speech went, "I think the 'rat smart thing' for us to do is to vote down this rat bill 'rat now.'" Florida Democrat James Haley suggested releasing "federally funded cats" in the cities instead. The rat bill was successfully revived at the end of the year as a part of a bigger spending bill, but its ignominious treatment in mid-summer foreshadowed the growing revolt against the relentless centralization of modern liberalism.

WITH THE TWIN WARS going badly, the atmosphere inside the White House oscillated between confusion, frustration, and stubborn optimism. Johnson's political compass was wobbling badly; he still thought the greatest threat to his agenda came from the Right. The New Left, now almost wholly galvanized by the Vietnam War, was moving in an asymmetrical direction from Johnson. It had set out, as one spokesman put it, to "murder liberalism in its official robes." For Johnson and many other liberals, this killing would seem a mystery to them, even as it unfolded in front of their eyes.

During 1966 and 1967 the New Left transformed itself in three ways. It changed from being an anti-war movement into an anti-American movement, actively siding with America's war enemy; it changed intellectually from being a critical movement into a movement of almost pure nihilist negation; and consequently it changed from being a protest movement into a movement of active resistance that would eventually embrace violence. The SDS promised to "open up a front in the mother country." *Ramparts* editor Peter Collier wrote: "We were the Americong." The sheer intensity of the New Left's activities assured itself of a long half-life in the American mind whose active residue is still evident today, yet it was in fact embarking down a dead-end road. It would quickly surrender what little moral authority it ever plausibly held. It increasingly evinced an attitude best described by C. S. Lewis 25 years before: "Peace matters more than honor and can be preserved by jeering at colonels." John P. Roche saw this coming, writing in 1965: "Leaving aside pacifism, on what grounds can one argue that our Vietnamese policy is *immoral?* (Not mistaken, but immoral.) There is only one other foundation for such a position, namely, that North Vietnam is a historically progressive regime confronted by a reactionary, imperialist creation in South Vietnam."[52]

The "New" Left had begun in the late 1950s as an attempt to distance radicalism from having to defend the Soviet Union—the albatross of the "Old" Left of the 1930s and 1940s. Between Khrushchev's admission of the Stalinist purges, the Soviet invasion of Hungary in 1956, and other outrages, western radicals found it impossible to continue their embrace of Soviet Communism. Thus began the familiar radical dodge that the Soviet Union was corrupt and did not represent "true" Marxist socialism. The Marxist ideology was substantially unchanged, but as former New Left leader David Horowitz explained, the New Left thought "we could create a new socialist vision free from the taint that Stalin had placed on the movement our parents had served. . . . As members of a new radical generation, our political identity was virginal: We could position ourselves as radical critics of American society without having to defend the crimes committed by the Soviet bloc."[53]

The New Left would not maintain its virginity for long, in part because of its eagerness to be seduced by the next huckster of socialist utopianism. In the 1960s the leading Lothario of the Left was Fidel Castro's Cuba, which New Left leaders stampeded to visit and embrace. The adoration of Castro and his regime began simultaneously with Castro's coming out as a dedicated Communist. Castro, historian John Patrick Diggins observed, was "a John Wayne of the Left."[54] In 1961 Saul Landau wrote in the *New Left Review* that "Cuba is the first purposeful society that we have had in the Western hemisphere for many years . . . where men have a certain dignity, and where this is guaranteed to them." The

Leftist crusaders for freedom always were quick to denigrate "bourgeois" freedoms such as free speech. "To the Cuban worker," Landau wrote, "free speech meant very little. The revolution is everything to them."[55]

The Old Left apologists for Soviet Communism in the 1930s used to attempt to associate their radicalism with the great tradition of the American democratic revolution with the slogan, "Communism is merely 20th-century Americanism," as though Samuel Adams and Leon Trotsky were somehow plausible kindred spirits. The New Left had no use for the American political tradition or its heroes such as Thomas Jefferson. By the middle years of the 1960s, Todd Gitlin admitted, "we found our exemplars and heroes in Cuba, in China, in the Third World guerrilla movements, in Mao and Franz Fanon and Che and Debray, most of all—decisively—in Vietnam."[56] A sojourn to Cuba became *di rigeuer* for Gitlin and countless other Leftists. Gitlin's description of his first-ever visit outside the United States in late 1967 captures the growing anti-American hatred of the New Left: "To breathe un-American air for three days felt to me like liberation."[57] It was during a trip to Cuba in 1964 that Jerry Rubin first coined the term "Amerika" that became a staple of New Left rhetoric. (Rubin attributed the term to Che Guevara, but the authenticity of this origin is dubious.).

It was a highly credulous New Left that traipsed through Cuba in those days, waxing rhapsodic about farm workers heading off to sugar cane fields singing revolutionary songs, and becoming positively rapturous when told how revolutionary guerrilla soldiers longed for the day they could put down their guns and pick up books of poetry. How enlightened, Leftists thought, compared to the average American factory worker, who longed to put down his tools only so he could pick up a Budweiser. Above all, Cuba's revolutionary vanguard constantly reiterated to their American visitors their "solidarity" with North Vietnam. It was a magnificent public relations effort on behalf of Ho Chi Minh. Whereas in early 1965 the SDS and other parts of the Left had still been split over whether the United States should withdraw from Vietnam immediately, by the end of 1966 the New Left was actively on the side of North Vietnam. *The New Republic*'s Andrew Kopkind succinctly described the change of view in 1967: "I was no longer merely 'against the war,' but struggling in solidarity with Vietnamese revolutionaries."[58]

The transfixation with the Vietnam War and the infatuation with America's enemies contributed to the swift intellectual decay of the New

Left. It was not enough for the New Left to argue that the war was immoral and that capitalism was an inferior and unjust social system. They needed a unified field theory to explain the supposedly moral and social bankruptcy of what appeared on the surface to be the most prosperous and successful nation on earth. The New Left embraced without discrimination (and without much intellectual rigor) every off-the-shelf radical critique of civilization available, beginning with Marx but also including Sigmund Freud, C. Wright Mills, Paul Goodman, and Norman Brown. The most influential critique, however, was found in the abstruse writings of Herbert Marcuse.

Marcuse offered an all-encompassing gloss on the Marxist idea of "false consciousness" that was perfectly suited to the vanity and intellectual insecurity of student radicals. Modern capitalist society, Marcuse argued, was so skillful at manipulation and oppression that most people did not even realize that they were being oppressed. Never mind formal freedoms such as are found in the Bill of Rights; oppression was so subtle and pervasive that virtually no one was truly "free." Anyone who did not see this was suffering from "false consciousness." Whatever subtlety might have been latent in Marcuse's teaching (the evidence suggests there wasn't much) was lost in the hands of crude student radicals. To them Marcuse's doctrine meant that the middle class was just as oppressed as blacks living under Jim Crow; there was no qualitative difference between a sharecropper and a certified public accountant. It was the ideal tonic to assuage students' liberal guilt as well as feed their paranoia. But it also signaled a sharp break for the student New Left, which had viewed itself in the *Port Huron Statement* that founded the SDS as a comfortable and privileged elite. Now, as SDS president Greg Calvert explained in early 1967, students discovered that they were *"one of the oppressed."* (Emphasis in original.) "[W]hite Americans as well as black Americans are beginning to recognize their common oppression."[59] Conveniently armed with this field theory of pervasive oppression that assigned central role in social change to intellectuals, the student movement could now see itself in heroic terms, rather than as just another critical movement.

As had been foreshadowed with the Free Speech Movement in Berkeley in 1964 ("Stop the machine!"), the university was now seen as just another cog in the oppressive bureaucratic system, brainwashing students into wanting middle-management careers and charge accounts. Here the paranoia and silliness kicked in to produce a seamless world in the radical mind. If the university were part of the oppressive apparatus, then issues such as dormitory hours and the Vietnam War were connected by the common thread of the oppressor state behind both. Even the much-cherished draft deferment system that enabled many students to avoid military service was revealed to be part of the massive system of oppression. The New Left seized upon a poorly phrased memorandum by Selective Service director Lewis Hershey, which noted that the draft had the collateral result of prompting many more young people to go to college than might otherwise have chosen to do so, which in turn would aid the nation's need for skilled manpower.[60]

In other words, the student deferment process was a conspiracy to expand the labor pool for corporate America. The oppressors had thought of everything! That the draft was expanded in 1966 to include college students whose grades were in the lower tier added to this paranoid perception, and contributed to the drive to reform or abolish the grading system. Where the grading system withstood the attack, sympathetic faculty began the process of grade inflation and dumbing down the curriculum. (The grading system, a popular account had it, was revised: A—excellent; B—good; C—average; D—below average; V—Vietnam.) The way was cleared not only for the burning of draft cards, but also for the sacking of universities themselves. In January 1967 SDS president Greg Calvert supplied the new direction for the movement in an article in *New Left Notes* entitled "From Protest to Resistance." In the spring of 1967 *New Left Notes* performed a similar service to the Left when it referred to the police as "pigs" for the first time. Violence was now embraced as a positive force, and the nonviolent roots of the movement in the civil rights struggle were forgotten. A new poster became popular in dorm rooms: Che Guevara.

To be sure, genuinely radical students were but a tiny minority of the total student body—5 percent at the very most—but they enjoyed the advantage of the publicity that accrues to the most extreme position and the loudest bullhorn. The radicals, Berkeley political scientist Aaron Wildavsky observed, could always count on "a significant stratum anywhere from ten to thirty percent of the student body, who lend their support in times of crisis."[61] Not to be underestimated, sociologist Robert Nisbet added, was the relief from the sheer boredom of student life that protests provided for ordinary, non-radical students. The street theater antics of the New Left appealed to liberals and unserious fun-loving students. Student health services typically reported a sharp decline in the number of students seeking psychological counseling during campus protests. (War protests were also thought to be good venues to get dates.) University of Wisconsin students and other protestors, for example, marched to a local air force base and attempted to make a "citizens arrest" of the base commander; in Detroit, a group of "white panthers" applied at city hall for a demolition permit to blow up the General Motors headquarters building. The refusal of the application, radicals solemnly complained, showed the futility of "working within 'the system.'"[62]

Almost totally absent from contemporary media coverage or the subsequent chronicles of the 1960s was the widespread evidence that most students were not "alienated" or deeply disaffected from American life, or even opposed to the Vietnam War. Indeed, the campus turmoil had a noticeable effect at the most fervent venues such as Berkeley, where applications fell by 21 percent in 1966 even as the baby boom demographic bulge was swelling the ranks of college students overall. So even as antiwar radicals practiced attention-getting street theater, one 1966 poll of University of Wisconsin students found that 72 percent supported the Vietnam War, with only 16 percent opposed.[63]

Other surveys reported the surprising fact that young and college-educated Americans supported the war more strongly than older, less-educated citizens.[64] At Indiana University, students donated more than 1,000 pints of blood for the war effort in three days in early 1966. At UCLA, a student group called VIVA (Victory in Vietnam Association) turned out 3,000 students to a pro-war rally at the same time an anti-war teach-in attracted only 800. At Yale University, 500 students objected in a petition to a New Left plan to send medical aid to North Vietnam. At Stanford, 70 percent of the student body voted in favor of allowing government agencies and Dow Chemical (a favorite target of antiwar protestors) to recruit on campus. Three-quarters of the student body at Washington and Lee University in Virginia signed a resolution supporting President Johnson, and the National Student Committee for the Defense of Vietnam gathered a half million student signatures on a pro-LBJ petition.

The April 1967 antiwar protest in New York's Central Park that attracted more than 100,000 people was followed three weeks later by a pro-war rally of 70,000 people. And the same October weekend that antiwar protestors got worldwide attention for surrounding the Pentagon, 95,000 turned out for a pro-war march in Newark, New Jersey. These gestures received very little media coverage (peaceful demonstrations are not news, the media said), while an anti-war letter to LBJ from student leaders at 100 colleges was reprinted in the *New York Times* and in *Time.*

The antiwar protest movement and the extreme radicalism it fed might have been contained were it not for its congruence with the simultaneous radicalization of the civil rights movement. Malcolm X had achieved notoriety for ridiculing "the so-called civil rights movement" and for his endorsement of violence through the slogan "by any means necessary." But the mainstream of the civil rights movement, anchored in the principles of American democracy and committed to the tactic of nonviolent protest, successfully marginalized Malcolm X and his separatist message during the early 1960s. When Malcolm X was assassinated by rival blacks in February of 1965, it might have seemed that the moderate elements of the civil rights movement were the only game in town.

But Malcolm X's militance lived on and began to spread widely, acquiring a momentum of its own with the onset of the urban riots starting with Harlem and Watts. Malcolm X had several would-be successors who would soon eclipse his fiery reputation and impact. The most flamboyant of these was Stokely Carmichael, who was born in the West Indies but raised in New York.

Carmichael quickly established himself, in Julius Lester's words, as "the Mick Jagger of revolution . . . Stokely fills the air with words like someone throwing flares to light up the sky."[65] Carmichael, 24 years old in 1966, had been active in the Student Nonviolent Coordinating Committee's voter registration efforts in Mississippi and Alabama in 1964 and 1965, and was elected chairman of the SNCC after a contentious election in May 1966. (He defeated the incumbent chairman, John Lewis, who is a congressman from Georgia today.) It was during a 1965 voter registration drive in Lowndes County, Mississippi—where no blacks were currently registered to vote—that Carmichael hit upon the symbol that would become an American legend. Bitter from the treatment of the Mississippi Freedom Democratic Party received at the Democratic National Convention the previous summer ("Liberal Democrats are just as racist as Goldwater," Carmichael had complained), Carmichael decided to register black voters to an independent third party. He needed a ballot symbol to match up with the Democrat donkey and the Republican elephant. He chose a black panther, "just the bogey to scare the white folks," historian Godfrey Hodgson observed, "lean, black, hungry, and dangerous."[66] Though Carmichael's efforts to form an independent black party in Mississippi quickly fizzled, the Black Panther name caught on.

Out in Oakland, California, Huey Newton and Bobby Seale drew up a platform for the Black Panther Party in the local office of the Community Action Program. The Black Panthers would quickly become the most celebrated efflorescence of the counterculture, mostly through the patronization of self-congratulatory white liberals. "The world of the Black Panther party," Tom Milstein wrote in *Commentary*, "might have been constructed by Kurt Vonnegut out of bits and pieces of Dostoevsky."[67]

Carmichael was quickly steering the SNCC away from its nonviolent, integrationist roots, and was edging closer to an open embrace of Black Nationalism. "Almost overnight," Milstein observed, "SNCC and CORE, which had formerly measured 'militancy' by the degree of commitment to integrationist ideals, reversed themselves and now equated militancy with fervid denunciations of liberals, honkies, middle-class Jews, and white America."[68] The SNCC, Carmichael announced, would not attend the White House conference on civil rights the following month. "We see integration as an insidious subterfuge for white supremacy in this country," Carmichael declared upon becoming chairman of the SNCC. "The goal of integration is irrelevant. Political and economic power is what black people have to have." Carmichael was also a misogynist, remarking that "the only position for a woman in SNCC is prone."[69] Martin Luther King, who helped found the SNCC in 1960, was alarmed. "I can't agree with the move toward a kind of Black Nationalism," King told the *New York Times* in a cautiously worded criticism of Carmichael.

The news media had been one of the greatest assets of the civil rights movement, providing an amplifier for the moral authority of King and other civil rights leaders who were attempting to claim the place of blacks in American society according to the principles of American democracy. But all protest movements suffer from the defect of having self-appointed leaders, and the media's penchant of glamorizing the most extreme among the self-appointed led them to focus the spotlight on Carmichael and the flamboyant Black Panthers. (By fall of 1966, Carmichael was being published in *The New York Review of Books,* among other elite outlets.) King and his allies had made it possible for black radicalism to go public. King was surely right that 90 percent of blacks were not radical anti-white nationalists, but there was no chance black militants could be moderated once unleashed. The news media was quick to pounce on this new militance and the split that was opening within the civil rights movement; the *New York Times,* with typical understatement, noted that "Observers have found SNCC generally to be more militant than the older civil rights groups."[70] And, as with the New Left, media coverage greatly exaggerated the true depth of the movement.

The embrace of Black Nationalism spelled the ruin of the civil rights movement as it had always understood itself. The civil rights movement was already reeling from Watts and other urban disturbances. The exact moment it turned the corner toward ruin could, however, be dated with the James Meredith march in June 1966. Meredith, who had been the first black student admitted to the University of Mississippi in 1962, planned to march from Memphis to Jackson, Mississippi, on behalf of voting rights. Meredith's march had not attracted a huge following (he had launched the march on his own initiative, without much attention or encouragement by civil rights organizations), and he began with a small entourage. But just across the Mississippi state line on Highway 51, Meredith was felled in an ambush by a shotgun blast.

Civil rights leaders including King rushed immediately to Memphis, determined to carry on Meredith's march and thinking it could help boost chances for new civil rights legislation then before Congress, just as the bloody Selma march the year before had aided the passage of the Voting Rights Act. At a meeting held in Centenary Methodist Church in Memphis, Carmichael argued that the time had come for blacks to seize power, since they outnumbered whites in the area. Further, Carmichael wanted whites excluded from the continuation of the march. King was dismayed. As he wrote of the meeting a year later: "I tried to make it clear that besides opposing violence in principle, I could imagine nothing more impractical and disastrous than for any of us, through misguided judgment, to precipitate a violent confrontation in Mississippi. We had neither the resources nor the techniques to win."[71] For the moment King succeeded. The militants backed down from threats of violence and the march would continue to be interracial. King returned to Chicago, where he was in the midst of a highly publicized effort to integrate housing.

But King's pleas for moderation proved to be unavailing. Along the way marchers punctuated their anger with a new chorus to "We Shall Overcome." The new chorus was "We Shall Overrun."

New lyrics were also offered for the tune of "Jingle Bells:"

> Jingle Bells, shotgun shells,
> Freedom all the way,
> Oh what fun it is to blast
> A trooper man away.[72]

When not singing, the marchers were chanting slogans such as "Hey! Hey! Whattyaknow! White people must go—must go!"

The emblematic moment came at a rally in Greenwood. Carmichael was arrested for defying an order not to pitch tents in a restricted area. At a rally of 600 people after his release on bail, Carmichael roared to the crowd: "This is the twenty-seventh time I have been arrested, and I ain't going to jail no more. The only way we're gonna stop them white men from whuppin' us is to take over. What we gonna start saying now is Black Power!" At this point another SNCC leader, Willie Ricks, led the crowd in a responsive chant:

> "What do you want?"
> "Black Power!"
> "What do you want?"
> "Black Power!"[73]

Black Power, Carmichael decided, would be the slogan for the rest of the march, replacing the slogan the civil rights movement had been using for the last several years—Freedom Now!

King rushed back to Mississippi, as his colleagues in his Southern Christian Leadership Conference (SCLC) struggled at damage control. King caught up with Carmichael and the march the following day in Yazoo City, where he was booed when he repeated his call for non-violence. Later that day, in a tense five-hour meeting, the final self-destruction of the civil rights movement commenced. "I pleaded with the group," King recalled, "to abandon the Black Power slogan. It was my contention that a leader has to be concerned with the problem of semantics. Each word, I said, has a denotative meaning . . . and a connotative meaning . . . Black Power carried the wrong connotations." In an echo of Malcolm X, Carmichael rejoined: "Power is the only thing respected in this world, and we must get it at any cost."[74]

Despite King's pleadings, Carmichael and his allies refused to back down. After scoring a small tactical victory by getting Carmichael to agree to drop both "Black Power" and "Freedom Now" as slogans for the march, King bent to the pressure. Carmichael told him: "Martin, I deliberately decided to raise the issue on the march to give it a national forum, and force you to take a stand for Black Power." King replied: "I have been used before. One more time won't hurt."

Whatever hopes King might have had for quelling black militance were dashed a few days later, when a white mob in Philadelphia, Mississippi (where civil rights workers Chaney, Schwerner, and Goodman had been murdered two years before), set upon the marchers with clubs and ax handles while local police looked the other way. A few days later it was the police themselves who set upon the marchers with tear gas and clubs in Canton. The Johnson Administration ignored pleadings from King to send Federal Marshals to protect the marchers. Amidst the local brutality and Washington's inaction, it is not hard to understand why King was increasingly powerless to contain the rage of black militants.

But instead of turning on whitey (which in reality they were powerless to do), the marchers began turning on each other. Egged on by Carmichael, the leaders decided that the NAACP would be excluded from the final rally of the march in Jackson. The SNCC would subsequently declare that "We are now aware that the NAACP has grown reactionary, is controlled by the black power structure itself, and stands as one of the main roadblocks to black freedom."

This split had been building for a while, and the controversy over Black Power that arose during the march was only a pretext for militants to declare their independence from the NAACP and King. It is instructive to compare the founding statement of the SNCC from 1960 with the position paper on "The Basis of Black Power" that SNCC issued in 1966 after the Meredith march. The founding statement was a short five paragraphs, containing just 157 words—shorter even than that model of brevity, the Gettysburg Address. The statement mentions "nonviolence" four times within its brief compass, and bases its hopes on the Judeo-Christian tradition and "the moral nature of mankind," which "nurtures the atmosphere in which reconciliation and justice become actual possibilities." There was no mention of race, and the SNCC went forward as an integrated civil rights organization. Indeed, it was under the banner and sponsorship of the SNCC that many white students went to the South to participate in the civil rights movement in the early 1960s.

After Carmichael assumed the chairmanship of the SNCC, all this changed. "The Basis of Black Power" was more than 2,000 words; neither "nonviolence" nor any appeal to justice appears. While the paper was careful not to call openly for the violent pursuit of power, it articulated a much more ominous direction for African-Americans: a self-defined alternate reality, separate from white America. "If we are to proceed to true liberation, we must cut ourselves off from white people. . . . we propose that our organization (SNCC) should be black-staffed, black-controlled, and black financed." By the end of 1966 all non-blacks had been ousted from membership in the SNCC, and Carmichael planned to change the name of the SNCC to the Negro Movement for Liberation.

The SNCC also became the first civil rights organization to come out against the Vietnam War. The Congress on Racial Equality (CORE) followed SNCC's lead, voting in 1967 to strike the term "multiracial" from its membership clause. This separatism also contained a rejection of middle-class American values that can be recognized as the germ of the so-called "multiculturalism" of today: "We reject the American dream as defined by white people and must work to construct an American reality defined by Afro-Americans. . . . Whites are the ones who must try to raise themselves to our humanistic level." As if any additional confirmation of Carmichael's contempt for America were needed, in 1967 he set off on a world tour of Communist nations, denouncing American imperialism on Radio Havana, predicting in Algiers the imminent start to violent revolution in the United States, and declaring in Syria his solidarity with the Arabs against Israel. And no tour of Communist garden spots would be complete without a drop-in at Hanoi, where Ho Chi Minh asked a bewildered Carmichael why American blacks did not return to their home in Africa. (Carmichael eventually did emigrate to Africa in the 1990s, taking an African name, Kwame Ture, and founding the All African People's Party in the West African nation of Guinea. He died there in 1998 at the age of 57.)

Civil rights leaders who had spent years building up the movement through litigation, incremental legislation, and painstaking public relations were loathe to see their hard-won progress thrown away, and courageously attacked the self-destructive course Carmichael and other militants had embarked upon. A month after the Meredith march finished, the NAACP's Roy Wilkins received front-page coverage when he declared that the NAACP could no longer cooperate with the SNCC (to which the NAACP had provided major financial support in the past) or any other group advocating Black Power. Black Power, Wilkins said, "means reverse Hitlerism, reverse Ku Klux Klanism, wicked fanaticism," and would lead to "black death."[75] The NAACP would later issue a statement saying "The time has come for speaking out loud and clear lest the entire race be branded as hate-mongers, segregationists, advocates of violence, and worse."[76] Bayard Rustin, no shrinking violet when it came to radical ideology (Rustin was a Marxist), said that "the separatist methods of the Carmichaels are no help to the American Negro."[77] In the pages of *Commentary,* Rustin argued that "'black power' not only lacks any real value for the civil rights movement, but . . . its propagation is positively harmful." But Rustin also could see how the Black Power movement was inevitably blending by degrees with the New Left: "'Black power' is a slogan directed primarily against liberals by those who once counted liberals among their closest friends."[78]

King and other older civil rights leaders were correct that the vast majority of American blacks were not attracted by the Black Power philosophy. A 1966 poll of blacks gave King an 88 percent approval rating, while Carmichael got a mere 19 percent approval rating.[79] Pat Moynihan wrote ruefully: "Read the election returns from Lowndes County. The great, guilty, hateful secret is that Negroes are not swingers. They are Southern Protestants. They like jobs in the civil service. They support the war in Vietnam, approve the draft, back the President. And all this in greater proportion than any other group in the nation."[80] There was ample survey data backing up Moynihan's perception; one survey of non-Southern blacks found that 81 percent thought things were getting better for blacks, and 70 percent thought that the day would come when whites fully accept blacks. These findings showed, Harvard's Edward Banfield wrote, "that most Negroes were neither sunk in hopelessness nor consumed with anger."[81]

Civil rights old-timers were right to complain that excessive news media coverage of black power radicals inflated their influence and following far out of proportion. But the news media love drama and conflict, so the intramural conflict over black power was irresistible for the media. The media, along with publicity-hungry academics, could also be relied upon to fan the flames of controversy by puffing up every preposterous interpretation of black experience that came along. The *New York Times,* for example, gave front page coverage to a psychiatrist who asserted that Black Power was actually the result of the sexual jealousy of black women. In a paper presented to the American Psychiatric Association, Dr. Alvin Poussant argued that "The Negro girls were often resentful and jealous of the attention which Negro men showed to the white girls. . . . The problem was further exacerbated because many of the white girls were extremely seductive, sometimes unknowingly, in their behavior." (Where was the feminist movement when it was needed?) Therefore, the Negro girls "usually were the most vociferous in demanding that whites be put out of the movement and were the strongest supporters of exclusive 'black consciousness.'"[82]

The allure of Black Power also proved irresistible to many liberals who liked nothing more than to have their liberal guilt confirmed in the most fulsome way. The more Carmichael and other radical blacks attacked whites, the more white liberals loved them, and rushed to express their "solidarity." The author and critic Susan Sontag, for example, went public with the claim that "The white race is the cancer of human history. It is the white race and it alone—its ideologies and inventions—which . . . now threatens the very existence of life itself." Black Power advocacy of a complete separatism from the white world had its convenient limits, however. Carmichael was soon receiving more than $1,500 per speech on college campuses, and H. Rap Brown received a large advance from Dial Press for a book on "his philosophy about racial questions."[83] The University of California at Santa Cruz granted a Ph.D. to black panther Huey Newton; his dissertation was titled "War Against the Panthers: A Study of Repression in America."

The apotheosis of what Tom Wolfe would savagely lampoon as "radical chic" came with conductor Leonard Bernstein's fundraiser for the Black Panthers at his Park Avenue home in 1969. "Wonder what the Black Panthers eat here on the hors d'oeuvre trail?" Wolfe asked in describing the scene.

"Do the Panthers like little Roquefort cheese morsels rolled in crushed nuts this way, and asparagus tips in mayonnaise dabs, and meatballs *petites au Coq Hardi,* all of which are at this very moment being offered to them on gadrooned silver platters by maids in black uniforms . . . ?" This was too much even for the *New York Times,* which editorialized that "The emergence of the Black Panthers as the romanticized darlings of the politico-cultural jet set is an affront to the majority of black Americans. . . . the group-therapy plus fund-raising soiree at the home of Leonard Bernstein, as reported in this newspaper yesterday, represents the sort of elegant slumming that degrades patrons and patronized alike."[84]

Black radicals may have been willing to take money from the honky, but they were not much enamored with the tendentious and indulgent New Left notion that white students were just as oppressed as Southern blacks. It was inevitable, then, that the New Left's ideology of seamless oppression and "participatory democracy" would turn around to bite them as soon as they attempted seriously to forge an alliance with black radicals. The hollowness and corruption of both movements became obvious in the fall of 1967, when 3,600 New Left activists assembled at Chicago's ornate Palmer House Hotel for the "National Conference for the New Politics."

The New Left had in mind generating momentum behind a third-party antiwar presidential ticket of Martin Luther King and Dr. Benjamin Spock. Black Power advocates had something else in mind. Blacks composed about one quarter of the delegates (transportation and lodging for black delegates was being subsidized by, among others, Martin Peretz, later the owner of *The New Republic*), but the question was moved that the convention should consider, as a show of good faith, whether blacks should be given greater voting power. Black delegates, who had formed their own caucus at the outset, wanted a great deal more. The Black Caucus issued 11 demands and an ultimatum that the demands be met by mid-day of the second day of the conference, or else they would walk out. (Separately they demanded that one-half of the front seats at the conference be roped off for them.) Among the demands: half the seats on all committees reserved for blacks; condemnation of Zionist imperialism; reparations for the historic exploitation of blacks; and "white civilizing committees be established immediately in all white communities to civilize and humanize the savage and beast-like character that runs rampant throughout America. . . ."

"We're being asked to flagellate our white consciences," said one delegate from Berkeley, while others compared the step to castration. "After four hundred years of slavery," one Jewish delegate said to the convention, "it is right that whites should be castrated."[85] The vote to accept the demands passed by a 3 to 1 margin, whereupon white delegates gave themselves an ovation for their broadmindedness. The afternoon's planned activities were cancelled in favor of a panel on black liberation featuring the SNCC's James Foreman. Foreman announced that the 50 percent committee representation quota meant that blacks had 50 percent of the general convention votes as well. "Is this a dictatorship?" a woman called out to Foreman from the convention floor. "Yes," Foreman responded, "I'm the dictator." *New York Times* reporter Walter Goodman noted, "Whites fairly tingled with pleasure under the whiplash of this demagogy." The conference ended three days later in disarray, the original objective of launching an anti-Johnson third-party movement lost amidst the posturing.[86] "Maybe," an editorial in *New Left Notes* after the convention mused, "the lesson is that, for a while, whites and blacks must organize separately in order to organize at all." Historian Ronald Radosh pointed to a different lesson: "Few realized that a new habit within the Left had been born, and would recur, that of willing subordination by white liberals and radicals to the demands and programmatic initiatives of radical blacks."[87]

The disturbing and dramatic upswing in urban unrest during 1966 and 1967 added a verisimilitude to the threats of Black Power activists. By the end of 1967, more than 150 cities had experienced rioting of some kind, usually touched off by seemingly random events but nearly always with a racial dimension. In Hartford, Connecticut, two days of rioting erupted after a black luncheonette owner threw out a black customer who had accosted a waitress. In Erie, Pennsylvania, two days of rioting occurred after police broke up a sidewalk craps game. Chicago rioted after the police shut off fire hydrants that cooled off neighborhood kids. Even tiny Waterloo, Iowa (population 75,000), with a black population of about 6,000, suffered two days of rioting after a young black was arrested for assaulting an elderly white man. The National Guard had occupied parts of eight major cities by the end of 1967, prompting James Q. Wilson to lament: "Americans have never liked to garrison troops in the central city, but we may have to reassess this position."[88]

Although liberals and civil rights activists chalked up urban unrest to the grinding poverty of the ghettoes, the Waterloo riot should have suggested that something else was amiss; black unemployment in Waterloo was 2.3 percent, well below the nation's already low 4 percent unemployment rate.[89] In New York City, where police quickly contained rioters rampaging on Fifth Avenue, four of the 23 arrested rioters turned out to be antipoverty workers from Harlem earning a respectable $90 a week in a federal OEO program.

The riots that most shocked the nation took place in Newark and Detroit within a fortnight of each other during the "long, hot summer" of 1967. In Newark, the arrest of a black cab driver named John Smith (who was a decorated World War II vet) was quickly exaggerated by other black cab drivers, who said over their taxicab radios that white police had killed a black driver. By midnight a crowd had gathered at the police station and started throwing rocks and bottles. Though police restored order by about 3 A.M., it did not last. The next four nights saw widespread looting and rioting that required 2,600 National Guardsmen to be put down. Some of the looting that took place spontaneously organized into highly efficient forms. Looters formed human chains often a block long near liquor stores, which were cleaned out starting with the best brands first. TV stores were equally popular targets. By the time it was over, 21 had been killed, 1,000 injured, and 1,600 arrested.

"That sort of thing can't happen here," civic leaders in Detroit were saying. Even radical black leaders seemed to agree; CORE's Floyd McKissick left Detroit off a list of cities he drew up that were most likely to experience racial trouble in 1967. Late on a Sunday night at the end of July, police raided a "blind pig"—an illegal after-hours bar—and arrested 73 black patrons along with the bartender. (The revelers were reportedly celebrating the return of two black soldiers from Vietnam.) Like Watts three years before, the police were about to close up the scene and pull out without incident when a bottle was thrown through a squad car window. It was the only spark needed for an explosion.

The rioting and looting that followed saw 14 square miles of Detroit destroyed by fire (but usually only after the stores in the neighborhood had been completely looted), and required 15,000 police, National Guard, and ultimately U.S. Army paratroopers dispatched by President Johnson to bring it to an end. Forty-one were killed, 347 injured, and

3,800 were arrested. Nearly 3,000 businesses were destroyed, and more than 5,000 people, mostly black, were left homeless. Damage was estimated at $500 million, more than ten times the damage of the Watts riot.

President Johnson decided that the issue of urban unrest needed high profile treatment, so he made a prime-time TV address a few days later calling for "an attack—mounted on every level—upon the conditions that breed despair and violence." The centerpiece of his speech was the announcement of a bipartisan commission to look into the causes and cures of urban unrest, to be headed by Illinois Governor Otto Kerner and New York City Mayor John Lindsay. It was the making of the Great Society's next big political debacle. "To me," LBJ aide Joseph Califano wrote in his memoirs, "the commission had the potential to be a political Frankenstein monster. . . . the President planned to load the commission with liberals who wanted more money spent on Great Society programs. . . ."[90]

Califano's premonition would not be confirmed until the commission completed his work nine months later, but there was ample reason for his worry (which LBJ dismissed out of hand at the time). Once again the anomalies of Detroit and Newark were overlooked. Both cities were *already* models of Great Society activism and rapidly increasing federal spending. Newark was spending $277 per capita to combat urban blight, ranking it first among the nation's largest cities. Unemployment had fallen by half over the previous five years.

Detroit, meanwhile, had garnered more than $200 million in federal grants, including $48 million in federal antipoverty funds and $3 million for Head Start programs designed specifically to stave off rioting. Moynihan admitted that "ravaged Detroit was, as it were, liberalism's city."[91] *Time* magazine had described Detroit Mayor Jerry Cavanaugh as "an imaginative liberal with knack for landing government grants," and elsewhere he was credited with having practically invented the "Model Cities" program. Cavanaugh had marched shoulder-to-shoulder with Martin Luther King and Detroit was the only city in the nation with two black congressmen. Black unemployment in Detroit had declined to 6 percent, down from 10.7 percent in 1960 (it was less than 2 percent among married black men).[92] Up to 90 percent of the rioters arrested in Detroit had prior criminal records, but an amazing 83 percent were employed at an average wage of $117 a week (about the median wage at that time), and half were members of the United Auto Workers union.[93]

And the Detroit riot was not a race riot in the old sense; whereas whites and blacks had violently clashed in riots in the 1940s, 1967's riot was an interracial affair, with white and blacks looting amicably side-by-side.

Many Republicans and conservatives pointed to the virtual threats Great Society liberals had made in support of their "Model Cities" legislation; if Congress were not forthcoming with funds, administration spokesmen had darkly warned, dozens of cities would "explode." Language like this, combined with the rabble-rousing of Black Power advocates, set up a self-fulfilling prophecy. Even Martin Luther King had acknowledged that "a prediction of violence can sometimes be an invitation to it."[94] But some, including President Johnson himself, suspected something more sinister at work, just as he had when Harlem had erupted in 1964. "When Johnson first called me in," recalled David Ginsburg, who directed the work of the Kerner Commission, "he was convinced that somebody had given an order for disruptions. How else to explain rioting in so many cities?"[95] FBI director J. Edgar Hoover had predicted in May that widespread urban violence could be expected over the summer, the result, the FBI thought, of deliberate Communist (and possibly foreign-supported) agitation.

Evidence for this view was mixed, at best. The *New York Times* had discounted the possibility of organized conspiracy. One *Times* reporter wrote that "all the racial explosions observed during the last two years seem to have been spontaneous. The agitators always flock to the scene immediately afterward."[96] Sure enough, Tom Hayden had rushed to Newark while the riot was underway and inserted himself into the mayor's crisis-management process. And the Justice Department, seeking to bring some kind of incitement-to-riot charge, found that few of the arrested rioters had crossed state lines. (Crossing state lines to incite a riot had been made a federal crime in 1966—again under the same "interstate commerce" power that was used to justify the Civil Rights Act.) However, a grand jury convened in Cleveland following that city's riot the year before concluded that the riot was "organized and exploited [by] trained and disciplined professionals." The grand jury had uncovered instances of radical agitators with specific plans and targets for rioting. Even Cleveland's new black mayor, Carl Stokes, was inclined to agree when another riot broke out in 1968, saying that the rioting "was not at all related to any kind of honest reaction to the environment at all," but "a planned, deliberate and previously contrived plot to damage." (The FBI had uncovered a plot by black nationalists to assassinate Stokes for being a "collaborator with the white oppressor.")[97]

We are not likely ever to know whether or to what extent organized agitation contributed to the urban rioting of the mid-1960s, though it is more than curious that it stopped almost as suddenly as it began, not coincidentally with the election of Richard Nixon as president. (Also, no city that had a major riot had a second one.) Certainly the combination of New Left/Black Power rhetoric and the mainstream exculpation of rioting generated by liberal guilt contributed significantly to the rioting in ways that can never be definitively measured or proved. But the effect of mass media should not be overlooked. These were the first urban riots carried on live television, which not only helped swell the number of rioters but also tipped them off about the movements of the police—and especially the non-movements of the police. Mass media helped spread rioting from city to city—a phenomenon that would be confirmed most vividly 25 years later when the Rodney King riot in Los Angeles had instant imitators in other cities simultaneously.

Edward Banfield observed: "By carrying vivid accounts of rioting to cities all over the country, television not only eliminated the necessity that would otherwise have existed for the independent discovery of certain techniques of rioting (for example, the use of firebombs) but also, and especially, it established the *possibility* of it." The role of demographics should not be overlooked either. Banfield's 1969 essay on the subject ("Rioting Mainly for Fun and Profit") noted that "Rampaging by teenagers has always been a problem in the cities. . . . Without a large supply of boys and young men, most of them lower-working or lower class, to draw upon, major riots would be impossible."[98] Rampages by whites and other non-black ethnic youths also took place on a smaller scale in the 1960s, but tended to draw little media attention and so never entered the public mind. The demographic cause is given further credence by the fact that riots were also occurring overseas. In a typical riot such as Detroit, half of the arrestees were between 19 and 24, and the reason the proportion wasn't even higher was that the shorthanded police tended to arrest those easiest to apprehend, which were usually older people. In the end, however, riots would not prove to be the most significant effect of the baby boom demographic bulge.

"Societies, no matter where they are," Pat Moynihan would reflect in 1972, "are mostly organized around the problem of how to get people from 14 to 24." In between these ages, he noted, "extraordinary turbulences take place."[99] The number of people in this volatile age group more than doubled during the 1960s, more than it had grown during the six decades of the twentieth century preceding it. Between 1890 and 1960, the 14-to-24-year-old cohort had grown by 12.5 million; during the 1960s it grew by 13.8 million. During the middle years of the 1960s, one new college was opened every week to meet the demand. In the 1970s the growth rate of this cohort plummeted back to 600,000, and was flat in the 1980s. This sort of demographic wave would portend a dramatic shock in any society. When it occurred simultaneously with a peculiar war and the full bloom of the university as an ideological hothouse, the result was bound to be dramatic. So shocked was the establishment that, Moynihan mused in 1967, "it may be argued that the nation is entering a period of political instability from which it will not emerge intact."[100]

So it was not surprising that in 1966 *Time* magazine selected the "under 25 generation" as its "Man of the Year" instead of a single individual. "This is not just a new generation," *Time* wrote, "but a new kind of generation." The youthful penchant for self-indulgence was receiving sanction from a pillar of the Establishment itself: "With his skeptical yet humanistic outlook, his disdain for fanaticism and his scorn for the spurious, the Man of the Year suggests that he will infuse the future with a new sense of morality, a transcendent and contemporary ethic that could infinitely enrich the 'empty society.'"[101] Perhaps *Time* was trying to put the best face on a phenomenon that neither it nor other leading lights of the World War II generation had anticipated nor understood.

Time must have had someone beside the New Left in mind by describing sixties' youth as disdaining fanaticism and scorning the spurious, and sure enough six months later *Time*'s cover took notice of the hippies. "The hippies," *Time* observed in July 1967 just as nearly 100,000 bedraggled youth were streaming into San Francisco for the "summer of love," "have emerged on the U.S. scene in the last 18 months as a wholly new subculture." The hippies and the "counterculture" they represented were more dismaying to middle-class parents than the antiwar movement and the New Left, and though the number of hippies was, like the antiwar movement, comparatively small as a proportion of young people (*Time* estimated their number at no more than 300,000 nationwide), their visibility and aggrandizement by the media heightened middle-class anxiety that America was coming apart. Joan Didion caustically remarked that the half-comprehending media "continued to report 'the hippie phenomenon' as an extended panty raid," and constituted "the most remarkable if unwitting, extant evidence that the signals between the generations are irrevocably jammed."[102] Historian Arnold Toynbee remarked that the rise of the hippies was "a red warning light for the American way of life."[103] Though the hippies were sympathetic to New Left ideology, they mostly eschewed politics and turned out for war protests, if at all, mostly to have a good time. Unlike the New Left, Moynihan observed, the hippies "seek not to change our society, but simply to have nothing to do with it."[104]

Time was hasty in suggesting that the hippie phenomenon was wholly unprecedented. Despite the new vocabulary, clothing, and music, the quest for innocent authenticity at the heart of the hippie experience was mostly a demographically exaggerated expression of the Rousseauian romanticism that erupts in nearly every generation. Thoreau, Emerson, and the Transcendentalists represented the high church version of this in the nineteenth century, while the "hobos," bohemians, and Beats represented the twentieth century version prior to the arrival of the hippies. Though the hippies may have appeared to be little more than hobos in tie-dye, they represented a revolt against the secular religion of America-middle-class liberalism. Moynihan thought the counterculture represented the first heresies of liberalism. "Who are these outrageous young people?" Moynihan asked. "I suggest to you they are Christians arrived on the scene of second-century Rome."[105] The conservative theologian Will Herberg offered a similar judgment, observing that the hippies resembled the "Adamites" of second-century Christianity, believing that "they had been restored to the sinless purity of before the Fall, in fact, to Adam's primitive innocence in Paradise."[106]

Like most enthusiasms for recapturing the "authentic" existence of sinless natural man, the hippies offered the latest iteration of the idea of "free love." Of equal importance with the sexual revolution was the explosion of the drug culture. The creation of the "new man" always presupposed the reshaping of consciousness at some level, but now the chemical means were available. For many hippies, drugs were simply a more potent means to a good time (and a way of striking back at the supposed hypocrisy of their alcohol-guzzling, cigarette-smoking, coffee-swilling parents), but the drug culture also offered grandiose metaphysical justifications. Timothy Leary became famous for touting LSD as a "cerebral vitamin." Hunter S. Thompson celebrated LSD in *Fear and Loathing in Las Vegas:* "There was a fantastic universal sense that whatever we were doing was *right,* that we were winning. . . . We had all the momentum; we were riding the crest of a high and beautiful wave."[107]

New Left figures managed to discern a political metaphysic to LSD; Michael Lerner (who 25 years later would briefly become the "politics of meaning" guru for First Lady Hillary Clinton) said "until you've dropped acid, you don't know what socialism is," and Emmett Grogan, the founder of San Francisco's Mime Troupe that achieved notoriety for its street theater, said that it was during his first LSD trip that he realized that "property is theft."[108] With the politicization of the drug culture, one student commented, "German idealism finally caught up with LSD, in the making of a lysergic *Gotterdammerung.*" By the time LSD was made illegal in 1966, an estimated 1 million people had tried it. But this was a fraction of the people who had used marijuana, which had been outlawed way back in the 1930s. *Time* magazine reported that "Some medical authorities and federal officials believe the drug will eventually be legalized."[109]

Herberg observed that "It is not innocent to pretend to an innocence impossible for man. . . . The hippie spectacle is a kind of Medusa head; but it will turn those who gaze upon it without adequate protection not into stone images, but into fools and simpletons."[110] The casualties of the sexual revolution and the drug culture showed up quickly. The rate of venereal disease in San Francisco during 1967's "summer of love" was six times higher than it had been in 1964. *Newsweek* noted that "Pregnancy becomes the most frequent serious side effect of pot."[111] At the peak of the "summer of love," San Francisco's public health authorities were treating 10,000 hippies for drug addiction, at a cost of $35,000 a month. Other casualties of hippiedom were not so lucky as to acquire a mere medical problem. One hippie attracted to Haight-Ashbury in 1967 was Charles Manson; it was amidst the communal atmosphere of the "summer of love" that he recruited much of his "family."

Even though the hippie scene would burn out in a few short years, the broader "counterculture" it represented immediately began to be assimilated into the mainstream of American life. It showed up first in retailing.

Most of the customers at the art and craft shops the hippies started were middle-class weekend gawkers come to Haight-Ashbury and similar neighborhoods to take in the free circus. Soon major department stores offered prefabbed tie-dye hippie fashions. But the Establishment against which the counterculture was supposedly rebelling displayed its weakness in its quick affirmation of the counterculture's supposedly noble and "idealistic" intention. "Indeed it could be argued," *Time* ridiculously concluded, "that in their independence of material possessions and their emphasis on peacefulness and honesty, hippies lead considerably more virtuous lives than the great majority of their fellow citizens."[112]

This rapid assimilation of the counterculture into the mainstream of American life was an early hint that the hippie counterculture more than the New Left would turn out to be the most significant legacy of the baby boom generation's coming of age. It would be a mistake, though, to suppose that the baby boomers started this *ex nihilo* in the 1960s, as was supposed in a Philip Larkin poem popular at the time:

> Sexual intercourse began
> In nineteen sixty-three
> (Which was rather late for me)—
> Between the end of the "Chatterley" ban
> And the Beatles' first LP

That the "old taboos" were dying out was a commonplace theme in the media and among social commentators since at least the late 1950s. The sexual revolution was already well advanced by the time hippies took it up. The Food and Drug Administration had approved the birth control pill ("The Pill") in June 1960, but at first many unmarried women had difficulty getting a doctor to give them a prescription. By 1967, though, nearly one-fifth of American women of childbearing age were on The Pill. "In a mere six years," *Time* declared in a cover story on The Pill, "it has changed and liberated the sex and family life of a large and still growing segment of the U.S. population."[113]

Advancing technology was outpaced only by advancing publicity. Masters and Johnson's *Human Sexual Response* was a best-seller in 1966, and *Playboy* magazine's monthly circulation topped 4 million copies. While Hugh Hefner's "Playboy philosophy" of unalloyed hedonism inveighed against "organized religion" as a repressive force that prevented man's natural spontaneous goodness from emerging, he also offered 25 percent discounts on subscriptions to members of the clergy and started a religion department in the magazine's pages, featuring essays by avant-garde theologians such as Harvard's Harvey Cox and the heterodox Bishop James Pike.

Although the sexual revolution would eventually come to be seen as predominantly a convenience for men, in the 1960s it had more than its share of women collaborators. Helen Gurley Brown set out to be the female analogue to Hugh Hefner with her book *Sex and the Single Girl*; her *Cosmopolitan* was for swinging single women what *Playboy* was for men. (*Cosmopolitan* is a good example of how the cultural revolution was quickly being assimilated into the mainstream; while *Playboy* was the sole brainchild of Hefner, *Cosmopolitan* was published by the venerable Hearst Corporation.) The rise of the sexual revolution coincided with the emergence of a more assertive feminism. Betty Friedan's 1963 book *The Feminine Mystique* had identified the middle-class housewife as yet another category of oppressed persons—the suburban family household, she wrote, was "a comfortable concentration camp"—and set the stage for feminism to emerge as still another claimant on the moral authority of the civil rights movement. It was *boredom* more than "oppression" that afflicted increasingly comfortable but restive housewives in the middle 1960s, but boredom makes for much less snappy copy. In 1967 feminism took political form with the founding of the National Organization for Women (NOW). NOW's "Bill of Rights" closely echoed the civil rights movement's legal aims (passage of the Equal Rights Amendment, for example). Although feminism was not ostensibly directed toward the loosening of moral codes, its most significant aim—the repeal of all laws restricting abortion—shows its harmony with the sexual revolution.

Yet nowhere was the rapid progress of the counterculture more evident than in the popular entertainment that started coming out of Hollywood in 1967, opening up the cultural split in middle America that has lasted right up to this day. The entertainment community rivaled the hippies in their fondness for drugs. "Taking LSD is more enriching than a trip to Europe," a young screenwriter told *Newsweek*.[114] Just as the hippies accelerated a sexual revolution that was already in progress, Hollywood was already primed to join the countercultural parade. In 1966, Jack Valenti left his job as a White House aide to President Johnson (he told Johnson when he left that he thought the debate over the Vietnam War was ebbing) to become president of the Motion Picture Association of America. "The first thing I did when I became president," Valenti wrote, "was to junk the Hays Production Code, which was an anachronistic piece of censorship that we never should have put in place."[115] Under his leadership the MPAA would develop a film rating system instead. But filmmakers would no longer face any prior restraints based on conventional pieties.

Throughout the mid-1960s, a number of low-budget films celebrated the counterculture, such as Roger Corman's *The Wild Angels,* which depicted Hell's Angels as yet another group seeking shelter under the civil rights umbrella. "We just want to be free to ride our machines," Peter Fonda's biker character protests to the yokel sheriff in the film, "and not be hassled by The Man!" (*The Wild Angels* cost $360,000 to make, but grossed $10 million.) While these and similar efforts were eminently forgettable, 1967 saw the appearance of two movies that, in the words of film critic Peter Biskind, "sent tremors through the industry."[116] The two films were *Bonnie and Clyde* and *The Graduate.*

Bonnie and Clyde not only romanticized the outlaw, but also broke new ground with the slow-motion, graphic violence by which the heroes meet their demise at the end of the film. The idea for *Bonnie and Clyde* had languished around Hollywood for years until Warren Beatty pushed it through. Even though Beatty and director Arthur Penn were behind the movie, it seemed bound for relative obscurity like the other countercultural films of its time. *Bonnie and Clyde* was originally scheduled for first release at a drive-in theater in Benton, Texas. It opened instead at the Montreal Film Festival that was running concurrent with Expo '67 (where, coincidentally, a large number of New Left antiwar activists had gone to meet with North Vietnamese representatives), and subsequently in New York.

Most critics were severe in their judgment. Bosley Crowther of the *New York Times* called it "a cheap piece of bald-faced slapstick that treats the hideous depredations of that sleazy, moronic pair as though they were as full of fun and frolic as the jazz-age cut-ups in *Thoroughly Modern Millie,*" and *Newsweek*'s Joe Morgenstern called it "a squalid shoot-'em-up for the moron trade."[117] Other critics such as *The New Yorker*'s Pauline Kael loved the film, however, and *Bonnie and Clyde* became an instant sensation—a "watershed picture," *Time* magazine said—that received ten Academy Award nominations. (It would end up winning only two.) "The wall came tumbling down after *Bonnie and Clyde*," director Arthur Penn reminisced to the *Los Angeles Times* in 1986. "All the things that were in concrete began to just fall away."[118]

The Graduate was an even more fulsome expression of the countercultural mood, with its satirical send-up of upper-class professionalism, materialism ("I only have one word of advice for you Benjamin: Plastics"), and morals. Director Mike Nichols offered the part of Mrs. Robinson to Doris Day, who turned it down because "it offended my sense of values." And Robert Redford was briefly considered for the lead role as Benjamin Braddock, but Nichols decided he wanted someone who could evince a more pathetic character, and settled on Dustin Hoffman instead. *The Graduate* was a flash point for the growing cultural divide. In New York City, Queens Councilman John J. Santucci, a Democrat, demanded that the Transit Authority remove from subways and busses posters for the movie that showed Hoffman in bed with Anne Bancroft (Mrs. Robinson). Constituents had complained that the posters were indecent. The Transit Authority bowed to the pressure and removed them.[119] This sense of restraint was winning its last battles in the entertainment industry. *The Graduate* ended up the top grossing movie of the year, taking in $44.1 million.

The year 1967 was also when the *Ed Sullivan Show* required the Rolling Stones to alter the chorus to their single "Let's Spend the Night Together." Mick Jagger fought back by rolling his eyes in an exaggerated grimace each time he reached the amended lyric, "Let's spend some *time* together. . . ." CBS censors forbid *The Smothers Brothers Comedy Hour* from using the word "mindblowing" in a sketch, and prohibited Pete Seeger from singing an antiwar song on the show in the fall of 1967—the first of many skirmishes the Smothers Brothers would have with CBS. (CBS finally pulled the plug on *The Smothers Brothers Comedy Hour* abruptly in 1969 and, as if to underline Newton Minnow's famous lamentation that TV is "a vast wasteland," replaced it with *Hee Haw*.)

While Hollywood was celebrating its newfound license to push the fringes of conventional standards, a funny thing happened: The number of people going to the movies began to plummet. Since 1953 weekly movie attendance had hovered between 40 million and 44 million people a week.

But between 1965 and 1969 weekly movie attendance dropped from 44 million to 17.5 million. Since most moviegoers are younger, the baby boom surge during these years should have boosted movie attendance. The case is difficult to prove, but a major reason may have been Hollywood's swing toward the counterculture. In 1965, Michael Medved points out, the best picture Oscar went to the family-friendly *Sound of Music;* in 1969, the best picture Oscar went to X-rated *Midnight Cowboy.*[120]

Meanwhile, John Wayne had been toiling for over a year to get a Hollywood studio interested in a movie treatment of Robin Moore's *The Green Berets,* a novel that celebrated the special forces in Vietnam. Studios turned him down because they thought that there were so few Americans who supported the war in Vietnam that any film celebrating troops there was bound to be a flop. Warner Brothers (which had backed *Bonnie and Clyde*) finally decided to back the movie, counting on Wayne's box-office draw. It didn't do well at the box office, though this may have been more on account of the movie's lackluster script and listless direction. The movie's title song, however, went to number one on the pop music charts, a sign that the old order, while perhaps passing from the scene, was not quite dead yet.

THAT THE NATION was moving toward a political crisis of the first order was not yet fully evident to the political class. In addition to the clash over the Vietnam War and the disillusionment with the Great Society, the widening cultural divide was rapidly emerging as the dominant backdrop for the nation's political life, a fact that Ronald Reagan and Richard Nixon understood equally. LBJ was largely oblivious, still believing as late as 1967 that the primary challenge to his presidency would come from the Right rather than the Left.

Responsible liberals were only beginning to grasp the disaster that was in store for them. Pat Moynihan saw the outline of their predicament, but was hopeful that the nation would emerge from this "troubled time . . . wiser and having demonstrated anew the deep sources of stability in American life." By 1967 Moynihan had come, like most liberal intellectuals, to oppose the Vietnam War, though he understood that Vietnam was the liberals' war, that it "most surely must be judged our doing," and therefore that liberal leaders should exercise restraint in their judgments against President Johnson. "The plain fact is that if these men

[Kennedy and Johnson liberals] got us into the current predicament, who are we to say we would have done better?"

About domestic affairs Moynihan's second thoughts took more concrete form. "Liberals," Moynihan told the Americans for Democratic Action, "must divest themselves of the notion that the nation—and especially the cities—can be run from Washington. . . . The old-time Tories had a point when they said you can't change human nature—for good or ill—with a bill-signing ceremony in the Rose Garden." This was heresy, but was only a warm-up for his third challenge: "Liberals must somehow overcome the curious condescension that takes the form of defending and explaining away anything, however outrageous, which Negroes, individually or collectively, might do." Liberals at this moment, Moynihan said, should consider entering an alliance with reasonable conservatives, in part because, he wrote separately, conservatives "are showing some of the toughness of mind and spirit associated with persons willing to persist in an unpopular cause."[121]

Liberals ignored Moynihan's advice, as usual. Edward Shils remarked years later that during the 1960s "Liberals would sooner see their society ruined than learn something valuable to its preservation from conservatism."[122] There was, however, one unlikely figure within the Democratic firmament who displayed some understanding of the liberal predicament: Robert F. Kennedy. Between having picked up the standard of his slain brother and subsequently falling to the assassin's bullet himself, Bobby Kennedy occupies a lofty position in the pantheon of liberal icons. Much of this iconography, however, can be seen as the posthumous attempt to see Bobby Kennedy as the lost rescuer for the liberal cause that was beginning to flounder. If only Bobby had lived, goes the wistful myth, he would have prevented liberalism's slide to disrepute and saved the Great Society and the Democratic Party.

Bobby Kennedy's protean political character provides ample material to lend verisimilitude to the myth, and in an ironic way the liberal myth might have been correct—Bobby might have helped restrain liberalism's worst impulses had he lived. His disillusionment with liberal elites has been a well-concealed aspect of his evanescent political ascent. Certain Kennedy gestures bolstered his stock among intellectuals prone to swooning before political idols, such as his penchant for quoting ancient and modern poets and philosophers, hobnobbing with foreign literati such as

Andre Malraux, and saying nice things about Che Guevara. He sought out a meeting with Staughton Lynd and Tom Hayden (just back from a celebrated visit to Hanoi), telling them that "We're in the same ballpark" on Vietnam. His solicitude for college students, especially the self-consciously "alienated," earned him the campus nickname "Ho Chi Bobby." "The near–New Left and the half-hippies," Andrew Kopkind wrote in the *New York Review of Books,* "hope that somehow Kennedy can create a world of love and pot and participation." Yet Kennedy at other times spoke scornfully, but mostly in private, about "peacenik professors" and "kooky intellectuals."[123]

These contradictions suggest that the full story is more complicated and subtle that the great liberal myth allows. Just as many liberal intellectuals and activists had distrusted his brother in 1960, liberals were wary when Bobby decided to seek elective office by running for the U.S. Senate from New York in 1964. He had never belonged to the Americans for Democratic Action, which was the *sine qua non* of liberal *bona fides* in those days. The memory of Bobby Kennedy's tutelage under Sen. Joseph McCarthy a decade before was unforgivable to many liberals. Bobby reciprocated, telling Anthony Lewis in 1965 that "What my father said about businessmen applies to liberals . . . They're sons of bitches."[124] A surprising number of liberal intellectuals, including Richard Hofstadter, Barbara Tuchman, and Arthur Schlesinger Sr., supported the liberal Republican incumbent, Kenneth Keating. Labor unions, still resentful of Kennedy's crusade against organized crime, naturally opposed him, but even the NAACP joined the anti-Kennedy bandwagon. But Kennedy didn't need any of these people. Bolstered by the family fortune, Kennedy's heavy advertising blitz blew Keating away by 720,000 votes.

Whether from ambition, a visceral hatred for Lyndon Johnson, a sense of family honor, or all of these factors, Bobby Kennedy became a leading critic of the Johnson administration, and thereby was able to dissipate the lingering liberal suspicion of him. Bobby had desperately wanted to be Johnson's running mate in 1964—Johnson had just as desperately wanted to shut him out—which, had it happened, would have ruined Bobby's political future (he would have had to play the Hubert Humphrey role and defend the Vietnam War), though it might have saved his life. The media, always eager for a star and a conflict, fixed upon Bobby's every move, usually to the disadvantage of LBJ. The *New York Times* routinely gave stories about Kennedy's doings more prominent coverage and page placement than concurrent stories about LBJ. Kennedy shied away from suggestions that he ready himself to challenge Johnson for the nomination in 1968, and he grudgingly professed public support for President Johnson, carefully calibrating his criticisms of the Vietnam War to keep his break from Johnson from being complete and open. But his highly publicized trips to South Africa and Latin American were clearly intended to burnish his image as a world leader more enlightened and worthy than Johnson. His cloying shyness—in sharp contrast to his brother John's outgoing self-assurance—made this ambiguous posture highly effective and alluring.

Although Kennedy's attack on Johnson's foreign policy can easily be viewed as a combination of conscience and opportunism, his criticism of the Great Society was more interesting and probably more sincere. Kennedy attacked the Great Society simultaneously from the Left and the Right. He complained that Johnson wasn't spending enough for the War on Poverty—"a drop in the bucket," he complained—but later said that the nation could not "afford to continue, year after year, the increases in welfare costs," and that the last thing the nation needed was "a massive extension of welfare services."[125] He offered a criticism of big-spending bureaucratic approaches to social problems that could have come from the pen of a conservative Republican; indeed, Reagan commented sharply in 1968 that "I get the feeling I've been writing some of his speeches. When he gets before the chamber of commerce he talks like Barry Goldwater."[126] At about this same time, the *New York Times* ran a feature entitled "Kennedy: Meet the Conservative." There is not, Kennedy wrote in his book *To Seek a Newer World,* "a problem for which there is not a program. There is not a problem for which money is not being spent. There is not a problem or a program on which dozens or hundreds or thousands of bureaucrats are not earnestly at work. But does this represent a solution to our problems? Manifestly it does not."[127] During the 1968 campaign, he came close to repudiating his brother's "New Frontier" legacy: "In the last analysis it should be in the cities and towns and villages where the decisions are made, not in Washington. . . . Solutions of the 1930s are not the solutions of today. The solutions of the New Frontier, of the early 1960s, are not necessarily applicable now."[128] In one of the last press releases before his death, Kennedy allowed that "the welfare system itself has created many of our fatherless families."[129]

Kennedy thought he had a better idea: a return more or less to the self-help philosophy of the original community action program. Rather than trying to run another version of this troubled approach through Congress and the federal bureaucracy, Kennedy decided to try a private-sector approach (or what in today's neologism would be a "public-private partnership") to revitalize the Bedford-Stuyvesant neighborhood of New York City. He sought out private foundation and corporate funds to support the Bedford-Stuyvesant Renewal and Rehabilitation Corporation. This non-profit corporation would be run by local community leaders, not Washington bureaucrats. What the poor needed were jobs and neighborhood economic development, not handouts, Kennedy stressed. Kennedy wanted to pass tax incentives for businesses to locate plants in distressed urban areas and to hire poor and unskilled workers—the same idea that would emerge under the name "Enterprise Zones" in the 1980s. Kennedy hoped this effort at community self-help would provide a model for rescuing the anti-poverty effort nationwide.

The Left was not impressed. Michael Harrington attacked the plan for "putting too much trust in private business, which remains motivated by profit." Andrew Kopkind wrote that "it may be a serious mistake to consider what Kennedy is doing—in Bedford-Stuyvesant as elsewhere—a healthy 'first step' toward significant change." The program, Kopkind thought, amounted to "elitist reform." Robert Scheer wrote in *Ramparts* that "The Kennedy plan, then, involves a return to the market economy, and he has described the Bedford-Stuyvesant projects in terms more reminiscent of Ronald Reagan than Herbert Lehman." Indeed, William F. Buckley Jr. praised Kennedy's effort as "sensible."[130]

Pat Moynihan had privately advised Kennedy that the project was a bad idea. He knew that the grievance mentality unleashed in the ghetto by the Community Action Program was likely to poison the well for Kennedy's pilot project as well, and the vindication of this worry was not long in coming. (Though friendly to Moynihan, Kennedy privately complained that Moynihan "knows all the facts and he's against all the solutions."[131]) The Bedford-Stuyvesant community corporation was launched in December 1966, but by March 1967 competing community factions who felt insufficiently represented within the community corporation turned on Kennedy. In a protest whose script, Jack Newfield wrote, "could have been written by Genet or Daniel Moynihan," local black activists attacked Kennedy and his recruits as "outsiders" and "colonialists." Reflecting the radicalism animating the Black Power movement, the protestors turned against their own; the "black bourgeoisie" was trying "to make it uptown on the backs of the brothers."[132] "These are the people we need to reach," the irrepressible Kennedy said after leaving the meeting.

The welfare state was not the only area where Kennedy had a latent conservative populist streak. Sensing the public mood in 1968 about urban unrest, Kennedy began touting his background as the "chief law enforcement officer" as Attorney General. Theodore White's quadrennial election chronicle for 1968 noted that Nixon seized upon the "law and order" theme after he found on the campaign trail in the spring that "a lot of these people think Bobby is more of a law-and-order man than I am." Later, Nixon remarked that "Bobby and I have been sounding pretty much alike" on major issues.[133]

The Bedford-Stuyvesant misadventure and Kennedy's heterodox views on the welfare state faded from view—and have in some ways been suppressed—as the mythology of Kennedy the Lost Liberal Hero came into being after his murder. The swirl of circumstance, family history, and the studied ambiguity of his own words will forever mark Bobby Kennedy as "enigmatic" to serious inquirers. It was this chameleon quality that made him such a compelling figure within the Democratic Party as 1968 approached. But it was doubtful that he really would, or could, challenge LBJ for the Democratic nomination. It seemed more likely that 1972 or 1976 (at which point Bobby would still only be 50 years old) would be the propitious moment. And his likely opponent already seemed evident: the other flashy newcomer to national politics, the man in the California statehouse. In fact, they would soon have their first (and only) head-to-head clash.

"AMAZINGLY ENOUGH," *Newsweek* magazine reported in May 1967, "with little more than his first 100 days in office scratched from the calendar, the quondam host of 'Death Valley Days' has managed to close one of the widest credibility gaps any politician ever faced."[134] Ronald Reagan indeed got off to a fast start in Sacramento following his midnight inauguration in January 1967, but it was not without its bumps. Three weeks into his term Reagan was embroiled in a controversy that augmented the enmity liberal intellectuals held for him: the firing of U.C.

Chancellor Clark Kerr. Kerr's position had weakened with the U.C. Board of Regents ever since the Free Speech Movement two years before, and it is likely that the Regents would have dismissed Kerr on that fateful February day even if Pat Brown had been re-elected the previous November. Kerr had a full measure of academic arrogance, and had been spoiling for a showdown with the regents. He asked for the February meeting with the regents in hopes of extracting a vote of confidence. Kerr was certain that the new governor, still warming up his chair, would shy away from such a visible fight. He was not the last person to make this mistake with Reagan.

Though California's governor is a member of the Board of Regents, few actually attended before Reagan. (Reagan attended regents meetings faithfully throughout his two terms.) When the Regents voted 14–8 to dismiss Kerr in a closed-door session (Reagan voted with the majority), it was immediately supposed that Reagan had engineered Kerr's ouster. After all, Reagan's famous slogan about student antics—"Obey the rules, or get out"—was immortalized in a sign on the wall in his capitol office. But in fact it was a Pat Brown appointee to the regents, Laurence Kennedy, who offered the motion to dismiss Kerr. Reagan was no fan of Kerr, but he would actually have preferred to delay the Kerr matter until later in the year because another crisis was looming much more prominently in his mind.

The state budget was a mess. During the campaign Reagan had attacked Governor Brown's spending "gimmicks." Now he was learning that the gimmickry had been much more extensive than even his oratorical flourishes suggested. Brown's administration had masked a growing budget shortfall during the election year of 1966 by accelerating tax collections and employing accrual accounting by which revenue was counted as in the bank even though it had not yet been collected. Brown's own outgoing finance director was candid about their plans had they been returned to office: "Raise taxes."

In Reagan's first few weeks in office California's state government was faced with a serious cash-flow shortage. As he later reflected, "I didn't know if I was elected governor or appointed receiver." For the year ahead, it appeared that the state's projected $5 billion budget would be nearly $1 billion short. Reagan followed his first instinct, and called for a 10 percent across-the-board spending cut in every state agency and spending program, which would still have left the budget at least $240 million short.

"Any major business can tighten its belt by 10 percent and still maintain the quality and quantity of its operation," Reagan said. "So too can government."[135] The 10 percent across-the-board cutback idea was a nonstarter, and made Reagan look like the amateur politician that he was. He compounded this gaffe by calling on state workers to volunteer to work on the Lincoln and Washington birthday holidays in February; the gesture backfired, with less than 2 percent of state workers responding to the challenge. But Reagan minimized the embarrassment of these ideas by aggressively pruning small but symbolically rich spending practices. He sold the state airplane, cut back on out-of-state travel by state officials, canceled plans to build a new 10-story state office building, froze the purchase of state automobiles, and began reducing the state workforce through attrition. "We are going to squeeze and cut and trim until we reduce the cost of government," Reagan said on his 100th day in office.

But no amount of cutting and squeezing and trimming was going to obviate the need for a big tax increase, and Reagan was quickly coming to grips with this unhappy fact. His handling of the issue was the first sign that Reagan was no lightweight, but in fact possessed genuine political skill. The temptation to adopt a posture of attack against the Democrat-controlled legislature would have been irresistible to a mere ideologue, but Reagan adopted a posture of compromise and cooperation from the outset. When Reagan first sat down with the Democratic Speaker of the Assembly, Jesse Unruh, the only issue between them was what form the tax increase would take. Reagan and Unruh were surprisingly like-minded: Both wanted to include some kind of property tax relief to soften the blow to the taxpayer. They both agreed that the state income tax would have to be hiked. The only sharp point of difference was over a typically Reaganesque point of philosophy. Unruh wanted to institute income tax withholding, which speeds up revenue collection. Reagan was adamantly opposed. "Taxes should hurt," he famously remarked, knowing that the act of having to write a large check to the government each year tended to concentrate the minds of voters on the need for limited government. Reagan held fast on the issue and won.

The $1 billion tax increase Reagan embraced was not merely the largest tax increase in California history—it was four times larger than any previous tax hike. "In the political intricacies of pushing through a revenue measure, the actor-turned-politician named Ronald Reagan had shown his competence as governor of California," wrote journalist Lou Cannon. [136] Democrats were similarly impressed. Unruh, who had not gotten along with Brown even though they were in the same party, told a Reagan aide after the tax bill passed: "Can you imagine what could have been accomplished up here when Brown was governor if I could have gotten the cooperation from him that I got from you people?"[137] Democrats also thought Reagan would reap the whirlwind of unpopularity when the first tax bills came due the following April. But the fact that Reagan had inherited the mess, along with his clearly and repeatedly expressed intent to shrink government as much as possible, built up a fund of goodwill with the public that deflected the public's annoyance with higher taxes. By the fall of 1967, polls showed Reagan with a 70 percent public approval rating. "How in the devil a governor can push through a billion-dollar tax increase and win popularity doing it is beyond me," a frustrated Democratic legislator told *Time* magazine.[138]

A handful of extreme conservatives blasted Reagan for midwiving the tax increase (which attacks actually helped Reagan with moderates), but for the most part conservatives were well pleased with Reagan because they had few doubts about his principles. "Now, there are some who would believe that with my recent change of occupation, I would change my tune," Reagan remarked in a speech. "But I want you to know that I am just as frightened of government, even though I am now a part of it, as I have been these many years, and I believe being frightened and concerned with the growth of government is legitimate." The tax bill he was forced to adopt, he underscored, "does not represent my philosophy of government. I still think the government of California costs the people of California too much." Reagan was not about to "grow in office," as the euphemism goes.

Although Reagan's handling of the budget mess incurred no lasting political liability, other controversies of his first year were more ambiguous. Reagan was forced to fire two senior staffers whose extracurricular homosexual activities threatened an embarrassment. Reagan's public denial of the episode was punctured by the press, thus extending the life of the story. While Reagan lost no sleep over this moral controversy, he was soon to make another decision that he would later profess to be his greatest regret. He would shortly sign a bill liberalizing California's abortion laws.

Prior to 1967 California law permitted abortion only to save the life of the mother, and the legislature had twice rejected a bill to widen the abortion statute. There is a strong likelihood that even had a reform bill passed before 1967, Pat Brown—a Roman Catholic—would have hesitated to sign it into law. But the clamor for more liberal abortion law was rising rapidly. Several states liberalized their abortion laws in the mid-1960s, including New York and Colorado. Proponents claimed that up to 100,000 illegal abortions took place in California each year. (There were only 517 legal abortions in 1967, according to state figures.) An illegal abortion trade flourished over the Mexican border. The existing restrictions were dealt a public relations setback when nine physicians were prosecuted for performing abortions on mothers with German measles, which can cause severe deformities in children. So when a new bill was proposed in 1967 to allow abortions in cases of rape or incest, in cases where there was "substantial risk" that the child would be deformed, and in cases where childbirth would impair the physical or mental health of the mother, the only meaningful opposition came from the Catholic Church. Reagan's legislative aides quietly signaled his support. Republicans supplied five of the seven votes to move the bill out of the Senate Judiciary Committee. It looked like smooth sailing.

Then Reagan wavered. His legislative aides suddenly shifted gears and worked behind the scenes to shelve the bill. The normally decisive Reagan said he was now "studying" the bill, and was worried about some of its "ambiguities." In a press conference he said, "I have never done more study on any one thing than on the abortion bill." He objected especially to the clause allowing abortions in the case of prospective birth defects—"not different from what Hitler tried to do," he remarked. The bill's sponsor agreed to remove the offending clause, and the bill passed the Senate by one vote, and the Assembly by a wide margin. Reagan still worried aloud about "loopholes," but he agreed to sign it into law. The number of legal abortions quickly jumped from 517 in 1967 to more than 100,000 a year. "Those were awful weeks," Reagan told Lou Cannon in 1969. His father-in-law, a surgeon, reportedly swayed Reagan toward signing the bill, but he still harbored misgivings. He was troubled by the slippery slope of the issue. "You can't allow an abortion on grounds the child won't be born perfect. Where do you stop? What is the degree of deformity that a person shouldn't be born? Crippled persons have contributed greatly to our society."[139] In the 1976 presidential campaign Reagan incautiously allowed that "there have to be loopholes" in any laws restricting abortion to allow for the priority of the life or health of the mother. This naturally set off a tempest in the burgeoning Pro-Life movement, and Reagan immediately wrote publicly to Congressman Henry Hyde in favor of the Human Life Amendment, explaining why he now considered his agreement to the abortion bill in 1967 a mistake:

> The only circumstance under which I felt [abortion] could be justified was self-defense, a concept deeply rooted in our laws and traditions. If a mother's life is endangered by her own unborn child, she has a right to protect her life. I do not believe, however, that abortion of a less-than-perfect child, or abortion for convenience sake or abortion because "a mistake" has been made can be justified.
>
> The bill I signed followed the self-defense concept. As time was to prove, however, it contained one flaw. The self-defense concept also included a provision in cases where a mother's mental health might be irreparably damaged. This required professional certification, but as we were to learn, it became subject to very liberal interpretation by some psychiatrists to justify abortions that should not have been made.[140]

The hesitancy over the abortion bill proved the exception to the most surprising trait Reagan showed as a novice politician: decisiveness. Lou Cannon read through the minutes of cabinet meetings, and observed that the minutes "reveal a Reagan who was not above admitting his ignorance about a major state issue but who displayed a ready decisiveness once he was presented with alternatives."[141] "There's no better time to make a decision than when it's right in front of you," Reagan liked to say.

Reagan's power of decision was the product of his supreme self-confidence combined with an unobserved discipline that tightly structured his working routine. It was Reagan's discipline that enabled him to keep regular business hours and get home by 6 P.M. most nights—a practice that also raised eyebrows among the workaholic political class. "Reagan," *Newsweek* observed five months into his first term, "is one of the most carefully programmed officials in America." In addition to regular meetings with his top officials to thrash out issues, Reagan relied upon a controversial managerial device: the one-page memo. Reagan required agency officials and staff to boil down a pending issue into a one-page format with the following four elements: the issue, the facts, reasoning, and recommendations. His cabinet secretary, William P. Clark Jr., had helped develop the routine. "It has been found," Clark said, "that almost any issue can be reduced to a single page."[142]

Reagan made as many as eight decisions in a hour during staff meetings, affixing an "OK, R.R." next to one of the alternatives presented in a memo. With this method Reagan had followed the practice of Churchill, who often demanded "on a single sheet of paper" memoranda from his cabinet about wartime issues, and also President Eisenhower, who had used the single-page memo format both as president and also as Allied Commander during World War II. But like Reagan's use of three-by-five cards for his speeches, his use of the one-page memo became a source of ridicule by sophisticates who thought the process of governing ought to be more laborious and complicated than this. (Of course Reagan didn't stick rigidly or blindly to this method; he often asked for additional analysis and argument about issues, which often resulted in the customary fat briefing books.) But the smooth-running results Reagan achieved tended to dissipate this criticism. The *New York Times* observed at the end of Reagan's first year in office: "He has turned out to be a man of some strength who likes to make decisions and makes them easily."[143]

Reagan's freshman year success in office immediately ignited speculation about the Republican presidential campaign in 1968. Reagan's potential had been obvious even before he was elected governor. The *New York Times'* Tom Wicker had written in July of 1966 that Reagan "may play the decisive role in the 1968 Republican Presidential maneuvering."[144] Reagan disclaimed interest in the presidency throughout 1967. "I am not a candidate for President," Reagan told *Time* magazine in April. "I've got a pretty big job right here."[145] Some in the media thought Reagan would have to run because, as Harry Reasoner explained in a one-hour *CBS Reports* special entitled "What About Ronald Reagan?", "this is probably his last chance at the White House. . . . For one reason or another, chiefly age, it's 1968 or never. . . ."[146]

Reagan privately had serious doubts about the whole idea, telling Lou Cannon later that "My feeling was that to go straight from Hollywood to governor and one year after you were there to be in a position of saying, 'I want to be President of the United States,' there was no way I could do that and be credible."[147] Reagan was also sincere in his belief that "the office seeks the man," and while he undoubtedly burned with ambition to seek the office, he wasn't certain it sought *him*. But by the middle of the summer the idea of Reagan's candidacy was acquiring a momentum of its own, and Reagan's tune became more ambiguous. He refused to make a Shermanesque statement categorically declining interest in the office. "Nobody else ever made this statement except Sherman, and it wasn't a particularly good idea for him," Reagan said.[148] At a meeting of the Western Governors' Conference in Montana in July, Reagan told reporters: "If the Republican Party comes knocking at my door, I won't say, 'Get lost, fellows.'"[149]

Throughout most of 1967 Michigan Governor George Romney was reckoned the Republican front-runner, and several polls put him slightly ahead of LBJ. Romney was regarded as a liberal Republican, and was thought perhaps to be running as a stalking horse for Nelson Rockefeller, whose own ambitions for 1968 were muted in the same way as Reagan's. But Romney suffered from a charisma gap. "Romney," *Newsweek* wrote in May 1967, "may be the first major political candidate of modern times to lose out because he is too boring. . . . Everywhere Romney goes he seems to bomb." Jack Germond wrote that when Romney visited New York, reporters complained that "There are eight million stories in this town, and we're stuck with the dullest." *National Review* observed in March 1967 that Romney had "a gaffe-proneness of Mr. Magoo dimensions"—a judgment that would be spectacularly confirmed five months later.[150] Nixon, regarded as a moderate but nonetheless acceptable to conservatives, was running hard, but was burdened with the stigma of being a two-time loser. The early line held that Nixon and Romney would cancel each other out in the Republican primaries. Leaving exactly who?

Time magazine offered their answer in an October cover story that featured Rockefeller ("For President") and Reagan ("For Vice President"). "A growing number of Republican officials," *Time* reported, "believe that the surest way to [win] in 1968 would be with a Rockefeller-Reagan ticket."[151] (*Newsweek* noted one drawback for this ticket: both candidates had been divorced and were on second marriages.) A Gallup Poll found that a Rockefeller-Reagan ticket would beat Johnson by a 57 to 43 margin—a larger margin than the Eisenhower landslides of the 1950s. Rockefeller had been careful not to characterize Reagan with the same broad brush with which he had tarred Goldwater. "When he [Reagan] gets engaged with the realities of being governor," Rockefeller said after Reagan's election, "you'll find he's no extremist." Rockefeller had reason to be delighted with *Time*'s suggestion; he was reported to fear Reagan even more than Nixon as a rival for the GOP nomination, and the potential pairing with Reagan would provide him a means to outflank Nixon on the Right. Reagan thought the arrangement might be acceptable—if the order on the ticket were reversed.

The 1968 nomination process was the last in either party where it was possible for someone to gain the nomination merely by being "available." Barely a tenth of the 1,333 delegates to be selected for the 1968 Republican convention would be chosen by the voters directly in primary elections. It made more sense in this environment, therefore, to run an undeclared campaign of "availability" rather than to become a direct contestant head-to-head against Nixon and Romney. Above all, conservatives feared that a Nixon collapse in the primary might pave the way for a liberal Republican—either Rockefeller or Romney—to capture the nomination.

A behind-the-scenes Reagan campaign was quietly taking shape. Reagan refused to file disclaimers for the Oregon and Nebraska primary elections, where fervent grassroots supporters had placed his name on the ballot. Reagan's clarity on the issues and his charisma had long made him the most popular draw among Republican audiences around the nation, and this demand provided him with a convenient excuse to travel the nation testing the presidential waters while raising millions for Republicans on the rubber-chicken circuit.

The book on Reagan was that while he was obviously superb with the set-speech, whether he could handle himself on his feet under pressure was still in doubt. An outburst of temper over civil rights during the 1966 campaign, and in a press conference following the dismissal of the homosexuals on his staff, kindled lingering doubts. His performance on the hustings in 1967 largely dispatched these doubts.

Reagan ironically received some of his best reviews for his appearances on hostile territory—college campuses. When a student audience at Colorado College cheered his call for ending the draft, Reagan asked, "Have you ever thought about transferring to Berkeley?" At Yale University, where Reagan visited for four days as a guest lecturer in December

1967, Reagan kept his cool in the face of deliberate provocations. Reagan again benefited from the overreaching and crude characterizations of his opponents. "Weren't people who held your views convicted at Nuremberg of crimes against humanity?", one student asked in a political science class. "Do you believe the governors of the other major states have been unwise in failing to veto as many O.E.O. grants for their states as you and Lurleen Wallace [George Wallace's wife, who was elected governor of Alabama when her husband's tenure of office ended in 1966] have done?" Reagan deflected these and other set pieces with his usual firmness and wit. "Do homosexuals have any place in government?", one student asked. "Well, perhaps in the Department of Parks and Recreation," Reagan quipped.

Reagan received a standing ovation from the Yale Political Union for his performance, and subsequent media notices were effusive. *Washington Post* columnist Joseph Kraft wrote that Reagan was a "dekooking agent" for the conservative wing of the Republican Party. Reagan's "oversimplification is not the awful thing so many of his critics have imagined." To the contrary, Kraft concluded, Reagan has "demonstrated that the concept of the straightforward citizen leader is not all reactionary hot air."[152] "Reagan Keeps Smiling at Yale Despite Sneers and Hostile Air," read the *New York Times* headline.

Reagan's most significant showing in 1967, however, came in a head-to-head television debate with Robert F. Kennedy in May. Reagan and Kennedy appeared on an unusual CBS news program called "Town Meeting of the World," billed as a bi-partisan discussion of America's image. CBS linked Reagan, speaking from a studio in Sacramento, and Kennedy, from a studio in New York, with a group of 18 students in London in what *Newsweek* called "the first eyeball-to-eyeball test of the two men who may very well meet on the road to the White House."

Most of the forum was devoted to the subject of the Vietnam War. Fifteen million Americans tuned in—and saw a confident, self-assured Reagan clobber a defensive and apologetic Kennedy. The problem for Kennedy—and the opportunity for Reagan—was that most of the students' questions were unremittingly hostile to the United States and sympathetic to North Vietnam. The tone was so insulting that CBS edited out 30 minutes of the taped program. (The one notable exception to the hostile tone was a question from the only American student on the panel, former Princeton basketball star, Rhodes Scholar, and later U.S. Senator Bill Bradley.) Kennedy could not conceal his essential agreement with the students' sharply worded attacks on U.S. policy in Vietnam; he couldn't even come to use the words "Viet Cong," referring instead to the National Liberation Front (the VC's formal name) as "the political arm of those who are providing most of the troops, most of the force, most of the effort in the south." When a student asserted that "While they're [the U.S.] spending 20 billion dollars a year destroying the country [Vietnam]," Kennedy interrupted: "You're wrong in your figures again—it's about $25 billion." The student pounded on the gaffe: "Oh, splendid, 25 billion dollars. . . ."

By contrast, Reagan challenged both the premises and the facts behind most of the hostile questions. When a student asserted that the late South Vietnamese leader Diem had imprisoned six million people, Reagan quickly retorted, "I challenge your history," reminding the audience that the South Vietnamese population was only 16 million people to begin with. Reagan had thoroughly prepared for the debate, reeling off facts and figures about Vietnam. But his greatest strength, as always, was his appeal to larger themes and principles. When a student asserted the moral equivalence between American democracy and Soviet Communism, and asked whether Barry Goldwater's "extremism in defense of liberty" wasn't indistinguishable from Stokely Carmichael saying "to hell with the laws of this country," Reagan defended crisply. He reminded the audience that the United States had held the monopoly on nuclear weapons at the close of World War II, but had not exploited the bomb for conquest. "Can you honestly say," Reagan asked, "that had the Soviet Union been in a comparable position with that bomb, or today's Red Chinese, that the world would not today have been conquered with that force?"[153] (This argument, which Reagan was fond of repeating well into his presidency, closely echoed Winston Churchill, who said in 1948: "What do you suppose would be the position this afternoon if it had been Communist Russia instead of free enterprise America which had created the atomic weapon? Instead of being a sombre guarantee of peace it would have become an irresistible method of human enslavement.")

"It was political rookie Reagan," *Newsweek* wrote, "who left old campaigner Kennedy blinking when the session ended." "The general consensus," David Halberstam wrote, "was that Reagan . . . destroyed him."[154] "Bob was talking to the students, [while] Reagan was talking to the American TV audience," a Kennedy aide admitted to a reporter. "That's why Reagan was the big gainer."[155] Reagan's office was deluged with thousands of letters of support for his "standing up for America." Kennedy was furious. He was heard to ask immediately after the debate, "Who the fuck got me into this?" Weeks later he came across the aide who did, Frank Mankiewitz, and said "You're the guy who got me into that Reagan thing."[156] Kennedy refused permission for Reagan to use portions of the program tape in the 1968 Oregon primary, where Reagan was on the ballot, and the debate disappeared into a black hole as far as Kennedy's camp was concerned. Arthur Schlesinger's 1,000-page biography of RFK makes no mention of the encounter.

When a young woman from Pennsylvania told Reagan that "Everyone back home wants you to be our next President," Reagan replied: "Dear girl, don't scare me! You scare me when you say that!" The only person more scared of the prospect were the liberals of both parties. George Gilder, hoping to revive liberal Republicanism as the head of the Ripon Society, wrote in *The New Leader* that Reagan's potential ascendance meant that "the national party would be consigned to permanent minority status."[157] Liberal Democrats were even more apoplectic. In December 1967 a group of liberals took out a full-page ad in the *New York Times* with the headline: "Johnson vs. Reagan? God help us."[158] As shaken liberals looked ahead to 1968, they could scarcely imagine a worse nightmare. They got one anyway.

CHAPTER FIVE

ANVIL: 1968

———

As 1968 BEGAN Lyndon Johnson considered not running for re-election, but he had reason to be optimistic if he did. The economy was heading into its 84th month of expansion, a new record. "Johnson Popularity on Upswing, Year-End Gallup Polls Discloses," the *New York Times* declared on page one on New Year's Day. LBJ's public approval numbers had bounced back from a low of 38 percent in October 1967 to a respectable 46 percent at the end of December. While the polls showed that LBJ would face a close race in a head-to-head contest against a Republican, he would win handily in the anticipated three-way race that included Alabama Governor George Wallace running as an independent. A *Fortune* magazine poll of 400 top corporate executives found 65 percent expected Johnson to win, though they would prefer Nixon. *Time* magazine named LBJ their "Man of the Year" for 1967. Despite all of the troubles at home and abroad, *Time* wrote, "the President's prospects are not all that gloomy. . . . The greatest Presidents are those who emerged during periods of severe strain, domestic or foreign. Johnson still has a chance to stand among them."[1]

Although liberals were dismayed about Vietnam (with the Americans for Democratic Action openly threatening to support a Republican in 1968), many prominent and influential liberals remained loyal to LBJ. "President Johnson will almost certainly be reelected in 1968," Pat Moynihan told the ADA the previous October. John Kenneth Galbraith looked to the balance sheet: "Our gains under the Johnson administration on civil rights outweigh our losses on behalf of [South Vietnam's] Marshall Ky."[2] Sen. Ted Kennedy offered the most unexpected show of support, telling Democrats at an Iowa fundraiser in the fall that "the voters are going to give President Johnson a vote of gratitude and confidence next year."[3] It was taken as a clear signal that Bobby Kennedy would not challenge Johnson for the nomination, as Bobby had been saying publicly and privately for months. Disaffected liberals, including many from the Kennedy circle, would have to settle for Minnesota Senator Eugene McCarthy to be their champion against Johnson in the Democratic primaries. Johnson had almost picked McCarthy to be his running mate in 1964; he had been Lady Bird Johnson's first choice. McCarthy didn't really think he had any chance to overtake LBJ. He merely hoped to do well enough to compel Johnson to adopt a peace platform at the Democrats' Chicago convention at the end of the summer. Early polls showed McCarthy trailing badly in New Hampshire, however. "We know who our nominees will be," the chairman of the Democratic National Committee, John Bailey, said on January 8. "I'm happy to be able to say the Republicans have all their bloody infighting to look forward to."[4]

Republicans, indeed, were feeling none too confident. Throughout 1967 Michigan Governor George Romney had been regarded as the strongest potential GOP nominee, though Nixon held a slight lead in polls of the GOP rank and file. Then, in late August, the often platitudinous and noticeably ineloquent Romney committed a suicidal gaffe. Romney had gone back and forth on the Vietnam War, hawkish and supportive of Johnson's policy one day, dovish and critical the next. He had gone to Vietnam in an effort to burnish his foreign policy credentials in 1965, and had said upon his return that the U.S. commitment to the war was "morally necessary and right." Had he changed his mind about that trip?, he was asked on a Detroit television show. Romney replied: "I just had the greatest brainwashing that anyone can get when you go over to Vietnam, not only by the generals but also by the diplomatic corps over there, and they do a very thorough job."

Romney's plausibility as a presidential candidate imploded instantaneously. "In a matter of hours," James Jackson Kilpatrick wrote, "commentators across the country were remarking acidulously that it certainly took a long time for George to get his brain back from the laundry."

Goldwater, whom Romney had pointedly refused to endorse even after Goldwater had captured the nomination in 1964, now got his revenge: "When you admit that you can be brainwashed, you're in trouble."[5] Democrats piled on, too. Eugene McCarthy displayed the wit that was shortly to become more widely known to Americans: "There was no need to brainwash the Governor. All he required was a light rinse." Romney lamely tried to reverse the damage: "I wasn't talking about Russian-type brainwashing; I was talking about LBJ brainwashing."[6] But it didn't wash. He dropped ten points in the polls, and never recovered. The *Detroit News,* which had long supported Romney, urged him to get out of the presidential race with a brutal editorial. Taking note of Romney's "inexplicable blurt-and-retreat habit," the *Detroit News* said the brainwashing comment illustrated Romney's "unfortunate incapacity to achieve stability and constancy in Presidential politics." The paper suggested that Rockefeller should be the Republican standard bearer.

The *Detroit News* was not unique in this view. New York Republicans awoke New Year's day to the following headline on the front page of the *New York Times:* "GOP Leaders Say Only Rockefeller Can Beat Johnson; 50-State Check Finds Nixon a Close Loser, and Reagan and Romney Routed." But Rockefeller, knowing that an open campaign would arouse the wrath of the Goldwater wing of the party, had repeatedly said he was not a candidate. No one doubted that he still hungered for the White House, however. His strategy was clear. If Nixon stumbled in an early primary, his candidacy would collapse, leaving the nomination wide open. Even if Nixon did well in the primaries, lingering doubts about Nixon might still result in a deadlocked convention, which would also open the door for Rockefeller. (Illinois Senator Charles Percy and New York City Mayor John Lindsay were also among the "mentioned," and of course Ronald Reagan was also pursuing the "availability" strategy.) In the meantime Rockefeller would throw his support behind the faltering Romney campaign.

Nixon remained the real question mark. Following his ignominious loss to Pat Brown in the California governor's race in 1962 (after which Nixon famously said, "This is my last press conference; you won't have Dick Nixon to kick around anymore"), *Time* magazine pronounced his political epitaph: "Barring a miracle, Richard Nixon can never hope to be elected to any political office again." Nixon's course over the following six years were one of the most remarkable political interludes in history, ranking with Churchill's "wilderness years" and Napoleon's exile to Elba. "Throughout this time," Nixon biographer Jonathan Aitken noted, "he prepared himself for his comeback with the discipline of a former heavy-weight champion returning to the ring."[7] His first move was counterintuitive: he left California. Having turned down lucrative offers to become chairman of Chrysler or Pepsi-Cola International, or president of the Dreyfus mutual fund group, Nixon settled on practicing law in New York. His prospective new law partners asked him, "Have you really given up politics?" Nixon answered: "Anyone who knows anything about politics knows that when you give up your base, as I've done in California, then you're finished."[8]

Nixon alone knew better. In addition to building the usual bank account of political chits by campaigning relentlessly for Republican candidates throughout the nation in 1964 and 1966, Nixon traveled the world (impressing Charles De Gaulle most of all—a difficult feat for an American) and applied himself to the serious study of philosophy and literature, reading more of the ancient and modern classics than most graduate students. Through it all he managed to carry on a serious law practice, even arguing a case before the U.S. Supreme Court in 1966, *Time Inc. v. Hill*. He lost, but received high marks for his performance before the Justices. The *Washington Post* wrote that Nixon had presented "one of the better oral arguments of the year."

From a survey of Nixon's relentless activity it is impossible to finger a decisive turning point in his political fortunes, but one key moment came in the summer of 1967 when Nixon and Reagan both appeared at the Bohemian Grove in Northern California. Nixon gave a carefully prepared overview of the world situation based on his extensive travels, and received a standing ovation. "By contrast," Nixon biographer Aitken wrote, "Governor Reagan was glitzy but lightweight. The many influential GOP power brokers present, including southern conservatives such as Senator John Tower of Texas, and Governor Claude Kirk from Florida, shared the consensus that there had been no contest between the two speakers. Nixon alone had sounded ready to win the White House and to lead the free world."[9]

Although Nixon was consolidating his strength with party regulars, there was still considerable doubt that he could shake his image as a two-time loser. While his imagination and insight shone in the area of foreign policy, the public, according to the polls, was more concerned about crime than Vietnam or other foreign issues, which was understandable given the 80 percent rise in crime since 1960. So Nixon was attempting to talk tough on crime.

But LBJ had a typically ambitious federal crime bill before Congress, and seemed poised to inoculate himself on the issue. Polls showed him with a slight lead over Nixon, and if the advantages of incumbency were factored in, he had reason to be confident of his re-election. Even the Vietnam War was looking more hopeful. "There is good reason to believe," *U.S. News and World Report*'s Saigon correspondent wrote in the magazine's first issue of 1968, "that this year is going to see the beginning of the end of the war here in Vietnam."[10]

On January 1, North Vietnam's foreign minister Nguyen Duy Trinh announced a significant concession of North Vietnam's conditions for negotiations with the United States. Trinh said that a halt in U.S. bombing of North Vietnam *would* open the way for negotiations to begin. Previously the North Vietnamese had said only that a bombing halt *might* lead to negotiations, and their other conditions, especially the inclusion of the Viet Cong as an official negotiating player, still applied. But now a diplomatic breakthrough seemed possible at last; Johnson's advisers apparently forgot or disregarded John P. Roche's prediction that North Vietnam would agree to open negotiations on the eve of the American election cycle for the purpose of exciting maximum mischief. Nonetheless, in the first week in January of 1968 it appeared that only a surprise could upend the LBJ re-election scenario. Thus began what would turn out to be America's single worst year since 1861.

ON JANUARY 5, the Joint United States Public Affairs Office in Saigon released to reporters the contents of a Viet Cong soldier's notebook that had fallen into the hands of U.S. intelligence two months before. The key passage read:

> The central headquarters has ordered the entire army and people of South Vietnam to implement general offensive and general uprising in order to achieve a decisive victory. . . . Use very strong military attacks in coordination with the uprisings of the local population to

take over towns and cities. Troops should flood the lowlands. They
should move toward liberating the capital city [Saigon], take power
and try to rally enemy brigades and regiments to our side one by
one. Propaganda should be broadly disseminated among the population in general, and leaflets should be used to reach enemy officers
and enlisted personnel.[11]

Because the VC soldier's notebook had been captured up near the De-
Militarized Zone (DMZ), not far from where North Vietnamese troops
were thought to be massing for an attack on the U.S. base at Khe Sanh,
U.S. intelligence dismissed the contents of the notebook as disinformation, as a means of diverting attention away from where the main blow
was expected to fall. Hence it received little emphasis by U.S. military
commanders in Saigon, and little notice in the news media. This was
merely one of the countless missed signals contributing to what Army
General Bruce Palmer later called "an allied intelligence failure ranking
with Pearl Harbor in 1941"—the surprise of the Tet offensive.[12]

On January 30, in the middle of the Tet holiday, North Vietnamese
regular army troops and Viet Cong troops struck in a coordinated attack
on 36 of South Vietnam's 44 provincial capitals, and 70 other towns in the
country. The North Vietnamese also unleashed a ferocious attack on the
U.S. base at Khe Sanh that lasted two months. The North Vietnamese
stormed the coastal city of Hue; it required some of the hardest fighting of
the war over the next month for U.S. Marines to retake the city. The most
stunning blow of the surprise attack was the guerrilla raid on the U.S. embassy in downtown Saigon. Nineteen Viet Cong commandos blasted a
hole in the perimeter wall of the embassy compound at 3 A.M., and killed
five U.S. GIs upon storming the embassy grounds. (Four South Vietnamese
policemen assigned to guard the embassy fled when the shooting started.)
U.S. forces killed all of the commandos within a few hours, but the episode, occurring amidst an unexpected and widespread offensive, was a severe embarrassment for the United States.

The Tet offensive proved to be the turning point of the war, delivering
a fatal blow to political support for the war in the United States. Even
though Tet was a disappointing defeat for North Vietnam in strictly military terms, it exposed the bankruptcy of U.S. war policy and aims in Vietnam, and prepared the way for America's eventual humiliation. The most

surprising aspect of the Tet offensive was that it was not really a surprise at all. Yet the episode shows how even a superior force can be taken by surprise both militarily and politically when it lacks the initiative in war. Since the North Vietnamese had the initiative instead of the United States, it was possible for their elaborate campaign of deception to succeed in maintaining the element of surprise, even though the United States discovered numerous details of the attack to come.

The complete battle plan for the Tet offensive has never been revealed, but it is evident that the plan for a major offensive against South Vietnam originated in the summer of 1967, following the death of North Vietnamese General Nguyen Chi Thanh. (Thanh is thought to have been killed in an American bombing raid in Cambodia, though rumors of assassination—which might have been disinformation—made the rounds.) North Vietnam used the cover of Thanh's funeral to recall its diplomatic corps to Hanoi for consultations. This was the first signal that U.S. intelligence missed. U.S. analysts assumed that the diplomatic recall was purely for the purpose of attending Thanh's funeral, forgetting that the only previous time such a wholesale diplomatic recall had taken place was immediately after the United States had committed its first ground troops in 1965. Some American analysts hoped that the diplomatic recall was a precursor to a North Vietnamese peace offer.

With the death of Thanh, General Vo Nguyen Giap became the unrivalled strategist for the North Vietnamese war effort. Giap ironically embraced Thanh's war strategy after having opposed it for two years; whereas Giap had previously advocated using primarily guerrilla tactics against the United States and South Vietnam, Thanh had advocated general main force action, which had led to the big (and losing) battles in the Ia Drang Valley in 1965. Now Giap decided that the time was ripe for a major conventional offensive. Giap and the North Vietnamese leadership came to this conclusion out of an odd combination of hard-headed realism and head-in-the-clouds Marxist ideology. They thought their military position was weakening, and would continue to deteriorate without some dramatic act. This calculation was largely correct. They also thought that the South Vietnamese government and the U.S. presence were so unpopular in the South that a broad-based attack would spark a spontaneous uprising of the South Vietnamese population, which would enable the North to sweep to a quick, decisive victory. This calculation was wholly fantastic, and would prove to be the undoing of the Tet offensive.

By September the signs of a new North Vietnamese initiative were starting to emerge. North Vietnam announced substantial new military aid agreements with both China and the Soviet Union. (There were nearly 4,000 Soviet "advisers" in North Vietnam at this time, some of them manning surface-to-air missile batteries.) U.S. and South Vietnamese forces soon began noticing that Viet Cong and North Vietnamese forces were equipped with new AK-47 assault rifles and B-40 rocket launchers. The North also increased the tempo of its propaganda activities.

One of the obvious difficulties with trying to carry off a surprise attack of this kind is that it is necessary to communicate the plan and its objectives to all of the Viet Cong cadres and "sleepers" in place in South Vietnam. It is obviously impossible in such a war to communicate with all the cadres by telephone or telegram. Yet the odd idiom of Communist propaganda and bombast is ideal for communicating a general outline of a battle plan concealed amidst a jumble of slogans and boilerplate jargon about smashing American imperialism and its South Vietnamese puppets. Ideological cadres understand the significance of such messages and could "decode" their meaning, while U.S. eavesdroppers were mostly just bored.

In September Radio Hanoi broadcast General Giap's battle message, "The Big Victory, The Great Task," which was in fact an outline for the Tet offensive. Americans and South Vietnamese listened as Giap's message said that the time had come for a major offensive against U.S. forces, but also including an attack on South Vietnam's cities. "U.S. generals," Giap said, "are subjective and haughty, and have always been caught by surprise and defeated." Key to Giap's strategy was the view that the United States would not decide to send major reinforcements beyond the already announced troop ceiling of 525,000. "The longer the enemy fights," Giap observed, "the greater the difficulties he encounters."

Knowing that Americans would hear Giap's war message, North Vietnam masked its seriousness with the first of several effective diversions. Days before the broadcast, North Vietnam struck hard at the United States base at Con Thien near the DMZ (using, among other new Soviet-supplied weapons, large gauge long-range artillery for the first time). The North Vietnamese judged—correctly, as it turned out—that the United States would make a connection between the broadcast of the battle message and the Con Thien siege. At the same time, North Vietnamese and Viet Cong forces stepped up the tempo of skirmishes along the Laos–Cambodia–South Vietnam border, successfully drawing U.S. forces away from the cities.

Throughout the fall the signs of a major attack continued to accumulate. In October the number of trucks observed heading south on the Ho Chi Minh trail jumped from the previous monthly average of 480 to 1,116. North Vietnam also announced in October that it would observe a seven-day truce from January 27 to February 3, 1968, in honor of the Tet holiday. Such truces had always been honored in the past—the North Vietnamese usually used the truce period (which typically meant a short halt in U.S. bombing as well) to resupply, and South Vietnam used truces to allow many of its troops to take a short leave. With the North's announcement of the Tet truce, the South Vietnamese army made plans to allow half of its troops to go on leave during Tet.

In November the number of southbound trucks spotted on the Ho Chi Minh trail jumped again, from 1,116 counted in October to 3,823—an eightfold increase over the previous year's monthly average of 480. A series of documents were captured that outlined the battle plan in general terms (including the notebook released to the media on January 5 mentioned previously). North Vietnam began conducting a swift and brutal purge of officials who urged negotiations with the United States rather than a military offensive. More than 200 officials, some of them very senior in the Communist Party and the government, were arrested and given long prison sentences. Some were executed. There would be no doves in Hanoi. Near the end of November a CIA analyst named Joseph Hovey circulated a memorandum to U.S. leaders including President Johnson that predicted a major North Vietnamese offensive against South Vietnamese cities in the coming months. Hovey's analysis was dismissed as unrealistic.

In December the signs intensified. The number of trucks seen on the Ho Chi Minh trail nearly doubled again, from 3,823 spotted in November to 6,315. On December 20 Gen. Westmoreland cabled a warning to Washington, explaining that the signs suggested that North Vietnam had decided "to undertake an intensified country-wide effort, perhaps a maximum effort, over a relatively short period." President Johnson, then in the midst of a state visit to Australia, warned that the desperate North Vietnamese might engage in "kamikaze attacks." But he made this warning privately to the Australian cabinet; no public acknowledgement was ever made in the United States that trouble might be brewing. Following North Vietnam's January 1 offer to negotiate in exchange for a bombing halt, Westmoreland judged that the prospective offensive was an attempt "to gain an exploitable victory before talks so that he might negotiate from a position of strength." This is exactly what the North Vietnamese had done to the French in 1954 at Dien Bien Phu.

With the memory of Dien Bien Phu prominently in mind, Westmoreland and U.S. leaders cast their eyes up to the large U.S. base at Khe Sanh, located in a northern province of South Vietnam not far from the DMZ. Four divisions of North Vietnamese regular army troops—more than 40,000 troops—were massing near Khe Sanh, where 5,000 U.S. and South Vietnamese troops were stationed, in what looked like a repeat of the Dien Bien Phu strategy. Westmoreland and U.S. intelligence thought that all this Viet Cong talk of an uprising in the cities was a diversion away from Khe Sanh, where the main attack was expected to fall. They had it exactly backward: *Khe Sanh* was the deception, intended to draw U.S. attention and resources away from the cities, and the United States largely fell for it. The U.S. calculation actually made good sense. U.S. intelligence knew that there was little prospect for a spontaneous uprising of the South Vietnamese populace, and couldn't believe that the North Vietnamese and Viet Cong believed it. (It turned out that many VC cadres on the ground in the South didn't believe it either, but never told their higher ups. Several VC officers captured during Tet told interrogators that they never expected an uprising in their assigned area, but carried out their attack in hopes that it would stir an uprising in other cities.) In an ironic way the blinders of Communist class struggle ideology helped serve the purpose of deception.

So even as more intelligence accumulated in January that an attack on South Vietnamese cities was a serious prospect, U.S. war planners continued to downplay the threat and misjudge the timing. On January 9 U.S. intelligence received a captured document that described a reorganization of the command structure of Viet Cong forces. "At the present time," U.S. analysts wrote, "no explanation is available as to the reason for this reorganization."

Caches of weapons and propaganda leaflets calling for an uprising were found near Saigon throughout January. Well-equipped VC sapper teams were caught infiltrating areas near U.S. bases. The National Security Agency, which collects and analyzes "signals intelligence" (SIGINT), reported that radio intercepts indicated preparations for attacks on cities in the central coast region of South Vietnam, and increased enemy activity near Saigon. But based on the predominance of radio traffic near the borders and the DMZ, the NSA still thought, along with Westmoreland, the main blow would come at Khe Sanh. Only General Fred Weyand thought that the action elsewhere might be significant. On January 10, Weyand, the commander for the southern region of South Vietnam including Saigon and the Mekong River delta, canceled plans to move troops in his sector toward the Cambodian border, and ordered 15 battalions to be redeployed near Saigon, a fortuitous move that greatly aided the defense of Saigon during Tet. But neither Weyand nor anyone else in high command thought that the attack would come during the Tet holidays, and over half of U.S. combat forces were detailed for the northern provinces, away from the cities.

As more signs and enemy troop movements were reaching a crescendo in mid-January, a new distraction occurred several thousand miles away. On January 10, the U.S. Foreign Broadcast Information Service published the transcript of a North Korean radio broadcast in which the North Koreans threatened to take action against U.S. Navy surveillance ships operating in international waters off North Korea, which patrolled there to keep tabs on the Soviet fleet operating out of Vladivostok. The threat was ignored.

Up until June 1967, lightly-armed U.S. spy ships enjoyed an escort of two destroyers. But the destroyers had been reassigned, and no notice of the North Korean threat was sent to the navy. North Korean harassment of U.S. spy ships was routine, so when North Korean PT boats began circling the U.S.S. *Pueblo* on January 23—as they had done several times in the previous few days—the *Pueblo*'s captain Lloyd Bucher saw no reason for special concern. But this day the North Koreans boarded the slow-moving *Pueblo,* whose top speed was 13 knots. The crew belatedly tried to smash much of its sensitive intelligence equipment and throw code and cipher books overboard, but the North Koreans still captured an estimated 600 pounds of classified information—an intelligence bonanza for the Soviets, who were en route to North Korea within hours of the *Pueblo*'s capture.

Most valuable of all, the Soviets received an only slightly damaged KW7 cipher machine off the *Pueblo,* which was the standard code equipment of the U.S. Navy. (The U.S. Navy took no chances, changing codes and cipher keys fleet-wide within hours. U.S. intelligence felt the KW7 machine would be of little use without the cipher keys and code books. Alas, the Soviet Union was already receiving U.S. naval code keys from the Walker family spy ring, which would not be broken until 1985. The Soviets were able to read U.S. Navy coded transmissions like an open book for much of that time.) Although it took over two hours to tow the *Pueblo* into North Korea's Wonsan harbor, the United States was powerless to come to the *Pueblo*'s aid. The four warplanes on alert at U.S. bases in South Korea were outfitted for nuclear weapons; it would have taken three hours to refit them for a close support mission. All other U.S. planes in the region were out of range. The *Pueblo* was the first U.S. Navy ship captured since 1807, during the Napoleonic wars.

The White House went into full crisis mode, assembling many of the same advisers and conveying much of the mood of the Cuban missile crisis six years before. Secretary of State Dean Rusk candidly called the *Pueblo*'s seizure "an act of war." Congress was in an uproar, with the notable exception of Senate Foreign Relations Committee chairman William Fulbright, who said we might find out what really happened "in two or three years. We're just now finding out what took place in the Gulf of Tonkin."[13] A Navy carrier battle group was dispatched to take up position off North Korea, and an assassination attempt against South Korea's president a few days later kindled additional fears that war might erupt again on the Korean peninsula.

President Johnson agreed to a limited call up of U.S. reserves—a move he had resisted for Vietnam—and a buildup of U.S. forces in the Far East, but decided to pursue a diplomatic solution to the *Pueblo* crisis. (The 83 crewmen were finally released 11 months later, after suffering torture and humiliation, and during which time North Korea missed few opportunities to taunt the United States. Captain Bucher was later tried in a naval court of inquiry for having given up the *Pueblo* without a fight.)

There has never been any proof that North Korea deliberately timed its seizure of the *Pueblo* as a diversion for North Vietnam's imminent offensive, though it is unlikely that it was a coincidence. (A Czech general who defected to the West in 1969 claimed that Soviet defense minister Andrei Grechko had spoken of plans to have North Korea seize a U.S. spy ship eight months before the *Pueblo* was taken. This might explain why Soviet intelligence specialists were so quickly on the scene.[14]) Even if the *Pueblo* capture didn't distract the United States in Vietnam, it threatened to disrupt the allied effort in South Vietnam in meaningful ways. Over two divisions of South Korean troops were deployed in South Vietnam, and plans were being made to send these troops quickly home to South Korea when Tet began.

The final clues that a serious attack against South Vietnam's cities was imminent came on January 28, when South Vietnamese forces captured 11 Viet Cong guerrillas in the central coast city of Qui Nhon. Their mission was to capture a radio station and broadcast two audiotapes announcing that the cities of Saigon, Hue, and Da Nang had been occupied, and calling for the population to rise up and overthrow the government. Under interrogation, the VC prisoners admitted that the attacks were to begin during the Tet holiday. The next day U.S. forces near Saigon captured two Viet Cong guerrillas who confessed that their mission was to guide main force troops in an attack on the city. Separately other U.S. units reported significant enemy troop movements around Saigon, Bien Hoa, and Da Nang. Westmoreland cabled to Washington on January 29 that "there are indications that the enemy may not cease military operations during Tet."

Notwithstanding the accumulation of intelligence pointing to an attack on South Vietnam's major cities, Westmoreland and other U.S. commanders continued to regard this prospect as no more than a diversion from Khe Sanh, where the North Vietnamese attack had already begun. Westmoreland did send out an alert to U.S. forces throughout South Vietnam, but it was not given special emphasis above the other alerts that had been given over previous months. (U.S. forces had been at a state of high alert nearly 50 percent of the time during the 12 months before Tet.) The allied ceasefire for Tet began at 6 P.M. January 29; South Vietnamese president Thieu left town for a vacation at the coast, and nearly half of South Vietnam's army went on leave. The North Vietnamese attack began just a few hours later, shortly after midnight.

The attacks that began in the early morning hours of January 30 were premature; several units of Viet Cong troops were not informed that the attack had been postponed 24 hours to January 31. But ironically this mistake may have actually reinforced the perception among U.S. command that these actions were a deception. Although Westmoreland reiterated his alert, warning of "the likelihood of immediate widespread attacks," they still underestimated the magnitude of the blow that was about to fall. Perhaps the commanders had cried "wolf" too often. Two hundred U.S. colonels in Saigon went to a pool party at bachelor officers' quarters the evening of January 30 (none of whom was aware that a major attack on Saigon was in prospect), and only one extra guard was stationed at the U.S. embassy, bringing the number of on-duty guards to three.

THE TET OFFENSIVE was a military failure—for the North Vietnamese. North Vietnam failed to take any major South Vietnamese city except for Hue, from which they were ejected within a month—but not until after massacring more than 3,000 South Vietnamese civilians, an episode only lightly reported by the media. Except for Khe Sanh, Hue, and one or two other locations, the enemy offensive was spent within a few days. By the end of February Hanoi was ordering a general retreat, which ironically happened to coincide with the moment of maximum pessimism in Washington. Out of a total attack force of 84,000 troops, nearly 50,000 North Vietnamese and Viet Cong were killed in Tet. These losses decimated the Viet Cong, destroying their command structure and morale among troops. Viet Cong offensive capabilities suffered and dwindled for the next three years; much of the rest of the war was fought by North Vietnamese regular army troops. Viet Cong defections increased dramatically in the aftermath of Tet. The United States suffered 1,100 dead; the South Vietnamese lost 2,300. Indeed it can be argued that General Giap botched the attack; having achieved tactical surprise, the attack was dispersed too widely, with not enough troops in any one location to score decisively.

The Tet offensive failed in part because one of the central premises—that South Vietnam's population would spontaneously revolt—was wrong. In fact, the lack of an uprising exposed the hollowness of North Vietnamese propaganda claims. But Tet *did* provoke an uprising—among U.S. elites, including the inner circle around President Johnson. Because of the prior political and public relations handling of the war at home, Tet demolished the illusion of control and progress.

Despite the battlefield outcome, a number of shocking vignettes from Tet had a powerful impact on American opinion and became etched in the American mind. Gallup Poll data suggest that between early February and the middle of March one-fifth of the people who had regarded themselves as "hawks" changed their minds and became "doves."[15] It is commonplace to refer to Vietnam as America's first televised war, but in fact prior to Tet few television reports contained much footage of actual close combat. With a few notable exceptions, most of the TV coverage was typified by correspondent stand-up shots in front of arriving or departing helicopters, or in front of U.S. patrols marching near a tiny village or rice paddy. Much of the "reporting" from Vietnam consisted of swapping stories and rumors in hotel bars in Saigon where journalists loitered. Most reporters had but limited exposure to real gunfire. Tet was different. Now the entire Saigon press corps could watch combat from their hotel window. American TV viewers could see the chaos and destruction in Saigon up close. And then there was the Eddie Adams photograph.

On the morning of January 31, the first full day of the Tet attack, Associated Press photographer Eddie Adams and a Vietnamese TV cameraman employed by NBC were wandering around Saigon getting photos and footage of the battle damage when they noticed a small contingent of South Vietnamese troops with a captive dressed in a checked shirt. From the other direction came Gen. Nguyen Ngoc Loan, chief of South Vietnam's national police. As Adams and the NBC cameraman aimed their cameras, Loan calmly raised his sidearm and shot the prisoner—a Viet Cong officer—in the head. Loan walked over to Adams and said in English: "They killed many Americans and many of my men." (It was not reported at the time that the prisoner had also taunted his captors, saying "Now you must treat me as a prisoner of war," and had been identified as the assassin of a South Vietnamese army officer's entire family.)

Adams' stunning photo of the prisoner's grimace as the bullet struck his head ran on the front pages of newspapers all across America two days later. Only the Associated Press reported Loan's remark to Adams that "They killed many Americans and many of my men." Most news accounts of the photo ignored this context; the drama of the picture was just too irresistible for most news organizations to try to put it in any kind of balanced context. NBC, which had only a silent film clip because no sound man had accompanied its cameraman, went so far as to embellish its TV broadcast of the episode by adding the sound of a gunshot. Tom Buckley, a writer for *Harper's* magazine, said Adams' photo was "the moment when the American public turned against the war."[16]

The visual shock of the Adams photograph (for which he was awarded a Pulitzer Prize) was soon matched by the journalistic interpretation of events. On February 7, Associated Press reporter Peter Arnett filed a story from the Mekong Delta town of Ben Tre, where hard fighting had inflicted severe damage and high civilian casualties. The third paragraph of Arnett's report quoted an unnamed U.S. major: "It became necessary to destroy the town to save it." The phrase proved an immediate sensation, and was picked up and amplified by the media echo chamber. The phrase came to be repeated countless times by other media outlets, and was adapted into an all-purpose slogan to describe hard action in other cities such as Hue. For many Americans, and not just those in the antiwar movement, it became an epigram that captured the disproportion between America's seemingly excessive use of firepower and our limited war aims. (Arnett refused to identify the source of the quote, but later revealingly referred to his source as "the perpetrator." *The New Republic* identified the source at the time as Major Chester L. Brown.)

Arnett's sensational quotation was only the beginning of the bad press the Tet offensive unleashed. "Rarely," wrote Peter Braestrup in his two-volume analysis of the press coverage of Tet (*Big Story*), "has contemporary crisis journalism turned out, in retrospect, to have veered so widely from reality. . . . To have portrayed such a setback for one side as a defeat for the other—in a major crisis abroad—cannot be counted as a triumph for American journalism."[17] Braestrup later went even further, describing media coverage of Tet as "press malpractice."[18] Media critics, especially conservatives, have long charged that antiwar bias emerged openly in the wake of Tet. Former *Los Angeles Times* and *Newsweek* correspondent Robert Elegant, who covered Vietnam for ten years, wrote that "For the first time in modern history, the outcome of a war was determined not on the battlefield, but on the printed page and, above all, on the television screen."[19]

The coverage of Tet can be charitably attributed as much to press incompetence and a journalistic herd instinct as to outright bias. There was no prior public warning that North Vietnam might launch some kind of serious attack, and given the Johnson administration's public relations campaign of the previous fall that "progress was being made," the element of surprise was important in shaping the shock value of the news coverage. But by 1968 much of the media was disposed to cover the war in the most negative light possible. David Halberstam plaintively confessed in *The Best and the Brightest,* that "we were on the wrong side of history"—a judgment he says he reached as early as 1963. It was not just the media that read the situation this way. Republican Senator George Aitken of Vermont, most famous for his remark that the United States should declare victory in Vietnam and go home, said, "If this is a failure, I hope the Viet Cong never have a major success."[20]

Above all, the Tet offensive exposed the fundamental weakness of Johnson's war policy: There was no clear strategy or timeline for ending the war, a point which antiwar critics in Congress reiterated in the media day after day. Even if the media had no bias about the matter, the act of merely reporting the rising crescendo of war criticism would have tilted the coverage in a negative way. The Johnson administration had set itself up for a press whipping, and it would have been a surprise if the media coverage had been otherwise. As Braestrup put it, "when the crisis came, Johnson was not given the benefit of the doubt, as Presidents usually are." Walter Cronkite expressed the surprise felt throughout the media when, after seeing the first bulletin about the Tet attacks on January 31, said, "What the hell is going on? I thought we were winning this war." Army Major Colin Powell, attending an Infantry Officers Advanced Course at Fort Leavenworth, was similarly stunned: "When I went to class that day, the atmosphere was one of disbelief, as if we had taken a punch in the gut."[21] (Powell would head to Vietnam for a second tour of duty six months later.) The "credibility gap" had become a yawning abyss; Tet may have been the point of no return for the growing public distrust of the federal government.

The *Wall Street Journal* was the first major media organ to weigh in against the war in the aftermath of Tet. On February 23 the *Journal* editorialized: "We think the American people should be getting ready to accept, if they haven't already, the prospect that the whole Vietnam effort may be doomed, that it may be falling apart beneath our feet." But it was Cronkite, "the most trusted man in America," who dealt the hardest media blow against the war. Cronkite had gone to South Vietnam after the fighting had subsided. In a special CBS news broadcast on February 27, Cronkite concluded his gloomy assessment: "We have been too often disappointed by the optimism of the American leaders, both in Vietnam and in Washington, to have faith any longer in the silver linings they find in the darkest clouds. . . . To say that we are mired in a stalemate seems the only realistic, yet unsatisfactory, conclusion. . . . It seems increasingly clear to this reporter that the only rational way out will be to negotiate."[22] Johnson, who was airborne in Air Force One at the time of the broadcast, took the blow personally when briefed about it later. If I've lost Cronkite, LBJ told aides, then I've lost the country.

The Cronkite broadcast opened the floodgates for the media to offer their judgments, as opposed to their reporting, about the war. Frank McGee of NBC, not to be outdone by rival CBS, on March 10 declared that "the war is being lost by the administration's definition," adding the by-now-familiar cliché spawned by Peter Arnett: "It's futile to destroy Vietnam in the effort to save it.[23] (Several months later an NBC producer proposed to correct the record with a three-part series showing that Tet had in fact been an enemy defeat. The idea was rejected by higher-ups at the network because, a senior producer said, Tet was seen "in the public's mind as a defeat, and therefore it was an American defeat."[24]) *Newsweek* piled on a few days later: "The Tet offensive . . . has exposed the utter inadequacy of the Administration's war policy. . . . Those who opposed the war can now find new reasons to justify their criticism."

Public opinion about the war held remarkably steady despite the tide of negative press. Although polls found that a rising plurality of Americans had for many months judged American involvement in the war to have been a "mistake," it is erroneous to suppose that this judgment meant that Americans were increasingly antiwar. What the polls failed to capture was the implicit reproach in the minds of many Americans toward Johnson's war policy; the center of American opinion held the commonsense view that the United States should have pursued a policy of "win or get out." This explains why polls during Tet showed declining approval for Johnson at the same time that support for the war remained steady or even rose (in some polls), as is typical in moments of national crisis. Even after the Cronkite broadcast and other negative press, a late February poll still found the antiwar candidacy of Eugene McCarthy attracting only 11 percent of the vote in the upcoming New Hampshire primary (though this poll was stale by the time it was published). It would take yet more self-inflicted wounds to ruin Johnson's prospects irretrievably.

IN SAIGON, Gen. Westmoreland was worried, as all competent commanders should be, about the risk of a "worst-case scenario" occurring at Khe Sanh and other U.S. positions in the northern provinces. But he also saw a huge opportunity: He thought he could win the war outright. Within days of the start of the Tet offensive, Westmoreland knew that the enemy offensive had suffered major losses and constituted a strategic defeat for North Vietnam. But U.S. forces were stretched thin, and Westmoreland wanted reinforcements, not only to bolster weak spots, but also, as he wrote to the Joint Chiefs of Staff on February 12, "to capitalize on [the enemy's] losses by seizing the initiative in other areas. Exploiting this opportunity could shorten the war."[25] Westmoreland wanted to go on the offensive in a big way, including ground operations against the Ho Chi Minh trail, raids against enemy sanctuaries in Laos and Cambodia, and even an invasion of North Vietnamese territory above the DMZ. "If I could execute those moves fairly rapidly following the heavy losses the enemy had incurred in the Tet Offensive," Westmoreland wrote in his 1976 memoirs, "I saw the possibility of destroying the enemy's will to continue the war."[26]

Westmoreland had no way of knowing that despite Johnson's tough talk in public about staying the course in Vietnam (LBJ was even contemplating asking Congress for a formal declaration of war), his inner circle was in the process of losing its nerve. Incoming Secretary of Defense Clark Clifford, reputed to be a hawk, was in fact turning decisively against the war, and would shortly use his influence to reverse LBJ's war policy. But General Bus Wheeler, chairman of the Joint Chiefs of Staff, had encouraged Westmoreland to ask for more troops. Three days into the Tet offensive, Wheeler cabled Westmoreland that "if you need more troops, ask for them." Westmoreland replied that he wanted the modest additional troops already scheduled for Vietnam to be sent immediately. Wheeler replied this would be done, but reiterated his previous encouragement for Westmoreland to think big: "I do not believe that you should refrain from asking for what you believe is required under the circumstances."

The commonsense reader will ask: Why was not the nearly 500,000 American personnel in place in South Vietnam sufficient to take the offensive against a less well-equipped and battered enemy force of less than 300,000? How could such a seemingly immense force be "stretched thin"? To the average American, the U.S. force level sounded enormous, an impression easily reinforced by the huge bomb tonnage (already by 1968 more than had been dropped on Germany in World War II) and artillery ordnance used so far. Few Americans realized that no more than 15 percent of the total force—about 80,000—were actually ground combat troops. The rest were all "support" personnel: supply sergeants and quartermasters, cooks, doctors, nurses, engineers, pilots, radio technicians, officers' club bartenders, mechanics, intelligence officers, janitors, and squads of clerks and statisticians to process the mountains of paperwork required by Pentagon whiz kids to feed into their computer models. The American war effort in Vietnam was carried out with an enormous logistical "tail," whose most characteristic expression was the large base camp complete with creature comforts such as movie theaters, swimming pools, and ice cream parlors. The greatest enemy facing American personnel in Vietnam, a reporter wrote, was not the Communists—it was boredom.[27] With such a lopsided "tail to teeth" ratio, U.S. and allied forces were arguably outnumbered.

Even for the richest nation in the world, this kind of effort took its toll on U.S. forces committed elsewhere. Because Johnson had refused to mobilize the reserves to keep overall U.S. military forces at full strength, the Vietnam effort had seriously weakened U.S. forces worldwide. The Vietnam War, Gen. Bruce Palmer wrote in his history of the conflict, "destroyed the U.S. 7th Army in Germany without firing a shot. It destroyed that army because we were so strategically out of balance we used the 7th Army as a replacement [pool] for Vietnam."[28] Active duty reserves in the United States were dangerously thin; only two-thirds of one division were available. Meeting Westmoreland's request for substantial new troops would require calling up the reserves, and using many of them to bolster weakened active duty forces elsewhere in the world so that trained troops could be used in Vietnam.

In order for Westmoreland to have the 108,000 new troops he wanted in Vietnam, total U.S. force levels would need to be increased by more than 200,000, so that reserve units in the United States and elsewhere could be replenished. Johnson and his advisers were conferring on Westmoreland's request in late February when the Cronkite broadcast hit the airwaves. Clifford and other Johnson advisers were against the troop request, and the turning of the media posed further difficulty for the idea. On March 8, Gen. Wheeler told a disappointed Westmoreland that the additional troops were unlikely to be forthcoming. The idea was virtually dead.

All of these deliberations were supposed to be secret, of course. But as so often happens with fast-moving events, there was a press leak that resulted in a muddled story. On March 10, two days after Wheeler told Westmoreland that the troop request was dead, the *New York Times* led with the bombshell headline: "WESTMORELAND REQUESTS 206,000 MORE MEN, STIRRING DEBATE IN ADMINISTRATION." The lead of the story, written by Hedrick Smith and Neil Sheehan, read: "Gen. William C. Westmoreland has asked for 206,000 more American troops for Vietnam, but the request has touched off a divisive internal debate within high levels of the Johnson Administration." Unnamed sources were quoted calling Vietnam "a bottomless pit," and the Tet offensive "a body blow." Ironically, Smith and Sheehan had emphasized the policy fight in their first draft of the story, but *New York Times* editors insisted that the number of troops involved—206,000—needed to be in the headline and in the lead of the story.

This outdated story, which, without context, reinforced the panicky view that the military situation in Vietnam was falling apart, spread like wildfire in newspapers across the nation within 24 hours. Seventy-two hours later the voters went to the polls in New Hampshire, and gave 42.4 percent to Eugene McCarthy (to Johnson's 49.5 percent). But 5,500 Republicans cast write-in ballots for McCarthy, bringing him virtually even with LBJ when all the votes were finally counted the next day. Even McCarthy's ebullient supporters were stunned. It was an earthquake immeasurable on the political Richter scale.

The timing of the New Hampshire vote amidst the general reaction to events in Vietnam and the specific controversy over the troop request lent verisimilitude to the view that the McCarthy vote represented a thumbs-down referendum on the war. But the full evidence presents a more complicated picture, suggesting that the vote reflected more a thumbs-down-on-LBJ vote than an antiwar vote. An NBC exit poll found that fewer than half the voters could correctly describe McCarthy's position on the war.[29] Later it was found that the largest plurality of McCarthy supporters before the Democratic nomination was decided switched their votes in November to George Wallace—hardly a "peace candidate."[30] There is even some evidence suggesting that many New Hampshire voters may have actually had a different McCarthy in mind when they cast their ballots. Following a speech to the Manchester Kiwanis Club, for example, McCarthy was presented the customary service club thank-you plaque with an inscription expressing "appreciation to Senator *Joseph*

McCarthy."[31] (Emphasis added.) No wonder Gene McCarthy attracted some hawkish votes.

But as with Tet, the media interpretation of the New Hampshire result proved inexorable. As if the McCarthy campaign weren't enough of a headache for Johnson, four days after the New Hampshire primary Robert F. Kennedy, having said there were no "foreseeable circumstances" under which he might run, jumped into the race. "The thing I feared from the first day of my presidency was coming true," LBJ wrote in his memoirs. "Robert Kennedy had openly announced his intention to reclaim the throne in the memory of his brother." Over the next six weeks, Johnson would gradually relent on his resolve over the war, and, facing certain defeat to McCarthy in the April 2 Wisconsin primary, he announced his withdrawal from the race on March 31, a halt to the bombing of North Vietnam, and the willingness to begin negotiations. In 10 weeks LBJ had fallen from the threshold of presidential greatness (according to *Time*) to the ignominious station of a reviled lame duck.

The triumphal myth of the antiwar movement ever since 1968 has been that the furor over Tet and the McCarthy upset in New Hampshire was the crucial turning point in their crusade to stop the war. At the instant LBJ withdrew from the race, the McCarthy camp felt as though it had deposed the king; outside the White House, a small gaggle of activists sang "We *have* overcome." "In a sense," Moynihan wrote of Johnson's decision to step aside, "he was the first American President to be toppled by a mob. No matter that it was a mob of college professors, millionaires, flower children, and Radcliffe girls."[32] Narratives of the struggle inside the White House, meanwhile, fix upon the dramatic turnabout of the so-called "Wise Men," which included former Secretary of State Dean Acheson, Supreme Court Justice (and LBJ confidant) Abe Fortas, and Generals Maxwell Taylor and Omar Bradley, who told Johnson on March 26 that the war was lost. Clark Clifford's self-dramatized realization that there was no plan to end the war, and his clandestine machinations inside the White House and the bureaucracy to force LBJ to capitulate, also receive great emphasis. And while these factors should not be slighted, they have come to eclipse the most fundamental reason why Westmoreland's troop request, and the general war policy, collapsed at this particular moment: The troop buildup would cost $2.5 billion immediately, and $10 billion in 1969. This cost was intolerable, because the richest nation in the world was staring into the abyss of bankruptcy.

AT THE SAME MOMENT the tumult over the Tet offensive was unfolding, "the most serious economic crisis since the Great Depression shook the Western world," in the words of economic historian Robert M. Collins.[33] In a nutshell, there was a loss of confidence and a near-panic over the U.S. dollar. In the old days, if bank depositors feared for their deposits and lost confidence in their bank, there would be a run on the bank. If the bank had enough reserves or could borrow dollars from another bank, the panic could be quickly dispelled. But what happens when the financial system is backed up by a central bank promising to redeem depositors with gold? If a crisis of confidence occurs, then you have not a run on a bank, but a run on a whole country's currency and gold reserves. This is what happened in 1968. The episode brought to an abrupt end the lofty promise of "growth liberalism" or the "New Economics," and set the stage for rising inflation and economic instability that took 20 years to remedy.

The crisis had been creeping up on the United States for the previous three years. Since 1965, the U.S. balance of payments deficit had crept up from $1.3 billion to $3.5 billion in 1967. The Johnson administration was especially alarmed in the last quarter of 1967, when the trade deficit spiked up to a $7 billion annual rate. The trade deficit had actually been higher in 1959 and 1960, reaching $3.8 billion in both of those years. But those deficits occurred in the context of a sluggish economy, with very low inflation. By contrast, at the end of 1967 economic growth continued to chug ahead at a rapid rate, and inflation was creeping up, setting off alarm bells about the value of the dollar overseas. Inflation had risen from 1.6 percent in 1965 to what was regarded as the ominous rate of 2.8 percent in 1967; inflation looked to be even higher in 1968 (it was: 4.8 percent). The American economy was in danger of "overheating." When Britain devalued the pound sterling by 14 percent in the fall of 1967 under similar circumstances, it immediately brought the dollar under pressure.

These events need to be understood against the backdrop of the Keynesian economic theory that ruled at the time. Keynes had famously written in 1936 that "Practical men, who believe themselves exempt from any intellectual influences, are usually the slaves of some defunct economist. Madmen in authority, who hear voices in the air, are distilling their frenzy from some academic scribbler of a few years back." Keynes was featured on the cover of *Time* magazine at the end of 1967—the first time the magazine had pictured a person no longer living on its cover—at the very moment the Keynesian theory began to unravel.

The Keynesian answer for fighting inflation is simply to choke off spending; the gold/dollar link is best defended by simply allowing fewer dollars to escape the nation's borders, thus lowering the number of dollars that have to be redeemed for gold. The Keynesian ideology spawned a number of quaint reflexes among liberals in those days. Johnson's Council of Economic Advisers actually wrote in 1965 that *monopoly* was the chief cause of inflation, and in 1967 the Department of Justice considered an antitrust suit to break up General Motors. Almost no one was paying attention to Milton Friedman's compelling case that growth in the money supply—and not spending *per se*—was the engine of inflation. Even though Friedman would win the Nobel prize for economics less than ten years later, and see his monetary theory accepted among central bankers throughout the world, in the middle 1960s "the financial press virtually ignored money growth," in the words of Allen Matusow.[34] Sure enough, the money supply had been growing at an annual rate approaching 7 percent in 1966, well above the historical non-inflationary average of 2.8 percent. An interest rate hike by the Federal Reserve in 1966 (which angered LBJ) slowed monetary growth, but not enough to stem the inexorable acceleration of inflation. Meanwhile, the Johnson administration was resorting to a policy that would later become popularly known as "jawboning," that is, exhorting businesses and labor unions to hold down wage and price increases to no more than the economy's general rate of growth. This advice was promptly ignored.

The Keynesian macro-managers were unwittingly on a monetarist track when they criticized the federal budget deficit as an engine of inflation. Though there is no correlation between budget deficits and inflation (the price level fell sharply in 1931 and 1932, Friedman pointed out, even though the federal government was running a huge deficit), the expanding budget deficits of the late 1960s were contributing background pressure for excess monetary growth. In the space of just four years the federal budget had gone from having surpluses as far as the eye could see—the cornerstone, remember, of the spending plans for the Great Society—to huge deficits. The federal deficit for 1967 was $8.6 billion (out of a total budget of $157 billion); early projections for 1968 placed the coming deficit at more than $30 billion.

How had this happened? Starting in 1965 federal spending began growing at double-digit rates. Even an economy growing at an unprecedented rate could not keep up with this fiscal explosion. The numbers: Federal spending in 1966 grew 13.7 percent, while the economy grew 9 percent; in 1967, spending grew 17 percent, while the economy grew 5 percent; in 1968, spending grew another 13 percent, while the economy grew 8 percent. It is commonly supposed that the Vietnam War was the primary component of this spending surge; but expenditures for Vietnam, though conspicuous, account for only about half of the spending increase, and in any case even Johnson would likely have spent even more for social programs had not the war intruded on his budgeting. (Defense spending during the Vietnam years was actually lower as a proportion of GDP than it had been during the Korean War.) But the war critics are right in one crucial respect. Johnson consistently low-balled the cost of the war. Not only had Johnson avoided directly explaining the war; he avoided paying for it too. He asked Congress for, and received, supplemental appropriations for the war in 1966, but he did not ask for any tax increases to pay for the appropriations.

He had lots of collaborators in this shell game. In 1965 McNamara had budgeted the war to be over by the end of 1967, even though Pentagon commanders were telling him otherwise. Nevertheless he low-balled the budget estimates. "Do you really think," McNamara told Tom Wicker of the *New York Times* when asked about this finagling in 1967, "that if I had estimated the cost of the war correctly, Congress would have given any more for schools and housing?"[35] Wicker was appalled by the conversation, but McNamara was right. In a contemporaneous interview in *U.S. News and World Report*, House Ways and Means Committee Chairman Wilbur Mills said, "I'm convinced that had we known in 1965 what we know now about the acceleration of the war in Vietnam, there would have been fewer of these new programs passed."[36]

As the chairman of the Congressional panel through which all tax bills must pass, Mills' views were important. When Johnson began to face the reckoning in 1967 and asked for a 10 percent income tax surcharge to keep the budget deficit from exploding, he ran straight into the implacable opposition of Wilbur Mills. No deal, Mills said. "I thought I knew the President well enough to know," Mills said, "that if we gave him ten billion dollars more money to spend, that he would spend it if we didn't tie his hands."[37] Mills, who might be considered the first "deficit hawk," infuriated Johnson by saying that there would be no *temporary* tax increase unless there were some *permanent* spending reductions to go with the new taxes. Fine, Johnson said. I'll start by canceling the construction of the new post office in Conway, Arkansas, which was in Mills' district. Undeterred, Mills killed the tax increase in his committee in October of 1967, and Congress went home for the year. (Mills reported that his mail had been running 99 to 1 against the tax hike. LBJ didn't get much support elsewhere, either; both the *New York Times* and the *Washington Post* editorialized against the hike.)

But as the new year approached, the exploding deficit and the balance of trade deficit were ominously converging. Seeing inflation rising in the United States and fearful of a devaluation of the dollar, foreign holders of U.S. dollars rushed to the gold window to redeem their dollar holdings. In the two weeks following the British devaluation of the pound in mid-November, net U.S. gold redemptions ran more than $75 million a day in the international gold markets. With the bad news that the trade deficit, the budget deficit, and inflation were all heading sharply higher in 1968, Johnson could not wait for Wilbur Mills to relent. He had to act.

On January 1, Johnson announced a series of economic steps that must surely strike contemporary readers as bizarre. In good Keynesian fashion, Johnson wanted to choke off the air supply for the dollar/gold redemption market by keeping dollars from going overseas. Hence, he asked U.S. corporations to reduce overseas investment by $1 billion and banks to reduce overseas lending by $500 million, even though both activities contributed to the nation's balance of payments bottom line in the fullness of time. But the clincher was Johnson's request that Americans not travel abroad in 1968, which would supposedly save $500 million. Johnson was prepared to put some teeth behind this idea, including perhaps an "exit tax" of up to $500 for travel to forbidden areas (Mexico and Canada would be exempted, which means that travelers would simply have embarked for Europe from Montreal), or perhaps a $6 per day tax levied on travelers' time overseas.

It might have been worse. Rumors began to circulate that Johnson would soon resort to wage and price controls. Such rumors had been swirling for two years, always denied by the administration. In early 1968 the Johnson administration put down the rumors with strong language that is worth noting in full, in light of what President Nixon would do three years later:

> Mandatory controls on prices and wages . . . distort resource allocation; they require reliance either on necessarily clumsy and arbitrary rules or the inevitably imperfect decisions of Government officials; they offer countless temptations to evasion or violation; they require a vast administrative apparatus. All these reasons make them repugnant.[38]

The travel ban never got very far, but the other measures, along with greater prospects for getting the 10 percent income tax surcharge through Congress, alleviated the panic in the international currency markets—for a while. In early March dollar/gold redemptions began heating up again, with daily gold outflows exceeding $100 million. Then the news of the massive troop request on March 10 blew the lid off. On Wednesday March 13, the gold outflow was $200 million. The next day, Thursday March 14, the gold outflow reached nearly $400 million. Federal Reserve chairman William McChesney Martin called his counterparts at European central banks to say that the United States might be forced to take the drastic step of closing the gold markets. Martin later described the episode as "the worst financial crisis since 1931."

Panicky administration officials feared that the loss on Friday might reach $1 billion, and asked the British to close the London gold market on Friday while central bankers convened an emergency meeting in Washington over the weekend. LBJ, meanwhile, pledged to defend the value of the dollar "to the last bar" [of gold]. But the credibility gap that plagued Johnson on Vietnam spilled over to international finance. One European banker commented in the press: "Every reassurance carries less assurance," while another European banker referred to the Johnson administration as "the grave digger of the dollar."[39]

What emerged from the weekend meeting was a patchwork scheme that essentially closed the "gold window" partway. (Nixon would complete the job in 1971.) First, dollar/gold redemptions would henceforth be limited to central banks only; speculators would have to resort to private exchanges to convert their cash to gold. The United States also made available 25 percent more of its gold reserves to defend the dollar. These and other moves eased the crisis, but also spelled the end of Johnson's war policy. It was a stunning irony. Johnson had begun the heavy bombing of North Vietnam in 1965 supposing that the destruction of that poor nation's limited economy would compel it to stop making war. But it was the U.S. economy that buckled under the strain.

"Someone had better tell the President," economist Edwin Dale wrote in *The New Republic,* "that if he puts into Vietnam the number of troops that now seem required to restore and improve the situation there, he may throw away the fruits of a generation of brilliant economic progress."[40] Dale needn't have fretted. Johnson was being told exactly this by the "Wise Men," most of his other top advisers, and congressional leaders. "The decision to halt the escalation of the war," Robert Collins concludes, "was as much economic as it was political or military."[41] The dollar crisis did provide Johnson with the necessary leverage to get Mills to relent on the income tax increase, which finally passed in June, but the episode also spelled the end of the Great Society. It was a startling turnabout. Johnson had entered office pressing for an income tax cut; he would leave office having pressed for an income tax surcharge. Even as the central bankers were meeting in Washington to save the dollar, Johnson was addressing a group of business leaders, saying, "We must tighten our belts. We must adopt an austere program." This from the man who four years before had confidently boasted that "We can do it all; we're the richest nation in the world."

That this boast was no longer plausible was brought home to Johnson by a bitter coincidence. Just as the economic crisis was unfolding in March, the Commission on Civil Disorders (the Kerner Commission), appointed the previous year to study and make recommendations following the summer riot season of 1967, reported in. Just as Joseph Califano had warned, the Commission urged government spending for social programs on an "unprecedented scale:" $11 billion immediately, and more than $25 billion by 1971. With Congress demanding a $10 billion spending *cut,* the Kerner report's wish list was dead on arrival. But more troubling than its advocacy of big spending was its sociology: "white racism," the report concluded, "is essentially responsible for the explosive mixture which has been accumulating in our cities since the end of World War II."

There was no proof or line of argument offered for this conclusion; it was a straight-out capitulation to liberal guilt.

Johnson ignored the report, refusing even to receive a copy publicly. He saw it as an implied criticism that his Great Society had not gone far enough. "As soon as I read it," Califano wrote, "I knew Johnson would erupt."[42] While Johnson ignored the report, the public did not. It received prominent media coverage, and sold 2 million paperback copies. (Though Illinois Governor Otto Kerner chaired the commission and gave it its colloquial name, the commission was in fact chiefly the brainchild of New York City's liberal Republican Mayor John Lindsay. Kerner later went to prison over a race track scam. Lindsay later became a Democrat.)

The economic crisis of 1968 would have repercussions for the next 20 years. This surprising turnabout also shattered one of the most deeply held myths of the Left: that the Vietnam War was motivated out of economic imperialism and a desire to pump up the U.S. economy. In fact, by 1968 the profits of most major defense contractors such as General Dynamics and Lockheed had fallen by half since 1965, and the day after Johnson announced his withdrawal and the bombing cutback, the Dow Jones Industrial Average jumped 20 points, a large move in those days.[43]

THE EUPHORIA on the Left over Johnson's March 31 decision not to run for re-election was short-lived, as the assassination of Martin Luther King in Memphis four days later plunged the nation into gloom. King's assassination started the 1968 riot season four months early. Rioting erupted in 125 cities in 29 states, with 46 people killed, more than 2,500 injured, and 21,000 arrested. Some of the worst rioting took place in Washington, D.C., where Stokely Carmichael gave an impassioned speech urging black people to "get a gun, because they [whites] are coming for you."

King's killing at the hand of (apparently) the small-time criminal James Earl Ray set off a fresh round of hand-wringing and breast-beating about the collective guilt—especially white guilt—of American society. Here was fresh evidence that America was an irredeemably sick society, just as the New Left had been saying. Benjamin Mays, emeritus president of Morehouse College (King's alma mater), said in his eulogy at King's funeral: "But make no mistake, the American people are in part responsible for Martin Luther King Jr.'s death. The assassin [at that point not yet apprehended] had enough condemnation of King and of Negroes to feel that he had public support."[44]

Stokely Carmichael went further: "Bobby Kennedy pulled that trigger, just as well as anybody else."[45] Black militants like Carmichael who had little use for King before his death had been handed a sharp two-edged sword: They had both a martyr useful for spurring white guilt, and a new reason to reject King's principle of nonviolent democratic reform. Washington D.C. civil rights leader Julius Hobson, for example, argued that "The next black man who comes into the black community preaching non-violence should be violently dealt with by the black people who hear him. The Martin Luther King concept of nonviolence died with him."[46]

In the emotion and anguish of the moment it hardly seemed propitious to gainsay the new heights of racial grievance rhetoric from black militants and the Left. There was one notable exception, however: The governor of Maryland, Spiro Agnew. Agnew was a liberal Republican who had been supporting Rockefeller for the GOP nomination. He was elected to the Maryland statehouse in 1966 with the editorial endorsement of both the *Washington Post* and the *Baltimore Sun*. He had even drawn favorable editorial notice from the *New York Times* for his pro civil rights record, having helped to pass Maryland's first open-housing law. Agnew had attempted to work with local black leaders to improve conditions in Baltimore, but when Baltimore rioted in the aftermath of King's killing—and after Carmichael had taken his road show through Baltimore telling blacks to be more militant—Agnew blew his top.

One week after King's shooting Agnew summoned local and state black leaders to a meeting in Baltimore, where Agnew berated them for their failure to repudiate Carmichael and other advocates of black militance. "I did not invite you here," Agnew said, "to recount previous deprivations, nor hear me enumerate prior attempts to correct them. I did not request your presence here to bid for peace with the public dollar. . . . The circuit-riding, Hanoi-visiting type of leader is missing from this assembly. The caterwauling, riot-inciting, burn-America-down type of leader is conspicuous by his absence." Agnew was just warming up. He cited the incendiary remarks of black militants that had appeared in the media, and added: "It is a deplorable sign of sickness in our society that the lunatic fringes of the black and white communities speak with wide publicity while we, the moderates, remain consciously mute. I cannot believe that the only alternative to white racism is black racism."[47]

Many of the attendees walked out in the middle of Agnew's jeremiad, and all were offended. News accounts of the tempestuous meeting caught the eye of Nixon campaign aide Pat Buchanan, however, who made a point of passing them along to his boss. Nixon had met Agnew for the first time a few weeks earlier and had been impressed, even though he failed to get Agnew's endorsement for the GOP nomination at the time. Taking on blacks in such a bold way, Buchanan and Nixon thought, showed that Agnew had some real stuffing.

COMING HARD UPON the shock of the King assassination were fresh indications that the downward spiral of campus politics was reaching a new depth. A week after King's killing, Columbia University president Grayson Kirk, in a speech at the University of Virginia in Charlottesville, said: "Our young people, in disturbing numbers, appear to reject all forms of authority, from whatever source derived, and they have taken refuge in a turbulent and inchoate nihilism whose sole objectives are destruction. I know of no time in our history when the gap between the generations has been wider or more potentially dangerous."[48]

Kirk's speech may not have been the origin of the phrase "generation gap," the first cousin of the "credibility gap," but events at his beloved university would soon give the phrase a much wider currency. Ten days after Kirk's speech, an open letter to Kirk appeared in the student newspaper, the *Columbia Spectator*, that sought to rebut Kirk's charge of student nihilism, but which ironically served more to confirm Kirk's view. The "generation gap," the letter said, is "a real conflict between those who run things now—you, Grayson Kirk—and those who feel oppressed by, and disgusted with, the society you rule—we, the young people." Even though the letter protested the charge of nihilism, it acknowledged "our own meaningless studies, our identity crises, and our revulsion at being cogs in your corporate machines." We aren't nihilists, the letter protested; we're *socialists*. The letter closed with an ominous note: "We will have to destroy at times, even violently, in order to end your power and your system. . . . I'll use the words of LeRoi Jones, whom I'm sure you don't like a whole lot: 'Up against the wall motherfucker, this is a stick-up.'"

Twenty-year-old Columbia junior Mark Rudd was the author of the open letter. Rudd was also the head of the Columbia chapter of the Students for a Democratic Society (SDS). He had cut three weeks of classes earlier in the year to make the obligatory radical pilgrimage to Cuba, and counted himself a leader among the SDS faction calling for the transition from protest to active (meaning violent) resistance. It took only 24 hours from the publication of his letter for his desire for direct action to be fulfilled.

Having set out a rage against The System, Columbia became the best-known scene of a protest in search of a cause, and the events that ensued provided a sharp contrast to the events at Berkeley four years earlier. The Berkeley Free Speech Movement had a superficially plausible basis (eliminating arbitrary restrictions on political activity on campus), and although the kind of trouble about to be experienced at Columbia and other campuses was prefigured at Berkeley in 1964, the Free Speech Movement had an air of virginal innocence compared to what came later. The Free Speech Movement, after all, had carried the *American* flag at the head of its procession to occupy campus buildings; by 1968, most campus protests marched under the Viet Cong flag.

Over the previous two years at Columbia, campus radicals had agitated against a series of issues, including class rankings for the draft, military and corporate recruiting on campus, and ROTC programs. None of these provided a critical mass for a campus-wide uprising, however. In April of 1968, though, a convenient issue presented itself that added a racial dimension to the campus atmosphere. It would be the only ingredient needed to push the campus to the flash point.

The issue was a new college gymnasium to be built on city-owned land adjacent to the campus and on the edge of nearby Harlem. Here was an issue that could excite black students and Harlem neighborhood activists alike ("Gym Crow" it was cleverly called), enabling the combination of civil rights fervor with the almost wholly white New Left. Hitherto the SDS at Columbia had failed in every attempt to get blacks involved in their activities. On April 23, the SDS finally persuaded Cicero Wilson, president of the Student Afro-American Society at Columbia, to speak against the gym at a rally whose original cause was to protest the potential expulsion of six students who had violated university rules a month earlier when they demonstrated against Columbia's minor research ties to the Pentagon.

About 1,000 students (including 300 counterdemonstrators with signs such as "Send Rudd Back to Cuba") were assembled at noon outside Low Library, which housed Kirk's offices, when Cicero Wilson blew the lid off with a by-now familiar Black Power mau-mau motif. Wilson seized upon the gymnasium controversy as a symbol for racism and revolt. "You white people will be responsible for a second civil war because of your ignorance and your inactivity. . . . How many black faculty do you see at Columbia? What percentage of the school population is black? [D]o you realize that when you come back, there may not be a Columbia University? Do you think that this white citadel of hypocrisy will be bypassed if an insurrection occurs this summer?"

Just as in the case of the New Politics conference the preceding fall, the white students who had just been categorically labeled as ignorant racists responded with sustained, enthusiastic applause. Within a few minutes, the rally transformed itself into a low-grade riot. Students attempted to take their protest inside Low Library, which the university administration, anticipating trouble, had prudently locked shut. With the mood of the crowd simmering, Cicero Wilson led a group of several hundred students to the gymnasium site, where they tore down some of the perimeter fencing and scuffled with police. With little to do at the construction site, the crowd returned to the main campus, where Mark Rudd came up with an idea to keep the protest roiling. Low Library was locked, but Hamilton Hall, another principal building in the middle of campus, was not. "Let's go!" Rudd shouted, and they did.

Thus began the week of the Columbia University crisis, which saw students and campus hangers-on occupy four more university buildings, including eventually Kirk's offices in Low Library (which were trashed). Along the way the predictable theater of the absurd unfolded. Black activists from Harlem evicted all whites from Hamilton Hall during the first night—they wanted to occupy the building by themselves—and the administration, fearing racial violence might spread to Harlem, shrank from calling in the police. This decision would prolong and deepen the crisis by several days.

The faculty and administration offered various compromises to the students, but the uncompromising radicals eschewed any deals. The faculty and administration were unable to grasp that student radicals regarded their uncompromising nature as their chief virtue. On the third day the great ambulance chasers of radical politics—Tom Hayden, Stokely Carmichael, and H. Rap Brown—predictably turned up at the scene. The students occupying the five campus halls declared them to be "liberated buildings," and immediately set out to form communal societies. "This was," Rudd wrote triumphantly afterward, "one of the first times in our experience that 'participatory democracy' had been put into practice."[49] In a touch of farce, a campus chaplain performed a wedding in one occupied building, declaring the couple to be "children of the new age."

With all efforts at reasonable compromise having failed, the police were finally called in a week later to clear the occupied buildings. A total of 712 were arrested, and 148 injured, as New York police, working class men who had little use for the nostrums of privileged students about class war, used riot tactics to subdue the campus. The irony of the police raid is that the black students and activists occupying Hamilton Hall surrendered peacefully; they didn't want a violent confrontation. The crisis did not end on April 30, however. A student strike of classes for the rest of the semester was declared, and classes came to a halt amidst a bitterly divided faculty. Two weeks later another round of building occupations began afresh. Hamilton Hall and two other buildings were occupied again. Fires set in one building destroyed 10 years' worth of research notes by a professor. Police arrested 255, and 66 students were suspended.

The aftermath of the Columbia crisis was in some ways more significant than the episode itself. Final examinations were cancelled, and year-end grades were improvised. Several hundred students walked out of commencement ceremonies in June, where the commencement speaker was the venerable historian Richard Hofstadter, whose most recent book was *The Paranoid Style in American Politics,* about the threat to American stability from the Goldwater movement and the radical Right. The administration ultimately capitulated to most of the radical student demands. Construction of the gymnasium was halted, research ties with the Pentagon were ended, and most of the criminal charges against the arrested students were dropped. Over the summer Grayson Kirk resigned.

Columbia became ground zero in the widening political-cultural divide of 1968. The national publicity of the Columbia crisis made the SDS a household name for the first time, and Tom Hayden publicly called for "one, two, many Columbias, so that the U.S. must either change or send its troops to occupy American campuses." He got his wish. Between January and June there were 221 major protests at 101 university campuses. In 59 cases students occupied a building in the Columbia style.[50] With each outbreak of campus unrest the Nixon campaign grew more confident of victory in November.

The "revolt of the overprivileged," as campus upheavals have sometimes been called, would redound to the benefit of the Nixon candidacy mostly because the reaction of establishment liberals was so weak and incoherent. Columbia appointed a "fact-finding" commission headed by Archibald Cox to review the incident and make recommendations for reform. The commission produced a pabulum-filled report that exemplified why old-guard liberals were held in equal contempt by both the New Left and conservatives. "The present generation of young people in our universities is the best informed, the most intelligent, and the most idealistic this country has ever known," the commission's report began. It got worse from there.

> It is also the most sensitive to public issues and the most sophisticated in political tactics. . . . Today's undergraduate and graduate students exhibit, as a group, a higher level of social consciousness than preceding generations. The ability, social consciousness, and honest realism [Honest realism? About people who scrawled on the walls of occupied buildings, "WE WANT THE WORLD AND WE WANT IT NOW!"—a slogan borrowed from the lyrics of a song by The Doors] of today's students are a prime cause of student disturbances. . . .
>
> At Columbia more than a few students saw the barricading of buildings in April as the moment when they began meaningful lives. They lived gloriously like revolutionary citizens of Paris.

Even more disturbing than this pandering to student pretensions was the commission report's tacit acceptance of the radical critique of "The System" and "The Establishment." "Many of these idealists," the report said after ticking off student grievances about Vietnam and racial injustice, "have developed with *considerable sophistication* the thesis that these flaws are endemic in the workings of American democracy." (Emphasis added. Rudd's "sophisticated" response to every invitation from the faculty to discuss his grievances was to shout "Bullshit!" into a megaphone.) Here, for all the world to see, was an official public display of the liberal Establishment losing confidence in itself. The report further anguished over the role of the university in modern society, and suggested that universities should "be actively engaged in social endeavor."

Other liberal intellectuals closer to the scene were not quite so woolyheaded as the Cox commission, and understood that the events at Columbia and other campuses were a disaster for liberalism. Columbia professor of government Herbert Deane, who had offered the prescient warning a year before about the likely destination of growing student nihilism, had a much more clear-eyed view of the intellectual and moral shallowness of the student radicalism:

> Again and again one is struck by the posture of complete self-righteousness and of unyielding moral absolutism in the attitudes and actions of the radical leaders. "I am totally right and completely moral, and you—if you disagree with me—are absolutely wrong and wicked. Therefore, there is no basis for any real discussion with you. You have no rights that I must respect, and you must agree to accept everything that I demand. If you fail to do so, I am justified in using any and all means to insure the triumph of right and justice, of which I am the embodiment and exponent." Faced with this complete moral certainty, one is tempted to cry out, in Cromwell's great phrase, "I beseech you, in the bowels of Christ, think it possible you may be mistaken."[51]

To Diana Trilling, wife of famed Columbia literary critic Lionel Trilling, the disaster for liberalism was clear:

> [T]he social and political message of the revolution was anti-liberal. The sit-in was anti-liberal in its lawlessness and its refusal of reasonable process. It was anti-liberal in its scorn for the entire liberal goodwill with which the largest part of the faculty tried to meet it. In fact, the demonstration was a demonstration *against* liberalism— more (if the two can be separated for purposes of comparison) than Mark Rudd's "bullshit" expressed a lack of personal respect for his teachers, it communicated the contempt of the revolution for any embodiment of liberal purpose, liberal hope and confidence such as the faculty predominantly represents.[52]

But for Deane and Trilling both, the worst effect by far was the boost the disturbances were giving to the *Right,* especially the Governor of California. Trilling: "And before [Columbia], in Berkeley, when the New Left was still young, the campus disorders had brought about the election of Reagan." Deane: "The most likely consequences of violent protests by the left, such as the demonstrations led by student 'revolutionaries,' are, therefore, a resurgence in ultra-right-wing movements and an even more widespread swing towards conservatism in this country. We already see ominous signs of these developments, such as . . . the surprising strength of the pro-Reagan forces across the nation. . . ."[53]

For the old liberals, the Mark Rudds of the world were a profound disturbance for university life, but Reagan represented a worse menace to society as a whole. In an ironic way they were proved correct. By 1980, the fires of the New Left long having burned out, Mark Rudd was a high school teacher in Arizona, while Reagan was on his way to the White House.

AT THAT MOMENT, however, it was not out of the question that Ronald Reagan might become president within 12 months rather than 12 years. The drama and turmoil of the Democratic Party's nomination struggle in 1968 has obscured and overshadowed the significance of the Republican intrigue that year. Nixon's long march to the nomination in 1968 seems in hindsight orderly and inevitable, especially in comparison to the Democrats' travails. In fact Reagan's stealth campaign for the GOP nomination posed the most serious threat to Nixon, but it ultimately helped Nixon unify the Republican Party in ways that have not been appreciated by the chronicles of that infamous year.

Nixon knew he would have to cope with two factors if he ran for the nomination in 1968. First, although Goldwater's trouncing in 1964 had badly bruised the conservative wing of the Republican Party, he knew that the conservatives were still the active core of the party, without whom he could not expect to win the nomination nor win the general election in November. Whoever the Republican nominee would be, it would have to be someone acceptable to the conservative wing of the party. This is why he knew that Rockefeller's chances were dim. While other Republican moderates shunned Goldwater and his supporters, Nixon shrewdly sought out and won Goldwater's active backing.

The second thing Nixon knew was that he would have to find a way to shake his image as a loser. He chose the high-risk strategy of entering nearly every Republican primary even though most delegates were chosen by party bosses, hoping that big wins would bolster his stature, but knowing that a single upset might bring his campaign to a crashing halt. (One primary he decided not to enter was California's; Nixon figured that it would be prudent to concede California's huge delegation to "favorite son" Reagan.) Most of the chronicles of Nixon's nomination drive portray Rockefeller as his chief rival, but in fact Nixon knew that his greatest vulnerability came from the Right.

"Reagan is a real contender," a Nixon aide told *U.S. News and World Report* in the fall of 1967. "His strength is vastly underrated by the Eastern press."[54] Nixon's camp had good reason to be worried. Reagan's supporters had hired F. Clifton White, the mastermind of Goldwater's successful nomination drive in 1964, to court delegates. If anyone could pull the rabbit out of the hat, it was Clif White. Reagan's California backers quietly chipped in nearly $500,000 for the campaign. Conservative activists immediately understood the significance of a potential Reagan candidacy. Although Nixon was "acceptable" to conservatives, there was still the worry that he might swing the Republican platform to the left, or that he would choose a liberal running mate such as New York Mayor John Lindsay, Oregon Senator Mark Hatfield, or New Jersey Senator Clifford Case. Frank Meyer wrote in *National Review*: "The solider the support for Reagan at the Republican convention, the greater the possibility that he may be nominated—but also the certainty that any liberal candidate can be vetoed; the assurance that, if Nixon is nominated, he will owe it to conservative support; and the guarantee that conservative control of the Republican Party will be consolidated."[55]

Reagan's strategy was harmonious with his circumstances. He rightly thought it would be presumptuous for a governor with barely 12 months on-the-job political experience under his belt to be a full-fledged candidate for president, yet his popularity with the grassroots of the party made the prospect of the nomination irresistible. His strategy was the political equivalent of the four-corner stall in basketball; he would try to delay Nixon's progress by appealing for party leaders to remain uncommitted while hoping for selected back-door scoring opportunities. He would allow his name to be placed on several primary ballots and hope that increasingly strong showings would give momentum to his undeclared candidacy.

Reagan never did achieve a primary breakthrough, finishing well behind Nixon in Nebraska and, most tellingly, in Oregon, where a serious TV advertising campaign had been run on Reagan's behalf. In June, Barry Goldwater wrote bluntly to Reagan that, having failed to make a primary breakthrough, it was time for him to fall in line behind Nixon. But there was still one plausible avenue down which Reagan might still capture the nomination—the South, where, one Washington reporter wrote, Reagan was regarded as "the greatest thing to come along since corn pone and hog jowls."[56] None of the southern states held primaries; their delegations were chosen the old-fashioned way—by party bosses. Throughout late 1967 and early 1968, Clif White flew southern delegates out to Sacramento to meet quietly with Governor Reagan, and the operation was building a solid core of sentimental support among Southern party leaders. Reagan also made a few careful forays into the South. "There's nothing more impressive than Ronnie Reagan behind closed doors," said Harry Dent, a leading South Carolina Republican. One of Reagan's most successful party appearances had taken place in Columbia, South Carolina, in September 1967, where 3,500 party faithful had paid $100 apiece to hear Reagan. His non-campaign managers cleverly arranged to have the speech telecast throughout the South. Reagan was also showing strength with party leaders in Texas and Kentucky.

"If emotion ruled the Southern delegates," journalists Lewis Chester, Godfrey Hodgson, and Bruce Page wrote in their epic book on the 1968 campaign, *An American Melodrama*, "at least 300 of the South's 334 convention votes would have been in Reagan's pocket the moment he declared his open candidacy."[57] It looked as though Reagan already had the South Carolina delegation in the bag, with others ripe for the picking. But Nixon was not without a Southern strategy of his own. In fact, he had not only been courting Southern Republicans longer than Reagan, he also had on his side the one person who was esteemed among Southern Republicans even more highly than Goldwater: Strom Thurmond.

Nixon knew that Thurmond, having run for president as an independent "Dixiecrat" in 1948, would be invaluable in staving off the third-party challenge of George Wallace, but as the Republican convention approached and Reagan's inroads in the South became apparent, Nixon turned to Thurmond to help secure his nomination. Nixon went to see Thurmond in

Atlanta in early June. Thurmond liked Reagan, but, like other practical-minded southern politicians, was favorably disposed to Nixon because Thurmond thought he could win. Nixon feared that Thurmond's condition for support would be a pledge to back off federal school desegregation efforts in the South. Thurmond no doubt would have liked such a pledge, but knew it was unrealistic. He wanted something else: a pledge from Nixon to develop and deploy an anti-ballistic missile system. Done deal, Nixon said. Thurmond turned around the South Carolina delegation at a meeting three weeks later. "I love Reagan," he told the delegates, "but Nixon's the one." As the convention approached and Thurmond's help became even more critical for Nixon, Thurmond exacted another pledge from Nixon: that the vice-presidential nominee would be someone "acceptable to all wings of the party." Translation: No northeastern liberals.

While Reagan's southern opening was seemingly closing up, the other shoe was also not dropping: Nelson Rockefeller was not succeeding in peeling off Nixon's support in the North. The worst blow may have been the Maryland delegation. Governor Agnew declared that it would go with Nixon. As the convention neared in early August, Nixon looked secure. Then, on August 5, as the convention began, the head of the California delegation, William Knowland, announced publicly that Reagan was at long last formally a candidate for the nomination. The California delegation, Knowland said, had passed a resolution declaring Reagan's candidacy; it looked like a draft, and enabled Reagan to say that he was responding to the call of the party.

"It was not long," Nixon wrote in his memoirs, "before a new catchword began making the rounds in Miami Beach: *erosion.*"[58] Reagan's formal announcement instantly galvanized Southern delegates who were privately pining for the man from California. "The lightning struck," South Carolina's Harry Dent said. "I have been in politics for I don't know how many years, and I have never seen anything like it."[59] Reagan was especially popular with the Florida delegation, whose women members reportedly were in tears when their party bosses told them they had to hold fast for Nixon. A Miami TV station sponsored a phone-in poll asking "yes" or "no" on Reagan for president. Reagan got 76 percent yes from Dade County, and 77 percent yes from Broward County. "All we need is one break," Clif White told reporters, "one state switching to Reagan, and we've got him."

With Thurmond struggling mightily to hold South Carolina and Florida, Reagan's best chance for a breakthrough was Mississippi. But Reagan ran into Clarke Reed, the head of the Mississippi delegation, and Reed had an old score to settle with Reagan. Reagan had left Reed's requests for help in his own gubernatorial race in 1966 unanswered, and Reed hadn't forgotten. "Perhaps you had better try where you have a few favors owing," Reed told Reagan over the phone.[60] The South was going to hold for Nixon.

The final count was Nixon 692 (only 25 more than necessary for the nomination), Rockefeller 277, and Reagan 182. Nixon's first ballot win at the convention was a close run thing, with lots of evidence that had he failed on the first ballot, a large portion of Southern delegates would have broken for Reagan on a second ballot. The heads of the Florida and South Carolina delegations had to impose the "unit rule" (requiring all delegates to vote as a block) to hold the Reagan-lovers in line for Nixon.

Reagan's late entry into the presidential race has always been regarded as "clearly a mistake," in the words of Reagan-watcher Lou Cannon. Reagan told Cannon years later that he had a "sense of relief" when Nixon won the nomination; he told Mike Deaver after the convention that "I wasn't ready to be President."

"In retrospect," Cannon concluded, "it is not so clear that the 1968 presidential campaign, 'bad chemistry' and all, was really a mistake for Reagan. In fact, it is possible to argue that he would not have wound up president without it. . . . Reagan came out of Miami Beach a loser. But his losing helped prepare him for the victories which lay ahead."[61]

There was another way in which Reagan's campaign served the party well. The Rockefeller-Reagan North-South pincer scenario had the fortuitous effect of damping down some of the intra-party ideological strife that had characterized past Republican conventions. Rockefeller and Reagan each hoped the other would deadlock the convention on the first ballot, and leave the way open to grasp the nomination on a succeeding ballot as delegates were free to vote their preference. This strange calculus led to a rhetorical ceasefire among all three major candidates. Nixon, seeking party unity above all, disdained to alienate the fervent supporters of both Reagan and Rockefeller, while Reagan and Rockefeller refrained from attacking each other. Thus the convention did not engage in the recriminations between the wings of the party that had struck such a sour note among Republicans in both 1960 and 1964. Indeed, Reagan went on to campaign for Nixon in 24 states in the fall campaign; he appeared in more states than Nixon did himself.

The one area over which the ideological struggle threatened to break out was Nixon's selection of a running mate, and Reagan's candidacy may have had an unseen effect on this matter as well. The Rockefeller faction wanted a northeastern liberal, while the Southerners wanted a Southerner. Thurmond wanted Reagan, but Nixon didn't want someone who would potentially overshadow him on the campaign trial, and Reagan wasn't interested in the number two spot anyhow. Word reached Thurmond that Nixon's first choice was liberal Oregon Senator Mark Hatfield. Thurmond sent back the word: Unacceptable. This may or may not have been a Nixon calculation to pave the way for Agnew, who could also have been regarded as a liberal.

It has been reported that Nixon had Spiro Agnew in mind for several weeks before the convention, and this widely ridiculed choice reflected shrewd calculation in many ways. As a border state governor with a strong civil rights record, Northern liberals had trouble finding obvious fault with Agnew. Indeed, Nixon prevailed upon Mayor John Lindsay to place Agnew's name in nomination. Agnew's tough recent stands on urban disorder gave him appeal to the South, where Nixon was hoping to contain Wallace. "If you put all the conflicting Republican elements into a computer," Nixon aide Stephen Hess wrote, "and programmed it to produce a Vice President who would do least harm to party unity, the tape would be punched SPIRO T. AGNEW."[62] Agnew's relative obscurity also had the benefit of enhancing Nixon's stature in a backhanded way. Nixon, campaign aide John Sears remarked, would have preferred to run by himself anyway. With Agnew on the ticket, Nixon had the next best thing. William F. Buckley Jr. observed that "There are those who believe that Mr. Nixon appointed Mr. Agnew as a sort of personal life insurance policy. No one, they reason, will pop off President Nixon while Vice President Agnew is around."[63]

THE IRONY of the 1968 campaign is that the Republican nomination was much more in doubt than the Democratic nomination, though the traumatic events surrounding the Democratic Party in 1968 have always conveyed the opposite impression. There was little chance that Vice President Hubert Humphrey could be denied the nomination, even though he did not enter a single primary. (Johnson dropped out too late for Humphrey to file to be on any primary ballots, and a write-in campaign would surely have failed.) Only 19 percent of Democratic convention delegates were selected by primaries in 1968; a *New York Times* canvas in April estimated that 70 percent of county chairmen in the Democratic Party were backing Humphrey.

By the time of the California primary, Humphrey had already secured the lopsided majority of the delegates from key states such as Ohio, Pennsylvania, Florida, and Texas. With Bobby Kennedy and Gene McCarthy splitting the vote in the various primaries they contested, it was unlikely that either could have demonstrated enough strength to Democratic Party bosses to topple Humphrey. McCarthy ran a diffident and disorganized campaign whose effectiveness unraveled with each passing week. It could be said that McCarthy ran his campaign in much the same fashion as LBJ ran the Vietnam War—with limited aims and a lack of ruthlessness to go for the kill. The conventional wisdom, both then and today, is that Bobby Kennedy was the real contender. Democratic Party insiders thought otherwise. On the morning of the California primary, Humphrey remarked to an aide: "I want Bobby to win big. Number one, there are too many party leaders opposed to him for him to have any real chance of winning the nomination. Number two, since Oregon [where Kennedy had lost to McCarthy], he can't use the argument that he went right through the primaries."[64] (Bobby didn't win big; his margin over McCarthy was only 5 percent—short of the landslide he needed.)

Twenty-four hours later Kennedy was dead. The assassination of Robert Kennedy two months after the killing of Martin Luther King has forever blurred and romanticized the memory of 1968. Like King's killing, Kennedy's killing set off a fresh round of America-bashing among liberals. "The world today," Arthur Schlesinger Jr. said the day after, "is asking a terrible question which every citizen of this republic should be putting to himself: What sort of people are we, we Americans? And the answer which much of the world is bound to return is that we are today the most frightening people on the planet."[65] Never mind that Kennedy's killer, Sirhan Sirhan, was a foreign-born radical whose diary said, among other things, "I advocate the overthrow of the current president of the fucking United States of America . . . I firmly support the Communist cause and its people."[66]

The more durable strain of romantic myth is that King and Kennedy's killings spelled the end of hope, the end of the dream, that America could redeem itself through politics. "With King and Kennedy dead," New Left historian Todd Gitlin wrote, "a promise of redemption not only passed out of American politics, it passed out of ourselves," and Carl Oglesby of the SDS said "When these two heroes were killed, the movement was silenced. The whole procedural foundation of our politics was shattered."[67] This is nonsense, an exercise in selective memory and convenient revisionism. Prior to their death the Left had little use for King, and no use for Kennedy. Kennedy especially was a threat to the New Left precisely because he appealed to the same youth constituency the New Left needed to survive and prosper. Kennedy's position on Vietnam was to the right of McCarthy (and was not that far different from the "Vietnamization" policy that Nixon later embraced). Tom Hayden has always made great show about attending RFK's funeral, holding his Cuban army cap in hand, tears streaming down his face. Yet only a few days before Kennedy was killed, Hayden had referred to Kennedy as "a little fascist." Hayden also taunted McCarthy supporters by asking "Why are you a whore for McCarthy?"[68] Kennedy had been booed at an early campaign appearance at the University of Pennsylvania; at another rough reception at Brooklyn College, a banner read: "Bobby Kennedy—Hawk, Dove or Chicken?" The Left in Berkeley spread the slogan before the California primary: "Don't waste your vote for Kennedy." Another reason the Left had contempt for Kennedy, besides his weak position on Vietnam, was the demagogic means he used to defeat McCarthy in the California primary. In a televised debate, the man with the posthumous reputation as a "racial healer" employed crude race-baiting to bash McCarthy. McCarthy had proposed moving poor people out of slums and closer to middle-class neighborhoods. Kennedy twisted McCarthy's unspecific idea into a stick: "You say you are going to take 10,000 black people and move them into Orange County." McCarthy had said no such thing, but the attack worked, propelling Kennedy to a narrow win.

Yet the fondly held view that Kennedy would have won the nomination and gone on to defeat Nixon in the fall is based on wishful thinking. Kennedy was disliked—hated may be a more accurate term—by two of the Democratic Party's most important blocks: organized labor, and the South. AFL-CIO leader George Meany wasn't even on speaking terms with Kennedy. These blocks, together with President Johnson's undying enmity, would surely have combined to deny Kennedy the nomination. "Nearly everyone is furious with Kennedy for what he is doing to the party," *The New Leader* observed right after RFK's entry; "In Congress . . . the reaction [among Democrats] to Kennedy's decision can be summed up in a word—panic."[69] Even Nixon remarked to an aide when Kennedy announced, "I'd be very surprised if Johnson let Bobby Kennedy have it on a platter."[70]

The popular outpouring of support for Kennedy on the campaign trail, usually carefully orchestrated by his campaign staff (and composed often of young people not then eligible to vote), masked a lack of enthusiasm for Kennedy among other large blocks of voters. A February poll of his (adopted) home state New Yorkers found that only 36 percent would vote for him again for the U.S. Senate there.[71] By spring, reporters Chester, Hodgson, and Page wrote, "resentment of Kennedy's candidacy was nowhere stronger than in his own home state."[72] McCarthy snagged most of New York's convention delegates. But even if Kennedy *had* won the nomination, it is far from certain that he would have beaten Nixon in November. President Johnson would likely have surreptitiously helped Nixon; Texas Governor John Connally (whom Nixon courted behind the scenes) might have openly done so, and swung that key state to Nixon. (Humphrey ended up narrowly carrying Texas.)

Then, finally, there is the issue of Chicago. Kennedy would not likely have been able to stop *that*.

A POPULAR SONG among disaffected radicals in the late 1960s was Gil Scott Heron's "The Revolution Will Not Be Televised," an attack on the commercial and mass media sublimation of the counterculture's wardrobe and style. Yet at the Democratic National Convention in Chicago in late August, the revolution—or as close as it ever came—*was* televised. That was the whole point. An estimated 89 million Americans watched as protestors clashed violently with Chicago police and National Guard troops on the streets (hence the chant on the last night of rioting: "The whole world is watching") while a few miles away, at the convention hall, the Democratic Party self-destructed. Most of the blame for the violence on the streets of Chicago was laid at the feet of Mayor Richard Daley's police; to this day, "police riot" is the phrase most strongly associated with the

Chicago convention. The Chicago police reacted to a calculated provocation, and, like the case of fighting schoolchildren where the second child to strike a blow is the one usually caught by the teacher, the media caught the police reaction and attributed it as the cause of the violence.

Few events of 1968 had been more fully foreshadowed than the three days and nights of rioting during the Chicago convention, yet it proved impossible to avert. Planning for the Chicago slugfest had begun the previous December among three allied factions of the New Left: The "Yippies" (short for "Youth International Party"), the National Mobilization to End the War in Vietnam (known as the "Mobe"), and the SDS. The Mobe wanted a peaceful protest similar to the march on the Pentagon the previous October, while the Yippies, the semi-serious street clowns of the New Left, wanted to have a music festival and create havoc in mischievous ways, such as putting LSD in the Chicago water supply (which, though attempted, failed because automated chlorination neutralized the LSD). The SDS, however, wanted a violent confrontation. The Yippies had even tried a dress rehearsal at Grand Central Station in New York City in March, when about 3,000 protestors occupied the station and had to be ejected forcefully by the police. The *Village Voice* commented that the riotous Grand Central Station protest "seemed to be a prophecy of Chicago." SDS leader Tom Hayden ended nearly every public statement in the winter and spring of 1968 with the slogan "See you in Chicago." On the eve of the convention, Hayden made his intentions even more clear: "We are coming to Chicago to vomit on the 'politics of joy.'"[73] It was to be, in the words of *Ramparts* editor Peter Collier, "the *Kristallnacht* of the New Left."

Contrary to popular belief then and now, the success of the antiwar candidacies of McCarthy and Kennedy made violent confrontation in Chicago *more* necessary to the Left, because the Left saw the McCarthy and Kennedy campaigns as a threat. After McCarthy declared his candidacy, the SDS warned against "the danger of cooption by liberal elements within the antiwar movement." Hayden wrote: "If radicals really believe that President McCarthy could not solve America's problems but only reveal the problems of liberalism, then McCarthy is even a better establishment figure to pressure and expose than Humphrey."[74] Yippie leader Jerry Rubin commented: "We expected concentration camps and we got Bobby Kennedy. I am more confident of our ability to survive concentration camps than I am of our ability to survive Bobby."[75] Mobe leader David Dellinger warned antiwar groups in April—at the flood tide of the McCarthy and Kennedy enthusiasm—that "It would be a mistake to think that the fight against the war can be won in the ballot box. It still has to be won on the streets."[76] To Hayden, the United States was an "outlaw institution under the control of war criminals," a "police state" requiring a confrontation with a "people's movement."

For Hayden and many others in the New Left, the cause for protest went far beyond the war; the entire social order of "Amerika" needed to be overthrown. Peace in Vietnam was not enough; it didn't matter who the Democrats nominated. Violent confrontation, Hayden thought, would be a "dramatic national experience" and a means "to make a leap of consciousness." The convention riot would serve as an anvil, against which to smash Democratic Party liberalism into a thousand bits. The irony about the New Left's comparisons of the United States with Nazi Germany is that the New Left was emulating the same strategy that the German Left had embraced in the 1920s—destroy the liberal center, and ride to power in the ensuing clash of the extremes. Hayden had described the strategy to Todd Gitlin several months earlier: "arouse the sleeping dogs on the Right."[77] The Left aided Hitler's rise to power in this fashion in the 1930s—much to their detriment—and in seeing Nixon as Hitler in 1968 the New Left proved it had learned nothing from their forebears.

Although many of the 12,000 protestors (the planners had boasted of 100,000) came to Chicago in the naive but sincere belief that they were going to stage a peaceful protest, the hard-core leaders of the Left knew it would be easy to manipulate the situation into a violent confrontation with police—and be able to blame the police. Chicago's police were notoriously aggressive toward protestors and rioters. Mayor Richard Daley had famously ordered his police to "shoot to kill" arsonists and looters during the riots that followed King's assassination in April. (It should be noted, however, that no one was shot during the convention riots.) The protestors had applied for a parade permit for 200,000 people to march on the convention hall, and an assembly permit for Grant Park on Michigan Avenue for 150,000 people—huge numbers that assured the permits would be denied, even if Mayor Daley had been inclined to grant them. One of the assembly permit applications had been wrapped in a *Playboy* "Playmate of the Month" centerfold, with the inscription: "To Dick, with love—the Yippies." The protest organizers were not above even attempting a little blackmail. At one point the organizers offered the city "to drop the whole thing" for a payment of $200,000.

The provocateurs knew that the police could be expected to act harshly when provoked; organizers had arranged for medical care for the anticipated injuries, and had instructed protestors to try to stay close to journalists so that police violence would be reported. Many protestors were armed with caustic items such oven cleaner, hair spray, and ammonia; 198 policemen were injured, many with chemical burns to the face and eyes. The provocateurs knew that the police would overreact when screamed at ("Fuck the pigs!") and when they were the object of thrown bags of excrement, but the Left knew they could rely on the media to amplify the situation as well.

According to some reports, the news media had advised Jerry Rubin where their cameras would be so that the provocateurs would know where to plan their activities. Democratic Senator Dale McGee said he witnessed a TV camera crew instigate a clash between National Guardsmen and one cell of protestors. Regardless of the veracity of these reports, it certainly helped generate media sympathy for the protest that the police injured 32 journalists and photographers. The Chicago police had it in for the media as much as they did for the protestors, because they understood class warfare better than the New Left did. They knew that the Left represented not the working class—such as the police themselves—but the elite "new class" that wanted to overturn institutions wholesale. As a police spokesman put it after the convention: "The intellectuals hate Mayor Daley because he was elected by the people, unlike Walter Cronkite."[78]

NBC declared the convention to be "an armed camp," and broadcast a "highlight" film that alternated scenes of street violence and scenes inside the convention hall of celebration over Humphrey's nomination, even though these events were not contemporaneous. But the damage was done. David Dellinger said: "It was a clear-cut victory because the police acted abominably and our people showed courage, aggressiveness and a proper sense of values."[79] Yippie leader Stew Albert said Chicago was "a revolutionary wet dream come true."[80] Hayden declared that intensive media coverage made the protest a "100 percent victory in propaganda." Just as he had declared in April that there should be "two, three, many

Columbias," Hayden now urged that the Movement should go on to create "one, two, three hundred Chicagos" around the country, or a "mini-Chicago" wherever nominee Humphrey appeared on the campaign trail.

But while the media sympathized with the protest, ordinary viewers across America did not. The general public did not share the verdict of the commission appointed to study the protest after the fact that it had amounted to a "police riot." A poll taken shortly after the riots found that 71 percent of Americans thought Chicago's security measures were justified; 57 percent thought the police had not used excessive force, while 25 percent thought the police had not used *enough* force.[81] Public sentiment about media coverage of the riot was even more lopsided. CBS received 9,000 letters criticizing the network's coverage of the riots by an 11 to 1 ratio. Several Democratic members of Congress demanded—and got—a Federal Communications Commission hearing to review media coverage of the riots.

As the protestors had intended, liberals in the Democratic Party were riven over how to respond to the riots. Unable or unwilling to make a distinction between the naïve peaceful protestors and the radical manipulators who made sure they were all caught up in the manufactured maelstrom of violence with the police, many Democratic Party liberals, intellectuals, and journalists decried that the Chicago police had beaten "our children." Sociologist Christopher Lasch thought Chicago showed that a "fascist mentality" was ascendant in America, which required a swing further to the Left by intellectuals. Senator George McGovern, watching a clash from his hotel room window, said: "Do you see what those sons of bitches are doing to those kids down there?"[82]

Connecticut Senator Abraham Ribicoff set off pandemonium when, in the course of placing Senator McGovern's name in nomination from the convention podium, he blasted the "Gestapo tactics" being used in the streets. A furious Mayor Daley screamed at Ribicoff: "Fuck you, you Jew son of a bitch, you lousy motherfucker go home." Humphrey, backpedaling furiously from his statement two years before that had he lived in a ghetto he could have led a pretty good riot himself, now turned into a hard-liner. After the convention Humphrey said it was time to "quit pretending that Mayor Daley did anything that was wrong. . . . There are certain people in the United States who feel that all you have to do is riot and you can get your way. I have no time for that."

Yet the riots outside the convention hall had an indirect influence on a quiet revolution going on inside the convention hall. There was great unhappiness among liberals in the Democratic Party over a nomination process that not only enabled Humphrey to capture the nomination without having entered a single primary, but that also generated a delegation that thwarted popular support for a change in the Democratic platform's position on the Vietnam War. (President Johnson and Humphrey had strong-armed delegates into defeating an alternative plank calling for a complete bombing halt and negotiations.) Under pressure from restive liberals, Humphrey and other party leaders acquiesced to the demand for a special party commission to reform the rules by which convention delegates were chosen. It would be headed by Senator George McGovern.

The commission was intended to "open up" the Democratic Party, but in fact the effect of the rules changes adopted in the aftermath of Chicago was to close the party to many of its traditional core constituencies and capture it for a new set of mostly left-leaning factions. In hearings held in 1969, activist groups complained to the McGovern commission that women and minorities were "underrepresented" in the convention delegation; women had composed only 13 percent of the delegates to the 1968 convention, and blacks only 5 percent. The now familiar cry went up: Discrimination! So when the commission issued its directive to state parties in late 1969, its first priority was "to overcome the effects of past discrimination by affirmative steps to encourage minority group participation, including representation of minority groups on the national convention delegation in reasonable relationship to the group's presence in the population of the state." Did this mean quotas? The commission said no—in a footnote—but in fact the commission's guidelines led immediately to quotas, as even McGovern himself admitted to a reporter: "The way we got the quota thing through was by not using the word 'quotas.'"[83]

So although more delegates to future conventions would be committed to candidates as a consequence of primary election results, the kind of people who would serve as the delegates would come increasingly from the ranks of younger, single- or narrow-issue constituencies, with views far to the Left of previous Democratic convention delegations. Four-fifths of the delegates who would attend the 1972 Democratic convention would do so for the first time. With so many newcomers, many old-time party regulars had to lose. The biggest loser: organized labor, which had been the traditional backbone of Democratic Party get-out-the-vote efforts in industrial states. "The rules being promoted were clearly the left's revenge for the 1968 riots," historian Ronald Radosh wrote in his history of the modern Democratic Party.[84] For the Left there would be no need to riot at future Democratic conventions; at the next convention, the riot would take place inside the convention hall, as we shall see.

IN THE AFTERMATH of Chicago a Nixon landslide in November seemed assured. Humphrey's "politics of joy" theme and "happy warrior" image seemed dissonant in the spring after King's assassination; after Chicago it seemed like a farce. Some polls showed Humphrey so far down it appeared that he might finish third, behind George Wallace, who showed surprising strength among some traditional Democratic constituencies in the North. A local of the United Auto Workers union in Michigan endorsed Wallace, for example, and he often drew larger, more enthusiastic crowds in the North than Humphrey. It had to be discouraging for the irrepressible Humphrey, one of the great campaigners of modern times. Humphrey, James Jackson Kilpatrick observed, "pours out speech like a Tastee-freez. . . If God had made him a canine, he would wiggle around like a hound dog having his belly scratched."[85] Around Minnesota the standard line on Humphrey was that he spoke at 120 words per minute, with occasional gusts of 180. Still another widely repeated story was that Humphrey was once invited to speak at a tree-planting ceremony, and by the time he finished he was standing in the shade. Humphrey's campaign was nearly broke, while Nixon was flush with money to pour into a heavy TV advertising effort. Having been done in by TV in 1960 through his poor image in the debates with John F. Kennedy, the 1968 edition of Nixon was determined to turn the tables. "Nixon," Joe McGuinniss wrote in his famous book *The Selling of the President*, "depended on a television studio the way a polio victim relied on an iron lung."[86]

The razor-thin narrowness of Nixon's eventual victory after such a commanding lead in the polls can be viewed as the result of the cardinal mistake of sitting on the ball and trying to run out the clock. To be sure, political analysts have always pointed to the 15 percent of the vote that went to Wallace as evidence of a decisive rejection of the Democratic Party's Great Society liberalism. It is supposed that much of the Wallace vote would have gone to Nixon had Wallace not been in the race, yet Humphrey's late charge that transformed the race into a dead heat going into election day (a Harris Poll actually had Humphrey in the lead) suggests that the electorate's voting habits die hard. Mid-campaign polls showed Wallace drawing two votes from Nixon for every vote he drew from Humphrey, and much of Humphrey's late surge probably came from putative Wallace voters, at least in the North. This can be seen especially in the results of voting for the House and Senate, where only modest Republican gains meant that Nixon would be the first president since Zachary Taylor in 1848 to not have his party control at least one house of Congress. But if the voters who "returned home" to the Democratic Party late in 1968 represent a regression to the mean, it may equally have been the case that the polarization of the electorate that began in the mid-1960s was not yet complete. The eggs had been broken, but the omelet wasn't ready.

The combination of Nixon's prior reputation as Red-baiting "Tricky Dick" and his subsequent disgrace on account of Watergate has tended to skew our view and judgment about his 1968 campaign, which marked a watershed for more than just its use of advertising and marketing techniques. Far more significant than Nixon's "law and order" theme was his rhetoric about what became known as "the silent majority"—"the forgotten Americans, the non-shouters, the non-demonstrators," Nixon called them in his nomination speech to the Republican convention. Political rhetoric about the "forgotten man" had been a staple of American politics since the late nineteenth century, but it almost always had an economic or class dimension, and was typically the province of populist liberals. Now it was to become increasingly the language of conservatives; Reagan had used this kind of language before Nixon did, remarking in a July 1968 speech that "There is an American out there who has been a forgotten man, perhaps because he asked little of government except freedom."[87] It was a new kind of conservatism that could appeal to the "forgotten man." This was the first look at a populist conservatism that was already successfully casting liberalism as an elitist extravagance. The 1968 campaign prefigured the new fault line of American politics for the next generation.

The reigning myth about 1968, however, is that it represented a last chance for the politics of "hope," as though intentions alone are sufficient to assure success. Especially among liberals 1968 has become, in the title words of Jules Witcover's book, "the year the dream died." Nixon and Agnew, in the words of Ted Kennedy, "appealed to the darker side, and what changed the political dialogue was this change to the darker side."[88] Because Martin Luther King and Bobby Kennedy were said to have appealed to "the nobler side of human nature," they would have been able to "bring the people together" and appeal to the "vital center." But what does this imply about the liberal bona fides of Hubert Humphrey, who had been one of the Democratic Party's early stalwarts for civil rights, long before anyone in the Kennedy family embraced the issue? The trashing of the real in favor of the imaginary belies the fact that the liberal dream was already a shambles before 1968. The events of 1968 foreclosed an era in American political life, but liberals have been in denial ever since.

Abiding faiths die hard, and the cause of Great Society liberalism would be able to persist in its denial because it would have the benefit of what modern psychobabble calls "an enabler"—Nixon. To liberals Nixon was the Prince of Darkness. Chester, Hodgson, and Page observed in their election chronicle that "there is no doubt that there exists in America a durable reservoir of hostility toward Richard Nixon."[89] The "New" Nixon said after the election that his theme was "Bring Us Together." How would he do it?

PART TWO

THE FAILURE OF RICHARD NIXON

CHAPTER SIX

THE EDUCATION OF
RICHARD NIXON

A FEW DAYS INTO the new administration in 1969, Nixon's chief of staff Harry Robbins Haldeman—better known simply by his initials H. R.—made the following entry in his diary: "Had Tim in the [president's] office, both of them pretty nervous." "Tim" was an Irish setter (full name: King Timahoe) that the White House staff had given Nixon as an inauguration present. Harry Truman had famously said that if you want a true friend in Washington, get a dog. Did the White House staff have a premonition of Nixon's fate, or were they merely attempting to revive the sentiment of Checkers, the spaniel forever associated with Nixon since 1952?

Several writers fixed upon this entry when Haldeman's diaries were published in 1994 as another example of Nixon's legendary awkwardness. Nixon was utterly incapable of small talk, and small talk is a prerequisite for politicians in ceremonial meetings with girl scouts and little leaguers. In this case Nixon seemingly couldn't even bond with man's best friend. Yet just the next day Haldeman noted Nixon's opposite capacity. "P. really handles new people well, i.e., the NSF [National Science Foundation] group," Haldeman wrote. "Knows just how to lead them on and establish rapport. Build their interest." Haldeman noted this contrast in an annotation he added to his diary before it was published: "This skill in handling new groups in stark contrast to his awkwardness, mentioned above . . . One of many interesting contrasts in Nixon's nature."[1] As has been oft noted, Nixon won many votes but little affection. He seemed the diametric opposite of the cliché that someone is "comfortable in his own skin." Who can forget the photo of Nixon walking on the beach in California—in wingtip dress shoes. A glance at the photo of Nixon in his late years, together with the four other living presidents, shows the other presidents standing Marine-corps straight, while Nixon stands pigeon-toed, his shoulders stooped as if in a conspiratorial caricature.

Haldeman's clipped prose offers an understatement, as pointing to "contrasting" attributes barely begins to scratch the surface of Nixon's character. Henry Kissinger wrote in 1999 that "I still remain mystified by the personality of the perhaps most complex President of the twentieth century. . . . It would take a poet of Shakespearean dimension to do justice to the extraordinary, maddening, visionary, and debilitating personality of Richard Nixon."[2] It was fashionable during the time of President Clinton to speak of "compartmentalization," but if ever there was a person for whom it was necessary to "compartmentalize," it was Nixon. His dark side is well known and endlessly recalled. Yet the talents and supreme ability that brought him to the summit of public life have faded beneath this massive shadow. Friend and foe alike have testified to his first class intellect. Milton Friedman, who met with Nixon on several occasions to discuss economic and social policy, wrote that "few if any [presidents] have had a higher I.Q. . . . He was also personally pleasant."[3] In his rare relaxed public moments he dazzled even the cynics of the news media. In 1992, a 45-minute off-the-cuff excursus on the world situation by the 80-year-old ex-president drew a standing ovation from a gathering of elite journalists. "They're still a bunch of shits," Nixon remarked to an aide as he made his exit.

There is no doubt that liberal hostility toward Nixon hardened him and aggravated his own animosities. Probably no president of the twentieth century took office with such a fund of hatred among his enemies and critics, most of which arose from his role in the exposure of Alger Hiss's espionage in 1948 and his "Red-baiting" campaign against Helen Gahagan Douglas in 1950. Liberals would never forgive these transgressions against good will and good taste. "The hatred he evoked in his political opponents," Kissinger observed, "was extraordinary even by the turbulent standards of American democracy."[4] "The *New York Review of Books*," Theodore White noted, "treats him as if he does not belong to the human race."[5] Nixon reciprocated, saying that his enemies should be "kicked in the groin." Nixon biographer Jonathan Aitken recalls the shock of incoming British Ambassador John Freeman in 1969 at the attitude toward Nixon among the Washington elite. When Freeman expressed respect for Nixon at a Georgetown dinner party, hostess Alice Longworth replied: "How extraordinary! Listen. The Ambassador thinks well of Mr. Nixon! Such a common little man!" Aitken's narrative adds: "And her guests roared with laughter."[6] (The irony of this story is that Freeman had been a harsh critic of Nixon in Britain—he had written that Nixon's 1962 defeat in California's governor's race was "a victory for decency in public life"—but later became a strong admirer of Nixon in the course of his diplomatic mission.)

Quite aside from the personal animosity Nixon generated, there was also an undercurrent that Nixon's election was a fluke, that his administration was somehow illegitimate, because, after all, the Democrats are the natural ruling party. Nixon was only the second Republican president since Hoover, and the first, Eisenhower, was discounted because his election was seen as a reflection of his personal popularity (Democrats had wanted him to run as *their* candidate before Ike declared himself a Republican), and not as a sign that Republicans had genuine appeal to a majority of voters. "The Eastern liberal establishment never really admitted the legitimacy of the Nixon administration," historian Paul Johnson wrote in 1988. "From the start, the media interests which spoke for the establishment treated the Nixon presidency as in some metaphysical sense an outlaw regime whose true, unconstitutional character would eventually be exposed."[7] Even Daniel Patrick Moynihan, who had urged Democrats in 1967 to work with thoughtful conservatives, shared this condescension toward Republicans: "The Republicans cannot govern on any sustained basis in America. They simply do not have the intellectual or moral basis on which to build consensus. . . . They had no program, far less a mandate to put one in effect. They had almost no thinkers, almost no writers. . . . Its periods in office have been and are likely to continue to be little more than interludes brought on by Democratic internal dissidence."[8] Michael Barone noted that in the Washington of Nixon's era "the phrase 'conservative intellectual' seemed very much an oxymoron."[9]

It is largely because of these hardened personal and political positions that conservatives then and now have tended to rally to Nixon's cause

while liberals maintain a blind hatred for him. In fact the Nixon public policy record would justify reversing these allegiances. Any other president
who compiled Nixon's domestic and foreign record would be regarded as
standing firmly in the liberal progressive tradition. The *New York Times*
praised Nixon near the end of his first term for his "abandonment of outmoded conservative doctrine." Johnson has gone down in the history books
as the big spender for social welfare programs, yet federal spending grew
faster during Nixon's tenure than during Johnson's. It was under Nixon
that social spending came to exceed defense spending for the first time. Social spending soared from $55 billion in 1970 (Nixon's first budget) to
$132 billion in 1975, from 28 percent of the federal budget when LBJ left
office to 40 percent of the budget by the time Nixon left in 1974.

Although Nixon would criticize and attempt to reform welfare, he
nonetheless approved massive increases in funding for other Great Society
programs such as the Model Cities program and the Department of Housing and Urban Development, even though top aides had urged him to cut
or eliminate many of these programs. Some of the changes in spending
policies that Nixon supported, such as automatic cost-of-living increases
for Social Security recipients and other entitlement programs, contributed
to runaway spending trends in successive decades. Federal spending for the
arts, which went mostly to cultural elites who hated Nixon, quadrupled.
Economist Herbert Stein, who served on Nixon's Council of Economic
Advisers, summed up this dubious record: "The administration that was
against expanding the budget expanded it greatly; the administration that
was determined to fight inflation ended by having a large amount of it."[10]
"What's a balanced budget worth in terms of votes?", Nixon once asked
an aide. "Fifty thousand votes in a national election, that's all."[11]

The explosion in spending was matched by an equally dramatic explosion in federal regulation—from an administration that regarded itself as
pro-business. The number of pages in the *Federal Register* (the roster of
federal rules and regulations) grew only 19 percent under Johnson, but a
staggering 121 percent under Nixon. In civil rights, Nixon expanded the
regime of "affirmative action" racial quotas and set-asides far beyond what
Johnson had done. In other words, Nixon consolidated the administrative
state of the Great Society in much the same way that President Eisenhower
(for whom Nixon served as vice president) consolidated the New Deal.
Ronald Reagan would run and govern as much against the legacy of Nixon

as he would the legacy of the Great Society, and it was a number of Nixon's administrative creations that would cause Reagan the most difficulty during his White House years. Yet at the same time Nixon deserves the credit for assembling the new political coalition of working class and ethnic voters who would later become known as "Reagan Democrats." Nixon was the first Republican to win a majority of working class, Catholic, and labor union voters, as well as voters with only a grade school education. In the political sense Nixon played Moses to Reagan's Joshua. This is Nixon's greatest paradox.

The key to understanding the Nixon paradox, several biographers have pointed out, may lie in the nineteenth century British Prime Minister Benjamin Disraeli. Moynihan recalls giving Nixon a list of the "ten best political biographies" that he thought Nixon should read, which list included Lord Charnwood's *Lincoln,* Alan Bullock's *Hitler,* and Robert Blake's *Disraeli.* Five weeks later Nixon said to Moynihan, "I've read them all. Now, about Disraeli . . ." Nixon identified with Disraeli on several levels. Disraeli, born a Jew in Christian England, knew that he was never quite "respectable."

"There was something about Disraeli," Robert Blake wrote, "which those who constitute that mysterious but nevertheless recognizable entity, 'the establishment,' could never quite countenance. . . . The charge of insincerity and lack of principle has often been made against Disraeli." Like Nixon, Disraeli had risen to the summit of British politics after early success and promise in public office had ended abruptly, with his prospects seemingly ruined. Randolph Churchill, father of Winston, once summarized Disraeli's life as "Failure, failure, failure, partial success, renewed failure, ultimate and complete triumph." Having been down and out after losing two elections within two years, Nixon could identify with Disraeli's experience. Blake's description of how Disraeli revived his and his party's political fortunes when both were at low ebb neatly tracked Nixon's experience in the mid-1960s: "Disraeli exploited this situation with cautious adroitness, mending the party machine, waiting shrewdly upon events, and above all attacking Gladstonianism for its radical implications. The old feuds in the party were forgotten . . . and Disraeli became . . . the leader around whom moderate opinion began to crystallize."[12]

But the real attraction for Nixon was intellectual. Disraeli was what would be called in today's oxymoron a "progressive conservative." Disraeli was the prime mover of the Reform Bill of 1867, which widened the franchise beyond the landholding class. It was a bold reform that the Liberal Party had dared not attempt when it held power. Conservative policy, Disraeli thought, was the policy of true progress. Disraeli is thought to have attracted much of the newly enfranchised middle class to the ranks of the Tory Party. The political lesson was not lost on Nixon. "You know very well," he said to Moynihan, "that it is the Tory men with liberal policies who have enlarged democracy."[13] This could easily serve as the motto for Nixon's first term.

To be sure, Nixon had many conservatives in his cabinet and on the White House staff. Some of his key aides and appointees included figures who would play central roles in the Reagan administration, including George Shultz, Caspar Weinberger, Martin Anderson, and Pat Buchanan. And many of Nixon's political instincts were straight Republican chamber of commerce–style conservatism. But the more dominant intellectual side of Nixon yearned to transcend the conventional categories. "I'm an intellectual, too," Nixon told a task force of scholars he assembled in New York after the election to advise him on social policy—a group, Nixon knew, among whom very few had voted for him.

Theodore White recalled his first meeting with Nixon before the 1968 campaign: "He'd been reading some things recently by this fellow Moynihan, for example—very good stuff; did I know Moynihan and what did I think of him?"[14] So it came as no surprise that one of Nixon's early staff appointments was the ubiquitous Moynihan to chair an Urban Affairs Council, which Nixon intended to be the equivalent in stature, importance, and function to the National Security Council. "Moynihan," Herbert Stein observed, "was Nixon's soaring kite reaching out for the liberal chic Eastern establishment, whose respect Nixon did not have but wanted."[15]

Moynihan was to be the Henry Kissinger of domestic policy. Though Moynihan had been a thoughtful critic of the Great Society, he remained a committed champion of government social programs. "We may well have been the most progressive administration on domestic issues that has ever been formed," Moynihan later commented. "It was amazing what he [Nixon] would say yes to. . . . It is not likely that the Nixon Administration will ever be credited for what it tried to do."[16] Moynihan privately viewed his role as defending the Great Society against the predations of narrow-minded Republicans until Democrats returned to power and fixed their previous mistakes. He quipped that he would last in the Republican administration "until [John] Ehrlichman discovers the Bureau of the Budget and [Bob] Haldeman produces a telephone directory."[17]

Yet to conservatives who hoped Nixon would lead a rollback of the Great Society, Moynihan was a worrisome appointment. The election returns of 1968 certainly expressed the public's dissatisfaction with the results of the Great Society. Between 1963 and the beginning of the Nixon presidency, the number of Americans who identified themselves as "liberal" in opinion polls declined from 49 percent to 33 percent.[18] Public opinion surveys found that although the public supported government programs to help the poor, at the same time the public wanted these programs to embody the work ethic. Welfare, the public thought, should be hard to get, and the growth of the welfare rolls in the mid-1960s had made it seem that it had become far too easy to get.

Most significant, from a conservative point of view, was the Gallup Poll finding in 1968 that for the first time more Americans thought "big government" rather than "big labor" or "big business" was the greatest threat to the nation's future. The political opportunity for Nixon to change the ground of the American political debate was clearly open to him. Nixon sounded the tocsin in his inaugural address, implicitly criticizing the rhetorical excess of the Great Society and the political conflagration it helped touch off: "America has suffered from a fever of words; *from inflated rhetoric that promises more than it can deliver;* from angry rhetoric that fans discontents into hatreds; from bombastic rhetoric that postures instead of persuading." (Emphasis added.)

"From the first days of my administration," Nixon wrote in his memoirs, "I wanted to get rid of the costly failures of the Great Society—and I wanted to do it immediately." Few lines in Nixon's campaign had been more enthusiastically received than his pledge to "get people off welfare rolls and onto payrolls." After taking office he resumed the theme: "Never in human history has so much been spent by so many for such a negative result."[19] But Moynihan cautioned Nixon against any aggressive pruning of the welfare state: "All the Great Society activist constituencies are lying out there in wait, poised to get you if you try to come after them: the professional welfarists, the urban planners, the day-carers, the social workers, the public housers. Frankly, I'm terrified at the thought of cutting back too fast."[20] Moynihan had urged Nixon to declare publicly, in words that would become a familiar refrain in the 1990s, that "welfare as we know it is a bankrupt and destructive system."

It is doubtful that Nixon had a clear idea at the outset of his first term about how he wanted to roll back the Great Society, and he would have as little success in quickly ending the War on Poverty as he did in quickly ending the Vietnam War. In his presidential campaign, Nixon had declared that "at the present time I do not see a reasonable prospect that I will recommend a guaranteed annual income or a negative income tax."[21] Yet that is exactly what he would end up proposing. A favorite cliché about Nixon is that "Only Nixon could go to China," because any liberal Democrat who tried such a thing would have been pilloried (perhaps especially by Nixon) for being "soft on Communism." "Nixon-to-China" has entered the political vocabulary as a simile for counterintuitive political initiatives. Welfare reform was in fact the first "Nixon to China" moment. "Anyone," journalists Vincent and Vee Burke wrote, "who had predicted that Richard Nixon would be the first president to propose a guaranteed annual income for families, coupled with wage supplements for poor fathers, would have been dismissed as mad."[22] How this came to pass, the strange fate the political process dealt Nixon's proposal, and the contrast with Governor Reagan's welfare reform efforts in California, provide a clear illustration of the shifting political fault lines of the time. It was a precursor to the debate that was not finally settled for another 20 years.

THE WELFARE PROBLEM that confronted Nixon in 1969 was this: Hitherto welfare (or AFDC—Aid to Families with Dependent Children), although federally mandated and partially funded by the federal government, had been tailored and run by the states individually. Benefit levels varied widely, with New York and California offering the highest benefit levels, and Southern states offering very low benefit levels. Not surprising to critics of welfare, New York and California together accounted for almost half of the national increase in the welfare caseload in the mid-1960s. Ten percent of New York City's population, and 20 percent of its children, were on welfare in 1969. There was agreement across the political spectrum that the current welfare system presented the poor with a set of perverse incentives. If an able-bodied father was in the house, a poor family was generally ineligible for AFDC. This rule naturally discouraged marriage and intact two-parent households.

Moreover, welfare was seen as a disincentive for work, in effect a 100 percent tax on earned income; if a poor person took a low-paying job, they would lose their welfare benefits. In many states, a father who worked full time at a minimum-wage job did not earn as much as the welfare, food stamp, Medicaid, and housing benefits paid mostly to nonworking welfare mothers. Meanwhile, the welfare caseload in 1969 and 1970 was continuing to soar, as welfare became easier and easier to receive. A Supreme Court decision in 1968 struck down one-year residency requirements in 40 states, most of which had required a recipient to live in a state for one year before becoming eligible for welfare. Residency requirements, the Court ruled, somehow infringed on "the right to travel." Now there was "instant welfare." Governor Reagan complained that the Court ruling "creates nothing less than a bonus for migrating to California merely to get on our relief rolls."[23] Poverty lawyers followed up this case with another successful lawsuit calling for automatic cost-of-living increases in welfare payments.

Although the nation's governors complained about the soaring cost of welfare driven in part by court cases and federal mandates, the incoming Nixon administration took this state of affairs as reason to federalize welfare even further, and adopt national standards. On the surface the case was compelling. The Great Society's basic strategy for poverty, as we have seen, was the services strategy—education, job training, in-kind services, and other indirect help that was supposed to equip people to move out of poverty on their own. It clearly wasn't making any progress; by 1969, while the nonwhite unemployment rate had fallen by half and overall poverty had fallen by 25 percent during the previous five years, the welfare caseload had doubled. Moynihan plotted these two trends on a graph for Nixon; the diverging lines became known as "Moynihan's scissors." "The more one knows about welfare," Moynihan wrote to Nixon, "the more horrible it becomes . . . the system destroys those who receive it, and corrupts those who dispense it."[24] "Much of the money being spent to alleviate poverty," Senator Abraham Ribicoff, a leading liberal, complained, "does not bring a single person out of poverty." Another leading liberal Democrat, Senate Majority Leader Mike Mansfield, concurred: "We may have passed too much legislation and spent too much money. I think it is time to reorganize and tighten our belts."[25]

In an amazing turnabout, Nixon decided to junk the services approach, and embrace the income strategy that the Democrats had rejected at the beginning of the Great Society. Nixon proposed to federalize welfare completely; henceforth the program would be administered by the Social Security Administration in Washington, which knew a thing or two about sending out checks. Most importantly, he wanted a work requirement; a non-working recipient had to sign up for job availability or job training. If the recipient refused, his welfare benefits could be cut off (though not benefits for his or her children, significantly). In order to remove the disincentive to take a job rather than a welfare check (Nixon had repeatedly criticized "a system which makes it more profitable for a man not to work than to work"), the new welfare plan would need to adopt an "income disregard," so that poor households would not lose all of their welfare benefits if the mother or father became employed.

The logic of these features pointed policy in the previously unthinkable direction: a guaranteed annual income. The plan that soon emerged would provide an income floor for intact families and the working poor: $1,600 for a family of four, plus $800 in food stamps. Other poverty programs, such as Medicaid and housing assistance, would be maintained. To provide an incentive for work, the first $720 of earned income would be excluded from the benefit calculation. (At that time, median family income was about $9,000 a year; the "poverty line" for a family of four was $3,900 a year.) By broadening eligibility to intact families and the working poor, Nixon's proposal would have added 12 million more low-income people eligible to the welfare rolls, at an additional cost of more than $4.4 billion a year. Because of Moynihan's high-profile position as head of Nixon's Urban Affairs Council, he was assumed then and still today to have been the author of the idea. In fact, Moynihan's role was mostly limited to supplying Nixon with analysis of what was wrong with the present system; it was a passel of mostly conservative aides who designed the features of the Nixon welfare plan, which, when unveiled, split conservatives down the middle.

The irony of a guaranteed annual income is that it had been rejected by Democrats in the Kennedy and Johnson administrations as a "crackpot" idea on its merits, as well as politically dangerous for Democrats. "The central political fact about the negative income tax [a more elegant name for a guaranteed income]," Moynihan wrote, "is that Democrats did not dare be the first to propose it. . . . [But] the negative income tax was a spanking good idea."[26] (Moynihan would later change his mind about the guaranteed annual income, writing to William F. Buckley Jr. in 1978 that "we were wrong about the guaranteed annual income! Seemingly it is calamitous. It increases family dissolution by some 70 percent, decreases work, etc. Such is now the state of the science, and it seems to me we are honor bound to abide by it for the moment."[27]) To some conservatives, including several prominent members of Nixon's inner circle such as Arthur Burns, the idea was equally unthinkable. But among many other influential conservatives the idea of a guaranteed annual income had a more respectable pedigree. Robert A. Taft—"Mr. Conservative"— had flirted with the idea as far back as 1948, and of course Milton Friedman had championed the idea of the negative income tax since the late 1950s. Other free market–oriented economists such as George Stigler (who also later won the Nobel prize) joined Friedman in backing the idea. Inside the Nixon administration, one of the key supporters of the Nixon plan turned out to be Secretary of Labor George Shultz, who would go on to become President Reagan's Secretary of State. (It was Shultz who first urged the work requirement idea on Nixon.)

In addition to the intrinsic policy attractions of the idea, Nixon the politician saw potential for political gain. The existing welfare programs were most unpopular with the demographic group that was most solidly Democratic—the working class. Lower middle-income and working-class voters expressed the most vocal resentment of what they saw as "welfare freeloaders." Nixon thought welfare reform would be his Disraeli moment, that an emphasis on the work requirement would be a political winner, peeling away votes from the Democratic Party at the next election. A number of shrewd political analysts agreed. One important figure in the White House didn't: Vice President Agnew. Agnew was among the conservative faction that hated the GAI plan. He cautioned Nixon: "It will not be a political winner and will not attract low-income groups to the Republican philosophy. The $6 billion estimated for the program will be greeted on the Hill with shouts of derision, and the liberal Democrats will propose that three or four times that amount should be spent."[28] Agnew didn't limit his efforts to persuasion alone; he actually tried to strong-arm Nixon out of the idea. As Agnew left a meeting to head to the Senate where it was thought his vote might be necessary to break a tie on a close vote for a defense bill Nixon wanted, Agnew turned and said: "Mr. President, if there is a tie may I telephone you before I vote and ask whether you've changed your mind about this welfare program?"[29] Nixon was not amused. Agnew later dutifully defended the proposal.

On August 8, 1969, Nixon announced his "Family Assistance Plan" (FAP) in a nationally televised address. He had come up with the name "Family Assistance Plan" at the last moment, and had not liked it very much. "It sounds kind of blah," Nixon complained. Nixon emphasized the work requirement in his speech, and downplayed the huge expansion of welfare that it entailed. Early editorial, political, and public reaction was favorable. *The Economist* of London said Nixon's FAP "may rank in importance with President Roosevelt's first proposal for a social security system in the mid-1930s."[30] A few of Lyndon Johnson's poverty warriors claimed that FAP had been their idea all along, even though in truth they had rejected the idea. Although some turbulence in Congress was to be expected, the prospects looked good. One eager sponsor of the Nixon plan was Texas Congressman George Bush. Yet despite the early auguries of success, within days Agnew's warning seemed prophetic.

The White House knew that even with the work provisions there would be some opposition from anti-welfare conservatives—one White House aide had suggested that the plan be called the "Christian Working Man's Anti-Communist National Defense Rivers and Harbors Act of 1969." Sure enough, many conservatives did oppose FAP, including Milton Friedman (because FAP supplemented rather than replaced other poverty programs such as food stamps, housing grants, Medicaid, and so forth). Nixon made the same political calculation that Johnson had made about Vietnam and the Great Society: "I thought the biggest danger would be the attack from the right," Nixon wrote in his memoirs. "I was in for a surprise."[31]

Sure enough, the rumble of liberal voices quickly built to a roar: Nixon's proposed level of benefits was too low. The guaranteed income level needed to be much higher. Several Congressional liberals, following the lead of the National Welfare Rights Organization (NWRO), declared that the income guarantee should be at least $5,500 for a family of four instead of Nixon's $1,600—a level that would have cost $71 billion, required a 78 percent income surtax, and made two-fifths of the population eligible for welfare. Nonetheless, the $5,500 level, Moynihan wrote, "became almost a talisman of advanced liberalism." (Senator George McGovern would eventually up the ante, however, calling for a $6,400 guaranteed annual income in 1972.) Nixon may have expected this, and no doubt calculated that this was an easily winnable argument. What no one had anticipated was the ferocity and tactics of the liberal attack, and how it would harmonize with the attacks on FAP from wholly different quarters, such as the U.S. Chamber of Commerce and organized labor.

It was not enough for liberal critics to charge that Nixon was parsimonious. It was the weak work requirement (which had been watered down in the drafting of the bill in Congress) that sent the entitlement-minded Left into paroxysms of outrage. Income, they thought, should be redistributed without any reciprocal obligation on the part of the recipients. The work requirement made FAP into "an act of political repression . . . a flagrant example of institutional racism" in the words of the NWRO. The president of the National Council of Churches called FAP "a racist bill." New York Congresswoman Shirley Chisholm said that FAP "hedges on involuntary servitude with its compulsory work qualification," and fellow New York Congressman William Ryan, echoing the entitlement mentality of the NWRO, said that "a guaranteed income is not a privilege, it should be a right to which every American is entitled."

Liberals who should have known better were cowed by the mau-mauing of the welfare-rights activists. "We can't take a position against the NWRO," a New York City welfare administrator said. "We *can't discuss* it."[32] Senator Eugene McCarthy called FAP the "Family Annihilation Plan," and allowed the NWRO to arrange a set of Senate hearings into FAP that turned into a show trial and protest rally. The packed hearing room erupted with raucous cheers and applause when a single welfare mother indignantly declared: "We only want the kind of jobs that pay $10,000 or $20,000 . . . we aren't going to do anybody's laundry or babysitting except for ourselves!" Another welfare mother who was also NWRO's vice chairwoman declared: "You can't force me to work! You'd better give me something better than I'm getting on welfare. I ain't takin' it."[33] "With the welfare mothers opposing it," McCarthy said, "it makes it easy to vote against." (McCarthy had proposed an income guarantee in his presidential campaign in 1968.)

The effect of the entitlement Left's mau-mauing was compounded by the opposition of organized labor. Within a week of Nixon's announcement of FAP, AFL-CIO president George Meany declared his opposition. Meany and other union leaders suspected that FAP was part of a backdoor strategy to undermine the minimum wage. "The AFL-CIO vigorously opposes the use of federal funds to subsidize the employers of cheap labor." The United Auto Workers said FAP would "subsidize sweatshop employers." The real trouble, however, came from a different sector of organized labor—the public employee unions. The one commendable aspect of FAP from a conservative point of view is that it would upset the current structure of the social service bureaucracy, the "caring professions" whose self-interest lies in having an ever-expanding caseload of welfare "clients" to serve. There were more than 30,000 unionized welfare administrators and caseworkers around the nation in 1969, and the proposal to federalize the program meant one thing: their jobs might disappear, or at the very least, they would become federal employees, which would mean giving up the superior benefits most of them enjoyed at the state level.

Jerry Wurf, the head of the American Federation of State, County, and Municipal Employees (AFSCME), complained to the Senate Finance Committee that under FAP the work week at welfare offices could "leap up" to 40 hours; currently local welfare office employees in some states worked a 32-hour week. "It is imperative," Wurf said, "that this bill guarantee complete employee protection against any loss of jobs, benefits, and collective bargaining agreements. . . ." The opposition from such an important segment of the Democratic machine made it even tougher for Democrats to support FAP.

Despite opposition from the Left, FAP might have passed in some form were it not for the determined opposition of one key conservative— Ronald Reagan. Nixon had hosted Reagan and his senior aide Ed Meese at a meeting at Nixon's western White House in San Clemente, where Moynihan presented Reagan with the conservative case for FAP. "Reagan and Meese were almost convinced," one Reagan aide recalls. But other Reagan staff members were reading the fine print, and presented a very different picture of FAP to Reagan, including that the number of welfare recipients would go up, and that the program would cost billions more than the current system. Reagan was incredulous, and decided to go into opposition. He directed his finance department to engage in detailed analysis of the cost and effects of FAP, which he used in his extensive lobbying effort against FAP. "Reagan probably received more information about the potential effects of FAP than Nixon ever did," Reagan aide Charles Hobbs wrote."[34]

Welfare reform should have as its principal aim the *reduction* of the number of people receiving aid, not a vast expansion of the rolls. "In California," Reagan told Congress, "one out of every twelve persons is now on welfare. The new bill will increase this ration to *one of every seven*, with every indication that it could deteriorate even further." Welfare reform should *save* the taxpayers money, not cost them billions more. While the White House projected that FAP would cost $4.4 billion more, Reagan argued that its true cost would be closer to $15 billion when the cost of all of the collateral social programs (such as Medicaid) whose caseload would grow in proportion to the welfare caseload. This would cost California taxpayers an additional $450 million at the outset. The work requirement was weak, Reagan rightly judged, and made it more profitable for many people to be on welfare rather than work. Reagan argued all of these points forcefully in testimony to the Senate Finance Committee, whose chairman, Sen. Russell Long, invited Reagan to appear. (Long also opposed FAP.)

Above all, Reagan opposed the idea that the government should guarantee an income. "I believe that the government is supposed to *promote* the general welfare," Reagan said in a TV debate on FAP, "I don't think it is supposed to *provide* it."[35] And Reagan objected to the federal takeover of welfare. Reagan was the only governor to vote against a National Governors Association resolution calling for a federal takeover of welfare. If welfare was centralized in Washington, Reagan knew, reform efforts would be difficult and there would be a bias toward increased spending in the future. "It would only be the first installment," Reagan observed. "Raising the annual family grant would become an election-year must." "If there is one area of social policy," Reagan began to say in his standard stump speech, "that should be at the most local level of government possible, it is welfare. It should not be nationalized—it should be *localized*."[36]

Although many governors were unenthusiastic about FAP, Reagan was the most aggressive in his opposition. He wrote several times to every governor and to the entire House and Senate, providing extensive analysis of why he thought FAP was a bad idea. Reagan became the leader of the conservative opposition to FAP, receiving thousands of letters of support, including one from Erza Taft Benson, president of the Mormon Church, urging Reagan to oppose "this socialistic program, which to me is one of the worst mistakes made by our current Republican administration."[37] (The correspondence file on FAP is one of the largest in the Reagan gubernatorial archives.) Were it not for his stalwart support for Nixon on other issues (especially Vietnam), Reagan might have risked a serious breach with the White House. Reagan had hesitated to oppose the president from his own party, but in the end was typically blunt. "I'm sure you know how painful it is to find myself in the position of opposing this measure," Reagan wrote Nixon after having failed to reach him by phone to tell him that he would publicly oppose FAP. "[But] we received no assurance of what, if anything, the administration intends to do to amend the Act accordingly."[38]

Most members of Congress sent routine courtesy responses back to Reagan. One Republican, however, wrote four single-spaced pages to Reagan defending FAP against Reagan's criticisms—George Bush. The exchange revealed much that later became evident about the character of both men. Bush hastened to embrace Reagan's principles that welfare reform should have as its goal the reduction of the number of people on welfare, a serious work requirement, and a removal of the incentives for family breakup. "Our disagreement is therefore not philosophical but factual," Bush wrote. Bush thought Reagan had his facts wrong. Bush challenged Reagan's view that FAP would cost $15 billion instead of $4.4 billion. (Virginia's Democratic senator, Harry Byrd, wrote to Reagan at the same time confirming Reagan's estimate.) Bush also thought the work requirement was sufficient, and reduced the incentive for family breakup.[39] Reagan, naturally, fired back at his future running mate, telling Bush that his (Reagan's) cost estimate was probably conservative. "The bill has a built-in capacity for cost expansion," Reagan told Bush. Reagan was not to be deterred by sophisticated arguments that FAP could serve conservative ends.

FAP managed to get through the House of Representatives, thanks mostly to the support of Ways and Means Committee Chairman Wilbur Mills and Republican Minority Leader Gerald Ford. But it died in the Senate, from a coalition of antiwelfare conservatives and liberals in thrall to the entitlement Left. Welfare reform was a dead issue by the time FAP finally expired for the last time in 1972. A Democratic president in the 1980s, Moynihan predicted, would successfully revive the idea. Not surprisingly, the unusual coalition that defeated FAP led to some unusual political fallout in the aftermath. In the Texas Senate election in 1970, Democratic candidate Lloyd Bentsen excoriated the Republican nominee for his support of "big welfare" and higher taxes that FAP supposedly represented. Despite the Republican candidate's protest that "anyone who tries to get to the right of me is going to fall off the edge of the earth," the attack was effective, and Bentsen handily defeated George Bush.

ALTHOUGH IT WAS NOT evident at the moment, the defeat of FAP marked a turning point in the history of American social policy. It marked the dead end of the slow march toward explicit, redistributive egalitarianism, which has always been the chief goal of the Left. But the Left was unable to recognize the folly of their own actions, or it might have taken a different attitude toward FAP. Moreover, had welfare been federalized and the principle of a guaranteed annual income established, the state-based welfare reforms of the 1990s would never have taken place. Reagan had argued during the FAP debate that Washington should get out of the way and let states take the lead in reforming welfare. Once again Reagan was a generation ahead of events. He decided to put his words into practice in California, understanding that if welfare could be successfully reformed in the nation's largest state, it would provide an example of why centralizing welfare in Washington through FAP was unnecessary.

The timing could not have been more propitious. While FAP was grinding its way through the legislative sausage factory in Washington from 1969 to 1972, California was confronting a welfare crisis. California's welfare rolls were growing by 40,000 a month in 1970. While California had 10 percent of the nation's population, it had 16 percent of the nation's total welfare caseload. Unless something was done, Reagan's finance department told him, a tax increase would be necessary to meet the added fiscal burden. Reagan made welfare reform a central theme of his successful re-election campaign in 1970, and set in motion a process that he would repeat 10 years later during his drive for the White House. He appointed a task force to produce a blueprint for welfare reform to be implemented during his second term. Reagan's language was tougher than Nixon's: "This study will place heavy emphasis on the tax-payer as opposed to the tax-taker; on the truly needy as opposed to the lazy unemployable."[40]

When Reagan's task force finished its report in the late winter of 1971, Reagan intended to address a joint session of the legislature to announce his reform plan. The Democrats blundered—not the first time Reagan had enjoyed this experience. The Democratic-controlled legislature refused Reagan's request—an act of intransigence that handed Reagan a golden opportunity to "go over their heads directly to the people." "This will be like the books banned in Boston," Reagan gloated to Ed Meese. Reagan arranged for a statewide telecast of the speech he had planned to give to the legislature—being able to bill it as "the speech the legislature wouldn't hear" enhanced media interest and attention. Reagan also set in motion a plan to organize grassroots groups around the state to build support for his plan. More than 120 local groups formed, backed up with staff loaned from the state Chamber of Commerce. Soon legislators were being deluged with thousands of letters urging support for welfare reform. But the real pressure was the threat of a ballot initiative in 1972; if the legislature refused to deal, Reagan would lead the initiative campaign.

Assembly Speaker Bob Moretti finally went to Reagan in June and asked Reagan (as Reagan told the story) to "stop your cards and letters." Moretti is reported to have said: "Governor, I don't like you, and I know you don't like me, but we don't have to be in love to get something worked out around here, and if you're serious about accomplishing some things, let's sit down and let's do it."[41]

"This meeting," Lou Cannon judged, "was the turning point that marked Reagan's transformation from communicator to governor."[42] There followed a week of face-to-face, morning-till-late-evening negotiations between Reagan and Moretti to work out a compromise on welfare reform, sessions that, *Los Angeles Times* reporter Bill Boyarski wrote, "told much about Reagan's willingness to work long hours, to master tedious detail and to compromise."[43] Reagan's skillful negotiating—the Democrats apparently forgot that Reagan had negotiated with tough-minded studio executives when he headed the Screen Actors Guild in Hollywood—shattered the low expectations and image of being lazy and uninformed. Reagan proved himself thoroughly able to argue the arcana of welfare law, and the details of how much low-income households spend for necessities. Reagan's team also employed the clever tactic of fighting hard for items they were willing to give away, while seemingly placing less emphasis on items that were on their "must-have" list.

The Democrats fell for the ploy, acceding more easily to the main requirements of Reagan's plan, and gaining "concessions" on the items Reagan was willing to deal away in the first place. Reagan's team came out of the negotiations with 80 percent of what they wanted in their reform package. (Reagan's most significant concession was an annual automatic cost-of-living increase for welfare benefits, a feature that would plague his successors in office as inflation soared in later years. He also was unable to get a permanent ceiling on annual welfare appropriations.) The final hurdle to implementing the welfare reform plan turned out to be the Nixon administration. Several of the changes Reagan had negotiated with the legislature required a waiver from the federal government's rules, which the Department of Health, Education, and Welfare (HEW) had the power to grant. HEW under Secretary Elliott Richardson was cool to the reform plan, with some of the HEW staff calling Reagan's work requirement "slave labor." Reagan personally lobbied Vice President Agnew and later Nixon himself for the waiver, which Richardson grudgingly granted in 1972.

The main improvement Democrats could claim was a 43 percent increase in the level of benefits for welfare recipients, and money for family planning. But Reagan had said all along that he wanted welfare to be adequate for the "truly needy," and he was quite willing to give higher benefits in return for tighter eligibility requirements to reduce the total number of welfare recipients. Reagan's design worked: the caseload, which had been rising by 40,000 a month, started falling by 8,000 a month. By July 1973 the caseload was nearly 800,000 lower than had been predicted before reform, with a savings of $1 billion (out of a total state budget of about $9 billion at the time).

The most significant aspect of Reagan's welfare reform was the themes he staked out—themes that sounded radical in 1970 but which would become the conventional wisdom in the 1990s. "There are those who say that welfare reform cannot be handled at the state level," Reagan observed in his stump speech on welfare. "They say we must turn it over to the federal government. I do not agree. I do not agree because some of the worst abuses you have read and heard about are the direct result of unreasonable, unrealistic federal regulations that become distorted by the time they are applied to individual cases."

But it was not the monetary cost of welfare that Reagan criticized, but its moral cost: "In a more basic sense, California and the United States cannot afford the moral and spiritual disintegration that the welfare system is subsidizing. . . . We should begin to measure the success of welfare not by how many additional people we put on the rolls each year, but by how many we restore to the dignity of self-sufficiency." Reagan noted that thousands of children had been abandoned by their fathers, who should be held accountable for child support. This was all anathema to those Reagan called "the professional poor, who view welfare as an acceptable lifelong career." (Reagan had in mind the NWRO, whom he singled out by name for attack.) Reagan's public teaching was as significant if not more significant than the actual legislative compromise. The *L.A. Times'* Boyarski offered this verdict: "What was important was that Reagan was able to marshal enough political power to change the rules of debate on welfare in California. . . . It was a political victory, a philosophical change for the state and an indication that Reagan, rather than being a mere compromiser, had become an effective negotiator in tough legislative confrontations."[44]

One thing Reagan's welfare reform couldn't change was the culture of social workers who run the local welfare offices. Because of this and other factors, welfare reform in California and elsewhere was only partially successful. While reform stemmed the tide of soaring caseloads, it did not change the fundamental culture of welfare dependency, household breakup, and joblessness. That would have to wait until the wave of state-based welfare reform in the 1990s.

The increasingly polarized politics of social policy in the early 1970s foreclosed the possibility of meaningful social policy reform for the time being. Social policy would need to find a fresh vista if it was to engage the public in a way that generated broad consensus to move forward boldly as had been the case with the Great Society a few years before. As it happened, a new social cause that had been slowly incubating was propelled to a prominence by a singular event that permanently changed the American conscience. As was the case with so many changes in modern America, the galvanizing event occurred in California.

ON JANUARY 28, 1969, on Union Oil Platform A five and a half miles off the California coast near Santa Barbara, oil drillers working a well 3,500 feet under the ocean floor needed to haul up the line to replace the drill bit. This is a routine procedure in oil drilling; in order to prevent gushers, drilling rigs pump a synthetic "mud" down the drill casing to maintain pressure equilibrium. On this day the Union Oil crew miscalculated and the well blew, sending a mix of crude oil and drilling mud over 100 feet in the air. A temporary cap did not work, and crude oil began leaking out new fissures on the ocean floor at a rate of 1,000 gallons an hour. Although Union Oil promised to have the leak plugged in 24 hours, the massive flow continued for 11 days before Union Oil was able to gain control, by which time more than 200,000 gallons had been spilled. It was the largest offshore oil blowout in U.S. history; the largest previous event, in 1965, had spilled 60,000 gallons of oil.

It did not take long for the winds and ocean currents to begin washing oil and dead wildlife onto the beaches of Santa Barbara, an affluent coastal community that at the time leaned Republican. What followed would become a familiar script for the new world of environmental politics—the public alarm and outrage, the callous remarks of corporate executives that fueled more outrage, recriminations against the government for allowing the catastrophe in the first place, lawyers racing to file lawsuits, gross exaggeration and doomsday predictions by the media, missteps and pledges of "action" by the politicians, and clean up efforts that may have done more harm than good.

The media did its best to distort and magnify the event. News reports repeated a description from the *Washington Post* of an oil slick "the size of Rhode Island," when in fact the slick was well less than half that size at its largest extent. Public sensibilities were further inflamed by a quote from Union Oil president Fred Hartley in the *New York Times* saying, "I'm amazed at the publicity for the loss of a few birds."[45] Editorial reaction was swift and severe. David Brinkley remarked on the *NBC Evening News* that "A few more remarks like that and Mr. Hartley could never be confirmed as Secretary of the Interior." Even the pro-business *Wall Street*

Journal jumped on Hartley's insensitivity. The only trouble was that Hartley didn't say it. His full remarks before the Senate Public Works Committee reveal a different context and meaning:

> I think we have to look at these problems relatively. I am always tremendously impressed at the publicity that the death of birds received versus the loss of people in our country in this day and age. When I think of the folks that gave up their lives when they came down into the ocean [in an airliner crash] off Los Angeles some three week ago, and the fact that our society forgets about that within a 24-hour period, I think relative to that, the fact that we have had no loss of life from this incident is important.[46]

Nixon's Secretary of the Interior Walter Hickel did his best imitation of the Keystone Cops, first asking the oil companies to suspend further drilling in the Santa Barbara channel, reversing himself the next day, and then re-reversing himself and shutting down the rigs again a few days later. Recriminations flew against the recently departed Johnson administration; Johnson's Interior Secretary Stewart Udall called the spill "a conservation Bay of Pigs," but Santa Barbarans pointed to his promise while in office that "No oil leases will be granted except under conditions that will protect your environment." Tempted by the lure of $600 million in oil royalties that would help balance the federal budget, the Johnson administration had granted the leases and quietly dropped its support of a proposal to make the Santa Barbara channel a wildlife sanctuary.[47]

Soon the media was thick with alarmist reports about the extent of the disaster and the successive catastrophes that were sure to follow. A hastily assembled White House panel of experts concluded that it might take 10 to 20 years to stop the still-seeping oil in the channel. Another group of experts forecast that with the number of rigs operating in the channel, a similar blowout could be expected to occur on average once a decade. Dire predictions of the permanent loss of wildlife and damage to the channel's ecosystem became a daily refrain. Santa Barbara braced for a major hit to its vital tourist industry. It took only five months for *Time* magazine, which had hyped the story when it first broke, to admit sheepishly that "dire predictions seem to have been overstated. . . . Now, four months later, the channel's ecology seems to have been restored to virtually its natural state."[48] (A University of Southern California study two

years later concluded that "damage to the biota was not widespread."[49])
The spill also became the occasion for perhaps the first episode of "eco-
tourism," as tourists by the thousands came to Santa Barbara to view the
scene firsthand. "I'm just waiting for the vendors to start selling ribbons
printed with 'We saw the oil slick in Santa Barbara,'" a federal pollution-
control official remarked. The local director of the Sierra Club, Fred
Eissler, sounded a note of glee: "We're delighted now that the rest of the
country can see us and learn a lesson from what's happening here."[50]

The Santa Barbara oil spill established a perverse pattern whereby
bad news was good news for the nascent environmental movement. A crisis such as Santa Barbara was an entrepreneurial opportunity. The crisis
entrepreneurs of Santa Barbara were quick to graft the sensibilities of the
New Politics to the issue. "We need a new politics," the Sierra Club's
Eissler told a beachfront rally of more than 1,000 people, "a politics of
ecology, based on reverence for the land and reverence for the man. What
we need is an environmental rights movement along with a civil rights
movement."[51] A grassroots group sprang into being: Get Oil Out, which
offered the handy acronym GOO. The American Civil Liberties Union
even joined the fray, filing a federal lawsuit that contended a clean environment was a basic human right.

The environment was not a wholly new issue in the late 1960s.
Rachel Carson's 1962 warning about the pesticide threat to wildlife,
Silent Spring, had been a sensation, and set in motion a train of events
that soon led to a ban on the pesticide DDT in the United States. President Johnson had championed several early environmental measures,
some of which were significant, such as early clean air and pesticide regulation, and some of which were more aesthetic, such as highway beautifi-
cation. But the environment was not yet seen as a mass political issue that
could capture and move the sentiment of the nation. Neither Nixon nor
Humphrey had talked about the environment in the 1968 campaign; at
that time "green power" still meant the Irish vote. Gallup didn't think the
issue was worth polling until 1965, and the early polls generated ho-hum
results. Gallup's first poll found that only 28 percent considered air pollution to be a serious problem (a Harris Poll reported a majority against
higher taxes and higher consumer prices to pay for environmental clean
up), while only 35 percent thought water pollution was a serious problem. By 1969, these numbers had risen to 69 percent and 74 percent.[52]

After Santa Barbara, environmental episodes were big news. In June, five months after Santa Barbara, a pile of logs, picnic benches, and other debris that had collected beneath a railroad trestle over the Cuyahoga River in Cleveland caught fire when sparks from a passing train ignited the kerosene and oil floating on top of the river. The fire burned for only 24 minutes, not long enough for the *Cleveland Plain-Dealer* to get a photo. Hence it was reported briefly in the back pages of the paper, and didn't attract much attention until months later, when a *National Geographic* magazine article on river pollution gave the episode fresh attention nationwide.

The reaction to the Cuyahoga River fire is an excellent illustration of what economists call the "wealth effect," that is, how the public demands higher environmental quality as society becomes more affluent and aware. The Cuyahoga, which the mayor of Cleveland had described as an "open sewer" as far back as 1881, had caught fire twice before, in 1936 and 1952. There was no fanfare or general outrage then; it was regarded as the price of progress. Such a price was no longer acceptable by 1969; the Affluent Society did not want to be the Effluent Society. The environment as a political issue was here to stay. In 1970 *Time* magazine named the environment "Issue of the Year" to go along with its Man of the Year (West German Chancellor Willy Brandt) and its sister publication *Life* soon designated the 1970s as "the environmental decade." California Assembly Speaker Jesse Unruh, Reagan's opponent for governor in 1970 and the originator of the phrase "Money is the mother's milk of politics," now had a corollary: "Ecology has become a substitute for the word 'mother.'"[53] On April 22, 1970, the first "Earth Day" was held. Wisconsin Senator Gaylord Nelson, one of the prime forces behind the first Earth Day, proclaimed: "Earth Day may be a turning point in American history. It may be the birth of a new American ethic that rejects the frontier philosophy that the continent was put here for our plunder." The issue was on its way. In the 1970 *Readers' Guide to Periodical Literature*, entries for the environment and related subjects take up less than a page and a half; in 1971, the entries required five pages.

Environmentalism appeared to be the perfect consensus issue to take the place of increasingly contentious social policy. Who, after all, is *for* polluted air and dirty water? Even the evil corporations of leftist lore must have some self-regard to not want to poison their customer base.

But on a deeper level, environmentalism would wreak havoc on both parties. Environmentalism is politically awkward for pro-business Republicans, and the fact that environmentalism as an ideology attracts considerable attention from the Left makes environmentalism a dubious cause for Main Street chamber of commerce Republicans. "Ecology," *New Republic* writer James Ridgeway said in 1970, "offered liberal-minded people what they had longed for, a safe, rational and above all peaceful way of seeming to remake society . . . [and] developing a more coherent central state. . . ."[54] These kinds of celebrations give conservatives the vapors, right down to this day. Sure enough, some conservatives announced their immediate opposition to ecology. The Daughters of the American Revolution unintentionally endorsed pollution with their poorly phrased complaint that "Subversive elements plan to make American children live in an environment that is good for them."[55] (The fact that the date designated for the first Earth Day—April 22—also happened to be Lenin's birthday further fueled the suspicions of the paranoid Right.) But other conservatives, including Senator Barry Goldwater, Senator James Buckley (Bill Buckley's brother), and even Ronald Reagan, joined the environmental bandwagon. Shortly after the first Earth Day, *National Review* sounded more like the Sierra Club than a conservative standard-bearer: "If [corporations] do not stop [polluting] we must find ways to compel them in some way to do so. . . . important people must be interfered with before notice will be taken of disagreeable facts. Instead of demonstrating on Fifth Avenue on behalf of baby seals, the saviors of the environment would get far better results picketing the country clubs of Nassau, Fairfield, and Morris counties."[56]

Reagan devoted fully a third of his 1970 state-of-the-state speech to the environment, declaring "the absolute necessity of waging all-out war against the debauching of the environment." Reagan wrote in *Nation's Business* that "the one major issue that is most likely to dominate the nation's political attention in the 1970s [is] environmental protection. . . . The bulldozer mentality of the past is a luxury we can no longer afford. Our roads and other public projects must be planned to prevent the destruction of scenic resources and to avoid needlessly upsetting the ecological balance."[57]

Reagan also pointed out that had Union Oil Platform A been in state waters instead of federal waters, stricter California drilling regulations would likely have prevented the blowout. Reagan's most widely recycled comment on the environment—"If you've seen one [redwood] you've seen them all"—was not a fair reflection of his record as governor. William Pemberton's mostly critical account of Reagan's political career notes that "Reagan's good record on environmental issues surprised liberals. He saved Round Valley from a huge dam project, protected the John Muir Trail from highway construction, established an ecological reserve program to maintain critical wildlife habitat, established an Ecology Corps, and took important actions to maintain and improve air and water quality."[58] Reagan's decision to block a dam planned for the Eel River on California's north coast stunned environmentalists and the business community alike. In addition to opposing the dam for environmental reasons, Reagan decided to stop the dam because it would flood a large area of Indian land including several grave sites of the Yuki Indians. "We've broken too many treaties [with Indians]," said the man who was supposedly insensitive to minorities. "We're not going to flood them out."[59]

Yet if environmentalism is counterintuitive for Republicans, it initially divided the Left, and would ultimately prove a subtle disaster for Democrats. The dilemma for the Left was clearly evident in the reaction to the first Earth Day in 1970. Many on the Left, Norman Podhoretz observed in *Commentary,* thought that "the whole issue of the environment represented a maneuver to distract the national attention from Vietnam and the problems of blacks."[60] Teach-ins on college campuses on Earth Day were viewed with alarm by the antiwar movement. Sure enough, Earth Day campus teach-ins occurred at more than 1,500 colleges, and employed all the antic street theater that went into antiwar demonstrations. Burying cars was a popular gesture at many Earth Day observances. At San Jose State University in California, students buried a new $2,500 automobile, while at Florida Technology University students put a Chevrolet "on trial" for poisoning the earth. When their attempts to smash the car with sledgehammers proved exhausting, they donated the car to the art department, which promised to make a sculpture project of it. "SDS chapters on many campuses," *Time* reported, "have also publicly embraced anti-ecology because President Nixon is publicly pro-ecology."[61] "Rallying around the ecology banner is the biggest assortment of ill-matched allies since the Crusades," sniffed *The New Republic* in an editorial about the "ecology craze." "Worst of all, of course, the ecology binge provides a cop-out for a

President and a populace too cheap or too gutless or too tired or too frustrated or too all of them to tangle harder with some old problems that have proved resistant and emotionally unsatisfying to boot."[62] Writing in *Science* magazine, Amitai Etzioni of Columbia University dismissed ecology as a "fad," and thought that "the newly found environmental dangers are being vastly exaggerated." Even if not exaggerated, Etzioni thought the environment was the wrong priority: "Fighting hunger, malnutrition, and rats should be given priority over saving wildlife, and improving our schools over constructing waste disposal systems."[63]

This criticism was mild compared to the blasts that came from black civil rights leaders. The most bitter attack came from Richard Hatcher, the black mayor of Gary, Indiana: "The nation's concern for the environment has done what George Wallace was unable to do—distract the nation from the human problems of black and brown Americans."[64] Whitney Young of the National Urban League was equally distressed: "The war on pollution is one that should be waged after the war on poverty is won. Common sense calls for reasonable national priorities and not for inventing new causes whose main appeal seems to be in their potential for copping out and ignoring the most dangerous and pressing of our problems."[65] A black militant in Chicago put it more bluntly to a *Time* reporter: "Ecology? I don't give a good goddamn about ecology!" The talk about population control that accompanied the first Earth Day was especially disconcerting to minority groups with high birth rates; they knew who the target groups for cutting birthrates would be.

But much of the ever-protean Left quickly embraced environmentalism. The lingering problem for traditional liberal Democrats, however, is that environmentalism in its most popular form is deeply pessimistic about the future, feeding the "limits to growth" mentality that is counter to the core of liberalism's historically pro-growth attraction to the working class. A liberalism that was already starting to appear dark and gloomy because of its social policy failures would soon embrace a pessimistic countenance toward economic growth that would prove at least as problematic for Democratic candidates as the seemingly anti-business effects of environmentalism was for Republicans.

The seeds of this political cognitive dissonance could be seen in the reaction to early environmental legislation. While many big business trade associations supported the creation of the Environmental Protection

Agency (chiefly because a single national regulatory body was easier to cope with than separate state agencies with different standards and regulations), the labor unions for auto workers and steel workers expressed dismay that their industries would be at the top of the list for expensive regulatory cleanups.

All of this would take a decade or more to play itself out. Meanwhile, environmentalism was a jump ball in domestic politics. Nixon tried to outflank the Democrats' point man on the issue, Senator Edmund Muskie, who, as Hubert Humphrey's running mate in 1968, was a leading contender to challenge Nixon for the White House in 1972. As chairman of the Senate Public Works Committee, Muskie had been the moving force behind the 1967 Clean Air Act, which so far hadn't produced much progress (or so it was commonly believed—data suggest that some forms of air pollution, especially sulfur dioxide, were falling sharply in the late 1960s). Muskie preferred an incremental approach to environmental legislation, and actually opposed having a one-size-fits-all national standard for air quality. But when the Nixon administration proposed a more ambitious clean air bill that would set national standards, Muskie was not going to be left behind, and a typical legislative-executive bidding war ensued. This was a bidding war that Nixon could not possibly win, as Muskie changed tactics and embraced a far-reaching bill that mandated national air quality standards *without regard to cost*. Nixon had wanted cost-benefit analysis to be at the heart of any regulatory strategy, but was not about to veto a clean air law that lacked such a feature. The environmental bidding war went well beyond just the Clean Air Act. Nixon proposed 36 different environmental laws—Congress turned down most of these—and proclaimed the first "Earth Week" in 1971. "Just keep me out of trouble on environmental issues," Nixon is reported to have said to his domestic policy adviser John Ehrlichman.[66] (Nixon does not make a single mention of the environment or the EPA in his 1,100-page memoirs.)

The coming of environmentalism marked more than just a turning point in domestic politics; it also marked a decisive turning point in the nature of government regulation with far-reaching constitutional implications. Hitherto the object of government regulation was to ensure *fairness*—fairness to competitors and potential competitors, and fairness to consumers. The regulatory goal of fairness was clearly a derivative of the idea of equal rights and equal opportunity that is central to American political life.

The new regulation starting in the 1970s was more ambitious and social in nature, and a marked departure from the old kind of regulation. Nixon's creation of the EPA, which was cobbled together from parts of other federal agencies by executive order, marked the beginning of a regulatory revolution. No other federal agency has ever been created in this fashion. Nixon had first wanted an act of Congress to create a cabinet-level Department of Environment and Natural Resources, but abandoned the plan because he feared congressional opposition. Others in the Nixon White House thought the new EPA should be more like the National Institutes of Health, conducting research and recommending environmental standards and strategies for Congress to incorporate in legislation. But Nixon wanted EPA to be an operating and enforcement-oriented agency. Ironically, the EPA that emerged would be a more powerful agency than a cabinet-level department, because unlike a cabinet department that is under the authority of the White House, the EPA would enjoy more independence as a mere *administrative* agency.

The most striking aspect of the EPA and other regulatory agencies created contemporaneously (such as the Consumer Product Safety Commission and the Occupational Safety and Health Administration) is that they were the first agencies with a mandate to range widely throughout the economy and set their own policy strategies largely without the deliberation of, or input from, Congress. The Consumer Product Safety Commission initially contemplated regulating swimming pools, tricycles, artificial turf, and women's platform shoes. The CPSC's first chairman, Richard Simpson, remarked that "It's possible to make this a complete witch-hunt. . . . I suppose if there were enough complaints about the hazards of wearing maxi-coats, we could even regulate length."[67] OSHA briefly became the laughing stock of Washington when it decreed that horseshoe-shaped toilet seats were unsafe and would have to be replaced. OSHA backed down in the face of ridicule.

Throughout the previous decades of the twentieth century, government regulatory agencies had always been highly specific to narrow aims and usually a single industry; the Securities and Exchange Commission and the Food and Drug Administration are good examples of the old kind of regulation. (The one prior exception to single-industry regulation—the Federal Trade Commission, created in 1916—is the exception that proves the rule. Its undefined, wide-ranging scope caused Congress and the executive branch to curb its power within a few years of its creation.) Not only was the EPA without specific statutory basis, but the term "environment" was never defined in Nixon's reorganization plan that created the agency. Nixon thought these matters should be left for the EPA's administrator to decide.

The trouble with leaving "the environment" undefined is that it leaves humankind's place in it ambiguous. Are humans part of "the environment," and therefore the object for whom the agency was created? (In other words, is the EPA just a glorified public health agency?) Or is "the environment" a transcendent category, in which case the EPA may regulate in the interests of nature herself? The lack of congressional deliberation and a specific statutory mission has made the EPA a battleground for the competing views of what "the environment" comprises. For example, some members of Congress in 1970 wondered whether the EPA might claim jurisdiction over population control (a Nixon-appointed commission had, after all, doubted whether rising population was of any future benefit to the United States).

Ironically, Muskie had proposed a bill in Congress that would have created an "Environmental Quality Administration." Muskie's bill would have demanded from Congress a detailed statement of the agency's goals and purposes, and would have included a congressional intent to balance environmental protection with economic growth, a proviso without which Muskie judged that the proposal would fail. Muskie's "EQA" would have been a more circumspect agency than Nixon's EPA. But Muskie's bill never even got a committee hearing. (A similar proposal in 1967 had been opposed by, of all people, Bobby Kennedy.)

Quite aside from the ideological battles that would swirl around the EPA and other new quasi-independent, economy-wide regulatory agencies was the question of how this new kind of regulation changed the relations of citizens to their national government. For under the new regulation, administrative questions that had always been strictly local in character were centralized in the federal bureaucracy. The EPA's earliest mission was essentially a public works program to build new sewers and water treatment plants throughout the nation. Hardly a single yard of sewer line was subsequently laid without the direct involvement and supervision of the EPA. The centralization of previously local decisions had a necessarily degrading effect on state and local government, and contributed to the rising sense of remoteness from government that has increasingly plagued American public life over the last generation. All of this happened, to repeat, largely without any kind of fundamental, substantive debate about the principles of the new regulation. As this regulation was extended further and further during the 1970s, a backlash would grow into a potent force.

In many ways the regulatory revolution was President Nixon's most profound legacy. "Probably more new regulation was imposed on the economy during the Nixon administration than in any other presidency since the New Deal," wrote Herbert Stein, who served on Nixon's Council of Economic Advisers.[68] Stein never bothered to count up the new agencies, or he would have removed the "probably" from the front of his sentence. Between 1970 and 1974, eight new independent regulatory agencies, and eight new agencies within the executive branch were created. In addition, 13 existing independent agencies, and 22 executive branch agencies, were substantially reformed and strengthened during these years. It represented a vast expansion and centralization of government power, reaching down to local and remote reaches of the private economy; these new or expanded agencies represent nearly three-quarters of the regulatory apparatus of the federal government. Certainly this was the aspect of "big government" that would prove the most vexing and intractable to the reformers of the Reagan administration 10 years later and to congressional Republicans today. This was not obvious then or now because of the murkiness surrounding the constitutional status of the new economy-wide "social" regulation and the abstract issue of the violation of the separation of powers implied by this kind of activity. Such abstruse questions do not make for good front page or TV news copy. The controversies over the nature and reach of federal regulation would remain relatively opaque for several more years. In the meantime, bread-and-butter economic policy was becoming a much more transparent and urgent preoccupation of the nation. And if Nixon's social and regulatory policy was baffling and frustrating to conservatives, his economic policy would turn out to be an even greater source of consternation.

THE ECONOMY has always been the political Achilles' heel for Republicans. The long shadow of Herbert Hoover reached all the way to the White House early in Nixon's first term. In retrospect it can be seen that Nixon's travails over economic policy represented the key transitional period in modern economic theory and practice, opening the way to the policies that successfully revived economic growth with low inflation in the 1980s and 1990s. But this was not evident to Nixon at the time, and the nation paid a fearsome price.

In the early months of the Nixon administration it appeared that the economy was getting back on track after the crisis of March 1968. Unemployment, which had been a tiny 3.5 percent on the eve of the 1968 election, had fallen to 3.3 percent by inauguration day in January. Nixon tacitly endorsed the Keynesian premise with the only sentence in his inaugural address that mentioned the economy: "We have learned at last to manage a modern economy to assure its continued growth." But after Nixon approvingly used the phrase "fine tuning" at an early press conference, his top economic advisers took him aside and said, "That's not what we do; that's what the other people believe in doing."[69] Nixon was restive with conventional economics, however; a fan of the long bomb in football, Nixon referred scornfully to the economics of "three yards and a cloud of dust."

The problem of the present moment was that inflation was running high; it had stood at 5 percent on election day in 1968, and has heading higher. Conventional Keynesian economics held that the only way to stem inflation was to dampen aggregate demand by raising taxes, cutting spending, or some combination of the two. The premise of this policy was embodied in the infamous Phillips Curve, which held that inflation and unemployment existed in an inverse relationship. Reducing one required putting up with more of the other. Keynesianism prescribed the economic equivalent of chemotherapy through the levers of government tax and spending policy, and was what Johnson had attempted with the 10 percent income tax surcharge in 1968.

Milton Friedman, the leader of the Monetarist school that argued that fiscal policy was irrelevant to inflation and unemployment, had correctly predicted that Johnson's tax increase would fail to stem rising inflation, and when his prediction was vindicated by events, people started taking notice of Monetarism as an alternative to Keynesianism. In a later age, Friedman's message might have been boiled down to a bumper sticker: "It's the monetary policy, stupid!" Although the importance of the Federal Reserve's monetary policy was becoming more evident, there was still a lot of murkiness about how policy should change. The Fed's inflation-fighting strategy of constricting monetary growth still seemed to operate according to the Phillips Curve, after all. Cutting the growth of the money supply would bump up unemployment to some extent. With unemployment at 3.3 percent, it seemed that a modest increase would be politically tolerable if inflation came down. Fed Chairman William McChesney Martin duly clamped down on the money supply.

Friedman's theory that steady monetary growth would achieve an equilibrium point, which he called the "non-accelerating inflation rate of unemployment" (NAIRU), was gaining acceptance among some of Nixon's White House advisers, especially Friedman's close friend, Labor Secretary George Shultz. Shultz and others convinced Nixon that a "steady-as-she-goes" policy of bringing inflation down first and then resuming a steady rate of monetary growth would restore the economy to its mid-1960s condition of full employment with low inflation. Sure enough, unemployment went up as the economy appeared clearly headed for a cyclical recession, long overdue after more than 90 months of expansion—a new record at the time. Unemployment unexpectedly jumped one-half percent in September; housing starts fell by a quarter.

With unemployment rising amid concern that monetary growth was too slow, Nixon succeeded at last in getting his man Arthur Burns installed as chairman of the Federal Reserve in January 1970. "The Fed has the fate of the economy in its hands," Nixon remarked after Burns' swearing-in. Burns led a sharply divided Fed to ease up on the tight money policy of the previous few months. While Nixon still hoped that a severe recession could be avoided (by spring the economy had suffered two quarters of declining output—the official definition of recession), a stubborn problem remained: Inflation had not come down. While unemployment hovered around 5 percent (it would reach 6 percent within a year), inflation was still running well over 5 percent. The nation was getting its first taste of unprecedented phenomena that would later be known as "stagflation"—slow growth with both high inflation and high unemployment.

As 1970 gave way to 1971, an inflationary spiral appeared to be gaining momentum, especially in the form of large wage increases for unionized workers. Construction industry wages went up nearly 20 percent in 1970; railroad workers gained a stunning 42 percent wage increase to be phased in over 42 months. A threatened strike led to a 30 percent wage boost for steelworkers over three years, which cascaded into an immediate price hike for steel products. (Private sector wage levels overall had risen

22 percent in the previous three years, but federal employee wages had risen by 35 percent during the same period. Perhaps Nixon was looking at the wrong culprit.) Corporate profits were eroding nonetheless. "For one of the rare times in U.S. history," *Time* magazine noted in 1971, "almost everyone feels less well off than he was several years ago." Suddenly the chattering classes began talking about the need for an "incomes policy," a wage and price review board of some kind, and perhaps even direct wage and price controls. *Newsweek,* among others, attacked Nixon's "Do-Nothing Economic Plan," and editorial cartoonists relished the theme of Richard Milhous Hoover.

The polls looked dismal. A Harris Poll in January had found 68 percent disapproved of Nixon's handling of the economy, with only 28 percent expressing approval. By summer Nixon's disapproval rating on the economy had slipped to 73 percent, and consumer confidence fell to its lowest level since 1957, with only 27 percent telling a Sindlinger poll that they wanted to see Nixon re-elected in 1972.

Democrats thought they saw a wedge. "Like piranha fish slashing at a wounded cow," *Time* observed in early August, "Democrats of all stripes were on the attack last week on the issue they now think will decide next year's election: the floundering U.S. economy."[70] Senate Majority Leader Mike Mansfield publicly came out in favor of wage and price controls. It wasn't just the Democrats; a number of prominent Republicans were beating the drums for drastic government action. David Rockefeller endorsed wage and price controls in May of 1971, and even Senate Republicans started pressuring the White House for some kind of "incomes policy." Twelve Republican senators announced plans to introduce legislation to create a wage and price review board of some kind. But Democrats, as always, were out ahead on the government remedy front. They pushed successfully in Congress to give Nixon the power to impose wage and price controls in what was seen at the time as a cynical attempt to corner Nixon. No one thought Nixon would actually invoke such power. In 1965 Nixon said "The lesson that government price fixing doesn't work is never learned." He had attacked wage and price controls in the 1968 campaign, and spoke often of his firsthand frustrations with wage and price controls during World War II. "I will not take this nation down the road of wage and price controls," Nixon reiterated, "however politically expedient that may seem."[71] But with an election looming barely 16 months ahead, some White House fingers were itchy to hit the panic button.

The itchiest trigger finger belonged to Treasury Secretary John Connally, the Texas Democrat with whom Nixon was fascinated and enamoured. Nixon had installed Connally at Treasury following the 1970 elections. (Nixon sent a miffed George Bush to be U.S. Ambassador to the United Nations as a consolation prize, as Connally had worked on behalf of Lloyd Bentsen to defeat Bush in the Texas Senate race.) "Connally's swaggering self-assurance," Henry Kissinger observed, "was Nixon's Walter Mitty image of himself. He was one person whom Nixon never denigrated behind his back."[72] "The arrival of Connally," Herbert Stein reflected, "contributed greatly to the probability that the Nixon administration would end with [wage and price] controls."[73]

Although Nixon was perceived in public as having a "Do-Nothing Economic Plan," behind the scenes he was maneuvering to counteract what he saw as sluggishness at the Fed. Although the Fed had eased up on the money supply, Nixon and his advisers feared it wasn't enough to get the economy growing again. Burns had unaccountably left the team, blaming the administration for the economy's sluggishness and publicly calling for some kind of incomes policy to thwart inflation. Nixon responded with a mix of high and low tactics. The low tactics involved having hatchet man Charles Colson call up prominent New York banker Alan Greenspan to get Greenspan to intervene with Burns. Greenspan sensibly declined to be part of such an intrigue. Colson then planted a false story in the media that Burns was seeking a raise in his own salary even as he was calling for restraint in wage increases for everyone else. Nixon had to undo the damage with a public statement defending Burns.

On a more substantive level, Nixon decided to do what he could to stimulate the economy with the federal budget. In January 1971 he submitted a big spending budget that would have made Lyndon Johnson blush. It deliberately planned for an $11 billion deficit. Budgets from the previous three years had come in with deficits as high as $25 billion on account of the war and deteriorating economic conditions, but none had set out to have a deficit as big as Nixon's prospective 1972 budget. He explained himself to Howard K. Smith of ABC News: "I am now a Keynesian in economics." It was like, an astonished Smith said later, "a Christian crusader saying, 'All things considered, I think Mohammed was right."[74] But Nixon meant it; he explained that he planned to spend as much as would be spent were the economy at full employment—the classic Keynesian prescription. Nixon had clearly expressed a preference to downgrade the fight against inflation for the sake of economic growth (and re-election).

George Shultz and others in the White House still held out hope that steady monetary policy would lead to revived economic growth and a moderation of the inflation rate. "What we need now to complete the treatment," Shultz told Friedman, "is the time and the guts to take the time, not additional medicine."[75] But the political pressure had become overwhelming, and time had run out for the gradual "steady as she goes" policy. Connally and several senior Treasury officials headed by Paul Volcker began quietly readying plans to impose a temporary wage and price freeze. All that remained was the timing of the plan.

Concern turned to panic in mid-August when rumors in the foreign currency markets that the United States might devalue the dollar touched off a run against the dollar very similar to what happened in March of 1968. The final straw came when Great Britain demanded a guarantee that its dollar holdings could be converted into gold by the United States at the existing fixed exchange rate of $35 an ounce. While Connally put off the British, Nixon hastily called for a weekend meeting of his economic team at Camp David to resolve the crisis. "This could be the most important weekend in the history of economics since March 4, 1933," Herbert Stein told William Safire as they boarded the helicopter for Camp David. It happened to be Friday the 13th.

The package that emerged over the weekend included "closing the gold window" and allowing the value of the dollar to float in the international exchange market, some tax cuts for business, and a 10 percent tariff on imports. The final element of the package was the one that captured the headlines and the imagination of the public: a 90-day wage and price freeze. It was ironically the least debated feature of the package over the weekend: Shultz's main argument against controls at the 11th hour— "How do you stop it when you start?"—was brushed aside as if it was a rhetorical question. Closing the gold window was the real centerpiece of the package, and represented the end of the post–World War II international monetary system known as Bretton Woods. Fed Chairman Arthur Burns opposed the move, predicting that the stock market would crash and that *Pravda* would have a field day by saying the abandonment of the gold standard was a sure sign of the collapse of capitalism. Above all, abandoning gold would signal the beginning of the rise of inflation over the rest of the decade.

Nixon stayed up all night on Friday the 13th writing his speech for national TV on Sunday evening. Though he hesitated about pre-empting *Bonanza*, he thought it was necessary to announce the freeze before the markets opened Monday morning. Nixon called his program the "New Economic Policy," apparently oblivious to the irony that Lenin had used the same banner for his economic reversal in the 1920s. Nixon's bold stroke caught everyone by surprise, and was a huge hit with the public. A Gallup Poll found 73 percent of the public approved of the freeze. Editorial reaction was effusive. The *Philadelphia Inquirer* praised Nixon for "an act of courage and statesmanship unparalleled by any U.S. chief executive for at least a third of a century," and the *Baltimore Sun* said Nixon had shown "an activist flexing of government muscles not seen since the early Roosevelt experiments."[76] Even the *New York Times* and the *Washington Post* approved. The Dow Jones Industrial Average jumped 32.9 points the day after Nixon's announcement, the biggest one-day jump in history up to that point. Democrats who had been calling for strong measures, and who had granted Nixon the authority to impose a freeze through executive order, were flummoxed. It was as if, a *Time* reporter put it, Nixon had "opened their closet and stolen their shoes." Having given Nixon the sole discretion and authority, congressional Democrats were not in position to share any of the public credit for the bold move.

Milton Friedman was practically alone in dissenting over the freeze. He wrote in *Newsweek* that Nixon "has a tiger by the tail. Reluctant as he was to grasp it, he will find it hard to let go. The outcome, I fear, will be a further move toward the kind of detailed control of prices and wages that Mr. Nixon has resisted so courageously for so long. . . . The result is likely to be more inflationary pressure, not less."[77] (About the only major newspaper that shared Friedman's view was the *Los Angeles Times,* which worried "whether we might be starting down the road to a permanently regimented economy.") But even Friedman came to admit later that political circumstances had become irresistible for Nixon. The public enthusiasm for price controls, Herbert Stein observed, "shows how shallow was the general support for the basic characteristics of a free market economy."[78] The free marketeers in the administration tried to put the best face on their defeat, telling *Newsweek:* "Well, we lost the race. But at least the people who are going to have to administer this whole mess—the controls and all—are people who genuinely believe in a free market and will try to get back to it as fast as possible."[79]

The obvious fallacy is that not even smart capitalists can make socialism work, and beneath the layer of public popularity, the freeze was a mess. The World War II Office of Price Administration (for which a young Richard Nixon worked briefly) required more than 250,000 paid and volunteer employees to operate. Nixon hoped to avoid "the establishment of a huge price control bureaucracy," and instead hoped to rely "on the voluntary cooperation of all Americans." This was a sham. If you didn't voluntarily comply, the government had the legal authority to make you comply. Among other federal agencies mobilized to police the freeze was the IRS, though the principal government enforcement agency was the Office of Emergency Preparedness, which was woefully unprepared for this emergency duty. A light touch of fascism emerged, as when the director of the Cost of Living Council said that "The citizen's role in this program is to rat on his neighbor if his neighbor violated the controls."[80] And although the freeze ended after 90 days, price controls of various kinds were to last for three years.

Soon the two government bodies (the Price Commission and the Pay Board) established to administer "Phase II" wage and price adjustments after the 90-day freeze ended were involved in arbitrary hairsplitting decisions about various kinds of products and whether their prices would be allowed to rise. Raw farm produce was exempted from the freeze and subsequent controls because of the seasonally fluctuating nature of the farm produce economy, but processed foods were not exempt. This led to some comic dilemmas that can only occur under bureaucratic control of the economy: raw cucumbers were exempt, but pickled cucumbers were not. Were shucked almonds considered "processed food"? (The answer was: maybe.) Oranges were exempt, but frozen orange juice would remain just that.

The program was so complicated that the Price Commission received 400,000 requests for clarification in the first two weeks. As always, clever operators found easy ways to get around price guidelines. Manufacturers, for example, simply made small modifications to products, called them "new," and charged a higher price. Some companies got around the wage guidelines through the simple expedient of "promoting" people to a new job description. There was no practical way the government could contain this kind of innovation and ingenuity in a modern economy.

In hindsight nearly everyone agrees that wage and price controls were a mistake. Nixon wrote in his memoirs that although controls were "politically necessary and immensely popular in the short run . . . in the long run I believe that it was wrong." The irony of the episode is that the steady-as-she-goes policy of gradualism was about to pay off. Historian Allen Matusow wrote that "There was a logic at work that would have unwound inflation in the months ahead even without controls." When inflation revived again in the months after the 1972 election, Nixon's policies seemed all the more ineffective. But it was only a prelude for the downward spiral of the rest of the decade. As Matusow has observed: "Through most of the rest of the 1970s the 6 percent unemployment rate and 5 percent inflation rate of 1971 would seem less the evidence of a failed policy than an outcome devoutly to be wished."[81]

One reason the 1971 unemployment and inflation rate would shortly be viewed with nostalgia is that the next great shock to the United States and world economy was imminent—the "energy crisis." The common perception is that the Arab oil embargo of 1973–74 and subsequent market discipline of the OPEC oil cartel caused the energy crisis of the 1970s, but in fact it was more a creation of government price controls and heavy regulation of the market for energy. What would have been a sharp but short adjustment in world energy markets was prolonged by government into a decade-long pandemic. This was the most important legacy of wage and price controls.

Government manipulation of the domestic oil market had a long pedigree. Oil import quotas had been in place since the late 1950s ironically because foreign oil was much cheaper than domestically produced oil at that time—about $2 a barrel, compared to about $3.30 a barrel in the U.S. (Foreign oil would remain cheaper right up until the Arab embargo in 1973.) It was thought necessary to prop up the domestic oil industry, so under the pretext of "national security" oil import quotas were imposed that limited the total amount of oil that could be imported, and allocated the quotas among refiners in the interest of fairness. Throughout the 1960s the problem in the domestic oil market was surplus, not scarcity; some states, like Texas, attempted to keep the market price up by limiting the number of days each month that oil could be pumped out of the ground. Amidst this stagnant price outlook for domestic oil, domestic oil exploration and production sagged.

By the late 1960s the market for petroleum began to tighten as energy demand grew rapidly in the United States and elsewhere. An energy shortage of some magnitude was on the way for the United States; by 1972 oil provided for nearly half of the nation's energy needs, and imported oil accounted for nearly 30 percent of the nation's total petroleum usage. Oil imports from the Middle East were soaring—they had grown by 50 percent in 1973 alone, and the price was up to about $3.50 a barrel. Soon, some experts predicted, the Soviet Union and its Eastern Bloc satellites might begin to import oil from the Middle East, which would exert upward pressure on the world market price. Some saw ominous portents in these trends. "What is going on today," a senior government official told *U.S. News and World Report* in 1969, "will turn the power politics of the world upside down."

Nixon's price controls had already had a highly disruptive effect on the energy market; prices for heating oil were frozen in August of 1971, when prices were typically low because of ordinary seasonal fluctuation in demand. Conversely, gasoline prices were frozen at their seasonal high point. By the winter of 1972, the nation had too much gasoline and not enough heating oil. At the time the Cost of Living Council administered these controls on the price of oil and petroleum products, its "energy desk" had no economists and little expertise in oil markets; in those days, Herbert Stein remarked, "an energy expert was a person who knew that Abu Dhabi was a place and Qaddafi was a person."

The rising price of imported oil had the effect of turning the U.S. government's oil price regulation scheme on its head: What was once used chiefly to keep the price of domestic oil *above* the world price in the interest of oil producers was now used to keep the price of domestic oil *below* the world price in the interest of consumers. Controlling the price of domestic oil created an obvious disincentive for new exploration and production in the United States, which would lead to growing dependency on foreign oil, so the regulators contrived a two-tier price scheme that further distorted the energy market. "New" oil could be produced and sold at the world market price, while "old" oil from existing sources would still be sold at the controlled price. To make sure that everyone from refiners down to individual gas stations got their fair share of oil and petroleum products at the controlled price (so that refiners with access to low-priced "old" oil wouldn't reap windfall profits over refiners who did not), the regulators devised a system for allocating "old" and "new" oil among refiners that, in Stein's phrase, became "an immense Rube Goldberg structure." These controls, Stein argued, would not have been so extensive had the entire wage and price control program of August 1971 not happened.

This control mechanism was already in place when the Arab oil embargo was announced in October of 1973. (In light of events 20 years later, it is ironic to note that Iraq did not join the other Arab nations in the embargo, and neither did Iran, a non-Arab nation.) By Christmas OPEC was able to dictate a price of $11.65 a barrel, a 470 percent increase for the year. Although the lifting of the oil embargo at some point in 1974 was a foregone conclusion, the Nixon administration dreaded the price jolt that higher oil prices would send throughout the entire economy. So in addition to expanding the price and supply controls, Nixon added a public relations component reminiscent of World War II: He asked that gas stations close on Sundays. As long lines became the norm at gas stations throughout the nation, the Senate came within eight votes of instituting wartime-style gasoline rationing. Nixon opposed rationing, but had the Bureau of Engraving and Printing print up 10 billion rationing coupons just in case. Letting the market adjust freely to the new world price was thought unacceptable; one government study predicted that gasoline would rise to more than $1.50 a gallon if controls were lifted. Better, in the name of fairness to the poor, to put up with gas lines and shortages than allow the market to clear. Allen Matusow notes that Canada took the opposite approach; its eastern provinces, almost wholly dependent on imported oil, did not impose price or supply controls, and saw its gasoline price stabilize at 59 cents a U.S. gallon. Canada had no gas lines.[82]

Nixon's entire price control scheme was eventually abandoned except for oil. Even as the world adjusted to higher-priced oil and supply began to even out, the U.S. system of price controls on oil were extended for the rest of the 1970s, a ticking time bomb that guaranteed a recurrence of the "energy crisis." With the price of oil and petroleum products held artificially low, American consumers reverted to their old preferences for big, low-mileage cars. Over the next five years, sales of smaller, high-mileage cars slumped, and the big car divisions of the automakers reported record profits.

IT IS TIME to catch up with the Cold War, which reached a major turning point in the Nixon years. The Cuban Missile Crisis of 1962 has come to be regarded as the key event leading to the first thaw in the Cold War 10 years later, and the aftermath of that infamous confrontation seems to lend verisimilitude to the conventional narrative. President Kennedy's guarantee that the United States would not invade Cuba was seen as a small *political* victory for the Soviet Union, but on balance the outcome was represented as a *military* humiliation for Soviet Premier Nikita Khrushchev. The Kennedy White House heavily spun the outcome that way, even to the point of concealing for a time that Kennedy had also agreed to remove American Jupiter missiles from NATO countries.

Indeed, Khrushchev's reckless Cuban "adventure" was ostensibly prominent among the reasons the Soviet Presidium ousted him in October 1964 in what Soviet scholar Adam Ulam called "a virtual coup d'etat," to be replaced by Leonid Brezhnev.[83] The records of that Presidium meeting remain closed to Western researchers, so the proportionality of the reasons for Khrushchev's ouster will remain murky. The breach with China apparently weighed heavily on the minds of the Presidium, and Khrushchev's "hare-brained scheme" in Cuba may have provided an additional superficial excuse to purge the last of the old Stalinist retinue from Soviet leadership, in order to make way for an ambitious younger cohort. Ridding themselves of Khrushchev's crude shoe-pounding bluster certainly enabled the Soviets to conduct themselves in a more low-key manner henceforth, although their international behavior changed little. Regardless, Khrushchev's bold gamble and subsequent ouster obscured the fact that Cuba's future as a Soviet ally—and military asset—was secured. The extremity of the crisis had the effect of making future Soviet activities in Cuba, such as frequent submarine and surface fleet visits, combat aircraft flights, and even small troop deployments, seem like small potatoes, not worth getting excited about.

The Cold War took its first steps toward détente in the aftermath of Cuba. In the spring of 1963 Kennedy gave a conciliatory speech about Soviet-American relations, which for the first time since the end of World

War II mentioned the Soviet contribution in the war effort. In the summer of 1963 the direct phone link known as the "hot line" was established to allow for instant communications. (During the Cuban crisis messages back and forth sometimes took several hours to get through.) Three days before he was shot in Dallas, Kennedy confided to a friend that he intended to be the first American president to visit the Kremlin after his presumed re-election in 1964.

The most important step, however, was the agreement on a long-delayed atmospheric nuclear test ban treaty in 1963. This opened a new chapter in the crusade for "arms control," which had limped through the 1950s as a sentimental cause but was now to become the principal focus of U.S.-Soviet diplomacy. Anxiety over "The Bomb" had led to the view that nuclear weapons themselves were an inherently destabilizing force in world affairs, and that peace therefore depended on arms control.

Early American proposals, from the Baruch plan for international control of nuclear technology to Eisenhower's "opens skies" proposal, were non-starters with the Soviet Union, and no responsible American government was going to enter an arms control agreement with the Soviets that could not be verified. But in the early 1960s Americans thought the coming of satellite technology meant that there was some prospect that arms control agreements might now be verifiable (notwithstanding the total secrecy of the Soviet Union, where even telephone directories remained state secrets). Kennedy established an Arms Control and Disarmament Agency within the State Department (which was later split off to be independent of State), thus ensuring that arms control ideology would have a bureaucratic advocacy interest in the perpetuation and expansion of "the process."

The arms control "community" (as it came to call itself) came to have a reflexive bias for accommodation and concession, even to the point of arguing that additional American military strength would be a source of worry to our allies. Arms control was necessary, in the first instance, to avoid an "arms race," which would be wastefully expensive as well as providing no additional security for either side. The central axiom of arms control theology was that the logic of mutual assured destruction (MAD) must be as compelling to the Soviet Union as it was to us, and therefore all negotiations should have a mutual acceptance of MAD as their premise. The Soviets would surely respond to our "restraint." No arms configurations or articulated strategic doctrine to the contrary from the Soviets could jar American arms control enthusiasts from this view. (The CIA would conclude in 1976 that "Mutual assured destruction as a desirable and lasting basis for a stable strategic nuclear relationship between superpowers has never been accepted in the USSR."[84])

This new momentum for arms control clashed directly with a nuclear modernization program that had begun under Eisenhower. The United States was in the midst of building 1,000 Inter-Continental Ballistic Missiles (ICBMs) and 40 missile firing submarines at the time of the Cuban missile crisis; the Soviets, by contrast, had a mere 14 deployable ICBMs at the time of the Cuban crisis. This situation was about to change dramatically. Whatever else the new guard in the Soviet Union may have had in mind by purging Khrushchev, it became evident within the next few years that the Soviet Union meant to close this gap so that they need never have to back down again on account of manifest nuclear inferiority. Indeed, it became apparent that the Soviet Union was aiming for superiority in strategic weaponry, which they might plausibly achieve because the end of the U.S. strategic buildup was in sight.

Throughout the rest of the 1960s American defense planners watched in dismay as the Soviets developed a new generation a long range ballistic missiles capable of carrying larger warheads, and which were deployed in hardened silos that would be difficult to attack. The CIA had predicted that the Soviets would respond to U.S. "restraint" by curtailing their own arms buildup. McNamara confidently declared that "the Soviets have decided that they have lost the quantitative" arms race, and that they "are not seeking to engage us in that contest. . . . There is no indication that the Soviets are seeking to develop a strategic nuclear force as large as ours." Instead, the Soviets set out to build a *superior* force with startling speed. It became apparent that by 1980 the Soviet Union would have the capability to deliver 5,000 warheads by missile at the United States. While the United States was targeting its new missiles at the Soviet Union's population centers in accordance with its new doctrine of deterrence through mutual assured destruction the Soviet Union was targeting U.S. military sites in what appeared to be a war fighting strategy.

The rise of the "arms control process" as the centerpiece of U.S.-Soviet relations proved to be the perfect talisman for the increasing demoralization of U.S. foreign policy. By the time Nixon assumed office in

1969, the political fractiousness that had made a ruin of domestic policy over the previous decade was also beginning to make a ruin of foreign policy as well. The Vietnam controversy was merely the catalyst for a wholesale attack on American foreign policy. The unpopularity of Vietnam provided cover for calls to reduce defense spending dramatically, even as a major Soviet arms buildup continued apace. More fundamental, the theoretical basis of American foreign policy—containment—came to be increasingly doubted by the mainstream Establishment, a clear sign that the fevers of the radical Left were contagious. Maybe, it was commonly heard, the tension in East-West relations really was just a matter of misunderstanding, or, even worse, maybe the Cold War was the fault of the United States in the first place. Above all, the popular line unfolded, we must understand that the Soviets are deeply "insecure"; Soviet leadership was supposedly divided between "hawks" and "doves" just like U.S. leadership, and therefore any bellicose noises from the West would only strengthen the hawks over the doves in the Kremlin.

Hence, as Henry Kissinger observed, "The new Nixon Administration was the first of the postwar generation that had to conduct foreign policy without the national consensus that had sustained its predecessors largely since 1947."[85] This circumstance ironically suited Nixon and Kissinger just fine, for they wanted to embark on a new direction based on a finely balanced sense of "realism." It would produce a highly ambiguous legacy. No one doubted Nixon's anti-Communist credentials, yet keepers of the anti-Communist faith who thought Nixon would stanch the growing demoralization of the West would be disappointed. Nixon thought that the end of the Cold War might be in sight, that a political settlement for permanent co-existence could be reached. Yet embracing co-existence as a *principle* instead of as a practical concession to military strength meant dropping the ideological competition between the West and its Communist enemies. "Our objective," Kissinger wrote in his memoirs, "was to purge our foreign policy of all sentimentality. . . . Co-existence on the basis of the balance of forces should therefore be within our grasp. . . ."[86] Here we see one of the paradoxes of modern American politics: Although ideological conservatives are the most fervent anti-Communists, mainstream Republicans, who typically represent a more practical, commercial-minded conservatism, tended to regard the Soviet Union in less ideological terms, sort of like, in Norman Podhoretz's memorable phrase, "a Federal Trade Commission with nuclear weapons." We can do business—literally and figuratively—with the Soviets according to this view.

Although Nixon's approach undoubtedly created new practical difficulties for the Soviet Union and its allies, the "de-moralization" of American foreign policy does not fit well with the historically moral character—the "sentimental" character, to use Kissinger's term—of America's place in the world. American foreign policy has always oscillated between idealism and realism; the two great American talents, D. H. Lawrence is reported to have said, are saving the world and fixing the plumbing. But over the long run the idealistic side must always dominate in a democracy founded on the universal creed that "all men are created equal." Abandoning the idealistic basis for anti-Communism in the long twilight struggle of the Cold War would be, William F. Buckley Jr. argued in 1970, "a callousing experience . . . a lesion of our moral conscience, the historical effects of which cannot be calculated, but they will be bad."[87]

These effects would work themselves out slowly over the next decade. In the near term, Nixon and Kissinger looked like geniuses, reaching the first major arms control agreement with the Soviet Union, opening relations with China, and plotting America's slow-motion withdrawal from Vietnam at the same time. Although Nixon and Kissinger were effective in incorporating the doctrine of "linkage" to their diplomacy (that is, requiring better Soviet behavior elsewhere in the world as a condition of improving relations), their accomplishments nonetheless exacted a share of America's moral capital, and required some twists and turns that seem more the result of chance than design.

THE "DEMORALIZATION" OF foreign policy was a tacit prerequisite for arms control negotiations, because arms control requires that political and military differences be converted into technical questions that can be supposedly resolved without reaching the fundamental causes of international division in the first place. Negotiating the first major arms control agreement in 1972 required the United States to give up the deployment of an anti-ballistic missile (ABM) defense system, which had been long in development, and which candidate Nixon had promised to deploy. The controversy over ABM had a long history prior to Nixon.

Under the sway of MAD and arms-control ideology, Johnson's Defense Secretary Robert McNamara argued that it would be more cost effective to emphasize the nuclear deterrent than it would be to continue to develop ballistic missile defense, which had been in development for more than a decade. (McNamara actually opposed ABM completely, but Congress insisted that ABM development and deployment be carried out.) It would simply cost too much money to deploy an ABM system to protect all the American cities that would be vulnerable to Soviet attack; even if all major cities were protected, McNamara told Congress, nuclear warheads could be exploded in the atmosphere some distance upwind from cities, with drifting fallout doing the dirty work nearly as effectively as a direct hit. Future ABM deployments, therefore, would be limited to protecting key American missile silos, airfields, and submarine bases, but not the American people. It would be a "thin shield," costing no more than $5 billion, and carefully described so as not to give reason for concern to the Soviets. McNamara emphasized that the "thin shield" would be principally designed to protect us from a Chinese nuclear attack, which was supposedly more likely than a Soviet attack.

A few Republicans, private citizen Richard Nixon among them, wondered why, at a time when the United States was spending $24 billion a year to protect the people of South Vietnam, the Johnson administration refused to spend a similar amount to protect the people of the United States. Liberals in Congress opposed even the "thin shield" proposal. Meanwhile, the Soviets began work on an ABM system of their own.

The problem with a limited ABM system is that making ABM a prop for the policy of mutual assured destruction ensured that political support for it would steadily erode. And indeed by the time Nixon was ready to push ahead with ABM deployment in 1969, the mood in Congress had changed. Why support an expensive system that won't protect constituents in your congressional district or home state? ABM became a surrogate for opposition to Vietnam; as Nixon himself put it, opposition to ABM "is the liberals' way of getting back at the generals for Vietnam."

Among the liberals leading the opposition were Senator Ted Kennedy and Minnesota Senator Walter Mondale. Mondale worried that the "uncertainties" would undermine deterrence, while Ted Kennedy, whose can-do brother had committed the nation to the technological challenge of the moon landing, argued against the ABM on grounds that it would be "the single most complex undertaking man has yet set for himself in his time on earth." A full-page newspaper ad read: "From the same people who brought you Vietnam: the anti-ballistic missile system."

Nixon won the legislative battle in the Senate by the barest margin in the fall of 1969—Vice President Agnew had to cast a tie-breaking vote. This turned out to be the high-water mark for ABM; subsequent Congressional votes pared back the system from the originally planned 12 sites to just two. This may have been a major turning point in Nixon and Kissinger's thinking; if Congress was not going to maintain a commitment to strategic superiority, then the United States needed to start making the best arms deal it could with the Soviet Union. Kissinger later admitted as much, telling *The Economist* magazine in a 1979 interview that "starting in 1970 our Defense Department was pleading with us to negotiate a freeze on the Soviets lest the disparity in numbers [of missiles and warheads] would continue to grow. We needed a freeze not only for arms control, but for strategic reasons."[88] The arms race was on, but only one side was running hard.

One of the liberal arguments against ABM was that it would kill the chances for an arms control agreement, which conveniently overlooked the fact that the Soviets had responded to longstanding U.S. invitation to negotiate during the Johnson administration only *after* Johnson had approved the "thin shield" ABM proposal. In 1969 the Soviets waited for the results of the ABM vote before responding to Nixon's invitation to begin arms talks, even though the Soviets themselves had called for arms talks on Inauguration Day. When the Americans and Soviets sat down for their first face-to-face negotiation in Helsinki in November 1969 (the talks that became known as SALT, for Strategic Arms Limitation Talks), the United States expected that the Soviets' top priority would be a limit on MIRV missiles (multiple independent re-entry vehicle—a euphemism for a missile that could carry up to ten nuclear warheads), of which the United States enjoyed technological superiority at the time. But the Soviets had little interest in the MIRV issue, chiefly because they were making great strides in their own MIRV technology. Instead, they were most eager to talk about limiting ABM systems. In fact, at first the Soviets wanted arms talks to focus *only* on ABM systems.

Nixon and Kissinger were in full accord with the arms control concept of mutual assured destruction, and were just as committed to the arms control process as their predecessors. U.S. defense planners foresaw a scenario in which the Soviets might field as many as 8,000 anti-ballistic missiles in their own ABM system, and thought this would upset the doctrine of mutual assured destruction. That U.S. security might be enhanced by a similar system of our own was rejected precisely because it conflicted with MAD doctrine. Nixon and Kissinger regarded the ABM as an ideal bargaining chip with the Soviet Union, and were only too happy to bargain ABM away in exchange for an interim framework for limiting (they thought) intercontinental ballistic missiles. A permanent balance of power between the two superpowers would lead to a more secure world, they thought, than defenses against missile attack.

The SALT-ABM Treaty of 1972 limited each side to just two ABM sites containing no more than 100 anti-missile missiles each. The idea of strategic defense was formally abandoned. Meanwhile, the treaty did not actually limit the number of missiles, but instead limited *launchers,* a distinction that allowed for plenty of mischief and wiggle room on both sides, especially as MIRV technology improved. The first SALT treaty was intended as an interim agreement (it was set to expire in the spring of 1977); the next round of talks, SALT II, would attempt more comprehensive limits on warheads and other means of warhead delivery. SALT II would drag on for seven years under two more presidents, resulting in an unsatisfactory treaty that was never even brought up for a ratification vote by the Senate. By that time, presidential candidate Ronald Reagan was preparing to rethink the premises of MAD, missile defense, and the arms control process. But at the time SALT I was signed and ratified in 1972, it seemed as though Nixon had turned a corner on superpower relations. The Soviets had indeed made arms control concessions in the laborious SALT negotiations in part because of deft Nixon maneuvers with a third power.

JUST A FEW WEEKS into the Nixon administration in 1969, James C. Thomson Jr., a State Department official under Presidents Kennedy and Johnson, wrote in *The Atlantic Monthly:* "The idea of a Washington-Peking détente under the presidency of Richard M. Nixon strains the imagination. Could anything be more bizarre than a Nixon-Mao summit?"[89] No

doubt Thomson had in mind not only the Red-baiting Nixon of long reputation, but also the Nixon who had opposed mainland China's admission to the U.N. as vice president because it "would make a mockery of
the provision of the [U.N.] charter which limits its membership to 'peace-
loving nations,'" and moreover "would give respectability to the Communist regime." China held reciprocal views about Nixon, calling him "a
cunning and crafty swindler and a murderer" when he became president.
But Nixon had been steadily modifying his views during his wilderness
years in the mid-1960s. As early as 1965, Nixon had told a U.S. embassy
official in Singapore that he thought a normalization of relations with
China was possible.

The most clear signal of a New Nixon came with his widely remarked upon 1967 article in *Foreign Affairs* on "Asia After Vietnam."
Nixon noted that the Communist world was starting to fragment, while
the non-Communist nations were evolving rapidly toward a condition
that Nixon described as "dynamic stability." Nixon was beginning to see
the dim outline of future opportunities, which the Johnson administration, wholly fixed upon Vietnam, and the Eurocentric foreign policy establishment were missing. Above all, Nixon wrote, "An American policy
toward Asia must come urgently to grips with the reality of China." He
further stated:

> Taking the long view, we simply cannot afford to leave China forever
> outside the family of nations, there to nurture its fantasies, cherish
> its hates and threaten its neighbors. There is no place on this small
> planet for a billion of its potentially most able people to live in angry
> isolation . . .
>
> The world cannot be safe until China changes. Thus our aim, to
> the extent that we can influence events, should be to induce change.[90]

Nixon wasted little time in setting things in motion after becoming
president. Within two weeks of inauguration Nixon sent a memo to
Kissinger: "I think we should give every encouragement to the idea that
this Administration is seeking rapprochement with the Chinese." Kissinger was initially skeptical or worse, telling his deputy Alexander Haig
that "Our leader has taken leave of reality. . . This crazy guy really does
want to normalize relations with China."[91] Early efforts to open a back
channel for communications were halting and even comical. One Chinese

embassy official in Poland fled fearfully when a U.S. diplomat tried to start a conversation with him at a Warsaw embassy reception. (Chou En Lai later told Kissinger that the unexpected advance had nearly given the Chinese diplomat a heart attack.)

Eventually Pakistan emerged as the principal back channel, though the Pakistanis who served as intermediaries insisted on the quaint practice of delivering handwritten notes in person to Kissinger in Washington, which further delayed an already slow process. (Pakistan would later pay a heavy price for their role in Nixon's China opening, as the Soviet Union would aid India's war effort that resulted in the breakaway of East Pakistan into Bangladesh.) Meanwhile, the United States began sending less and less subtle public signals of their objective, the most significant being the president's 1970 Foreign Policy Report, which referred to China for the first time as the "People's Republic of China" instead of "Communist China" or "Red China." Nixon also ordered the U.S. Information Agency not to produce any material critical of China. Meanwhile, China's ritualistic attacks on American "imperialism" in Vietnam and elsewhere conspicuously started to omit any unflattering personal references to Nixon, while references to Soviet leader Brezhnev continued with their usual tartness.

The project of opening to China took on new urgency as 1969 progressed, when it appeared that China's border skirmishes with the Soviet Union might erupt into full-scale nuclear war. The exact circumstances of the Sino-Soviet border clashes were obscure to Westerners. Kissinger had originally accepted the "fashionable view" that the Chinese were the aggressors in the border skirmishes, but by summer he had changed his mind. The Soviets were deploying massive forces along the Chinese border, and constructing new airfields in Soviet-occupied Mongolia. Satellite intelligence photos showed that several of the most recent clashes took place close to a Soviet railhead but hundreds of miles from any Chinese railhead. "It occurred to me," Kissinger later wrote, "that Chinese military leaders would not have picked such an unpropitious spot to attack."[92] But Kissinger also realized that if the Soviet Union was the aggressor, the United States had a golden opportunity.

Then in August a Soviet diplomat who was lunching with a mid-level State Department official dropped a bombshell into their conversation: What would the U.S. reaction be if the Soviet Union attacked China's nuclear facilities? For a long time the Soviet Union assumed that in any

Sino-Soviet war the United States would take the side of the Soviet Union, and perhaps even aid the Soviet war effort. After all, the Johnson administration seriously considered a preemptive strike against China's nuclear facilities in September 1964 (at the same time they were publicly attacking Goldwater as a reckless adventurer), and went so far as to record in a memorandum that "We believe that there are many possibilities for joint action [against China] with the Soviet Government if that Government is interested."[93] Dean Rusk even took up the idea with Soviet Ambassador Dobrynin, who demurred.

But by 1969 circumstances had changed sufficiently that the National Security Council, whipped to a frenzy by the Soviet query, decided that in the event of a Sino-Soviet war the United States would now take the side of China. This was not unlike the centuries of British policy toward the European continent, in which Britain sought to ally itself with the weaker powers against the strongest imperial power, and above all not to allow a hostile power to control the channel ports of Europe's "low countries" in the Netherlands. The advent of nuclear weapons is too commonly thought to have made geographic considerations of strategy quaint if not obsolete. But the growing nuclear and conventional power of the Soviet Union bolstered its position as the "geographical pivot of the world," as the great British strategist Halford Mackinder called the Eurasian land mass. Now the Chinese could be deployed in the West's containment strategy against this surging Eurasian giant.

The Chinese undoubtedly made a similar strategic calculation. The conventional wisdom in the West was that American presence in Vietnam was inherently threatening to China, and although China publicly said it wanted the United States out of Vietnam, it dawned on Nixon and Kissinger that "China desperately wanted us *in* Asia as a counterweight to the Soviet Union." In fact Vietnam was rapidly evaporating as a serious issue with the Chinese because they were able to perceive that Nixon's Vietnam strategy was a slow-motion bug-out. The Chinese, Kissinger wrote with scarcely concealed bitterness, understood Nixon's Vietnam policy better than Harvard Yard. But if Vietnam was receding as a serious point of contention between the two nations, the issue of Taiwan remained paramount for the Chinese. They were determined to exploit the U.S. opening to achieve the maximum concessions. At one of the earliest diplomatic contacts in Warsaw in 1970, the United States indicated to the Chinese that the United States was ready to make concessions over Taiwan, perhaps starting with China's prospective U.N. membership. Even the notoriously calculating Kissinger reflected that "No government less deserved what was about to happen to it than that of Taiwan. It had been a loyal ally; its conduct toward us had been exemplary."

With this preemptive American concession out of the way at the outset, there began an elaborate game of cat-and-mouse between the United States and China to reach an arrangement for a real meeting of the nation's principals. Through the slow but secure Pakistani back-channel (Nixon and Kissinger still had not told Secretary of State William Rogers of their Chinese overtures), the United States had made some progress toward an invitation for a high-level exchange, and hopefully a summit involving Nixon himself.

Taiwan was the Chinese sticking point, of course. The Chinese struck an intransigent pose, demanding the complete severance of U.S. support for Taiwan. In the early months of 1971 the Chinese fell silent, failing to respond to Nixon's latest messages. During this interval the Chinese showed that they could be as skillful at subtle political maneuvering as Americans. The announcement that China's Ping-Pong team would participate in an international tournament in Japan in April of 1970 raised eyebrows within American diplomatic circles, as the Chinese had deliberately isolated themselves from Japan above all.

Toward the end of the tournament the Chinese stunned the American team with an invitation to visit China after the tournament was over. The out-of-the-loop State Department reported to the White House: "Though we have no way of being sure, this invitation may be intended at least in part as a gesture in response to recent U.S. initiatives." (It is hard to say whether Taiwan or the U.S. State Department suffered the greater humiliation from the entire China episode.) The U.S. Ping-Pong team was astonished to be received formally by Chou En-lai himself in the Great Hall of the People. During the visit, a Chinese official sidled up to an American reporter and inquired whether several prominent Democrats including Senators Ted Kennedy, George McGovern, and Edmund Muskie (Nixon's likely opponents in the 1972 election) might be interested in being invited to China. The subtle message—that China might deal with Democrats instead of or in addition to Nixon—was not lost on the White House, which quickly scrambled to press upon the Chinese the necessity of dealing with Nixon alone.

A few weeks after the Ping-Pong team's visit, the Chinese responded at last, softening slightly their demanding language about Taiwan and inviting a U.S. emissary to come to Beijing to prepare the way for Nixon to visit. Nixon and Kissinger huddled over who should go. One suggestion was U.N. Ambassador George Bush, or perhaps Nelson Rockefeller. One person ruled out was Secretary of State Rogers; Nixon wanted the world to know that this was his triumph alone, and not the product of the foreign policy establishment. (So complete was Nixon's distrust of the State Department that he insisted only Chinese interpreters be used on his visit. But translators were somewhat redundant, as Premier Chou En-lai was nearly fluent in English.) Nixon wanted the trip to be secret no matter who went, so he settled upon Kissinger himself as the emissary. Kissinger's secret July trip to Beijing by way of Pakistan, which involved Kissinger faking a stomach ailment and "recuperating" at a secluded mountain retreat outside Islamabad to mislead the press as to his whereabouts, was the first great episode contributing to the subsequent Kissinger mystique.

Kissinger was clearly captivated, so to speak, by his Chinese hosts. "Chou En-lai," Kissinger wrote, "was one of the two or three most impressive men I have ever met. Urbane, infinitely patient, extraordinarily intelligent, subtle, he moved through our discussions with an easy grace that penetrated to the essence of our new relationship as if there were no sensible alternative. . . . Two ideological enemies presented their respective views on the world with a frankness rarely achieved among allies and with a depth that one experiences only in the presence of a great man."[94] Kissinger showed up in Beijing with a fat briefing book to guide his negotiations; Chou had but a single sheet of paper with a few notes. Kissinger quickly put his fat briefing book away, and he laid gifts at the feet of his Chinese hosts, including high-resolution spy satellite photos of Soviet military assets, as well as communication intercepts. By this and other gestures the Chinese were reassured that the United States regarded China as a strategic bastion in Asia against the Soviet Union rather than a fratricidal Communist twin of Moscow. This, as much as the status of Taiwan, was the primary Chinese objective of the opening to the United States.

Kissinger was less successful in making progress on the chief U.S. objective—getting China's help in settling the Vietnam War. China demurred at all U.S. requests for intermediation. Chou argued not implausibly that any Chinese pressure on Hanoi would push North Vietnam closer to Moscow, even though China was at that moment supplying North Vietnam with most of its weapons and munitions. But the Chinese contact would have the effect of giving Nixon a freer hand in prosecuting the military side of the war in 1972 in the teeth of a new offensive and stalled negotiations.

Even as Kissinger's secret meetings were underway in Beijing, Nixon was hinting at forthcoming events back home. In an extraordinarily wide-ranging and plaintive speech about America's foreign and domestic circumstances before a convention of journalists in Kansas City (about which more shall be said in due course), Nixon slipped in a subtle reference to his forthcoming China opening that is heavy with irony when read against the backdrop of more recent Sino-American relations:

> . . . U.S. policy must be, in the long run, ending the isolation of Mainland China and a normalization of our relations with Mainland China because, looking down the road—and let's just look ahead 15 to 20 years—the United States could have a perfectly effective agreement with the Soviet Union for the limitation of arms; the danger of any confrontation there might have been almost totally removed.
>
> But Mainland China, outside the world community, completely isolated, with its leaders not in communication with world leaders, would be a danger to the whole world that is unacceptable, unacceptable to us and unacceptable to them. So, consequently, this step [of opening to China] must be taken.

Ten days later Nixon requested network TV time to make the announcement that he would visit China in 1972. "Rarely," *Time* magazine marveled, "had official Washington ever kept so momentous a secret so well."[95] Nixon took only 90 seconds for his announcement, a rare instance of a politician using understatement to enhance the shock value of a bold move. Nixon sought to reassure Taiwan—and its vocal American supporters—by saying that "our action in seeking a new relationship with the People's Republic of China will not be at the expense of our old friends," but this was a pretense that fooled no one. Taiwan's ambassador to the United States was only given notice 20 minutes before Nixon's TV announcement. Other allies, including South Vietnam's Prime Minister Thieu, were given no notice at all. "What are they up to?" Thieu asked one of his American-educated advisers. "Well, Mr. President," the adviser answered, "I think they are giving up on us."[96]

The Soviets were the most shocked, though they surely knew through intelligence sources of Kissinger's secret negotiations. Playing the China card had its desired effect on the Soviets. The Soviet Union had been dragging its feet regarding U.S. overtures for a Nixon-Brezhnev summit and several other matters. But with the China announcement, Kissinger observed, "negotiations deadlocked for months began magically to unfreeze." The Soviet Union "was suddenly anxious to create the impression that more serious business could be accomplished in Moscow than in Peking."[97] Within weeks of Nixon's announcement, a long-sought agreement to settle the problem of Berlin was concluded, and an agreement over technical measures to prevent an accidental nuclear launch by either side was reached. And the Soviets were suddenly eager to arrange a summit as soon as possible.

While the China card shook the Soviet Union, it also evidently set off a fierce dispute within China's ruling circles, perhaps culminating in a full-scale power struggle and purge. Most of China's top military commanders were replaced shortly after Kissinger's first visit, and China's defense minister, Lin Biao, was killed in an airplane crash in Mongolia in September. (Biao was widely considered to be Mao Tse-tung's successor as Communist Party chairman.) The circumstances of the crash remain murky to this day, with widespread rumors that a disaffected Lin Biao was en route to the Soviet Union with transcripts of the Kissinger-Chou discussions, and perhaps that the plane had been shot down. Most of China's senior leadership disappeared from public view for several days during this same time, and all Chinese aircraft were grounded. The annual October 1 parade celebrating the Chinese Revolution was abruptly cancelled. But Chinese communications regarding Nixon's forthcoming visit were uninterrupted, so there was no way for the United States to judge how serious the internal crisis might be.

The first fallout from Nixon's surprise announcement was not long in coming. In the fall, the United Nations General Assembly voted to oust Taiwan and seat mainland China at the U.N. The United States had hoped vainly for a transitional formula in which both Chinas would be offered seats (which Mainland China would decline), but U.S. allies who had backed America's Taiwan policy saw little reason to carry on in the aftermath of Nixon's announcement. Every NATO ally voted against the United States and in favor of an Albanian resolution to seat Mainland China. U.S. allies made the self-interested calculation that if the United States was going to open itself up to expanded trade with China, they weren't going to be left behind on account of fealty to Cold War doctrine. The humiliation of Taiwan was accompanied by dancing and cheering in the aisles of the U.N. General Assembly by Third World representatives gleeful at having handed a defeat to the United States. (It would be the first of many U.N. humiliations of the U.S. in the coming decade.) Conservatives in the United States were furious.

Though conservatives had expressed strong misgivings about Nixon's China trip when it was announced, Nixon had taken great care to minimize their criticism. He had actually gotten Senator Barry Goldwater to endorse the venture, while other conservatives such as Texas Senator John Tower muted their criticism with the hope that Nixon would be able to use China to help end the Vietnam War. Nixon appealed personally to Governor Reagan to travel to Taiwan as Nixon's personal representative for Taiwan's annual National Day festivities. "I think he [Reagan] always had some lingering regrets about having been used in this way," Reagan aide Richard Allen later told journalist James Mann, "but his reasoning was that when the president asked him to do something, he [Reagan] was going to do it for him."[98]

The conservative misgivings would grow to open revolt as the contours of Nixon's trip unfolded in February of 1972. Nixon arrived at the Beijing airport to a very spare reception. There was no crowd and no music or fanfare beyond the playing of the two countries' national anthems. It was "an all but desolate scene," according to William F. Buckley Jr., who was among the press entourage. The Chinese took some steps to remove obvious insults or provocations, such as renaming Beijing's Anti-Imperialist Hospital (so named because it had been built by the Rockefeller Foundation before the revolution) the Friendship Hospital. But other small gestures seemed designed to reinforce the revolutionary destiny of Chinese Communism. American reporters couldn't help noticing that the American flag was always slightly smaller than the Chinese flag when they were displayed side-by-side. Nixon and his entourage were also made to sit through a Chinese ballet that acted out the liberation of landless proletarians oppressed by a "running dog despotic landlord." "It was as if," Buckley wrote, "at a White House conference of African presidents, we had taken them over to Kennedy Center to see a ballet of Li'l Black Sambo."[99]

If conservatives were offended at the symbolism that attended the public events of the summit, they would have been apoplectic had they known what passed between Nixon and Mao behind closed doors. The transcript of the Nixon-Mao meeting was not made public until many years after the summit. It reveals a positively obsequious Nixon. (Nixon's meeting with Mao was not certain even as *Air Force One* was en route to China, supposedly because of Mao's ill health, and occurred with only short notice after Nixon had been in China for several days.) It was evidently a stiff and awkward conversation much of the time, no doubt aggravated by the problems of translation and unfamiliar colloquialisms. Most of the recorded conversation appears to be mere banter from the Chinese side, with jocular deflections of every Nixon attempt to broach a serious subject. Perhaps it was a canny Chinese tactic to make Nixon concede as much philosophical ground as possible. Mao joked that "I like rightists . . . I am comparatively happy when these people on the right come into power." Mao may have been mixing flattery with subtlety, nodding toward Nixon's conservative reputation while expressing kinship with the stern authoritarianism Mao shared with such "rightist" figures as Francisco Franco.

Nixon took Mao literally, however, responding that "I think the important thing to note is that in America, at least at this time, those on the right can do what those on the left talk about." (Nixon was not unaware of the saliency of the slogan that later came to be popular—"Only Nixon could go to China.") Nixon told Mao that "What brings us together is a recognition of a new situation in the world and a recognition on our part that what is important is not a nation's internal political philosophy. What is important is its policy toward the rest of the world and toward us." This statement represented a complete repudiation by Nixon of the Western view that totalitarian Communist revolutions are morally odious and illegitimate because they violate the universal democratic principle of government by consent. The Nixon of the ideological "Kitchen debate" with Khrushchev was long gone. Mao said little in direct response, but he apparently liked what he heard. Mao joked that in the case of ultimate world revolution, perhaps Nixon and Kissinger would not be among those who would be overthrown, because "if all of you are overthrown we wouldn't have any more friends left."

Given the relentless rhetorical concessions based on "realism" that Western leaders had made to Communist leaders since Yalta and before, it is not difficult to see why Communist leaders could easily persist in the view that their creed, or at least their style of government, represented the tide of the future. Though William F. Buckley Jr. did not know what had passed between Nixon and Mao, the public remarks of the trip led him to write: "We have lost—irretrievably—any remaining sense of moral mission in the world." When Nixon compared Mao and the Chinese revolution to George Washington and the American Founding in a toast, a reporter remarked to Buckley: "That should dispel the last suspicion that there is a trace of ideological conviction left in Richard Nixon."[100]

But Nixon's concessions were more than merely rhetorical. The Shanghai Communiqué Nixon signed at the end of the trip affirmed Beijing's claim over Taiwan: "The United States acknowledges that all Chinese on either side of the Taiwan Strait maintain there is but one China and that Taiwan is a part of China. The United States Government does not challenge that position." The Communiqué went on to announce that all U.S. military forces would be withdrawn from Taiwan, and called for a peaceful settlement of the Taiwan issue. The final language of the Communiqué actually came from some two decade–old State Department talking points, and Kissinger repaired behind the ambiguities of the Communiqué to defend it.

Our defense treaty with Taiwan, Nixon and Kissinger reaffirmed upon their return to Washington, remained in force. In the short run, Nixon partisans argue, Nixon bought time for Taiwan. China would not want to jeopardize its newfound relationship with the United States by any precipitous act toward Taiwan. As trade and other contacts increased, the value of good relations with the United States would only grow. Or so the theory went. Yet it is not clear that the U.S. concession over Taiwan, however ambiguously made, was necessary to secure the U.S. aim of aligning China with itself against the Soviet Union, and it bears repeating that Nixon got little or no help from the Chinese over Vietnam. Even the *Washington Post* concluded that "Weighing the concessions made by the President, many observers here feel that the Chinese got the better of the bargain. . . ." Other newspapers were more sarcastic; *The Detroit News* reported, "They got Taiwan, we got egg rolls." Kissinger bitterly rejected these criticisms in his memoirs. It was the beginning of open hostilities between Kissinger and conservatives.

The reaffirmation of the Taiwan defense treaty was insufficient to stop a growing conservative revolt against Nixon. Nixon speechwriter Pat Buchanan was reportedly "morose" on the long plane ride back from China, and nearly resigned over the Shanghai Communiqué. (By 1976 Buchanan would offer a sweeping judgment on the failure of Nixon: "Looking back on the budget, economic and social policies of the Republican years, it would not be unfair to conclude that the political verdict of 1968 had brought reaffirmation, rather than repudiation, of Great Society liberalism.") Conservatives had already publicly broken with Nixon a few weeks before the China announcement was made.

In July 1971 a group of eminent conservatives led by William F. Buckley Jr. and New York Conservative Party Chairman J. Daniel Mahoney issued a public declaration withdrawing their political support for Nixon. Conservative activists were consciously following the same playbook that toppled LBJ in 1968, and "draft-Reagan" committees began to be organized. The conservative weekly *Human Events* reported: "an increasing number of conservatives are beginning to think the unthinkable: that a Nixon defeat in 1972 might not be so catastrophic after all. These conservatives reason that it would be better to have a liberal Administration, with all the consequences that might bring, than to permit Richard Nixon to destroy the Republican party as a vehicle for conservatism."[101] Even in the aftermath of the 1972 Nixon landslide, *National Review* was disconsolate: "In the first four years of the Nixon era American conservatism has been largely smothered as a distinctive doctrine and movement."[102] And Gaylord Parkinson, the influential California Republican who coined the so-called "11th Commandment"—"Thou shalt not speak ill of a fellow Republican"—violated his own rule, saying Nixon "has reversed his position on every issue affecting our economy and national security."[103]

The White House publicly dismissed the conservative revolt as being limited to "a bunch of disgruntled intellectuals," noting that no office holders had endorsed the declaration. "Barry Goldwater, Ronald Reagan, and Strom Thurmond are backing the President," a White House staffer told columnist Kevin Phillips. "They're not part of this thing." One elected official who publicly distanced himself from the conservative revolt was William F. Buckley's own brother, James L. Buckley, then serving in the U.S. Senate from New York. "While I share many if not all of their concerns," Sen. Buckley said in a press statement, "I am not prepared to join them in a declaration of non-support." Another elected official who dismissed the revolt was the GOP National Chairman, Kansas Senator Bob Dole: "Sooner or later these conservatives are going to look at the alternatives. . . . And there aren't any alternatives on our side. Nixon's the nominee." Dole could say this with confidence because Reagan was assiduously avoiding the grass-roots enthusiasm for his candidacy. At the suggestion of the White House, Reagan began charging $25,000 for speaking appearances as a way of dampening the draft-Reagan forces.

Although the China trip, coming on the heels of wage and price controls and the Family Assistance Plan, was the last straw for conservatives, it was in fact a turning point for Nixon with the general public. Just as wage and price controls were immensely popular, so too the China trip was a public relations boost. A Harris Poll found the public in favor of the trip by a 69 percent to 19 percent margin. After having trailed his putative Democratic challengers in the polls throughout the middle months of 1971, Nixon began 1972 back in the lead. *Time* magazine named him "Man of the Year," and bestowed the kind of encomiums that conservatives would later come to disparage as "strange new respect," in which media praise is always bestowed for movement to the left.

Nixon, *Time* rhapsodized, was proving to be "refreshingly flexible and disconcertingly unpredictable. . . [U]nless he provides a great deal of fresh ammunition, Nixon-hating will become a bore."[104] (As to supplying "a great deal of fresh ammunition," Nixon would not disappoint on this score.) On the heels of the China announcement the long-sought summit with the Soviet Union was also arranged. His program of "Vietnamization," though frustratingly slow, was showing promise that it might work out. By 1971, U.S. combat deaths had fallen by 50 percent from their peak in 1968, and South Vietnamese pilots were flying twice as many missions as American pilots. Troops were coming home at a rate of one division a month; more than half of America's ground forces had been brought home by the end of 1971. Nixon had succeeded in establishing himself as a colossus of world affairs. Domestic circumstances were quite different, however, and had a direct relation to the shaping and outcome of Nixon's foreign stratagems.

CHAPTER SEVEN

EXHAUSTION:
THE SHAPING OF THE 1970S

THE AMERICAN PEOPLE and its leaders can be forgiven for feeling disoriented as the 1970s began. No one was more disoriented than Nixon and his administration, and it is out of this confusion and insecurity that the seeds of Watergate can be seen. Nixon won the 1968 election in part because he represented to the disgusted middle class a point of resistance to the social turmoil of the 1960s. Confronting the forces of radicalism and disorder was a top priority for Nixon, yet his effort was confused, defensive, and ineffective, chiefly because of Nixon's own insecurities and confusions.

"Nixon's convictions," Kissinger wrote, "while firm and—in foreign policy—carefully thought out, did not seem able to sustain him unless they resonated not just with public acclaim but with the approval of the classes he admired and despised at the same time."[1] What Nixon failed to appreciate was that the Establishment itself was in such turmoil that it was incapable of giving him even grudging respect. As Kissinger bitterly reflected: "So it happened that a majority of the Old Establishment—the men and women who had set the direction and tone for American foreign policy for a generation—came to insist on the defeat of their own country in order to purify it."[2] There may have been little Nixon could have done to combat this directly, but his passive-aggressive approach to this problem was one of his greatest weaknesses.

A startling and unappreciated aspect of Nixon's character and presidency is that Nixon hated confrontation. "Nixon abhorred face-to-face disagreements of any kind," Kissinger noted.[3] This may have been another reflection of a deep insecurity or lingering sense of inferiority, no doubt aggravated by the disrespect accorded to him by so many in the media and Establishment elites. This led his staff to pre-arrange all meetings meticulously to avoid argument and surprises. The staff supplied Nixon with "talking points" for all meetings, and the outcome, including what his interlocutors would say, was pre-arranged as far as possible. Nixon largely avoided public confrontations with his enemies and critics. Instead he brooded in private, venting his animosities to his close staff and friends, as is well known from the Oval Office tapes.

Nixon's approach to the domestic crisis again contrasts sharply with Reagan, who was grappling with the same set of troubles as governor of California. Reagan relished confrontation. "People who come up against him think he's a *dumb* movie actor," a Reagan friend told *Newsweek* in 1970, "and they wind up in pieces."[4] Above all, Reagan carried out his own crusade against the counterculture with his typical good humor, a trait noticeably absent from anything Nixon did.

As the 1960s gave way to the 1970s, it would have required a very discerning eye to recognize that the nation was turning a corner. By 1973 Pat Moynihan would reflect that "most of the events that tore American society almost apart (or so it seemed in the 1960s) arose from conditions unique to the decade in which they occurred. They had not ever existed before. They will not ever exist again."[5] A montage of the transition from the 1960s to the 1970s would record the debut of *Sesame Street* on "educational television" (as it was known then) in 1969, and the launch of ARPANET (Advanced Research Project Agency Network) at UCLA to link up military-related computer functions. ARPANET was the first step toward what would become the Internet. In 1970 Texas Instruments introduced the first pocket electronic calculator at a retail price of $400. In 1971 the fledgling Intel Corporation produced its first computer microprocessor, model 4004. Boeing produced the first 747 jumbo jet planes. Cigarette advertising was banned from television at the end of 1970; the following year, consumption rose by 12 billion cigarettes. Jack Weinberg, the author of the phrase, "Don't trust anyone over 30," turned 30. New York Jets quarterback Joe Namath emerged from a hospital following knee surgery wearing a smiley-face button and helped propel the symbol into a ubiquitous emblem of the decade. (Bergdorf-Goodman offered smiley-face gold cuff links for $80.) Jimi Hendrix and Janis Joplin both died of drug overdoses. "Do the Funky Chicken" was a hit pop song, the advance guard for the imminent Age of Disco. The Bureau of the Census reported that 143,000 unmarried couples were living together, up from 17,000 in 1960. The number of unmarried couples living together (which the Census Bureau would come to classify officially as POSSLQs— "Persons of the Opposite Sex Sharing Living Quarters") would soar in the 1970s, and a 1971 Yankelovich Poll found that 34 percent of the public believed marriage was obsolete. Between 1969 and 1973, the proportion of the public who thought premarital sex was wrong dropped 20 points in the Gallup Poll, from 68 percent to 48 percent.[6] The sexual revolution was gaining traction.

Having survived a helicopter crash in 1968 during his second tour of duty in Vietnam, Army Major Colin Powell was studying for an MBA at George Washington University, where he would receive all A's except for a single B grade in computer logic. He would shortly be picked to be a White House Fellow, serving in the office of the director of the Office of Management of Budget, Caspar Weinberger. (One of Powell's interviewers in the selection process was Milton Friedman.) Marine Second Lieutenant Oliver North shipped out to Vietnam for his first action since graduating from Annapolis in 1968. Marines in his rifle platoon described North as "utterly fearless." On May 28, 1970, Lieutenant Colonel Norman Schwarzkopf, then on his second tour in Vietnam, went to rescue a patrol trapped in a minefield on the Batangan Peninsula. He earned his third Silver Star for rescuing a private whose leg had been blown off when the unlucky soldier stepped on a mine. Newt Gingrich, having completed his Ph.D. in history at Tulane University, became an assistant professor at West Georgia State College in the fall of 1970.

New Year's Day of 1970 found Bill Clinton in Moscow. He was finishing his second year as a Rhodes Scholar at Oxford University. Clinton had sidestepped a draft notice through a deferment the previous year, and Nixon's new draft lottery system now provided him with an escape hatch from his tentative commitment to enter an ROTC program at the University of Arkansas Law School. Clinton's August 17 birth date drew number 311 in the draft lottery for 1970, leaving him easily clear of being called into service. He would go to Yale Law School in the fall instead. There he would meet Hillary Rodham, who chose Yale Law over Harvard Law in part because a Harvard law professor had brusquely told her that "We don't need any more women." (She had also declined a job offer from community organizer Saul Alinsky.)

Hillary Rodham had received a standing ovation from her fellow Wellesley graduating class the previous spring when, as student commencement speaker, she hectored Sen. Edward Brooke, the black Republican senator from Massachusetts who was on hand to receive an honorary degree. *The Washington Post* described her remarks as a "mild rebuke," but many alumni thought she had been exceedingly rude. *Life* magazine decided to run her photo as an "example of the best and brightest" of the young generation. Her first year at Yale Law found her in the eager defense of several Black Panthers jailed on murder charges. She had the blessing of the Establishment; the president of Yale, Kingman Brewster, remarked at the time that he doubted a Black Panther could get a fair trial in America. He was ironically correct; the New Haven Panthers were acquitted.

Despite the evidence of material progress and the signs that the worst of America's social upheavals was over, a sense of pessimism took firm hold over the nation. A Princeton public opinion poll in 1971 found that a substantial majority of Americans believed that the nation had "lost ground" over the previous decade. The one major demographic segment that thought the nation had made progress was, significantly, black Americans, evidence that civil rights and economic gains were not unnoticed by ordinary black Americans. That didn't stop Senator Walter Mondale from remarking in 1971 that "The sickening truth is that this country is rapidly coming to resemble South Africa."[7]

It was not just among the protest Left that the putative decline of America was becoming axiomatic. Pessimism was perhaps nowhere stronger than among America's "chattering class" in the Establishment. "[T]he dominant characteristic of the American Establishment today," Edmund Stillman wrote in *Commentary,* "is exhaustion—exhaustion of ideas, exhaustion of will, and most damaging of all, exhaustion of the power to generate popular faith in its ideas."[8] *Time* magazine sensed in 1970 that "There is a vague anxiety that the machine of the 20th century is beginning to run out of control," while *The New Republic* thought that

"We seem to be in one of those long periods when civilization is in decline."[9] Shirley MacLaine said in 1972 that "Right now the social soul of America is so sick that even the overthrow of a political regime may be insufficient." The musings of an overheated Hollywood starlet might be dismissed, but similar sentiments were expressed by supposedly sober eminences such as James MacGregor Burns, who also said in 1972: "The nation is essentially evil and the evil can be exorcised only by turning the system upside down."[10]

The reaction to the moon landing in 1969 is a good example of national exhaustion and liberal guilt at work. The moon landing had been set out as a lofty goal by the liberals' hero, John F. Kennedy, and the actual landing on the moon was an occasion of national pride and celebration for most Americans. Here, amidst the rubble and gloom of the 1960s, was something that had gone splendidly right. Many leading liberals, however, could only sniff that while the moon landing was undeniably impressive, the money would have been better spent on social problems on Earth. The popular cliché of the time went: "Any nation that can land a man on the moon can [fill in the blank]." (The total cost of the decade-long moon landing project was less than three months' worth of federal spending for social programs in 1969.)

A 25-person delegation from the Poor People's Campaign, led by Rev. Ralph Abernathy (Martin Luther King's successor), came to the *Apollo 11* launch at Cape Canaveral "to protest America's inability to choose human priorities," while Senate Majority Leader Mike Mansfield said that "The needs of the people on earth, and especially in this country, should have priority. When we solve these problems, we can consider space efforts." Even the brother of the man who issued the call to go to the moon, Sen. Ted Kennedy, expressed weariness with the space program: "I think after [the moon landing] the space program ought to fit into our other national priorities."[11] (At the moment he spoke these words Kennedy was the presumptive Democratic nominee against Nixon in 1972. Polls showed him to be the preference for nearly two-thirds of rank-and-file Democrats. Since Inauguration Day he had assumed the leadership of the opposition to Nixon and was making all the moves one would naturally expect of a presidential candidate. He was elected to the Democratic leadership in the Senate, ousting the incumbent, Sen. Russell Long, from his perch as Senate Majority Whip. While *Apollo 11* was en route to the moon, however,

Kennedy's presidential ambitions went over the side of the road along with his car at Chappaquiddick.)

Above all, the nation's weariness with the Vietnam War constituted the chief source of the nation's exhaustion, and most deeply constrained Nixon's scope of action. By the middle of 1969 Vietnam had become the nation's longest war, and war deaths surpassed the Korean War total. The U.S. troop level peaked at 543,000 in the spring of 1969. Nixon shared the nation's frustration, but dared not openly show it. That Nixon had advertised a "secret plan" to end the war during the 1968 campaign is a commonplace of Nixon lore, but this is a myth, owing mostly to a wire service story that intuited such a plan.[12] Nixon said no such thing; the phrase "secret plan" was used by a questioner to Nixon in a New Hampshire town meeting, but attributed to Nixon in a UPI story that was only belatedly corrected. But Nixon had to treat the issue carefully; it hardly served his purpose to refute the story and say he had no plan. Instead Nixon said, quite reasonably, that he didn't want to undercut President Johnson's negotiations through any campaign statements he might make. In fact Nixon wasn't sure what to do about the war.

Nixon's inclination was to emulate the strategy Eisenhower had used to bring the Korean War to an end—threaten to escalate. It was too late, however. President Johnson's unilateral bombing halt in October 1968, and the opening of the Paris peace talks, represented a turn in the course of the war that could not be easily reversed. Media coverage of the war had turned overwhelmingly negative; by these late years reporters who had staked out a negative view of the war had a perverse interest in seeing the United States *lose* in order for their interpretation to be vindicated. Johnson's disastrous lead negotiator at the Paris talks, former New York Governor Averill Harriman, had become the de facto leader of the peace process faction, publicly arguing after Nixon's inauguration that what was needed for the peace talks to succeed was more U.S. "restraint" on the battlefield. This was nonsense, but it attracted considerable media support and provided sustenance to the antiwar movement.

Nixon secretly threatened Hanoi that he would escalate the war by the fall of 1969 if there was no progress in the peace talks, but the North Vietnamese, carefully gauging American opinion, not only decided to call Nixon's bluff, but launched an offensive in the spring of 1969. It would be their last for three years. Harriman led the chorus of Establishment voices attributing the North Vietnamese offensive to U.S. intransigence. "If the United States would take the lead in scaling down the war," the hapless Harriman said, "the enemy would follow suit." Rightly worried about the political fallout of a major war controversy in the early months of his administration, Nixon flinched, deciding against renewed bombing of North Vietnam, a decision Nixon later described as "my biggest mistake as President."[13]

North Vietnam remained confidently intransigent at the peace talks, biding their time while America's patience steadily ebbed. Captured documents indicated that North Vietnam was preparing to revert to the long-term guerrilla strategy they had employed a decade earlier, in order to conserve manpower and supplies while protracting the war. Nixon realized that he would have to settle for a drawn-out strategy of his own; he would seek to build up South Vietnam's capacity to carry on the war by itself while gradually withdrawing U.S. forces. Nixon no doubt believed in the strategy, but it could also turn out to be a slow-motion bug-out.

The irony of the situation, which is still largely unappreciated to this day, is that the war situation was improving markedly for the United States as Nixon became president. This was not Nixon's doing as much as it was the change in strategy that the new commander, General Creighton Abrams, adopted upon succeeding General Westmoreland in 1968. Abrams junked Westmoreland's manpower-intensive "big unit" war of countryside "sweeps" and heavy use of bombing and other firepower that often inflicted more damage on friendly South Vietnamese people and towns than the enemy. The mindless exercise of "body counts" was out; providing perimeter security for the populations in towns and villages and interdicting enemy supplies were in.

"The tactics changed within 15 minutes of Abram's taking command," one senior commander told military historian Lewis Sorley.[14] American casualties immediately declined by a third, and made possible Nixon's "Vietnamization" policy of gradual troop withdrawal. By 1971, the South Vietnamese army had grown to twice the size it had been when the United States first escalated its presence in 1964. Abrams stabilized the war in a way that might have made the war sustainable at vastly lower cost in terms of both money and lives had it been adopted at the outset. This was the strategy the military had rejected four years before as being too passive and unmanly.

It was too late for a change in strategy and tactics to rescue the war effort. There was, after all, no change in America's war aims. Nixon never seriously considered conventional victory over North Vietnam, and without the old-fashioned goal of defeating the enemy it became increasingly difficult in the face of determined domestic opposition to explain why the United States was killing *anyone* in Vietnam. The momentum of public sentiment, not to mention the organization and energy level of the antiwar movement, had turned the corner against continuing the war.

Polls showed that a majority of Americans by 1969 believed the nation had been mistaken to get involved in Vietnam, though a large majority, often as high as 75 percent in some polls, opposed a unilateral pullout, evidence that national honor remained an important commodity for most Americans—more so than Congress. A congressional resolution calling for an immediate pullout from Vietnam failed, but Congress did repeal the Tonkin Gulf resolution, which was the initial authorization for a wider war back in 1964. The rising congressional opposition to the war was beginning to exact a wider toll on foreign policy; if we can't get out of Vietnam in the midst of the fighting, some congressional leaders thought, maybe we can reduce U.S. commitments elsewhere in the world before a new conflict arises. Senate Majority Leader Mike Mansfield offered a resolution calling for the immediate withdrawal of U.S. troops in Europe, which caused consternation among our neglected NATO allies.

More and more oracles of the Establishment publicly came out against the war; two of the biggest blows came when Bishop Fulton Sheen, a noted conservative and anti-Communist, came out against the war in 1969, along with Notre Dame University's influential president, Father Theodore Hesburgh, whom Nixon had appointed to the U.S. Commission on Civil Rights. The doubts about the legitimacy and morality of America's effort in Vietnam wasn't just limited to clerics and disaffected liberal intellectuals. Even General David Shoup, the former Commandant of the U.S. Marine Corps and a highly decorated World War II hero, wrote in *The Atlantic* that "America has become a militaristic and aggressive nation."[15]

In such circumstances the change in U.S. battle tactics counted for naught, while every fresh battlefield setback or report of U.S. misconduct—whether genuine or exaggerated—set off a new firestorm at home. The military continued committing gaffes of the "destroy the village in order to save it" variety. After days of hard fighting in 1969 to capture what became known as "Hamburger Hill," the hill was abandoned, and a commander remarked that "Hill 937, as a piece of terrain, was of no tactical significance."[16] "Then why waste American lives to take it?" the average American back home sensibly wished to know. (Fifty-six U.S. soldiers had been killed in the assault on the hill.)

Even effective military operations backfired or failed. In the fall of 1970, the United States staged a daring raid deep inside North Vietnam in an attempt to rescue 70 American POWs in the Son Tay prison. The raid involved flying five HH-53 heavy-lift helicopters from Thailand (which required a delicate mid-flight refueling to reach the camp), carrying a 56-man assault team. The team practiced the raid 175 times. Extensive intelligence photos had been gathered. Despite these extensive preparations, two of the helicopters carrying the main assault teams landed at the wrong site, though they killed or wounded an estimated 200 Chinese and Russian military advisers. (China reportedly threatened to cut off aid to Hanoi if they could not defend themselves better.)

The assault team made quick work of the North Vietnamese forces when they finally made it to the correct site of the prison—but there were no American POWs to be found. They had been moved four months before. The Defense Intelligence Agency knew this, and had passed the news along to the Joint Chiefs of Staff, who inexplicably decided to go ahead with the raid anyway. Out of 91 rescue attempts made throughout the war, only a single American POW was successfully rescued.[17] (This rescue fiasco would be repeated at the end of the decade in Iran.) In typical Pentagon-speak, an Army general proclaimed that the raid "was a complete success with the exception that no prisoners were rescued."[18] The raid did have some small benefit. Word of the raid reached American POWs in other camps, and boosted their morale.

The worst trouble came from Cambodia. In 1969 the United States began bombing North Vietnamese bases in Cambodia. Cambodia, ostensibly a neutral country, was little more than a "gun-running syndicate" (in the words of John P. Roche) at that time, but the fiction of respecting a nation's neutrality led the United States to conduct the bombing without public acknowledgement, though Nixon did keep congressional leaders informed throughout, contrary to popular perception. The United States had legal right under international law to operate in Cambodia; the

Hague Convention of 1907 gives belligerents the right to take action against the enemy in a neutral nation if the neutral cannot prevent the enemy from using the neutral's territory. Cambodia's ruler, Prince Norodim Sihanouk, angry at North Vietnam's encroachment on his sovereign territory, had given the United States the green light to attack the North inside his borders in a conversation with President Johnson's envoy, Chester Bowles, in late 1968.

The bombing was kept quiet because Nixon wanted to allow Sihanouk to save face and be able to deny knowledge of both the North Vietnamese presence and the American bombing. North Vietnam tellingly didn't blow the whistle to the international antiwar movement, because it would have had to admit that it was violating a neutral country. A strange coincidence of political interest came together to keep the Cambodian bombing "secret." Naturally it did not remain secret; acting on a leak, the front page of the *New York Times* described the Cambodian bombing campaign on May 9, 1969. The story attracted little attention and caused only a faint ripple of protest at the time, but Nixon was furious about the leak anyway, which was only one in a series of never-ending leaks that drove him to distraction. (*National Review* quipped: "Henry Kissinger can't tell [CIA chief] Dick Helms his latest martini formula without it being in print an hour later."[19]) Nixon wanted something done to stem such leaks; he ordered wiretaps—which were not thought to be illegal at that point; the Supreme Court had not yet ruled on the issue—and increased political intelligence gathering by and among his staff. Hence the White House unit known as the "Plumbers" came into being.

The worst blow to the legitimacy of the American war effort came in 1969, when investigative journalist Seymour Hersh broke the story of the My Lai massacre. Hersh revealed that in March 1968, shortly after the Tet offensive, an Army platoon under the command of Lt. William Calley swept through the village of My Lai in search of Viet Cong, who seemingly drifted in and out of South Vietnamese villages and hamlets at will. Calley's platoon was not atypical of the condition of many army units in the field. In 1968 almost a quarter of U.S. battlefield deaths were caused by booby-traps and mines. Calley's unit had lost 42 men to booby traps, snipers, and mines in the month before the My Lai sweep. Calley's platoon, which had received an abbreviated training period before being put into action, should have been taken out of the line for some relief. The army's frustration at their inability to stem this problem, and the suspected collaboration of South Vietnamese villagers with the Viet Cong, led to the rise of a "kill them all" attitude among some units.

That's exactly what Calley's platoon did during a day-long killing spree at My Lai. By the end of the day, 567 men, women, and children were dead. There were apparently no Viet Cong in the village. A few soldiers in Calley's platoon refused to obey the order to kill civilians. One GI shot himself in the foot to get out of the killing; he was the only American casualty of the day. A helicopter pilot who flew to the scene in the middle of the massacre (and who rescued 16 children) alerted senior commanders of what had taken place. The army attempted to cover up the massacre, but it was inevitable that word would leak out. A year later, with rumors and second-hand reports of the massacre circulating in Washington, the army began an investigation, which discovered, among other things, that an army photographer had caught much of the massacre on three rolls of film. The army indicted Calley for killing 109 Vietnamese civilians. He was convicted in 1971, after a four-month trial.

Needless to say, news of the My Lai massacre set off paroxysms of rage in the antiwar movement, and fresh fuel for the flourishing war crimes industry. Most Vietnam historians conclude that My Lai was an isolated incident, but it lent verisimilitude to the antiwar movement's characterization of the U.S. war effort as little more than a genocidal rampage. Because of My Lai, other supposed atrocities, such as pushing Viet Cong prisoners out of airborne helicopters, were widely believed and became easy bait for the news media. Yet not a single instance of pushing an enemy captive from a helicopter was ever confirmed. (The single instance that was photographed was staged with a dead body. The soldier who took the photo mailed it to his girlfriend back in the United States along with a made-up story about an interrogation.)

Other sensational charges were disproved entirely, though often not until after they received wide publicity. In 1971, for example, the media offered itself as a megaphone for the war atrocity claims of Lt. Col. Anthony Herbert, whom the *New York Times* described as "the most decorated American soldier in the Korean war," a falsehood that the *Times* could easily have discovered with minimal fact-checking. *Time, Newsweek,* and the television networks all credulously reported Herbert's claim of having witnessed or heard firsthand of 21 war crimes a single airborne brigade had committed in 1968 and 1969. To their credit, CBS's *60 Minutes* eventually exposed Herbert's story as "a kaleidoscope of truth, half-truth, and falsehood." Herbert had in fact been dismissed from his army command in Vietnam because his superiors judged him "totally unfit to be an Army officer."[20]

The record shows that far from whitewashing troop misconduct, the United States was fastidious in enforcing its code of conduct. More than 200 army personnel, and 77 marines, were convicted of serious crimes in Vietnam. Ninety-five of the army convictions, and 27 of the marine convictions, were for murder or manslaughter of Vietnamese.[21] (The comparable North Vietnamese or Viet Cong figure was zero.) Perhaps any war that received such intense publicity would be widely perceived as excessively barbaric, but by comparison Vietnam was much less destructive of civilian life than other wars. Civilians accounted for 42 percent of war deaths in World War II, and 70 percent in the Korean War, but only 30 percent in Vietnam, according to estimates Guenter Lewy analyzed in his book *America in Vietnam*. "[T]he Vietnam war during the years of active American involvement was no more destructive of human life, both North and South, than other armed conflicts of this century and a good deal less so than some, such as the Korean war," Lewy concludes.[22]

My Lai also became exhibit A for the widespread perception that discipline and morale problems had been pervasive since the very start of the war effort. In fact, discipline and morale didn't begin to erode until late in the war—*after* the United States began its slow-motion bug-out. It was always difficult to tell soldiers to risk their lives so that the United States could gain a better negotiating position; it was even harder to ask soldiers to risk the supreme sacrifice when it was clear the United States was abandoning the field of battle. The method of U.S. troop withdrawals, organized by Gen. Westmoreland, who had been kicked upstairs to Army Chief of Staff in the wake of the Tet offensive, contributed to the problem. Westmoreland insisted on sending home the troops who had been in Vietnam the longest, which removed some of the most experienced troops and disrupted cohesive units. (Abrams had favored sending home complete and intact units, but Westmoreland overruled him.)

Then, too, the general erosion of America's military manpower was beginning to tell in the late years of the war. The army had rejected Calley the first time he had tried to join in the early 1960s, but by the time

Calley applied again in 1966 after he had fared poorly in junior college, the manpower-strapped army sent him off to Officer Candidate School, where Calley finished near the bottom of the class. Had the United States used a military draft that was not riddled with so many exemptions and deferments, or had the reserves been fully mobilized, it is unlikely that a person of Calley's marginal leadership ability would have been in charge of a platoon.

Along with charges of misconduct in the field there would come the charges of misconduct in Washington. On June 13, 1971, the *New York Times* published the first installment of the secret Pentagon study of the origins and decision-making of America's Vietnam policy—the "Pentagon Papers." Daniel Ellsberg, one of McNamara's disaffected whiz-kids, leaked the study to the *Times*. Once again the wrong lesson was learned. The Pentagon Papers confirmed that the Johnson administration had deceived Congress and the public, preparing for a wider war while denying that escalation was in prospect. This the war critics made out as proof of the inherent mendacity of the U.S. government. "The famous credibility gap," Hannah Arendt wrote, "has suddenly opened into an abyss."[23]

But the blame lay properly with Johnson; Johnson's deception began with himself, and was borne of the mistaken idea that Vietnam could be a "limited war," resolved rationally through the use of "graduated pressure." Since the Pentagon Papers exposed the machinations of the preceding Democratic administrations, the Nixon White House was briefly tempted to use the Papers to score partisan political points. But cooler heads understood that the precedent of using leaked documents for partisan purposes would forever undermine the nation's already fragile foreign policy consensus, and would in turn threaten future administrations. The Justice Department went to court to get an injunction blocking further publication of the Pentagon Papers, but lost.

It is matter of continuing controversy whether Ellsberg's disclosure of the Pentagon Papers damaged U.S. security (for example by assisting Soviet code-breaking efforts), and it is arguable that Henry Kissinger over-reacted to the episode. But the episode makes clear that the Nixon administration needs to be regarded as a *wartime* administration, as Nixon historian John Taylor has long argued. The losing court battle to keep government secrets from being published seemed symbolic of the entire frustrated effort in Vietnam. For all of these reasons, Nixon felt constrained in what he could do. Between the condemnation of the war by the Establishment elites in their salons and on the op-ed pages, and the protests carried out on the streets and campuses, it was not unsurprising that Nixon would underestimate the latent support of what he himself called "the silent majority."

Lavish media coverage of the antiwar movement, amidst the general encomiums to the "idealism" of the young generation, made it seem as though the antiwar movement engaged the sympathy of a broad spectrum of the American people. In fact, the antiwar movement was even more unpopular with most Americans than the war itself, a fact a few on the Left, such as Todd Gitlin, recognized. "As the war lost popularity," Gitlin wrote, "so did the antiwar movement." A Gallup Poll in 1969 found a whopping 82 percent in favor of expelling student demonstrators from their colleges or universities.[24] A few mass expulsions would have quieted down the campuses in a hurry, but pusillanimous university administrations never broached the idea. A defining moment occurred in May 1970, when a group of union construction workers in New York, whose long hair hanging out from their hardhats demonstrated how countercultural styles had been assimilated into the middle class, beat up antiwar demonstrators on Wall Street. (Six of the workers were arrested for battery.) The episode greatly cheered Nixon.

The dual unpopularity of the war and the antiwar movement is a not atypical expression of the cognitive dissonance that is often found at the heart of public opinion. Nixon's appeals to the innate patriotism of the nation, and his and Vice President Agnew's attacks on the news media, were largely effective on the occasions when they made them. But Nixon concluded that although the silent majority might back him, he could not prosecute the war with a free hand with the cultural and media establishments of the nation against him. There is some evidence to suggest that the North Vietnamese understood and exploited this circumstance. Years after the war a North Vietnamese official told *The Wall Street Journal:* "It [the antiwar movement] was essential to our strategy. Every day our leadership would listen to world news over the radio at 9 A.M. to follow the growth of the American antiwar movement. Visits to Hanoi by people like Jane Fonda and former Attorney General Ramsay Clark and ministers gave us confidence that we should hold on in the face of battlefield reverses. We were elated when Jane Fonda, wearing a red Vietnamese dress, said at a press conference that she was ashamed of American actions in the war and that she would struggle along with us."[25]

The antiwar movement was more than happy to oblige Hanoi, which contributed to its growing unpopularity with middle-class Americans who also hated the war. At the same time the antiwar movement was in high dudgeon over My Lai and other American war crimes, every denial and excuse was offered for the much greater atrocities the North Vietnamese and Viet Cong committed. The antiwar movement usually justified Communist atrocities by reference to the desperateness of their situation, that is, having to confront the United States. When reports of mistreatment of U.S. POWs began to circulate, the antiwar movement and its sympathizers in the media rushed to deny the veracity of the reports. Wilfred Burchett wrote that "it is a tribute to the discipline and truly civilized outlook of the Vietnamese people that pilots have been humanely treated from the moment of their capture."[26]

The literary critic Susan Sontag, following a visit to North Vietnam during which she spoke to no POWs, reported on her return that "The North Vietnamese genuinely care about the welfare of the hundreds of captured pilots and give them bigger rations than the Vietnamese population gets, 'because they're bigger then we are,' as a Vietnamese army officer told me, 'and they're used to more meat than we are.'"[27] North Vietnam, she added, "is a place which, in many respects, *deserves* to be idealized."[28]

Seymour Hersh, who broke the My Lai story, said that reports of brutality by a released POW "seriously distorted and misrepresented the prison conditions inside North Vietnam." The antiwar "mobilization" leader David Dellinger called it "the prisoner of war hoax," and Richard Barnett of the Institute for Policy Studies, an influential leftist think tank in Washington, testified to a House Committee that "the evidence of [POW] mistreatment is itself highly suspect."

When former Attorney General Ramsay Clark went to Hanoi in 1972, Lt. Commander David Hoffman was "persuaded" by his North Vietnamese captors to meet with Clark by being hung by his broken arm. John McCain refused to meet with another set of American "visitors"— he believes they were Jane Fonda and Tom Hayden—and was beaten, had an arm and leg broken, his ribs cracked, and teeth knocked out as punishment. Clark returned to the United States to tell a Senate committee that prisoners were well-treated, well-fed, and got plenty of exercise. When the POWs finally came home in 1973, some on the Left claimed that their injuries had been inflicted by American doctors for propaganda purposes. (They were hard pressed to explain, however, the severe weight loss among the supposedly well-fed POWs.)[29] The radical Catholic priest Daniel Berrigan, true to the last, protested that "we are over-publicizing the war criminals who are coming home."[30]

The irony is that just as the antiwar movement was attaining it greatest clout with the media and Establishment elites, it was beginning to dissipate, as the New Left itself was beginning to crack up. Nixon's first term in office saw a gradual tapering off of protest activity, punctuated by occasional flashes of fury such as after the Cambodian incursion of 1970, when Ohio National Guard troops killed four students at Kent State University. The Left has always made great hay about FBI infiltration and the clandestine efforts of the Nixon administration, through the "Huston Plan," to bait the New Left into self-destructive behavior that would discredit the New Left with the public. Most of these infiltration efforts were ham-handed, and were unnecessary anyway; the New Left was so far around the bend that it self-destructed without outside pressure. The new extremes of leftist violence the nation experienced starting in 1969 were in fact the death spasms of a movement whose essential nihilism would always consume itself and require that it find new targets to sustain its energy.

By the summer of 1969, the most prominent student organization, the Students for a Democratic Society, came apart in a comic orgy of radical purity, with rival factions denouncing each other for being insufficiently revolutionary. Paul Berman remarked that the SDS had become "Students for a Dictatorial Society," which was more literally true than he meant.[31]

Out of the ashes of this crack-up would come more ashes—real ashes from bombings by the "Weatherman" (who later changed their name to the "Weather Underground" to be gender-neutral) that sought to "bring the war home." They promised to employ "the classic guerrilla strategy of the Vietcong . . ." The Weather Underground borrowed their motto from a Bob Dylan lyric: "It doesn't take a weatherman to know which way the wind blows." Less violent Leftists coined their own rejoinder: It doesn't take a rectal thermometer to tell who the assholes are. Sure enough, a cell of the Weather Underground blew themselves up by accident in Greenwich Village in 1970. "The Revolution," elements of the Left confidently believed, was imminent; if not this year, then surely 1970 would see "The Revolution" come into being. "There were soporific discussions about parallels between 1970 and 1917," *Ramparts* editor Peter Collier recalls. "To invoke The Revolution," Todd Gitlin wrote, "was to claim title to the future. . . . The Revolution was an eschatological certainty, a given, a future already unfolding."[32]

The growing talk of "The Revolution" provided cover for the advent of the third and terminal phase of campus protest activity. Campus protest had evolved a long way since the Berkeley Free Speech Movement, when students marched peaceably with the American flag and claimed their rights under the First Amendment. The more militant disruption seen at Columbia in 1968, where the occupation of buildings was the central tactic, now gave way to tactics designed to provoke police violence, radicalize moderate students on the sidelines, and shut down universities entirely. By 1969 and 1970 these tactics had evolved into an art form.

The first stage involved making a set of confrontational "non-negotiable demands" of the university administration, always so outlandish that the university could not possibly give in. Stage two involved using the university's refusal of the demands to indict the university itself—see, the university is part of the evil War Machine. Protest leaders force the university into punishing them for rule violations. Sit-in and building occupations are called for, which have as their goal forcing the university to call in the police (who will hopefully have to smash a few student skulls with their batons), which is stage three.

Berkeley's John Searle described the dynamic: "The introduction of the police is regarded as the ultimate crime that any university administration can commit. . . . In the face of the sheer horror of the police on campus, the opposition to the movement, especially the opposition among the liberal and moderate students, becomes enfeebled and usually collapses altogether." Searle called this protest tactic "left-McCarthyism."[33] In 1969, this scheme extended even to Harvard and Cornell Universities. In all, 448 universities experienced student strikes or were shut down that year. At Cornell, the university was shut down in 1969 by armed black radicals demanding autonomous "black studies" programs and segregated dormitories, among other things. The university leadership cravenly capitulated before armed force, while Harvard arrested protestors and gave in to their demands simultaneously. *Time* magazine noted that there was "a growing feeling throughout the nation that the rebels have at last gone too far."[34]

The furthest fringes of radical protest were not satisfied with merely shutting down a campus. There were nearly a hundred bombings, attempted bombings, or acts of arson on college campuses during the first six months of 1969; a favorite target was campus Reserve Officer and Training Corps (ROTC) offices. The worst bombing occurred at the University of Wisconsin in 1970, when a bomb in a science building killed a graduate student working in the building late at night. The Weather Underground's plan to reprise the events of the 1968 Chicago convention through the "Days of Rage" was a bust; only a few hundred rowdies showed up in Chicago, and were quickly rolled up by Chicago police after a petulant frenzy of window smashing. Nixon's move to change the draft to a lottery system, a prelude to abolishing the draft entirely, began to cut off the oxygen supply of the antiwar movement. The apolitical cohort of students who opposed the war simply to save their own skin stopped attending the protest rallies, except for the purpose of getting dates.

Despite the growing violence and palpable absurdity of leftist politics, the Establishment's indulgence of youthful protest continued to grow, and constituted the greatest expression of the Establishment's exhaustion and declining self-confidence. The National Commission on the Causes and Prevention of Violence, appointed by President Johnson in the aftermath of the events of 1968, reported back in 1969 that campus upheaval "mirrors the turmoil . . . and the economic and social imbalances which bitterly divide the American people today." Others divined a moral equivalence at work: "Freedom of expression in America," President Kennedy's speechwriter Theodore Sorenson warned, "particularly on our college campuses, is under increasing pressure from the New Left and the Old Right," as though Herbert Marcuse and Ronald Reagan were equally responsible for starting college conflagrations.[35]

The National Council of Churches sanctified student violence on the grounds that "God is in some way present in the midst of these movements, and we would be prepared to see in them His creating of a new order."[36] Silly clerics are one thing, but the approbation of the revolutionary character of youth culture extended to the highest reaches of the nation's leadership. The very liberal Supreme Court Justice William O. Douglas caused a furor when he wrote in 1970 that "Violence has no constitutional sanction, but when grievances pile high and most of the elected spokesmen represent the Establishment, violence may be the only effective response." Britain's King George III, Douglas elaborated, "was the symbol against which our founders made a revolution now considered bright and glorious. We must realize that today's Establishment is the new King George III. Whether it will continue to adhere to his tactics, we do not know. If it does, the redress, honored in tradition, is also revolution."[37]

Republican Minority Leader Gerald Ford took to the floor of the House of Representatives to give a 90-minute speech calling for the impeachment of Douglas. A few old liberals spoke up against the tide. In a memo to Nixon, Pat Moynihan commented: "Someone should be pointing out that when an upper-middle-class Ivy Leaguer says something particularly outrageous, official America is supposed to respond that 'he is trying to tell us something.' But when a young construction worker says something in response, we are to conclude that he is a dangerous neofascist who must be silenced." Among liberal intellectuals, historian Henry Steele Commager was practically alone in denouncing campus leftists as "Luddites of this generation," and warning that "academic freedom is being destroyed from within."

Even Nixon unwittingly contributed to the indulgence of countercultural protest when he appointed a commission to study campus disturbances headed by former Pennsylvania Governor William Scranton, who had been one of Goldwater's liberal Republican rivals in 1964. The report the commission produced in the fall of 1970 was every bit as fatuous about the roots and nature of student radicalism as was the Cox report on the Columbia University episode in 1968. Like the Cox report, the Scranton report validated the youthful pretensions to moral superiority and higher insight about "The System." The report found that the "counterculture" was the repository of "high ideals," whose members "stress the need for humanity, equality, and the sacredness of life." The student protesters represented a "new culture," rebelling against their "elders entrapped by materialism and competition . . . prisoners of outdated social forms." The report, Norman Podhoretz observed, "accorded a kind of *de jure* diplomatic recognition [of the counterculture] by the United States government itself," and established the counterculture "as a legitimate entity in American life, an alternative mode of living and thinking which, the Report comes very close to declaring explicitly, is superior to that of everyone else."[38] Vice President Agnew, in a phrase Pat Buchanan most likely coined, called the Scranton report "pablum for the permissivists." Nixon was furious with the outcome, and did his best to suppress the report he had commissioned.

LIKE TANGLED DEBRIS left on the riverbank after a flood, the receding tide of the New Left deposited long-lasting residue on American culture and public life. The most significant residue was radical feminism and other variations of what has become known as "identity politics." These represented the long-term institutionalization of New Left sensibilities. It signaled the beginning of a now familiar process by which grievance groups—feminists, ethnics, homosexuals, and so forth—were granted specialized curricula on campus that were short on substance but heavy on the theme of "oppression," and special commissions and offices in government to perpetuate group consciousness. Starting for the first time with the 1970 census, for example, people of Hispanic origin were classified as a separate ethnic group; previously people of Hispanic origin had been classified as "Caucasian," just as Italians, Greeks, Slavs, Armenians, Jews, and other immigrant groups had always been (and still are).

Feminists had made a splash by protesting the Miss America pageant in Atlantic City in 1968, which featured perhaps the first episode of public bra-burning. Among other complaints at the 1968 protest: Miss America represented "a Military Death Mascot." By 1970 feminism lurched forward as yet another schism within the Left. Feminist author Robin Morgan let out a blast against "the counterfeit Left, counterfeit, male-dominated cracked glass mirror reflection of the Amerikan Nightmare." "White males," she charged, "are most responsible for the destruction of human life and environment on the planet today. . . . Women are the real left." *Ms.* Magazine debuted in 1971; its editor, Gloria Steinem, declared in the first issue that "Eliminating the patriarchal and racist base of the existing social system requires a revolution, not a reform." The National Organization of Women (NOW) was still fledgling in 1970, with only 3,000 members and about 100 local chapters. While the radicals dominated the headlines, behind the scenes the quiet signs of change were occurring. In June 1972, the first woman rabbi in the United States was ordained in Cincinnati, and the following month the FBI swore in its first two female agents. (J. Edgar Hoover had died just three months before.)

The most important feminist totem was the Equal Rights Amendment (ERA), which Congress passed by lopsided majorities (only eight no votes in the Senate, 24 no votes in the House) and sent to the states for ratification in 1972. The amendment was seemingly simple and straightforward: "Equality of rights under law shall not be denied or abridged by the United States or by any state on account of sex." The Republican Party had backed the ERA in its platform since 1940; Nixon supported the ERA, as did his successor, Gerald Ford. The near-unanimity of support for the ERA extended even to Ronald Reagan, who wrote in January of 1972 to Barbara Trister, president of Theta Sigma Phi: "I am in full support of the Equal Rights Amendment, and will be pleased if you are able to find a use for my name in attracting additional support."[39] Reagan was squarely in the mainstream of public opinion; polls showed that the ERA enjoyed the support of two-thirds of Americans.

Thirty-three states voted to ratify the amendment in the first 18 months after Congress passed the amendment, but 38 states are required for ratification, and after the initial flurry the ERA began running into trouble. With the rise of judicial activism in the 1960s, generating court rulings untethered to any common sense rendering of statutes or the Constitution, second thoughts began to arise about the potentially sweeping effects of the ERA in the hands of lawyers and judges. Could the amendment be used to ban separate bathrooms, men's clubs, or require admitting women into combat roles in the military? State legislators began to receive a torrent of mail opposing the amendment—most of it from women. Armed with these growing doubts, momentum swung against the ERA. It was rejected in Oklahoma, Vermont, and Connecticut; in the latter state, 10 of the 18 women in the state legislature voted against ratification. Then three states voted to rescind their ratification, which some constitutional scholars doubted was permissible. Congress voted to extend the ratification deadline in 1978, but no more states approved the ERA and the ratification effort expired in the early 1980s.

It is not clear that women needed the ERA for its main equitable goals. A commonplace claim made at the time of the ERA debate was that women were paid only 59 cents for every dollar a man was paid. (It was fashionable during the early stages of the ERA for feminists to wear buttons reading "59¢.") This type of statistic is still put forth today as a supposed measure of the inequality of the sexes, though today the claimed figure is about 80 cents. This so-called "wage gap" was the cornerstone of what feminists call "the glass ceiling." But the wage gap ignores major differences in job qualification, tenure of work experience, and other relevant factors. Economist June O'Neill commented that "When earnings comparisons are restricted to men and women more similar in their experience and life situations, the measured earnings differentials are typically quite small."[40] More to the point, between 1960 and 1994, women's wages grew 10 times faster than men's wages.

Measures of women's participation in higher education and the advanced professions also show a rapid rate of change and near-parity with men as a group. Women outnumber men in four-year colleges and universities today, and women now earn about 55 percent of all Bachelor's and Master's Degrees awarded in the United States. The story is similar in the advanced professions. In 1970, women earned fewer than 10 percent of all medical degrees; by 1995 women earned more than 40 percent of medical degrees. Other advanced professional degrees—such as law, dentistry, MBA—show similar huge jumps in participation by women.

It is precisely because of these trends, which tended to make the ERA unnecessary or superfluous to most women, that the feminist movement degenerated into a fever swamp, discerning omnipresent "oppression" of women in increasingly subtle and obscure ways similar to Herbert Marcuse's "repressive tolerance" that was so inspirational to the New Left a decade earlier. Most women had little use for this kind of paranoia (though the new feminist attitude proved useful to professional women as a tool to be picked up and laid aside as needed), and it was ultimately women turning against the ERA that finished it off. Feminist author Sylvia Ann Hewlett lamented in 1986: "It is sobering to realize that the ERA was defeated not by Barry Goldwater, Jerry Falwell, or any combination of male chauvinist pigs, but by women who were alienated from a feminist movement the values of which seemed elitist and disconnected from the lives of ordinary people."[41]

Feminists did not have the gender identity stage to themselves in the 1970s, however; gay pride was soon crowding in front of the footlights.

IN 1969 NEW YORK'S statutes included a law requiring that anyone in a public place wear at least three pieces of clothing "appropriate to one's gender." Such laws provided New York City police with the authority to raid and close up gay bars, which they did frequently. At 1:20 A.M. on a June evening in 1969 New York police made a sweep of the Stonewall Inn, located on Christopher Street just off 8th Avenue in Greenwich Village, which was a favorite spot for drag queens and petty drug dealing. Police raided the Stonewall Inn regularly, but this time the gay clientele of Stonewall did not go quietly into the night, or into the paddy wagon. As with most riots, it was impossible to determine what set off the conflagration. According to one account, a crowd started throwing rocks and bottles at the police after someone in the paddy wagon kicked a policeman in the chest with a fishnet stocking–clad leg. As the melee grew, the police were forced to retreat and call for the riot squad.

The gay population was not cowed by the tough riot squad that showed up, and hence began three days of low intensity rioting in Greenwich Village. It was perhaps the first time a riot had featured a heel-kicking chorus line:

> We are the Stonewall girls
> We wear our hair in curls
> We wear no underwear
> We show our pubic hair . . .
> We wear our dungarees
> Above our nelly knees![42]

Stonewall became the gay equivalent of the Montgomery bus boycott, and marked a turning point for "gay pride." The anniversary of the Stonewall riots became, gay writer Randy Shilts wrote, "the high holy day of the national gay movement." Gay rights as a political movement came fully into the open starting with Stonewall, and it is a measure of its progress that the Stonewall Inn is now listed as an official site on the National Historic Register. Homosexuality gained rapid acceptance in the 1970s. Another major milestone occurred in 1974, when the American Psychiatric Association removed homosexuality from its roster of mental illnesses.

MORE SIGNIFICANT than the rise of identity politics and the corruption of higher education was the entertainment industry's growing embrace of the countercultural Left's insurrection against middle-class values and styles, which had been well underway since the mid-1960s. Mostly this was manifest in a continuing erosion of standards and taboos. In August 1969 *Playboy* magazine published its first photograph showing pubic hair. In 1970, *M*A*S*H* became the first major motion picture to use the word "fuck" in its dialogue. Intended as a thinly veiled satire against the Vietnam War, *M*A*S*H* was written by Ring Lardner Jr., one of the "Hollywood Ten" writers blacklisted for being a Communist in the 1950s.

A few major movies cut against the grain, such as *Dirty Harry*, Clint Eastwood's vehicle for criticizing the permissive attitude toward crime that was pervasive among liberals in the late 1960s. *Dirty Harry*, film critic Richard Grenier later observed, "was the first popular movie to talk back to liberalism," and was a hit with conservatives. (This was during the period that Reagan liked to joke that a liberal's idea of being tough on crime was to give longer suspended sentences.) Early in the film, Eastwood's character, Inspector Harry Callahan, who incredibly affected complete ignorance of a suspect's due process rights, quizzes his new young partner about his education. A degree in sociology from San Jose State University. "Oh, you'll go far," Eastwood sarcastically replies. The movie also directed a blast against the decisions of the Warren Court such as *Miranda*. "Well, I'm all broken up about that man's rights," Eastwood says with derision and sarcasm when the district attorney informs him a murderer cannot be prosecuted. *Dirty Harry* was a box office hit, but its sequels consciously adopted more liberal themes as if to offer penance for the first film's reactionary character.

Patton, which lionized the aggressive war fighting spirit of World War II General George S. Patton, won the best picture Academy Award in 1970. However, the film was originally going to be titled *Patton: Salute to a Rebel*, in order to attract the youth market. *Patton* represented a complete turnabout for its star, George C. Scott, who had played a lunatic general in *Dr. Strangelove* six years before.

For the most part, though, the main current of popular entertainment continued to embrace and celebrate the styles and mores of the counterculture, and entertainment became increasingly politicized. *The New*

Yorker's legendary film critic Pauline Kael wrote in 1970 that "Many of the best recent American movies leave you feeling there's nothing to do but get stoned and die. . . ." Kael had *Easy Rider* mostly in mind. After the appearance of *Easy Rider*, which glorified the cocaine trade as well as the outlaw biker lifestyle, comedian Buck Henry remarked that "Now the children of Dylan were in control."[43] *Time* called *Easy Rider* "one of the ten most important motion picture events of the decade." The Georgia State Senate condemned *Easy Rider* in a 1969 resolution because "heroin-selling, pot-smoking, LSD-taking motorcycle riders are portrayed as the good guys while those folks who comprise a portion of the 'silent majority' are made to look like creeps in the hayloft."[44] Such rearguard protests disappeared into oblivion. (*Easy Rider* also signaled a new phase of rock and roll music, when Steppenwolf, in "Born to Be Wild," provided the moniker for the dominant electric guitar style pioneered by Led Zepplin: "I can see the lightning/*Heavy-metal* thunder. . .")

No show better demonstrated the change in entertainment industry perspectives and tastes since the days of *Father Knows Best* than the advent of the TV show that might easily have been called *Father Knows Least*. In the late 1960s veteran Hollywood producers Norman Lear and Bud Yorkin, whose credits included *The Andy Williams Show* and *The Dinah Shore Show*, were looking for a vehicle for new style of TV situation comedy. Lear and Yorkin learned of a hit British comedy, *Till Death Do Us Part*, about a British family of modest means headed by a bigoted father who clashed with his live-in son-in-law. Lear and Yorkin bought the American rights to the show, and persuaded ABC to back a pilot for a show they wanted to call *Those Were the Days*. ABC was unimpressed even after the pilot episode was reshot, and dropped the show. CBS, which had dropped *The Smothers Brothers Comedy Hour* because of its controversial political content, liked Lear's pilot, however, and after some retooling and a name change, the show debuted as *All in the Family* on Tuesday, January 12, 1971, starring veteran actors Carroll O'Connor and Jean Stapleton.

This was clearly going to be "A Show With a Message." An announcement ran before the premier: "The program you are about to see is *All in the Family*. It seeks to throw a humorous spotlight on our frailties, prejudices, and concerns. By making them a source of laughter we hope to show—in a mature fashion—just how absurd they are." CBS added extra operators to its switchboard the night of the premier, expecting a flood of angry phone calls. The main character, Archie Bunker, was intended to represent the semi-educated, working class Everyman who dominates the American electorate. Each week Archie proved himself an equal opportunity abuser of all minorities, letting loose a torrent of racial epithets including spic, Mick, Hebes, Polacks, fairies, fags, Chinks, coloreds, black beauties, jungle bunnies (but, significantly, never "nigger"), among other epithets. Most pervasive of all was his habitual description of his wife Edith as a "dingbat." Network executives resisted Lear's desire to let Archie say "goddamnit."

Although Archie had the best comic lines, he was clearly the loser in the didactic, set-piece arguments with his graduate-school educated, Noam Chomsky–quoting son-in-law, Mike Stivic, ably played by Rob Reiner. "Archie's dilemma," actor Carroll O'Connor explained, "is coping with a world that is changing in front of him. . . . But he won't get to the root of the problem because the root of the problem is himself, and he doesn't know it."[45] In other words, the vast American working class consists of ignoramuses.

Because of its lively writing and its loud acting style (which bordered on shouting through most episodes), *All in the Family* quickly became the highest rated show on television. Yet its satirical intent backfired to some extent. Far from becoming a figure of contempt and derision as intended, Archie Bunker became a folk hero character for many Americans who identified themselves with his simple prejudices. A 1973 survey found that Archie Bunker's face was the most recognized face in America, and "Archie Bunker for President" bumper stickers became a popular item. Archie Bunker's name was actually placed in nomination for vice president at the Democratic National Convention in Miami in July 1972. O'Connor, a long-time Hollywood liberal, despised being stopped by fans on the street and praised for "telling the truth for a change" with his portrayal of Archie.

Meanwhile, civil rights leaders were not amused. The Urban League's Whitney Young called it "a new low in taste," and deplored "the creative liberals who find racism a fit subject for television comedy."[46] (A better role model for moving beyond racism, Young suggested, was the new governor of Georgia, Jimmy Carter.) The Anti-Defamation League said

Archie was "too enjoyable" and that the show made "bigotry tolerable." the *New York Times* echoed this criticism.

Not for the first time, Americans ignored the critics on all sides, and *All in the Family* became, in the words of television chronicler Alex Mc-Neil, "the most influential show in TV history." One reason people of all ideological descriptions liked *All in the Family* is that they knew Archie's crude bigotry was largely an anachronism, something out of the "Amos 'n' Andy" era. Not very many real bigots actually spoke that way any more. The time of *All in the Family* can be considered a transitional moment on the way to our current world of politically correct sensitivity to all distinctions among people and groups. In 1968, Calvert Whiskey had cancelled $30,000 in advertising after an Indian civil rights group complained about the ad's visual image of a warbonneted Indian chief praising Calvert's "firewater," and in the early 1970s Stanford University changed its team name from "Indians" to "The Cardinal" in order not to give offense to native Americans.

Amidst this rising climate of increasing racial and ethnic sensitivity, conservative and working class viewers embraced Archie's character partly out of nostalgia, while liberals delighted in his being the embodiment of ignorance. The point is, for all its "cutting edge" image, *All in the Family* succeeded because it was following and affirming changes in American sentiment that were well established by 1970. By 1970 polls and other measures showed dramatic changes in public attitudes about race and ethnicity. Between 1964 and 1970, for example, the number of blacks elected to public office nationwide had jumped from 103 to 1,469. (By 1994 the number had grown to 8,406.)[47] In this respect, Hollywood is largely a lagging indicator of social change.

All in the Family nonetheless broke the dam in Hollywood, spawning numerous socially conscious (the social conscience was invariably liberal) imitators. Over the course of the 1970s few "family" sitcoms depicted intact, two-parent families with normal kids. Single moms and divorced or dysfunctional households were now the rage. Many of them were developed by Norman Lear himself. One new Lear show, *Maude,* was a spin-off of *All in the Family.* Maude, played by veteran actress Bea Arthur, was Edith Bunker's sharp-tongued, liberal-minded cousin, and was brought in as a guest star on *Family* as a reinforcement for Mike against the irrepressible Archie. Once spun-off into its own show, *Maude* shot to the top ten in the Nielsen ratings. *Maude* pressed the envelope for the feminist viewpoint; in one episode, Maude made having had an abortion a point of pride.

This was one instance where Hollywood was a concurrent rather than lagging indicator of social change. By the early 1970s abortion was slowly and quietly working its way up the judicial ladder. Several states, including New York, had gone through bitter debates over liberalizing their abortion statutes—New York in 1970 changed its law to allow abortion in cases of rape, incest, or pregnancies that threatened the life or health of the mother. The bill passed by a single vote in the legislature. Demographers noticed an immediate drop in New York's birthrate. By 1971, 11 states had liberalized their abortion laws, though few allowed abortion-on-demand. In 1971 federal District Court Judge Gerhart Gesell ruled that "a woman's liberty and right to privacy . . . may well include the right to remove an unwanted child." It was an opinion obviously cast to draw appellate review of the broadest grounds of the issue.

There was, however, no widespread recognition that abortion would come to be a central preoccupation of judicial politics. Nixon set out to put a more conservative cast on the Supreme Court by appointing "strict constructionists," that is, jurists who would construe the Constitution narrowly or in accordance with the "original intent" of the Founders. But the Senate rejected Nixon's first two nominees, Clement Haynsworth and G. Harold Carswell, because they were thought too conservative and Southern-leaning. When Nixon then appointed Judge Harry Blackmun from Minnesota in 1970, *Time* magazine wrote that "There is little likelihood that Blackmun will be criticized for his judicial philosophy or specific decisions," while *U.S. News and World Report* speculated that Blackmun would bolster the "'conservative' power" on the Court.[48]

Strict constructionism? "I don't know what it means," Blackmun told a reporter. Blackmun was swiftly confirmed, and would go on to demonstrate his lack of care for constitutional construction by writing the 1973 *Roe v. Wade* decision that mandated abortion-on-demand in all 50 states. *Roe*, it was thought, would end the horrendous practice of "back alley" abortions, yet the Centers for Disease Control reported that in 1972, the year before *Roe*, there were just 39 deaths from illegal abortions, while there were 27 deaths from legal ones.[49] There had been 480,000 legal abortions in 1971. After *Roe*, the number of abortions nearly tripled, to as many as 1.5 million a year. The *New York Times* opined that *Roe* had "settled the issue" once and for all, but just the opposite was true: Abortion henceforth became one of the most contentious national issues.

OF ALL THE cultural path-breaking of the late 1960s and early 1970s, one episode still commands fascination today: Woodstock. Part of the enduring fascination with Woodstock was the unprecedented scale of the event. Promoters hoped for 120,000 people; when 400,000 showed up (with many thousands more physically unable to get to the rural site), it not only made Woodstock the 22nd largest "city" in America (and the third largest in New York state), but may well have constituted the largest gathering in history at that time. The organizers were wholly unprepared for the massive throng. Food ran out within hours of the first day, though drugs remained in plentiful supply throughout. The "miracle" of Woodstock is that such an enormous throng didn't descend into riotous chaos. That nearly all the crowd was stoned throughout has seldom entered into the explanations for the peaceful nature of the crowd.

Woodstock set off a fresh round of self-congratulation about the idealism of the young generation. The absence of destructive chaos was taken as evidence of the moral superiority of the counterculture's rejection of middle-class materialism. It was, in Abbie Hoffman's words, "the birth of the Woodstock Nation and the death of the American dinosaur."

"This festival will show," Woodstock organizer Michael Lang said, "that what this generation is about is valid . . . This is not just about music, but a conglomeration of everything involved in the new culture."[50] The *New York Times* thought Woodstock was "essentially a phenomenon of innocence," while *Time* magazine chirped that Woodstock

> may well rank as one of the significant political and sociological events of the age. . . . [T]he revolution it preaches, implicitly or explicitly, is essentially moral; it is the proclamation of a new set of values. . . . With a surprising ease and a cool sense of authority, the children of plenty have voiced an intention to live by a different ethical standard than their parents accepted. The pleasure principle has been elevated over the Puritan ethic of work. To do one's own thing is a greater duty than to be a useful citizen. Personal freedom in the

midst of squalor is more liberating than social conformity with the trappings of wealth. Now that youth takes abundance for granted, it can afford to reject materialism.[51]

The New Left was not thrilled with the spin surrounding Woodstock because it suggested that the revolution of youth was far less political than cultural. After all, the New Left had struggled to get a mere 10,000 to come to Chicago the summer before. "Our frivolity maddened the Left," one concertgoer remarked. "We did not even collect pennies for SANE [Society for the Abolition of Nuclear Energy]." Abbie Hoffman was booed when he attempted to offer some political remarks: The Who's Pete Townshend whacked Hoffman with his guitar to get him off the stage.[52] But the ever-protean ideological Left managed to adapt. Leftist writer Andrew Kopkind wrote that Woodstock represented

> a new culture of opposition. It grows out of the disintegration of old forms, the vinyl and aerosol institutions that carry all the inane and destructive values of privatism, competition, commercialism, profitability and elitism. . . . For people who had never glimpsed the intense communitarian closeness of a militant struggle—People's Park or Paris in the month of May or Cuba—Woodstock must always be their model of how good we will all feel after the revolution. . . . [P]olitical radicals have to see the cultural revolution as a sea in which they can swim.[53]

A surprisingly sympathetic account of Woodstock in *National Review* noted that Woodstock was "a moment of glorious innocence, and such moments happen only by accident, and then not often. . . . [T]hese accidental bursts of aimless solidarity do not last forever."[54] In fact the purported innocence and new moral world of Woodstock would prove as evanescent as the summer showers that cooled off the concertgoers at Max Yasgur's farm. A few months later the attempted sequel to Woodstock at California's Altamont Pass ended violently when the Hells Angels hired as stage security proved they were not yet ready to be part of the Age of Aquarius. The Hells Angels beat a concertgoer to death just a few feet in front of Mick Jagger, who was in the middle of singing "Sympathy for the Devil." In contrast to the encomiums to Woodstock, there was little media commentary suggesting that Altamont showed a dark side of the counterculture.

IT IS WHEN one views Nixon's approach to the domestic crisis of the nation that the full idiosyncrasies of his character and intellect are most fully revealed, and the contrast with the way Reagan confronted a similar mood a decade later most striking. Though Nixon liked to think of himself as resisting the exhaustion of the Establishment, on a fundamental level he was himself symptomatic of it. On the surface no one could seem more opposed to the Spenglerian cloud of American pessimism than Richard Nixon. Rhetorically he exuded a visceral rejection of the negativism that gripped much of the nation. In announcing the controversial Cambodian incursion in 1970, which ran counter to his "winding down the war" policy and touched off a new frenzy of anti-war protests, Nixon emphasized that it was crucial that America not come to be seen as a "pitiful, helpless giant." More significant was his call for the "silent majority" of Americans to resist the tide of negativism and protest, a slogan that seemed to generate a spontaneous outpouring of public enthusiasm.

While the antiwar movement erupted in fresh frenzy after Cambodia, Nixon's public approval rating went up six points. In a spontaneous moment Nixon once referred to antiwar protestors as "bums," and yet in one of the most bizarre episodes in his presidency Nixon showed his sentimental side. When thousands of antiwar protestors streamed to Washington in 1969, Nixon made a spur-of-the-moment early morning trip to the Lincoln Memorial, where, with minimal Secret Service protection, he attempted to establish a sympathetic rapport with angry student protestors. "I know that probably most of you think I'm an S.O.B.," Nixon told the students, "but I want you to know that I understand how you feel." His attempts to connect with the students through questions about college football and recollections of the rigors of college coursework met with mixed success, while the absent news media, angry about not having been apprised of this venture, were severely critical.

This was the Nixon of his small-town, up-by-the-bootstraps origins, whose celebration of America as the land of hope and opportunity is the hallmark of Main Street Republicanism. To borrow the ancient Greek imagery, this represented Nixon's passions, while his intellectual side—his reason—was in conflict. For there was a strong pessimistic strain to Nixon's intellectual outlook. Perhaps he had absorbed it from his acquaintance early in his career with that great pessimist Whittaker Chambers, who thought the cause of Western democracy was doomed to be overrun eventually by the Communist revolution. Nixon's pessimistic outlook may also have been subtly reinforced by Kissinger, whose much vaunted "realism" can easily be made out to be a cover for an acquiescence in American decline, as we shall see in chapter 9. Indeed this may explain some of the attraction Nixon had for Kissinger.

The odd combination of Nixon's philosophical pessimism and Republican Main Street boosterism was on full display in a remarkable and underappreciated speech Nixon made to a convention of media executives in Kansas City in July 1971. Nixon had made several briefings to regional news executives, but this one went far beyond the others in its philosophical depth. The speech offers great insight into Nixon, and was as much a harbinger of the decade of the 1970s as it was a comment on the present moment. In fact, Nixon's Kansas City speech can be regarded as one of the decade's rhetorical bookends, along with President Jimmy Carter's infamous "crisis of confidence" speech in 1979.

Speaking extemporaneously without a prepared text, Nixon took square aim at the "negativism, defeatism, [and] sense of alienation" that was dominant in the American mind at the moment. "I don't want to sound here like a moralist or preacher, although I have great respect for preachers and moralists. This Nation needs moral health. By moral health, I use the term in a very broad sense." Nixon directly challenged the notion, "raised often in your editorial columns," he chided the media executives, that "the United States cannot be trusted with power . . . because we engage in immorality in our foreign policy." Nixon utterly rejected the defeatism behind the distrust of American power, and offered the typical politician's refrain about the innate sources of strength and goodness to be found among America's citizens in the "Heartland." Yet between these two points of resistance Nixon offered a curious affirmation of thesis that America was in decadent decline. My favorite building in Washington, Nixon explained, was the National Archives building, "because it has the appearance of the ages there" and because it "is simply one that holds the Constitution, the Bill of Rights, the Declaration of Independence, the great documents that started the Nation at the beginning."

But then came the curious part. In his off-the-cuff remarks Nixon's syntax seemed to confuse the pillars of the Archives building with the founding documents it holds as the pillars of the American regime:

> Sometimes when I see those pillars I think of seeing them on the Acropolis in Greece. I think of seeing them also in the Forum in Rome, great stark pillars—and I have walked in both at night, as I have walked down by the Archives at night from time to time.
>
> I think of what happened to Greece and to Rome and, as you see, what is left—only the pillars. What has happened, of course, is that great civilizations of the past, as they have become wealthy, as they have lost their will to live, to improve, they then have become subject to the decadence which eventually destroys a civilization.
>
> *The United States is now reaching that period.* (Emphasis added.)

No president had ever publicly spoken this way before. It turned out that Nixon, too, was a cultural pessimist. But Nixon accurately expressed the fact that the nation's discontent was not limited to, or defined by, the Vietnam experience alone. Though Nixon viscerally rejected defeatism and opposed the decadent spirit he saw at work in American cultural life, he seemed not to have any idea of what to do about it. Nixon's mixed and confused view of the American prospect bore out an evaluation Whittaker Chambers made in 1960, when he wrote to William F. Buckley Jr. about a recent lunch with Nixon: "If he were a great, vital man, bursting with energy, ideas (however malapropos), sweeping grasp of the crisis, and (even) intolerant convictions, I think I should have felt: Yes, he must have it [the presidency], he must enact his fate, and ours. I did not have this feeling . . . So I came away with unhappiness for him, for all."[55]

Chambers added an afterthought: "Of course, no such man as I have suggested now exists? Apparently not." Chambers did not live to evaluate the character and resolve of Ronald Reagan (who would award the Presidential Medal of Freedom posthumously to Chambers in 1983), but at the time Nixon was having his crisis of confidence in the American prospect, Reagan was starting to show the very kind of "intolerant convictions" that Chambers thought necessary.

GOVERNOR REAGAN characteristically took a different approach to the cultural crisis of the moment. Like Nixon, Reagan had sometimes made his own comparison between contemporary America and decadent ancient Rome. Reagan's analysis, while perhaps not faithful to Gibbon or other conventional narratives of Roman history, placed the blame for Rome's decadence on the effect of high taxes, inflation, and eroding morals of the middle class. It was intended to be a familiar and suggestive account. For Reagan, one faction stood above other causes of Rome's decline:

> Among the teachers and the scholars there was a group called the Cynics who let their hair and their beards grow and wore ragged and old clothing. They professed indifference to worldly goods and heaped scorn on what they called the culture of middle class values. (Now, I'm still talking about *Rome*.)[56]

Reagan refused to be swayed by the elite approbation of youth culture, to grant any concession to the America-in-decline viewpoint, or concede any blame for his generation. "The leaders of today's so-called establishment did not have to listen in a classroom lecture or make a field trip to the ghetto to learn about poverty. We lived it in the depths of the Great Depression. The horrors of war are not just a subject for a term paper to a generation that sent its finest young men to fight at Omaha Beach. . . ." Most significantly, Reagan refused to indulge the moral earnestness of the protest Left and its moderate liberal sympathizers. In testimony about campus unrest to the House Committee on Education and Labor in 1969, Reagan attacked the "mythologies" of the

> well-meaning apologists for anti-social behavior . . . who seek to make their excuses acceptable through sheer repetition. . . . To rationalize their permissiveness and appeasement, administrators themselves often promote myths which confuse those both on campus and off. They speak disparagingly of a "generation gap" at a time when too many parents are in awe of, and tend to imitate, their own children. They speak of a "new breed with wisdom and conscience" at a time when research has clearly indicated a social and emotional immaturity of youth to a degree previously unknown.[57]

If there was a "generation gap," it was entirely the fault of the younger generation. To the contrary of both Nixon and the New Left, Reagan asserted:

We have been picked at, sworn at, rioted against and downgraded until we have a built-in guilt complex, and this has been compounded by the accusations of our sons and daughters who pride themselves on "telling it like it is." Well, I have news for them—in a thousand social science courses they have been informed "the way it is not" . . . As for our generation I will make no apology. No people in all history paid a higher price for freedom. And no people have done so much to advance the dignity of man. . . . We are called materialistic. Maybe so. . . . But our materialism has made our children the biggest, tallest, most handsome and intelligent generation of Americans yet. They will live longer with fewer illnesses, learn more, see more of the world and have more successes and realizing their personal dreams and ambitions than any other people in any other period of our history—because of our "materialism."

Reagan, it is clear, was not the kind of man who would ever have—or comprehend in others—a "mid-life crisis."

Reagan met the agitation of the Left with his typical combination of toughness and humor. His toughness cheered the general public that was exasperated with protest, while his humor deflated the moral pretensions of the Left. Reagan bluntly referred to campus protestors as "cowardly little fascist bands." He also ridiculed protestors. "I had a nightmare last night," Reagan said in his standard after-dinner speech, "I dreamed I owned a laundromat in Berkeley." He also claimed to have thought of a new way to fight smog: "Stop burning down the schools."

Reagan naturally attracted fierce criticism for his blunt rhetoric and stern action. *The Los Angeles Times* called him "anti-intellectual," and the co-chairman of the California Democratic Party said that Reagan's response "has been so oppressive and so indiscriminate in its application that he has done enormous damage to the colleges and universities of this state." Reagan set off a firestorm, however, with a comment on campus protest in April 1970. Answering a question about New Left campus tactics before a meeting of the California Council of Growers in Yosemite, Reagan said: "If it takes a bloodbath, let's get it over with. No more appeasement." Liberals howled with indignation. Assembly speaker Jesse Unruh, Reagan's opponent for re-election that fall, said that Reagan "had forfeited any right to hold public office." Others complained that Reagan was actually inciting violence on campus. Even Reagan's friends at *National Review* worried that "the potential for political disaster here is huge."

Yet it was Reagan's candor that polls showed to be his most admired trait among the public, and Reagan was taking the Left at its word that its goal was violent insurrection against the Establishment. Most politicians glossed over the implications of the Left's rhetoric (never mind their tactics), drawing fine distinctions between civil disobedience (good) and violence (bad). These are exactly the kind of distinctions that Reagan, in his simple way of looking at things, thought amounted to little more than moral evasion and false sophistication attempting to mask the necessity for hard decisions. The timing seemed to be unfortunate. It was less than a month later that the Ohio National Guard fatally shot four students at Kent State. Yet this episode showed that Reagan's hard line was close to the heart of public sentiment; a *Newsweek* poll found 57 percent of the public blamed the students for the incident, and other polls found a majority sided with the Ohio guardsmen (who were later acquitted in a trial).

California naturally saw more than its share of campus turmoil and violence in 1969 and 1970. Student rioters at UC Santa Barbara burned a Bank of America branch to the ground in Isla Vista, the bank being the most prominent symbol of corporate capitalism available to be trashed. UCSB was also the scene of several campus bombings; one exploded in the faculty club and killed a maintenance man. Undeterred, several faculty members declared their support for a new course, "On the Tactics and Practice of Guerrilla Warfare at UCSB and the Santa Barbara Community."

Berkeley, too, experienced an incident that, like other Berkeley events, took on legendary dimensions. In 1969 the University razed a block of apartment buildings it had bought in 1967 between Dwight and Haste Streets, a few blocks away from the main campus. There was no definitive word what the University intended for the land. Rumors ranged from a new dormitory to a parking lot. While the land sat empty, a group of street people sodded and landscaped the land in early April, thereby performing, *National Review* commented, "the first constructive action of their lives." The university administration, however, was seemingly intent on proving that it had learned nothing from is mishandling of the Free Speech Movement five years earlier, and promptly panicked. On May 15 a university work crew descended on the lot, trampled the shrubs and plants, and put up a nine-foot fence around the lot. The University intended to build a soccer field on the site, the administration explained, soccer being "a sport which at Berkeley ranks right up there with cock-fighting," one observer noted.

The fenced lot was immediately dubbed "People's Park," and became a cause celebre for both the protest Left and regular students annoyed with the high-handedness of the administration. People's Park was turned into a symbol of the evil of the Establishment; protestors tried to tear down the fence, and the usual provocateurs incited protestors to start throwing rocks and bottles at the police. Reagan didn't hesitate to dispatch the California National Guard to quell the campus; their efforts included the first ever air raid on an American university when they dispatched three helicopters to spray tear gas down on a protest rally. "Those who want to get an education, those who want to teach," Reagan said in a 1969 press conference, "should be protected in that at the point of a bayonet if necessary."

BERKELEY'S EMINENT PHILOSOPHY professor, John Searle, wrote in 1969 that "A confident administration bent on defending intellectual values, and consequently determined to destroy the power of its essentially anti-intellectual adversary, can generally win."[58] Reagan emphatically agreed with Searle, remarking contemporaneously that "the university can dispose of the threat [radicals] represent in a week if they will take a stand." This is what finally happened at the scene of the most protracted and significant university upheaval in California, which occurred at San Francisco State College. In 1968 black militants decided to shut down UCSF—a campus of 18,000 students at the time—if the university did not immediately act on 15 "non-negotiable demands," which included a black studies department wholly autonomous from the university administration, and open admission for all black applicants. Black activists alone might not have been able to shut down San Francisco State, but other factions immediately joined up; the SDS naturally, but also a faction of the faculty and the local chapter of the American Federation of Teachers union, which the SFSC faculty had rejected as its bargaining unit, but which saw the fracas as an opportunity to regain their status.

At first the scene played out according to the standard script. SFSC president Robert Smith—the college's sixth president in eight years—temporized and evaded, and then stepped down in the closing months of

1968 after a faculty teaching assistant, who also happened to be the Black Panther's "minister of education," beat up Smith in his office. Into the breach the trustees appointed a diminutive, 62-year-old professor of semantics to be acting president of the college—Samuel Ichiye Hayakawa. Hayakawa quickly showed that he was made of sterner stuff than his witless predecessors in the president's chair. He drew nationwide publicity when he climbed onto a sound truck from which protestors were shouting obscenities through a microphone, knocked a protestor to the ground who stood in his way (Hayakawa weighed only 145 pounds), and ripped out the wiring of the sound equipment, which the protestors were unable to repair.

On another occasion Hayakawa brought a bullhorn to the protest, and shouted back at demonstrators. He also did not hesitate to call in police in large numbers to arrest protestors who disrupted classes. "In a democratic society," Hayakawa said in justifying his recourse to the police, "the police are there for the protection of our liberties. It is in a totalitarian society that police take away our liberties." He took activists at their word that their demands were "non-negotiable," and refused to negotiate. A star was born, and he would serve as a complement to Reagan's tough approach to campus troubles. Like Reagan, he referred to campus protestors as a "gang of goons and neo-Nazis," and criticized the hypocrisy of campus liberals who expressed sympathy for the extremism of black radicals. Hayakawa attacked "the intellectually slovenly habit, now popular among whites as well as blacks, of denouncing as racist those who oppose or are critical of any Negro tactic or demand. We have a standing obligation to the 17,500 or more students—white, black, yellow, red and brown—who are not on strike and have every right to expect continuation of their education." For such forthright resistance to the tides of campus disruption, the state university board of trustees, with Reagan in the lead, removed "acting" from Hayakawa's title in the spring of 1969, making him president in fact.

REAGAN'S PUBLIC APPROVAL ratings with California voters soared to 78 percent at one point in 1969, up sharply from the year before. This was the New Left's gift to Reagan. "Every time he shakes his finger at one of those mobs," a supporter remarked to *Newsweek,* "it gets him 10,000 votes." A Reagan campaign aide told the *New York Times:* "Campus unrest is an issue between Reagan and the people with nobody in between. They understand what he's saying. Reagan is a polarizing politician, much more than Nixon. With Nixon, there are all shades of gray, but that's not the way Reagan operates—he lays it out there." A Field Poll found that Reagan's strongest point with the public was that he "speaks his mind, [and is] honest, sincere, straightforward, decisive." For a time in 1969 Democratic fundraisers in California thought Hayakawa, who described himself as a "liberal Democrat," would be their best challenger against Reagan in 1970. Hayakawa was uninterested (he would be elected to the U.S. Senate in 1976 after having switched parties to become a Republican), so the job of opposing the popular Reagan fell to Assembly Speaker Jesse Unruh, the pot-bellied, mustachioed pol who is credited with originating the phrase, "Money is the mother's milk of politics."

The trouble for Unruh was that few of the Democratic Party's milk cows produced for him in 1970, while Reagan headed into the campaign with a vast war chest. Short of money and issues alike (he could hardly claim he would be tougher on campus unrest or welfare cheaters than Reagan), Unruh was compelled to employ a guerrilla campaign to attract free media. Many of his stunts fizzled. He attempted to bring attention to Reagan's wealthy backers by holding a press conference on the front lawn of Reagan "kitchen cabinet" member Henry Salvatori, charging that Reagan's tax reform ideas would entail a windfall of more than $5,000 to wealthy people like Salvatori. Salvatori, who Unruh's advance team thought was out of town, complicated Unruh's spectacle by charging angrily out his front door to confront Unruh: "Oh you ass, stop being so silly!" Unruh succeeded in getting lots of press coverage, but the stunt backfired. Reagan reacted with his typical cool: "I can remember when the worst thing you had on your front lawn was crabgrass." But it was nice, he also quipped, that he had an opponent who made house calls.

Unruh's campaign never recovered its bearings after this stunt, and Reagan's re-election was never in doubt, even though polls detected a late Democratic surge in California that was probably more part of the national trend than due to Unruh's efforts. Even the *Los Angeles Times*, which had rapped Reagan's handling of campus unrest (calling Reagan "an anti-intellectual political reactionary"), endorsed him again: "The great majority of Californians are people of the center—moderate, reasonable people who want pragmatic solutions to real problems. The

Governor's conduct in office has shown his growing awareness of these realities and a growing flexibility in meeting them."

Reagan coasted to re-election with a half-million vote margin—far smaller than his 1966 landslide, but still comfortable in an election that did not otherwise go well for Republicans in California or elsewhere in the country. Republicans lost the California Senate seat of Reagan's pal George Murphy, as well as their slim majority in the state legislature. The "emerging Republican majority" didn't. Despite Nixon's determined effort to capture Congress (he traveled more than 17,000 miles in 22 states campaigning on behalf of Republicans in the fall of 1970), the deteriorating economy dashed hopes that Republicans could build on their gains of 1968. Reagan's win in California was one of the few bright spots for the GOP on election night. The GOP lost 11 governorships elsewhere, and nine seats in the House of Representatives. Republicans scored a few breakthroughs. The Republicans did gain two seats in the U.S. Senate, but had hoped for many more. One of the pickups was in Tennessee, where Republican William Brock narrowly defeated incumbent Senator Albert Gore, the first time a Republican had won a Tennessee Senate seat in decades.

At the same time Reagan was being handily re-elected in California, in a sunbelt state on the other coast there were signs that the much heralded, post-civil rights "New South" was starting to emerge. *Time* magazine took note of this trend in a 1971 cover story featuring the new governor of Georgia, Jimmy Carter, who looked, *Time* noted, "eerily like John Kennedy from certain angles."[59] (The president of the Coca-Cola company had lobbied *Time* to put Carter on the cover.[60]) State Senator Jimmy Carter had won in a landslide against a weak Republican candidate in 1970, having already vanquished former Democratic Governor Carl Sanders in the Democratic primary by a similarly large margin. Carter, *Time* said, "is both product and destroyer of old myths. . . . a man as contradictory as Georgia itself." Carter had eschewed ideological labels during the campaign. "I believe I am more complicated than that," he replied when asked whether he was liberal, conservative, or moderate. But upon becoming governor he revealed himself to be more liberal than his campaign suggested, prompting even one of his media consultants to remark that "I was not aware that Carter was far more liberal than the campaign we were waging."[61]

"The time for racial discrimination is over," Carter declared in his inaugural address, which, coming from the state that had just passed through four more years of segregationist Lester Maddox as governor, marked a significant departure. Carter had a record of support for desegregation in the legislature, and as governor he placed a portrait of Martin Luther King Jr. in the state capitol. But he had run a subtle and vicious race-baiting campaign against Sanders in the Democratic primary, a sign that Carter had a streak of Machiavellian ruthlessness. Under Georgia's state constitution governors were limited to one term, so the ambitious, 46-year-old governor was already setting his sights on higher office. Most observers assumed this entailed a run for the U.S. Senate in 1974 when Carter's term as governor was over, but Carter had a more audacious notion. By the fall of 1971, not yet even a year in office, Carter and his inner circle were thinking about the White House.

Despite *Time*'s fulsome praise for Carter in 1971, there was no speculation in 1971 that he might have a future in national politics. While Carter would not appear on the media radar screen again for some time, Reagan's future was a constant source of speculation. Reagan had promised not to seek a third term as governor in 1974. Maybe he would seek the Senate seat currently held by liberal Democrat Alan Cranston. Nixon worried that Reagan might challenge him for the Republican presidential nomination in 1972. It was supposed that 1972 might be Reagan's only realistic window for the Oval Office. Stephen Roberts expressed the conventional wisdom in the *New York Times Magazine*: "In 1976, the reasoning goes, Reagan would be 65, and too old to run." At election time in 1970, *Newsweek* wrote that "By every normal measure, Ronald Reagan ought to be entitled to any political future he wants," but also noted that he might be too old to run for president in 1976. A close aide said, "The Presidency? Oh, he's not interested. Four more years and I think you'll see Ronald Reagan riding one of his horses off into the sunset."[62]

His second term got off to a rocky start. Reagan's opponents made an issue of Reagan's personal state income taxes in 1971; Reagan hadn't paid any in 1970, on account of investment losses and perfectly legal tax shelters relating to his real estate. The media pounced on the story and kept Reagan on the defensive for several weeks. "When a guy's built on celluloid," Democratic State Senator George Moscone said, "he goes up fast, but he burns out quickly." By the end of 1971, *Newsweek* had changed its assessment of Reagan. *Newsweek*'s story, "Ronald Reagan's Slow Fade," ended with the judgment that "the somber truth is that Sacramento may mark the end of Ronald Reagan's political road."[63] Reagan, too, was thought to be exhausted, and was written off again. How could a man well into his sixties, with such a traditionalist perspective, possibly reverse America's exhaustion and fallen confidence? By the time Reagan was ready to step into the breach to answer that question, America's exhaustion had given way to an even worse calamity—the crisis of Watergate.

CHAPTER EIGHT

WATERGATE AND

ITS AFTERMATH

———➤●◄———

I T WAS A FORMER banjo player named Richard Drew who invented
adhesive masking tape for the 3M company in 1925, while an engi-
neer named Marvin Camras developed magnetic recording tape after his
successes with wire recording devices in World War II. Like the slipping
pebble that starts an avalanche, by a strange coincidence the use of both
kinds of tape set in motion the nation's most acute constitutional crisis
since the Civil War.

To this day no one can say for sure what the Watergate burglars were
after when they were discovered on that fateful June night in 1972, but
their plan began to unravel when Watergate night security guard Frank
Wills stumbled across a stairwell door whose bolt had been taped open.
This is not unusual in office buildings, where movers and maintenance
crews often tape open doors to make entry and exit to the elevators and
suites easier. But when Wills came by on his rounds after midnight and
found the door taped open *again,* he knew something wasn't right and
called Washington, D.C., police. Police arrested five men (James McCord,
Bernard Barker, Eugenio Martinez, Frank Sturgis, and Virgilio Gonzalez)
in the sixth floor offices of the Democratic National Committee. They
were dressed in business suits, wore surgical gloves, and carried an assort-
ment of paraphernalia that included 39 rolls of film, two spotlight bulbs,
an extension cord, a small battery, a screwdriver, a roll of black tape, four
sponges, a pair of needle-nose pliers, a key to a secretary's desk in the

office, and several thousand dollars in cash. Notebooks were also found, containing cryptic references to the White House, along with the names and phone numbers for E. Howard Hunt and G. Gordon Liddy, who would be arrested and charged several weeks later for their role in planning the break-in. Strangely, accounts differ as to whether electronic listening devices ("bugs") were found in their possession; this turned out to be the *second* time the team had been inside the DNC Watergate offices, and this second trip was ostensibly to fix a previously planted bug that wasn't working. One reason the bug wasn't working is that someone had already removed it days or weeks before the burglars came back—one of the many anomalies of the Watergate story.

When it emerged a few days after the "burglary" that the burglars had connections to the CIA, the White House, and the Committee to Re-Elect the President, it was evident that a scandal of some dimension might unfold. The conspiratorial food chain led eventually up through President Nixon's senior staff to the Oval Office and Nixon himself. The entire affair might have remained limited to the five burglars and a few White House aides had it not been for Nixon's use of the second kind of tape—the magnetic recording kind. Nixon might never have been driven from office without evidence indicating his early knowledge of the Watergate cover-up, and the tapes provided the so-called "smoking gun" that was the final blow to his presidency. The infamous tape of June 23, 1972, captured Nixon, Haldeman, and John Dean discussing how to use the CIA to try to head off the FBI's investigation into Watergate. The attempt failed, and the investigation went ahead. Yet the conversation alone was thought sufficient evidence of conspiracy to obstruct justice.

The final irony of this Tale of the Tape is that Nixon was appalled when President Johnson explained the Oval Office taping system to him before he took office in 1969. Nixon ordered the taping system removed, but reinstalled another taping system in February 1971, after his concern for leaks and the accuracy of notes of decisions taken in innumerable Oval Office meetings, along with his desire to use the tapes as an *aide memoire* for his inevitable post-presidency writings, got the better of him. Nixon's taping system differed in one significant way from Johnson's: while Johnson had to turn his taping system on manually (which means he could be selective about what was taped), Nixon's was voice-activated. It vacuumed up everything that took place in Nixon's offices. Haldeman decided to install a voice-activated system because Nixon was notoriously inept with mechanical devices. Just more than 4,000 hours of conversation were taped by the time the system was shut off following its inadvertent public disclosure during the Senate Watergate hearings in 1973. Less than 10 percent of the tapes have been released to the public so far.

The culpability of Nixon in the Watergate cover-up is a supposedly well-established fact of the Watergate affair. What might be called the "Standard Heroic Account" of Watergate finds its wellsprings in Nixon's much-exaggerated "paranoia," (i.e., Nixon's fixation that his enemies were out to get him). The operation to plug leaks through the "Plumbers," along with the wiretapping and intelligence gathering efforts against the Left and other targets, is said to have melded with an overzealous effort at opposition research against Nixon's Democratic opponents in the 1972 campaign season that culminated in the Watergate break-in. Because earlier operations of the Plumbers—such as the break-in at the office of Dr. Lewis Fielding, Daniel Ellsberg's psychiatrist—had been illegal, it was feared that any probe of the Watergate affair would expose the entire underside of White House activities, which is exactly what happened over the next two years.

The Standard Heroic Account of the Watergate saga played out over two years as an epic struggle between the truth-seeking crusaders in Congress, the Justice Department, and the media against the villains in the White House trying to cover it all up, complete with a "Saturday Night Massacre" (when Nixon fired special prosecutor Archibald Cox and attempted to close down the investigation), missing or tampered evidence (the unexplained 18½ minute gap in a key Oval Office tape), hush money (cash payoffs to Howard Hunt and others), mystery figures ("Deep Throat," the still-secret source for *Washington Post* reporters Bob Woodward and Carl Bernstein), and betrayals (White House counsel John Dean, whose 1973 Senate testimony first implicated Nixon in the cover-up). With Nixon's resignation in August, 1974, the outcome of Watergate is regarded as a triumph of American constitutional democracy. The combination of a vigilant media and an aroused Congress supposedly showed that "the system works."

The Standard Heroic Account as plain narrative will doubtless be the main account for the annals of history, and therefore will not be retold in its fullness here. Yet many key aspects of Watergate remain mysterious or controversial, and what Hollywood calls "the back story" has never been widely understood. Who in the White House actually authorized the break-ins? Nixon's Attorney General and re-election campaign manager John Mitchell received the blame, but denied to his dying day that he ordered or approved either the burglary or the cover-up. Did Nixon know about the break-in beforehand? Most historians think not, yet Nixon speechwriter Bryce Harlow once remarked that Watergate happened because "Some damn fool got into the Oval Office and did what he was told," meaning that Watergate occurred because of the "paranoid" atmosphere Nixon generated around him.[1] What were they hoping to learn by bugging the Democratic National Committee? National committee offices are bureaucratic institutions, far removed from the inner circle of key decisions of presidential campaigns. The quadrennial campaign chronicler Theodore White wrote that the DNC "might more aptly be described as the central stationery supply closet of the party. . . . A good clipping service would have provided the Committee to Re-Elect with more information than any number of wiretaps."[2] By the time of the first Watergate break-in, it was known that Sen. George McGovern would be the Democratic nominee against Nixon, and there was little significant information that could be learned about his campaign at the DNC offices. G. Gordon Liddy is reported to have wanted to bug McGovern's campaign office, but McGovern had retained 24-hour security after the office had been burglarized by someone else (apparently a routine burglar after valuables, and not a political operation). Who was "Deep Throat?" Woodward refuses to say, more than 25 years later. Most fundamentally, what factors gave rise to the bugging operation in the first place? The number of conflicting accounts, strange anomalies, and conspiracy theories now rivals the Kennedy assassination.

The leading explanation of Watergate, which was given by, among others, G. Gordon Liddy, who headed the burglary team, is that the Nixon campaign wanted to see what information Democratic National Committee chairman Lawrence O'Brien might have had about Nixon, and particularly Nixon's connections to eccentric billionaire Howard Hughes or to a Greek tycoon, Thomas Pappas, whose secret contributions to Nixon's campaign would have been embarrassing if publicly revealed. This is the explanation that was generally accepted for most of the decade following Watergate. There is a startling anomaly, however, that casts doubt on this explanation: According to some accounts, O'Brien's office was never bugged (other accounts say a bug was planted, but didn't work), and the burglars were caught far from O'Brien's office on that fateful night. The original bug the burglars thought had malfunctioned—but which had in fact been removed—had been placed in the office of a low-level subordinate employee who was seldom at the office.

A more outlandish explanation that is gaining respect as time passes holds that at the root of the Watergate break-in was an attempt to gain embarrassing information about a call girl ring that had ties to someone working at the DNC. From this supposition, which rests on a web of circumstantial evidence, the threads of the story go in several directions. According to some accounts, the burglary team was after information about potentially prominent Democratic clients of the call girl ring, which information the Nixon campaign could use for public embarrassment or private blackmail. (The White House may also have worried about Republicans who might have been clients of the ring.) One variation of the story, propounded by author Jim Hougan in 1984, holds that the CIA was clandestinely involved in the burglary and deliberately botched the effort so as to avoid exposing the call girl ring. Why else, skeptics have asked, would veteran CIA agent James McCord do something as stupid as tape a door open a second time, which would be an obvious tip-off to Watergate security? Why the CIA would wish to do this is murky, but is said to have involved agency suspicions that Nixon was trying to exert too much control over the agency, which Nixon disliked. A faction of the military is also alleged to have helped exploit Watergate as a means to derail Nixon's arms control efforts. (This was, coincidentally, the line the Soviet press adopted.) "If we didn't know better," Nixon remarked on one of the famous tapes, "[we] would have thought it was deliberately botched."[3]

By far the most elaborate and problematic variation of this story holds that John Dean was the mastermind of the break-in, and was attempting to cover up connections his fiancee and future wife Maureen Biner had with the call girl ring. Len Colodny and Robert Gettlin argue this and much more in their controversial 1991 book *Silent Coup*. Colodny and Gettlin further maintain that the military, alarmed at Nixon's policy of détente and arms control, exploited Watergate to force Nixon's removal from office, and that Alexander Haig, who was Kissinger's deputy from 1969 and later became Nixon's chief of staff in

1973, was "Deep Throat." It was Haig who remarked during the unraveling of the Nixon presidency that some "sinister force" was responsible for the nefarious events at the White House; Colodny and Gettlin make a persuasive case that Haig himself was that "sinister force." Some of Colodny and Gettlin's evidence is compelling, while other conclusions require assumptions and leaps of logic that are less convincing. Yet, as Nixon scholar Joan Hoff writes, "*Silent Coup* has made all other books about the origins of Watergate obsolete."[4]

As interesting and provocative as these cloak and dagger accounts of the story may be, it obscures the fact that Watergate could not have happened without the previously established momentum for political spying and dirty tricks, (i.e., the creation of the "Plumbers" in the aftermath of the Pentagon Papers leak). Nixon's "paranoia" is always attributed as the ultimate cause for the "climate" that gave rise to such unsavory activities occurring in the White House. While the standard explanation is not wrong, it is worth recalling Delmore Schwartz's counsel that "just because you're paranoid doesn't mean they're not out to get you." The nation was divided as at no time since the Civil War, and Nixon indeed had political enemies. He meant to defeat them, and they knew it. A ferocious and possibly decisive political clash was coming. But then came the blunder of Watergate, which diverted attention away from the main contest Nixon wanted to fight. Watergate became a surrogate battle, a dramatic—and traumatic—sideshow that diverted attention away from the main clash and deepened the nation's existing divisions.

It is on precisely this point that *all* of the accounts of Watergate miss the nature and deeper significance of the political clash that served as the backdrop of the affair, and how the aftermath of Watergate changed the operation of government in subtle but profound ways. While the sleuths of history attempt to peel away the tantalizing missing details suggested previously, it is in the more abstract arena of Watergate's effect on the constitutional structure of government where the most important revisionism remains to be done. The reaction to the *temporary* constitutional crisis brought about by Nixon's misdeeds (temporary because he would have been gone from the White House by 1976 anyhow) was a *permanent* constitutional crisis in the form of the powers that Congress and the bureaucracy usurped from the executive branch during its post-Watergate weakness. Watergate didn't just change our standards of ethics in government; it changed how the Constitution works. Far from showing that "the system works," Watergate introduced significant new distortions into our system that Ronald Reagan was largely unable to affect despite two popular landslide elections, and which persist today.

To understand all of this, it is necessary to recapture the full splendor and ideological animosity of the 1972 presidential campaign, and how the aggressive political agenda of the victorious Nixon threatened the institutional bastions of liberalism in a way that fueled their already existing hatred for the man. The 1972 campaign widened divisions that first started appearing in 1968, and which still had not fully closed by the end of the century.

NINETEEN SEVENTY-TWO opened with the prospect of a close election ahead in November. January polls showed Nixon locked in a tight three-way race with Democratic front-runner Sen. Edmund Muskie of Maine and Alabama Governor George Wallace, whom everyone expected to make another third-party run. A federal judge in Richmond, Virginia, had issued a ruling in January 1972 that held that desegregation would require merging suburban and inner-city school districts, busing suburban children to inner city schools, and vice versa. A similar ruling had also come down in Detroit. Wallace's main issue appeared to have national potential. (The Supreme Court would reverse these decisions in June, but not until after the Wallace factor had played out in the primaries.) Nixon's forthcoming trips to China and the Soviet Union would surely help, but inflation and unemployment, though gradually coming down, were still uncomfortably high. Among the fever swamps of the New Left, a popular rumor made the rounds that Nixon would cancel the November election and declare martial law.

Yet the political peril in 1972 lay chiefly with the Democrats, not Nixon. A few observers noted this at the outset of the campaign. "The Democratic Party is today in greater danger of flying apart than at any time since the Civil War," A. James Reichley wrote in *Fortune* magazine in February. "All sorts of issue groups . . . now insist on judging Democrats by strict doctrinal standards, rather than by comparison with what the Republicans are prepared to offer." Reichley thought this state of affairs constituted a "time bomb" inside the party waiting to go off, and he predicted before the first primary ballot was cast that the Democrats would probably go for an ideological liberal. "A middle-of-the-road Democrat—probably the only kind that could be elected President this year—would find himself besieged on all sides by demands that he could not possibly fulfill."[5]

There was no shortage of Democrats from every side of the road willing to test the proposition. At one point near the beginning of the year as many as 15 Democrats declared their interest in running for the nomination to face Nixon, but following the withdrawal of Sen. Ted Kennedy after Chappaquiddick, Muskie was the clear favorite. As late as a week before the New Hampshire primary, *CBS News* was estimating that Muskie already had 1,199 delegates in the bag—only 310 short of the number necessary for the nomination.[6] Muskie had acquitted himself well as Hubert Humphrey's running mate in 1968, and had burnished his image during Nixon's first term. As chairman of the Senate Public Works Committee (later renamed the Senate Environment and Public Works Committee) Muskie had been, along with Wisconsin Sen. Gaylord Nelson, the preeminent Democrat for the new cause of environmentalism. Muskie was a traditional Democrat of moderate liberalism, but he also packed an acerbic wit and a quick temper. When a group of gay rights activists picketed an early campaign meeting, Muskie reacted strongly, telling his staff, "Goddamn it, if I have to be nice to a bunch of sodomites to be elected president, then fuck it."[7] This was not Muskie's only tergiversation. At a press conference a few months later, Muskie threw out Gloria Steinem, who had shown up as a reporter for her new *Ms.* magazine. "How did this girl get in here?" Muskie bellowed after Steinem asked an impertinent question about Muskie's previous support for the Vietnam War. "Get her out of here!"[8] (Muskie wasn't the only Democrat to express traditional—feminists would say chauvinist—views about women. McGovern's campaign manager, Gary Hart, remarked later in the year: "Women don't have the experience or ability to organize. . . . Do you lower your standards in the midst of a campaign like in the midst of brain surgery and try to equalize social ills?"[9] Yet Hart eschewed the traditional hierarchy in running the McGovern campaign, favoring what he called "concentric circles" of management.)

Muskie made two big mistakes—one strategic and one personal. He went into the campaign season with an old-fashioned front-runner strategy, which was wholly unsuited to the turbulent times of the early 1970s. "If he was long at the bank and on the letterhead," Theodore White observed, "he was short, depressingly short, in ideas."[10] "Muskie is not coming on like gangbusters," Joseph Kraft wrote in late 1971 "He is coming on the way Ohio State plays football, slowly and methodically, doing one thing at a time with just enough momentum to keep going forward. His public campaign is almost invisible."[11] (It as an ironic metaphor, since number one ranked Ohio State had been upset by Stanford's aggressive passing attack in the most recent Rose Bowl.) Aside from the environment, which was still a nascent issue in 1972, Muskie's other legislative enthusiasm was civil service reform—hardly a gut-grabber for the general public. Between the political climate of the country, and the ferment in the Democratic Party in the aftermath of 1968, there would be a premium in 1972 for candidates who spoke in broad, challenging themes. Whereas only about 20 percent of Democratic convention delegates were selected through primaries in 1968, reform of party rules had upped the number to about 60 percent in 1972. (It was precisely because of this more populist bias of the nominating process that Wallace decided to run in the Democratic primaries instead of as an independent.) Moreover, the reform rules that mandated de facto quotas for convention delegates meant that the 1972 nominating process would tilt to the Left. The signs of this leftward movement in the party—the progress of what activists self-consciously called "The Movement"—had been clear for a while. The 1970 convention of the Michigan state Democratic Party produced a platform calling for amnesty for draft evaders, reduced criminal penalties for drug use, and U.S. "reparations" to North Vietnam. The Washington state Democratic convention that same year called for a moratorium on missile building and for the nationalization of railroads. They also endorsed a primary challenger to their state's popular, but moderate, Senator Henry Jackson.

Muskie's New England propriety combined with his front-runner strategy produced a bland campaign vulnerable to setbacks. It only took one setback to derail Muskie, and it occurred early in the campaign season. The ferociously conservative Manchester *Union Leader* newspaper, which went to 40 percent of New Hampshire households, had published scurrilous attacks denigrating Muskie ("Moscow Muskie" the paper called him) and his outspoken wife, but topped even this a week before the New Hampshire primary by publishing a spurious letter claiming that Muskie had laughed at an ethnic slur against French Canadians. This was the infamous "Canuck" letter, produced by Nixon's dirty tricks squad.

Muskie erupted in rage, and performed a public meltdown. Standing on the back of a flatbed truck outside the *Union Leader,* Muskie shook with fury as he lashed out at *Union Leader* publisher William Loeb, calling Loeb a "liar" and a "gutless coward." His voice choked and shook with emotion. Snow was falling steadily as Muskie raged. Wait—were those *tears* streaming down his cheeks, or just melting snowflakes? To the TV audience watching on the network news broadcasts, it appeared Muskie was crying, and perhaps he was. On the network newscasts that same night, viewers also saw Nixon on his triumphant China trip—a stately contrast to Muskie's wrath.

Muskie's erosion dated from that moment. Muskie "won" the New Hampshire primary a week later with 46.4 percent of the vote, but polls a few weeks earlier had placed him at 65 percent or better. As in 1968, the winning margin wasn't enough to prevent a fatal hemorrhage. Who would pick up the pieces of the crumbling Muskie campaign? Prior to New Hampshire the punditocracy would surely have fingered Sen. Hubert Humphrey, Sen. Henry Jackson, or Gov. Wallace as the main contenders if Muskie stumbled. But New Hampshire fixed the spotlight on a dark horse, the senator from South Dakota.

George McGovern was the first Democrat to announce his candidacy, in January 1971—the earliest announcement in campaign history. Perhaps he was trying to average things out, having announced his candidacy in 1968 just days before the Chicago convention. First elected to the Senate in 1962, McGovern was one of the most decent and gentle souls in American public life. "He comes on like Muzak," James Jackson Kilpatrick observed, "which descendeth like the gentle dew."[12] His gentleness would constitute his greatest weakness in 1972; like Barry Goldwater and elements of the kooky Right in 1964, McGovern became flypaper for the most vocal liberal and leftist enthusiasms then convulsing on the American scene. Not that he was without firm left-liberal convictions of his own. He blamed the Cold War chiefly on the United States and the West, writing in his autobiography that "Without excusing the aggressive behavior of the Soviets in Eastern Europe after 1945, I have always believed that we not only overreacted to it but indeed helped to trigger it by our own post–World War II fears."[13] But neither was he the reckless or naïve radical he seemed by election day. He had been a B-24 bomber pilot in World War II—an experience that earned him a Distinguished Flying Cross and a hatred of war—and later earned a Ph.D. in history, writing his dissertation on the tactics business had used to smash labor unions in the west. (McGovern was the only Ph.D. serving in the Senate at the time.) "I am not a pacifist," he would protest late in the campaign; "It's a dangerous world, and some people only understand force."[14] But by election day in November 1972, McGovern had become almost unrecognizable amidst the maelstrom he unleashed.

McGovern's central insight was that he could harness "The Movement" to gain the Democratic nomination. At the core of The Movement was a belief in what it called the "new politics." The new politics described an approach that emphasized ideology over vested interest, and the morality of intention over the morality of result. The ideologically motivated were thought to be morally superior to the practical politician who was solicitous of how interest groups would be affected by any proposal, and who understood that the road to hell is often paved with good intentions. The big cause of the moment and the rallying point for the new politics was naturally the Vietnam War. Although the antiwar movement and related ferments on the Left were a minority position in the nation, they could provide the solid core of support necessary for a prolonged nomination contest. Yet it would be McGovern's misfortune that he could not control the same "Movement" he rode to the nomination. With a few notable exceptions, McGovern caved in to the demands of many of the liberal interest groups he used on the road to the nomination, acquiring along the way a number of positions that would haunt him in the general election campaign.

McGovern, for example, entered the campaign season with the position that abortion was a matter that should be left to state legislatures (which is the default *Republican* position today), and although he resisted attempts at including a pro-abortion plank in the Democratic platform in 1972, he gradually conceded to the pro-abortion views of insurgent feminists. (Muskie and Humphrey, it is worth adding, both opposed abortion. "I am not for it," said Humphrey. "It compromises the sanctity of life," said Muskie.[15] The Rev. Jesse Jackson had an even tougher opinion at that time, describing abortion "as too nice a word for something cold, like murder."[16]) The paradox of the McGovern campaign, Theodore White observed, was that it became impossible to tell whether McGovern was the creation of his movement, or its creator. "We were always subject to this pressure from the cause people," McGovern's campaign manager Frank Mankiewicz told White after the election. "If I had it to do all over again, I'd learn when to tell them to go to hell."[17] McGovern himself later protested that he was not a McGovernite, and admitted that when he opened the party's doors (through the quota-based delegate rules changes), 20 million Democrats walked out. He was unable to counter the image that Republican Senator Hugh Scott indelibly attached to him as "the candidate of acid, amnesty, and abortion."

McGovern was considered a second- or even third-tier candidate throughout 1971. He stood at 3 percent in polls in January 1972. "George McGovern has as much chance of being elected President as Harold Stassen," Bill Buckley wrote in January. But with the antiwar movement billowing his sails, McGovern campaigned hard in New Hampshire. He spent 24 days in New Hampshire before the primary, while Muskie only spent 13. McGovern ran a strong second to Muskie, gaining 37.2 percent of the vote to Muskie's 46.4 percent. Moreover, Democratic turnout in New Hampshire was up by more than a third over the 1968 vote. McGovern beat Muskie handily in white collar and college towns, while Muskie carried the working class precincts of the state.

Although McGovern was in the catbird seat immediately after New Hampshire, it was not a foregone conclusion that he was a genuine front-runner. In 1972 the nomination process was still a long, drawn-out affair, unlike today's "front-loaded" primaries that settle the issue by early March. In 1972 it was still the case that the nomination might not be settled until the last primary in California in June. The next primary after New Hampshire was in Florida, then inflamed over the prospect of widespread busing. The busing issue in the Florida primary revealed the widening fissures in the Democratic Party. Sen. Henry Jackson joined Wallace in opposing busing, while Muskie, McGovern, and Humphrey all supported it. Florida would be George Wallace territory, even though Muskie was well organized in Florida, with 26 campaign offices throughout the state and a large budget. A Muskie comeback was thought not out of the question. Wallace indeed scored a solid victory in Florida, gaining 42 percent to Hubert Humphrey's 18 percent for second place.

Muskie managed only a feeble 8.9 percent; his candidacy was over. A popular bumper sticker read: "Vote for Muskie or He'll Cry." The McGovern campaign was suspected as the source. Muskie didn't cry, but he did react badly, saying "The Florida returns reveal to a greater extent than I had imagined some of the worst instincts of which human beings are capable."[18] Exit polls, however, found that 40 percent of black voters had cast their ballot for anti-busing candidates.[19] McGovern was at the back of the pack with a mere 6.2 percent, but no other liberal candidate had shown strength, which was McGovern's hoped-for outcome in Florida.

With no other left-liberal contender in prospect, McGovern rolled to an easy victory in the next primary in Wisconsin, which had gone heavily for Gene McCarthy's antiwar campaign four years before. Wallace finished second. But it was in Wisconsin that some of McGovern's articulated ideas began to become ugly barnacles on his campaign. Back in January McGovern had given a speech in Ames, Iowa, calling for higher income taxes on upper incomes and steep taxes on inheritances (a 77 percent tax rate on everything above $500,000). To the objection that such a tax policy might discourage investment, McGovern's people responded: No problem—the government will make up the slack by investing more itself. But the heart of McGovern's scheme was an annual $1,000 government grant to every man, woman, and child in the country. It was McGovern's version of a guaranteed annual income (he had proposed a $6,500 guaranteed annual income in Congress in response to Nixon's FAP proposal, but had backed away from the bill by 1972). This was the origin of the infamous "Demogrant" proposal. The idea had emerged from a position paper an academic had written for the campaign months earlier, and no one had worked out the nitty-gritty details of how much the plan would cost or how it would be financed. The media paid little attention to the January speech, but McGovern's Democratic rivals would make sure it received wider attention later. McGovern fueled the controversy with his populist attacks on wealth. McGovern thinks of wealth, William F. Buckley Jr. noted, "the way the ladies who formed the Anti-Saloon League thought of booze: as inherently wicked, and the more of it you have, the more wicked you are."

In addition to much higher taxes on the rich, another place the money for the Demogrants might come from was the defense budget. McGovern was starting to offer some specifics to go with his antiwar rhetoric. Not only would he bring home all U.S. forces from Vietnam within 90 days of becoming president, McGovern promised, but he would also set out to cut the defense budget by 37 percent, with the savings going to social programs. Military manpower would be cut by nearly a third, requiring the removal of two divisions from Europe and the complete withdrawal of U.S. forces in Korea and elsewhere in the Pacific. The Air Force would scrap nearly half of its bombers, while the Navy would be pared back to from 15 to six aircraft carriers. The F-14 and F-15 fighters, then under final development, would be cancelled altogether. All of this was possible, McGovern thought, because "The challenge to the free world from Communism is no longer relevant."[20] "I don't like Communism," McGovern said, "but I don't think we have any great obligation to save the world from it."[21] The United States, McGovern told *Playboy* magazine, is "paranoid" about the Soviet Union. Moreover, McGovern attacked "the Establishment Center" for having "led us into the stupidest and cruelest war in all history." (McGovern had been among the near-unanimous Senate vote in favor of the Gulf of Tonkin resolution in 1964. He said he regretted his vote as soon as the next day.)

The antiwar movement was in a state of rapture over McGovern's positions, and the phones rang off the hook in McGovern campaign offices all over the country as the antiwar movement signed up in droves to help his campaign. He won an outright majority of 52 percent in the Massachusetts primary at the end of April, where student turnout was especially heavy (Muskie had polled over 40 percent in Massachusetts as late as the end of February, but finished a dismal second to McGovern with 21 percent). Humphrey won the Pennsylvania primary the same day, which established him as the main rival for McGovern among moderates and liberals in the party. McGovern fought Humphrey to a draw in the Ohio primary (Humphrey, 41.4 percent; McGovern, 39.3 percent), but won the Nebraska primary. The mid-May primaries in Maryland and Michigan now loomed large. Although McGovern had the lead in the all-important delegate count, he was still a long way from the majority needed to secure the nomination. As of early May Humphrey had actually received more total votes in all the primaries combined (2.6 million to McGovern's 2.1 million). George Wallace, however, had received the most Democratic primary votes so far—3.3 million—and was polling well in Maryland and Michigan. His anti-Washington appeal was showing surprising strength in the North; Wallace's attacks on Washington made Ronald Reagan seem a benign moderate by comparison. Washington, Wallace said, was run by "hypocrites, uninterested politicians, and briefcase totin' bureaucrats who can't even park their bicycles straight." If Wallace won Maryland and Michigan, it would postpone the final reckoning between McGovern and Humphrey to the winner-take-all California primary in June. It was still thought at the beginning of May that Wallace could not possibly get the Democratic nomination no matter how many primaries he won, and might well run again as an independent in November. This was Nixon's nightmare more than the Democrats. Polls in mid-May put McGovern within 5 percent of Nixon: Nixon 40, McGovern 35, Wallace 17. This was a doable race for McGovern.

"In May," Michael Barone wrote, "Nixon had quite possibly been on his way to losing. By June he was pretty clearly assured of winning."[22] Two events occurred within the span of a week that transformed the entire campaign and reversed Nixon's fortune. The day before the Maryland and Michigan primaries, Wallace was shot in Laurel, Maryland; he survived, permanently paralyzed, and won the Maryland and Michigan primaries partly on a wave of voter sympathy. But his candidacy was over. November would now offer a head-to-head race between Nixon and the Democratic nominee. The other event took place a few days before Wallace's shooting, starting once again halfway around the world.

IN THE EARLY MONTHS of 1972 American intelligence in South Vietnam began picking up the telltale signs that a major offensive from North Vietnam was in preparation. Heavy truck traffic down the Ho Chi Minh trail had been observed in the second half of 1971, indicating the prepositioning of supplies, followed by the massing of troops near the De-Militarized Zone (DMZ). By this point U.S. forces were down to less than 100,000, but only about 5,000 were ground combat personnel. Whenever and wherever the blow came, it would be a test of Nixon's "Vietnamization" policy; the South Vietnamese army would have to prove it could take a punch. By this time South Vietnam's army had more than doubled in size over the previous six years, to more than 1 million troops, with another million men organized into local self-defense forces. Peace talks between the United States and North Vietnam had broken off. The United States had invited North Vietnam to resume the Paris talks, and any offensive the North launched now was undoubtedly intended to provide the North with a stronger negotiating position in Paris, as well as disrupt the American political cycle in the same way the Tet offensive did in 1968.

Fourteen divisions and 26 regiments of North Vietnamese troops launched the attack on March 30, 1972, shortly before Easter—a total force of 120,000 troops backed by hundreds of Soviet-made tanks and artillery pieces. General Giap botched the attack in the exact same fashion as he had botched the Tet offensive four years before. The offensive was dispersed into three different regions: the northern provinces near the DMZ; the central highlands, where the North hoped to cut South Vietnam in half just as they had tried—and failed—in 1966; and in the southern provinces west of Saigon. A single offensive, or at most two, might have succeeded in capturing an integral portion of South Vietnam or in smashing the South Vietnamese army in a decisive trial of strength. Giap's divided offensive wreaked havoc in all three areas, but was not in the end successful in any one of them.

It took six months for this outcome to be clear, however. The early weeks of the offensive were ominous for South Vietnam. Some South Vietnamese forces dissolved in chaotic retreat as NVA forces overran Quang Tri province and its capital city, Quang Tri, near the DMZ. South Vietnamese forces in the city of An Loc, west of Saigon, were surrounded and needed to be supplied by airdrops. The NVA's central highlands offensive looked potent. (The battle for Quang Tri provided another of the indelible images that Americans forever recall: the sight of 9-year-old Kim Phuc, running naked down a highway, her back seared with napalm. Associated Press photographer Nick Ut won a Pulitzer prize for the photo, which ran in papers worldwide. The antiwar movement literally had its poster child, and used the image to decry American barbarism in Vietnam. In fact, the bomb that injured Phuc was dropped by a South Vietnamese aircraft, after having been wrongly told that civilians had evacuated the area. In the confused battlefield scene, a number of South Vietnamese troops were injured along with Phuc. Far from being a deliberate attack on civilians as the antiwar movement suggested, the bombing was a common accident of war. Phuc went on to become a Communist propagandist, traveling to Cuba after the war to learn Spanish and English. "I'm proud of the picture," Phuc told a reporter in 1997 after she was named to a United Nations post, "because that picture stopped the war."[23])

North Vietnam had rightly calculated that Nixon could not reintroduce a large number of American troops to blunt the offensive. But Nixon could resume large-scale bombing, which is exactly what he did starting on April 6. The United States flew more than 5,000 sorties in South Vietnam over the next few weeks, pulverizing NVA troops in several key areas. U.S. air strikes, especially from B-52s, are thought to have killed half of the estimated 100,000 NVA troops lost in the Easter offensive. (South Vietnamese forces, by comparison, suffered 10,000 killed and 33,000 wounded.) For the first time, there were set piece battles with fixed fronts, which allowed for the most effective use of air power in the entire war. By this time the new generation of laser-guided "smart bombs" were coming on line, making American air power more precise than it had been in Rolling Thunder and other previous bombing campaigns. (For example, on their first try U.S. planes took out a North Vietnamese bridge that had survived *800* previous air attacks.) Without American air power, South Vietnam's forces would not have been able to hold out. Under the American air umbrella, South Vietnam's forces regrouped and rallied.

A more decisive moment, however, occurred in early May, when Nixon decided that his current steps were insufficient. In order to cut the supply lines for the attacking NVA forces, the bombing campaign would have to be expanded aggressively into North Vietnam. For the first time in the long history of the war, U.S. air power was unleashed on significant targets in and around Hanoi, and Haiphong harbor was mined as well as bombed, to cut off supplies for the NVA forces in the south. President Johnson had always placed these targets firmly off limits, and it was widely reported that both Kissinger and Defense Secretary Melvin Laird opposed Nixon's move. This constituted a major turning point in the war: Nixon shocked the North Vietnamese and American critics of the war alike. Nixon went on national television to explain his decision: An American defeat in Vietnam would encourage aggression throughout the world. By stressing the prospect of an *American* defeat, Nixon tied the fate of his entire foreign policy to the efforts of the South Vietnamese army on the ground, and he knew it. Strictly as a military matter, the bombing and mining of Haiphong harbor would take months to choke off supplies to the NVA troops in the field in the South; Nixon's move was clearly intended for the "moral effect" it would have on the political and battlefield situation. The French magazine *L'Express* captured the drama of the moment in a headline: VIETNAM: NIXON JOUE QUITTE OU DOUBLE—"Nixon Bets Doubles or Nothing."

Political reaction was fierce. McGovern led the charge, saying that Nixon was "reckless" and embarking on "a flirtation with World War III." Other Democratic leaders echoed McGovern. Muskie said that Nixon's move "is risking a major confrontation with the Soviet Union and . . . is jeopardizing the security interests of the United States." New York Congressman Edward Koch called Nixon "an international law-breaker."[24] Jane Fonda called a press conference upon returning from a visit to Hanoi (where she had posed, beaming, on an antiaircraft gun), accusing Nixon of "genocide, biocide, ecocide, and perhaps even meteocide," whatever that is.[25]

Nixon thought it possible that the Easter offensive might do to him what Tet did to Johnson—force his abdication from the presidency. "[U]nder these circumstances," Nixon wrote in his diary, "I had an obligation to look for a successor."[26] In addition to the political reaction from liberals and the media, Nixon was jeopardizing the Moscow summit, scheduled to be held just two weeks later, and at which Nixon was intending to sign the long awaited SALT arms control treaty. On the second day of the bombing of Haiphong harbor, U.S. warplanes hit four Soviet merchant ships. The Soviets promptly denounced U.S. "gangster activities." The summit seemed doomed. Nixon felt he had no choice but to risk having the Soviets cancel the summit. "I determined I could not go to the U.S.S.R. if the North Vietnamese offensive was continuing. . . . The summit would be a dismal failure. . . ."[27] Kissinger wrote that "I, the Soviet expert on my staff, as well as the CIA and the State Department, all expected the Soviets to cancel the summit."[28]

Within days the outcome of Nixon's gambit became apparent, and it was a happy surprise. The Soviet Union apparently wanted a summit with Nixon (and an arms control treaty) more than they wanted to side closely with North Vietnam; the Soviets communicated through channels that the invitation to Nixon was still good. Nixon arrived in Moscow as scheduled on May 22, less than two weeks after his defiant speech about Vietnam, and signed the SALT treaty. (Nixon ordered the dismantling of one of America's two antiballistic missile defense installations the next day.) In the United States, opinion polls showed substantial public support for Nixon's hard-line steps. A Lou Harris Poll found 59 percent supported Nixon's move, with only 24 percent opposed. Other polls placed the favorable numbers as high as 70 percent. The campuses, significantly, remained quiet, signifying the waning strength of the campus protest movement.

The reaction to Nixon's bombing offensive against North Vietnam showed that the nation still had a measure of resolve about the war, and agreed with Nixon that America's honor was not a bargain-basement commodity to be dealt away at the negotiating table. The North Vietnamese offensive was thus a political gift to Nixon: The contrast with McGovern's proposal for an immediate, unilateral withdrawal—a surrender and abandonment of an ally—was drawn in the starkest terms. The episode turned McGovern's dovishness into an albatross.

A closer look at Nixon's tough move, however, revealed a remarkable weakness. Having said in late April that "we will never surrender our friends to Communist aggression," Nixon on May 8 outlined terms that amounted to a slow-motion surrender of South Vietnam, and mitigated the moral effect of the intensive bombing campaign. The United States, Nixon said, would withdraw all forces within four months of a cease-fire and the release of American POWs. In other words, the United States would not seek to emulate the Korean settlement, which left a permanent American garrison as a tripwire against any future incursion from the North. Internationally supervised elections could follow, thus allowing "a political settlement between the Vietnamese themselves." Nixon's most significant concession was to omit any demand for a withdrawal of North Vietnamese forces from South Vietnamese territory. The North could keep their forces on the ground wherever they might be at the time of a cease-fire. Nixon rightly called these "generous terms." *National Review* called it "tacit surrender," noting that Nixon's terms "guarantee Hanoi's achievement, in due course, of the aims of its protracted conflict."[29] To be sure, these terms presented a dilemma for the North: Nixon clearly wanted out, and placed American withdrawal as a higher priority than securing the lasting independence of Vietnam. But these or even better terms would likely be available to them later if they persevered on the battlefield and consolidated more territory. The prospect of achieving the complete humiliation of their hated foe, as they had done to the French 20 years before, may also have been irresistible. The North's steely countenance under the intensive bombing bore out John P. Roche's comment to Lyndon Johnson in 1967 that the North Vietnamese "like Lenin at the time of Brest-Litovsk would negotiate in cold blood for whatever goals he considers realistic—even if bombs were coming down his chimney." As events unfolded, the North would eventually be vindicated in its doctrinaire stance.

NONE OF THIS was apparent or inevitable as spring gave way to summer in 1972. McGovern might still have had a chance at making a close race with Nixon, had he and his party not embarked on a course of self-destruction over the summer. McGovern added new woes to his public image with some carelessly chosen words in a *Playboy* interview implying that Ho Chi Minh could rightly be compared to George Washington. This was arguably no more egregious than Nixon's comparison of Mao Tse-tung and George Washington on his Beijing trip, except that American soldiers were not in the field against Mao as they were against Ho. But the biggest blow to McGovern came not from the reaction from the Right or the center, but from the delayed-fuse charges that Hubert Humphrey attached to him in California.

California's June primary was the next to last of the campaign. McGovern was still far short of the number of delegates necessary for a first-ballot nomination heading into the primary, but if he won there it would give him the momentum he needed to get over the finish line. It would also be the last, best chance for the ABM (Anybody-But-McGovern) faction of the Democrats. Humphrey went all out. In a series of three televised debates, Humphrey attacked McGovern from the right, slashing at McGovern's "confiscatory" tax proposals, his $1,000 per person guaranteed income scheme, and his severe defense cuts. Humphrey's frenetic energy, normally his greatest asset, made him seem harsh and strident, while McGovern came across as the nice guy, even though he was vague in his responses to Humphrey's charges. Most damaging was his admission that he really didn't know exactly how much his $1,000 per person proposal would cost. McGovern suggested that income taxes would go up slightly for households earning more than $12,000 a year—but more than 40 percent of American households earned more than $12,000 a year.

McGovern won the primary narrowly—44.3 percent to Humphrey's 39.2 percent. McGovern swept up all of California's delegates under California's winner-take-all rules, which magnified his win. But beneath the momentum it provided heading into the convention in July, there were some worrisome signs. Polls before the first debate with Humphrey put McGovern 20 points ahead; what had happened to shrink the margin to five? McGovern ran poorly in working-class areas of California; Humphrey ran between two and three to one over McGovern in blue-collar areas of Los Angeles. Humphrey's attacks on McGovern had resonated among this core group of Democratic voters. McGovern had overlooked the most salient political trait of working class Democratic voters—if they were not rich now, they hoped they or their children some day would be. McGovern's soak-the-rich proposals, especially his steep inheritance tax, was as an obstacle to their dreams. Humphrey turned out to have field-tested the Republican strategy to defeat McGovern.

The media started to scrutinize McGovern's half-formed ideas more closely. *Time* magazine called McGovern's proposals "A radical economic scheme reminiscent of the days when Huey Long promised to make 'every man a king.'"[30] *The New Republic* said McGovern's program "is notable neither for logical consistency nor irresistible political appeal." The *Washington Post*'s Nicholas von Hoffman called McGovern's welfare ideas "horrendous," "a pernicious extension of the power of the state." The business community was sounding the alarm; the Dow Jones Industrial Average dropped sharply the day after McGovern won the California primary, and the financial community started warning of a "McGovern market." *Time* came back for another bite two weeks after its "Huey Long" comment, calculating that McGovern's proposals for expanded welfare, universal government health care, and other social programs would cost a staggering $165 billion a year (at a time when the total federal budget was still about $250 billion a year), requiring massive tax increases that no one thought realistic, including McGovern himself. (*Time* was even more emphatic about McGovern's defense and foreign policy proposals: "But the net effect of McGovern in the White House would likely be that the U.S. would be living more dangerously."[31])

Even though McGovern's brain trust included the best that Harvard, Yale, and MIT had to offer (which was precisely the problem, economist Melville Ulmer wrote in *The New Republic*), they hadn't thought through many of McGovern's proposals in sufficient detail. *Time*, which depicted McGovern as Robin Hood in a composite drawing, reported that McGovern was "horrified" at the size of the tax increase that would be necessary, and "sent the whole program back to his economists for redrafting."[32]

McGovern's team amazingly came back with a proposal for a flat-rate income tax—a popular *Republican* idea in the 1990s—but it was too late. Second thoughts were becoming third and fourth thoughts among many Democratic leaders. Just as many establishment Republicans publicly abandoned Goldwater in 1964, leading establishment Democrats began publicly dissociating themselves from McGovern even before the convention. "This man's ideas aren't liberal," huffed union stalwart (and faithful Democrat-backer) George Meany of the AFL-CIO; "This man's ideas are crazy."[33] The AFL-CIO would sit out the November election. Why spend our money, Meany asked, "to help a political party commit suicide?" Sen. Robert Byrd said in June that he had always supported the Democratic ticket, but would have to reconsider with the case of McGovern. Philadelphia Mayor Frank Rizzo said that he had a "standing order" for a one-way ticket to Australia if McGovern won. The Republicans, sensing a golden opportunity, moved quickly to set up "Democrats for Nixon."

The second and third thoughts among establishment Democrats would become full blown panic during the party's convention in Miami. The convention, dominated by the youth "Movement" that had propelled McGovern to the nomination, was a week-long vindication of political philosopher Michael Oakeshott's explanation of why "politics is an activity unsuited to the young":

> Everybody's young days are a dream, a delightful insanity, a sweet solipsism. Nothing in them has a fixed shape, nothing a fixed price; everything is a possibility, and we live happily on credit. There are no obligations to be observed; there are no accounts to be kept. Nothing is specified in advance; everything is what can be made of it. The world is a mirror in which we seek the reflection of our own desires. The allure of violent emotions is irresistible. When we are young we are not disposed to make concessions to the world; we never feel the balance of a thing in our hands—unless it be a cricket bat. . . . Since life is a dream, we argue (with plausible but erroneous logic) that politics must be an encounter of dreams, in which we hope to impose our own.[34]

If this passage had been read to any of the delegates in 1972, most would have missed the irony and said, "Right on, man!"

The combination of the party reform rules (quotas) that McGovern had promulgated combined with the intensity of the McGovern movement in 1972 produced the most turbulent convention in modern history. As the convention opened, McGovern's people boasted that it would be "the most representative group ever gathered in one spot in our party's history." It was in truth highly unrepresentative of the Democratic Party and its core constituencies. The convention was skewed to upper income, highly educated, ideologically oriented groups. "The 1972 Democratic convention," sociologist Lewis Feuer wrote, "was the first in American history that could be called the 'Convention of the Intellectuals.' Miami saw the transformation of the Democratic into the Intellectuals' Party."[35] Eighty-six percent of the delegates were attending their first convention. Nearly a quarter of the delegates were under 30 (Arizona had two delegates who hadn't turned 18 at the time they were selected in the spring); 31 percent of the delegates earned over $25,000 a year (the comparable figure for the U.S. population as a whole was 5 percent). A disproportionate number had advanced degrees. Delegates from organized labor had plummeted from their number at the 1968 convention, while the number of women delegates had risen from 13 percent in 1968 to 38 percent. Only 30 of the 255 Democrats in Congress attended the convention. One Democratic House leader who skipped the convention was Tip O'Neill of Massachusetts. And the party's most recent president, Lyndon Johnson, was a non-person at the convention, never mentioned at the podium. As LBJ aide Jack Valenti put it, LBJ was "expunged from the Democratic party with the same kind of scouring effectiveness that Marxist revisionists use to rewrite Communist history."[36] (It is also worth noting that McGovern never mentioned John F. Kennedy in his acceptance speech.) There were no farmers in the Iowa delegation, only a handful of Poles or Italians in the Illinois delegation, no elected official among the Virginia delegation, while nine members of the New York delegation were associated with a gay rights group. Two welfare mothers were on the Washington, D.C., delegation, and two Native Americans (the media called them "Indians" at the time) anointed the delegation from McGovern's home state of South Dakota. California's delegation included actress Shirley MacLaine, who remarked that her delegation "looked like a couple of high schools, a grape boycott, a Black Panther rally, and four or five politicians who walked in the wrong door."[37] She meant it as a compliment. One old time Democrat remarked that the key decisions were still made in smoke-filled rooms, "only the smoke smelled different." The *Village Voice* ratified this observation: "There was enough grass to satisfy Man O'War."[38]

The Democrats had chosen Miami as their convention site in 1972 for the same reason the Republicans had chosen it again: The main convention sites were across a causeway from the mainland, which made it easier for police to prevent any large Chicago-style protest or riot from forming. It was unnecessary. In Ben Wattenberg's memorable phrase, "There won't be any riots in Miami because the people who rioted in Chicago are on the Platform Committee."[39] The Leftist writer I.F. Stone agreed: "It was joy to be at the Democratic convention this year. . . . I felt I had lived to see a miracle. Those who had been in the streets of Chicago were now, only four years and one convention later, in the delegates' seats in Miami."[40] Just to make sure, though, Jerry Rubin, one of the leaders of the Chicago riots who was inside the convention hall in 1972, told a reporter: "If George McGovern doesn't win the nomination, we are going to have Chicago right there on the convention floor."[41] Wrecking the Democratic Party may have been what many "new politics" activists had in mind all along. *Rolling Stone*'s Hunter S. Thompson wrote that "the only way to save the Democratic Party is to destroy it."[42]

It wasn't easy to tell the difference between a riotous disruption and the course of events that occurred on purpose. Even though McGovern's opposition had been crushed, the convention was a chaotic affair that damaged McGovern deeply. The McGovernites decided to expel the duly-elected Illinois delegation simply out of spite at Mayor Richard Daley (who led the delegation, as he had for the last four conventions) for his role in the 1968 Chicago convention. A delegation led by Jesse Jackson, who despised Daley for having slighted him in Chicago affairs, was installed, even though Jackson had neither voted in the Illinois primary nor was even a registered Democrat at the time. A black labor leader complained that Jackson was a mere TV militant who "couldn't lead a vampire to a blood bank."[43] McGovern campaign strategist Frank Mankiewicz cringed at the effect of ousting Daley: "I think we lost Illinois tonight."

States were seated on the convention floor, and the roll was called, in random order, so as not to discriminate on the basis of alphabetic order.

The spirit of "participatory democracy" had taken over, which meant that every "cause" group demanded—and received—its moment in the spotlight. The convention sat until nearly 5 A.M. the first night, and until 6:20 A.M. the second night, as a parade of feminists, homosexuals, and peace activists went before the microphone and TV cameras to plead their cause. "The convention," Theodore White wrote, "gave the sense of a movement rushing through and beyond the political and cultural limits all politicians had up till now accepted."[44] McGovern's convention managers were able to beat back floor votes for radical ideas, but they had effectively lost control of the all-important show business side of the convention. Chaos turned into catastrophe on the last night of the convention, when McGovern was to give his nomination acceptance speech before a prime time television audience of nearly 18 million homes. But first there was the formality of voting for the vice presidential nominee. McGovern had chosen Sen. Thomas Eagleton of Missouri, about whom more in due course. Normally confirming the nominee's choice for running mate is a quick affair, usually accomplished by a quick roll call or sometimes a voice vote of acclamation. But in the year of the runaway convention, "open politics" required that other candidates, or their enthusiasts, receive equal time to plead their case directly to the convention floor. Feminists demanded that a woman's name be placed in nomination, and every nutball constituency and street theater artist got into the act. Among the names placed in nomination for the vice presidency were Ralph Nader, Cesar Chavez, Jerry Rubin, Benjamin Spock, Mao Tse-tung, and even Archie Bunker. By the time the circus was put down, it was nearly 3 A.M. Fewer than 4 million households were still tuned in at that hour to hear McGovern's acceptance speech, in which he unveiled his signature theme, "Come home America." It was prime time only in Guam, and past deadline for most of the morning papers. One American who stayed up late to hear McGovern's speech was Nixon, who shook his head in amazement at the incompetence the spectacle revealed. Nixon remarked that the "scene had the air of a college skit that had gotten carried away with itself and didn't know how to stop."[45]

The fevers of the convention floor found expression in the 26,000-word platform the convention produced. Joyce Milton described the 1972 platform as "a liberation movement wish list," while A. James Reichley argued that it signified that "The Democrats have now chosen to be the party of discontent. Farewell forever to Hubert Humphrey and the politics of joy!"[46] "We are not sure if the values we have lived by for generations have any meaning left," said the introduction. One thing the 1972 Democrats did believe in, however, was rights—lots of them. "The Democratic Party in 1972 is committed to resuming the march toward equality," which entailed enumerating the claims and demands that various constituencies called "rights." Included were "The right to be different, to maintain a cultural or ethnic heritage or lifestyle, without being forced into a compelled homogeneity . . . The rights of people who lack rights: Children, the mentally retarded, mentally ill and prisoners, to name some . . . [and] the development of new rights of two kinds: Rights to the service itself and rights to participate in the delivery process." The platform also called for quotas and the expansion of bilingual education. Mainstream Democrats recoiled in disgust; a few had tried to head off the disaster. Jimmy Carter, who on the eve of the convention had declared McGovern's views "completely unacceptable," had proposed that a platform committee of just four people—McGovern, Muskie, Humphrey, and Wallace—be given the job of crafting the party's stands on the issues, but was rebuffed.

One right conspicuously absent from the platform was abortion. The right to abortion-on-demand was the chief cause of feminists at the convention, but McGovern managed to keep an explicit abortion plank off the platform. (The platform did, however, endorse the Equal Rights Amendment, which Congress had sent to the states earlier in the year.) McGovern placated feminists by pledging verbal support for a woman's right to choose. Yes, McGovern conceded under pressure, abortion should be a matter of personal conscience. But he wouldn't embrace abortion-on-demand. There must be regulating legislation, McGovern thought: "You can't just let anybody walk in and request an abortion."[47]

The abortion issue was also the dog that did not bark in the controversy over McGovern's running mate, Thomas Eagleton. McGovern's selection of Eagleton was as haphazard as his $1,000 per person Demogrant idea. McGovern and his team had put off consideration of a running mate until the convention. McGovern hoped that Ted Kennedy could be persuaded to accept the number two slot, but he refused. Now McGovern instructed his team to come up with a list of names for him to consider. (One person who came to Miami wanting the vice presidential nomination was not on the list: Jimmy Carter.) Sargent Shriver, a Kennedy brother-in-law, was on the list, along with Boston Mayor Kevin White, Larry O'Brien, and a handful of others, including Missouri Senator Thomas Eagleton. Few of McGovern's people knew any of these names personally, and there was little time for any kind of background check beyond a few cursory phone calls. Shriver was out of the country on a trip to the Soviet Union, and had to be scratched from consideration. McGovern then settled on Mayor White. The name was sent out to be vetted with the usual interest groups and party chieftains. Word came back from Massachusetts that Ted Kennedy was cool to the idea; opposition to White emerged from other corners of the campaign, including John Kenneth Galbraith. With the deadline approaching and having been turned down by others on his list, McGovern settled on Eagleton, his Senate colleague with whom McGovern had had few conversations. No, Eagleton told McGovern's aides; there are no skeletons in my closet.

When it emerged over the succeeding weeks that Eagleton had been hospitalized three times for depression, and had received electroshock therapy ten years before, Eagleton's candidacy imploded. McGovern's maladroit handling of the Eagleton matter—first saying that he was "1,000 percent for Tom Eagleton and have no intention of dropping him from the ticket," but then having surrogates call publicly for his withdrawal when it was clear Eagleton could not be sustained—added to the perception that McGovern was a less than competent politician. "It was," Theodore White wrote, "possibly the most damaging single *faux pas* ever made by a presidential candidate."

The fuss over Eagleton obscured the most remarkable political fact about his selection: Eagleton was staunchly anti-abortion, and would have been categorically unacceptable to future Democratic conventions for that fact alone. He was the last pro-life Democrat to appear (however briefly) on the national ticket. By 1992, the Democratic Party would refuse to allow pro-life Pennsylvania Governor Bob Casey to speak to the Democratic National Convention, yet the media would portray the Republican Party as intolerant of any diversity of views.

Other campaign gaffes followed hard upon the Eagleton affair, the most damaging of which was the Salinger mission to Paris. Pierre Salinger had been passed over to be vice chairman of the Democratic National Committee after McGovern had promised him the post during the convention. Then, a few days later, McGovern asked Salinger if he would chase down the truth of a report passed along by the antiwar movement that the North Vietnamese would like to meet with an emissary from the McGovern campaign. Perhaps, it was suggested, North Vietnam might release some POWs on McGovern's behalf. It was foolish for McGovern to entertain the idea; no good could possibly have come from it. Even if Hanoi agreed to release some POWs, the Nixon campaign would unmercifully exploit the "interference" with ongoing negotiations, and many Americans would conclude that the nation's enemy was taking sides in the election. It might even be against the law; the seldom-enforced Logan Act of 1799 makes it a crime for private citizens to engage in diplomacy. But Salinger went off to Paris anyway, and met twice with the North Vietnamese. Salinger told the North Vietnamese that they should make peace with Nixon right away. Perhaps disappointed that Salinger offered no concessions, at the second meeting they informed Salinger that no POWs would be released. The story of Salinger's mission inevitably leaked out, and when confronted with the story, McGovern tried to deny that Salinger had gone to Paris on his behalf. "Pierre Salinger had no instructions whatsover from me," McGovern told the press. The press responded by increasing the harshness of its criticism of McGovern. The *Miami Herald* said that McGovern "for all his melodic contortions can't even charm a garter snake."

McGovern made one last attempt to rescue his tarnished image and convince Americans that he was not a naïve or dangerous radical in world affairs with a prime-time TV speech on October 10. McGovern laid out his timetable for bringing American forces home from Vietnam and ending the war. While many war-weary Americans might have accepted McGovern's elegant proposal to bug out, most were offended by the additional point that McGovern insisted on including in his speech over the objection of his campaign strategists: amnesty for draft dodgers. This proposal was deeply unpopular even among most Americans who opposed the war, but who nonetheless thought no person should be allowed to decide which obligations to their country they would refuse to honor.

The emotions the amnesty issue evoked merely highlighted how the McGovern campaign served to widen the cultural divide in the country. In the 19th century Benjamin Disraeli had described the class division in Britain with the slogan "two nations," and in 1962 Michael Harrington had written movingly of poverty as "The Other America." By 1972 "the other America" more aptly described the vocal faction that elevated doubt and cynicism about American institutions into a principle; a second nation, or national character, was taking its place in the public life of America. Increasingly the two nations of America would lead separate lives, as exemplified by *New Yorker* film critic Pauline Kael's famous remark that she couldn't understand how Nixon could have won the election, because she only knew one person in New York who had voted for him. (Kael's actual quote: "I live in a rather special world. I know only one person who voted for Nixon. Where they are I don't know. They're outside my ken. But sometimes when I'm in a theater I can feel them."[48]) While Nixon and other Republicans wore American flag lapel pins, the McGovernites found appeals to patriotism repellent, and wore the flag— if at all—upside down. Theodore White observed that "At McGovern headquarters, the word itself, 'patriotism,' was a code word for intolerance, war, deception . . . and phrases like 'peace with honor' actually did make them gag."[49] In contrast to the countercultural appearance of Democrats at their convention, White counted only three delegates to the GOP convention who wore beards. "The California delegation to the Republican convention," White noted, "was so different from the California delegation to the Democratic convention that it might have come not from a different state, but a different country or different era. . . ."[50] The full bitterness of the gulf between the "two nations" can be seen in the extreme language that McGovern employed in the frustrating closing weeks of his futile campaign. The same man who had made an indirect favorable comparison of Ho Chi Minh and George Washington in June was by the fall directly comparing Nixon with Adolf Hitler. Watergate, McGovern said, "is the kind of thing you expect under a person like Hitler."[51] At least two other Hitler comparisons were offered during the late weeks of the campaign, along with the blanket statement that Nixon had "conducted an evil administration." "No presidential candidate in modern history," columnist Stewart Alsop wrote in the *Washington Post*, "has imputed to his rival such foul and evil motives."[52]

"There would be a permanent residue of the McGovern campaign," Theodore White wrote in 1973. He had no idea how fully this judgment would be vindicated. While McGovern would not come close to going to the White House in 1972, his campaign offered an entrée into politics for a number of people who would make it into the White House two decades later. Twenty-six-year-old Bill Clinton was the co-director of the McGovern campaign in Texas. His live-in girlfriend, Hillary Rodham, spent the summer in Texas with him before returning to Yale in the fall for her final year of law school. Hillary worked on voter registration efforts, and at least one observer thought that she—and not Bill—would have a brilliant political future.[53] But Bill was already telling people who would listen that he planned to return to Arkansas, run for governor, and eventually president. Another top McGovern campaign aide was Tony Podesta, who would later serve as White House chief of staff for President Clinton. Clinton would appoint McGovern's convention delegate manager, Rick Stearns, to an Appeals Court judgeship. Dozens of other McGovernites filled the ranks of the Clinton administration.

NIXON WON A 49-state landslide on November 7, losing only the reliably liberal citadels of Massachusetts and the District of Columbia. He won 60.7 percent of the popular vote, just slightly below LBJ's 61.1 percent landslide in 1964. Nixon garnered the votes of 37 percent of Democrats, 51 percent of union members, and 53 percent of Catholics. He trailed McGovern in New York City by only 82,000 votes; he had lost the Big Apple by 800,000 to Humphrey in 1968. The rout was especially apparent in the South, where only one out of eight whites voted for McGovern. McGovern's campaign expected that they would win three-fourths of the 18- to 24-year-old voters, most voting for the first time, but they barely got half. The election result was a thumping rejection of liberalism, the "new politics," and the counterculture. The Left took this rejection with its usual grace. One columnist wrote: "The people, as always, voted their fears, their pitiful hopes, and their meanest prejudices." Socialist Michael Harrington attributed the landslide to "a reactionary, utterly erroneous myth about the United States" which "coincided with the false consciousness of the majority of the people."[54]

The weakness and latent radicalism of the McGovern phenomenon and the sweeping dimensions of Nixon's victory conceal a major enigma. Landslides of this magnitude usually have party-wide coattails—Roosevelt in 1936, Johnson in 1964, and Reagan in 1980. Nixon had virtually no coattails; although Republicans gained 12 seats in the House of Representatives (leaving them still in the minority by 51 seats), they lost two Senate seats, including such seeming stalwarts as Gordon Allott in Colorado and Margaret Chase Smith in Maine. The GOP did equally poorly on the state level, losing six seats in the California state Assembly, for example, while the number of GOP governors fell to 19, down from 31 in 1968—"a prolonged landslide in reverse," commented Seymour Martin Lipset. "So far as any change in the ideological balance indicated by shifts in its membership," *National Review* lamented, "[the 93rd Congress] may be a degree or two left of the 92nd."[55] Political scientists took these results as evidence of "de-alignment," that the phenomenon of "split ticket" voting that had first been observed in the 1968 election was becoming the predominant trait of the electorate. But Nixon had deliberately eschewed campaigning for a *party* victory; he campaigned mostly for a personal victory instead, and gave the public little reason why they should vote for Republicans below him on the ballot.

This was extremely odd because, as Henry Kissinger pointed out, the 1972 campaign was "a contest as close to being fought on ideological issues as is possible in America . . . The American people for once had chosen on philosophical grounds, not on personality."[56] Nixon didn't just emphasize the differences on foreign policy and Vietnam between himself and McGovern. "Richard Nixon campaigned in 1972," Theodore White observed, "against central power, against the idea of the omnipotent President doing his will from Washington. He was for returning home power to the people in their communities." Standard Republican small-government fare. But if these were issues dear to Nixon's heart, why not press for an across-the-board party victory?

If ever there was an opportunity for a Republican standard-bearer to press for a partisan realignment, this was it. Democrats had been fearing since the convention in July that McGovern would lead the entire party over a cliff, and had expected to take a drubbing down the ticket. It hadn't happened. In fact, the election featured not only split-ticket voting, but the anomaly of fewer votes being cast for president than for state and local candidates in 42 states. Typically a handful of people who turn out to vote for president don't bother voting for state and local candidates, leaving the vote total for president higher than for state and local candidates. In 1972 it appears that many habitual Democratic voters didn't vote for McGovern, but remained loyal to the rest of the ticket. Nixon might not have been able to change this, but he didn't even try to make a connection in the public mind between the radicalism of McGovern and the general direction of the Democratic Party.

Nixon campaigned for a personal victory on purpose. Nixon was so aloof from Republicans that his campaign severed most ties with the Republican National Committee, and the RNC's chairman, Sen. Bob Dole, couldn't get an appointment to see Nixon throughout the entire campaign. After trying for months to get an appointment to see Nixon, a senior White House aide called Dole on the phone late one afternoon, saying, "Hey, Bob, do you still want to see the President?" "When?" asked Dole. The reply: "Tune in on channel 9; he's coming up on the tube in ten minutes."[57]

This was fully in keeping with Nixon's predilection to run as a lone wolf. "I'm not going into the states for the purpose of supporting Senate or House candidates," Nixon told Theodore White in September, "the way FDR did or the way I did in 1970."

"Then," White asked, "there will be no Truman-style 'Give 'em Hell' campaign against the Democratic Congress?"

"'No, sir,' he [Nixon] said vehemently."[58]

According to White's account, Nixon had his eye on foreign policy in the second term, and didn't want to alienate Congress. Nixon hoped that he could restore the pre-Vietnam consensus about foreign policy, and, as he flattered White, "I have to not have drawn the sword on the Congress I'll be working with. . . . A mistake in domestic affairs isn't necessarily fatal—but in foreign policy it is fatal." That Nixon cared less for domestic policy than foreign policy is not a man-bites-dog insight, but White (among others) seems to have taken Nixon's personal victory on behalf of foreign policy strategy at full face value. White recalled that in 1967 Nixon had told him that "I've always thought this country could run itself domestically without a President; all you need is a competent Cabinet to run the country at home."[59] In fact the wily Nixon had been as deeply frustrated with his own Cabinet during the first term as he was with Congress. The personal mandate he sought for—and claimed—in the 1972 election was intended to provide him with the political clout to govern over and around both the Cabinet and the Congress. The man liberals derided as "Tricky Dick" indeed had another trick up his sleeve. In this lay his undoing. He provoked the furies of established liberalism.

A FORMER UNDERSECRETARY of the Deptartment of Health, Education and Welfare during Nixon's first term named Richard Nathan recalls overhearing a conversation on a crowded plane in the spring of 1973: "Nixon, Haldeman, and Ehrlichman are on the verge of taking over the government."[60] This "plot" to "take over" the government had begun the morning after the election when a grim-faced Nixon met with his Cabinet and staff, and turned what should have been a light moment of celebration into a shock. ("I am at a loss to explain the melancholy that settled over me on that victorious night," Nixon wrote several years later.[61]) Nixon asked that all Cabinet members, and their top appointees, submit their resignations. Then Nixon left for Key Biscayne.

Pro forma requests for resignations at the start of a second term are not unusual, but this time it was clear that many would be accepted. "My action was meant to be symbolic of a completely new beginning," Nixon explained later in his memoirs. Nixon watchers have long pointed to this episode as a supposed example of Nixon's capriciousness and pettiness. But Nixon had set his sights on a large project—gaining real control of the executive branch bureaucracy—and this would require a wholesale reorganization of executive branch personnel and offices. During his first term Nixon was deeply frustrated about the inability of the White House to rein in the independence of the bureaucracy and get the multitudinous agencies to adopt Nixon's policies. The typical problem all presidents face is that their top appointees "go native," or get "captured" by the agencies or departments they run, and often become advocates for the agency against the policy designs of the president.

During his first term Nixon had tried several strategies to bring the bureaucracy to heel. He thought he might employ the same administrative strategy that had been so effective in neutralizing the State Department—operating foreign policy through Kissinger's National Security Council instead of State—and started a White House Domestic Policy Council under John Ehrlichman. But the domestic bureaucracy was too large and diffuse to command in this fashion, so Nixon's next strategy was "revenue sharing," a proposal to send tax revenues back to states and localities with fewer federal strings attached. Congress had little enthusiasm for a spending program that would enable governors and mayors to claim most of the credit for federal pork, so the program was enacted more in name than in substance. Congress made sure that it—and the bureau-cracy—called the shots with revenue sharing.

Above all Nixon came to see that even if he appointed the most fiercely loyal people to the top administrative slots, the massive number of career civil servants could thwart the policy designs of the president. Civil servants who are supposed to be the neutral instruments to carry out the policy of the elected branches are anything but neutral in practice. A White House aide summed up Nixon's frustration to a *Wall Street Journal* reporter in 1972: "President Nixon doesn't run the bureaucracy. It took him three years to find out."[62] "We have no discipline in this bureaucracy," Nixon complained to Ehrlichman on one of the Watergate tapes. "We never fire anybody. We never reprimand anybody. We never demote anybody. We always promote the sons-of-bitches that kick us in the ass."[63]

As Nixon contemplated his second term, he knew that different and more permanent controls over the bureaucracy were necessary. Even before the election, Nixon was starting to implement his new tougher domestic policy strategy. Shortly before the election Nixon vetoed a clean water bill that he considered too expensive. In a foretaste of spending battles to come, Congress overrode his veto before election day. He was starting to refer to many federal programs not as objects to be "reformed," but as "failures" that should be cut. In his second inaugural address Nixon set out his intention bluntly: "[A] new era of progress at home requires turning away . . . from condescending policies of paternalism—of Washington knows best."

This was not the Disraeli-inspired Nixon of 1969. Between his inaugural address and other public statements, it was clear that the second Nixon term was going to be much more conservative. His next budget proposal called for eliminating more than 100 programs, while holding total spending growth to a relatively parsimonious 8 percent. Suddenly the reason for the attacks on the liberal media, and the articulation of the "silent majority" theme, began to come into sharper focus. Nixon was proposing nothing less than upending the established political alignment.

The significance of Nixon's conservative turn was not lost on the liberal establishment. The *New York Times* huffed that Nixon's second inaugural address heralded "a reversion to the do-nothing Federal Government and every-man-for-himself ideology of the Hoover era."

Michael Novak, fresh from writing speeches for McGovern running mate Sargent Shriver in the 1972 campaign, wrote that the Establishment "knew that for the first time since Andrew Jackson, a President had arisen who genuinely threatened both the economic and symbolic power of the Eastern elite."[64] *National Review* applauded Nixon's embrace of the principles of the "silent majority," but warned of the ferocity it would provoke: "Nixon must realize that any attempt to move as he proposes to do will inflame the other constituency. The people at OEO and HUD, assorted poverty bureaucrats, the education lobby, the counter-Pentagon over at HEW, the liberal press and its allies, will put up the heat. They will burn up the phone wires and flood the corridors of Congress."[65] This would turn out to be an understatement.

HERE THE NARRATIVE should pause briefly to explain why Nixon's initiative was more significant than the usual partisan battle over policy priorities and spending levels. Gaining more effective control of the large federal bureaucracy may seem on the surface as simply a large managerial or organizational problem. But the problem is not one of mere scale, i.e., that the federal government has grown too large for any one chief executive to control meaningfully. The expansion of the permanent centralized bureaucracy has undermined some of the central principles of democratic government itself. This is an obscure problem, because it involves the constitutionally ambiguous ground of the nature of the administrative functions of government and the shared powers of the executive and legislative branch. Over the decades Congress has delegated considerable legislative authority to executive branch agencies (some of them nominally "independent" of both the president and Congress), while maintaining a large measure of control through the appropriation and oversight process. Public administration textbooks portray bureaucratic administrative agencies as the neutral playing field wherein the tensions between the separated powers of the legislative branch and the executive branch are worked out in practice. Congress legislates and appropriates for each executive branch agency, yet the president and his appointees run the various agencies.

But is the president merely to be the manager of Congress's expressed intent, or is the president, as the only person in American government elected by *all* of the people, supposed to reflect the preferences of the people by imposing his own policy preferences on the executive branch? The president is, after all, the only political figure in the American system who is responsible to all of the people, rather than to a local district or single state, as congressmen and senators are. If the president cannot exert any meaningful authority over the bureaucracy, then the people cease being the final arbiter of policy to some extent, and render presidential elections less significant as a means of expressing change in national policy. As presidential scholar Clinton Rossiter put it, "The President is the American people's one authentic trumpet . . . a clear beacon of national purpose." If Nixon was powerless to act on campaign promises to change the bureaucracy, he could not keep his compact with the people. He could not implement his electoral mandate. Even President Franklin Roosevelt, the author of much of the modern government bureaucracy, ironically held this view. In 1937 Roosevelt complained:

> The plain fact is that the present organization and equipment of the executive branch of the Government defeats the constitutional intent that there be a single responsible Chief Executive to coordinate and manage the departments and activities in accordance with the laws enacted by Congress. Under these conditions the Government cannot be thoroughly effective in working, under popular control, for the common good.[66]

Nixon understood this problem clearly, though his complaint against the bureaucracy went beyond Roosevelt's, for he also understood that by the early 1970s, the bureaucracy had become the partisan instrument of governance for the Democratic Party. Democrats, as the party of liberalism, favored enlarging centralized administration as its chief instrument of policy, while Republicans generally favored reducing centralized power and bureaucracy. Not surprisingly, Democrats dominated the ranks of the permanent bureaucracy. A 1970 survey published in the *American Political Science Review* found that only 17 percent of senior career bureaucrats were Republicans, while 47 percent were Democrats; the remaining 36 percent were independents who, the survey's authors concluded, "more frequently resemble Democrats than Republicans." The authors concluded: "Our findings document a career bureaucracy with very little Republican representation but even more pointedly portray a social service bureaucracy dominated by administrators hostile to many of the directions pursued by the Nixon administration in the realm of social policy." A separate study estimated the proportion of Republicans among the foreign service at 5 percent.[67] As Nixon put it with rare understatement, "Democratic institutions naturally resist a Republican President."

Enacting policy through semi-independent and congressionally dominated bureaucracies made liberal policy changes permanent and beyond the reach of electoral majorities. Yet this also means that people are no longer governed by their consent. To expect Republican presidents to be bound by the administrative designs of Democrats was effectively to have narrowed, if not ended, partisan competition in American public life. Worse, to a large extent bureaucratic government had begun to have a petty corrupting effect on Republicans in Congress by this time, because the bureaucracy, through pork barrel spending and other means, made it in the interest of individual congressmen of both parties to defend and even enlarge it, because it was the chief means of their re-election. The bureaucracy was less and less accountable to the president with each passing year. This state of affairs effectively prevents the president from governing. This is why Nixon's battle was with Congress itself as much as it was with the Democratic Party, and is one reason why Nixon felt he had little to gain by campaigning for a Republican congressional majority in the 1972 election. In fact, Nixon's increasing independence from the main body of the Republican Party even led him at one point after the 1972 election to contemplate founding a new political party.

The institutional differences between the executive branch and the legislative branch had come to be as significant as party differences in Nixon's mind. By 1973, Nixon wrote, "I had concluded that Congress has become cumbersome, undisciplined, isolationist, fiscally irresponsible . . . and too dominated by the media." What was needed, Nixon thought, was to "break the Eastern stranglehold on the executive branch and the federal government." Nixon's plan to break the bureaucracy required that he break Congress as well. "[A]rmed with my landslide mandate and knowing that I had only four years in which to make my mark," Nixon wrote in his *Memoirs,* "I planned to force Congress and the federal bureaucracy to defend their obstruction and their irresponsible spending in the open arena of public opinion. . ." Nixon wrote in his diary at the time: "This is going to be quite a shock to the establishment, but it is the only way, and probably the last time, that we can get government under control before it gets so big that it submerges the individual completely and destroys the dynamism which makes the American system what it is."[68]

By declaring his intent to control, and reduce in size, the structure that maintained the power of the Democratic Party, Nixon would be launching one of the most bitter political fights in American history. Nixon knew that he had "thrown down a gauntlet to Congress, the bureaucracy, the media, and the Washington establishment and challenged them to engage in epic battle."

NIXON MADE his intent clear in the opening days of his second term. "I intend to stand for the general interest," he said in his first press conference, by inference asserting his station above Congress as a barometer of the popular will. He deliberately snubbed Congress by being the first president since Woodrow Wilson who did not deliver his State of the Union message in person in 1973. His written message set out the stakes:

> Throughout the middle third of the 20th century, power flowed to the center at every level of American government. . . . The vigor and independence of State and local government ebbed as Washington's power grew. . . . Now the age of centralism in American Government is ending.[69]

Nixon announced that he was going to set up on his own authority and without congressional approval the "supercabinet" structure that Congress had rejected in 1971. (In 1971 he had submitted to Congress an executive branch reorganization plan that would have created a "super-cabinet" of four large domestic departments—Natural Resources, Human Resources, Community Development, and Economic Affairs—headed by "supersecretaries" whose formal job titles would be "Counselor to the President." This title would put the "supersecretaries" inside the White House rather than the bureaucracy, and thus make them more responsive to the president. Congress was not amused, and the proposal died quickly.) This would threaten Congress's control over executive agencies, and is what prompted the remark cited earlier that "Nixon, Haldeman, and Ehrlichman are on the verge of taking over the government." But Nixon's main chosen battleground would be the federal budget itself. Control federal spending, and you control the oxygen supply for the bureaucracy. Nixon's proposed budget for the 1974 fiscal year included steep cuts in numerous domestic social programs.

But Nixon wasn't going to wait until the next budget. He started his attack on spending immediately. He froze spending for housing and urban development programs, suggesting that the money be sent back to the states through revenue sharing instead. When Congress overrode his veto of the Federal Water Pollution Control Act, which had appropriated $18 billion for water treatment, Nixon announced that he was going to invoke the presidential power of "impoundment"—he was going to re-fuse to spend the appropriated money. There is no more direct way of taking on Congress and the bureaucracy than impoundment. Presidents going back to Thomas Jefferson had impounded duly appropriated funds. Nixon pointed out that while his impoundments came to 3.5 percent of total spending in 1973, President Kennedy had impounded 7.8 percent of the budget in 1961 and 6.2 percent in 1962, while LBJ had impounded 6.7 percent in 1967. Yet the power was thought to be narrow in scope, as funds could be impounded only if the purpose for which they were appro-priated had become obsolete, or for some other reason of timing. Jeffer-son had impounded funds Congress appropriated for the construction of naval warships because the threat of war with Britain and France had eased. A 1969 legal memo from the Justice Department interpreted the impoundment power narrowly (the memo was written by Assistant At-torney General William Rehnquist). Yet Nixon signaled that he intended to make the widest use of impoundment: "I have nailed my colors to the mast on this issue; the political winds can blow where they may."[70] By the beginning of 1973, Nixon had impounded funds for over 100 federal pro-grams, each with an interest-group or local constituency behind it. More impoundments were promised to follow if Congress didn't shape up. Members of Congress in both parties rightly feared that "shaping up" might involve being defeated for re-election; pork-barrel spending was the chief means of assuring their re-election, and a reduced ability to deliver pork diminished the attachments of the interests who help keep them in office. Hence their fury at Nixon.

IN THE MIDST of Nixon's developing strategy to reform Congress and the bureaucracy, there occurred a convulsion that in hindsight can be seen to have provided the final measure of enmity between Nixon and his enemies that sealed their determination to get rid of him by any means. The Vietnam War, thought finally to be over any day, suddenly sprung back to life with a fury unmatched throughout the long history of the war.

The antecedent to this convulsion needs to be recalled. The last American combat troops had been withdrawn in August. By September the North Vietnamese offensive begun the previous spring had fully spent itself. The South Vietnamese had retaken the northern provincial capital of Quang Tri, and were mauling North Vietnamese troops elsewhere. American intelligence thought that it would be at least 18 months before the North could mount another offensive. In October, a breakthrough in the Paris peace talks had come at last. North Vietnam accepted Nixon's longstanding proposal for a cease-fire in place. The North dropped their persistent demand that Thieu be removed as prime minister of South Vietnam and replaced by a coalition government (which was the functional equivalent of saying, "hand us over the government on your way out the door"); they agreed to an international peacekeeping body to monitor the cease-fire, and they agreed that South Vietnam could continue to receive U.S. aid. American POWs would be released without linking them to the release of Vietcong prisoners held by South Vietnam, while the United States would withdraw all its remaining forces from the South.

The terms were actually *better* than Nixon and Kissinger thought they would ever get, and certainly far better that the war's critics in the United States thought possible. But many important details were still to be worked out. The North Vietnamese, who normally dragged out discussion of even the smallest point, were now suddenly in a hurry. They wanted the treaty signed by October 31—just days before the U.S. presidential election. They had evidently made the calculation that they would get better terms from Nixon if they bargained in the shadow of the imminent election. The North Vietnamese were shrewd observers of the American political scene, often quoting the American press and antiwar politicians at the Paris negotiations. "I would like to quote a sentence from Senator Fulbright to show you what Americans themselves are saying," Le Duc Tho would say to Kissinger. "I have heard it before," Kissinger would drolly reply. That Nixon would be overwhelmingly re-elected was obvious in late September, and a triumphantly re-elected Nixon might be harder to deal with. (Nixon actually didn't want an election-eve settlement, knowing it would roil the election scene.) Yet despite the risks of an accelerated timetable, the United States agreed to try.

There was one hitch on the U.S. side, but it was a big one: South Vietnam. Since the United States was negotiating on behalf of South Vietnam, Prime Minister Nguyen Van Thieu needed to sign off before the United States could complete the treaty. This was a matter of some delicacy. A combination of shame and honor prevented the United States from imposing a unilateral solution on its long-suffering ally. North Vietnam and the antiwar movement had long charged that Thieu was merely an American puppet; if Nixon forced the agreement on him it would vindicate the claim. As an honest broker, the United States felt honor bound to present to the North Vietnamese whatever objections and changes Thieu demanded. Thieu zeroed in on the most glaring weakness of the draft agreement—not requiring the withdrawal of all North Vietnamese troops from the South—and later added 68 other changes he wanted made in the agreement. "We failed early enough," Kissinger reflected, "to grasp that Thieu's real objection was not to the terms but the fact of *any* compromise. . . The South Vietnamese, after eight years of American participation, simply did not feel ready to confront Hanoi without our direct involvement."[71] Thieu's outrageous insolence and stonewalling exasperated Nixon and Kissinger, and made it impossible to complete the agreement by the October 31 deadline. Instead of heading to Hanoi in late October to complete the treaty, Kissinger headed back to Washington. Before leaving Kissinger cautioned Thieu that while the United States would present Thieu's demands to North Vietnam, they were prepared to reach agreement with the North without the participation of the South if necessary. Moreover, Kissinger warned Thieu, once news got out that South Vietnam had blocked a treaty, congressional support for South Vietnam would collapse, and all American aid cut off.

North Vietnam, seeing their timetable slip away, may have reached the same calculation. "There was no doubt that the Communists had infiltrated the Saigon government," Nixon wrote, "and that Hanoi was therefore aware of our warnings of congressional fund cutoffs in January."[72] Thus far the negotiations and the tentative treaty were secret, but on October 26 North Vietnam went public with news of the treaty, broadcasting the main points over the radio, and, taking no chances, leaking the story to the *New York Times* through French sources. It was another masterful maneuver by Hanoi. The premature public release of the news had the effect of further isolating Thieu, and forcing the United States into taking a public position. Kissinger called a press conference and affirmed the news with the fateful words, "We believe that peace is at hand."

It wasn't. At the follow-up negotiations to iron out the "technical details" in November and early December, which Kissinger thought would take no more than two or three days, the October agreement came unstuck.

Thieu's demands were totally unacceptable to the North, though the United States did not intend to press any of them beyond a formal recitation. Meanwhile, the North Vietnamese introduced new demands and conditions (such as limiting the international supervisory force to just 250 people), dragged their feet over terms of returning U.S. POWs, and withdrew some of their earlier concessions. Kissinger was stunned, and described the new countenance of the North as "insolence, guile, and stalling." North Vietnam's lead negotiator, Le Duc Tho, would agree verbally to a change one day, and then in written drafts of the agreement withdraw the concession a day later. Nixon told Kissinger to pass along a threat, which, stripped of the normal diplomatic courtesies, amounted to saying: If you think I was tough in May, imagine what I might do to you now that the election is over. Le Duc Tho told Kissinger on December 13 that he needed to return to Hanoi for "consultations." North Vietnam didn't think Nixon was bluffing, and began evacuating Hanoi. Kissinger made a straightforward public statement blaming the North Vietnamese for the breakdown of negotiations, but said nothing about what the United States was going to do about it.

There has always been speculation that Hanoi's stalling tactics arose because of an internal fight in Hanoi's politburo. But it may have also reflected hardheaded calculation. From the North Vietnamese point of view, stalling for time and riding out a resumption of American bombing seemed an eminently sensible risk. Over the course of a few weeks, they came to see that there was a prospect of a clear-cut victory. They could reasonably guess that Nixon was desperate for a settlement, and might well accept weaker terms. (If Kissinger's memoirs are taken at face value, Nixon was willing to settle for weaker terms than Kissinger demanded at the negotiating table.) Although Nixon had won a landslide election, Congress was more dovish than ever. Already the Senate had voted in the summer of 1972 for a cutoff of funds for the war and for immediate U.S.

withdrawal; more of this could be expected if the settlement talks dragged on or collapsed. (They were fundamentally right about this calculation, as we shall see.) North Vietnam may have thought growing tensions between the United States and South Vietnam might lead to a complete breach. Having forced the United States in to a public position that a peace treaty was within reach, the North Vietnamese knew that Nixon would pay a fearsome political price if negotiations now collapsed.

North Vietnam underestimated Nixon's resolve. On December 14 Nixon ordered the resumption of intensive bombing. "The order to renew bombing the week before Christmas was the most difficult decision I made during the entire war," Nixon wrote later. Kissinger had urged Nixon to make a national TV address, as he had in May and other previous occasions, to rally public opinion in favor of renewed bombing. Nixon rejected the idea. In his diary Nixon wrote: "Expectations have been built so high now that our failing to bring the war to an end would have a terribly depressing effect on this country, and no television speech is ever going to rally the people."[73] There was probably another reason: Nixon thought massive bombing without comment from him would have a larger psychological effect on North Vietnam. A cardinal error of the American war effort from the start was to couple force with plaintive declarations of restrained and peaceful intent, a sure signal to North Vietnam that they had little to fear. Nixon had also secretly promised Thieu that if North Vietnam ever violated the terms of the cease-fire agreement, the United States would undertake "swift and severe retaliatory action." Here was a chance to show both South and North what that meant.

This time would be markedly different. The bombing campaign would not be limited to peripheral targets far removed from Hanoi. Nixon, according to his own recollection, told the Chairman of the Joint Chiefs of Staff, Admiral Thomas Moorer: "I don't want any more of this crap about the fact that we couldn't hit this target or that one. This is your chance to use military power effectively to win the war, and if you don't, I'll consider you responsible." For the first time in the war, B-52s were used to bomb Hanoi, starting on December 18. For obvious reasons, "Linebacker II," the official code name of the air campaign, became known publicly as the "Christmas bombing." Over the next 10 days, the United States flew round the clock, with squadrons of B-52s taking off from Guam even as returning bombers were landing. The United States flew 729 B-52 sorties, and more than 1,000 fighter-bomber sorties, hitting transportation terminals, rail yards, power plants, airfields, and other military targets. The North Vietnamese fired nearly 1,250 antiaircraft surface-to-air missiles (SAMs) in defense. Fifteen B-52s and 11 fighters were shot down. Because of Nixon's decision not to make a statement of any kind, the bombing had begun without public notice by the United States. The media got its first reports of the bombing from North Vietnam. When asked, all Defense Secretary Laird would say was "Air operations are being conducted throughout North Vietnam at the present time."

The reaction was ferocious. Opponents of the war, who had by this late date virtually exhausted the critical vocabulary, seized upon the image of supposed B-52 "carpet bombing" to level the most extreme charges of the entire war. The *New York Times* called the bombing "terrorism on an unprecedented scale," and said the first two days of bombing alone were the "equivalent of the Hiroshima bomb." (This was wildly inaccurate.) *Times'* columnist Tom Wicker said the United States had "loosed the holocaust" on North Vietnam. The *Washington Post* also embraced the theme that the bombing amounted to "terrorism," calling it "the most savage and senseless act of war ever visited, over a scant ten days, by one sovereign people upon another." On *CBS Evening News,* commentator Eric Severeid said the object of the bombing could only be "the mass killing of civilians." (Reagan, in a personal call to Nixon to express his support, mentioned that under the circumstances of World War II, CBS News might be charged with treason.) The foreign press was even more strident. Sweden's Prime Minister Olof Palme compared the bombing to Nazi atrocities. The London *Daily Mirror* said the bombing was "an act of insane ferocity, a crude exercise in the politics of terror." The *Guardian* said "Mr. Nixon wants to go down in history as one of the most murderous and bloodthirsty of American Presidents," and *La Opinion* in Buenos Aries carried the headline: "U.S. Carries Out Most Complete Plan of Destruction in Human History." Although the United States was targeting military and not civilian sites, the media credulously reported North Vietnamese claims that the United States was deliberately striking civilian targets. A hospital located adjacent to a military airfield was hit in an early raid, and dominated news and commentary for the rest of the bombing campaign. An analysis of news coverage by the major news outlets in the United States found that coverage of civilian damage ran two to three to one over coverage of military damage.[74] Antiwar groups immediately began raising funds to help North Vietnam rebuild.

Congressional Democrats were not to be outdone by the media, and engaged their own hyperbole. Sen. McGovern called it "a policy of mass murder . . . the most murderous bombardment in the history of the world," and Iowa Sen. Harold Hughes said "the only thing I can compare with it is the savagery at Hiroshima and Nagasaki." Democrats charged that Kissinger's October pronouncement that "peace is at hand" was not just premature but a deliberate, cynical ploy to sway the election. (That it was North Vietnam who first announced a prospective treaty on election eve was conveniently forgotten.) Beyond the hyperbole, critics of the war were certain that the bombing would only prolong the war.

There were few public expressions of support for Nixon reported in the media. What was most striking, however, was the dog that did not bark: There was no explosion of mass protests as there had been after Cambodia in 1970—a clear sign that the antiwar movement in the United States was a spent force, a fact that was probably not lost on Hanoi. The subdued reaction of the Soviet Union and China—Hanoi's patrons and suppliers—must have also been a sobering portent. On December 28, after nine days of bombing (there was a bombing halt for Christmas Day), the North Vietnamese signaled their willingness to return to the negotiations in Paris. The North significantly didn't require a bombing halt as a precondition of returning to the table. They knew Nixon was not a pushover like Johnson. But Nixon ordered the bombing halted anyway. He had made his point.

Only months later did information emerge showing that the media coverage of the Christmas bombing was not simply inaccurate, but bordered on hysteria. Contrary to the popular image that the B-52 was an imprecise bombing platform that raked down indiscriminately in a half-mile wide by two mile long strip, by 1972 B-52s were capable of much more accurate bombing. (How accurate is still classified.) U.S. pilots were under orders not to deviate from carefully plotted bombing runs under threat of court-martial, partly to avoid civilian casualties, and partly because countermeasures to North Vietnamese surface-to-air missiles (SAMs) were more effective if the planes remained in tight formation. Most importantly, B-52s were not used for most targets in central Hanoi and Haiphong; fighter-bombers, using laser-guided bombs, were used for these targets. On January 4, a week after the bombing ceased, the North Vietnamese reported their losses: 1,318 killed in Hanoi, 305 killed in Haiphong—certainly far from the "mass killing of civilians" the media claimed had occurred. In fact, it was one of the lowest casualty totals of any bombing campaign in the history of warfare, and makes evident that the United States had indeed targeted military sites. The Hanoi death toll, the *Economist* noted, "is smaller than the number of civilians killed by the North Vietnamese in their artillery bombardment of An Loc in April or the toll of refugees ambushed when trying to escape from Quang Tri at the beginning of May. That is what makes the denunciation of Mr. Nixon as another Hitler sound so unreal."[75] (One reason for the small death toll was that by the time the bombing started on December 18, two-thirds of the population of Hanoi had been evacuated.) In March, *New York Times* reporter Malcom Browne acknowledged that "the damage caused by American bombing was grossly overstated by North Vietnamese propaganda," and the *Baltimore Sun*'s Peter Ward agreed that "evidence on the ground disproves charges of indiscriminate bombing."[76] The critics who claimed the bombing would prolong the war were proved wrong. North Vietnam returned to the negotiating table on January 8. It took only four days to complete a treaty (it contained substantially the same terms that had been agreed to in October), which was signed on January 27, on which date the cease-fire took effect.

Military experts will forever debate whether the Christmas bombing compelled the North Vietnamese to settle and end the U.S. involvement in the war. Many experts argue that Linebacker II was little more effective than previous bombing campaigns, at least in strict military terms. Admiral Thomas Moorer, chairman of the Joint Chiefs of Staff at the time, argued fervently that the bombing made the decisive difference. "I am convinced that Linebacker II served as a catalyst for the negotiations which resulted in the ceasefire. Airpower, finally given its day in court after almost a decade of frustration, confirmed its effectiveness as an instrument of national power—in just 9½ flying days."[77] (Moorer made these remarks in 1973 in a speech to a then-obscure naval aviators annual convention in Las Vegas known as "Tailhook.") Moreover, the Christmas bombing lent credence to those who argued that a similar intensive bombing campaign might have ended the war in 1965. Retired Air Force

General T.R. Milton wrote in 1975 that the Christmas bombing was "an object lesson in how the war might have been won, and won long ago, if only there had not been such political inhibition. . . . The Christmas bombings of 1972 should have taken place in 1965."[78] Testimony from POWs in Hanoi suggests the Christmas bombing had a significant moral effect on the North Vietnamese, which was Nixon's primary intention. Admiral James Stockdale, by December 1972 a prisoner for nearly seven years, offered the most compelling eyewitness account in support of the effect of the Christmas bombing:

[A] totally contrasting atmosphere swept the city about an hour after dark on that December 18 night in 1972. As first we (in the very center of Hanoi in Hoa Lo prison) thought it was a regular tactical raid of the sort that came every few nights. The bombs hit out where they usually hit—in the railroad yards, power plants, and airfield areas. Some of the prisoners did detect higher level explosions early in the bombardment, but it wasn't until these explosions were still being heard 20 minutes later that the cheers started to go up all over the blocks of that downtown prison. This was a new reality for Hanoi. These were big explosions—and the bombs kept coming! Though landing thousands of yards away, they shook the ground under us and plaster fell from the ceilings. The days of Mickey Mouse were over! Our wonderful America was here to deliver a message, not a self-conscious stammer of apology. "Let's hear it for President Nixon!" went the cry from cell block to cell block, all around the courtyard.

. . . [T]he bomber stream continuing to roll right on like Old Man River was a message in itself: proof that all that separated Hanoi from doomsday was an American national order to keep the bombs out on the hard targets. We prisoners knew this was the end of North Vietnamese resistance, and the North Vietnamese knew it, too. . . .

One look at any Vietnamese officer's face told the whole story. It telegraphed accommodation, hopelessness, remorse, fear. The shock was there; our enemy's will was broken. The sad thing was that we all knew that what we were seeing could have been done in any ten-day period during the previous seven years, and saved the lives of thousands. . . .[79]

At the time the bombing ended on December 28, North Vietnam was nearly out of antiaircraft ordnance. Further U.S. bombing would have met little resistance. On the other hand, there were few military targets left to hit. The United States would have had to begin bombing river dikes to inflict further damage on North Vietnam without intentionally targeting civilians. It might be said that Nixon was lucky the North Vietnamese decided to bargain, given the mood of Congress; conversely, given the military realities of the moment, Nixon's grim determination, and the lack of mass protest from the antiwar movement, perhaps it was the North Vietnamese who were lucky.

With the signing of the peace accord at the end of January the war was finally over for the United States. It had cost 56,146 American lives and $140 billion dollars. U.S. airplanes dropped eight million tons of bombs in the course of the war—twice as much as had been dropped by Allied forces against Germany and Japan during World War II. The war's effects on the American economy would linger for the rest of the decade. Its political effects would linger even longer. The end of the war brought no peace for Nixon. Nixon's claim, plausible at the moment, that he had achieved the goal of "peace with honor" was bitterly resented by both the pro–North Vietnamese faction of the antiwar movement as well as congressional critics of the war whose stance on the war Nixon had now proven wrong. Rather than admit that Nixon's toughness and resolve had been vindicated, the critics now disingenuously charged that Nixon could have had the same peace agreement as far back as 1969, and had prolonged the war needlessly. This is nonsense, but it received the sanction of oracles such as the *Washington Post* and other editorial pages and became the new stick with which to beat Nixon.

While Nixon was riding a wave of popularity for finally ending U.S. involvement in Vietnam—his approval ratings reached 70 percent in January—Congress began a determined assault against the executive branch. The anger provoked by the Christmas bombing cannot be understated. Coupled with Nixon's provocations over the budget, the reaction in Congress was ferocious. John Connally, who had run the "Democrats for Nixon" effort during the campaign, told Nixon in January that the mood on Capitol Hill was "the most vicious I have ever seen. They are mean and testy."[80] Between the budget actions and the war policy, George McGovern said that America under Nixon was "closer to one-man rule than at any time in our history," while Sen. Hubert Humphrey said Nixon's budget policy and impoundments had generated a "constitutional crisis."

A convenient constitutional rationale for opposing Nixon arrived on the scene at this moment: the "imperial presidency." The imperial presidency thesis was exactly the opposite of how the real balance of power had shifted between the executive and legislative branches of government, as was discussed previously. Moreover it represented a breathtaking hypocrisy on the part of the liberals who advanced the theme. Hitherto liberal intellectuals had championed executive power, and agitated for more of it. Harold Laski wrote in 1940 that "The President of the United States must be given the power commensurate to the function he has to perform," and Henry Steele Commager wrote in 1941 that "No strong Executive has yet impaired the fundamentals of our constitutional system or of our democracy." As recently as 1965 James MacGregor Burns wrote that "Presidential government, far from being a threat to American democracy, has become the major single institution sustaining it—a bulwark of individual liberty, and agency of popular representation." Norman Podhoretz went right to the heart of the matter: "Indeed, the Presidency would never have grown to 'imperial' proportions without the encouragement and support of liberals, who encouraged and supported it precisely (though not exclusively—there were also domestic considerations) because such a Presidency was necessary to the carrying out of an interventionist foreign policy."[81]

But now came the venerable liberal historian Arthur Schlesinger Jr.'s *The Imperial Presidency*, charging Nixon with being a "genuine revolutionary," whose "piratical administration" was bent on establishing a "plebiscitary Presidency," or "a quasi-Gaullist regime in the United States." Colorful language for what liberals had previously championed. Nixon was right to complain in his memoirs that liberal fondness for strong presidential power seemed to last only so long as a liberal was in the White House. It was to no avail. The litany of real and alleged presidential perfidy over Vietnam stretching back through the "secret" bombing of Cambodia to the Gulf of Tonkin incident lent verisimilitude to the foreign policy side of the "imperial presidency" theme, and Watergate would soon come to supply the seamier side of the domestic side of the argument.

Moving ahead under the popular banner "No more Vietnams," Congress launched a fresh assault to usurp more power from the executive branch under the guise of curbing the "imperial presidency." The

Senate moved with the most swiftness. In January the Senate passed the War Powers Act, which limits the power of the president to commit U.S. forces in combat—an Act which, while still on the books today, is certainly unconstitutional and will be declared so as soon as any president decides to challenge it. Nixon vetoed the Act when it finally reached his desk in the fall of 1973, but Congress overrode his veto. Much less noticed were the congressional steps taken in areas wholly unrelated to war powers and foreign policy. Democrats in the Senate pressed forward with a measure to reduce the president's ability to invoke executive privilege. A number of steps were taken to assert congressional supremacy over fiscal policy. In February the Senate voted to require Senate confirmation of the budget director, a position that had always been filled by the president without confirmation before. Requiring Senate confirmation is a step toward exerting greater congressional oversight; Congress can command confirmed appointees to appear before endless hearings, which serve as effective intimidation. In the aftermath of Watergate Congress took additional steps to solidify its supremacy over spending and the executive branch bureaucracy. In 1974 Congress passed the Budget and Impoundment Control Act, which established new administrative authority for Congress. Congress didn't even try to dress up what it was after. The official legislative history of the act says that its purpose was to "*assure congressional budget control;* provide for the congressional determination of the appropriate level of Federal revenues and spending."[82] (Emphasis added.) In other words, Congress wanted to make bloody sure that no future president could execute his fiscal policy goals if those goals conflicted with the spending wishes of Congress. Impoundment would be a thing of the past, and the executive branch lost control over even the timing of spending. The act's effects were immediate: Spending for non-defense discretionary projects, which is where most "pork barrel" grants and construction projects are to be found, had grown by only 7.3 percent a year under Nixon. But in 1975, the first fiscal year after the Budget Act passed, discretionary spending soared 26.4 percent. The overall growth rate of federal spending jumped, from 8.5 percent per year during the ten years before the act to 9.6 percent per year during the ten years after the act. The federal budget as a proportion of GDP also jumped significantly as a result of the act. From 1964 to 1974, federal spending averaged 19.4 percent of GDP; from 1977 to 1987, federal spending averaged 22.7 percent of GDP.[83]

IT WAS WATERGATE, though, that made these changes seem necessary and legitimate. The lingering question of Watergate at the beginning of Nixon's second term provided the fulcrum for Congress to assert itself effectively. McGovern had tried to make an issue of Watergate in the campaign, but got nowhere. One poll before the election found that the public regarded Watergate as routine political spying by a 70 to 13 margin, while another poll found that 57 percent of the public thought political spying was a common occurrence.[84] (And even after the dramatic Senate hearings began in the summer of 1973, the TV networks were deluged with calls from viewers angry that regular daytime programming— mostly soap operas—was preempted.) House hearings into Watergate in the fall of 1972 went nowhere. The story was about to disappear off the back pages of the news.

The Senate was more determined than the House, however. One of the Senators who was most offended by Nixon's aggressive budget strategy was North Carolina's Sam Ervin, who called it "executive usurpation of legislative power." Therein lies the thread that unraveled Nixon's fortunes. Ervin pressed hard for a resolution to create a select committee to investigate illegal and unethical conduct in the 1972 campaign. Majority Leader Mike Mansfield, whose anger at Nixon was aggravated to the breaking point by the Christmas bombing, helped press the resolution on the full Senate. The resolution passed 77–0. Republicans, knowing that LBJ had bugged Goldwater in 1964 and Nixon in 1968, failed in their attempt to have the inquiry broadened to include those previous campaigns. Ronald Reagan commented caustically that a bugging was small potatoes compared to Democratic dirty tricks like stealing elections with dead voters in Illinois, as was alleged to have happened in 1960.

What followed was two years of oscillating bombshells, irony, and a lynch mob mentality among the perennial Nixon-haters. Norman Mailer expressed the views of most liberals when he remarked in 1974, "We won't be happy until we cut Richard Nixon's heart out and hold it high on the summit of the Presidential pyramid while an ooh goes up from the crowd."[85] Republicans were initially confident that the hearings would exonerate Nixon. When Justice Department prosecutors pondered how to corroborate John Dean's testimony implicating Nixon in the cover-up, they contemplated—but rejected—putting a "wire" on Dean in hopes of getting Nixon on tape. When several months later White House aide Alexander Butterfield blurted out in a deposition to the Senate Watergate Committee that Nixon taped his conversations, Democrats and Republicans alike thought this admission must have been deliberate because Nixon knew the tapes would exonerate him. A few Democrats thought that they might be heading into a set-up. Nixon for a time thought the tapes would exonerate him, too, which is one reason he did not immediately destroy them. There was also a good deal of ironic foreshadowing as well. Young Hillary Rodham was a member of the House Judiciary Committee's staff working on the articles of impeachment against Nixon. And in the congressional election campaign of 1974, a first-time candidate for Congress running in Arkansas argued: "I think it is plain that the President should resign and spare the country the agony of this impeachment and removal proceeding. I think the country could be spared a lot of agony and the government could worry about inflation and a lot of other problems if he'd go and resign." The candidate was Bill Clinton. He lost.

The institutional dimensions of Watergate became more explicit when the story moved from the Senate inquiry of 1973 to the House Judiciary Committee's impeachment hearings in 1974. The Judiciary Committee significantly voted *not* to limit its impeachment accusations to "unlawful activities." While Republicans on the Judiciary Committee argued that the standard for impeachment must be a finding of some *illegal* conduct by Nixon, Democrats argued for a broader standard of *political* misconduct. "The issue here is broader than criminality," Democratic Congressman William Hungate argued.

One of the articles of impeachment the committee drew up was directed at Nixon's budget impoundments. Though the Judiciary Committee voted down the article, as legal scholar Stanley Kutler observed, "the fact that impoundment had risen to the respectability of being considered grounds for impeachment measured the furies Richard Nixon aroused in Congress."[86] The final irony of Watergate is that the Republicans' insistence that impeachment must rest on an illegality proved Nixon's final undoing. When the infamous June 23 "smoking gun" tape provided superficial grounds for involving Nixon in a conspiracy to cover up Watergate, his last Republican support crumbled.

WHETHER NIXON COULD have succeeded in bringing Congress to heel and taming the bureaucracy will never be known. His aggressive strategy proved stillborn because of Watergate. As his political troubles mounted in the spring of 1973, Nixon quickly abandoned his budget-fighting strategy in hopes of appeasing the congressional wolfpack. The drawn-out drama of Watergate and the relentless, pervasive demonization of Nixon over the years since has almost wholly obscured the deeper sources of the bitterness and passion that lay behind the episode. Watergate was more of an institutional than a legal crisis, which was further aggravated by having the two branches of government controlled by different parties. Watergate became a surrogate means of fighting out the institutional and partisan differences between the executive branch and Congress—a dimension that was completely absent from the impeachment of President Bill Clinton 25 years later, and which helps explain the very different character and outcome of that affair. At stake in the background of Watergate was whether the president would be subordinate to Congress, and Watergate provided Congress with the means to cloak its assertion of supremacy. "I gave them a sword," Nixon remarked to David Frost years later, "and they stuck it in. And they twisted it with relish. And I guess if I had been in their position I'd have done the same thing."[87]

This is probably the last time that we can get government under control, Nixon had written. Columnist Nicholas von Hoffman commented perceptively after Nixon's resignation: "What Richard Nixon contemplated doing was actually running the government, something no president in seven decades has attempted."[88] One of Gerald Ford's first acts upon assuming the presidency following Nixon's resignation was to undo Nixon's administrative reorganization scheme. The result of Watergate was to create an imperial Congress, and this institutional imbalance constituted Ronald Reagan's most significant obstacle as president a decade later. (Reagan wouldn't be the only chief executive hobbled by the imperial Congress. The post-Watergate changes would wreak havoc on Jimmy Carter's administration too.) The changes in the balance of power between the branches made the Watergate impeachment drama a mere sideshow from the standpoint of constitutional substance.

THESE WERE THE long-run consequences of Watergate. A postscript about the immediate consequences is required before the narrative can jump ahead.

In one of those stranger-than-fiction coincidences, the three shows the networks had to cancel to carry Nixon's resignation speech were: "The Taste of Ashes" (NBC), "The Nature of Evil" (ABC), and "The Last Man" (CBS). The Postal Service announced the following week that they would not replace the 41,000 pictures of Nixon in post offices; they only budgeted for presidential photos every four years, and needed to economize. Madame Tussaud's Wax Museum in London removed Nixon's figure. Henry Kissinger's wax figure continued on display, one of the museum's most popular attractions.

The adverse public reaction to President Ford's unconditional, preemptive pardon of Nixon a month later, along with rising worries about the economy, transformed what was sure to be a bad-midterm election for Republicans in to a disaster. Republicans tried to make a virtue of their difficult situation, running a TV ad with the slogan, "When has it been easy to be a Republican?" Republicans lost 43 House seats and four Senate seats. Democrats went to 62 to 38 in the Senate, and 291 to 144 in the House. The Democratic Senate could break any Republican filibuster, while the House could override a presidential veto without a single Republican vote. (And they did, often.) Republicans who had stuck up for Nixon until the very last were especially punished. Republican Congressman Earl Landgrebe of Indiana, for example, had said, "I'm sticking by my President even if he and I have to be taken out and shot." He lost. For the second time in ten years the death knell of the Republican Party was sounded, as the GOP sunk to the same low level it had been after the Goldwater debacle. George Bush, who had succeeded Bob Dole as chairman of the Republican National Committee in 1973, bravely went around the country during the fall campaign trying to disassociate the Republican Party from the misdeeds of the White House, but to no avail. Dole himself was barely re-elected to a second term in the Senate. Many Republican candidates in 1974 dropped their party affiliation from their advertisements, such that if someone saw an ad from a candidate that didn't mention the candidate's party, it was safe to assume that the candidate was a Republican.

Among the new faces elected to office were Michael Dukakis as governor of Massachusetts, Jerry Brown as governor of California (replacing Ronald Reagan), astronaut John Glenn as U.S. Senator from Ohio, and McGovern's 1972 campaign manager, Gary Hart, as U.S. Senator from Colorado. Hart ran a conservative campaign, running against gun control and busing, and in favor of capital punishment. He won narrowly.

Hart's conservative campaign was an anomaly among Democrats, and the numbers of seats Democrats won understate how dramatically the election changed the character of Congress. Because of the high number of House members who retired in 1974 (Democrats mostly because of age, Republicans mostly out of discouragement), the largest number of new Representatives—92—in a generation were elected that fall. Watergate had provided the impetus for organizing and accelerating the generational transition within the Democratic Party. Seventy-five of the 292 House Democrats—a quarter—were freshmen; half of the Democratic caucus in the House had been elected since 1970. The "Watergate babies," as they became known, were infused with a liberal, and in a few cases radical, reformist zeal formed in the crucible of the antiwar movement and tempered by the convulsion of Watergate. The official Democratic Party magazine, *The Democratic Review,* estimated that the incoming representatives were more than twice as liberal as the Democratic members they replaced.[89] A *Washington Post* survey asked the incoming Democrats, "What nation, if any, do you consider a threat to world peace?" The largest plurality, 27 percent, thought the *United States* was the leading threat to peace, with only 20 percent naming America's principal adversary, the Soviet Union, along with Israel.[90]

The liberal insurgency provided the critical mass to pass a number of reforms to the House's seniority and committee system that had been talked about for years. The most significant was selecting committee chairs by secret ballot, rather than by seniority. This one measure broke the dominance of Southern Democrats, who, by dint of longer seniority because the South had hitherto seen little partisan turnover, tended to dominate committee chairmanships. This one reform alone guaranteed that the House would be far more liberal. McGovernism, so thoroughly rejected at the polls two years before, now reigned triumphant in the legislative branch. Watergate, in other words, gave the left wing of the Democratic Party a reprieve and a second lease on life.

Another organizational reform—expanding the number of subcommittees and the size of congressional staff (which grew by 124 percent in the decade after the 1974 election)—enabled Congress to extend its control over executive branch agencies and departments. Before these reforms went into effect, for example, Defense Department affairs were the province of just four congressional committees. Over the next few years, even as the defense budget was shrinking, congressional management and oversight of the Pentagon grew to 24 committees and 40 subcommittees. The number of defense officials summoned to testify to these committees jumped threefold, to more than 500 hearings a year. These committees began demanding dozens of reports from the Pentagon, such as, for example, a report on the retirement benefits of Philippine scouts. In 1970, the Pentagon had to furnish Congress with just 36 reports. By 1980, the number had increased to 231, and by 1988, to 719. The proliferation of subcommittees offered another benefit to House members. Nearly every Democrat was a chairman of a subcommittee. "It became commonplace in the House," a staff member quipped, "that if you forgot a Democrat member's name, you could safely call him 'Mr. Chairman,' because he was sure to be chairman of something."[91]

THE OTHER POLITICAL complication to arise from Watergate concerned the fate of Ronald Reagan. More precisely, the resignation of Vice President Spiro Agnew on account of bribery and corruption charges changed the political landscape for Reagan. It is impossible to know what course events would have taken under different circumstances, but it is likely that had an undamaged Agnew, who was very popular with the conservative movement, succeeded Nixon in 1974, Reagan might never have made a run for the White House in 1976, and hence probably not in 1980 either. The accession of Gerald Ford to the vice presidency in 1973 changed all of Reagan's calculations, though the decision to run in 1976 was not automatic. As House Minority Leader Gerald Ford had a solidly conservative reputation. He had sat on the dais at *National Review*'s tenth anniversary dinner celebration in 1965, shortly after he had become House GOP leader, and had earned affection among conservatives for his attempt to collar Justice William O. Douglas, as discussed in the previous chapter. A Reagan candidacy would thus split the conservative movement as well as the Republican Party. Both ran against Reagan's instincts.

But even before this threshold could be crossed, there were more immediate political milestones for Reagan to consider. Polls showed his popularity with Californians remained intact at the end of his eight years as governor. When Reagan left the governorship in January 1975, the *Los Angeles Times* editorialized that Reagan had proven himself "an accomplished practitioner in the art of government, a proven administrator and a polished and potent force in conservative national politics."[92] His rival in the 1970 election, Assemblyman Jesse Unruh, offered a balanced assessment of Reagan as his term in office ended: "As governor, I think he has been better than most Democrats would concede, and not nearly as good as most Republicans and conservatives might like to think. As a politician, I think he has been nearly masterful." Unruh hastened to make clear that he was not softening his opinion of Reagan, adding that "I do not like Ronald Reagan."[93]

On the surface there is considerable merit to Unruh's observation that Reagan's rule in California was "not nearly as good as most Republicans and conservatives think." The state budget had more than doubled during Reagan's tenure, from $4.6 billion to $10.2 billion. Per capita taxes had increased from $426 to $768. However, more than half of the gain in state spending and taxes can be attributed to inflation, and the state's rapid population growth during those years assured that overall spending would grow substantially. Another measure of government is the number of state employees, which grew by 14 percent during Reagan's rule, slightly less than the rate of California's population growth. While Reagan's record could be considered mixed from a dogmatic conservative point of view, the *Baltimore Sun* still concluded that "the Reagan years represent the first attempt by any large government in this country (federal, state, or local) to do less for people, not more." In his last press conference—the 409th of his governorship—Reagan summed up: "I still think of myself as someone who took time out in my life . . . to present the viewpoint of the people. In other words, we've never come over to thinking of ourselves as 'we the government.'" It was this attitude, more than the arguable details of the results of his governance, that kept Reagan in good stead with conservatives.

What to do next? Perhaps, Reagan's inner circle thought, he should run for the U.S. Senate in 1974 against first-term incumbent Alan Cranston, or, if he ruled out a White House run in 1976, for the second California Senate seat then held by another first-term liberal Democrat, John Tunney. But Reagan ruled out a Senate race by the spring of 1973. "There's nothing I can do in the Senate for what I believe in that I won't be able to do anyway," Reagan is reported to have concluded. Nancy Reagan's lack of enthusiasm for the life of a Senate wife is said to have been also important in the decision.[94] A third term as governor was open to Reagan and would have been a natural way to extend his political viability on the national scene, but Reagan had pledged to serve only two terms, and had even supported an attempt to adopt a state constitutional amendment limiting a governor to two terms. (The attempt failed. Voters adopted term limits for all state offices in California by initiative in 1990.)

Reagan and his inner circle were already looking ahead for a plan by early 1974, with more than a year to go in his governorship. If Reagan were to be in position to run for president, a national political effort would need to begin immediately after Reagan left office in 1975. The object was to consolidate Reagan's position as *the* national leader of conservatives, and secondarily to bolster his foreign policy credentials. "Always," Peter Hannaford wrote in a February 1974 memo, "the number one objective must be: Stay out of trouble."[95] Perhaps, Reagan's insiders pondered, Reagan should seek out the leadership spot with a high-profile national organization such as the U.S. Chamber of Commerce or the Red Cross. Maybe Reagan should start his own political organization called "Alert America." Both of these ideas were eventually rejected in favor of something simple. By July of 1974, with Nixon's resignation imminent, Reagan's political strategy was coming into focus. The obvious idea emerged: turn Reagan's ability as "the great communicator" into a cottage industry that would double as a political organization. By election day in November of 1974, while Republicans were getting killed, Reagan's strategy was set in motion. As Mike Deaver and Peter Hannaford explained in a strategy memo:

> Conservative Republicans are disturbed at Ford's efforts at 'consensus' government and accommodations toward the left.... [Reagan's communications program] could provide an excellent vehicle for coalescing conservative thought during 1975 and for testing the potential strength of a Presidential bid, without RR overtly stepping out of the "mashed potato circuit" role he has described for himself.[96]

Deaver and Hannaford estimated that Reagan could generate nearly $400,000 a year in lecture fees, radio commentaries, newspaper columns, and other media activities. Roughly half of the revenue would support a small staff and outreach activities (especially direct mail), leaving Reagan with an annual income of $200,000. The plan worked exactly as laid out. Reagan's newspaper column ran in 175 papers, reaching an audience Peter Hannaford estimated at more than 15 million readers. Seventy-one radio stations had signed up for Reagan's commentaries by Christmas of 1974; eventually 200 stations took Reagan's broadcasts, exceeding the initial projections. Reagan's 1975 net income came in at $282,253 according to disclosure forms released during the 1976 campaign. Peter Hannaford wrote first drafts of many of the newspaper columns, which Reagan would revise before publication. Reagan himself, however, wrote most of the radio commentaries, as well as his stump speeches. Speaking invitations were not in short supply: Reagan would turn away 3,000 requests in 1975.

In his last hurrah as governor, however, Reagan attempted to establish a permanent legacy for himself in California. When Reagan raised income taxes in 1967 to close the $1 billion deficit Governor Pat Brown had left him, Reagan said he hoped the tax hike would prove temporary, and that he could reduce taxes later. By 1973 the state had piled up an $800 million surplus. Reagan wanted to return the surplus to the taxpayers either through a rebate or a tax cut. Democrats, who controlled the legislature, wanted to spend the surplus. One legislator told Reagan that returning the surplus to taxpayers would be "an unnecessary expenditure of public funds."

When it became clear that the legislature was not going to agree to rebate the surplus, Reagan turned up the heat. He decided to promote a comprehensive tax and spending limitation amendment to the state constitution. He knew that, even if the present surplus was rebated, the next governor, or the governor after that, could go back to business-as-usual, raising taxes and increasing spending. With a tax and spending limitation amendment to the state constitution, he would not only get the surplus rebated, but would set the state on the course of permanent tax reductions and tight spending limits. It would be his crowning achievement as governor, and would provide an example of fiscal responsibility that Reagan could run with in a national campaign. The initiative, which went before California voters in November 1973, was Proposition 1.

Proposition 1 was an embryonic model of the supply-side economic thinking that would later be central to Reagan's economic policy as president. Proposition 1 included an immediate 7.5 percent reduction in the state income tax and eliminated the income tax altogether for families earning less than $8,000. It would also impose a requirement for a two-thirds vote of the legislature to pass any tax increase. But the toughest feature of Prop. 1 would have limited total state spending to no more than 7 percent of personal income in the state. In 1973, state spending was about 8.75 percent of personal income; Prop. 1 would have lowered this to 7 percent of personal income over a 15-year period. An "Economic Estimates Commission" would be established to determine the amount that could be appropriated each year. (By way of comparison, the state tax burden reached nearly 12 percent of personal income—and the state surplus had grown to nearly $4 billion—by the time of Proposition 13 in 1978, which is one reason why that measure passed by a landslide.) Even with the 7 percent "fiscal straightjacket," Reagan pointed out that the state budget could still double in 10 years and triple in 15, as California's population and personal income grew.

As soon as Reagan's forces had gathered the signatures to qualify Prop. 1 for the November 1973 ballot, the legislature was suddenly in a mood to compromise about rebating the surplus. Democrats offered to rebate the surplus through a one-time 20 percent to 35 percent income tax cut, along with a temporary one-cent cut in the sales tax. Reagan agreed to the compromise, but pressed ahead with Prop. 1 anyway, even though the compromise may have blunted some of the urgency to pass Prop. 1.

The well-funded opponents of Prop. 1, mostly public employee unions threatened by spending limits, deployed a clever and effective argument: If state spending is capped, local taxes will have to go up. Opponents claimed that local governments "from counties to mosquito abatement districts" could impose their own income taxes under Prop. 1. Reagan and his forces were unable to counter this argument effectively. Then, on the eve of the election, Reagan blundered. He was asked about Prop. 1's complicated terms: "Do you think the average voter really understands the language of this proposition?"

The ever-candid Reagan replied: "No, and he shouldn't try. I don't either."

The opponents pounced, getting an ad on TV within 24 hours repeating Reagan's words with the tag line: "When a proposition's chief sponsor doesn't understand it, it's time for the rest of us to vote no."

Proposition 1 lost, 54 percent to 46 percent. "It was a victory for political demagoguery," Reagan reflected, "a triumph for the unsubstantiated charge that sounds convincing in a thirty-second television commercial but which does more to confuse than inform."[97] Reagan took solace in the fact that two-thirds of the people who voted against Prop. 1 did so thinking they were voting against higher taxes. The constituency for a tax revolt, Reagan thought, is clearly there to be mobilized. The opponents of Prop. 1 also used a line of argument that would later become a broken record for Reagan in Washington: that an income tax cut would be a "giveaway to the rich." Although the *Los Angeles Times* gave a lukewarm endorsement for Prop. 1, it also ran a cartoon depicting "Reagan Hood," robbing the poor to give to the rich.

In hindsight it is easy to see that with Prop. 1 Reagan was once again ahead of his time. (He was also musing aloud at that time about the desirability of a flat-rate income tax—a leading conservative issue 25 years later.) Five years after Prop. 1 California passed Proposition 13 by a landslide. Proposition 13 cut property taxes in half, imposed Prop. 1's two-thirds majority requirement to raise taxes, and launched the "tax revolt" around the nation. Throughout the 1980s and 1990s tax limitation amendments would prove popular in states with the initiative and referendum process. Michigan adopted a Prop. 1–style cap on spending, at 9.48 percent of personal income in the state. By the late 1990s, 13 states had joined California in imposing a supermajority requirement to raise taxes.

None of the conditions that fueled the rise of the tax revolt were fully evident or predictable in 1973. What helped propel the tax revolt in the latter half of the 1970s was high inflation, which boosted property tax bills and pushed people into higher income tax brackets, even as their inflation-adjusted income was steadily falling. With the defeat of Prop. 1, not for the last time it seemed Reagan's moment might have passed.

The end of direct U.S. involvement in Vietnam and the resignation of Nixon might have been thought at the time to have closed the chapter of the disruption of American democracy, and a return to normality. To the contrary, it marked not an end but merely the transition point to what might be called the "middle period" of discord in America. This discord of the 1960s was not over. The furies Vietnam and the New Left unleashed would have a long half-life, extending a shadow over the rest of the 1970s and beyond. As America moved toward the celebration of her bicentennial in 1976, it seemed that conditions were propitious for a reassertion of American optimism and confidence. Instead, the next few years saw a deepening of America's distemper, and at the same time the conservative movement began to coalesce in decisive ways that set the stage of Reagan's eventual victory in 1980. To this story we now turn.

PART THREE

THE COMING OF
RONALD REAGAN

CHAPTER NINE

DÉTENTE AND
ITS DISCONTENTS

THE JOB OF PICKING UP the ruins of Watergate and healing the nation's divisions fell to Gerald Ford. Ford has always been portrayed as something of a hapless figure: Think of how he is called "good ol' Jerry Ford" or how comedian Chevy Chase mercilessly lampooned his many pratfalls. Yet Ford was far from hapless. In fact he possessed a strong, solid character reflective of the heartland district in Michigan from which he came. "Eisenhower without the medals" is how Ford was often described.

It was Ford's misfortune to preside, without benefit of popular election, at the moment when the United States reached low ebb. In many respects the Ford-Carter years were the time of maximum peril for the United States and its allies in the West. It can also be recognized as a crucial early turning point in the political realignment to come, when the threads of what became the Reagan movement began to organize and rally. Recounting the travails that afflicted the abbreviated Ford administration are essential to understanding why and how Ronald Reagan mounted his challenge for the White House in 1976—a campaign that turned out to be a dress rehearsal for his successful campaign in 1980.

Gerald R. Ford Jr.'s real name was actually Leslie Lynch King—he had taken his adoptive father's name in the 1920s—and the only thing less likely than a man named Leslie becoming President of the United

States was Gerald Ford's ascension to the Oval Office. Nixon had reportedly included Ford on his list of potential running mates in both 1960 and 1968, but Nixon may simply have been returning a favor, as Ford had been among congressional Republicans who urged Eisenhower not to dump Nixon from the ticket in 1956. The irony of Ford's appointment to the vice presidency following Agnew's resignation in the fall of 1973 is that Ford, after 25 years in the House, was seriously considering retirement from politics in 1974. Nixon's first choice for vice president was John Connally, while party regulars recommended either Gov. Nelson Rockefeller or Gov. Ronald Reagan. Congressional Republicans suggested Ford. Congress was not about to confirm Connally (who at that time was still being investigated for Watergate-related matters), Rockefeller, or Reagan, and provide the Republicans with a strong incumbent president for the 1976 election. The Democratic House Speaker Carl Albert told Nixon that Ford was the only confirmable choice. In other words, Congress, sensing its power, dictated its choice for the executive branch. Ford accepted, despite the misgivings of his wife, Betty.

Ford's plain-spoken, middle-American countenance—"I'm a Ford, not a Lincoln," was his modest proclamation—was a welcome relief for the Watergate-weary nation after Nixon finally resigned in August 1974. Like most incoming presidents, Ford was greeted with a wave of public support and congressional goodwill, magnified by the fact that he had come from the ranks of the House. Ford, Pat Moynihan wrote, was "the most decent man I had known in American politics."

"Our long national nightmare is over," Ford told a relieved nation. But the good mood vanished abruptly when, barely a month in office, Ford pardoned Nixon for any and all crimes he might have committed, even though no indictments had yet been brought (and might not have ever been brought, if special prosecutor Leon Jaworski can be taken at his word). It was a supreme and necessary act of mercy, which even Nixon-hating liberals have come over time to admit. But the timing was awkward for Ford. "Will there ever be a right time?" Ford asked when his aides second-guessed him.

Congressional Democrats and media cynics, deprived of the final prize of seeing Nixon before a jury, thought the fix was in; Nixon had named Ford to the vice presidency in return for a promise of pardon. Congressional Democrats called for an investigation, and darkly hinted that another impeachment might be necessary. Ford denied any pardon deal, and took the extraordinary step of testifying before the House Judiciary Committee's Subcommittee on Criminal Justice—the first president since Lincoln to appear before Congress. Perhaps Ford had little choice. His dramatic appearance and denials blunted the congressional uproar and derailed the momentum for an investigation that would have tied the White House in knots for months, but it was also another subtle indication and encouragement of congressional dominance.

Ford had already divided and upset Republicans with his choice for the vice presidency. According to one account, the White House had conducted a quiet survey of Republicans leaders for their recommendation, and the leading pick was George Bush.[1] Bush's closest political allies, led by James Baker, were openly lobbying the White House to get Bush the appointment. But Jules Witcover's account of the episode said that "Everyone knowledgeable in Republican politics considered Bush incompetent to be President," while Bush's biographer, Herbert Parmet, relays the worry of senior Ford aides that "the nation's top leaders 'regarded [him] as intellectually light.'"[2]

Regardless of how seriously this perception weighed on Ford's mind, Bush's chances were undone when *Newsweek* reported that Bush's 1970 Senate campaign in Texas had received $100,000 from a Nixon "slush fund." Watergate special prosecutor Leon Jaworski later cleared Bush of any wrongdoing, but it did not come in time to help his veep chances. So Rockefeller, whom Nixon had recommended to Ford at the time of his own resignation, got the nod. As a consolation prize, Ford offered Bush his choice of the two top ambassadorships—England or France—but also mentioned that the post at the new U.S. liaison office in China was available. Bush chose the China post. It seemed a more interesting challenge, and, as a friend told Bush biographer Herbert Parmet, Bush wanted "to get as far away from the stench of Watergate as possible."[3]

Meanwhile, Reagan and his supporters mounted a quiet but serious effort to get him the appointment. Reagan said that Ford's choice ought to come from among the governors rather than from Congress, which meant either him or Rockefeller, and further that the appointment should be someone who supported "the philosophical mandate" of the 1972 election, which meant him and not Rockefeller. The chairman of the California Republican Party sent telegrams to the party chairmen in the other

49 states urging them to back Reagan for the vice presidential appointment. Ford attempted to placate Reagan by offering him the cabinet posts at the Department of Transportation and, later, at Commerce, and also the ambassadorship to England. Reagan declined, reportedly insulted at the offers.

The problem with Rockefeller was that, as Pat Buchanan put it in an interview a decade later, "there was no one who could rattle the cages of the Right like Nelson Rockefeller."[4] (The irony is that Buchanan, still on the White House staff after Nixon's resignation, had backed Rockefeller for the appointment. Appointing Reagan or Goldwater to the veep slot, Buchanan thought, would "cause a mighty rupture in the liberal establishment and tear up the pea patch with the national press corps." Rockefeller, on the other hand, would meet with media approval.[5]) Rockefeller's abiding interest in becoming president was no secret. Indeed he was widely thought to have been making plans to run against Agnew in 1976 to succeed Nixon until Watergate upended everyone's plans. The conservative wing of the Republican Party thought the fix was in. It was feared that Ford, having hinted privately that he was undecided about running for the Oval Office in his own right in 1976, would hand off the nomination to Rockefeller.

"Mr. Ford's first big appointment has become his first big albatross," William Safire wrote in the *New York Times*. Even before Congress confirmed Rockefeller, Safire predicted that Ford would have to dump Rockefeller from the ticket in 1976, whereupon "Democratic candidates will charge that Rockefeller is being dumped to 'placate the right wing.'"[6] Lou Cannon concurred in his chronicle of Reagan's rise: "More than any other single act of Ford's, or indeed all of them combined, it was the selection of Rockefeller which fueled national interest among conservatives in a Reagan candidacy."[7] (Though it should be added that Ford's outspoken wife, Betty, contributed mightily to conservative dislike with her candid comments on *60 Minutes* about her son's and daughter's potential marijuana use and premarital affairs, as well as her fulsome endorsement of abortion.)

The Rockefeller appointment did serve as a sign of Ford's confidence and self-assurance. In order to induce Rockefeller to accept the appointment, Ford had even promised Rockefeller a substantial role in crafting domestic policy—a promise that proved inherently impossible to keep. A less secure person—Nixon, for instance—would never have wanted such a large figure as Rockefeller at his elbow. Ford, Henry Kissinger observed, "was sufficiently self-assured to disagree openly, and he did not engage in elaborate maneuvers about who should receive credit" (which is an indirect slap at Nixon).[8] Only a person with such self-assurance could step into the devastated Oval Office, unelected, with no transition period to work out his own priorities, having to accept his predecessor's White House staff, Cabinet, and ongoing initiatives, and function as well as Ford did. Because Ford lacked the full legitimacy or moral authority that comes with having won a national election, he was at a profound disadvantage against an assertive Congress. But Ford's greatest handicap was that he was not equal to the supreme political demand of the television age—he was not a great communicator. He wasn't even a good one.

George Will put the problem succinctly: "Rhetorical skills are not peripheral to the political enterprise; and they are among the most important skills a person can bring to the presidency. . . . Ford is a passable head of an administration, but an unsatisfactory chief of state. A President is the chief articulator of collective aspirations, or he is not much. He is articulate, or he is inadequate. . . . There never has been a great inarticulate President. Ford is the most inarticulate President since the invention of broadcasting. . . . [A]n inarticulate President is like a motorcycle motor installed in a Mack truck."[9] Ford's 1976 campaign strategist Stu Spencer put the matter to Ford even more succinctly in an Oval Office conversation: "Mr. President, as a campaigner, you're no fucking good."

Ford's physical clumsiness didn't help. Ford was arguably the most athletic man ever to be president, but he repeatedly tripped, fell, or bumped his head, usually in the presence of cameras, reviving Lyndon Johnson's slur that "Jerry Ford can't fart and chew gum at the same time." Reporters joked that not only should Ford not have played college football without a helmet, but he shouldn't play president without one, either. Maybe he's trying to sew up the klutz vote, comedians joked. Even major news media made jokes about Ford. "The only thing between [Vice President] Nelson Rockefeller and the presidency," *Time* magazine quipped, "is a banana peel." (But both Rockefeller and Ford tripped when they walked together into the Senate chamber for Rockefeller's swearing-in ceremony.)

Behind the scenes, the record shows, Ford was a sure-footed and decisive leader, but his physical clumsiness seemed a metaphor for his handling of domestic issues. Ford inherited an economy that was deteriorating rapidly. Inflation was skyrocketing to unprecedented levels. The price level jumped 3.7 percent in just the *month* of July 1974. Unemployment was heading toward 7 percent. It was the deadly and unprecedented combination that came to be known as *stagflation.* The federal deficit was projected to balloon to $51.9 billion (out of a $350 billion budget), at that time an unheard of and alarming level.

Orthodox economics held that policy can fight inflation or unemployment, but not both at the same time. Ford chose the fight the former, and proposed to dampen inflation with the orthodox remedy of a tax increase. He proposed a one-year, 5 percent surtax on business and upper-income individuals to close the deficit and dampen inflation at the same time. Ford's economic advisers, a group that included Alan Greenspan and William Simon, argued that fighting inflation was more important than fighting unemployment, which they viewed as a cyclical phenomenon. Inflation was the more pervasive threat to the long-term health of the economy. They were undoubtedly right, but the short-run political cost of putting inflation ahead of unemployment was always heavy for Republicans, especially since the inflation-fighting priority compelled Ford to deny that the nation was in a recession. Ford struggled vainly to change the subject from unemployment. At the announcement of his tax surcharge proposal, Ford wore a campaign-style button that read: WIN. The button, Ford explained, stood for "Whip Inflation Now," which was the name of a volunteer organization to which Ford hoped citizens would enroll. (More than 100,000 amazingly did. Millions more requested WIN buttons.) It was one of the dumbest stunts in the annals of democratic propaganda.

Proposing to raise taxes on the eve of the 1974 congressional election was just the blow Republicans needed to complete their wipeout. Congressional Democrats called for the opposite—a tax cut. It was perhaps the last time Democrats would be in the vanguard of cutting taxes while conservatives, hewing to deficit-fighting orthodoxy, opposed a cut; a decade later, Democrats calling for a tax cut would be a man-bites-dog story line.

Ford bowed to the inevitable, abruptly reversed course, and proposed a tax cut in early 1975. What about the deficit? Ford's economic advisers, including Greenspan, argued that the cut would not swell the deficit because the economic stimulus from the tax cut would generate new revenue. It was the first tentative step by Republicans toward the "supply side" economics that would become central to Reaganomics. No one recognized its full political potential at the time. Even second-term Rep. Jack Kemp thought that the tax cut should be offset by a budget cut of equal proportions.

Democrats immediately upped the ante, calling for a much larger tax cut than Ford wanted and rejecting any of Ford's proposed spending cuts (other than defense, which Congress had cut already), which threatened to swell the deficit to over $100 billion. Ford pondered a veto, but realized Congress would override it. So Ford rolled over and accepted the Democratic tax cut of $28 billion over one year in March 1975. Out in California, Ronald Reagan criticized Ford for embracing the tax cut and departing from Republican deficit-fighting orthodoxy.

THE SAGGING ECONOMY was the lesser of Ford's travails. The greatest misfortune of Ford's tenure in office was having to preside over the last chapter of the long Vietnam saga, which resulted in the final collapse of South Vietnam. It was not simply that a long-suffering American ally was defeated that made the episode so ignominious, but the fact that, in the grips of a mood of self-flagellation, the United States refused to come to the aid of an ally whose survival had been the bipartisan commitment of five presidents. The repercussions and recriminations from the fall of South Vietnam would last more than a decade, well into the Reagan years.

Americans on all sides of the Vietnam controversy have consoled themselves ever since that the fall of South Vietnam was inevitable. While corruption, military ineptitude, poor leadership, and flagging morale doubtless weakened South Vietnam's prospects, their defeat was by no means foreordained. It required the United States deciding to look the other way as well. "There is no doubt in my mind," Kissinger wrote, "that, with anything close to an adequate level of American aid, they would not have collapsed in 1975."[10] Kissinger's views must be properly discounted as those of an interested party, but other Vietnam scholars and military experts such as Guenter Lewy and Col. David Hackworth share his view.[11]

North Vietnam had begun violating the 1972 Paris accord practically before the ink had dried. The agreement left 140,000 North Vietnamese troops on the ground in South Vietnam. Soviet arms shipments to North Vietnam increased fourfold (the United States thought, or hoped, that détente would restrain the Soviets), and Hanoi began augmenting its forces with fresh troops and new weapons—tanks, heavy artillery pieces, anti-aircraft rockets, and so forth. North Vietnam paved the Ho Chi Minh trail into a four-lane highway. Both actions violated the peace treaty, which said each side could only *replace* damaged or lost equipment. Kissinger, on a follow-up visit to Hanoi in February, warned Hanoi to stop. Hanoi, it was revealed after the war, had embarked on a long-range plan to conquer South Vietnam by 1976 or 1977—depending on what the U.S. reaction was. Hanoi studied Nixon's moves closely during these months.

Nixon had no illusions about North Vietnamese intentions, but had promised South Vietnam's President Thieu that "if Hanoi fails to abide by the terms of this agreement it is my intention to take swift and severe retaliatory action. . . . We will respond with full force."[12] By which Nixon meant he would send the bombers again. In late March of 1973, after the last American POWs had come home from Hanoi, Nixon issued his warning publicly: "North Vietnam should have no doubt as to the consequences if they fail to comply with the agreement." When stepped-up U.S. intelligence reconnaissance flights showed no abatement, Nixon in April decided to unleash a heavy bombing attack on North Vietnam.

Nixon knew that resuming the bombing of North Vietnam would ignite a domestic firestorm, but he was willing to persevere. But Watergate was beginning to unravel. Just as he was readying the decision to resume bombing, Nixon learned that John Dean was talking with Watergate prosecutors. Sensing the lifeblood draining from his presidency, Nixon stayed the bombing order. It was downhill from there. By August Congress had voted to prohibit any further U.S. military activity in southeast Asia; Nixon couldn't bomb after that if he had wanted to without provoking a constitutional crisis. The War Powers Act, passed in November 1973, when Nixon's position had eroded to the vanishing point in the aftermath of the "Saturday Night Massacre," further constricted Nixon's options for assisting South Vietnam. His promises to intervene on South Vietnam's behalf were rendered impotent.

As if tying the hands of the American president weren't enough, Congress (Kissinger consistently refers to "the McGovernite Congress" throughout his memoirs) moved to constrict U.S. aid to South Vietnam as well. The Paris Treaty had allowed the United States to provide military aid to South Vietnam on a "replacement" basis (that is, one-to-one replacements for equipment damaged or destroyed) as well as economic assistance. In 1973, the first year after the signing of the Paris Treaty, U.S. aid amounted to $2.2 billion. But at the end of the year Congress cut the level of aid for 1974 in half, to just over $1 billion, and in 1974 cut aid even further, to just $700 million for 1975.

Kissinger and America's Ambassador to South Vietnam, Graham Martin, pleaded with Congress that such drastic cuts in aid would "seriously tempt the north to gamble on an all-out military offensive." Congress was unmoved, despite the fact that many congressional leaders had been on record supporting aid at the time the treaty was signed in January 1973. But following the election of "the McGovernite Congress" in 1974, "suddenly," as Kissinger put it, "collective amnesia set in." So fully had Congress turned against South Vietnam that 72 members of the House voted against a resolution condemning North Vietnam for its aggression in the South. Even Sen. Henry "Scoop" Jackson, perhaps the most stalwart liberal supporter of the war effort, threw in his lot with the doves, coming out against further aid to South Vietnam, and for further cuts in the defense budget.

Inflation and the onset of the energy crisis magnified the cuts in the level of American aid, such that the lower level of aid was no longer sufficient to replace military equipment on a one-to-one basis. Even as the tempo of the war increased—South Vietnamese losses in 1974 were greater than in 1968, the year of the Tet Offensive—ammunition and fuel dwindled. The net firepower of the South Vietnamese forces fell by more than half because of bomb and ammunition shortages, and its mobility was cut in half. Air force sorties dropped 40 percent, as a third of South Vietnam's airplanes were grounded for lack of fuel and spare parts.[13] Why, Kissinger complained, can we give $1 billion to Israel for defense, and not the same to a country where 50,000 Americans had given their lives? (That South Vietnam lacked an effective Washington lobby and domestic voting block seemed to escape the savvy strategist.) Having come to the aid of South Vietnam a decade before because of John F. Kennedy's proclamation that America "would pay any price, bear any burden," by 1975 America decided that it would pay no price, not even the price of writing a check.

North Vietnam, meanwhile, was closely studying every political twist in the United States and could not believe their good fortune. Throughout the steady buildup in the South, North Vietnam's leaders "heatedly discussed" (according to one North Vietnamese account) whether the United States would resume bombing or send troops back to Vietnam if the North launched large-scale attacks. Their plan called for slow escalation and victory by 1976 or 1977, but with an increasingly prostrate Nixon and a supine Congress, Hanoi was able to accelerate its timetable. At a North Vietnamese leadership conference in late 1974, the record showed later, it was concluded that immediate victory was within reach: "The Watergate scandal had seriously affected the entire United States and precipitated the resignation of an extremely reactionary president—Nixon."[14]

Vietnam can be regarded as the last casualty of Watergate, but it can also be thought of as the first casualty of détente, about which more in due course. Although Kissinger is right to complain of the "McGovernite" tilt in Congress, it is also true that détente neutralized many moderate and conservative members of Congress who might have heeded Kissinger's pleadings for aid. As the conservative Democratic Congressman Walter Flowers of Alabama explained, "[My constituents] don't have any feeling of guilt. They say we're arm in arm with the big Communists in Russia and China but fighting the little Communists in Indochina tooth and nail. I can't justify any more military aid."[15]

As South Vietnam struggled into the early months of 1975 still hoping for additional American aid, President Thieu decided to consolidate his remaining strength by ordering a retreat of his best forces from the central highlands to the coast. It was a strategic error, setting off a panic among the population and emboldening North Vietnam to press their offensive harder. The rout was on. In Washington President Ford was still trying—*begging* would not be an inaccurate term—to get Congress to offer $722 million in additional aid for South Vietnam. It was not clear at this late hour whether the aid could be sent in time, even if Congress approved it.

It was a moot point. Congressional leaders were willing to make a supplemental appropriation, but only for the evacuation of Americans still in South Vietnam. "I will give you large sums for evacuation, but not one nickel for military aid," New York's Republican Senator Jacob Javits told Ford. Senator Joe Biden went further, saying he was against spending

U.S. funds to evacuate South Vietnamese officials and dependents whose service to the United States would make them obvious targets for North Vietnamese reprisals: "I will vote for any amount for getting the Americans out, but I don't want it mixed up with getting the Vietnamese out."[16] Senator Claiborne Pell suggested sending South Vietnamese exiles and refugees to Borneo: "It has the same latitude, the same climate, and would welcome some anticommunists. . . ."[17]

Although Congressional opinion was supine, the antiwar movement exulted not only about their own success, but about the imminent triumph of North Vietnam. At the Academy Awards ceremony in 1975, the producer of the winner of the Oscar for best documentary, the pro-Hanoi film *Hearts and Minds,* said "Isn't it ironic that we are here at a time just before Vietnam is about to be liberated?" (*Hearts and Minds* includes Daniel Ellsberg remarking, "We aren't *on* the wrong side; we *are* the wrong side.") Then he proceeded to read to the audience a telegram of congratulations from the Vietcong. Susan Sontag exulted: "One can only be glad about the victory of the DRV [North Vietnam] and the PRG [Viet Cong]. . . . It would have been disheartening if America had its way with Indochina."[18]

So craven had congressional opinion become that the Pentagon bucked when Ford ordered an aircraft carrier to sail through the South China Sea as a pro forma show of force. Some of Ford's own senior staff wanted to disassociate Ford from the 11th hour efforts to stand by South Vietnam, which many on the staff thought privately was occurring at the behest of Kissinger, anxious to preserve his own honor. As North Vietnam closed in on Saigon, Ford went to Tulane University on April 23 for a long-scheduled speech. In his speech was a phrase that had not been reviewed through the normal channels at the State Department or the National Security Council. "Today," Ford declared, "America can regain the sense of pride that existed before Vietnam. But it cannot be achieved by refighting a war that is finished as far as America is concerned." Ford's declaration took Kissinger by surprise. Ford was throwing in the towel, too.

At the time Ford said this, however, the U.S. evacuation from Saigon had not begun in earnest. Evacuations are difficult maneuvers, compounded in this instance by the political necessity of keeping up the appearance of support so long as any chance of additional Congressional aid remained. The biggest practical problem is how to evacuate without setting off a panic. Both considerations caused the United States to delay its evacuation until the last moment, a delay that observers have blamed on the desire of Kissinger and U.S. Ambassador to South Vietnam Graham Martin to preserve appearances to the bitter end.

Faced with a desperate scramble as the final attack on Saigon commenced, the United States even asked the Soviet Union to restrain North Vietnam long enough for the United States to get out. The North hinted to the Soviets that they would comply, and then proceeded to step up their attack, shelling an airport that was a principal evacuation site. And so unfolded the scene of America's final flight from Saigon, forever memorialized in the photograph of Americans and Vietnamese climbing a ladder atop the American embassy to a waiting helicopter. Over 6,000 Americans and South Vietnamese were airlifted from the embassy roof over an 18-hour period. The helicopter had been a symbol of American power in Vietnam; during the evacuation, the decks of navy ships offshore became so overcrowded that 15 helicopters were pushed over the side into the ocean, which seemed a fitting way to express the final frustration with the entire war effort in Southeast Asia. The embassy rooftop ladder captured in the famous photograph by UPI photographer Hubert Van Es now rests as an exhibit in the Gerald Ford Presidential Library in Grand Rapids, Michigan. Why Ford would want such an ignominious memento remains a mystery.

Even as late as 1999, Kissinger professes to be puzzled by the denouement of the war: "For the sake of our long-term peace of mind, we must some day undertake an assessment of why good men on all sides found no way to avoid this disaster and why our domestic drama first paralyzed and then overwhelmed us."[19] America had lost 58,000 lives in defense of South Vietnam, along with 3,706 airplanes, and 4,866 helicopters. South Vietnam suffered 245,000 dead. Hanoi later estimated that its dead totaled 1.4 million.

IT WAS DIFFICULT at that moment to see how Ford's promise that "America can regain its pride," let alone honor, could be realized. South Vietnam was not the only venue of American humiliation. Cambodia had fallen little more than two weeks before Saigon to the Communist (and

North Vietnamese–backed) Khmer-Rouge. The United States had backed the current government, which had overthrown the Communist regime in 1970. But Congress also cut off U.S. aid to Cambodia, and as the Khmer Rouge closed in on the capital city of Phnom Penh, Cambodian leaders expressed the same sense of betrayal as South Vietnam.

Cambodia's President Suakham Khoy sent an appeal to Ford: "For [a] number of years now the Cambodian people have put their trust in America. I cannot believe this trust was misplaced and that suddenly America will deny us the means which might give us a chance to find an acceptable solution to our conflict."[20] No aid was forthcoming, and U.S. diplomatic overtures were rebuffed. In the current climate of opinion in the United States, more aid, even for self-defense, was thought perverse.

Two weeks before the final collapse of Cambodia, Anthony Lewis wrote in the *New York Times:* "What future possibility could be more terrible than the reality of what is happening in Cambodia now?" It was, Lewis wrote a few weeks later, only our "cultural arrogance" that led us to believe that "our way of life must prevail." *New York Times* reporter David Andelman wrote that the vast majority of Cambodians "do not voice any concern about such issues as the shape of a peace or possible postwar reprisals," while another *Times* reporter, Sydney Schanberg, wrote that "it is difficult to imagine how their lives could be anything but better with the Americans gone."[21] Sen. Alan Cranston said that "the 'bloodbath' that some people fear after the fighting stops if the [Khmer Rouge] insurgents take over is only conjecture." The *Los Angeles Times* said the aid cutoff was "for the good of the suffering Cambodians themselves." Columnist Joseph Kraft asked, "Does it really matter whether Cambodia goes Communist?" And after South Vietnam followed Cambodia's fall, the *New York Times* carried a news story, datelined Phnom Penh, with the headline: "Indochina Without Americans: For Most, a Better Life."[22] The coming of the Khmer Rouge was beyond their imagination.

Cambodians who had fought the Khmer Rouge knew better, but showed themselves braver than America. The U.S. ambassador to Cambodia offered to evacuate Cambodian leaders, but, as Kissinger wrote, "To our astonishment and shame, the vast majority refused," even though they knew their refusal meant certain death. The former prime minister, Sirik Matak, replied caustically:

Dear Excellency and Friend:

I thank you very sincerely for your letter and for your offer to transport me towards freedom. I cannot, alas, leave in such a cowardly fashion. As for you, and in particular for your great country, I never believed for a moment that you would have this sentiment of abandoning a people which has chosen liberty. You have refused us your protection, and we can do nothing about it.

You leave, and my wish is that you and your country will find happiness under this sky. But, mark it well, that if I shall die here on this spot and in my country that I love, no matter, because we all are born and must die. I have only committed this mistake of believing in you.

Please accept, Excellency and dear friend, my faithful and friendly sentiments.

Sirik Matak

The Khmer Rouge captured Matak, shot him in the stomach, and left him to die of his wounds three days later.

Matak was among the minority of Khmer Rouge victims who were shot. Because of a shortage of ammunition, most of the hundreds of thousands massacred in the aftermath of the Khmer Rouge revolution were clubbed to death, hung, or stabbed.[23] No one knows how many people were killed in the charnel house of "Democratic Kampuchea" (as Cambodia was renamed) from 1975 and 1979. Credible estimates run as high as 2 million (out of a total population of about 8 million).[24] The Communist tyrant at the head of the Khmer Rouge, Pol Pot, claimed in 1979 that "only a few thousand Cambodians have died as a result of the application of our policy of bringing abundance to the people." In fact the murderous rampage was the deliberate policy of Pol Pot and the Khmer Rouge, which launched their rule by abolishing money and ordering the entire population of cities to evacuate to the countryside within 24 hours.

The unspeakable bloodbath in Cambodia prompted a round of recriminations in the West, where defenders of American intervention had predicted a Communist bloodbath in the wake of American withdrawal, while the antiwar Left, a large segment of which advocated a Communist victory, had denied the prospect of Communist repression. In Vietnam the conquering Communists at least had the good graces to conceal their repression in the form of "re-education camps," to which nearly a million people were sent after the fall of Saigon.[25] But the Cambodian atrocity was undeniable. So it became necessary for the Left to contrive a way to blame the Cambodian charnel on . . . *the United States.*

The bizarre argument, given credence in the film *The Killing Fields* in the mid-1980s, goes as follows: The U.S. bombing campaign and subsequent "incursion" in Cambodia in 1969 and 1970 destabilized the country and triggered the civil war that, over the next five years, drove the Khmer Rouge into a "mad rage," according to British author William Shawcross, thus provoking their murderous spree after they finally prevailed in 1975. It was an argument that, stripped of its casuistry, reduced to, "The devil made me do it," with the devil in this case dressed in an Uncle Sam costume. "This bizarre expression of self-hatred," Kissinger wrote, "makes as much sense as blaming Hitler's Holocaust on the British bombing of Hamburg." But it was a convenient way for liberals and the antiwar movement to overlook their own naiveté about the consequences of their policy and the nature of Khmer Rouge ideology, which was western Marxism.

Shawcross later expressed second thoughts about the attitude of the antiwar Left toward Indochina, writing in 1994: "[T]hose of us who opposed the American war in Indochina should be extremely humble in the face of the appalling aftermath: a form of genocide in Cambodia and horrific tyranny in both Vietnam and Laos. Looking back on my own coverage for *The Sunday Times* of the South Vietnamese war effort of 1970–75, I think I concentrated too easily on the corruption and incompetence of the South Vietnamese and their American allies, was too ignorant of the inhuman Hanoi regime, and far too willing to believe that a victory by the Communists would provide a better future. But after the Communist victory came the refugees to Thailand and the floods of boat people desperately seeking to escape the Cambodian killing fields and the Vietnamese gulags. Their eloquent testimony should have put paid to all illusions."[26]

The Marxism of the Khmer Rouge was even more problematic for the American Left than their barbarism, because if the role of ideology in the Khmer Rouge terror was acknowledged, it held the most searching consequences for the main Cold War struggle with the Soviet Union and its allies. In fact the Khmer Rouge leaders had learned their Marxism in the West, chiefly in Paris. The leader of the Khmer Rouge, Pol Pot, had gone to Paris in 1948 as an engineering student, but quickly fell under the spell of the French Communist Party. So thorough was his infatuation with the French Left that he chose Bastille Day for his wedding in 1956. Pol Pot's real name had been Saloth Sar; his chosen name "Pol Pot" meant "the original Cambodian," suggesting how seriously he viewed himself as an Adamite figure. His preoccupation with Marxist social engineering led him to fail his electrical engineering courses three years in a row, thereby losing his scholarship and prompting his return to Cambodia, whereupon he quickly rose through the ranks to become leader of the Cambodian Communist Party.

Other leaders of the Khmer Rouge had been his comrades in Paris, and had learned their doctrinaire Marxism just as thoroughly. Khieu Samphan, Pol Pot's chief deputy, had written a doctoral thesis in Paris embracing the Leninist-Stalinist practice of massive population relocation as a primary tool of reshaping society. When an Italian journalist asked Samphan about the large number of Cambodians killed, Samphan answered, "It's incredible the way you Westerners worry about war criminals."[27] Suong Sikoeun, another Khmer Rouge leader, explained that "I was very influenced by the French Revolution, and in particular by Robespierre. It was only one step from there to becoming a Communist. Robespierre is my hero. Robespierre and Pol Pot: both of them share the qualities of determination and integrity."[28] Pol Pot and his comrades thought Mao's "Great Leap Forward" (which had resulted in widespread famine in China) had been too modest and incomplete. They would show the world how "real socialism" was accomplished, with a Super Great Leap Forward.

The Left, with a few honorable exceptions such as Joan Baez, maintained a rigid denial about the aftermath of the fall of Vietnam. Conservatives took bitter pleasure in embarrassing the Left by recalling their predictions of Vietnam's bright, prosperous, and peaceful democratic future under Communism. Stanley Hoffman, for example, wrote in *The New Republic* that Hanoi's collectivism "is likely to produce greater welfare and security for its people than any local alternative ever offered, at a cost of freedom that affects a small elite." Hoffman's "small elite" comprised a million people sent to re-education camps (where 50,000 died), and another 2 million who took to boats to flee the country. The antiwar cleric Jim Wallis would later dismiss the visible evidence of the boat people with the remark that "Many of today's refugees were inoculated with a taste for Western lifestyle during the war and are fleeing to support their consumer habit in other lands."[29] By the end of the 1970s the Leftist charade of misdirection and denial was so rapidly unraveling and unconvincing that even the arch-dove Sen. George McGovern, who in 1975 had called for *returning* refugees to Vietnam, called for a U.S. invasion of Cambodia to end the genocide.

REVISIONIST HISTORIANS TWO or three generations from now are likely to begin making out the argument that the United States *won* the ultimate victory in the Vietnam War, and that it should be seen as the turning point of the Cold War. At this point such an interpretation will excite raised eyebrows if not ridicule. Yet even today, at a remove of over 20 years, and with the end of the Cold War providing the benefit of hindsight, it is possible to make out an argument that the United States didn't suffer unequivocal defeat in Vietnam.[30] At the moment of South Vietnam's final collapse, it seemed not only that the United States had lost, but that the "Domino Theory," a derivative of the containment doctrine, had been wrong, in which case the Cold War itself was misconceived. That no other southeast Asian nation fell to communist aggression, as had been feared in the 1960s, is perhaps a *vindication* of the Domino Theory.

Singapore's Prime Minister Lee Kuan Yew, speaking to a joint session of Congress in 1985, argued that America's long effort in Vietnam bought precious time for the rest of the region to solidify itself, turning a row of fragile dominoes into pillars of economic and political strength in the region, and formidable bastions against the further expansion of Communism in any form. The 10-year American effort in Vietnam can be seen then to have made Hanoi's eventual triumph a Pyrrhic victory. In fact, the drawn out war resulted in the exhaustion of guerrilla Communism in Asia. The aftermath of the fall of Saigon saw Communist nations turn against each other, as Vietnam invaded Cambodia in 1978, and as border skirmishes with China in 1979 threatened to erupt into full-scale war. Today, as billboards for the American Express card start to sprinkle the skyline in Ho Chi Minh City (the new name for Saigon), the poverty of

Vietnam and North Korea contrasts starkly with the rest of the region's booming prosperity. A commonplace half-jest of the 1970s, when the German and Japanese economies were outperforming the U.S. economy, is that the surest route to prosperity was to lose a war with the United States, after which the United States would help the prostrate nation rebuild. Vietnam today may wish that it had experienced such a fate.

None of this was predictable in 1975, however. To the contrary, as defeats in large-scale warfare are seldom isolated in their effects, the denouement of Vietnam entailed a loss of American standing in the world, just as the liberal internationalists of the Kennedy and Johnson administrations had predicted. It has been fashionable over the years to speak of "traumatic stress disorder" among troops who fought in Vietnam. The United States could be said to have suffered from the same psychological trauma in the immediate aftermath of Vietnam. Thailand, the most obvious domino of the region, decided that they would be better off without American help, and promptly ordered all U.S. forces to depart from Thai soil. "The United States," Thailand's foreign minister Chatichai Choonhavan caustically declared, "does not have any morals at this point. They have already pulled out from Cambodia and South Vietnam, so we are going to have to depend on ourselves." An anonymous Thai foreign ministry source was even more blunt: "If we cling to the United States we'll lose whatever bargaining power we have in the region—and we've already lost most of it."[31]

The greatest fear of American policy makers is that Japan would begin to wobble, and sure enough Japan started making neutralist sounds. A Japanese foreign ministry official remarked that "Japan, too, must rectify her position of having relied excessively on the United States." The South Korean National Assembly passed a resolution asking for additional U.S. military aid as a way of confirming that the United States remained committed to the defense of South Korea. Even Philippine President Ferdinand Marcos declared that "Closer links with the Communist states are the only way to ensure our security and survival." Syria's dictator Hafez Assad said to Kissinger, "You sold out Vietnam and Cambodia. Why should we not suppose you will also sell out Israel?"[32]

The doubts about America were not limited to Asia. *The Spectator* of London said "It is now doubtful how long American commitment to Europe will last. . . . All around the world American horns are being drawn in." *The Economist,* in a cover leader entitled "The Fading of America," wondered aloud whether "the Indochina rout will now make every ally of the United States doubt whether it can believe in promises of American support. . . . The past month's events make the question of American credibility a genuine one."[33] Sir Robert Thompson, the Australian officer who spent much of his adult life in Vietnam, lamented that "The American retreat before Moscow, like that of Napoleon, is beginning to litter the route with corpses." A senior party leader of West Germany's Christian Democratic Union said publicly that "If Berlin were attacked tomorrow I am not absolutely certain that the United States would intervene." His fears were well-founded. A Lou Harris poll taken shortly before the fall of Saigon found that only 34 percent of Americans would favor American intervention if the Soviet Union moved on Berlin. Only 27 percent favored aiding Israel if it were about to suffer defeat at the hands of the Arabs.[34] Small wonder Reagan complained that "Our word is not trusted for the first time in two hundred years."

All around the world democracy was in retreat. In Europe it was feared the Italian Communist Party might win the next election, while Portugal, following a Communist-led coup, seemed poised to become an adjunct member of the Eastern bloc, which might provide the Warsaw Pact with a strategic position on NATO's crucial Mediterranean flank. With Italy and Portugal teetering on the brink, France and Spain might not be far behind, and instability in Greece always made the cradle of democracy questionable. Freedom House's annual survey of free, partly free, and unfree nations found the largest decline in freedom around the world in the two-year period of 1974–1975. The percentage of the world's population Freedom House rated "free" declined from 35 percent in 1974 to 19.8 percent by the end of 1975; 44.9 percent of the world's population was rated "unfree." By the end of 1975 only about two dozen genuine multi-party democracies were left in the world, while six new pro-Soviet dictatorships could be counted. *The Collapse of Democracy* by *Economist* magazine foreign affairs editor Robert Moss went to the top of the bestseller list on both sides of the Atlantic. Pat Moynihan ruefully reflected: "Neither liberty nor democracy would seem to be prospering—or, in any event, neither would seem to have a future nearly as auspicious as their past." It was the attitude of much of the world, Moynihan concluded, that democracy "has simply no relevance to the future. It is where the world was, not where it is going."[35]

While the erstwhile dominoes of East Asia held steady, a new line of dominoes started teetering in Africa. Even as the Soviet-armed forces of North Vietnam were closing in on Saigon, reports started coming in from Africa that Soviet advisers and large quantities of Soviet weapons were showing up in Angola, which was then locked in a bitter civil war. The Soviets were arming, and the Cubans were training, the Marxist faction in the war, known as the MPLA. Before long, regular Cuban troops started showing up and joining directly in the fight; they appeared to be Moscow's mercenaries. An East German paratroop regiment would join the Cubans in Angola in 1978. The ultimate object of Soviet strategy was undoubtedly to bring pressure on South Africa, which, if toppled, would be a major strategic loss for the West.

Ford wanted to send $28 million of "covert" aid through the CIA to the anti-Communist faction in Angola, UNITA, which Ford could do on his own executive authority with discretionary funds. The CIA had wanted $100 million, but Ford calculated that this figure would arouse too much congressional opposition. He might as well have gone for the whole wad. Congress, citing all of the clichés about America sliding down the slippery slope to intervention, passed an amendment to the Defense Department appropriation banning any funds for Angola unless specifically approved in the budget by Congress. (The Tunney and Clark Amendments, as they were known, were the precursor to the Boland Amendments in the 1980s that would hamstring President Reagan's Central America policy.)

Aid to Angola, like aid to South Vietnam, was cut off completely. Kissinger and Ford reacted bitterly. "For the first time in the Cold War," Kissinger wrote, "the United States would capitulate to a Soviet-sponsored military adventure." Ford charged the Senate with an "abdication of responsibility" that "will have the gravest consequences for the long-term position of the United States and for international order in general. . . . Responsibilities abandoned today will return as more acute crises tomorrow."[36] (At the same moment, Soviet military aid to Syria and the Palestinian Liberation Organization was proving instrumental to the destruction of Lebanon, which, under the current circumstances, the

United States could only protest verbally.) While UNITA, generously supplied by South Africa, was never completely vanquished from the field, Cuban troops used Angola as an African beachhead, spreading their presence into Ethiopia, Somalia, and South Yemen over the next few years.

In the midst of an increasingly bleak geopolitical situation, the end of Vietnam and the cuts in the defense budget were signs that American military strength might be ebbing as well. That the travails of Vietnam had dissipated America's armed forces became apparent two weeks after the fall of Saigon, when Cambodia seized an American merchant ship, the *S.S. Mayaguez* in international waters. As the *Mayaguez* steamed slowly toward the Cambodian coast, the White House, wanting to avoid the prolonged spectacle and humiliation of the *Pueblo* seizure in 1968, ordered the military to plan an immediate rescue mission.

The United States had few military assets within reach of the scene, which complicated mission planning. Only 14 heavy-lift helicopters could be located within reasonable distance of the scene—too few for a serious assault and rescue force to be deployed—and one of them crashed en route to the staging area in Thailand. Moreover, neither reconnaissance flights nor other intelligence sources could determine where the ship's crew was being held. The *Mayaguez* was finally spotted at anchor near the offshore island of Koh Tang, about 35 miles off the Cambodian mainland, but the whereabouts of the crew could not be determined. Since the United States didn't know whether the crew had been taken off the ship, the Pentagon decided to launch a two-pronged attack: the *Mayaguez* would be boarded from a U.S. Navy vessel, while Marines would land by helicopter on Koh Tang island. An air raid on the mainland would be made to pin down Cambodian air power (which consisted mostly of propeller-driven airplanes—no match for American jets), along with air patrols between Koh Tang island and the coast to forestall any effort to move the *Mayaguez* crew to the mainland.

Several of the patrol aircraft spotted "caucasians" on the deck of a fishing boat heading for the mainland port of Kompong Som. It was indeed the *Mayaguez* crew. Even though American aircraft shot across the bow and even sank three other fishing boats nearby, the boat with the crew continued on its way to Kompong Som harbor. The sighting of the crew was passed along the chain of command all the way up to the White House, where the decision was made to proceed with the mission as originally planned—the attack on Koh Tang island and the boarding the *Mayaguez* offshore.

The boarding of the *Mayaguez* went easily—because it had been abandoned. Meanwhile, the Cambodians decided, perhaps under diplomatic prompting from the Chinese, to release the *Mayaguez* crew on a Thai fishing boat, which immediately steamed for the American destroyer *U.S.S. Wilson,* waiving white flags to keep from being fired upon. The *Wilson* took the crew aboard, and signaled Washington that all 39 crew members were safe.

But the helicopters carrying the Marine assault force for Koh Tang island, where intelligence sources knew the crew was not located, were already en route, and no one thought to call off the raid. It was a costly fiasco. U.S. military intelligence thought the island was lightly defended at best, but instead it was garrisoned by a contingent of close to 300 Cambodian soldiers, heavily armed with AK-47 rifles, twin Soviet 12.7mm machine guns, 20mm antiaircraft guns, and shoulder-fired rocket propelled grenades. Not only was the assault force of 180 Marines outnumbered and outgunned, they didn't even have tactical maps of the island. U.S. intelligence didn't have any. So the Marines landed at the wrong places, were widely scattered and pinned down under heavy fire. It took hours, because of the limited number of helicopters available, to send reinforcements. Since there was no one on the island to rescue, the purpose of the mission became mere survival while awaiting extraction from the beaches. By the time it was over two and a half days later, 68 men had been killed or wounded in an operation that was unnecessary. Twelve of the 13 helicopters used in the mission were destroyed or severely damaged.[37] President Ford's public approval rating shot up 11 percent because he had shown "toughness."

The enthusiastic public response to the *Mayaguez* episode showed that there was a strong reserve of popular sentiment among Americans to resist the tide of defeatism and pessimism in the wake of Vietnam, a current that Ronald Reagan was soon to discover and exploit in connection with the Panama Canal. Yet the gross failures of intelligence, communications, and decision making in the *Mayaguez* debacle highlighted a troublesome issue. Never mind America's *will* to fight—if America did decide to make a stand, *could she win?*

Knowledgeable observers were increasingly doubtful that the United States had the capacity to prevail in any large-scale engagement with the Soviet Union and its proxies. Adjusted for inflation, U.S. defense spending in the Nixon-Ford years (1969–1977) fell by 42 percent. The large margin of nuclear and conventional superiority the United States enjoyed at the time of the Cuban Missile Crisis was gone. The rapid build-up of Soviet nuclear forces had been accepted as a positive development by the arms control theologians besotted with the doctrine of "mutual assured destruction." But Soviet conventional forces were also racing ahead, such that superiority in Soviet conventional forces along with nuclear forces could now be projected in the near future.

The first time this new vulnerability came home to American decision-makers occurred in the Yom Kippur War of 1973.

ON OCTOBER 5, 1973, the CIA's daily bulletin commented on Egyptian military exercises on the west bank of the Suez Canal, just across the canal from the Israeli-occupied Sinai peninsula: "The exercise and alert activities . . . in Egypt may be on a somewhat larger scale and more realistic than previous exercises, but they do not appear to be preparing for a military offensive against Israel." The very next day, the CIA's daily bulletin reiterated its judgment that "For Egypt a military initiative makes little sense at this critical juncture." Before the ink was dry, 70,000 Egyptian troops and 800 tanks started rolling across pontoon bridges over the Suez. Syria launched a simultaneous surprise attack in the Golan Heights to Israel's northeast.

The attack had been carefully planned for months, yet Egypt achieved complete surprise not only over the CIA, but also Israel, which had shrugged off the large-scale military maneuvers taking place on two of its borders. Even the sudden evacuation of Soviet dependents from Egypt and Syria the day before the attack began failed to raise eyebrows in Washington. Tel Aviv foresaw the attack a few hours before it began, but, having been warned by the United States not to launch a pre-emptive attack against Arab forces, had to wait for the blow to fall. Both the Israelis and the CIA had neglected the great maxim of Sun Tzu: "All warfare is based on deception." At first, the CIA thought it impossible that they had been deceived, and reported to President Nixon that Israel must have started the fighting.

Egypt and Syria had launched the war for political purposes, to show the Arab world—and Israel—that Israel was not invulnerable, and therefore to compel Israel into negotiating a settlement of Arab demands. U.S. strategy in the crisis was to stall for time until Israel could reestablish the *status quo ante*, at which point the "peace process" could begin. It was expected that Israel would quickly turn the tables on their Arab attackers and win a decisive victory as they had in the 1967 six-day war. But things didn't go as easily as predicted. Five days into the war Israeli diplomats in Washington passed along the grim news to Secretary of State Henry Kissinger: Israel's losses had been "staggering and totally unexpected." The Egyptians and Syrians, armed with Soviet surface-to-air missiles, had shot down 49 Israeli warplanes. Worse, Israel had lost 500 tanks—400 of them on the Egyptian front in the Sinai. The Arabs had forced upon Israel a war of attrition, which the tiny nation could not afford.

Meanwhile, U.S. intelligence reported that a major Soviet airlift of supplies to Egypt and Syria was underway, consisting of 140 flights in a four-day period. Israeli Prime Minister Golda Meir was so panicked that she proposed to come immediately to Washington to meet with President Nixon and beg for supplies. If other Arab nations, sensing Israel's panic, joined Egypt and Syria in the attack, a major war might ensue, and would probably draw American and Soviet forces into battle before it was over. The United States decided upon an immediate airlift to Israel. (Worried about adverse Arab reaction to emergency American arms shipments, Governor Reagan, who received regular security briefings from Kissinger, offered Kissinger a practical suggestion: "Why don't you say you will replace all the aircraft the Arabs claim they have shot down?"[38])

After three weeks of hard fighting, Israel managed to turn the tables on their Arab attackers. They had driven deep into Syria and forced the Egyptians back across the Suez canal. The Israelis were preparing to move on Damascus, and had encircled the Egyptian army east of the Suez canal, when the Soviet Union issued an ultimatum: Either the United States get Israel to accept a cease-fire, or the Soviets would come directly to the aid of their Arab clients. The United States had already been pressing Israel to accept a cease-fire, but the Soviet gambit was a sobering moment because it brought home in vivid terms the erosion of U.S. force capabilities relative to the Soviet Union. The fact that U.S. intelligence confirmed that seven Soviet airborne divisions were mobilized and on alert added to the seriousness of the moment. It was, Nixon wrote later, "the most serious threat to U.S.-Soviet relations since the Cuban missile crisis." Nixon had no choice but to place U.S. military forces on worldwide alert, which his critics charged was a cynical ploy to distract attention from Watergate. (Nixon's Watergate weakness—the Yom Kippur War coincided with the furor of the "Saturday Night Massacre" firing of special counsel Archibald Cox—undoubtedly figured into the Soviet calculations.)

The cease-fire fortunately stuck, so the confrontation was avoided. But there was no avoiding the changing geostrategic realities of the moment. The Mediterranean had always been regarded as an Anglo-American lake, and Western strategists laughed off the occasional Soviet declaration that the United States should withdraw from the Mediterranean. During the Yom Kippur War, the United States stopped laughing. What most alarmed American strategists at that moment was the realization that Soviet capabilities in the region had grown to the point where the United States might well lose a confrontation with Soviet forces.

Most startling was the Soviet presence in supposedly "non-aligned" Yugoslavia, where, in addition to air bases made available to Soviet military aircraft, Soviet submarines were routinely putting into port for "repairs." The Soviet airlift to Egypt and Syria made heavy use of these Yugoslavian bases, and every nation in the region, including NATO ally Turkey, granted overflight rights to Soviet planes. (The single exception was the Shah of Iran, who said no to the Soviet request.)

Meanwhile, the U.S. airlift had to confine its supply flights to Israel carefully within the international air corridor over the Mediterranean because Greece, Turkey, Italy, and Spain refused to grant landing or overflight rights to U.S. planes. Libyan planes had fired on an American transport aircraft a few weeks before the war. (Portugal grudgingly granted permission to use the Azores for a transit stop only after Nixon sent a blunt message.) The Chief of Naval Operations, Admiral Elmo Zumwalt, candidly explained the score to the *Washington Post*:

> The United States had to back down in the face of a Soviet ultimatum, partly because Gorshkov [commander of the Soviet navy] had U.S. ships outnumbered in the Mediterranean, 98 to 65, and could have attacked U.S. carriers with airplanes flying from four directions. Soviet planes had bases in Egypt, Syria, the Crimea, and

Yugoslavia [and could have used Libya as well]—virtually surrounding the U.S. 6th Fleet in the Mediterranean, while we didn't have a
single land base in the area because none of America's allies would
allow their land or airspace to be used to help Israel.[39]

"The odds are very high," Zumwalt concluded, "that they would
have won and we would have lost." The U.S. Navy, the public learned,
had fewer ships than it had in 1939, before the outbreak of World War II.
Meanwhile, the Soviet navy, which had until the mid-1960s been chiefly a
coastal protection force, had begun to evolve into a blue-water force
with large capital ships and a rapidly expanding submarine force. In the
Syrian-Jordanian crisis of 1970, the United States moved its fleet to the
eastern Mediterranean and threatened to intervene in order to pressure
Moscow to make the Syrians halt their drive into Jordan. In 1973, the Soviets were able to turn the tables. Nixon and Kissinger could rightly boast
that their diplomacy with the Arab states had marginalized the Soviets'
political position in the Middle East, but at the end of the day diplomatic
strength rests on strategic (military) strength.

The erosion of relative American strength was not limited to the navy
in the Mediterranean. The *New York Times'* military analyst Drew Mid-
dleton concluded in 1976 that the U.S. and NATO would *lose* a conventional war in Europe. James Schlesinger, who served Nixon and Ford as
director of the CIA and as secretary of defense, warned that "The pace,
the dynamism, the momentum of the Soviet effort vastly exceeds that of
the U.S." General Alexander Haig, who had moved on from the White
House to become NATO commander in Europe, warned that "the explosion of Soviet military capabilities far exceeds the requirements of a
purely defensive posture . . . We are getting to the fine edge of disaster."
An unnamed "high-ranking" European official told *Newsweek* that if the
facts about the military imbalance were widely known, it would "provoke widespread panic."[40] Adam Ulam, a prominent scholar of Soviet affairs, wrote that "The Soviet Union has under Brezhnev achieved—it
would be both dangerous and ungenerous for us to deny it—the leading if
not yet the dominant position in world politics."[41]

In addition to building more hardware (three times as many tanks per
year, and nine times as many artillery pieces, than the NATO countries),
the Soviets were acquiring far-flung bases from which to operate. The

American abandonment of South Vietnam provided the Soviet navy with a first-class, American-built port in Cam Rahn Bay, while ports and bases in Angola seemed the logical outcome of their efforts to back the MPLA. Far from denying this bleak assessment as Western paranoia, Soviet foreign minister Andrei Gromyko celebrated that Eastern Bloc forces had "a visibly increased preponderance" that might enable the Eastern Bloc "to lay down the direction of international politics." Soviet Premier Leonid Brezhnev went even further, declaring in a 1973 speech in Prague:

> We are achieving with détente what our predecessors have been unable to achieve using the mailed fist. . . . We have been able to accomplish more in a short time with détente than was done for years of pursuing a confrontation policy with NATO. . . . Trust us, comrades, for by 1985, as a consequence of what we are now achieving with détente, we will have achieved most of our objectives in Western Europe. We will have consolidated our position. We will have improved our economy. And a decisive shift in the correlation of forces will be such that, come 1985, we will be able to extend our will wherever we need to.[42]

Brezhnev's remarkable speech received almost no notice in the Western press. (Reagan was one person who did take note. He referred to Brezhnev's speech in his radio commentary on arms control in 1978 and 1979.)

It was at this moment that a ferocious argument occurred within the U.S. intelligence community about the extent of the Soviet military building program, an argument that was soon to spill over into the national discourse about defense and foreign policy. And thrust into the middle of the dispute was—George Bush. Following the congressional investigations of the Central Intelligence Agency in 1975—an episode begun after the CIA's internal review of potential Watergate-related misdeeds leaked to the media—Ford wanted to install a new director at the agency. Bush was reluctant to take the job, writing to Kissinger that "I do not have politics out of my system entirely, and I see this as the total end of any political future."[43] Bush told reporters in Beijing: "If anyone can conceive of this [CIA] job as a springboard to political fortune, well, he's been hallucinating."[44]

The appointment was controversial both on Capitol Hill and within the CIA. Since Bush had served recently as chairman of the Republican

National Committee, it was thought his appointment veered close to making the CIA directorship a partisan appointment. Bush promised Congress that he would abandon his political ambitions, and Ford likewise pledged that Bush wouldn't be his running mate in 1976. Bush proved to be very popular with career CIA employees, who were initially wary. As one longtime career officer told author Anne Hessing Cahn, "At his first official appearance Bush was greeted with icy politeness. Within ten days he had everyone eating out of his hand. He had great rapport with people."[45] Bush's popularity at the agency perhaps reflected an undue deference for CIA careerists, given the agency's miserable record of prognostication of key trends and events.

Cleaning up after the CIA's alleged perfidy, such as the cartoonish assassination plots against Fidel Castro in the early 1960s, were the least of Bush's troubles. For years the CIA's annual projections of Soviet military strength, known as NIE (for "National Intelligence Estimate) 11-3-8 had consistently underestimated the extent of Soviet efforts to augment their military forces. In the late 1960s the CIA would increase its estimate of the number of nuclear missiles it expected the Soviets to deploy, and each year the Soviets exceeded the upper-bound estimate.

"Surely no failure of American intelligence," wrote Angelo Codevilla, a former senior staff member of the Senate Intelligence Committee during the 1970s, "compares in seriousness to this NIE's misprision of the size, scope, and purpose of Soviet strategic forces between 1965 and 1979."[46] The CIA estimates were clearly guilty of "mirror imaging," that is, imputing to the Soviets the same strategic thinking that guided American policy, namely, the idea of MAD (mutual assured destruction). Since under the doctrine of MAD strategic superiority is impossible, the CIA assumed that the Soviet Union would not strive for a numerical advantage over U.S. strategic nuclear forces. Codevilla succinctly summarizes the problem:

> Between 1973 and 1976, when it became undeniable that the Soviet Union was building the capacity to deliver at least three silo-killing warheads on every American missile silo (plus every other American strategic target) while using only about half of its missile force, the NIEs argued that the Soviets were not really preparing to fight, survive, and win a war; that even if they were, they would not soon succeed; and that if they did succeed, it would not matter.[47]

The most forceful proponent of this thesis was Kissinger, who re-marked at a Moscow press conference in 1975: "What in the name of God is strategic superiority? What do you do with it?" Kissinger came to regret these poorly chosen words. The CIA was merely tailoring its analy-sis to confirm the biases of it superiors, which is not atypical of Washing-ton bureaucracies. In this case, the CIA reports were tailored to support the arms control process.

By 1975 the obvious incongruity between the CIA's estimates and the reality of Soviet buildup was too great to overlook. The critiques of emi-nent scholars such as Albert Wohlstetter and Richard Pipes came to the at-tention of both outgoing CIA director William Colby and members of the President's Foreign Intelligence Advisory Board (PFIAB). Colby was trou-bled by the inaccuracy of the NIEs, and ordered a review of mistakes in past NIEs with an eye to improving the process. The report concluded: "The most obvious shortcoming was the failure of past estimates to foresee the degree to which the Soviets would not only catch up to the U.S. in num-ber of ICBMs but keep right on going."[48] Meanwhile, the CIA, the Defense Intelligence Agency (DIA), and some other federal agencies had embarked on a fresh analysis of Soviet military spending. Up until then the CIA had estimated that the Soviets spent 6 percent of their GDP on defense, about the same proportion of defense spending as the United States. But since the Soviet economy was thought to be just half the size of the U.S. economy (in truth it was only about one-fifth as large), this meant that the Soviets were spending only about half as much as the United States.

There were too many glaring anomalies for this figure to be taken se-riously. As Codevilla put it, "How could the Soviets, on about half the money spent by the U.S., maintain five times as many tanks as the U.S., 2.5 times the manpower, twice as many submarines and aircraft, an an-timissile defense, and an air defense with 10,000 radars, 12,000 surface-to-air missile launchers, etc., while the U.S. had no antimissile system and only vestiges of air defense?"[49] As if these anomalies weren't sufficient to discredit the CIA's previous estimates, a defector brought a text of a Brezhnev speech in which Brezhnev boasted that military spending was 15 percent of Soviet GDP. After an exhaustive process to determine the actual size of the Soviet's opaque command economy (which economist Nick Eberstadt described as "the largest single project in social science re-search ever undertaken"), the CIA grudgingly increased its own estimate to 12 percent, but the DIA argued that the real number was closer to 30 percent. (In the fullness of time—after the end of the Cold War and the collapse of the Soviet Union—it became apparent that the Soviet Union had been devoting as much as 70 percent of GDP toward the military in the 1970s.) This meant that real Soviet defense spending was considerably larger than American defense spending. As the DIA testified to the Senate Appropriations Committee: "By most of the available measures, American power is declining and Soviet power is rising. No one can say precisely where the peril points lie as this process unfolds. But if real expenditures by the United States remain constant or continue to fall, while real Soviet outlays continue to rise, the peril points will occur in the relatively near future."[50]

Colby had rejected a PFIAB proposal for an independent outside group of experts to prepare a competitive analysis of Soviet capabilities and intentions based on access to the same intelligence information that went into the CIA's official NIE. But new director Bush disagreed with Colby, and set in motion the infamous independent group that came to be known as "Team B." Both the CIA's regular analysts, "Team A," and the outside "Team B," would work independently and be given access to the same raw information. At the conclusion of their work each team would exchange drafts, after which the president's national security adviser (by this point Brent Scowcroft had replaced Kissinger as national security adviser) would evaluate the results of the "experiment."

Team B examined more than just the number of missiles or their "throw weights" (which was a centerpiece of arms control controversies in the 1970s). Team B thought Soviet missiles were more accurate than previous estimates, and that Soviet efforts at civil defense were more extensive. Team B's conclusions were stunning. "The evidence suggests that the Soviet leaders are first and foremost offensively rather than defensively minded. . . . While hoping to crush the 'capitalist' realm by other than military means, *the Soviet Union is nevertheless preparing for a Third World War as if it were unavoidable. . . . Within the ten year period of the National Estimate the Soviets may well expect to achieve a degree of military superiority which would permit a dramatically more aggressive pursuit of their hegemonial objectives. . . .*" (Emphasis in original.) When Team B met with the official Team A at CIA headquarters in the fall of 1976, the result was a "disaster" for Team A, which emerged from the meeting "badly mauled" according to Team B's leader Richard Pipes. "The champion of Team A had barely begun his criticism of team B's effort, delivered in a condescending tone," Pipes recalled 10 years later, "when a member of Team B [Paul Nitze] fired a question that reduced him to a state of catatonic immobility: we stared in embarrassment as he sat for what seemed an interminable time with an open mouth, unable to utter a sound."[51]

Pipes' account has been criticized as partial and self-serving, but the result of the exercise was beyond dispute: Team A's official NIE 11-3-8 was much tougher than previous NIEs. In the final report appeared the judgment: "[T]he Soviets are striving to achieve war-fighting and war-survival capabilities which would leave the U.S.S.R. in a better position than the U.S. if war occurred." "I strongly suspect," Pipes wrote, "that George Bush intervened to have Team A substantially revise its draft to allow for Team B's criticism." Nevertheless it was the Team B report that made news (even though the report itself remained classified for 18 years, portions of it leaked to the press) and became a rallying point for anti-détente forces.

Some evidence suggests Bush was embarrassed by the Team B report and regretted having supported the exercise. He opposed making outside competitive analysis like Team B a regular feature of CIA assessments. (The Republican Party's 1980 platform, however, called for establishing competitive intelligence assessment as a regular practice at the CIA.) If true it was probably out of loyalty to his employees at the CIA. Yet Pipes claimed that Bush privately agreed with Team B's assessment: "I do recall attending a dinner somewhere in 1977 [by which time Bush was a private citizen again] at which Bush spoke to a large audience and fully identified with the Team B point of view."[52] Needless to say, one person whose embrace of Team B was unequivocal was Ronald Reagan. With the election of 1980, Team B would become Team A.

THE TEAM B exercise wasn't completed until just after the 1976 election. But even before the Team B exercise was finished, discontent with détente was in full bloom. The Soviet military buildup meant that arms control was failing. The first SALT treaty had not appreciably slowed the Soviet buildup (and in fact did not prevent a single offensive weapons system from being developed or deployed), and the prospective successor treaty, SALT II, would not appreciably slow the Soviet buildup either. Soviet mischief in the Third World made a farce of the other half of détente. At the 1972 Moscow summit where Nixon signed the first SALT treaty, the two nations also signed a statement of "Basic Principles of U.S.–Soviet Relations," which supposedly pledged both superpowers to the necessity of avoiding confrontation, the imperative of mutual restraint, a rejection of attempts to exploit tensions to gain unilateral advantage, the renunciation of claims of special influence in the world, and the willingness to co-exist peacefully and build a long-term relationship.

These principles were, in Kissinger's words, "reference points against which to judge actions and set goals." These "Basic Principles" gave tangible benefits to the Soviets, especially trade credits at favorable interest rates as well as arms control terms within which it could continue its buildup, but yielded only intangible benefits to the United States. Détente may have helped the United States in the Middle East, but was of no help in the main goal the United States sought—Soviet assistance in achieving an honorable settlement to the Vietnam War. Yet there was little reason for the Soviets to help the United States in Vietnam. They knew that the North was likely to win after the United States departed, which made it costless to agree to the Basic Principles. Not only did the Soviet Union continue to supply arms in large quantities to Hanoi (which they denied whenever the United States brought up the matter), but their arms shipments to Africa and elsewhere clearly violated the spirit of détente. Détente achieved little or nothing to slow the aggrandizement of the Soviets' geostrategic position, or to deter them from chipping away at the periphery of the West.

In the 1950s a prominent Harvard professor had warned that for the Soviet Union, détente and "peace offensives" could be turned on and off to serve Soviet purposes. The chief effect of peace offensives, this academic warned, would be to divide and weaken domestic opinion in the West. For the Soviets, this author warned in 1965, "peaceful co-existence is never advocated for its own sake. It is justified primarily as a tactical device to overthrow the West at minimum risk."[53] The academic who issued these prescient warnings was none other than Henry Kissinger. Even William Shawcross, Kissinger's *bete noir* on the Left, argued that "the very structure of détente and its concessions to Soviet needs and Soviet power actually liberated the U.S.S.R. and gave it more freedom for an adventurist foreign policy."[54] One of the Soviet Union's senior strategists,

Gen. Dimitri Volkonogov, confirmed that the younger Kissinger was correct in a circular distributed to the Red Army in 1977:

> Détente among governments intensifies rather than weakens ideological combat. Peaceful coexistence does not signify an acknowledgement that the capitalist system, with all its social vices, is eternal; nor does it constitute peaceful cohabitation of socialism and capitalism; *rather it creates fresh opportunities* for stepping up the struggle against imperialism. (Emphasis added.)

The disharmony between the stated objective of easing superpower tensions through arms control negotiations, expanded trade, and other engagements, and the actual behavior of the Soviet Union and its proxies made Kissinger the flash point of domestic controversy—*just as he himself predicted years earlier.* As Warren Nutter observed, "Secretary Kissinger hails agreements that Professor Kissinger would have strenuously opposed."[55] Détente came to be seen as simply a fancy French word for appeasement, a point Norman Podhoretz vividly made when he wrote that Kissinger "often sounds like Churchill and just as often acts like Chamberlain."[56]

To many Americans, not just on the Right, the period of the mid-1970s was coming to resemble nothing so much as Britain in the 1930s. AFL-CIO president George Meany told the Senate Foreign Relations Committee: "Détente means intensification of ideological warfare. Détente means an undermining of NATO. Détente means ultimate Soviet military superiority over the West. Détente means recognition by the West of the Soviet Union's ownership of Eastern Europe."[57] The founders of the influential bipartisan Committee on the Present Danger began to think that these troubled years should be regarded not as the Post-War Era, but as a new Pre-War Era. Paul Nitze, the dean of American arms control diplomats who resigned from the SALT II negotiating team in protest of the weak agreement he saw coming from the SALT II round, warned in *Foreign Affairs* that "There is every prospect that under the terms of the SALT agreements the Soviet Union will continue to pursue a nuclear superiority that is not merely quantitative but designed to produce a theoretical war-winning capability."

There is no doubting Henry Kissinger's keen intellect and formidable skills as a negotiator. Kissinger can, and does, claim the vindication of history; after all, the Cold War worked out right in the end. But did superpower events unfold because of Kissinger's designs, or in spite of them?

In a 1978 essay about the sources of Kissinger's thought, Peter Drucker concluded: "[T]he more history I read, the more I become convinced that the genius foreign minister is a disaster for his country."[58] Judging whether Drucker is right requires a considerable digression, for the problem Kissinger and détente posed would be central to the course of world events for the next 15 years, and would constitute the central dilemma of foreign policy in the Reagan presidency.

HENRY KISSINGER WAS the most consequential and celebrated secretary of state in the twentieth century, and perhaps in all of U.S. history. Kissinger's influence and mystique are such that he continues to command public attention after more than 25 years out of office, showing up on *Nightline* and on the feature pages of leading newspapers and magazines whenever a foreign policy episode comes to the fore.

Kissinger was about the only close Nixon associate to escape Watergate with his reputation and prestige undamaged, even though Kissinger's conspiratorial nature contributed to the paranoid White House atmosphere. It was the concern for national security—Kissinger's portfolio—that set in train the events that led to Watergate. In fact, Kissinger ordered wiretaps liberally on his own subordinates and other White House staff he suspected of leaking. It was ironically Watergate that propelled him to the head of the State Department. Nixon hated the State Department, and had run foreign policy through Kissinger out of the White House during his first term. But as the entire White House staff became convulsed with Watergate in 1973, Nixon saw that the only way for Kissinger to avoid being fully caught in the maelstrom was to make him secretary of state. But such was Kissinger's value to Nixon that he stayed on concurrently as national security adviser, maintaining his White House office along with his suite at Foggy Bottom, and, more important, still reporting to Nixon every day.

Kissinger would be loathe to admit it, but a large part of the favorable publicity he received resulted from liberal sublimation: Liberals who detested Nixon found Kissinger a handy vehicle to give credit for the foreign policy achievements they welcomed, such as the opening to China and the beginning of détente. The other part of his popularity owed to his talent for prevarication, for empathizing with whatever person or group whose company he kept at that moment. One early biographer noted that "Hawks and doves alike thought they had found a kindred spirit in Henry," while another observer notes that "his style explains why he has proven singularly adept at manipulating and neutralizing potential critics on both the Right and the Left. There is something for almost everyone in Kissinger's writings, save possibly for an unreconstructed Wilsonian."[59]

On the eve of resignation Nixon implored Ford that Kissinger was indispensable, which was something of an understatement. Kissinger was consistently more popular with the public than either Nixon or Ford, which made him unassailable. Ford couldn't have dismissed him even if he had wanted to (which he didn't). The week Saigon fell, a Gallup poll found the public gave Kissinger a 56 percent approval rating, versus only 25 percent who disapproved. He consistently ranked higher than Nixon and Ford on the list of the public's most admired people. In 1973 and again in 1974 Kissinger was chosen the world's most admired man in a Gallup year-end survey, ahead of Billy Graham and President Ford. George Will wrote that "The nearly total collapse of confidence in Mr. Ford has made Henry Kissinger an even more important figure than he has been for the last six years. He seems to be the source of whatever legitimacy attaches to this Administration."[60] A contestant in the 1974 Miss Universe pageant said Kissinger was "the greatest person in the world today." The final irony of Kissinger's popularity is that for most of Nixon's first term, the White House refused to let TV or radio broadcast Kissinger's voice, for fear that his heavy German accent would put off middle-American constituents in the heartland. Yet his thick accent was a central part of his subsequent mystique.

Kissinger was among the throng of disaffected Germans who fled Nazi Germany for the United States in the 1930s. The conundrum of Henry Kissinger is that he seemed to have brought with him a middle-European outlook on world affairs, which, by his own admission, sits uneasily with the moralistic traditions of American foreign policy. The American experience is completely alien to the European mind, as exemplified by the remark attributed to Georges Clemenceau that "Americans have no capacity for abstract thought, and make bad coffee." European thinking is defined by balance-of-power "realism," which values stability or equilibrium above all else, while America, owing to the soaring principles of its founding along with its favorable geographical circumstances, has always had, in Kissinger's words, "a traditional sense of universal moral mission." The maxim for European foreign relations is *raison d'e-tat*—reasons of state, that is, self-interest. There is no shorthand maxim for America's foreign outlook, but it might be—if we spoke French— *raison droit* or perhaps *etat de droit,* that is, reasons of morality, or a state based on right.

This turns Clemenceau on his head, for the basis of America's moral outlook on the world was what Lincoln called "an *abstract truth,* applicable to all men at all times," namely, that great sentence from the Declaration of Independence that begins "We hold these truths to be self-evident, that all men are created equal. . . ." Yet even democratic idealists understand the real world mismatch between principles and power, such that President John Quincy Adams felt compelled to declare early in the history of the republic that although the United States was a friend of liberty everywhere, she was a defender only of her own. This is precisely the problem for European-minded realists like Kissinger: The native idealism of America coupled with her geographical isolation made her susceptible to unpredictable swings between interventionism and isolationism. As Kissinger put it, America's emphasis on democratic principle has created "an historical cycle of exuberant overextension and sulking isolationism." This volatility, Kissinger thought, unsettles the international equilibrium and is ultimately dangerous to the maintenance of peace.

Kissinger's doctoral thesis at Harvard, later published under the title *A World Restored,* dwelt on the diplomatic achievements of Count Metternich of Austria, whose grand design for Europe at the Congress of Vienna in 1815 ended centuries of virtually non-stop war in Europe and provided a stability that lasted 100 years. The key to this achievement was the finely calibrated balance of power among nations, leading to a stable equilibrium. Statesmen with an eye toward long-term stability have to meliorate the two main threats to international equilibrium: imbalances of military power, which tempt nations to aggression, and the rise of "revolutionary" states whose ideological zeal to overturn the established order causes them to disregard the realistic appreciation of equilibrium. The task of international relations, Kissinger thought, was to get revolutionary nations to accept the legitimacy of the established order, and thereby become "legitimate" nations themselves.

Communist nations in the twentieth century were explicitly revolutionary, of course, but, from Kissinger's point of view, *so was the United States* whenever it conducted foreign policy according to its democratic idealism rather than self-interested realism. In his semi-candid moments, Kissinger regarded the United States as an immature great power, perhaps not worthy of being trusted with the world's moral and political destiny. "Rather arrogantly," he once wrote, "we ascribed our security entirely to the superiority of our beliefs rather than to the weight of our power on the fortunate accidents of history and geography."[61] In Kissinger's framework, we should distinguish between "revolutionary" and "legitimate" nations; if a nation did not seek to follow its revolutionary beliefs in the international arena, it could then be accepted as a "legitimate" state. The clear implication is that the United States needed to set aside its understanding of the Cold War as an irrepressible conflict between freedom and tyranny.

By announcing at the outset of the Nixon presidency that foreign policy would now replace an era of confrontation with an era of negotiation, Nixon and Kissinger we acting on the theory that through diplomacy (especially arms control negotiations), the "revolutionary" Communist nations could be gradually transformed into "legitimate" nations with an interest in equilibrium. In one of his early press briefings in 1969, Kissinger made clear the implications of his understanding for the practice of American foreign policy: "We have always made it clear that we have no permanent enemies and that we will judge other countries, *and specifically countries like Communist China,* on the basis of their actions and not on the basis of their domestic ideology."[62] (Emphasis added.) "We moved toward China not to expiate liberal guilt over our China policy of the late 1940s but *to shape a global equilibrium.*" (Emphasis added.) Kissinger was now getting to play Metternich, but with the entire world instead of Europe as his diplomatic canvas.

Kissinger can be compared with Churchill, the firm anti-Communist whose own European-style realism was expressed in his famous remark, made after Hitler invaded the Soviet Union in 1941, that "if Hitler invaded hell, I would at least make a favorable reference to the devil in the House of Commons." But Churchill's realism never led him to abandon his basic distinction between civilization and barbarism, and understood that the object of stability, which could only be assured through the force of arms and a commitment to containment, was the eventual civilizing of the barbarous tyrannies of the Communist world (which is also the thinking at the heart of George Kennan's famous outline of the idea of containment in 1947).

Kissinger's analytical framework for international equilibrium requires him and his policy to embrace moral relativism by rejecting moral judgments of the character of regimes. Kissinger intimates this relativism as early as 1961, when he wrote that "Our best thought is required for adjusting to new conditions in a new world where the *truths of one decade became the obstacles to understanding of another.*" (Emphasis added.) Not only is this impossible for democracies to do without betraying their core principles of liberty and human rights, but it is also impossible for revolutionary regimes such as the Communist Soviet Union to do as well.

The Italian writer Luigi Barzini offered a sagacious observation about this problem in 1983: "The United States' and the Soviet Union's sense of historical mission is their principal *raison d'etre*. In fact, when they occasionally try to betray their heritage, they risk not mere loss of prestige and foreign followers, but above all internal demoralization, disintegration, and possibly dissolution."[63] This is exactly what began to happen to the United States under Kissinger's détente, and what ultimately happened fully to the Soviet Union with the advent of *glasnost* in the late 1980s.

Churchill might agree with and approve of Kissinger's diplomacy, given the change in the balance of power wrought by the Soviet arms buildup of the 1960s and 1970s. Indeed, Churchill foresaw as early as 1950 the need to establish an equilibrium—though based first and foremost on Western military strength—with the Soviet Union and its allies, and Churchill eschewed any idea of "rollback" that was popular with some conservatives in the 1950s. Kissinger's immense talents might well have complemented a rhetorical anti-Communist such as Churchill—or Ronald Reagan. (Kissinger had great respect for Churchill, but said Churchill "was not a chess player.")

Détente began under Nixon with the premise that the Soviet Union faced twin difficulties that would become acute crises in the fullness of time: Communist ideology was losing its attractiveness, including even within the Soviet Union, and the Soviet economy was faltering and would not keep up with the West. In other words, time was on our side. But with the demoralization that befell the United States in the aftermath of Vietnam and Watergate, détente could be further defended on the grounds that he deployed his diplomatic skill to mitigate the damage these adverse events were inflicting on American foreign policy.

Kissinger is correct in portraying the aftermath of Vietnam as another phase of "sulking isolationism," but such a posture was disastrous in the face of an aggressive Soviet bloc and a restive Third World. In other words, it might be said that Kissinger was playing from a bad hand, but bluffing his way along with sufficient skill that he maintained America's tenuous position until Ronald Reagan was able to come in the 1980s and rally America once again. This is the essence of Kissinger's argument in the final volume of his memoirs, *Years of Renewal.*

The trouble with this argument is the strong evidence that Kissinger was a historical pessimist who thought that the United States was in irreversible decline, such that his diplomatic task was not so much bluffing with a bad hand, but seeking the best terms he could get for his bankrupt client. Kissinger has always strenuously denied the charge, but the evidence against him is strong. In *A World Restored,* Kissinger wrote that "perhaps Metternich's policy should be measured not by its ultimate failure, but by the length of time it staved off ultimate disaster." Years before he became a national figure he laid out an historicist determinism with a definite pessimistic bent:

> The United States is at a point in its historical development where it
> has mastered much of its physical environment. . . . Any society faces
> a point in its development where it must ask itself if it has exhausted
> all the possibilities of innovation inherent in its structure. When this
> point is reached, it has passed its zenith. From then on, it must de-
> cline, rapidly or slowly, but nonetheless inevitably.[64]

Kissinger evidently still held this view during his years in high office, telling James Reston of the *New York Times* in 1974 that "As a historian you have to be conscious of the fact that every civilization that has ever existed has ultimately collapsed. History is a tale of efforts that failed, of aspirations that weren't realized, of wishes that were fulfilled and then turned out to be different from what one expected."[65] In his 1961 book he added that "only a heroic effort" can stave off decline. Did Kissinger think he and Nixon were the heroes performing this effort? Kissinger told Reston: "I think of myself as a historian more than a statesman."

Just as the controversy over détente was reaching a crescendo in 1976, Admiral Elmo Zumwalt went public with the story that Kissinger had confided his pessimism about America's prospects during a train ride the two had shared to West Point in 1970. Zumwalt's account held that:

> Dr. Kissinger feels that the U.S. has passed its historic high point like so many earlier civilizations. He believes that the U.S. is on the downhill and cannot be roused by political challenge. He states that his job is to persuade the Russians to give us the best deal we can get, recognizing that historical forces favor them. He says that he realizes that in the light of history he will be recognized as one of those who negotiated terms favorable to the Soviets, but that the American people only have themselves to blame because they lack the stamina to stay the course against the Soviets who are "Sparta to our Athens."[66]

Kissinger hotly denied Zumwalt's account, calling it a "fabrication," and that Zumwalt had misunderstood what he had said. "I am going to nominate the good admiral for the Pulitzer Prize for fiction," Kissinger told a press conference. "I do not believe the United States will be defeated. I do not believe the United States is on the decline." Zumwalt, then preparing to run for the U.S. Senate in Virginia, must be discounted as an interested party with an axe to grind against Kissinger, so his story should not be accepted at face value.

However, there is corroborating evidence in support of Zumwalt's thesis. Kissinger aides Peter Rodman and Helmut Sonnenfeldt both subsequently confirmed that Zumwalt did not invent the exchange.[67] *Partisan Review* editor William Barrett wrote that "I had that same conversation, or a very similar one, with Kissinger several times during the summer of 1952," when Barrett was a visiting scholar at Harvard. (At the time, Kissinger deeply impressed Barrett: "This young man will go far," Barrett predicted; "He will end up by becoming dean."[68]) William Safire records in his memoir of the Nixon White House that Kissinger was always trying to get Nixon to read Spengler's *Decline of the West.* (Whether he succeeded is unknown, but in his later years out of office Nixon expressed a fascination for the declinist insights of Hegel and Nietzsche.) And a few weeks before the Zumwalt episode, the West German magazine *Der Spiegel* reported that at a dinner with European journalists Kissinger had predicted that within a decade all Europe would be "Marxist-dominated."[69] The story caused a flurry of alarmed commentary in the European press, but received scant notice in the United States.

KISSINGER'S PRIVATE INTELLECTUAL pessimism might be of little account had it not been perceived as the basis of his enthusiasm for the Helsinki accords of 1975. Since the mid-1950s the Soviet Union had proposed that a "European Security Conference" be held to work out a new "collective security" agreement for Europe as well as a formal resolution of World War II issues. Their pre-conditions for holding the conference were preposterous: The United States was to be excluded from the conference, and the dissolution of NATO would be primary on the conference agenda. It was a crude attempt to divide the Western alliance—so crude that it was never taken seriously. Then in 1969 the Soviet Union dropped these conditions, which it termed a "concession," though a concession to reality should never be confused with an act of magnanimity. The formal "Conference on Security and Cooperation in Europe" finally began in July 1973.

The central strategic problem in Europe during the Cold War was the fate of divided Germany, and the nature of any prospective reunification between East and West Germany. A united, "neutral" Germany would favor Soviet interests and complicate the task of defending the rest of western Europe, and hence was unacceptable to the West. But the Soviets were not about to give up East Germany if it meant its incorporation within NATO.

The conference wasn't going to be able to resolve this issue, of course, but it could establish "principles" upon which future diplomatic maneuverings might take place. West Germany especially wanted a clause endorsing "the peaceful change of frontiers"—a code phrase not only for reunification with East Germany but also for prudent border adjustments with Poland. The Soviets would only accept the clause if the treaty also included the principle of "inviolability of frontiers"—a code phrase for recognizing existing borders. The inevitable compromise subsumed both principles beneath the right of every nation to join or leave alliances. While this clause represents a tacit repudiation of the "Brezhnev Doctrine" (which held that no Communist nation would be allowed to become non-Communist and would be prevented by force of arms from doing so, like Czechoslovakia in 1968, or Hungary in 1956). On the other hand, this clause seems a concession to the Soviets, since no Eastern bloc nation could realistically leave the Warsaw Pact without Soviet permission, while NATO countries, being democracies, could leave the alliance, as France did in the 1960s.

The deeper problem with the "inviolability of frontiers" clause is that it represented a *de facto* recognition of Soviet dominance of Eastern Europe. Kissinger saw this as no more than a concession to reality, since there was no prospect of a military liberation of Eastern bloc nations, and the tradeoff of having the Soviets agree to the principle of de-alignment outweighed the concession to military reality. But especially in the case of Lithuania, Latvia, and Estonia—three independent nations the Soviets absorbed by brute force in the 1940s—the acknowledgement of "inviolability of frontiers" ran counter to American policy, especially the annual congressional observance of "Captive Nations Week," which was specifically intended to remind of the three Baltic nations.

While the security section of the Helsinki Accords was problematic, the two other main sections (or "baskets" as they came to be called) were thought to be more favorable to the West. The second "basket" called for expanded trade between East and West, which Kissinger and others thought served the détente strategy of "engagement," that is, increased commercial ties would moderate Soviet behavior. Critics charged that the Soviets got the best of this deal, too, with favorable credit terms helping to bail out their antiquated command economy. But it was "Basket 3," concerning "free movement of peoples and ideas," that Kissinger thought represented the biggest diplomatic victory for the West. Basket 3 pledged the signatories to respect human rights within their borders, and became the basis for the various Eastern European human rights groups such as Czechoslovakia's Charter 77 that became a locus of liberalizing activism in the 1980s. Again, the conservative critics pointed out, a pledge to observe human rights means little in regimes without a free press or a judicial process to secure human rights. The Helsinki Accords prompted Ronald Reagan's first public criticism of Ford: "I am against it, and I think all Americans should be against it."

The final oddity of the Helsinki Accords (so named because Ford, Brezhnev, and other chiefs of state signed it at a summit in Helsinki in August 1975) is that it was not a formal treaty with legally binding enforcement mechanisms, so its significance was mostly symbolic and psychological. And although Kissinger makes a strong case that the Helsinki Accords worked to the advantage the West in the fullness of time, the symbolism and psychology of the moment signaled American weakness and Western accommodation. For just as President Ford was readying to sign the Helsinki Accords, he embarrassed himself and reinforced the suspicions of the critics of détente by refusing to meet with Aleksandr Solzhenitsyn.

Solzhenitsyn's significance cannot be understated. His *Gulag Archipelago* was a turning point in the intellectual life of the Cold War—a mortal wound to the socialist faith. It is worth recalling the testament of the French intellectual Bernard-Henri Levy, whose break with the French Left (Levy had been a leader of the French Socialist Party) came about because of his reading Solzhenitsyn:

> I have learned more from reading *The Gulag Archipelago* than from many erudite commentaries on totalitarian languages. I owe more to Solzhenitsyn than to most of the sociologists, historians, and philosophers who have been contemplating the fate of the West for the last thirty years. It is enigmatic that the publication of this work was enough to immediately shake our mental landscape and overturn our ideological guideposts. . . . All Solzhenitsyn had to do was *to speak* and we awoke from a dogmatic sleep. . . .
>
> That the Gulag is not a blunder or an accident, not a simple wound or aftereffect of Stalinism; but the necessary corollary of a socialism which can only actualize homogeneity by driving the forces of heterogeniety back to its fringes, which can aim for the universal only by confining its rebels, its irreducible individualists, in the outer darkness of a nonsociety. No camps without Marxism, said [Andre] Glucksmann. We have to add: No socialism without camps, *no classless society without its terror truth.*[70] (Emphasis in original.)

Yet Solzhenitsyn's exile from the Soviet Union was more than just a literary-intellectual event. Before his exile liberals in the West embraced

Solzhenitsyn, hoping that his limited success in publishing in the Soviet Union was a sign that the long hoped-for liberalization of the Soviet Union was possible. Solzhenitsyn dashed these hopes with his categorical denunciation of Marxism ("There can be no moral form of socialism," he said in his Nobel Prize acceptance speech) combined with an extreme anti-liberalism that quickly alienated him from his liberal champions in the West. Worse, he was also a fierce critic of détente. His greatest champion in the West turned out to be the AFL-CIO, which, under the leadership of George Meany, remained staunchly anti-Communist even as other liberal organizations had turned away from anti-Communism. Solzhenitsyn made front page news with a stinging speech to the AFL-CIO in June 1975, which Meany had scheduled deliberately before Ford left for Finland to sign the Helsinki Accords. Neither Ford nor Kissinger would attend the dinner, though the anti-détente Secretary of Defense James Schlesinger and U.N. Ambassador Pat Moynihan did. Solzhenitsyn minced no words: "The Communist ideology is to destroy your society." He implored the United States to stop selling food and technology to the Soviet Union—a cornerstone of détente—and to stop signing treaties. Above all, he assailed the spiritual and moral weakness of the West:

> The principal argument of the advocates of détente is well-known: all of this must be done to avoid a nuclear war. But after all that has happened in recent years, I think that I can set their minds at ease, and your minds at ease as well: there will not be any nuclear war. What for? Why should there be a nuclear war if for the last 30 years they have been breaking off as much of the West as they wanted—piece after piece, country after country, and the process keeps going on.[71]

After Solzhenitsyn first arrived in the United States, President Ford had "informally indicated" (in the words of Solzhenitsyn biographer Michael Scammell) that he would be interested in meeting Solzhenitsyn if he ever came to Washington. But after Solzhenitsyn began his public attacks on détente, it became impossible to Ford to meet with him without seeming to endorse his critique. The White House initially said "scheduling problems" prevented a visit, an unpersuasive excuse that was amended to an even less persuasive excuse. Solzhenitsyn, the White House said, was in the United States "to promote his books," and the president did not wish to lend himself to "commercial purposes." The week before, however, Ford had posed for photographs on the White House lawn with "the cotton queen" and soccer star Pele. Some White House aides muttered about Solzhenitsyn's mental stability, while Ford privately called Solzhenitsyn "a goddamned horse's ass."

Finally the White House came clean, admitting that Ford decided against meeting with Solzhenitsyn "on the advice of the National Security Council," which meant Kissinger. Kissinger issued a statement saying that "From the point of view of foreign policy the symbolic effect of that [meeting with Solzhenitsyn] can be disadvantageous." Kissinger had lobbied the Soviets to allow Solzhenitsyn to go into exile, and promised Soviet Ambassador Anatoly Dobrynin that the United States would not exploit Solzhenitsyn for political purposes. From his point of view, he was only living up to his end of an honest bargain. Solzhenitsyn returned the snub, attacking Ford for signing the Helsinki Accords, which he said represented "the betrayal of Eastern Europe, [and] acknowledging officially its slavery forever."

Ford's snubbing of Solzhenitsyn ignited a firestorm of criticism. "Not even Watergate," George Will wrote, "was as *fundamentally* degrading to the presidency as this act of deference to the master of the Gulag Archipelago."[72] William F. Buckley Jr. poured forth contempt for Ford: "For a horrible moment one was tempted to wonder whether Mr. Ford knew who Aleksandr Solzhenitsyn was." Even the *New York Times* took editorial notice of Ford's "appeasement." And if the mishandling of the Solzhenitsyn affair were not enough, a few months later an even larger blunder occurred—the so-called "Sonnenfeldt Doctrine," which more than any other single factor cost Gerald Ford the election of 1976.

THE "SONNENFELDT DOCTRINE" arose out of a seemingly routine episode in London in December 1975. Kissinger had given an overview of American foreign policy on Europe and East-West relations at a meeting of American ambassadors. Kissinger's long-time deputy, Hal Sonnenfeldt, whose current job was counselor to the State Department, delivered follow-up remarks the next day to fill in some "gaps" in Kissinger's remarks. Then a few weeks later Sonnenfeldt asked an aide to prepare a summary transcript of his presentation. Therein lay the makings of disaster.

According to the summary transcript, Sonnenfeldt told the assembled ambassadors:

With respect to Eastern Europe, it must be in our long-term interest to influence events in this area—because of the present unnatural relations with the Soviet Union—so that they will not sooner or later explode into World War III. This inorganic, unnatural relationship is a far greater danger to world peace than the conflict between East and West. *So it must be our policy to strive for an evolution that makes the relationship between the Eastern Europeans and the Soviet Union an organic one.* (Emphasis added.)

The tempest over the "Sonnenfeldt Doctrine" surpassed the Solzhenitsyn affair. Rowland Evans and Robert Novak wrote that the Sonnenfeldt Doctrine "put the U.S. on record for the stabilization of the Soviet empire," while C. L. Sulzberger, editor of the *New York Times,* wrote that "The idea sent shivers up my spine." Reagan was the most blunt, saying that Kissinger and Sonnenfeldt were saying that "slaves should accept their fate."

Whatever could Sonnenfeldt have had in mind with the phrase, an "organic" relationship? Kissinger and Sonnenfeldt argued that by "organic" they merely meant "normal," that is, a relationship not defined by force of arms and occupation. It was not clear whether Sonnenfeldt had even used the term "organic" in his oral remarks that started the controversy. It had been quiet U.S. policy under Nixon to shower attention and rewards upon any Eastern Bloc nation that showed any small steps of independence from Moscow. In other words, if the Soviet Union insisted on maintaining the charade that Eastern European nations were free and independent, than the United States would play along with this fiction and treat them that way. If Soviet military domination could be slowly ended, Eastern European nations would gradually carve out a wider sphere of freedom for themselves, not unlike Finland, Kissinger explained. The goal of American policy, in other words, was exactly the opposite of what the critics claimed the Sonnenfeldt Doctrine implied.

But this explanation did not sit well with how Kissinger and Sonnenfeldt explained it to the ambassadorial corps. Another passage from Sonnenfeldt's presentation was arguably worse than the "organic" passage:

The Soviets' inability to acquire loyalty in Eastern Europe is an unfortunate failure, because Eastern Europe is within their scope and area of natural interest. It is doubly tragic that in this area of vital interest and crucial importance it has not been possible for the Soviet Union to establish roots of interest that go beyond sheer power.

Kissinger tried to dismiss the episode as simply overheated ideological partisanship. "If there were truly a new doctrine of this administration," Kissinger said with his familiar mix of hauteur and ego, "it would not be named after Hal Sonnenfeldt."

Yet even if Kissinger is correct that the popular perception of the "Sonnenfeldt Doctrine" grossly misconstrued the subtle design of U.S. policy, it nonetheless laid bare the core defect of Kissinger-style détente. The entire premise of democracy is that, as the Declaration of Independence puts it, "government derives its just powers from the consent of the governed." Therefore, any polity that does not derive its powers from the consent of the governed is *ipso facto* illegitimate. A practical distinction must obviously be made with any armed nation, making it "legitimate," because it is *necessary,* to engage in negotiations. But it is different thing to accept a regime as politically legitimate simply because it is well-armed. The Sonnenfeldt Doctrine's "organic" understanding of international relations blurs all questions about moral distinctions beneath the fog of a value-free, social scientific approach to understanding different regimes, which is why it became gradually accepted in the Western media and academia to refer to tyrannical dictators and elected prime ministers alike as "leaders."

Remember the Sonnenfeldt Doctrine; it shall make a return appearance in chapter 11.

Kissinger bitterly resented the attacks of his critics, especially from "neo-conservative" intellectuals who had switched from Left to Right. These critics, Kissinger complained, wanted "a return to a militant, muscular Wilsonianism." While admitting later that his rhetorical performance was not what it might have been, Kissinger argues that "the United States, just emerging from Vietnam, in the midst of Watergate and later with a non-elected President, was not in a position to conduct a crusade; in fact, to attempt to do so would have torn the country apart even further. . . . In the early 1970s, the option of what later became the Reagan policy did not exist."[73] Kissinger grudgingly admits in his memoirs that "Reagan proved to have a better instinct for America's emotions by justifying his course in the name of American idealism." Kissinger's judgment that domestic opinion was so thoroughly desiccated and inflamed in the mid-1970s is well-founded (even *National Review* admitted in 1976 that "Kissinger's pessimistic view of history may, in fact, be valid"[74]). Yet was it really beyond the capacity of Kissinger and Ford to reinvigorate the nation with some old time religion? Never mind Reagan's challenge: An example right under Kissinger's nose suggests that the real problem was Kissinger's inherent pessimism, which blinded him to the necessity of America's categorical imperative.

IN FEBRUARY 1974 Pat Moynihan, then serving as U.S. Ambassador to India, gave a lecture in Washington that evinced exactly the opposite outlook from Kissinger. In what might be interpreted as a veiled slap at Kissinger (whose style, Moynihan wrote elsewhere, "was that of the Politburo"), Moynihan asked: "[A]re we not adopting much the same course [of diminished enthusiasm for Wilsonian principles] at the silent behest of men who know too much to believe anything in particular and opt instead for accommodations of reasonableness and urbanity that drain our world position of moral purpose?" Wilsonian idealism was indispensable to America, Moynihan argued:

> There will be no struggle for personal liberty (or national independence or national survival) anywhere in Europe, in Asia, in Africa, in Latin America which will not affect American politics. In that circumstance, I would argue that there is only one course likely to make the internal strains of consequent conflict endurable, and that is for the United States deliberately and consistently to bring its influence to bear on behalf of those regimes which promise the largest degree of personal and national liberty. . . . We stand for liberty, for the expansion of liberty. Anything less risks the contraction of liberty: our own included.[75]

Moynihan fundamentally agreed with the critics of détente, arguing later that détente "*was* a form of disguised retreat, carried forward in a rapture of exalted dissimulation by persons whose assumption was that the American people would not face reality." This was deeply wrong, Moynihan thought. "The electorate was quite capable of confronting the dangers of the time, so long as this was accompanied by some assertions of our strengths."[76] The place to do this, Moynihan argued, was the

United Nations and other international forums, where Communist and anti-American "non-aligned" nations were having a field day assailing the West.

"It is time," Moynihan wrote in a widely noted article, "that the American spokesman came to be feared in international forums for the truths he might tell," such as the fact that most of the Third World regimes that tub-thumped for various human rights resolutions at the U.N. didn't show the slightest respect for human rights at home. So weak was American prestige at the U.N. at that time that the United States couldn't even get South Korea's application for membership in the U.N. General Assembly considered. A *New York Times* headline captured the mood: "MOYNIHAN CALLS ON U.S. TO START 'RAISING HELL' IN U.N." Ford and Kissinger agreed, and Moynihan was appointed U.S. Ambassador to the U.N. in April 1975, the very month Vietnam and Cambodia fell.

Hypocrisy is perhaps the last moral failing in the modern world that has not (yet) been transmuted into an alternative lifestyle, and Moynihan relished shining the spotlight on Third World hypocrisy at the U.N. Observing that the median length of time since the government of average U.N. member nation had been overthrown was just 11 years, Moynihan declared that "We are not here to hear totalitarian dictators lecture us on how to run a democracy." More: Perhaps U.S. aid to Third World nations that voted against us at the U.N. should be cut. "Let the Tanzanians get their aid from the same capitals from which they got their politics," Moynihan said. When a U.S. mission officer passed along to Moynihan a query from a delegate from a Third World nation asking, "Are you threatening us?" Moynihan replied: "Tell him yes." Moynihan's tenure coincided with the nadir of the U.N., the infamous resolution equating Zionism with racism. If the Third World couldn't get directly at the United States (though not for lack of trying, such as a resolution condemning U.S. colonialism and repression in Puerto Rico), and couldn't expel Israel outright, a resolution that amounted to a *de facto* equation of Zionism and Nazism would do nicely as a humiliation for the West. It passed by a wide margin, after which followed "a long mocking applause" by the Third World nations that had engineered the vote. Moynihan walked over to the Israeli U.N. Ambassador and said, "Fuck 'em."

As Moynihan had foreseen, America loved his confrontational attitude. Mail to the American mission at the U.N. ran higher than at any time since the Cuban Missile Crisis. Nearly 30,000 letters came to the U.N. during Moynihan's tenure of less than a year; only 200 were critical. This proved to Moynihan that while "elites were exhausted, the country was not." The U.N. ambassador from Mauritius confessed that most other delegates "lived in positive dread of his [Moynihan's] manners, his language, and his abuse." Most important for the politics of the moment, Ronald Reagan, not yet a declared presidential candidate, began quoting Moynihan's U.N. speeches. (*National Review* even suggested that the Democratic Party ought to nominate Moynihan for president.) The mere mention of Moynihan's name and deeds generated prolonged applause at Reagan's public appearances.

But if the people loved Moynihan's performance, there was a formidable segment of elite opinion, including within the State Department and the Ford White House, that did not. A more diplomatic ambassador, the critics charged, might have succeeded in tabling the Zionism-equals-racism resolution and spared the United States and Israel the humiliation of their lopsided defeat. Ford and Kissinger publicly and repeatedly affirmed their support for Moynihan, though, as James Reston noted in the *New York Times,* "they couldn't be too hard on Mr. Moynihan, without giving Ronald Reagan of California a compelling argument in the coming Presidential election." If Moynihan was going to be eased out, it would have to come by a route even more indirect than is typical for Washington.

The public repudiation of Moynihan, therefore, came from the most unexpected source: Britain's U.N. Ambassador Ivor Richard. In a speech to a mostly American audience at the United Nations Association in New York, Richard took clear aim at Moynihan without naming him directly: "I don't see [the U.N.] as a confrontational arena in which to 'take on' those countries whose political systems and ideology are different from mine. I spend a lot of time preventing rows at the U.N.—not looking for them. Whatever else the place is, it is not the OK Corral and I am hardly Wyatt Earp. There is nothing whatsoever to be gained by ideological disputations of the most intense sort which one is probably going to lose anyway."

Richard later confirmed to Moynihan that his speech reflected official British policy and sentiment. Moynihan immediately suspected that Kissinger was behind the attack, which Kissinger naturally denied. But neither did Kissinger nor anyone else in the White House criticize

Richard's speech, an omission that spoke volumes. (Kissinger's voluminous memoirs contain scant mention of Moynihan—an omission suggestive of Kissinger's jealousy of Moynihan's popularity and clarity.) Following yet another publicized breach with Kissinger in January, Moynihan resigned, and geared up for a successful run for the U.S. Senate from New York, which had probably been his object all along.

The significance of Moynihan's departure is that he was the last prominent critic of détente within the Ford administration, as Ford had cashiered Defense Secretary James Schlesinger in November 1975. Ford first denied there were significant differences between Schlesinger and Kissinger, and, when this explanation failed the laugh test, admitted that the two didn't get along. The firing of Schlesinger and Moynihan's departure meant that Ford was throwing in his lot with the party of détente. Ford perhaps thought he could placate conservatives by dumping Rockefeller a few weeks earlier—which Ford later called the most cowardly act of his political career—but it was to no avail. Even Reagan publicly commented that Ford had treated Rockefeller shabbily. But détente was in ruins by this time; Ford himself decided not to conclude the SALT II treaty with the Soviet Union because he feared that it would fall victim to election-year politics. Yet there existed no one in the Ford administration with the imagination or energy to chart another course. As Moynihan summarized the problem, "Those seeking accommodation with rising Soviet power simply would not believe that in the end the Russians could be deterred by the threat to them of American argument and exposition."[77]

THERE WAS ONE other person who believed this, of course. How very opposite is Kissinger's entire mien from Ronald Reagan's constant refrain that "America's best days are ahead of her." This discontent over détente and the disillusion in the aftermath of Watergate came right on the eve of America's bicentennial in 1976, which had the effect of magnifying the troubles of the moment. With its affinity for historical reflection, the bicentennial year became the occasion for the open expression of pessimism about America's future for thinkers on all parts of the political spectrum. "In 1776 the United States was so to speak nothing; but it promised to become everything," the conservative scholar Harry Jaffa wrote in a typical reflection of the time. "In 1976, the United States, having in a sense become everything, promises to become nothing."[78] For the socialist

Daniel Bell, the "American Century" was over: "Today, the belief in American exceptionalism has vanished with the end of empire, the weakening of power, the loss of faith in the nation's future. There are clear signs that America is being displaced as the paramount country."[79] Bell added the question that was on the minds of many observers: "Can we escape the fate of internal discord and disintegration that have marked every other society in human history?"

The ruin of détente and America's concomitant loss of confidence in our bicentennial year thus became the most compelling rationales for Reagan's presidential campaign in 1976. But it didn't start out that way. Instead, Reagan began his campaign for the White House by repeating one of his biggest mistakes. It was a mistake that, in hindsight, might be said to have made him president.

CHAPTER TEN

THE DRESS REHEARSAL:
REAGAN'S CHALLENGE

———⟶⟶◆⟵⟵———

WILL HE or won't he?
That was the question on the minds of political watchers during the first half of 1975. There seemed little doubt that Ronald Reagan was preparing to mount a challenge to President Ford in 1976. Throughout 1975 Reagan barnstormed the country, "Paul Revering" the nation, as Reagan liked to put it. His speeches, press statements, broadcasts, and other political appearances generated over 100 print media stories a week. Such was the demand for Reagan that he enjoyed the luxury of being able to charge for his speaking appearances (which frequently doubled as fundraisers for some local Republican organization), making him perhaps the first candidate in history to collect a paycheck for his *de facto* campaign activities. "The Reagan non-campaign," *Newsweek* wrote in the spring, "still carries about it more nearly the aura of a Billy Graham crusade than of a classic political canvass."

Yet Reagan's candidacy was not the sure thing the subsequent story line would make it seem. According to several narratives, Reagan was genuinely reluctant to run. "Reagan really was reluctant," one insider told reporter Jules Witcover. "He didn't have that burning, that gut desire to be president that Jimmy Carter and Richard Nixon have. . . . He wasn't dying to do it."[1] (Which traits, it might be said, highly recommended him for the job.) He worried first and foremost that he might fail.

His prospective candidacy faced long odds. No incumbent president since Chester Arthur in 1884 had been denied his party's nomination.

Reagan trailed Ford by a wide margin in head-to-head matchups in opinion polls. Some of Reagan's most prominent backers during his years as governor, such as Henry Salvatori, were sticking with Ford. More significant was that Barry Goldwater, whose cause Reagan purported to inherit, was backing Ford. A failed candidacy would put him at risk of becoming the new Harold Stassen. "I'm not going to make a fool of myself," he told an adviser. Reagan's pollster Richard Wirthlin had said that Reagan wouldn't run unless national polls were encouraging: "The governor is not interested in running just as a spoiler. And he will not run just to exert pressure in pulling Ford toward the conservative side. If he's going to run, he wants to feel he has a shot at winning the whole thing." He took seriously the prospect of dividing the Republican Party, as well as his familiar injunction of "Parkinson's Law,"—"thou shalt not speak ill of another Republican." But the larger imponderable was whether he should run as a Republican at all.

In the aftermath of Watergate the Republican Party was at low ebb. After the drubbing of the 1974 election, pollsters found that the proportion of voters who identified themselves as Republicans had fallen to an all-time low of 18 percent. "The first thing that comes to people's minds about the Republican Party," pollster Robert Teeter told the stunned leadership of the Republican National Committee, "is that it's the party of big business and that it's rich, organized and wealthy." A majority of voters regarded Republicans as "untrustworthy" and "incompetent." When Teeter asked what voters found good about the Republican Party, two-thirds couldn't think of anything. The halls of the Republican National Committee, George Will wrote, "resemble the set for a disaster flick, a political *Poseidon Adventure.*" Was the Republican nomination even worth having?

Reagan's quandary was compounded by the fact that his ideological convictions ran against the grain of both political parties at that moment. His dislike of détente set him at odds with the current inheritance of the Republican Party, while his opposition to deficit spending and bureaucratic regulation set him against the Democratic Party. Maybe, it was suggested, since Reagan was set against the course of both parties, he should head a new third party. *National Review* publisher William A. Rusher was the leading voice urging this course upon Reagan, reasoning that a majority could be forged between the Goldwater and Reagan wing of the Republican Party and the George Wallace wing of the Democrats. Kevin Phillips, author of the 1968 book *The Emerging Republican Majority,* suggested that conservatives should forget the Republican Party and back an independent Reagan-Wallace ticket in 1976. William F. Buckley Jr. agreed. "Who cares, really, about the Republican Party? Its soul is the property of the Ripon Society, and a few of the older members of the Council on Foreign Relations." Calling the current Republican Party "an administrative convenience for a few politicians," Buckley speculated that "If Reagan ran for President on an independent ticket, he would get a higher percentage of the vote than the Republican Party would get if it were led by any other American."

Reagan appears to have considered the idea briefly. Caught off guard by a reporter's question in the fall of 1974, Reagan said of the third party idea: "There could be one of those moments in time, I don't know. I see statements of disaffection of people in both parties." But by election day of 1974 Reagan had closed the door: "I am not starting a third party. I do not believe the Republican Party is dead. I believe the Republican Party represents basically the thinking of the people across the country, if we can get that message across to the people. I believe that a third party movement has the effect of dividing the people who share the same philosophy and usually winds up, because of that division, electing those they set out to oppose." Reagan, Lou Cannon noted, would rather win an election than charge a windmill, and his political advisers (and major donors) convinced him that his chances were best in the GOP.[2] The following February Reagan gilded the point in a speech to the annual banquet of the Conservative Political Action Convention in Washington: "Is it a third party we need, or is it a new and revitalized second party, raising a banner of no pale pastels, but bold colors which makes it unmistakably clear where we stand on all of the issues troubling the people? Americans are hungry to feel once again a sense of mission and greatness." *No pale pastels* came to be Reagan's signature theme on the stump over the coming year.

Reporters asked Reagan at nearly every speaking appearance—which meant two or three times a week—whether he was going to run, and he routinely deflected the questions, saying he was not a candidate. Because

Reagan's public relations and media machine doubled as a campaign-in-waiting, he had the luxury of putting off a formal announcement longer than ordinary candidates could. Even as Reagan demurred, a formal campaign slowly began to take shape. Reagan finally established an "exploratory committee," the precursor to a formal campaign, in July. Senator Paul Laxalt of Nevada agreed to serve as the chairman of the campaign. Laxalt was quietly telling conservative groups and campaign donors that Reagan would make an announcement by October.

Conservative activists were restless and impatient, however. A Reagan supporter told *Newsweek* in the spring: "We're disgusted with him for not making the commitment. He's our man, but he just won't come in." The Young Republicans said that if nothing happens by Labor Day, they would have to reassess their position. The weekly conservative tabloid *Human Events* ran the headline, "Reagan: Time to Fish or Cut Bait." The first semi-official word came in a direct mail fundraising letter from Citizens for Reagan in early September of 1975: "The Reagan for President campaign is under way!"

Ford was now feeling the heat from both wings of the party. In early September liberal Republican Senators Charles Percy of Illinois, Clifford Case of New Jersey, and Jacob Javits of New York went to the White House to urge Ford to moderate his conservative positions and not give in to the pressure from Reagan. But two days later, on a West Coast political trip that included stops in Reagan's home turf in California, Ford sounded like an echo of Reagan: "We believe that the American people have grown weary of government's overblown promises and overbearing controls." Ford sought to blur the differences between himself and Reagan, telling Walter Cronkite in an interview that "I don't believe there's any serious differences between Governor Reagan and myself." Ford surged in the GOP polls, even in California. By October, the month before Reagan announced, the Gallup poll had Ford opening a 23-point lead over Reagan among Republicans. Reagan even trailed Ford by 9 points in his home state of California in an August poll.

In the end the decisive factors that led to the judgment that Reagan had a realistic chance of winning were Ford's political weakness and Reagan's perception of Ford as a weak leader. Reagan thought Ford was too accommodating to Congress (even though Ford was racking up a record number of vetoes), chiefly because Ford had been in Congress too long. Reagan was also encouraged by mid-year poll found that only 49 percent of Republicans said they wanted Ford to run again, which helped offset the polls showing Reagan trailing Ford among Republicans. But the polls were increasingly volatile. On the eve of Reagan's announcement, he was back ahead of Ford in one poll by a 1 percent margin.

Reagan formally announced his challenge to Ford on November 19, 1975, at a press conference in Washington, followed by a whirlwind of campaign stops the same day in Miami and New Hampshire, the site of the first two primaries Reagan planned to contest. (Ford had already announced his candidacy in July, the same week that Reagan established his "exploratory committee.") In his announcement speech at the National Press Club in Washington, Reagan attacked government for its destructive dominance of the economy: "Government at all levels now absorbs more than 44 percent of our personal income. It has become more intrusive, more coercive, more meddlesome and less effective." Reagan also decried America's military weakness, but then zeroed in on the heart of the problem: "In my opinion, the root of these problems lies right here—in Washington, D.C. Our nation's capital has become the seat of a 'buddy' system that functions for its own benefit—increasingly insensitive to the needs of the American worker who supports it with his taxes." (This rhetoric was nearly interchangeable with what Jimmy Carter was saying on the stump, as we shall see.) Reagan then crisply answered press questions for about 20 minutes.

Reagan then headed for Miami, though his departure was delayed at the airport because President Ford was giving an outdoor speech at a location on the Mall that required temporarily closing a runway at National Airport so that jet noise would not disturb the speech. In Miami a mentally disturbed man pointed a toy gun at Reagan. The Secret Service instantly intervened, but the scene dominated the headlines and press coverage of Reagan's Florida appearance. This was an unfortunate distraction, because Reagan's announcement speech in Florida (and the next day in New Hampshire) differed significantly from his Washington remarks. He began these speeches by quoting the Bible: "If the trumpet gives an uncertain sound, who shall prepare himself to the battle?" More interesting, however, was a long passage that took direct aim at the legacy of the New Deal:

Back in the Depression years there were those who promised to overcome hard times. Franklin Delano Roosevelt embarked on a course that made bold use of government to ease the pain of those times. Although some of his measures seemed to work, he was soon moved to sound a warning. He said, '. . . we have built new instruments of public power in the hands of the people's government . . . but in the hands of political puppets of an economic autocracy, such power would provide shackles for the liberties of our people.'

Unfortunately that warning went unheeded. Today, there is an economic autocracy, born of government's growing interference in our lives. Yet Washington, for all its power, seems powerless to solve problems any more.

It is worth pausing here to take note of Reagan's heterodox views of Franklin Roosevelt and the New Deal. Reagan is often represented attempting to repeal the New Deal and the legacy of FDR. Reagan delighted in annoying New Deal fans with reminders that he cast his first vote for president for FDR in 1932, but he really infuriated liberals with his assertion that it was he, rather than modern liberals, who was the legitimate heir to Roosevelt's legacy. To be sure, there is a studied ambivalence and ambiguity to Reagan's relationship to the New Deal, which was most clearly expressed with his oft-recalled remark that fascism was the basis for much of the New Deal. The ambiguity is also seen in his announcement speech above. The remark that "some of his measures *seemed* to work" (emphasis added) suggests agreement with the conservative criticism that most New Deal measures were ineffective or even counterproductive.

Yet Reagan has a stronger case for his affinity with FDR than is usually acknowledged, which points to an originality of Reagan's thinking for which he seldom gets credit. Reagan pointed to aspects of FDR's thought that liberal and conservative partisans conveniently overlook precisely because of their partisanship. Roosevelt said in 1935 words about welfare that found their close echo in Reagan in the 1970s and 1980s: "The lessons of history, confirmed by the evidence immediately before me, show conclusively that continued dependence upon relief induces a spiritual and moral disintegration fundamentally destructive to the national fiber. To dole out relief in this way is to administer a narcotic, a subtle destroyer of the human spirit. . . . It is in violation of the traditions of America."

In his stump speech throughout 1975 and 1976, Reagan attacked the permanent government in the following manner: "Who determines policy in this country? The truth is it is not those we elect, but those who are frozen into permanency in Civil Service jobs. Policy comes from these bureaus and agencies. Congress has before it 30,000 proposals for new laws and agencies and if most of them got lost on the way to the printer, we would be better off." Few noticed how closely this followed a remark of FDR's on the importance of not establishing a permanent bureaucracy: "We need trained personnel in government. We need disinterested, as well as broad-gauged, public officials. This part of our problem we have not yet solved, but it can be solved and it can be accomplished without the creation of a national bureaucracy which would dominate the national life of our governmental system." And it is nearly forgotten than FDR drew back from the full implications of his attacks on "economic royalism." "Let me emphasize," FDR said in 1944, "that serious as have been the errors of unrestrained individualism, I do not believe in abandoning the system of individual enterprise."

It is for continuities such as these that presidential scholar Richard Neustadt could write that Reagan was "a New Deal Republican." And, as hard as it might be for Democratic partisans to swallow, FDR would have understood it as well. But this perspective requires the benefit of hindsight. Neither in 1976 nor in 1980 was it possible even for Reagan's sympathizers to recognize this dimension to his challenge. At the moment the direct criticism of the New Deal reinforced the impression of Reagan as a turn-back-the-clock conservative or reactionary.

THE MAJOR MEDIA unsurprisingly greeted Reagan's announcement with a great harrumph. *New York Times* columnist James Reston thought Reagan's candidacy was "patently ridiculous." "The astonishing thing," Reston added, "is that this amusing but frivolous Reagan fantasy is taken so seriously by the news media and particularly by the President. It makes a lot of news, but it makes no sense."[3] *The New Republic*'s John Osborne wrote, "Ronald Reagan to me is still the posturing, essentially mindless and totally unconvincing candy man that he's been in my opinion ever since I watched his first try for the Republican nomination evaporate in Miami in 1968."[4] Elsewhere in *The New Republic*, Richard Strout offered the familiar judgment that "Reagan is Goldwater revisited. . . . He is a divisive factor in his party." Ditto *Harper's* magazine: "That he should be regarded as a serious candidate for President is a shame and an embarrassment for the country at large to swallow."[5]

The *Chicago Daily News* editorialized: "The trouble with Reagan, of course, is that his positions on the major issues are cunningly phrased nonsense—irrationally conceived and hair-raising in their potential mischief. . . . Here comes Barry Goldwater again, only more so, and at this stage another such debacle could sink the GOP so deep it might never recover."[6] *Time* magazine said much the same thing: "Republicans now must decide whether he represents a conservative wave of the future or is just another Barry Goldwater calling on the party to mount a hopeless crusade against the twentieth century." *Newsweek* was less condescending, but no less dismissive, describing Reagan as "a man whose mind and nerve and mediagenic style have never been tested in Presidential politics and may not be adequate to the trial."

Many moderate and liberal Republicans joined the media alarm. The Ripon Society huffed that "The nomination of Ronald Reagan would McGovernize the Republican Party." Vice President Nelson Rockefeller dismissed Reagan as "a minority of a minority," and charged that Reagan "has been taking some extreme positions." Senator Jacob Javits devoted an entire speech to an attack on Reagan. Reagan's positions were "so extreme that they would alter our country's very economic and social structure and our place in the world to such a degree as to make our country's policy at home and abroad, as we know it, a thing of the past." Senator Charles Percy issued a statement calling Reagan's candidacy "foolhardy," and predicting Reagan's nomination would lead to "crushing defeat" for GOP: " It could signal the beginning of the end of our party as an effective force in American political life. I only hope that the Reagan candidacy will not tempt President Ford to match the Reagan rhetoric, or—worse yet—to act on it." Reagan reacted to Percy's fit with his usual aplomb: "Sometimes I believe moderation should be taken in moderation."

Yet even some conservatives had doubts. Columnist James Jackson Kilpatrick wrote in *National Review* that "Reagan's image remains inchoate. . . . At the outset of his campaign, his image is largely that of the role-playing actor—pleasant on stage, but ill-equipped for the real world beyond the footlights. Reagan does not yet project the *presidential* image. He is not seen as a serious man."[7] And William Loeb, editor of New

Hampshire's conservative *Manchester Union-Leader* newspaper whose endorsement was highly valuable in the first primary state, wrote that Reagan "lacks the charisma and conviction needed to win." If domestic observers were dubious about Reagan, overseas the reaction was more serious. Former Defense Secretary James Schlesinger returned from a visit to China to report privately to Reagan's camp that the People's Republic "hankered" for a Reagan victory, believing that he would be more resolute about the Soviet Union than Ford.[8] The Soviet Union may have agreed with this assessment. *Pravda* attacked Reagan in terms not much different from American media commentators, saying he was "a dinosaur from the 'cold war' . . . reminiscent of Dulles. . . . It is strange that there are still fish in the sea that are tempted by this putrid bait."[9]

THE BEGINNING OF Reagan's formal campaign was soon overshadowed by a delayed-fuse charge that he had set two months before. In a September speech to the Executive Club of Chicago, Reagan had unveiled a sweeping reform program that called for devolving numerous programs from the federal government to the states. The speech was called "Let The People Rule." It was a wide-ranging speech with serious theoretical content about the nature of modern American government. Its most significant passage is never recalled:

> The states and local communities have been demeaned into little more than administrative districts, bureaucratic subdivisions of Big Brother government in Washington, with programs, spending priorities, and tax policies badly warped or dictated by federal overseers. . . . Even so liberal an observer as Richard Goodwin could identify what he correctly called the most troubling political fact of our age: that the growth in central power has been accompanied by a swift and continual diminution in the significance of the individual citizen, transforming him from a wielder into an object of authority.

This could have been adapted straight from Alexis de Tocqueville's *Democracy in America*. Had Reagan continued on this level of generality, the speech would have been quickly forgotten. Instead, Reagan proposed a serious specific course of action which, in the judgment of Lou Cannon, "prevented Reagan from winning the Republican presidential nomination of 1976."[10]

Mere reform or "streamlining" at the federal level wouldn't work, Reagan knew. "What I propose," Reagan said in the part of the speech that was widely repeated, "is nothing less than a systematic transfer of authority and resources to the states—a program of creative federalism for America's third century." What arrested attention was the specificity of Reagan's proposal. It is usually a mistake to be too specific in national campaigns because, as George Will noted at the time, "Political campaigns are not seminars: the truth gets its hair mussed." Rather that staking out a general theme which would allow for the usual political wiggle room, Reagan offered a precise bottom line: "The sums involved and the potential savings to the taxpayer are large. The transfer of authority in whole or in part in all of these areas would reduce the outlay of the federal government by more than $90 billion."

The speech attracted scant attention in the news media or elsewhere, with one exception—the Ford campaign. In a supreme irony, Ford had selected Stuart Spencer, the man who had managed Reagan's first campaign for governor 10 years before, to run his presidential campaign. Spencer had fallen out with Reagan's inner circle since the 1966 race, and readily signed up with Ford partly as a way of settling old scores. Spencer immediately saw the possibilities for using Reagan's $90-billion budget cut against him. Reagan's plan had the same political Achilles' Heel as his Proposition 1 in 1973: If the federal government was going to turn over programs to the states to run, then the states would have to pay for them. And that would mean increases in state and local taxes. For a low-tax state like New Hampshire, site of the first primary, even the potential for tax increases was anathema. The Ford campaign pounced, blanketing New Hampshire with the word that Reagan's plan would require a state income tax or sales tax. (New Hampshire at that time had neither tax.) Ford's campaign manager Bo Callaway said Reagan "wants to see elderly people thrown out in the snow."

Reagan was immediately on the defensive when he most needed to be on offense. Never mind that Reagan had called for "a systematic transfer of authority and resources" to the states, or that the plan exempted Social Security, Medicare, and other old-age programs. That part of Reagan's idea was lost in the media criticism and Ford campaign attacks that followed. By the time of Reagan's formal announcement of his candidacy in mid-November, his $90-billion budget cut idea was big news. Tom Wicker of the *New York Times* wrote that "the ill-conceived Reagan plan . . . would be as damaging to him as George McGovern's inexplicable $1,000 'Demogrant' scheme was to him in 1972." Evans and Novak wrote that the plan "threatens to be an albatross around his neck." *Time* magazine said Reagan's $90-billion proposal was "superficial," "unworkable," and showed that Reagan had a "lack of intellectual capacity." Conservatives also expressed misgivings. George Will dumped on the idea, and *National Review,* while wholly supportive, worried that it presented "a serious tactical problem" for Reagan.[11] *Human Events,* while praising the speech as "audacious" and "revolutionary," nonetheless concluded that "Even many outspoken conservative politicians will probably shy away from embracing the Reagan formula, fearing the ferocity of special interest groups in the 1976 election."

It didn't help that Reagan's staff was slow in coming up with a detailed analysis of how the plan might work in practice. As the cliché goes, success has many fathers but failure is an orphan. Reagan's senior campaign aides later disavowed prior knowledge of the speech, which the young Jeffrey Bell wrote, and said they "knew immediately" that they were in trouble. Yet most of this same inner circle had traveled with him to Chicago to hear him deliver it because it was a brand new speech that they expected would generate fresh media attention.

How Reagan handled the imbroglio revealed much about his character that later became familiar. A conventional political analyst would ask: *How could Reagan have made the same political mistake just three years after the defeat of Proposition 1?* The answer is: *only someone who believed deeply in the principle at stake.* Rather than obfuscate and trim in the fashion of ordinary politicians, Reagan came out swinging, defending the principle of the proposal even if he wasn't sharp on the details. Reagan understood instinctively that the more accountability can be localized, the more natural political forces will constrain taxing and spending. Since the federal government pays for 62 percent of New Hampshire's welfare costs, Reagan was asked on ABC's *Issues and Answers, Won't your plan require a state tax increase?* "Isn't this," Reagan replied, "a proper decision for the people of the state to make?" On the stump in New Hampshire Reagan used the issue as an opportunity to step up his attack on Washington and tell his success stories of welfare reform and tax rebates in California. *Contra* George Will, Reagan proceeded to give a seminar on federalism. His new standard stump speech in New Hampshire went right at the problem:

> I predicted at the time [of the $90 billion speech] that we would expect to hear screams of anguish from the carpeted anterooms and offices in Washington. Bureaucracy has a built-in instinct for the preservation and reproduction of its own kind. My prediction has come true. The well-orchestrated chorus of doom-criers, their voices amplified in this political season, have predicted every plague but a plague of locusts if such a plan were adopted. They said there would be increased local taxes, the elderly would be thrown out into the snow, and there would be a fiscal disaster if we moved to reduce the size and power of the Washington bureaucracy. . . .

From there Reagan recounted the California welfare reform story, and the subsequent budget surplus that was returned to the people through the tax rebate. The critics, Reagan reminded people, said that that couldn't be done then, either.

"There is nothing in my plan," Reagan concluded,

> which would require states to have either a sales tax or an income tax. . . . Approximately one-third of federal revenues come from the federal personal income tax. A portion of this tax, presently paid by the citizens of New Hampshire—and everyone else for that matter— could be earmarked and kept in each state instead of making a round trip to Washington and back minus the "freight charge."

And with his typical ironic flourish, the former Democrat also cited the famous Democrats of the past who expressed support for devolving power and responsibility from Washington. FDR, Reagan reminded audiences, "said the federal government should get out of the business of welfare," while John F. Kennedy "protested against centralizing all authority in Washington." Then he quoted from an Eisenhower-appointed blue ribbon commission on intergovernmental relations: "Whenever possible, decisions to spend and decisions to tax should be made at the same government level, thus encouraging financial responsibility." One of the commission members who signed onto this principle was none other than Hubert Humphrey, Reagan delighted to point out. Even President Ford himself, Reagan noted, had suggested a small scale version of the same idea with his federal budget proposal that some Medicaid and education programs be turned back to the states. See, went the tacit message, *I'm in the mainstream.* By implication, Ford had thrown in his lot with the Washington "buddy system." "If they [the Ford campaign] want to make decentralization the issue," a Reagan aide told *National Review,* "we're delighted."[12]

In addition to sticking with his core beliefs, Reagan's offensive on behalf of the $90 billion speech had the virtue of resonating with voters. National polls showed that voters supported the principle of Reagan's devolution plan by 59 to 31 percent. Voters thought state government more responsive than the federal government by 67 to 19 percent.[13] The issue was even polling well in New Hampshire. The mistake of the $90 billion speech was in choosing the specific bottom-line figure of $90 billion, which allowed his critics to pin him down with having to explain or deflect endless specific attacks, which kept him off his game plan. It was not a mistake Reagan would make twice.

If the $90 billion speech was an albatross weighing down Reagan, you wouldn't have known it from his performance on the stump. Reagan turned 65 three weeks before the New Hampshire primary, and although he sometimes looked "noticeably tired" at the beginning of the day (according to *The New Republic*'s John Osborne), "he seemed to gather vigor as the days proceeded." A *Boston Globe* reporter observed that "the old Gipper," campaigning hatless and coatless in the New Hampshire winter, was still going strong late in the day "while the reporters and photographers slowly turned grey with fatigue and cold." "His physical endurance was amazing," said a *National Review* reporter; he looked "a dozen years younger than he actually is." Mostly Reagan made fun of his age, telling an audience outside a fire station that he had always wanted to be a fireman—"back when horses were still pulling the engines."

Republican faithful who had seen Reagan at party banquets for the previous decade knew that he had the best shuck and jive routine in American politics, but it was new to average voters and much of the national press corps. Like any accomplished performer or entertainer, Reagan warmed up his audience with his stock anti-government jokes before delivering his serious themes. He would tell the shopworn story of the bureaucrat at the Bureau of Indian Affairs found sobbing at his desk.

"What's wrong?" a co-worker asked. "My Indian died." "Can you imagine," Reagan would add, "how miserable we'd be if we got all the government we paid for?" New Hampshire crowds loved it.

For any unbiased observer watching the scene, Reagan's performance should have dispelled the commonplace notion, which persists to this day, that he was merely a scripted performer dependent on his 3 × 5 cards. Throughout New Hampshire Reagan took questions from the audience, often for an hour or more. His best performance of the whole New Hampshire campaign occurred at Dartmouth College, where, anticipating the hostility of a predominantly liberal college audience, Reagan began by saying, "As General Custer said, 'Don't take any prisoners.'" (This may also have been a veiled reference to Dartmouth's mascot—a Native American "Indian"—that was controversial at the time and which Dartmouth later dropped.) Toward the end of the audience questioning several members of the self-styled People's Bicentennial Commission (PBC), a leftist group that sought to sully the nation's 1976 bicentennial observances, asked Reagan a series of questions about the American founding and the supposed hypocrisy of modern democracy. PBC activists had followed Reagan throughout New Hampshire, and attempted repeatedly to embarrass him with hostile questions. At Dartmouth, Reagan turned the tables.

"I've been answering a lot of your questions and for a change I'd like to ask you one." Reagan proceeded to quote a widely-publicized statement by the PBC's leader, Jeremy Rifkin, to the effect that America's revolutionary leaders should be equated with modern revolutionaries such as Mao, Lenin, and Che Guevara. "Do you agree with that?" Reagan asked. There is no more certain way to stir up a college audience than to engage in this kind of challenge. Left-leaning members of the audience cheered loudly as the names of Communist luminaries were mentioned. After his brawls with the campus Left in California, Reagan was ready. "I'm disappointed," he said. "I don't associate those Americans with the genocide and the dungeon states brought about by Lenin and the others." The audience erupted in cheers and applause.[14] He could hardly have gotten better opponents from central casting.

Reagan's vigorous campaigning propelled him into a 12-point lead in New Hampshire in January, a month before the primary. Nationally, in fact, Reagan had surged 31 percent in the polls in the three weeks following the November announcement of his candidacy, rocketing past Ford in a stunning reversal of their positions. Reporters gradually came to see that Reagan's candidacy was more than just an act. "The effect of this news," Jules Witcover wrote, "was immediate and devastating, especially among knowledgeable politicians who had been sensing that such a development might occur."[15] *The New Republic*'s previously dismissive John Osborne wrote shortly before the New Hampshire primary that "The Reagan insurgency represents a serious threat in part because his anti-Washington, anti-government ideology strikes a responsive chord in the country today."[16] Osborne now thought that Reagan would beat Ford in New Hampshire, and probably take the GOP nomination.

Ford made the same mistake that countless Democrats and liberals had made: He badly underestimated Reagan, admitting later to journalist Elizabeth Drew, "I didn't take Reagan seriously." Ford's campaign surrogates, especially campaign manager Bo Callaway, tried the same playbook that California Democrats had used: Reagan is an extremist who can't be trusted. This only provided Reagan with another opportunity: If the Ford administration thinks I'm an extremist, he asked, why did they offer me two cabinet posts and an ambassadorship? Callaway soon lost his job.

"There is little question," *Time* magazine observed, "that Reagan had outorganized and outdazzled Ford." Reagan made more than 200 appearances in 17 days of campaigning in New Hampshire. Yet a sitting president, even an unelected one, is not without formidable campaign assets, and Ford used his advantages deftly. Ten days before the primary Ford made a two-day swing through the state, and planned to return just before primary day. Ford's campaign operated a massive phone bank that contacted 60,000 Republican households, tallying loyal votes and targeting the undecideds for follow-up efforts.

Reagan's pollster, Richard Wirthlin, came in with poll numbers six days before the primary showing Reagan four points ahead (down from 11 points a week earlier), but with a large undecided vote. The undecideds, Wirthlin judged, would probably break for Ford, meaning the primary was too close to call. Reagan's chances depended on a final effort down to the wire. For one thing, Ford was coming back before election day. And Reagan's most potent campaign weapon was—himself. But Reagan's campaign manager John Sears didn't show Wirthlin's poll to Reagan or anyone else. Reagan's campaign was feeling confident—so confident that they publicly predicted victory and decided to stop campaigning. One Reagan supporter, former Governor Meldrim Thomson, predicted on "Meet the Press" that Reagan would win by five points. On the weekend before the primary, Reagan was campaigning in Illinois. It was a fatal miscalculation.

Former New Hampshire Governor Hugh Gregg was the state chairman and principal organizer of Reagan's campaign in the Granite State, and Gregg thought it was not necessary for Reagan to campaign further. Gregg also thought it would be easier to mobilize the election day get-out-the-vote drive without the distraction of Reagan appearing in the state. Some of Reagan's other campaign strategists agreed for different reasons, believing that Reagan's "star quality" risked being diminished by over-exposure, making him seem like just another grasping politician. (In fact Wirthlin's polls found that Reagan's movie connection was a net plus with voters and not the handicap the political class has always thought it to be.) Wirthlin later told Lou Cannon that he had a "sinking feeling" when he heard during the weekend before the primary that Reagan was in Illinois instead of New Hampshire.

Reagan jumped to an early lead in the vote count on election night, February 24. Some time before midnight, with Reagan leading Ford by a slim 52 to 48 margin, Reagan allowed himself to be photographed holding an early edition newspaper with the headline showing him in the lead. But then the count tightened. At 12:49 A.M., Ford went ahead for the first time, by five votes. When the final count came in a few hours later, Ford had edged Reagan by 1,317 votes, 54,824 to 53,507. It was the first time Reagan tasted defeat in an election. Wirthlin had been right; the undecided voters broke strongly in Ford's favor. (It is possible that Reagan actually won more votes than Ford. In a quirk of the New Hampshire ballot, voters elect *delegates* rather than the candidates themselves, and due to a mixup in delegate slates nearly 5,000 ballots were invalidated for having voted for two different Reagan delegate slates. Most if not all of these ballots probably were for Reagan, which would have given him a comfortable margin. In addition, 1,500 Democrats cast write-in votes for Reagan, which didn't count in the vote total.)

The Ford campaign couldn't believe its good luck. Had Reagan won, Ford would have been on the ropes and perhaps knocked out of the race in the same fashion as LBJ in 1968. "As a result [of losing New Hampshire]," *National Review* reported, "the whole Reagan game plan is now in doubt."[17] The next primary was Florida, where Reagan expected to do well. Reagan had hoped that beating Ford with a one-two punch in both New Hampshire and Florida would force him from the race and assure such momentum that a late entry could not wrest the nomination away. (Nelson Rockefeller, Charles Percy, and John Connally were rumored to be interested in entering the race to challenge Reagan if Ford dropped out.) Early polls had the race neck-and-neck, but after New Hampshire Ford surged to a 17-point lead in the Sunshine State.

Reagan became enmeshed in a new round of defensive campaigning in Florida. Ford's campaign continued to hammer on the $90 billion speech, but also brought into play some of Reagan's old statements about Social Security. Needless to say, the so-called "third rail" of American politics is thermonuclear in Florida. (Thirty-eight percent of Republican voters in Florida in 1976 were over 65.) Reagan thought he had learned from Goldwater's mishandling of Social Security in 1964. Reagan always thought that Goldwater was ahead of his time, on this as on other issues. In 1976 it was ironically Reagan who was ahead of his time, talking about reforming Social Security along the lines that became commonplace in the late 1990s. But even the "Great Communicator" couldn't make voters swallow this political camel in 1976.

"I've always believed that you say the qualifier first," Reagan told Jules Witcover as a preface to his views on Social Security. "If you say, 'Now look, let's make it plain; the first priority must be that no one who is depending on [Social Security] for their non-earning years should have it taken away from him, or have it endangered. It is endangered today by the shape it is in.' So then you go on and say, 'Now, the program is out of balance. Down the line someplace, can come a very great tragedy of finding that the cupboard is bare. Before that happens, let's fix Social Security.'"[18] Social Security, he reminded audiences, was $2.5 trillion out of actuarial balance. As president, Reagan said, he would appoint a commission to study how to ensure the long-term solvency and reform of the program (which is in fact what he did in 1981).

One of Reagan's ideas for reforming Social Security was to have some of its funds invested in the stock market, "in the industrial might of nation's economy." Voters weren't ready to contemplate this idea in 1976; the stock market had only recently recovered from its worst swoon since the Great Depression, and was still below its 1970 level. Worse, it allowed Ford's campaign to attack Reagan from the right, asserting that *government* ownership of stock would amount to "wild-eyed socialism," as it would give the federal government controlling interest in every industry in the nation. (This is exactly the idea President Clinton briefly contemplated in 1998.) Reagan had not yet contemplated the idea that individuals might control their own accounts rather than the government. Ford himself entered the fray, saying Reagan's idea "is the best blueprint for back-door socialism that I ever heard."[19] Along with the $90 billion speech, Reagan had a new issue on which he had to play defense at nearly every stop. Even for the Great Communicator the general rule of politics applies: If you're on defense, you're losing. In this case, Reagan was now being whipsawed as a right-wing extremist and a back-door socialist.

Reagan was not only on defense; he was also playing to small crowds, many of whom turned out hopefully to see Jimmy Stewart or Efrem Zimbalist Jr., whom Reagan's campaign had hoped (and apparently announced) might make some campaign appearances. Ford, by contrast, was starting to get the hang of how to campaign from the White House. In addition to milking Air Force One for all it was worth, Ford began handing out pork barrel projects throughout the state: a new veterans hospital and a convention center for Orlando; a mass transit system for Miami, defense contracts for major Florida firms, and a faster naturalization process for Cuban immigrants. Ford appeared before nearly 100,000 people in two days in his first campaign swing. And he returned for a second trip before primary day.

One reason Reagan found it hard to press the offensive was his reluctance to attack Ford directly, heeding his famous adopted 11th Commandment that "Thou shalt not speak ill of another Republican." "I will not put aside the 11th commandment for anyone," Reagan had said when he announced his candidacy. Throughout the New Hampshire campaign, and in the early days of the Florida effort, Reagan always dodged direct questions about Ford's performance in office, and tried hard not to make a direct attack on Ford. "I've made no list of differences between us," Reagan had said at his November announcement of his candidacy. "I'll campaign on what I think should be done and the proposals that I would make, what I believe the philosophy of government should be. I'm sure the President will campaign in the same way. Then it will be up to the American people to draw the distinction where there are differences and to make their decision. We will run our campaigns in a gentlemanly manner. I think of Jerry as a friend, and I think he thinks of me the same way." Then in Oregon a week later Reagan had promised, "I personally will do nothing divisive in the coming campaign."

But Reagan was going to have to eat his words if he was to turn around the race. Permutations of "The Speech" were not cutting it with enough voters. Reagan and his advisers decided they had no choice but to begin attacking Ford. And détente was the issue they chose to use against Ford, in part because détente could be blamed on Kissinger (and by implication on Nixon), thereby softening the attack. "Despite Mr. Ford's evident decency, honor, and patriotism," Reagan began saying in early March, "he has shown neither the vision nor the leadership necessary to halt and reverse the diplomatic and military decline of the United States."

It was perhaps surprising that it took Reagan so long to make détente a central theme of his campaign. Reagan had been working out his opposition to détente for a long time. A governor's "Cabinet Issue Memo" from early 1974—before Ford replaced Nixon—laid out the ground of Reagan's critique. The memo, written by Jeff Bell (author of the "$90 billion budget cut" speech) said: "The main substantive effect of détente has been a sapping of morale among our own allies. . . . European leaders increasingly doubt the credibility of the U.S. deterrent." But the memo also warned of the political hazards of attacking détente directly: "The word [détente] itself is politically unassailable. . . . The Governor's goal should be to accept détente as a potentially good idea, but to define the kind of détente which he favors and which will mean something." Above all, "détente cannot work in a context of U.S. military weakness."[20]

Reagan's attack on détente began in Orlando:

Ford and Kissinger ask us to trust their leadership. Well, I find that more and more difficult to do. Henry Kissinger's recent stewardship of U.S. foreign policy has coincided precisely with the loss of U.S. military supremacy. . . . Under Messrs. Kissinger and Ford this nation has become the Number Two military power in a world where it is dangerous—if not fatal—to be second best. . . . All I can see is what other nations the world over see: collapse of the American will and the retreat of American power. There is little doubt in my mind that the Soviet Union will not stop taking advantage of détente until it sees that the American people have elected a new President and appointed a new Secretary of State.

Reagan also began attacking the ongoing negotiations to turn back ownership of the Panama Canal to Panama, accusing Ford of duplicity and deception in the public description of the state of negotiations. "When it comes to the canal," Reagan concluded, "we built it, we paid for it, it's ours, and we should tell Torrijos [Panama's ruling general] and company that we are going to keep it!"

At first the Panama Canal line drew only tepid applause. But a few days later before a retirement community in Sun City, "bedlam broke loose" (according to Jules Witcover) when Reagan ended his "we are going to keep it" line. According to campaign aide David Keene, "Reagan, who knows his audience very well, was so taken aback that he lost his place." Suddenly Reagan had his new wedge issue. Keene succinctly and correctly explained the visceral resonance of the Canal issue: "It said more about the American people's feelings about where the country was, and what it was powerless to do, and their frustration about the incomprehensibility of foreign policy over the last couple of decades."[21]

The campaign suddenly came to life, and tracking polls showed Reagan gaining on Ford. But it came too late. Although Reagan closed the previous 17-point gap, Ford nonetheless carried Florida on March 9, 53 to 47 percent. Reagan's weakest showing was among the elderly; Ford garnered 60 percent of GOP voters over 65 years old. Ford was on a roll; one new poll showed him leading Democratic front-runner Jimmy Carter by eight points in a head-to-head matchup.

From Florida the campaign moved on to the Illinois primary a week later on March 16. Illinois was the state of Reagan's birth, but Illinois was also near enough to Ford's home state of Michigan to be considered home turf. It didn't help that the Republican senator from Illinois, Charles Percy, attacked Reagan as an extremist, while most of the state's Republican congressional delegation also backed their former House colleague and minority leader. Ford began to counterattack Reagan on foreign policy, even as he began to shift in Reagan's direction. Before the Chicago Council on Foreign Relations Ford quoted George Washington, though he might as easily have quoted Reagan: "Our policy of peace through strength is not something that I have recently invented. It is something we first found in our history books when we read George Washington's wise counsel, and again I quote: 'To be prepared for war is one of the most effectual means of preserving peace.'"

Henry Kissinger also lashed out at Reagan in a Boston speech, and issued a 10-page rebuttal to Reagan's charges: "The basic interests of the United States are permanent and ought not to reflect presidential campaigns." In January, Ford had told NBC News that "I think it would be very unwise for a president—me or anyone else—to abandon détente. I think détente is in the best interest of this country. It is in the best interest of world stability, world peace . . . and politically, I think any candidate who says abandon détente will be the loser in the long run." But by the time of the North Carolina primary, Ford stated: "I don't use the word 'détente' any more." Reagan's foreign policy attacks were clearly drawing blood.

But not enough blood. Ford bested Reagan 59 to 40 in Illinois; Ford also won uncontested primaries in Massachusetts and Vermont, bringing his record to 5 – 0. With each primary his margin over Reagan had widened. Reagan professed himself "pleased" at getting 40 percent of the vote in Illinois; as several campaign aides put it to reporters, only someone who had survived making as many bad movies as Reagan could remain plucky in the face of the numbers. "Ronald Reagan," William F. Buckley Jr. wrote after Illinois, "has lost his fight for the presidential nomination," and suggested that Reagan consider being Ford's running mate. Republican congressional leaders and several governors called publicly for Reagan to withdraw in the name of party unity. Ten of the eleven living former chairmen of the Republican National Committee issued an appeal for Reagan to drop out. (The one former RNC chairman missing from the list was George Bush, whose current position as CIA director prevented him from joining the fracas.) Reagan summarily rejected party pressure, dismissing it as White House–sponsored, which was undoubtedly true. Ford himself joined the chorus, saying publicly that Reagan should drop out. The pressure was a mistake. "As soon as I heard the Ford remark," Reagan told *Time* magazine a few weeks later, "I knew it would backfire on him."[22] Ford's people underestimated Reagan's stubbornness, and the pressure to withdraw only stiffened Reagan. None of them wanted me to run in the first place, so I'm not going to pay any attention to them now, Reagan said. "Tell him [Ford] to quit." Yet Reagan's campaign manager John Sears met secretly, and without Reagan's knowledge or approval, with Ford's campaign chairman Rogers Morton a few days after Illinois, to discuss terms for Reagan's withdrawal from the race.

Both Ford and the press corps figured Reagan would be finished off in the next primary in North Carolina. "Without recognizing it," Lou Cannon wrote afterward, "Reagan had now reached a moment in his own political career as fully critical as the time he gave his famous speech for Goldwater in 1964." Reagan showed a steely determination that his otherwise genial countenance led many people to believe he was empty or shallow at his core. At every campaign stop Reagan would be asked when he was going to drop out, and every time Reagan defiantly said he was going to continue the campaign. Moreover, he refused to answer follow-up questions on the issue, insisting he would only answer questions about something else. Sometimes there would be long, awkward pauses until a reporter would mercifully change the subject. When Cannon joined the chorus asking Reagan when he would quit, Reagan turned on him, saying "You, too, Lou? I'm not going to quit." At a meeting of his senior campaign staff, all of whom were currently working without pay and thought the campaign would soon end, Reagan struck the same defiant note. "I am taking this all the way to the convention in Kansas City," Reagan told his staff, "and I'm going even if I lose every damn primary between now and then."[23] There were 21 more primaries to go. "We were all slightly stunned," Martin Anderson recalled. "[I]t may have been this determination," Lou Cannon acknowledged, "that made Ronald Reagan the President of the United States. . . . North Carolina was the turning point of Reagan's political career."[24]

Reagan had a major asset in North Carolina: the political machine of freshman Senator Jesse Helms. Helms' campaign apparatus was able to turn out large crowds, and Reagan's speeches found their old bounce. He stepped up his attacks on Ford and Kissinger, typically reversing the order of their names—"Dr. Kissinger and Mr. Ford"—as if to suggest none too subtly that Kissinger was playing a Svengali role in the Ford White House. Ford's domestic record came into Reagan's crosshairs; Ford, Reagan pounded away, was responsible for the largest budget deficit in history (an argument that would obviously come back to haunt Reagan a decade later). He also managed some typically Reaganesque barbs: "If [Ford] comes here with the same list of goodies as he did in Florida, the band won't know whether to play 'Hail to the Chief' or 'Santa Claus is Coming to Town.'" The campaign spent heavily to put Reagan on television throughout the state. One small but telling episode is worth recalling: Reagan refused to allow the Helms organization to send a mailing to Republican voters attacking Ford for saying that black Republican Senator Edward Brooke of Massachusetts might make a fine vice president. Reagan never wanted to win an election on a racial appeal.

Ford was so confident of victory that he only spent two days campaigning in North Carolina, in the process giving arguably his most soporific speech ever. David Gergen had been brought in to help punch up Ford's speechwriting department, but it didn't avert the banal effort Ford made in Charlotte to the State Annual Convention of the Future Homemakers of America on March 20: "I regret that some people in this country have disparaged and demeaned the role of the homemaker. I say—and say it with emphasis and conviction—that homemaking is good for America." More: "The old values of caring and sharing have not gone out of date. I share your strong belief that every individual counts and that we are all involved in each other's lives." Jules Witcover said that the speech was "so vapid as to be ludicrous." One of Ford's own campaign aides admitted that "It was in North Carolina that Ford became a crashing bore." (Following this debacle, the Ford campaign hired a joke writer from New York.)

Still, Reagan was unable to predict that he would win, saying that he would be satisfied with a "strong showing." A *New York Times* headline read: "REAGAN VIRTUALLY CONCEDES DEFEAT IN NORTH CAROLINA." Reagan and his senior aides left North Carolina on primary day for Wisconsin, where the next primary would be held a week later. Reagan was in the middle of a speech to Ducks Unlimited in La Crosse when the first returns came in from North Carolina showing him ahead of Ford. Mindful of how his early lead in the New Hampshire vote count had slipped away, Reagan and his staff kept a low-key attitude and made no public statement. The final returns weren't available until Reagan was on the plane back to California: Reagan 52, Ford 46. Easing up in North Carolina, Ford's people would say later, was the single biggest mistake of the nomination campaign.

Although Reagan turned things around in North Carolina, he still trailed Ford badly in the delegate count, and worse, was over $1 million in debt. The campaign decided even before the North Carolina breakthrough on a bold step that Reagan had favored all along: a national TV address with Reagan making a pitch for funds from the conservative faithful. The campaign plunked down $100,000 to buy time on NBC. The speech was a success; 40,000 letters poured into Reagan's campaign headquarters, containing $1.5 million in contributions. But the TV effort meant skipping the Wisconsin primary the week after North Carolina, which in retrospect was a mistake. Reagan won 45 percent of the vote in Wisconsin, but no delegates.

The venue for the next primaries now shifted out West, where Reagan expected all along to be strongest. Texas was Reagan's most appealing target. The Lone Star state allowed crossover voting, and Reagan's campaign purposely targeted George Wallace voters among Democrats (Wallace, beaten handily by Jimmy Carter in every primary, had already dropped out). During the Texas campaign Reagan began using a signature line in his appeal for crossover votes: "I was a Democrat most of my adult life." Ford and the Republican establishment professed outrage. Imagine! Seeking Democratic votes! (As if a Republican could win the White House without Democratic votes. It was a controversy revived during John McCain's campaign in 2000.) The idea of "Reagan Democrats" had not yet entered the political lexicon.

Meanwhile, Ford didn't help matters with another gaffe in San Antonio, where he was handed a tamale which he bit through without removing the corn husk. The *New York Times* saw fit to print a photo of Ford's *faux pas* on the front page, along with the caption: "The snack was interrupted after the first bite so that his hosts could remove the corn shucks which serve as a wrapper and are not supposed to be consumed." The episode reinforced the unfair image of Ford as a dim and bumbling president. (When Jimmy Carter was asked after the election what the most important lesson he learned from the long campaign, he said: "Always shuck your tamales.")

Reagan clobbered Ford in Texas, winning every congressional district and capturing all 96 delegates at stake. Reagan also started showing strength in states that chose convention delegates by caucus or convention. Three days later Reagan swept Ford in Indiana (where Democratic crossover votes again helped run up Reagan's vote), Alabama, and Georgia. Reagan captured 130 of the 139 delegates at stake in these contests. But the biggest blow came four days later, when Reagan upset Ford in Nebraska, this time in a state without crossover voting, by a 55-to-45 margin. Ford had led Reagan by more than 20 points in the polls two weeks before the Nebraska primary, and the meltdown of his large lead set off the panic alarm in the Ford campaign. Ford's campaign chairman Rogers Morton was photographed on primary night sitting behind an array of empty liquor bottles (most of whose contents had been drained by journalists, not Ford campaign staff), remarking that "I'm not going to rearrange the furniture on the deck of the *Titanic*." The photograph and caption with this quotation ran in newspapers across the country. It was not the Ford campaign's finest visual moment.

Suddenly Reagan had won five primaries in a row, and had pulled ahead in the delegate count. In addition to winning more votes and delegates, Reagan started topping Ford in campaign contributions, too. Now the speculation began that Ford might drop out. Ford issued a Reagan-sounding denial: "Anybody who gets the impression that we're going to quit is crazy as hell." A group of congressional leaders went to the White House to meet with Ford and declare their support, but at least one member, probably House Minority Leader John Rhodes, suggested to Ford that Kissinger announce that he would not be part of a second Ford administration, and perhaps that he ought to go right away. Ford rejected this suggestion. A few days later, though, Kissinger told a television interviewer that he "would prefer" not to stay on if Ford won the election. A Harris poll found Kissinger remained highly popular with the general population, with a 55 percent approval rating.

The road ahead looked grim for Ford, as most of the remaining primaries were out West, where Reagan would be strong. The immediate worry was Michigan, Ford's home state. If he lost to Reagan at home, it would be all over. Polls showed Ford with only a slim lead, and Michigan allowed crossover voting. Wallace had received 800,000 votes in the 1972 Michigan primary; if Reagan attracted a major proportion of these, he could easily win. It didn't happen. Although 400,000 Democrats crossed party lines to vote in the Republican primary, the majority went for Ford, helping him to a landslide 65-to-34 percent win over Reagan on May 25. Ford also won the Maryland primary, which Reagan had not contested. Yet Reagan remained ahead in the delegate count.

What followed from May until the Republican convention in July in Kansas City was a see-saw battle. Ford narrowly won the Kentucky primary, 51-to-47 percent, which deprived Reagan of 27 delegates he had won at the state party convention. (Although Reagan had won 27 of Kentucky's 37 delegates at the state convention, a quirk in Kentucky's process bound all the state's delegates to support the winner of the primary election on the convention's first ballot.) In Tennessee, Reagan committed another Goldwater-style mistake, saying that selling off the Tennessee Valley Authority "would be something to look at." The Ford campaigned pounced on the statement, and Reagan lost Tennessee by only 2,000 votes out of 250,000 cast. (It was also around this time that Reagan repeated to *Time* magazine his old theme that "Fascism was really the basis for the New Deal."[25])

On the day of the last primaries in early June, Reagan trounced Ford as expected in California, 66-to-34 percent, while Ford prevailed in Ohio and New Jersey. Ford tried to use the "warmonger" tactic against Reagan in California, hoping to capitalize on another off-the-cuff remark in which Reagan suggested the possible use of U.S. troops in Africa against the Cubans. Ford's campaign ran a tough TV ad with the slogan, "Governor Reagan couldn't start a war. President Reagan might."

At the end of the primaries, Reagan had won more votes than Ford by a narrow margin, 50.7 percent to 49.3 percent. With the delegate count neck-and-neck, the battle now turned to the few remaining caucus and convention states, and to courting uncommitted delegates. Reagan did well in caucuses in Washington, Missouri, Iowa, Colorado, and Utah, though Ford swept North Dakota and Delaware along with Minnesota, the latter by means of strong-arm tactics. The job of nailing down uncommitted delegates for Ford fell to Texan James A. Baker III, whose previous political experience had been with George Bush's failed Senate campaign in 1970. Ford began pressing the advantages of incumbency to the hilt, inviting uncommitted delegates to the White House, having cabinet members listen to their concerns about pet projects, and even providing seven uncommitted New York delegates with prime seating on the deck of an aircraft carrier for the tall ships sailing exposition during the July 4 bicentennial celebration. Ford, Jules Witcover wrote, "functioned like some Chicago alderman hustling to keep his job by old-fashioned ward-heeling."[26] The best Reagan could do was to invite uncommitted delegates to visit him in a hotel suite. Ford sought to begin healing party divisions and blunt Reagan at the same time by hinting he might like to have Reagan as his running mate. Reagan emphatically repeated that he was not interesting in being vice president.

It was evident on the eve of the convention that neither man had enough delegates to assure nomination on the first ballot. Delegate counts varied, with the *New York Times* giving Ford 1,102 to Reagan's 1,063, with 1,130 needed to win. This circumstance clearly favored Ford, though Ford's people knew that if they didn't win on the first ballot (presumably through the abstention of a handful of delegates), many wavering delegates would break for Reagan on the second. Reagan's campaign knew it, too. Ford's full court press was even succeeding in peeling away a few Reagan delegates on the eve of the convention. Reagan's only chance to win was some kind of Hail Mary play to woo uncommitted delegates or extend the voting to a second ballot.

John Sears thought he had the answer. Reagan should name his running mate in advance of the convention. Since Reagan was strong in the South and the West, political calculus suggested that a running mate from the upper Midwest or Northeast would help Reagan most in a general election. Some weeks earlier Reagan had instructed his senior campaign staff to begin vetting potential running mates, so the campaign already had its "A" list underway. Sears own first choice was even more audacious than the tactic itself: Nelson Rockefeller![27] It is doubtful Rockefeller could have been persuaded, but the matter was moot. Sen. Paul Laxalt knew the idea would be a non-starter. Other names of political figures from the Northeast were considered, including a young second-term congressman from Buffalo, Jack Kemp, and former Attorney General William Ruckelshaus. Kemp was rejected as too young and unknown. Rucklelshaus was not entirely ruled out, but Sears zeroed in on what he considered a better prospect: Pennsylvania Senator Richard Schweiker. In addition to his geographical attractiveness, Sears thought Schweiker could peel away as many as 70 of Pennsylvania's convention delegates (47 of Pennsylvania's delegates were officially "uncommitted" at that point, though thought to be leaning to Ford)—enough to put Reagan over the top. Sears and Sen. Paul Laxalt arranged to meet Schweiker in Washington, where they popped the question. Schweiker, who didn't even know how to pronounce Reagan's name correctly (he kept referring to him as "Ree-gun"), accepted.

The next step was convincing Reagan to make the offer formally. Sears and Laxalt had gone to Schweiker and offered him the second spot without Reagan's knowledge! The trouble with Schweiker is that he was known as a liberal Republican, siding so solidly with organized labor that he was the only Senator to receive a 100 percent rating from the AFL-CIO in 1975. Schweiker was arguably as liberal as Jimmy Carter's running mate, Sen. Walter Mondale. His vote rating from the liberal Americans for Democratic Action (ADA), 89 percent, was identical to Sen. George McGovern. Like McGovern, Schweiker had opposed the Vietnam War, voted against Nixon's missile defense plan, against two of Nixon's Supreme Court appointments, and in favor of overriding all 14 of Nixon's vetoes (for which he earned himself a place on Nixon's infamous "enemies list"). He voted against Ford's program to deregulate energy markets, and in favor of breaking up "big oil." He was also a notorious big spender, having voted repeatedly to raise federal spending, and even co-sponsoring the original liberal Humphrey-Hawkins full employment act (the bill that Reagan had said a few weeks earlier was "a design for fascism"). No wonder McGovern was able to remark later that if Schweiker didn't make it onto a Reagan-led GOP ticket, he could succeed McGovern as president of the ADA. A more incompatible running mate for Ronald Reagan could hardly be conceived if central casting had been asked to fill the spot with a total opposite character to Reagan's lead.

But Schweiker opposed gun control, opposed abortion, and was always in the forefront of Captive Nations resolutions in Congress (which tacitly put him in the anti-Kissinger camp), which gave him just enough cultural conservative credentials, Sears and Laxalt thought, to be acceptable. But there was Reagan's professed antipathy toward traditional notions of "ticket balancing." "I do not believe," Reagan had said during the primaries, "you choose someone of an opposite philosophy in hopes he'll get you some votes you can't get yourself, because that's being false with the people who vote for you and your philosophy."[28] Just a few days before meeting Schweiker for the first time, Reagan had reiterated the point even more forcefully when asked by reporters what the reaction would be if Ford picked another northeastern liberal like Rockefeller to be his running mate. "It would be a foolish mistake," Reagan said. "Ford would lose the South, and a lot of Republicans might not work for him." Yet now Reagan was to contemplate the same maneuver.

Sears, Laxalt, and Schweiker quickly arranged to see Reagan in Los Angeles. Schweiker flew out incognito under the name of one of his Senate office staff members. As Schweiker waited in the Beverly Wilshire Hotel, Sears and Laxalt made the case to Reagan at his Pacific Palisades home. Reagan liked the sound of the idea, and wanted to meet Schweiker immediately.

Schweiker and Reagan talked for six hours the following day. Reagan took an instant liking to Schweiker, especially his religious convictions (Schweiker was a Catholic) and his family values (Schweiker was the father of five). Schweiker assured Reagan that he could support Reagan's positions in the campaign and as vice president. He further assured Reagan that he was not at heart a big spender, and favored private sector solutions to social problems. "You know, I have a strong feeling," Reagan told Schweiker, "that I'm looking at myself some years ago" (apparently referring to his own liberal past). Schweiker said, "Well, I'm no knee-jerk liberal." Reagan replied: "And I'm no knee-jerk extremist." At that point Reagan formally offered Schweiker the vice presidential nomination.

Reagan publicly announced his selection of Schweiker a week later, just days before the GOP convention opened in Kansas City. As expected, all hell broke loose, but mostly against Reagan. *Time* magazine described the move as "one of the most astonishing and bizarre turnabouts in a campaign full of surprises." Ford didn't believe the news when he first heard it. "I thought someone was pulling my leg," Ford said later. Reagan's campaign was startled by the vehemence with which conservatives reacted against Schweiker, and Reagan was on the defensive. "I am not going to pretend, nor is he, that in every area we are in complete agreement," Reagan said on August 6. "He has represented a blue collar constituency, essentially a labor constituency, but I have found that when principle dictated going counter to that he was not a rubber stamp for them." How was Reagan's selection of Schweiker any different that Ford's selection of Rockefeller? Or of Carter's selection of

Walter Mondale? The latter comparison did the most damage, and the Reagan campaign hastily composed memos to show that Schweiker's Senate voting record was not indistinguishable from Mondale's.

The whole point of the conservative movement starting with Goldwater was to purge the Northeastern wing of the Republican Party, and here was Reagan giving the liberal wing a seat near the head of the table. Furthermore, the Schweiker pick would give Ford more latitude to select a liberal running mate—perhaps even to bring back the dreaded Rockefeller. Angry letters from Reagan supporters flooded the campaign office in Los Angeles. One letter, written with the thick script of a black marker, simply said, "Dear Governor Reagan: Schweiker?!?! For God's sake!!!"

Conservatives leaders were no less harsh. Howard Phillips of the Conservative Caucus blasted Reagan, saying Reagan had "betrayed the trust of those who look to him for leadership." Sen. Jesse Helms swallowed hard and stuck with Reagan, calling the Schweiker pick "a coalition with the widest wingspan in all history." George Will was less charitable, writing that Mondale's liberalism "is a sliver more or less advanced than Schweiker's (more or less, depending on whose micrometer does the measuring). . . . If the Reagan-Schweiker ticket is a political coalition, then sauerkraut ice cream is a culinary coalition." Illinois Congressman Henry Hyde likened the move to "a farmer selling his last cow to buy a milking machine," while Mississippi Congressman Trent Lott switched from Reagan to Ford in anger over the Schweiker pick. "It's the dumbest thing I ever heard of," said Congressman John Ashbrook. James Jackson Kilpatrick wrote in *National Review:* "In that last misjudgment, no matter how plausible it seemed in conception, Reagan lost his purity; he was no longer Galahad in quest of the Holy Grail, but Lancelot panting for Guinevere."[29] It didn't help that Jimmy Carter said, "I think he [Schweiker] is a good man." And the *Washington Post* praised Schweiker's pick, calling the move "dazzling" and "wise."

Reagan's strategists thought it was possible they might lose some Southern delegates, and sure enough, the Mississippi delegation, hitherto tenuously pledged to Reagan, seized upon the Schweiker pick to defect to Ford, which its leader, Clarke Reed, had wanted to do anyway. Meanwhile, the expected gains among Northeastern delegations failed to materialize. Schweiker couldn't budge any Pennsylvania delegates, despite four telephone conversations with the leader of the delegation, Drew

Lewis, who was a close friend of Schweiker's. (Both Schweiker and Lewis would serve in President Reagan's cabinet in 1981.) Despite his friendship with Schweiker, Lewis stuck firmly with Ford and lost only one delegate to Reagan.

The Schweiker gambit was widely perceived for what it was—an act of desperation. Although it failed to break the delegate hunt in Reagan's favor, it nonetheless kept the drama of the convention alive when otherwise it might have been over before it began. Reagan was not without a few more cards to play at Kansas City. Reagan's forces attempted to force a rule change requiring Ford to announce *his* vice presidential selection before the presidential balloting took place. If he could break Ford's putative delegate majority on this question, it might expose Ford's weakness. This gambit failed, too, and Reagan's forces were left with the faint hope that they might break the convention open with a platform fight over détente. The Reagan forces submitted a platform plank called "Morality in Foreign Policy" which was, Jules Witcover observed, "a thinly veiled slap at Kissinger," who was being kept under "political house arrest" at the Kansas City convention. (Kissinger only appeared publicly on the last night of the convention, when the contest was over.) The plank saluted Solzhenitsyn, thereby reopening that old wound, and took direct aim at the Helsinki accords: "Agreements that are negotiated, such as the one signed in Helsinki, must not take from those who do not have freedom or the hope of one day gaining it." Much to Kissinger's annoyance, the Ford team swallowed hard and accepted the plank, thus preventing the humiliation of losing a floor fight on the platform. James Baker later observed that the Reagan forces erred by not making the plank more specific (such as repudiating the Panama Canal negotiations or China policy, or calling for Kissinger's dismissal) and obviously unacceptable to Ford. Had Ford lost a floor battle over the platform, Reagan might yet have drawn the inside straight he was seeking.

The final balloting for the nomination was close but anticlimactic, with Ford beating Reagan by the narrow margin of 1,187 to 1,070. Even though Reagan lost each maneuver, he nonetheless dominated the convention in many other ways. The most important was the party platform, which Reagan's forces transformed. Many of the changes Reagan's forces pushed through seemed merely semantic—calling for a "superior" national defense over a "strong" national defense as Ford's first draft called for—but the cumulative effect was to make the platform a full-throated conservative manifesto. Rather than call for dealing with the "root causes" of segregation (original draft language, indistinguishable from liberal rhetoric), Reagan's forces put through an endorsement of a constitutional amendment prohibiting forced busing. They won a change on the welfare platform from endorsing a "more rational distribution of welfare money" (draft language) to "we oppose federalizing welfare. . . . we also oppose the guaranteed annual income concept and any programs that reduce the incentive to work."

On gun control Reagan's forces changed the language from "eliminate the supply of cheap, available handguns . . . with such federal law as necessary" to "we support right of citizens to keep and bear arms. We oppose federal registration of firearms. Mandatory sentences for crimes committed with lethal weapons is the only effective solution to this problem." An endorsement of a constitutional amendment permitting school prayer was also adopted. But the most significant platform plank was an endorsement of the Human Life Amendment that would reverse the *Roe v. Wade* decision that made legal abortion on demand. The original draft of the platform was silent on abortion, and Ford, who was pro-choice, opposed the plank. However, Senator Bob Dole, the temporary chairman of the convention, supported it.

Reagan failed to capture the nomination, but his capture of the party's soul was nearly complete. This became most evident on the final evening, when, after Ford's nomination acceptance speech, Ford waived for Reagan to come down to the podium for the all-important "unity" tableau. (Ford had practiced his speech for two weeks but it still came out like . . . like Jerry Ford. Murray Kempton wrote that "He remains a long way from ceasing to remind us of Kafka's image of the candidate about whom it was no longer possible to tell whether he was outlining his program or crying for help.") With nearly half the delegates having voted for Reagan, and perhaps a majority secretly preferring Reagan, a unity gesture was essential. It turned out to be the most electric moment of the convention.

Accounts differ as to the sequence of events and whether Reagan had prior knowledge that Ford would invite him to the convention podium to offer some remarks. According to Martin Anderson's narrative, Reagan had declined an early invitation to appear on the platform with Ford at the end of the convention, but with Ford waving to him, the crowd cheering, and Ford emissary Bryce Harlow appearing at the door to Reagan's box asking him to come down, Reagan had little choice.

"But what will I say?" Reagan asked Mike Deaver.

"Don't worry. You'll think of something," Deaver replied.[30]

The disbelief of the veracity of this account derives from the sustained burst of eloquence that followed, eloquence which Reagan's many critics thought him incapable without a script. Reagan spoke for six minutes without notes or a teleprompter, and, had the speech come two days earlier, might have swayed the delegates to change their mind. "There was a palpable sense in the hall," Reagan's biographer Edmund Morris told PBS television in 1998 (but, curiously, did not say in his biography), "that we've nominated the wrong man."

Reagan started out repeating some of his familiar stump themes from the primary season. "I believe the Republican Party has a platform that is a banner of bold, unmistakable colors with no pale, pastel shades." That was easy to say: It was largely *his* platform. Reagan followed with a ritualistic attack on the Democrats.

With this formulaic pronouncement, it would seem appropriate—it is likely that Ford expected—that Reagan would stop. But then Reagan started, with a slight awkwardness and a hitch at the beginning, to tell a story. And as the story grew the hall became increasingly quiet and solemn:

> If I could just take a moment . . . I had an assignment the other day. Someone asked me to write a letter for a time capsule that is going to be opened in Los Angeles a hundred years from now, on our tercentennial. It sounded like an easy assignment. They suggested I write something about the problems and issues of the day and I set out to do so, riding down the coast in an automobile looking at the blue Pacific Ocean out on one side and the Santa Ynez mountains on the other, and I couldn't help but wonder if it was going to be that beautiful a hundred years from now as it was on that summer day.

Reagan-watchers will immediately recognize that this is same story that he started to tell at the end of his second debate with Walter Mondale in 1984, but which was cut short by the network moderator because Reagan had run out of time. Observers at the time said "Huh?" about

Reagan's rambling, unfinished anecdote. All they needed do was recall the scene in Kansas City, where Reagan finished the story:

> And suddenly I thought to myself, if I write of problems they'll be domestic problems, of which the president spoke here tonight, the challenges confronting us, erosion of freedom that has taken place under Democratic rule in this country, the invasion of private rights, the controls and restrictions on the vitality of the great free economy that we enjoy. These are the challenges that we must meet.
>
> And then there is the challenge of which he spoke, that we live in a world in which the great powers have poised and aimed at each other horrible missiles of destruction, that can, in a matter of minutes, arrive in each others' country and destroy virtually the civilized world we live in.
>
> And suddenly it dawned on me.
>
> Those who would read this letter a hundred years from now will know whether those missiles were fired. They will know whether we met our challenge. Whether they have the freedoms that we have known up until now will depend on what we do here.
>
> Will they look back with appreciation and say, 'Thank God for those people of 1976 who headed off that loss of freedom, who kept our world from nuclear destruction?'
>
> And if we fail, they probably won't get to read the letter at all because it spoke of individual freedom and that won't be allowed to talk of that or read of it.
>
> This is our challenge. And this is why, here in this hall tonight, better than we've ever done before, we have got to quit talking to each other and about each other, and go out and communicate to the world that we may be fewer in numbers than we've ever been but we carry the message they're waiting for.

Turning to Ford, Reagan ended: "We must go forth from here united, determined, that what a great general said a few years ago is true, 'There's no substitute for victory,' Mr. President."

Vice President Rockefeller rushed to shake Reagan's hand, saying "Beautiful, just beautiful." As Reagan made his exit, TV cameras panned around the convention hall searching in vain for a dry eye. A Reagan campaign aide remarked that "Ford has just given the future of the party to Reagan." It did not escape notice that Reagan had never mentioned Ford directly in his remarks.

And then it was over. Reagan had appeared near tears himself earlier in the day when making farewell remarks to his campaign staff. In a slightly hushed voice, Reagan concluded: "Don't get cynical because, look at what you were willing to do and recognize that there are millions and millions of Americans out there who want what you want, that want it to be that way, that want it to be a shining city on a hill." Reagan's voice broke a little. Nancy Reagan turned away from cameras to hide her visible tears. Reagan gave a half shrug, seemingly overcome with emotion and unable to continue, and walked out of the room. Clarke Reed, chairman of the Mississippi delegation whose swing to Ford was pivotal in Reagan's defeat, had turned up for Reagan's farewell remarks, and was heard to say "I've made the worst mistake of my life."[31] Reed was right. Four years later, after Reagan won the White House, Reed was frozen out of the administration, while Drew Lewis, whose demonstration of loyalty in holding the Pennsylvania delegation for Ford, was rewarded with the cabinet post at Transportation.

THE FINAL CONVENTION battles revealed much about Reagan's character, including his quick embrace of bold strokes (the Schweiker pick), his loyalty and stubbornness (Schweiker offered to withdraw when conservatives raised a ruckus, but Reagan refused, telling Schweiker "I'm not going to leave this convention with my tail between my legs, and neither are you"), and his broad historical vision (the meditation on the problem of nuclear weapons in his impromptu convention speech clearly presaged his negotiating strategy—arms *reduction* rather than control—as president in the 1980s). He also showed a sense of his own power in his handling of the vice-presidential nomination.

It would have made the most sense for Ford to have Reagan as his running mate, since Reagan had won so many primaries with Democratic crossover votes. And for most conventional politicians, especially at age 65 with uncertain prospects of reaching the summit of the party again, the number two spot would seem highly attractive. Not only did Reagan repeatedly and publicly refuse, but he made it a condition of meeting with

Ford at the convention that Ford not ask him to be the running mate. Most of Reagan's close advisers thought Reagan would have accepted out of duty had Ford pressed him (and Reagan later said as much), but Ford honored Reagan's demand. And then Reagan used the meeting to exercise a veto over several prospective running mates from the liberal wing of the party, especially Elliott Richardson. Sen. Robert Dole, however, met with Reagan's enthusiasm. Dole, for his part, had thought he might be a possible running mate—on a Reagan-led ticket. One final note: In drawing up his list of potential running mates, Ford became the first nominee to give serious consideration to a woman: Ambassador Anne Armstrong of Texas. Armstrong's name was eliminated from consideration when Ford's test polls showed that voters would look negatively on a woman running mate. Feminism had a ways to go yet.

There was not much joy among the Republican faithful as they left the Kansas City convention. Polls showed President Ford trailing Jimmy Carter by 30 points. Carter was the political phenomenon of the decade, and it seemed Ford had little chance even to make a close race. The eventual closeness of the contest was only a superficial sign of the continuing volatility of the political scene.

DURING ONE OF HIS lowest points in the "wilderness years" of the 1930s, Winston Churchill wrote: "If we look back on our past life we shall see that one of its most usual experiences is that we have been helped by our mistakes and injured by our most sagacious decisions."[32] Had Reagan won the nomination in 1976 yet lost to Carter in November (polls in the summer showed him trailing Carter by a larger margin than Ford), it is doubtful that he would have been able to capture the GOP nomination again in 1980. But perhaps he would have defeated Carter. It is possible to play out a number of counterfactual scenarios based on the premise of a Reagan presidency in the late 1970s, as Reagan would surely have handled inflation, Iran, Central America, the energy crisis, and arms control very differently than Jimmy Carter did. Yet dealing in counterfactuals is always fatuous, and in Reagan's case it is just as easy to conjure plausible scenarios of ruin and disaster. Could Reagan have gotten any of his legislative programs through the lopsided Democratic majority in Congress? Would Reagan have had to send U.S. troops to quell an uprising in

Panama when he cancelled treaty negotiations over the canal? William F. Buckley Jr. always considered this a likely possibility, and concluded that the luckiest thing to happen to Reagan was *losing* the Panama Canal fight in 1978; had the United States rejected the treaties and had to quell violence in the Canal Zone, Reagan would have been blamed. Regardless of where the balance of judgment comes down on such speculation, Reagan's experience can be said to parallel Churchill's in some respects. Just as Churchill's exclusion from the government in the late 1930s absolved him of the blame for the calamity he had predicted and thereby left him in an unassailable position in 1940, so too Reagan's return to the political wilderness in 1976 would turn out to his advantage in 1980.

At the moment, however, Reagan's future prospects looked dim. At 65, this seemed his last hurrah, though this had been said before. *Newsweek* magazine, which had run the headline "Ronald Reagan's Slow Fade" in 1971 (see chapter 7), now offered a reprise: "Into the Sunset." The concluding line of Reagan's convention speech—"There is no substitute for victory," *Newsweek* wrote, "could also turn out to be a epitaph for his own political career." The post-mortems on the mistakes of the Reagan campaign began to roll in. The $90 billion speech and his early pullout from campaigning in New Hampshire were obvious mistakes. Failing to contest several primaries could also be said to have cost him the nomination; just a handful of delegates from a few of the uncontested states would have made the difference. The Schweiker pick, while perhaps keeping the outcome uncertain, had tarnished Reagan's image as the principled leader of the conservative movement. Throughout media comment ran the thought that Reagan might conceivably run again in 1980, but at close to 70, it was unlikely he could succeed. This had been his moment, and the moment had slipped away.

National Review, Reagan's chief media cheerleader, faulted Reagan for not running a more aggressive campaign against the liberal wing of the party: "From its beginning, the Reagan challenge was inhibited by deference to the sensibilities of the impotent, vestigial wing of the party. . . . The very meaning of his rebellion entailed the destruction of that older Republican Establishment, now clustered around Ford. It meant insurgency against it. . . . The Reagan strategy sought to avoid a direct and bruising collision with its real opponents."[33] Still another *National*

Review writer wondered whether it was not poor strategy and tactics that undid Reagan, but the prospect that times had passed him by, that Reagan was washed up:

> Reagan seems somewhat out of step with the new political stirrings, a man very much of the Sixties. Reagan is most vividly remembered against a backdrop of chaos, with scenes from Berkeley and the characters from the New Left. But the backdrop has changed dramatically. . . . [P]erhaps he was simply the right man for the wrong time; the issues to which he addressed himself and the language in which he addressed them seem a throwback to a very recent but rapidly fading past. . . .
>
> It is difficult to say this, and especially difficult for one who is a long-time Reagan admirer. For a decade he has been a central symbol of everything that is best in what we call the conservative movement, and if his approach and his ideas are obsolete, then so are those many of us who believe in him. And it's never much fun to be a middle-aged anachronism.[34]

The present moment belonged not to Reagan, but to the other sunbelt phenomenon, Jimmy Carter, whose rise to political prominence was even more sudden and extraordinary than Reagan's. Like Reagan, Carter promised to reverse America's sour mood. He would, instead, make America's distemper worse, and provide the perfect foil for Reagan's comeback in 1980.

CHAPTER ELEVEN

THE EDUCATION

OF JIMMY CARTER

———➤●◄———

I N FEBRUARY 1975, Marie Jahn, the Recorder for Plymouth
County, Iowa, was retiring after 38 years on the job. Local Democrats
wanted to give her a testimonial dinner, complete with a speaker of national prominence. The only person they could get to come cheaply was
the little-known former governor of Georgia. For his part, Jimmy Carter
was delighted. Carter's strategists had singled out the early Iowa caucuses
as a neglected opportunity to win some convention delegates and campaign momentum. Carter had been looking for opportunities to wholesale himself to Iowa Democrats, but the Jahn testimonial dinner was the
best he could do so far.[1] The chair of the Iowa Democratic Party had told
Carter to "forget about Iowa—it's not your kind of state." Carter ignored
this friendly advice, and visited Iowa another seven times in 1975. In January 1976, Carter put the Iowa caucuses, and himself, on the national political map by winning 28 percent of the vote. (Carter actually finished
second behind an "uncommitted" delegate slate, but "uncommitted"
can't be elected president.)

Eagerly attending a testimonial dinner for a minor local functionary
no one in Washington had ever heard of was typical of Carter's go-
anywhere, meet-anyone style of campaigning that brought him from obscurity to the White House. Carter's ascension in 1976 is often explained
as a fluke of the post-Watergate political climate. Nathan Miller, author of
a book about America's 10 worst presidents, wrote that "Electing Jimmy

Carter president was as close as the American people have ever come to picking a name out of the phone book and giving him the job."[2] This is unfair. Although Carter exploited the post-Watergate moment with great skill, to judge him a fluke does a disservice to his relentless determination. His extraordinary stamina led political reporters to call him "the first bionic candidate." "Jimmy Carter's creation of a national organization from scratch between 1974 and 1976 was a work of brilliance," is Chris Matthews' more creditable judgment.[3] The real amazement of Carter was that he foresaw *before* Watergate what characteristics the voters would most desire in a candidate in 1976. Watergate was a bonus.

The idea to run for president was hatched midway through Carter's term as governor. After being spurned as a potential running mate for McGovern, Carter's close friends and aides thought to themselves, why not run for president? In September 1972, Carter's young political aides Hamilton Jordan, Jody Powell, and Peter Bourne went to Carter with their audacious plan. Jordan had worked out the nuts and bolts of how Carter could reach the nomination. First, Jordan wrote in a now-famous memo, position yourself as the alternative to George Wallace on the Right, and Ted Kennedy on the Left. (Both Kennedy and Wallace were presumed to be the front-runners in the Democratic Party in 1976.) Second, run in every primary, which Jordan later likened to "running for sheriff in 50 states." Third, begin cultivating the national media, a prelude to generating the all-important national coverage of any early primary breakthroughs. Above all, Carter's main selling point would be his personal charm, and his emphasis of personal character over particular issues. "I don't think we underestimated what a long shot it was," Powell said, "but we saw how it could be done."[4]

Still, as veteran political reporter Jules Witcover put it, "The idea of Jimmy Carter running for President was absurd on its face." It was, Witcover reiterated, a "seemingly ludicrous proposition that the country should put itself into the hand of a peanut-farming one-term former governor of a Deep South state."[5] "Unlikely" seemed like the kindest word that could be used to describe Carter's prospects. Zachary Taylor had been the last Southerner elected President—in 1848. Even Carter's friends and family were startled. When Carter told his family that he intended to run for president, his mother reportedly asked, "President of what?" Atlanta businessman Marvin Shoob recalls that when he came to a 1974 luncheon to discuss Governor Carter's intention to run for president, Shoob assumed Carter was aiming for the presidency of the Atlanta Chamber of Commerce.[6] Carter himself admitted that "we were at first embarrassed about the use of the word 'president.'" Carter's obscurity was confirmed when he appeared on the syndicated TV game show "What's My Line?" He stumped the panel, which not only didn't recognize him, but failed to guess he was a state governor. When pollster George Gallup drew up a list of 38 potential Democratic presidential candidates in 1975, Carter's name was not on the list.

It was inevitable that the smiley-face decade would produce a smiley-face candidate, and Carter's most prominent attribute was a grin toothier than a Cheshire cat. Like the Cheshire cat of Lewis Carroll, what lay behind the grin was mysterious. Hamilton Jordan referred candidly to what he called Carter's "weirdness factor." He was the first president to use his nickname ("Jimmy," instead of James Earl) when being sworn in as president, and also the only man to ever hold the job who had filed a UFO sighting report with the Air Force. (He was also the first president who was born in a hospital.) His family story seemed like a rejected script for a sequel to *The Beverly Hillbillies*. Carter had the unlikely background as a peanut farmer (although his principal business was actually peanut *warehousing*—much more lucrative than growing), and his cousin Hugh Carter operated a large worm farm.

More unusual was his religious faith. Carter was a "born-again" Southern Baptist who had gone on evangelistic missions to Pennsylvania and Massachusetts following his loss in the governor's race in 1966. His sister, Ruth Carter Stapleton, was a faith-healer of some prominence within fundamentalist Christian circles. The phenomenon of "born-again" evangelicalism was breaking large on the American scene in the mid-1970s, and Carter rode the wave. Pollster George Gallup labeled 1976 the "year of the evangelical," and a *Newsweek* cover story entitled "Born Again!" observed that "Carter's dramatic capture of the Presidential nomination has already focused national attention on the most significant—and overlooked—religious phenomenon of the '70s: the emergence of evangelical Christianity into a position of respect and power."[7] (This was perhaps the last time evangelical Christianity would be treated in a positive light by a major media organ.)

It was this dimension of Carter's persona that provided him with the mystique that captured the public imagination in 1976, and almost certainly it was the votes of "born-again" Christians that made the margin of difference in a close election. Since the Civil War, evangelicals had never given the majority of their votes to a Democratic presidential candidate. Typical of evangelical enthusiasm for Carter were the words of the Rev. Lou Sheldon, who became nationally famous in the 1980s for his ultraconservative Traditional Values Coalition: "God has his hand upon Jimmy Carter to run for President. Of course, he's wise enough not to be presumptuous with the will of God. But he's moving in the will of God."[8] And the Rev. Pat Robertson trekked to Carter's home in Plains, Georgia, to tape a laudatory segment for his fledgling TV show, "The 700 Club."

Carter was a walking example of the enigmatic biblical injunction to render unto Caesar what is Caesar's and render unto God what is God's. Carter was fond of saying "My religion is as natural to me as breathing," yet at one point in the 1976 campaign Carter said he was "concerned" that people were putting too much emphasis on his profession of faith. "I did not want to mix in religion and my duties as president," he told Peter Bourne before the fall campaign.[9] Yet Carter also told his fellow Baptists that "There's no doubt in my mind that my campaign for the presidency is what God wants me to do."[10] Then there was the studied ambiguity of Carter's signature theme in his stump speech: "If I had to sum up in one word what this campaign is about, that word would be *faith*. The American people want to have *faith* in their government." The invocation of "faith" was clearly a carefully thought-out crossover word; it served as an explicit appeal to his co-religionists, and also to the non-believing masses who had lost confidence in government. Above all, both believers and non-believers, it was tacitly suggested, could have faith in Jimmy Carter. It laid the foundation for Carter's most grandiose promise: "I'll never lie to you." After Johnson and Nixon, after Vietnam and Watergate, the nation wanted a saint. Carter's religion allowed him to assert the requisite sainthood indirectly. His 1976 campaign speechwriter Patrick Anderson sensed that Carter's private belief was "that he had been 'born again' not only in a religious sense but in a political sense."[11] True to the last, Carter's post-presidential memoirs are titled *Keeping Faith*.

The complexity and contradictions of Jimmy Carter were not limited to the uneasy status of his religious belief. The same man who could say "I'm basically a redneck" was also given to serving up quotes from neo-orthodox theologians such as Karl Barth, Paul Tillich, and Reinhold

Niebuhr. He also liked to quote America's favorite pop theologian, Bob Dylan. Carter was an intensely serious man (he claimed to have read Tolstoy's *War and Peace* at age 12), but there was a superficiality in the way he employed these intellectual blurbs. His favorite quote from Niebuhr was, "The sad duty of politics is to establish justice in a sinful world." Why is establishing justice a "sad duty," unless there is an ineluctable understanding that in a sinful world, establishing perfect justice is impossible, and therefore that politics has inherent limits? Carter never offered any reflections on this problem, which is central to the relation of religion and politics.

Following a conversation with Carter about theology during the campaign, the liberal journalist (and former seminarian) Garry Wills observed: "For a bright and educated modern man, dealing with the thing he says matters most to him, he shows an extraordinarily reined-in curiosity. It suggests a kind of willed narrowness of mastery." Years later, after Carter left the White House, Wills returned to this theme, writing that Carter's "narrow and repetitive intensity of his thought about religion . . . was one key to the personal narrowness that remains one's lasting impression of him in the presidency."[12] William F. Buckley Jr. would later summarize the problem with Carter thus: "Mr. Carter's difficulty is his overweening idealistic appetite combined with the humiliation of living in a sinful world."

The "narrowness" that Garry Wills and others discerned in Carter was more than just a reflection of his quirky intellect. Beneath the toothy grin and behind the Baptist piety was a hard-bitten toughness that at times verged on ruthlessness. Patrick Anderson described him as a combination of Machiavelli and Mr. Rogers. The *Washington Post*'s Sally Quinn observed: "The conventional image of a sexy man is one who is hard on the outside and soft on the inside. Carter is just the opposite."[13] Fellow Southern Baptist Bill Moyers said, "In a ruthless business, Mr. Carter is a ruthless operator, even if he wears his broad smile and displays his southern charm."[14] Speechwriter Bob Shrum, who left Carter's campaign after just 10 days because of his doubts about Carter's veracity, said "There were no private smiles."

The reputation for ruthlessness came not only from his alleged campaign dirty tricks in his Georgia elections, but from his slipperiness about the issues, and about his own ideological makeup. "I was never a liberal," Carter told Georgia voters in the governor's race in 1970. "I am and have always been a conservative."[15] (Carter received only 7 percent of the black vote in the 1970 Democratic primary.) In the run-up to the 1976 campaign, Carter variously described his philosophy as "benevolent conservatism" or "enlightened conservatism." Even after he became president, Carter would periodically proclaim that "I am a very conservative Southern businessman by heritage."[16] He touted as his chief accomplishment as governor of Georgia a sweeping reorganization of the state's administrative structure. Carter described it as "a revolution in state government that got rid of 278 of 300 state agencies and reduced administrative costs by 50 percent."

It was the same kind of thing you might expect from Ronald Reagan. In fact, Carter had used some of Governor Reagan's same methods, such as enlisting a team of private sector business executives to suggest changes to the state's management structure. Judging the results of this effort was difficult. Skeptics pointed out that while the number of state agencies went from 300 to 22, it may have represented nothing more than a consolidation of the organizational chart with a still larger bureaucracy. The number of state employees under Carter grew 30 percent during his four-year term, and total state spending grew nearly 60 percent. Still, on the basis of this experience Carter promised that as President he would cut the number of federal agencies from 1,900 to 200. Which ones and how, he could not specify.

Yet his plan to downsize the Washington bureaucracy was only a small particular of his general theme, which was to portray himself as an anti-establishment outsider. He began his early stump speeches: "I am not a lawyer, I am not a member of Congress, and I've never served in Washington." It took chutzpah for a Democrat to attack the capital city that Democrats had dominated for the last generation, but Carter carried it off with aplomb. It was not entirely an act. When he ventured to the House of Representatives chamber to deliver his first address to Congress in 1977, it was also the first time he had ever been inside the U.S. Capitol. His attacks on Washington were virtually indistinguishable from Ronald Reagan's own stump speeches of 1976.

Reagan: "Our nation's capital has become the seat of a buddy system that functions for its own benefit—increasingly insensitive to the needs of the American worker who supports it with his taxes. Today it is difficult to find leaders who are independent of the forces that have brought us our problems—the Congress, the bureaucracy, the lobbyists, big business, and big labor."

Carter: "The people of the country feel they've been betrayed. . . . The competence of government is not an accepted characteristic any more. No matter what a person hopes to do ultimately in life, no matter what his top hope or aspiration may be, he feels, generally, that Washington is an obstacle to the realization of that hope. . . . We know from bitter experience that we're not going to get the changes we need simply by shifting around the same group of Washington insiders. . . . Washington has become a huge, wasteful, unmanageable, insensitive, bloated bureaucratic mess."

Other Carter themes could have come straight from the speeches of Reagan. The income tax code, Carter said with deliberate southern drawl, "is a *dis*-grace to the human race." He promised welfare reform with a conservative tinge: "There ought to be a 'work incentive' aspect built in," and "we should remove from welfare those people who can work full time." "We should decentralize power," Carter added. "When there is a choice between government responsibility and private responsibility, we should always go with private responsibility." Reagan could hardly have put it differently, or better.

However much Carter's campaign resume may have made him seem like an outsider, by 1976 he had become a consummate insider of the American Establishment, which is merely the parent company of the Washington Establishment. During his years as Georgia governor Carter sought every opportunity to make connections with the wider world outside Georgia. He made trade missions to Europe and the Far East, making sure to meet foreign leaders. He ingratiated himself with David Rockefeller, and won Rockefeller's appointment to represent the United States on his prestigious Trilateral Commission. By far the most important assignment Carter sought was the chairmanship of the Democratic National Committee's campaign effort on behalf of Democrats in the 1974 election. The campaign chairmanship is normally an honorary position, but Carter saw it as an opportunity to travel the country laying the groundwork for his 1976 presidential campaign. He paid special effort to get on the good side of Chicago Mayor Richard Daley, and the effort paid off when Daley publicly endorsed Carter at a crucial moment in the 1976 primaries. The irony is that DNC general chairman Robert Strauss picked Carter partly because he thought Carter was one person who would not use the post to promote himself to party leaders around the country. Strauss admitted later that his appointment of Carter "let the Trojan Peanut into the National Committee encampment."[17] Carter's political positioning was a parallel of the New Testament injunction that Christians should be *in* but not *of* the world; by 1976 Carter was *in* the Establishment, but could claim he was not *of* it.

Carter's presentation of himself as a pious outsider served to mitigate the weakness of his regional identity and his limited experience in public office, which consisted of a single term as a state senator and a single term as governor—surely one of the thinnest resumes of any modern American president. Yet a number of persistent traits seemed to belie his image of a straightforward, upright character.

In 1979 he attracted public attention by remarking at a press luncheon that if Sen. Ted Kennedy challenged him for the Democratic nomination in 1980, he (Carter) would "whip his ass." This was old hat to journalists who had covered Carter in 1976, when "kiss my ass" was Carter's frequent and favorite epithet. "I'm glad I don't have to kiss his ass," Carter said of Ted Kennedy in May 1976, when he (Carter) was closing in on the nomination. When a journalist asked Carter what would he do if a member of his Cabinet lied to Congress, Carter snapped, "I'd fire his ass."[18] These departures from "born again" piety were nothing compared to the cognitive dissonance his famous *Playboy* interview generated six weeks before the November election. It wasn't simply the oddity of Carter confessing to virtual adultery by having "lusted in his heart" after women—this was orthodox New Testament teaching for evangelicals and fundamentalists, even if the sophisticates of the media didn't recognize it. It was his deliberate use of crude language in discussing the subject that startled.

> I've looked upon a lot of women with lust. I've committed adultery in my heart many times. This is something that God recognizes I will do—and I have done it—and God forgives me for it. But that doesn't mean I condemn someone who not only looks at women with lust but who leaves his wife and *shacks up* with somebody out of wedlock.
>
> Christ says, "Don't consider yourself better than someone else because one guy *screws a whole bunch of women* while the other guy is loyal to his wife." (Emphasis added.)

"Screws a whole bunch of women" is not a common translation of the Gospel passage about adultery. It was language not far removed from the Nixon Watergate tapes. And at the same time the *Playboy* interview was out, Norman Mailer quoted Carter in the *New York Times Magazine:* "'I don't care if people say _____,' and he [Carter] actually said the famous four-letter word that the *Times* has not printed in the 125 years of its publishing life. He got it out without a backing up of phlegm or a hitch in his rhythm." Was Carter's language a deliberate attempt to appeal to the hip readership of *Playboy* and the secular readers of the *New York Times?* Was he trying to send the signal *I'm not a freak?* Was he trying to ingratiate himself with the macho Mailer and *Playboy*'s interviewer, the secular and very left wing Robert Scheer?

Politicians at this high level typically choose their words carefully, and though all of them commit a "gaffe" from time to time, it is possible to see a pattern in Carter's gaffes that suggest his sense of political calculation and subtle advantage overrode his sincerity. The biggest flap of his campaign occurred in April 1976 when, during questioning about integration issues, Carter blurted out: "I see nothing wrong with ethnic purity being maintained. I would not force a racial integration of a neighborhood by government action." The reporter conducting the interview, Sam Roberts of the New York *Daily News,* buried the quote in a jump paragraph that appeared on page 134 of the paper. Rather than disappearing, however, the phrase "ethnic purity" ignited a firestorm. Under fierce questioning four days later, Carter poured gasoline on the fire: "What I say is that the government ought not to take as a major purpose the intrusion of alien groups into a neighborhood simply to establish their intrusion." This catapulted the story onto the front page of the *New York Times* and onto the TV network news. "Ethnic purity" and "alien intrusion" were red flags to liberals and civil rights groups, and Carter had to work mightily to mend fences.

But was it an unintentional slip? This flap arose after Carter had vanquished Wallace in the Florida primary, and on the eve of a series of crucial northern primaries in states where Wallace had done well previously. Careful observers noted that while Carter included Martin Luther King Jr. on his roster of great Americans, he conveniently omitted King's name before audiences of Southern or suburban whites. Carter knew that Democrats had been losing the votes of suburban voters in the North because

of busing and integration. Carter's aides denied the implication when reporters pressed the question. Yet Patrick Anderson recalled "Another
time, at a rally in West Virginia, he [Carter] told a dumb joke about some
tourists in Miami who started yelling 'Hialeah!' (the race track) instead of
'Hallelujah!' in church. Reporters immediately asked me if he could possibly be unaware that a West Virginia audience might take that as 'a Jew
joke,' since at certain levels of southern humor all visitors to Miami are
assumed to be Jews."[19]

Then there was Carter's elusiveness on major issues. "On a range of
issues," Jules Witcover wrote, "he showed all the elusiveness of a scat-
back."[20] Carter had a way of making a refusal to give a plain answer to a
direct question an act of political morality. He could carry off the most
audacious contradictions with a confidence bordering on belligerence.
Despite his explicit attacks on Washington as "a bloated bureaucratic
mess" and an "obstacle to hope," Carter asserted to a stunned press conference in Washington that "I'm not anti-Washington; I've never made an
anti-Washington statement."[21] Typical of Carter's ability to straddle was
his handling of the abortion issue in the Iowa caucuses. The 1976 election
was the first presidential election since *Roe v. Wade,* and the politics of
the issue were still crystallizing. But there were over a half million Roman
Catholics in Iowa, so when Carter met with Catholic clergy, he emphasized that he opposed abortion as a matter of personal conviction, and
though he would not support a constitutional amendment banning abortion, he would support a "national statute" regulating abortion, whatever
that meant.

"I would prefer a stricter ruling" was his comment when asked about
Roe v. Wade. This was good enough for pro-lifers in Iowa, some of whom
spoke up from the pulpit that Carter was their man. No one knew that he
had written a forward to a book, *Women in Need,* that advocated abortion rights, or that he had encouraged the plaintiffs in *Doe v. Bolton,* the
Georgia abortion rights case that had been the companion to *Roe v.
Wade,* or that he had supported abortion as a part of Georgia family
planning programs as governor.[22] Witcover summarized the incident:
"Carter's handling of the abortion issue in Iowa was a signal of things to
come. He would display a talent for being on two sides of an issue that
both dismayed and frustrated his opponents. In a political society accus-
tomed to having its leading figures neatly compartmentalized as liberals

and conservatives, Carter defied such categorizing."[23] William F. Buckley Jr. wrote that "Carter's position on abortion is more variously conjugated than French irregular verbs."

So who was the real Jimmy Carter? Neither Carter's rivals nor the media could figure him out, or out how to punch through the veneer. Patrick Anderson says that in Carter's home town of Plains, neighbors said of him that after an hour you love him, after a week you hate him, and after 10 years you start to understand him. Anderson added that anyone who didn't have a personality conflict with Carter, didn't have a personality. "Carter was never a regular guy," Anderson added; "the sum of his parts never quite added up to that. . . . Carter talked his way into the presidency, yet in some profound way he never learned the language of men."[24]

Liberals distrusted him, despite his soothing reassurances that he was in sympathy with their goals. "This independent stance of his," Rep. Mo Udall, his principal rival on the left during the primaries, "may just be a camouflage for a 'closet conservative.'"[25] Mark Shields, then working as an adviser to Udall, complained that Carter "has more positions than the *Kama Sutra.*" Bob Dole, Gerald Ford's running mate, tried to pin Carter as a liberal, calling him "southern-fried McGovern." "Carter's like Gatsby," a journalist told *National Review*; "I don't know where he comes from."[26]

Figuring out the "real Carter," *The New Republic*'s Richard Strout wrote, became "the greatest manhunt in political history. . . . I have never seen a candidate like him."[27] George Will observed that "Carter seems to believe that the way to keep knowledge pure is to keep it scarce."[28] A major labor union leader told the *Washington Post*'s David Broder: "I don't know who he is, where he's going, or where he's been."[29] Reg Murphy, editor of the *Atlanta Constitution* during Carter's years as governor, was less intrigued, calling Carter "one of the three or four phoniest men I ever met."[30] Chris Matthews described Carter as "a country slicker."[31] Steven Brill summarized the growing unease of the press with his observation that "His is the most sincerely insincere, politically antipolitical, and slickly unslick campaign of the year."[32]

Even Willie Sutton, of bank robbing fame ("Because that's where the money is") got in on the act, saying of Carter that "I've never seen a bigger confidence man in my life, and I've been around some of the best in the business."[33] Jokes about Carter's fuzziness began appearing in the media. When his father asked him if he had chopped down the family's beloved peach tree, went one popular gag, Jimmy replied, "Well, perhaps." Comedian Pat Paulsen quipped that "They wanted to put Carter on Mount Rushmore, but they didn't have room for two more faces."

Yet it worked. It might not have worked had not Carter enjoyed the luxury of having the liberal opposition in the primaries divided among *five* candidates. Carter had discovered how to succeed at being all things to all people, at least for the moment. Carter made more campaign promises than any successful presidential candidate in history (his staff counted more than 200; a complete list prepared by his staff required 111 pages).[34] Exit polls in the primaries showed that even people who voted for Carter were unsure of his stands on the issues. Carter's own pollster Pat Caddell found *on election day in November* that "fifty percent of the public still does not know where Carter stands on the issues."[35]

A *New York Times*–CBS poll on the eve of the Democratic convention in July found that 52 percent of the public thought Carter was a conservative, while a Harris poll in late September found that Carter "comes across as more conservative to conservative voters, more middle-of-the-road to middle-of-the-roaders, and more liberal to liberals."[36] Even *National Review* thought Carter had some conservative promise. Former Agnew speechwriter John Coyne wrote that "There are many things to recommend Carter. As a devout Christian, he is also a dedicated anti-Communist. As a firm believer in the afterlife, he can be counted upon not to attempt to build the perfect society here on earth."[37]

It is a mistake to dismiss Carter's performance as simply skillful wishy-washiness. Carter's straddling ability kept the Democratic Party's conservative Wallace wing from openly splitting from the liberal McGovern wing. Another pure-blooded liberal nominee like McGovern would surely have lost to Ford (Carter's plunging lead in the fall campaign coincided with voters coming to see that he was not a conservative), and precipitated a cataclysmic crisis in the party. Bridging the two wings of the party was a considerable achievement, which he accomplished by subsuming the liberal wing of the party beneath his campaign of character over issues. This presented a terrible dilemma for liberals and liberalism, for it enabled liberalism to postpone confronting its problems for another decade. Few liberals understood the truth of political scientist Walter Dean Burnham's judgment at the time: "Carter's nomination by the Democratic party will virtually certify that activist liberalism, as a national political force, is now in receivership."[38] Carter's reliance on liberals to staff his administration enabled the liberal wing of the party to persist in failing to recognize its difficulties and to consolidate its near-complete dominance over the Democratic Party.

Even though Carter had never topped 54 percent in any contested primary, did not win a single head-to-head race, and lost eight of the last 15 primaries, he nevertheless went into the Democratic convention with a solid lock on the nomination. Sixty-four percent of delegates told an NBC survey that they had "reservations" about Carter, but it was too late; a series of "Stop Carter" movements among party liberals never gained traction. This weakness enabled Carter to maintain his studied distance from liberals; he turned down Ted Kennedy's offer to place Carter's name in nomination at the convention. He kept up his "just folks" image right into his nomination acceptance speech, which began: "My name is Jimmy Carter, and I'm still running for president." He enjoyed a seemingly insurmountable 30-point lead in the polls over either Ford or Reagan (whose contest had not yet been decided at the time of the Democratic convention). Patrick Anderson commented: "If he had packed up that night and flown home to Plains and gone fishing until election day, he might have won by a landslide."

"Unfortunately," Anderson added, "he campaigned."[39]

IT WAS INEVITABLE that a nominee whom 95 percent of the public had never heard of a year before would suffer erosion in the polls as election day neared. Hamilton Jordan had predicted in July that the race would be neck-and-neck by election day. What was not inevitable was the many ways Carter found to squander his big lead. "Carter's course," *National Review* observed on October 1, "has resembled that of a football team which, after a dazzling string of pre-season victories, throws away the winning game plan and adopts an inferior one for the actual season."[40] "It may be that Jimmy Carter was overexposed," Ken Bode wrote in *The New Republic,* "that his message of love, trust and goodness began to curdle among those voters given the largest doses."[41]

The vagueness on the issues that had served Carter so well in the primaries began to plague him as the fall campaign unfolded. The prevarications of the spring became prejudicial in the fall. Repeatedly he was asked for details of his proposal for "sweeping tax reform" that he promised in the spring would be forthcoming "after the convention." Repeatedly Carter answered, "I just can't answer that question because I haven't gone into it. . . . It is just not possible to do that on a campaign trail." Some sloppy phrasing about raising taxes on those above "the median income" seemed to imply that Carter would raise taxes on more than half of American households, and was quickly disavowed. Carter was alternatively for defense cuts, but also for military strength, for dé-tente, but for being tougher on the Soviets, against abortion, but against any effective restrictions on abortion, for new social spending, but also for a balanced budget and against tax increases. More and more media accounts were starting to dwell on Carter's "flip-flops."

Then there were the tactical mistakes on the stump. Carter promised a "blanket pardon" (which he somehow distinguished from amnesty) to Vietnam draft dodgers—in a speech before the conservative American Legion. The audience of 15,000 erupted in loud boos, and Carter had to stop speaking until the Legion convention chairman could gavel the audience into silence. The scene was the lead story in the next day's news. In another speech Carter said that according to the teachings of his church, homosexuality was a sin. It was one thing to say this in the Bible belt states such as Iowa or Alabama, but Carter gave this speech in *San Francisco,* where it could hardly have motivated the gay community to lend him enthusiastic support.

At the traditionally lighthearted and strictly nonpartisan Al Smith dinner in New York in October, Carter stepped over the line with brazenly partisan remarks. "Carter Booed at Al Smith Dinner" was the lead headline of the next day's news coverage. The aforementioned *Playboy* interview was the biggest mistake, cutting into his support among women and evangelicals. The Rev. W. A. Criswell of Dallas, Texas, pastor of the largest Southern Baptist congregation in the nation, promptly endorsed Ford. Carter did display one of his few flashes of humor over the *Playboy* episode. When asked by a reporter for his reaction to the interview, Carter replied that he hadn't read it yet. "I looked at the other parts [of the magazine] first," he told the New York *Daily News.*

The sensational sex talk of the *Playboy* interview overshadowed a more significant political gaffe contained elsewhere in the same interview. At the very end of the interview, Carter had said, "I don't think I would ever take on the same frame of mind that Nixon or Johnson did—lying, cheating and distorting the truth." Johnson may have been an unpopular figure among liberal Democrats, but to equate him with Nixon was stepping into a deep pile of trouble. Lady Bird Johnson was furious, and Carter was about to campaign in Texas. Arriving in Houston, Carter tried to suggest that *Playboy* had conjured up an unfortunate "paraphrase" or "summary" of his remarks. But the phrase was a verbatim quotation, captured on tape. Reporters were outraged. "The candidate who promised never to tell a lie had told a whopper," Patrick Anderson wrote.

Was this another of Carter's Freudian slips, like "ethnic purity," or was this another subtle indication of Carter's above-it-all attitude that caused him to remain deliberately aloof from other Democrats throughout the campaign? In local campaign stops Carter eschewed the familiar photo opportunity with the local Democratic congressional candidate, and seldom endorsed the local Democrat in his remarks to crowds. It was as if he was running as a virtual Independent. Democrats around the country reciprocated Carter's aloofness. The *Washington Post* commented: "Even now, as Carter crisscrosses the country, the old-time Democratic politicians greet him more often than not like a naturalized Martian rather than as a fellow soldier." "It's not that Carter's a Southerner," one Democrat was quoted; "it's him; and he's a strange guy, and people seem to sense it too."[42] "If I have to take Carter I'll take him, but I'll have to swallow hard," Pennsylvania Democratic state Senator Martin Murray said, "He scares the hell out of me."[43] "There is enough in the Carter record, as governor and campaigner, to make us apprehensive," *The New Republic* editorialized in endorsing Carter "with reservations."[44]

Worried liberals consoled themselves with the thought that at least Walter Mondale was on the ticket. "With Mondale's designation," *The New Republic* reassured itself, "the slate is bonded 100 proof liberal."[45] The *New York Times* financial page certified this judgment with the headline: "Sag in Stocks Laid to Mondale: Democratic Ticket Regarded Warily on Wall Street."

But more significant than his slips and deliberate aloofness from the Democratic Party was Carter's undercurrent of meanness, which dismayed even his closest advisers. Hamilton Jordan tried to persuade Carter to stop attacking "the Nixon-Ford administration." "The phrase 'Nixon-Ford administration,'" Jordan told Carter in a memo, suggests a very conscious effort on your part to equate Ford, the man, with Nixon, the man. This does not and will not wash with the American people and I believe will be generally interpreted as a personal attack on the integrity of Gerald Ford. When I watched you say that on the news recently, it sounded out of character for you. It certainly did not sound like the man who wanted to put Watergate behind us and unite the country.[46]

But Carter didn't let up on this or other slashing attacks on Ford. "Richard Nixon was bad enough," Carter said on the stump in Indiana in late September, adding, "It's been worse the last two years."[47] "There was an undercurrent of malice in the Carter world," Patrick Anderson observed, while Jules Witcover scored "Carter's extraordinary churlishness."

By October, the effect of Carter's smile was wearing off. He was losing about a half-point a day in the polls. By mid-October, the race was a dead heat. Ford had even closed the gap in the South. No one had ever closed such a large gap in the polls in so short a time, not even Hubert Humphrey in 1968. The race, *National Review* observed, was now between a crippled hare and a stumbling tortoise. Whoever made the last mistake would lose.

FORD'S CAMPAIGN HAD decided early on to embrace a "Rose Garden strategy" that would attempt to display Ford as an on-the-job statesman. The strategy worked, though Ford's campaign was not without its share of troubles and mishaps. Old allegations that Ford had received improper favors while minority leader in the House dominated news headlines until the Watergate special prosecutor cleared Ford of the charges. Ford's Secretary of Agriculture Earl Butz foolishly told a racist joke to Pat Boone and John Dean at the Republican convention, which Dean gleefully included in an article for *Rolling Stone* magazine in late September. Ford had to fire Butz. The razor tongue of running mate Bob Dole was expected to be an asset, but the mordant wit that charmed the Beltway (especially the media) bombed on the campaign trail. Then, as if determined not to allow Carter to have a monopoly on crudity, at a Dole campaign rally in Binghamton, New York, Vice President Rockefeller let a gang of hecklers get the best of him. As if finally letting loose after all the years of abuse he had taken from all parts of the political spectrum, Rockefeller grinned broadly and extended his middle finger—as press cameras captured the gesture for posterity. Some newspapers (but not the *New York Times*) ran the photo on the front page.

To most voters these troubles were dismissed as the usual background noise of campaign season, and did not reflect seriously on their estimation of Ford's judgment. Campaign strategist Stuart Spencer had warned Ford in August that "Because you must come from behind and are subject to so many constraints, no strategy can be developed which allows for any substantial error." The debates gave Ford the opportunity to do just that.

The Ford-Carter debates of 1976 were the first since the Nixon-Kennedy debates in 1960. Because of the legend and effect of the Nixon-Kennedy debates, where the superficiality of Nixon's appearance trumped the substance of the encounter, most presidential candidates would just as soon not have them. (Surveys of the first Nixon-Kennedy debate found that those who listened on the radio judged Nixon to have won, while those who viewed the debate on TV judged Kennedy the winner.) But as Ford was so far behind at the time he issued the challenge to debate, he seemingly had little to lose. And for the confident challenger, stepping into the ring against the incumbent president lends instant stature. The Ford-Carter debates have set a precedent for all subsequent elections. But the modern debates are scarcely debates at all. Under the famous Lincoln-Douglas format of 1858, each candidate would hold forth for as long as an hour at a time rebutting the other candidate, and each candidate would pose questions to the other. Modern presidential debates are more like joint press conferences, "about as satisfying as a completed sneeze," observed George Will, while *The New Republic* called the debates "grounds for emigration."

The Ford camp was sufficiently nervous that they insisted on a deep drinking glass well on the podium to guard against Ford knocking over his water. The first debate in late September had gone well enough for Ford, with Carter seeming stiff, nervous, and deferential. Post-debate polls judged Ford the winner, and his surge in the polls continued.

The second debate in San Francisco in early October was dedicated to foreign policy issues, and on the surface figured to favor Ford as well. Yet it was a tricky moment for both candidates. Carter had called for defense cuts, which appeased liberals, but made him vulnerable to the traditional Republican charge that Democrats are weak on defense and East-West relations. But Carter effectively blunted this charge by attacking détente from the right, even going as far as to air a TV ad in Texas quoting Reagan on foreign policy to show the similarity of Carter's views to conservative Southern voters. The Democratic platform criticized Ford's détente as little more than "bad bargains, dramatic posturing, and the stress on general declarations. . . . We must avoid assuming that the whole of American-Soviet relations is greater than the sum of its parts, that any agreement is superior to none, or that we can negotiate effectively as supplicants." (Pat Moynihan helped write the foreign policy section of the Democratic platform.)

Polls showed that a large majority of Americans thought we had been going too easy on the Soviet Union; a *Newsweek* poll at the time of the second Ford-Carter debate found 73 percent agreed with the statement that the United States had "made too many concessions to the Soviets." But the same poll found a majority approved of Henry Kissinger's job performance—a reflection either of his powerful personality or the cognitive dissonance of American public opinion. Could Ford find a way to get some of Kissinger's popularity and mystique to rub off? Carter made a point of baiting Ford in the debate, charging that "As far as foreign policy goes, Mr. Kissinger has been the president of this country."

The kind of subtlety and obfuscation that served Kissinger well in State Department press conferences and congressional testimony won't do for a televised presidential debate, but that's what Ford had in mind to try. Ford's campaign could guess that the controversial Helsinki Accords might come up, perhaps in the context of the "Sonnenfeldt Doctrine," discussed in chapter 9, that caused so much trouble earlier in the year. The National Security Council prepared the following answer for Ford's debate briefing book:

> I am baffled by this talk about a Sonnenfeldt Doctrine in Eastern Europe. You can't have it both ways. I have visited Poland, Romania and Yugoslavia as President. Our relations with and support for the countries has never been stronger. I don't see how you can talk about conceding Soviet domination in light of this record.

This was a weak answer. In a three-hour rehearsal the night before the debate, Ford offered a stronger answer when National Security Adviser Brent Scowcroft posed the Helsinki question:

The policy of this government at the present time is to recognize the independence, the sovereignty, and the autonomy of all Eastern European countries. This has been the policy of this United States since after World War II. The President of the United States believes that those countries are independent and sovereign. And we feel that all other Eastern European nations and Baltic nation countries are in the same category. The so-called Sonnenfeldt Doctrine never did exist. And I can assure you that we do not recognize any sphere of influence by any power in Europe at the present time.

But when the *New York Times'* Max Frankel posed the question to Ford in a long and convoluted form during the debate the next evening, Ford botched it with an equally convoluted answer that culminated with the clunker that "There is no Soviet domination of Eastern Europe, and there never will be under a Ford administration."

Say what? Could Ford really be saying that the Captive Nations were no longer captive? Frankel couldn't believe his ears. Up in the control booth, Brent Scowcroft, doing a quick tally of more than 30 Soviet divisions stationed in Eastern European nations, turned white.

Frankel asked a quick follow-up question to see if Ford had misspoken and wished to elaborate. "[D]id I understand you to say, sir, that the Russians are not using Eastern Europe as their own sphere of influence and occupying most of the countries there and making sure with their troops that it's a Communist zone. . . ?" At this point Ford should have heeded the maxim attributed to the British politician Denis Healey, which he called "Healey's First Law of Holes,"—if you're in one, stop digging. Ford didn't know Healey's First Law.

I don't believe, Mr. Frankel, that the Yugoslavians consider themselves dominated by the Soviet Union. I don't believe that the Romanians consider themselves dominated by the Soviet Union. I don't believe that the Poles consider themselves dominated by the Soviet Union. Each of those countries is independent, autonomous; it has its own territorial integrity. And the United States does not concede that those countries are under the domination of the Soviet Union. As a matter of fact, I visited Poland, Yugoslavia, and Romania, to make certain that the people of those countries understood that the

President of the United States and the people of the United States are
dedicated to their independence, their autonomy, and their freedom.

Carter pounced on Ford's gaffe: "I would like to see Mr. Ford convince the Polish Americans and the Czech Americans and the Hungarian
Americans in this county that those countries don't live under the domination and supervision of the Soviet Union behind the Iron Curtain."
Over the next few days Carter compared Ford to George Romney, conveying the none-too-subtle double criticism that Ford was under the
brainwashing of Kissinger, and was too dumb to know it. *Newsweek* ran
the headline: "Jerry Ford Drops a Brick." "Never during his presidency,"
The New Republic observed, "had he so completely and disastrously misspoken." William F. Buckley Jr. observed that "the last contender for the
Presidency to make such a statement was Henry Wallace, some of whose
speeches were written for him by Communists."

This gaffe represented the final farce of détente. In Paris, a group of
Eastern European dissident intellectuals that included Romanian play-
wright Eugene Ionesco issued a statement bitterly criticizing Ford: "In reality Ford's slip merely comes down to the fact that he said out loud what
he thinks—or, rather, what Kissinger and Sonnenfeldt think for him." The
Sonnenfeldt Doctrine, so carefully disavowed earlier in the year, had
come back to bite Ford a second time. It was an object lesson in what
happens when subtlety is allowed to replace moral clarity in foreign policy. Reagan frequently got himself into trouble with his mouth, but verbally liberating Eastern Europe was not the kind of blunder he would
have made in a thousand years.

Yet the manner in which Ford's whopper played out in the media
over the next few days demonstrates how the media "spin" about debates
is equally important to the substance of the debates themselves. Ford's
pollster Robert Teeter reported some chin-pulling findings from his tracking polls. A small sample of voters surveyed within the first 24 hours after
the debate judged Ford to have won by a margin of 11 points. But over
the next three days, as the news media was thick with the theme that Ford
had committed a howler, voters judged Carter the winner, by 12 points
the next day, 27 points the day after, and 45 points by the weekend. It
didn't help that Ford wouldn't take the necessary step to stop the hemorrhaging, stubbornly refusing to admit that he had misspoken for a full

five days, by which time the damage was done. His surge in the polls promptly stalled, and Carter opened up some daylight again.

Carter's final margin over Ford on election day was 50.1 to 48 percent, but it was even closer than that. Carter's large majority in the South pushed him past the 50 percent mark; outside the South, Carter lost the popular vote to Ford. A switch of 8,000 votes in Ohio and Hawaii would have given Ford a slim majority in the electoral college. Ohio is home to a large population of Eastern European immigrants, and before Ford's clunker in the second debate polls showed Ford running well with these ethnic voters, perhaps in part because Carter's Southern Baptist evangelicalism didn't sit well with these mostly Roman Catholic voters. Exit polls showed that a quarter of independent voters made up their mind in the last five days before the election. An unpublished CBS poll found that Reagan would have run slightly better than Ford, but would still have lost narrowly. A significant finding of the poll was that Reagan would have won more Democratic votes than Ford, but would have lost some moderate Republican votes.

Republicans fared poorly all the way down the ticket. Republicans lost one House seat, on top of the 43 they had lost in the post-Watergate election of 1974. The Democrats' House majority of 292–143 was nearly as large as it had been after Johnson's landslide over Goldwater in 1964. The Senate remained unchanged, with a 62–38 Democratic majority. Democrats outnumbered Republicans in state legislatures more than 2 to 1—5,116 Democrats to 2,368 Republicans. The GOP held a majority in both houses of only four state legislatures—Colorado, Idaho, South Dakota, and Wyoming—down from 20 states in 1968, and held only 12 governorships, down from 32 in 1968. Only 24 percent of all voters were registered Republicans, the lowest since the party was formed in the 1850s.

The election produced, in the words of Michael Barone, "Democratic [Party] government as far as the eye could see." Among the winners in 1976 were Albert Gore Jr., elected to the House of Representatives in Tennessee; Bill Clinton, elected Attorney General in Arkansas (he had supported Jerry Brown instead of Carter in the primaries); and Pat Moynihan, elected to the U.S. Senate in New York, defeating incumbent Sen. James Buckley, Bill Buckley's brother. (Among the other GOP losers was first-time congressional candidate Newt Gingrich.) CIA director George Bush also has to be reckoned another winner in an odd way.

Bush, on the job barely a year at Langley, wanted to stay on at CIA under Carter. Bush went to Plains, Georgia, after the election to brief the president-elect on intelligence matters and offered to remain. But Carter was too distrustful of Bush's partisan Republican past, and did Bush the favor of dismissing him. Had Bush stayed on as Carter's CIA director, the foreign policy disasters of the Carter years would have foreclosed Bush's future in Republican politics.

Once again the death knell of the Republican Party was being sounded. Carter's Pollster Pat Caddell told Carter that "The Republican Party seems bent on self-destruction. . . . They have few bright lights to offer the public." Mark Siegel, executive director of the Democratic National Committee, crowed that "The Republican Party is dying [and it] can't bounce back any more. It has the brain wave of a dead person." Neutral observers were hardly more sanguine. *New York Times* political writer Warren Weaver wrote that the Republican Party was "perhaps closer to extinction than ever before in its 122-year history." Political scientist Carl Everett Ladd wrote in *Fortune* magazine: "The important question is: Which way are things tending? For the Republicans during this past decade and a half, they have been trending downward—so steeply, in fact, that by now the trend has begun to reshape U.S. political life as a whole. . . . For the political system as a whole as well as for the party itself, the really important erosion of Republican strength is the one that has taken place during the 1960s and 1970s."

Kevin Phillips, having predicted that the Republican Party was on the cusp of creating a new majority in 1969, now concluded that the Republican Party was approaching "critical non-mass." The Ripon Society wondered whether in retrospect the Nixon victories of 1968 and 1972 weren't "like an aberrant remission for the GOP from a case of increasingly severe leukemia." Conservative electoral disappointment, Georgetown University professor Jeane Kirkpatrick wrote eight years before she became a Republican, "is probably a chronic condition." Murray Kempton said that the Republicans "have become the inert party, and the size of the inert vote is by now incalculable, since we have no way yet to measure how far their numbness extends to the rest of us." Robert Novak said the election was "a continuation of the long descent of the Republican Party into irrelevance, defeat, and perhaps eventual disappearance." Even leading Republicans agreed with these grim diagnoses. The GOP House Minority Leader John Rhodes told *Time* magazine: "If the GOP does not experience a significant change in political fortunes by 1978, it is likely to go the way of the Whigs."[48]

These judgments would prove to be wrong for a simple reason: Carter and his lopsided Democratic majority in Congress would have to govern. *National Review* presciently observed shortly after the election: "When Carter has to face as President the policy decisions he could fudge during the campaign, the divided character of the Democratic Party will surface with a vengeance. The ingredients for internecine warfare remain only too obvious."[49] This is exactly what befell Carter, starting on Inauguration Day, if not before.

WHEN THE NEW Speaker of the House, Thomas P. "Tip" O'Neill, arrived for Carter's inaugural dinner on January 20, 1977, he was stunned to find himself and his guests seated at the furthest table in the balcony, far away from the new president. "The next morning," O'Neill wrote in his memoirs, "I called Hamilton Jordan and said, 'Listen, you son of a bitch. When a guy is Speaker of the House and his family gets the worst seats in the room, he figures there's a reason behind it. I have to believe that you did that deliberately.' 'If that's the way you feel about it,' he replied, 'we'll give you back the three hundred dollars.' 'Don't be a wise guy,' I said. 'I'll ream your ass before I'm through.'"[50] From that moment on, O'Neill referred to Carter's top aide as "Hannibal Jerkin."

O'Neill's bad seats were not an oversight; Jordan had put him in the back of the room on purpose, as a none-too-subtle signal of his contempt for the Democratic establishment he and Carter's campaign had routed in the long march to the White House. (In 1979 Jordan offered O'Neill a groveling apology for his arrogance.) But the low opinion of Congress wasn't limited to Jordan. Carter himself had scant respect for Congress, apparently considering it little more than a swollen version of the Georgia state legislature that he regarded contemptuously during his single term as a state senator, and which he successfully steamrollered during his governorship. In his first meeting with Speaker O'Neill before Inauguration Day, Carter said as much, telling the Speaker that when the Georgia state legislature had blocked him, he went over their heads to the people, and would not hesitate to do so with Congress. "I can talk to your constituents easier than you can," Carter said.

O'Neill was shocked, asking Carter, "You don't mean to tell me you're comparing the House and Senate with the Georgia legislature? Hell, Mr. President, you're making a big mistake." As O'Neill put it in his memoirs, "I tried to explain how important it is for the president to work closely with the Congress. He didn't seem to understand." O'Neill tried to make it simple, pointing out to Carter that three-fourths of the members of the House had run *ahead* of Carter in their districts in the election, and would not hesitate to run *against* Carter in the future if necessary. It was to no avail. The stubbornness that had served Carter so well during the long drive to the White House would typify his relations with a Congress dominated by his own party. Carter, political scientist Charles Jones observed, "was almost incapable of saying anything nice about members of Congress even as he traveled among their constituents."[51]

Although Tip O'Neill wrote in his memoirs that Carter was the smartest public official he had ever known, his administration was "like a bad dream." Senator Daniel Inouye (D-Hawaii) echoed O'Neill's complaint: "There were very few happy moments between the Democratic leadership and Carter."[52] In a chapter of Carter's own memoirs entitled "My One-Week Honeymoon with Congress" (it is arguable that it lasted even a week), Carter blamed Congress for the trouble, noting that the majority of its House members were newly elected in the last four years, and that most Democrats had never served under a Democratic president before. He never did grasp the incompetence of his administration's relations with Congress. (In one celebrated example, when the Japanese prime minister was hosted at a White House dinner, the White House neglected to invite California's Japanese-American congressman Norman Mineta because they thought Mineta was Italian.)

Carter made a bad start even worse when, barely a month into his administration he threatened to veto a public works bill unless nearly two-dozen water projects were cancelled. Carter was correct about the pork barrel nature of these projects (which were often environmentally unsound as well), but he announced his veto threat without any prior consultation with congressional leaders, or any attempt at compromise. Congress first learned of Carter's threat the same way the public did: in the morning newspaper. "I've never been so upset in my whole life," one House committee chairman sputtered. "I just read it in the paper."[53]

It is difficult to understate the completeness of the disaster of Carter's presidency. As we shall see, his domestic policies antagonized the liberal wing of the Democratic Party, while his foreign policies angered the conservative wing of the party. Unable to fly with either wing, Carter became the albatross of the Democratic Party. In addition to shredding his base within the party, there was his very style of governance, as suggested above. Carter's poor relations with Congress made apparent that the piety of Carter's election campaign had become self-righteousness when the time came to govern.

The populist aspect of Carter's persona was, however, initially popular with Americans. Upon taking office Carter embarked upon, as George Will put it, "a pompous crusade against pomp," because "some people seem to think silver trumpets and 'Hail to the Chief' caused Watergate." Carter chose to be inaugurated in a plain business suit instead of formal wear. He walked down Pennsylvania Avenue with his wife and daughter—much to the consternation of the Secret Service—eschewing the presidential limousine. (When he arrived at the White House, he didn't know how to get to the Oval Office; the Secret Service had to show him the way.) He sold the presidential yacht *Sequoia,* and ordered two cabinet members and their staffs who went along on his first state visit to Europe to move from four-star hotels into cheaper accommodations. He ended the playing of "Hail to the Chief" when he entered banquet halls and speaking venues, and circulated a memo to government offices instructing "that the official presidential photograph be limited to those places where absolutely necessary," which was not especially helpful guidance. He chose to go without a White House chief of staff because he wanted everyone to have "direct access" to the Oval Office. He gave his first televised address in a cardigan sweater beside a White House fireplace, self-consciously recalling FDR's radio "fireside chats." "The populist temper of the times," Will observed, "rewards a President who, with a flourish, bans ruffles and flourishes."

One of Carter's most "down-to-earth" gestures was agreeing to do a call-in radio broadcast with Walter Cronkite. Entitled "Ask President Carter," the calls were obviously not carefully screened. The program produced such gems as:

CALLER: Two questions: Would it be possible to eliminate the word "drug" from drugstore advertising? Also, when new drugs are invented, they always use the word "drug." Why not use the terminology "medication?" Maybe it would discourage drug abusers. What do you think?

THE PRESIDENT: I think that's a good idea. . . .

CALLER (Mrs. Dehart): Well, I really had more of a favor to make than a request. . . . I have been reading about vitamin B17, Laetrile. And I feel that the people in this country should be permitted to use this treatment in this country. I realize that the AMA says it's not been proved safe, but for a terminal patient, who is not going to live and has a chance to live with it, I don't see how it could be dangerous. And hospital insurance does not cover treatment not authorized by the AMA, and most hard-working people in this country cannot afford treatment that's not paid under insurance benefits. And if a person has money available to leave the country for treatment in one of the 17 countries where the cancer specialists use this successfully, they have a chance of recovery. And a lot of people even from my area have done this. What I want to say is that we need your help and the government's help in taking this vitamin out, that it's made available to the American people.

THE PRESIDENT: All right. Mrs. Dehart, I might let someone from the Department of HEW give you a call Monday and talk to you about it further. And you didn't ask me a question, but I have heard about the controversy. I know that in some of our neighboring countries, I think Mexico, you can buy the Laetrile and be treated with it.

CALLER: That's right.

THE PRESIDENT: Why don't you let me have someone call you Monday, if you don't mind. It wouldn't help much if I called you, because I'm not a medical doctor and I'm not familiar with it. Would that suit you okay?

CALLER: Yes, sir, it would. . . .

CALLER (Mr. Went): The question, Mr. President, is, would it be possible for you to accept an invitation from the governor of Minnesota or Mayor Geller of Granite Falls to be the speaker on National President's Day?

THE PRESIDENT: Mr. Went, I doubt it. . . .

CALLER (an 11-year old girl): Why doesn't Amy go to a private school?

THE PRESIDENT. She goes to the public school and did in Georgia when we lived there as well. She enjoys it very much, and I have a very strong commitment to the public school system and don't have anything against the private school system. But I think it helps the public schools in Washington, D.C., to have the president's daughter go there. . . . I hope sometime perhaps, Michelle, you can come and visit with Amy. . . .

The NBC comedy show *Saturday Night Live* deftly satirized this episode by portraying Carter talking down a drug-tripping caller.

These populist touches helped obscure even further Carter's ideological fuzziness. During the campaign Carter had promised to balance the budget by the end of this first term, and said he would approve no new spending programs that were incompatible with this goal. But he also endorsed several expensive spending ideas during the campaign—mostly as a way of placating the liberal wing of the party. Liberals were certain that Carter would acquiesce in new activist government programs once in office, and were shocked to discover that Carter *really meant it* about balancing the budget. This was heresy to orthodox liberalism, and Carter's relatively conservative fiscal governance was the source of a large part of his troubles with liberals. Democratic Senator Alan Cranston of California leaked to the media the liberal unhappiness over Carter's stinginess. "Many liberals in his own party," wrote Robert Shogan of the *Los Angeles Times,* "complain that he is the most conservative Democratic President since Grover Cleveland."[54] Carter relished the discomfort he caused liberals with this pledge. "I wish you could have seen the stricken expressions on the faces of those Democratic leaders when I was talking about balancing the budget," Carter told biographer Peter Bourne.[55]

It wasn't just members of Congress that Carter upset. Carter charged his Secretary of Health, Education, and Welfare, Joseph Califano, with

the task of coming up with a welfare reform plan. Califano didn't take seriously Carter's condition that any reform plan had to be accomplished at
current funding levels. When Califano presented Carter a set of options
that all cost billions more, Carter exploded: "Are you telling me that
there is no way to improve upon the present system except by spending
billions of dollars? In that case, to hell with it! We're wasting our time."[56]
(Carter eventually relented, sending a welfare reform plan to Congress
that he said would cost an additional $2.8 billion a year. When the Senate
Finance Committee estimated that Carter's plan would cost nearly
$15 billion more—a 70 percent increase over the current cost—the plan
quickly died.)

Carter's main gimmick for controlling federal spending was something called "zero-based budgeting." The idea was simple—in fact, it
sounded more like something Ronald Reagan might propose. At the beginning of the annual budget cycle, each agency and every program
would start "from the ground up," justifying each item in its budget as if
beginning from zero, rather than using the usual "current services" approach to budgeting where the previous year's budget figure was the base-
line upon which a spending increase was inevitably added. The idea
rested on the naïve belief that bureaucrats, so instructed to justify their
spending (Carter sent a memo in February of 1977 to all agencies requiring them to adopt zero-based budgeting henceforth), would aim sincerely
to reduce their own budgets and increase efficiency. It is not clear that the
idea had really worked during Carter's governorship of Georgia, but there
was no way such a system could be made to work with the federal
budget. Bureaucracies have too many methods of interring ideas they find
inconvenient. It is an idea that can work only with a high degree of centralized review, which is clearly impossible with the federal budget. Carter
imported the idea from the business world, where it has been a mixed
success. In Washington it flopped.

What most upset liberals, especially Sen. Ted Kennedy, was Carter's
refusal to back a comprehensive national health insurance plan that
would cost upwards of $100 billion a year. During the campaign Carter
had endorsed national health insurance, but in office proposed a slow,
piecemeal approach to the issue. The government "cannot afford to do
everything," Carter said, postponing even the introduction of a bill until

1979. (What Carter eventually proposed in 1979 was a hospital cost-containment measure that got nowhere.)

Barely four months into his first term, liberals were braying publicly against Carter. The AFL-CIO, the U.S. Conference of Mayors, and the Americans for Democratic Action all charged Carter with betraying his campaign promises. Michael Harrington complained that the Carter administration was "opposed to the principles of the New Deal." Vice President Mondale privately sympathized with the liberal dismay. Sen. George McGovern attacked Carter at the annual convention of the ADA for "trying to balance the budget on the backs of the poor and the jobless," while ADA national director Leon Schull threatened that if Carter continued on his present course, "the liberal movement, with the ADA in the forefront, will go into the opposition" just as it had with LBJ. In 1978 an Oval Office meeting between Carter and members of the Congressional Black Caucus turned into a shouting match, as Carter rebuffed demands for more spending on urban programs. Sen. Ted Kennedy warned that "the party that tore itself apart over Vietnam in the 1960s can tear itself apart today over budget cuts in basic social programs."[57]

Carter's fiscal conservatism initially paid off for him. His professed fiscal conservatism was matched with a cultural conservatism, if not Puritanism. "For those of you living in sin," Carter told his staff, "I hope you'll get married. For those of you who've left your spouses, go back home." His most quixotic gesture was his criticism of *People* magazine for encouraging the fixation on celebrity. The rhetorical centerpiece of his tax reform plan was the elimination of the deductibility of the "three-martini lunch," which excited many a smile. The puritanical "three-martini lunch" crusade prompted one of Gerald Ford's few genuine witticisms: "The three-martini lunch is the epitome of American efficiency. Where else can you get an earful, a bellyful, and a snootful at the same time?" Barry Goldwater quipped that "None of us had a three-martini lunch until Carter was elected."

A CBS–*New York Times* poll found that whereas 32 percent of voters thought Carter a liberal before the election, only 20 percent thought him a liberal in April 1977. Another poll found that half of the voters who had voted for Ford approved of Carter. Carter's balanced budget talk led House Republican leader John Rhodes to say that "The President sounds so Republican I'm overwhelmed."[58] Even Ronald Reagan seemed to think Carter might not work out too badly, writing a newspaper column entitled "Let's Give Carter a Chance." *Congressional Quarterly* noted that at Carter's first State of the Union speech, his statements on limited government "were greeted numerous times by applause, but frequently that applause was led by the Republicans in the House chamber, who obviously found much in the speech that could be applauded."[59] A study of network news and newspaper coverage in his first few months in office found that 85 percent of the criticism of Carter in those media had been instigated by Democrats.[60] Arthur Schlesinger Jr. complained bitterly: "He's a Republican. He has the temperament of a small businessman who happened to become President." *The New Republic* found that its pre-election reservations about Carter had been justified: "The administration has a remarkable record. Almost everything it proposes turns to ashes." Vice President Mondale said years later that "I never understood how Carter's political mind worked. Carter's got the coldest political nose of any politician I ever met."[61]

As his political fortunes with his own party soured, Carter's fiscal discipline—though not his fiscal rhetoric—quickly went by the wayside. He began to acquiesce to larger spending increases in order to appease liberals. After holding the deficit to a comparatively small $40 billion in fiscal year 1979 (Ford's last deficit had been $53 billion, down from a staggering $73 billion in fiscal year 1976), in 1980 the deficit swelled back up to $73 billion.

Carter attempted to compensate for his stiff personal skills and bad relations with Congress by adopting a crushing routine, working as much as 80 hours a week and reading as many as 300 pages of paperwork every night. It is doubtful that such a heroic workload was either productive or helpful in guiding his staff. It took six months before Carter would give up personally reviewing all requests to use the White House tennis court.[62] (Carter denied supervising the White House tennis court at a 1979 press conference, though his denial confirmed the perception that he was the Micro-Manager-in-Chief: "I have never personally monitored who used or did not use the White House tennis court. I have let my secretary, Susan Clough, receive requests from members of the White House staff who wanted to use the tennis court at certain times, so that more than one person would not want to use the same tennis court simultaneously, unless they were either on opposite sides of the net or engaged in a doubles contest.")

Between his work habits and his deliberate plain touch, it was remarked that the United States had elected its first national city manager, or, as one reporter put it, "McNamara with religion." Carter flooded Congress with ambitious legislative and reform programs: tax reform, health care, welfare reform, campaign finance reform, urban aid, and other ideas poured forth from the White House. Even Ted Kennedy, the avatar of activist government, observed that "Carter's reforms are lined up bumper-to-bumper." There was no hierarchy or priority among Carter's initiatives. He rejected advice that his administration was overloading Congress and trying to do too much. "It's almost impossible for me to delay something that I see needs to be done," Carter wrote in his diary after his first week in office. Carter's entire legislative program was not surprisingly ground to dust or stalled in Congress.

Carter's poor relations with Congress have been attributed to the combination of his hauteur and the growing institutional aggressiveness of Congress that was discussed in chapter 8. Although these factors are important in explaining Carter's difficulties, there was a deeper crosscurrent at work: the changing ideological outlook of the American people, a changing outlook that liberals either would not or could not recognize. The country was rapidly becoming more conservative, and liberalism was starting to exhibit deepening signs of intellectual and political exhaustion as it lurched toward a contradictory incoherence.

The liberal establishment was slow to perceive the seriousness and extent of the rising conservative tide. In retrospect it is clear that the election results of 1974 and 1976 were more of a reaction to Watergate and the poor economy than an affirmation of liberal ruling doctrine, but liberals failed to see this, and were lulled into a false sense of security. The University of Michigan's annual survey of public attitudes found that trust in government had fallen from 64 percent in 1964 to just 22 percent in 1976.[63] This was only one aspect of liberalism's increasing elitism and distance from the main currents of American life. In 1976 Seymour Martin Lipset of Stanford University and Everett Carl Ladd of the University of Connecticut released a survey of 3,600 college professors which found that self-identified liberals were more likely to drive foreign cars while moderates and conservatives tended to drive American cars. Ninety-eight percent of Saab drivers, and 76 percent of Porsche drivers, for example, voted for McGovern in 1972, while 49 percent of GM drivers voted for Nixon. Lipset and Ladd concluded: "If I were a Democratic precinct worker and I wanted to get people to the polls who are sympathetic to my candidate, I'd pick houses with foreign cars in front."[64] Yet it is liberals who talk most about the plight of the American auto worker.

Liberals thought the election of Jimmy Carter in 1976, despite its narrow margin and Carter's conservative campaign themes, represented the end of the Republican interregnum, and the resumption of activist government. Vice President Mondale's chief of staff Richard Moe said this openly: "We thought that the Nixon years were just an interruption of the normal—the standard way of doing things which was the Kennedy-Johnson years."[65] Liberalism may have been held in popular disrepute because of the McGovern experience and the bitter legacy of the 1960s, but among liberals in 1976 there was no lack of self-assurance. For liberals, after the go-go Kennedy-Johnson years, when the economy enjoyed the longest expansion in U.S. history, the Nixon-Ford years seemed like a sequel of the Eisenhower years, when the economy grew slowly and suffered several recessions. The New Frontier liberals of the 1960s thought the sluggish economy of the 1950s was due to Republican refusal to increase federal spending, and the activist liberals of the mid-1970s were still in thrall to Keynesian doctrine. On the surface they seemed to have a point: Unemployment during the Kennedy-Johnson years fell to a low of 3.5 percent, while inflation stayed mostly below 3 percent. Unemployment under Ford, by contrast, reached 8.5 percent in 1975, with inflation reaching 8 percent at its peak. Many liberals thought the travails of inflation and the energy crisis in the 1970s revealed the defects of the private market economy (rather than the effects of government distortions of markets, especially for energy), and were aggravated by Nixon and Ford's reluctance to stick with aggressive wage and price controls, as well as their opposition to regulating or nationalizing the energy industry. A liberal Democratic administration, it was assumed, would know how to do this.

Among liberals in the mid-1970s the idea that open markets could better solve economic problems was still held in disdain, while the idea of national management of the economy, if not national economic planning that verged on socialism, was still very much alive. In the summer of 1975 *Time* magazine expressed the doubts of liberalism with a cover story asking "Can Capitalism Survive?" "National economic planning is an idea whose time has come," the socialist Michael Harrington (who at that time was a Democratic congressman from Massachusetts) wrote in *Harper's* magazine. Harrington thought national planning should be the central issue of the 1976 presidential campaign. And indeed the 1976 Democratic platform carried a plank that read: "Of special importance is the need for national economic planning capability."

There was a powerful intellectual current among a few economists in favor of centralized economic planning. The Russian-born economist Wassily Leontief had been awarded one of the first Nobel Prizes for economics for his work on "input-output" models, a technique by which the overall economic effects of changes in investment and output from a single sector of the economy could be estimated. It seemed like the ultimate refinement of Keynesian general equilibrium theory, promising to provide government with the long-sought "black box" by which to perfect "fine-tuning" of the economy. (Friedrich Hayek, whose work constituted the refutation of Leontief, won the Nobel Prize for economics the year after Leontief, but was mostly ignored in America except among conservative economists.)

A good example of how this thinking played out can be seen in the debate over several proposals for federal employment programs. One of President Franklin Roosevelt's last campaign promises in 1944 had been to guarantee the right to a job to every American worker. In 1975 a group called the "Initiative Committee for National Economic Planning" convinced Sen. Hubert Humphrey and liberal Republican Sen. Jacob Javits to introduce a bill to achieve this goal at last by instituting a federal economic planning board that would produce six-year plans every two years. (Apparently five-year plans sounded too much like the Soviet Union.)

Although this bill went nowhere, the prospects seemed more realistic for the "Full Employment and Balanced Growth Act of 1976," more popularly known as the Humphrey-Hawkins Act because of its two chief sponsors, Sen. Humphrey and Rep. Augustus Hawkins of California. There was already a "Full Employment Act" on the statute books dating back to 1946, but it set full employment as a "goal," and not as firm or enforceable commitment. Humphrey-Hawkins promised to change that. It set a goal of achieving 3 percent unemployment within four years through a coordination of government programs and a guaranteed federal job for each worker if the private economy failed to achieve the 3 percent goal. The original draft of Humphrey-Hawkins included a clause allowing a worker to sue the federal government if the government did not find or create a job for him or her. This was too much even for the AFL-CIO, which declined to support Humphrey-Hawkins.

It is typical legislative strategy to start with a full-blooded proposal in hopes that you can get half or more of what you want in the inevitable compromises involved in getting a bill passed into law. This method is especially congenial to the liberalism, however, because the successive iterations and compromises gradually deliver the whole loaf one slice at a time. Some form of Humphrey-Hawkins would likely pass, and would be, in the approving words of investment banker Felix Rohatyn, "the first step toward state planning of the economy."

The enthusiasm for national economic planning wasn't limited solely to liberal Democrats. John Sawhill, President Ford's director of the Federal Energy Administration, had publicly endorsed the idea of national economic planning in 1975. (Ford fired him shortly after.) Most Republicans, though, were naturally aghast at Humphrey-Hawkins; the chairman of Ford's Council of Economic Advisers, Alan Greenspan, strenuously opposed it. Ford would have vetoed Humphrey-Hawkins if it had passed in anything close to its original form.

A few orthodox liberal economists were worried about the inflationary potential of a full employment program along the lines of Humphrey-Hawkins, but others dismissed this concern. Walter Heller, President John F. Kennedy's chief economic adviser, said the bigger budget deficits necessary to bring about full employment wouldn't risk inflation because the new money would only be putting idle men and machines back to work. A much watered-down version of Humphrey-Hawkins finally passed in 1978 (the crucial compromise was giving inflation an equal priority with unemployment), and it proved to be not a first incremental step toward economic planning and social democracy as liberals had hoped; rather, it proved to be the high-water mark for large-scale government management of the economy.

Though Humphrey-Hawkins and the idea of national economic planning represented an attempted revival of the can-do "growth liberalism" of the 1960s, by the time President Carter took office liberalism was rapidly coming to embrace its opposite: the "limits to growth." Partly this was an influence of the rapidly growing environmental movement, which, in its early days, was much taken with the 1972 Club of Rome book *The Limits to Growth*. The book offered a gloomy argument that natural resource depletion and rising pollution threatened mankind's long-term future unless economic growth was slowed or stopped. *The Limits to Growth* had the benefit of fortuitously appearing at the same time that commodity shortages were becoming chronic. *Newsweek* magazine in 1973 ran a cover picture of an empty horn of plenty with the ominous headline: "Running Out of Everything?" Most of the commodity shortages of the early 1970s were the result of the Nixon price controls discussed in chapter 6, and by 1976 the Club of Rome repudiated its own argument, recognizing that conquering poverty and preserving world peace would require a lot of economic growth.

The idea of the limits to growth has remained a core concept of environmentalism nonetheless, and became the new visage of liberal guilt. For some varieties of the liberal mind, gloom is exhilarating, and the limits to growth offered a large-scale sequel to the Vietnam War. Carter embraced the limits to growth view in his inaugural address, noting that "We have learned that 'more' is not necessarily 'better,' that even our great Nation has its recognized limits." Margaret Thatcher, among many others, noted the trouble with this, writing that Carter "had no large vision of America's future so that, in the face of adversity, he was reduced to preaching the austere limits to growth that was unpalatable, even alien, to the American imagination."[66] Liberalism is historically an optimistic creed, and having open doubts about growth was a disaster for liberalism. In the space of a decade, the central governing challenge of liberalism had transformed from allocating abundance to rationing scarcity. *National Review* took note of this problem as the Carter administration unfolded: "The profound negativism of the liberal wing of the Democratic Party is alien to the American tradition. The Democratic coalition could be split like a coconut on these issues. The Republicans, if they presented themselves as the party of growth, optimism, and expanding possibility could surely seize the high ground from the presently deeply divided and artificial Democratic coalition."[67]

Liberalism's contradictory embrace of the old-time government activism and the "limits to growth" ideology was the central cause of the incoherence of the Carter administration's domestic policy. Carter wanted both to balance the budget, but stimulate the economy. Since he didn't want to stimulate the economy with the old-fashioned Keynesnian elixir of more deficit spending (the existing deficit was thought to have pushed up interest rates), he instead encouraged the Federal Reserve to lower interest rates by expanding the money supply. The money supply had already been growing at the rate of about 11 percent a year by 1977—a rate of money growth that monetarist economists warned was too high—up from 7 or 8 percent in 1974–75. A parade of liberal economists, along with the Joint Economic Committee of Congress, were trotted out to argue that the money supply wasn't growing *fast enough*. "We need faster monetary growth," said economist and Carter adviser Lawrence Klein. "Government programs to stimulate the economy do not need to contribute to inflation." *Time* magazine had recommended that the Federal Reserve "should pump out as much money as might be needed to keep interest rates relatively stable." Carter's Fed chairman, G. William Miller, obliged. The result was accelerating inflation, which eventually became domestic equivalent of Vietnam.

Taking note of this monetary indiscipline, *National Review* predicted in 1975: "Nobody is even talking, anymore, about getting inflation below 6 or 7 percent. Having established that level as a politically viable floor for inflation, the discussion now centers on how rapidly we should take off from that point toward double-digit rates—and, of course, another big recession."[68] Inflation rose from 7 percent in 1977 to 9 percent in 1978 and the dollar began to plunge in the international currency exchanges. Polls in 1978 found that Americans now rated inflation as the most important national problem. Liberals had a blind spot for the dangers of inflation, as well as deep confusion about its source. Sen. McGovern argued that "the principle source of inflation now is oligopolies such as the oil and steel cartels which can raise prices regardless of demand or supply."

True to form, Carter tried to explain inflation as a moral problem afflicting the people: "It is a myth that the government itself can stop inflation." Rather, inflation was a reflection of "unpleasant facts about ourselves," of "a preoccupation with self" that retards the willingness of Americans "to sacrifice for the common good."[69] The chairman of the White House Council on Wage and Price Stability, Barry Bosworth, echoed Carter in blaming inflation on the private sector: "If government has any part to play in fighting inflation, it must have a role in private wage and price decisions."[70] At no time did Carter mention the money supply, or the government's role in running the treasury printing press.

The Carter administration proceeded to fight inflation through "jaw-boning," which meant giving an official scowl to businesses and labor unions who sought price and wage increases. In 1979, inflation soared further to more than 12 percent. With the prime rate nearing 20 percent and signs that inflation might begin spiraling to Latin American levels, Carter was forced to dismiss Miller and replace him with Paul Volcker, who immediately jacked up interest rates to curb monetary growth. Michael Harrington, who had looked forward to national economic planning as the cornerstone of an American Fabian socialism just a few years before, now admitted that "the conventional wisdom of the 1960s has been shattered by inflation."[71]

Carter's approach to the disrupted energy market of the mid-1970s was equally disastrous. (The wreck of his energy policy should have been apparent from an omen on Inauguration Day, when a solar-heated reviewing stand in front of the White House performed miserably, leaving most of its crowd visibly shivering.) Carter decided that the troubled energy sector of the economy should be regarded as a national crisis of the highest order, verging on "national catastrophe" unless drastic steps were taken. In a televised address Carter declared that "We must face the fact that the energy shortage is permanent," and described the imperative of an ambitious energy policy as the "moral equivalent of war," which yielded the unfortunate but highly symbolic acronym MEOW. If the energy crisis was the "moral equivalent of war," just who was the moral equivalent of the enemy? For most ordinary Americans it was the Arab oil sheiks and their OPEC cartel, but the conventional wisdom of liberalism in the 1970s held fast to Pogo's observation: The American people were the enemy, because of our profligate, energy-wasting lifestyle.

Carter proceeded to commit the same mistake that President Bill Clinton committed with health care reform in 1993: He developed a massive plan behind closed doors with little or no outside input. Neither his top economic advisers nor members of the cabinet were apprised of the details of the plan before its release. "The plan was conceived in secrecy by technicians," the *New York Times* reported, and it "reflected a detached, almost apolitical attitude." The architects of the energy plan "functioned as if they were a self-contained unit and their task was as hush-hush as the Manhattan Project."[72] The energy plan Carter produced contained a contradictory and complex mixture of tax incentives for conservation along with tax incentives to develop new supplies of energy. The populist cornerstone of the plan was a "gas guzzler tax" on large automobiles, then as now a popular target of enlightened people, along with a rebate for "efficient" smaller cars. (In answer to objections that such a plan would boost sales of foreign cars, the Carter administration proposed import restrictions.) Carter opposed the simple option of deregulating the market for domestically produced oil and natural gas. Not only would price controls on oil be continued, but a whole new set of complicated price controls on natural gas would be instituted. On the whole it was a technocratic plan beyond the wildest imagination of the frothiest New Dealer.

Carter's energy plan required four phonebook-sized volumes to spell out. House Speaker Tip O'Neill "took one look at it and groaned" when the White House delivered it to his office. O'Neill managed to shepherd Carter's energy plan through the House, but it was dead on arrival in the Senate. The Senate emasculated Carter's plan, carving it into 113 separate bills, finally passing a shriveled compromise for Carter's signature in the fall of 1978, almost 18 months after Carter had announced his plan. By then energy markets had calmed down. The most concrete result of Carter's energy plan was the creation of the cabinet-level Department of Energy, which quickly came to have a budget that rivaled the combined profits of the major oil companies, though it produced neither a single barrel of oil nor kilowatt of electricity.

If Carter's energy plan was an incoherent hodgepodge of big government nonsense, his attitude toward regulation of other basic industries was occasionally just the opposite. Carter advanced several deregulation initiatives, starting with the airline industry. To be sure, the momentum for deregulation began under the Ford administration, but Carter carried it through with equal enthusiasm. Prior to 1978, the federal government dictated routes and fares to any airline that flew interstate, which covered all airlines except a couple of small carriers who operated only in California and Texas. The Civil Aeronautics Administration (CAB), the regulatory agency that oversaw the airline industry, sometimes took several years to approve an airline's request to begin service on a new route.

The CAB itself noted the irrationality of this scheme, and became perhaps the first regulatory body ever to advocate it own abolition. Carter also set in motion the deregulation of the trucking industry, which would culminate in the eventual abolition of the Interstate Commerce Commission. Sen. Ted Kennedy was curiously one of the co-sponsors of the legislation to deregulate trucking. His rhetoric sounded like Adam Smith. "The problems of our economy," Kennedy said in 1978, "have occurred not as an outgrowth of laissez-faire, unbridled competition. They have occurred under the guidance of federal agencies, and under the umbrella of federal regulations." Political cynics thought his support of trucking deregulation owed more to the desire to punish the Teamsters Union for its support of Nixon in 1972.

There were, however, exceptions. On the whole the Carter administration ushered in a wholesale expansion of regulation. The Federal Register grew from 63,629 pages when Carter took office to 87,012 by the end of 1980—an all-time record high that was not matched again until the regulation-happy closing days of the Clinton administration. The regulatory burden would have been even higher had not Congress rejected Carter's proposal for a cabinet-level consumer protection agency and several other regulatory proposals. In 1978, General Motors grabbed headlines when it claimed that it spent more in a single year ($1.6 billion) to comply with federal regulations than it cost to run the entire U.S. government for the first 75 years of the nation's existence. GM added that the paperwork alone required 20,000 "person-years" to fill out.[73]

DEMOCRATIC POLLSTER Richard M. Scammon remarked after the 1976 election that, "There is nothing wrong with the Republican Party that 12 percent inflation won't cure." But more than the ineptitude and bad fortune of Jimmy Carter would be necessary to prepare the way for the coming of Ronald Reagan. In the long run it would not suffice simply for Republicans to hope for Democratic blunders. To find its way out of the wilderness, the GOP was going to need to figure out what it was all about, and find a way to communicate its antipathy to liberal governance, and constructive alternatives, in a way that a majority of voters would find appealing.

The intellectual groundwork for a conservative counter-revolution was beginning to reach a critical mass. One of the most important milestones was the 1976 Nobel Prize for economics, which was awarded to Milton Friedman. Liberals reacted with typical condescension, mixed with amazement. "To some," Melville Ulmer wrote in *The New Republic,* "it seemed as incongruous as a peace prize for Idi Amin, or a literature prize for Spiro Agnew. . . . [Friedman] is a hyperactive extremist of the right. . . . Is a modern restatement of the 1776 thesis of Adam Smith worthy of a Nobel Prize in economics?"[74] A group of fellow Nobel Prize winners including Linus Pauling wrote to the *New York Times* that Friedman had disqualified himself for any such honor because he had offered economic advice to the military rulers of Chile. A few liberals had more perception of Friedman's originality and brilliance. The liberal economist Paul Samuelson praised Friedman as "the *architect* of much that is best in our conservative tradition and not just the *expositor* of that viewpoint." (Emphasis in original.) As far back as 1971, Pat Moynihan commented that "If you were to ask me to name the most creative social-political thinker of our age I would not hesitate to say Milton Friedman."[75]

Yet by far the most significant development on the Right was the advent of a new tax-cutting philosophy that is said to have begun with a drawing on a restaurant napkin.

One day in 1974, the story goes, economist Arthur Laffer went to lunch with a Treasury official (other accounts say the lunch was with White House chief of staff Richard Cheney) at the Two Continents restaurant, and drew an inverted U-shaped curve on a napkin to illustrate the sensitivity of tax revenue to tax rates. With tax revenue on the vertical axis and tax rates from zero to 100 percent on the horizontal axis, Laffer illustrated how tax revenues would start to fall as tax rates increase beyond a certain point. Laffer argued that with income tax rates reaching 70 percent, the United States was on the downhill side of the revenue curve. IRS data tended to confirm at least part of Laffer's thesis: The 70 percent tax bracket in 1978 brought in only $1.7 billion in revenues— enough to run the government for about two days.

High-income individuals avoided paying these high rates through a variety of tax shelters, many of which represented a sub-optimal use of capital. The higher brackets of the income tax code were designed decades earlier to soak the very rich, but with inflation and expanding prosperity an increasing number of middle-class taxpayers were starting to fall into the higher reaches of the tax brackets. In the 1950s, a family earning the median income was taxed at a rate of 11.8 percent; by 1976 a family earning the median income was taxed at a rate of 20.2 percent. In the 1950s only 12 percent of all taxpayers were in brackets above 22 percent, but by the late 1970s nearly half were.[76] This inexorable "bracket creep" was reducing incentives to produce and was causing inefficient asset allocation as more and more people sought to avoid income taxes through tax shelters.

Cut tax rates, Laffer argued, and the economy would boom, along with tax revenues. A cut in income tax rates, Laffer argued, would actually generate more revenues from higher-earning individuals; empirical data from past income tax rate cuts supported Laffer's argument. The "Laffer Curve," as the infamous napkin sketch came to be known, became the intellectual basis of "supply-side economics." (Although Laffer came up with the curve, it was Herbert Stein who came up with the name "supply-side economics" in a 1976 academic paper.)

The only problem with this story is that it apparently didn't happen. Laffer told Martin Anderson that he has "no recollection whatsoever of drawing on a napkin."[77] The restaurant where the episode supposedly took place, the Two Continents, uses expensive cloth napkins, not suitable for drawing of any kind. But regardless of the provenance of the Laffer Curve, it represented a double-barreled repudiation of the political economy of liberalism. Orthodox "demand-side" Keynesianism held that total output was a function of aggregate demand, which was the sum total of private and public sector spending. Orthodox Keynesianism held that a tax cut might stimulate the economy if it raised aggregate demand, but raising demand beyond a natural equilibrium would surely stimulate inflation. In liberal orthodoxy, in other words, taxes should be cut only if aggregate demand was falling below the equilibrium level.

Supply-side economics turned the Keynesian presumption on its head, arguing that cutting taxes would change the incentive structure of the economy such that total output would grow. If total output grows, the risk of inflation diminishes. Supply-side economics was a revival of one of the older axioms of classical political economy that was attributed to the nineteenth century French economist Jean Baptiste Say. "Say's Law" can be simply stated: Supply creates its own demand. Supply-side economics had explosive political implications. It provided conservatives with a means of seizing the initiative on the central issue of

American politics—economic growth. Congressman Jack Kemp and Delaware Senator William Roth proposed a 30 percent cut in income tax rates in Congress in 1978; from that moment on, "Kemp-Roth" became a rallying cry for conservatives, and, *Newsweek* observed, had made Kemp "an overnight dark-horse candidate for President."

Liberals who worship at the shrine of progressive income tax rates hated the implication that lower marginal tax rates would generate higher revenues from the rich. Liberals were apoplectic when supply-side advocates began pointing to the impressive results of President John F. Kennedy's tax cuts in the early 1960s. But the most profound impact of supply-side economics was also its most subtle: Supply-side economics represented a fundamental rejection of the "limits to growth" viewpoint that had come to be the dominant theme of liberalism. Suddenly it was conservative Republicans who were able to say, "Let's get this country moving again," and it was liberal Democrats who took on the crabbed countenance of Herbert Hoover.

Deep income tax cuts without cutting federal spending first went against the grain for many fiscally conservative Republicans. Remember—Barry Goldwater had voted against the Kennedy tax cut in 1964 precisely because he thought it would swell the federal budget deficit. The supply-side theory that tax cuts would generate higher revenues through increased economic activity was as yet untested and, for many orthodox conservatives, unconvincing. One leading Republican who required no convincing of the economic merits was Ronald Reagan. Once again Reagan could generalize from his own experience. "Back in 1936, we used to make three or four or five movies a year and we loved it," Reagan was quoted as saying. "But in 1940 the wartime emergency surtax went up to 96 percent at the top of the scale and my agent told me, 'You can't make more than one movie a year.' So what happened is that instead of working for the whole year, we sat around the Brown Derby looking for oil deals."

The Kemp-Roth tax cut proved surprisingly popular in Congress in the months before the 1978 mid-term elections, so much so that Speaker Tip O'Neill had to resort to a parliamentary double-cross and party-line arm-twisting to kill its momentum. But the income tax cut was not the only "supply side" idea on the march. In the spring of 1978 Republicans proposed to cut the capital gains tax in half, from 49 percent to 25 percent. The Steiger amendment, after its sponsor, Wisconsin Congressman

William Steiger, didn't initially seem to have much chance of reaching the House floor for a vote. The House Ways and Means Committee, which would have to move a tax cut to the floor, had 25 Democrats to only 12 Republicans. The committee was a graveyard for conservative proposals. Even Steiger didn't think much of the chances for his bill: "I thought it would be a measure whose time hadn't come." On the table, instead, was President Carter's tax reform proposal. Having declared repeatedly that the income tax was a "disgrace to the human race," Carter proposed a tax reform package that would *increase* capital gains taxes, and that would reduce income tax rates only for low-income groups. Middle- and upper-class taxpayers would pay higher taxes under Carter's plan; Carter wanted the tax code to be *more* steeply progressive than it already was.

But then a political earthquake struck: the passage, by a two-to-one landslide, of California's Proposition 13 in June, which signaled the beginning of the "tax revolt." Carter attacked Proposition 13 with the revealing prediction that "There's no doubt about the fact that unemployment will go up in California, as government workers are laid off because of stringent budget requirements." (In fact California's economy boomed in the aftermath of Proposition 13. And the Congressional Budget Office predicted that Proposition 13 would bring about a slight reduction in the rate of inflation in California.) Other reactions to Proposition 13 were no less incredulous and uncomprehending. Senator George McGovern worried that the tax revolt "has undertones of racism." North Dakota tax commissioner Byron Dorgan, who later became a U.S. Senator, said Proposition 13 was "a vote for latent prejudice." The *Washington Post*'s Meg Greenfield said the message of Proposition 13 could be summarized in the headline: "California to Liberal Government: Drop Dead," while her *Post* colleague Haynes Johnson said the vote was an "exhibition of widespread public mean-spiritedness." For other liberals the portents of Proposition 13 were ominous. Tom Hayden argued that "the economics of the New Deal died in California on June 6."

Reagan had often spoken of igniting a "prairie fire" that would sweep the nation, and Proposition 13 appeared to be the catalyst he had long expected. Within days of California's June vote, tax-cutting initiatives were in the works in 20 other states. Within two years, 43 states had implemented some kind of property tax limitation or relief, 15 states had lowered their income tax rates, and 10 states moved to index their state income taxes for inflation. Perhaps the biggest shocker came in Massachusetts, the citadel of enlightened liberalism, which voted in September in favor of Proposition 2½, which cut property taxes in the same manner as Proposition 13. Governor Michael Dukakis had said that Massachusetts voters were too "sophisticated" to go for something like Proposition 13, so the voters showed him the door, too. Dukakis lost the Democratic primary to a conservative Democrat, Edward King. In an exhibit of how out of touch the major media was with the mood of the time, *Newsweek* magazine had lauded Dukakis in 1977 as a symbol of "the pragmatic new conservatism" in state houses around the country, yet Dukakis had raised taxes and made Massachusetts' tax burden the fifth highest in the nation. (*The New Republic* had a clearer assessment of Dukakis, calling him a "tight and humorless climber.") "There's real anger out there," Dukakis perceived the morning after his defeat.

Most politicians understood that they needed to get out of the way. The most remarkable about-face came from Governor Jerry Brown. Brown had attacked Proposition 13 before the vote as a "a rip-off" and "a consumer fraud," but after the vote acted as if he had invented Proposition 13. "Limiting the public sector is the message of Proposition 13," Brown said, adding with a straight face that "The historic mission of the Democratic Party is to curb government spending." Brown cruised to an easy re-election. "You can never underestimate the ability of the Democrats to wet their finger and hold it to the wind," Reagan said.

The tax revolt swiftly upended the dynamic of the tax issue in Washington. Democratic Rep. David Obey of Wisconsin said that Proposition 13 had caused "panic in this House." Members of Congress had learned from talking with constituents that what they meant by "tax reform" was "tax relief." A Roper Poll in the summer of 1978 found a majority regarded their income tax burden as "excessively high." One feature of the tax system was especially rankling—*bracket creep*. Bracket creep was extremely popular in Washington, however, because it amounted to an annual tax hike without having to vote to raise tax rates, and indeed offered the political bonus of being able to vote for "tax relief" every few years, even though taxpayers were barely staying even. Inflation was also pushing up the value of assets, especially houses, imposing large capital gains tax liabilities on middle-class households. When 62 Senators became co-sponsors of the Steiger amendment, the only question was not whether a capital gains tax cut would pass, but how large it would be.

Carter threatened to veto any capital gains tax cut and denounced it as "a plan that provides huge tax windfalls for millionaires and two bits for the average American. . . . The Steiger amendment is the greatest hoax ever perpetrated on the American people." Treasury Secretary Michael Blumenthal called it "the millionaires' relief act of 1978," because supposedly 80 percent of its benefits would go to taxpayers with incomes above $100,000. The *Washington Post*'s news coverage parroted the liberal line, with headlines such as "TAX CUTS, ENDING A TRADITION, WOULD TILT AWAY FROM POOR," and the *Post*'s editorial page decried the capital gains tax cut as "an offense to public morality." But one argument that didn't get much of a hearing was that a capital gains tax cut would increase the federal budget deficit. To the contrary, the stimulative "supply-side" benefits of a capital gains tax cut became one of its strongest selling points. An influential study from Chase Econometrics predicted that cutting the capital gains tax in half would generate 440,000 new jobs and reduce the Federal deficit by $16 billion by 1985. "It's actually revenue producing and will offset inflation," argued economist Martin Feldstein, president of the National Bureau of Economic Research. (*Business Week* magazine, on the other hand, worried that tax cuts would "touch off an inflationary explosion that would wreck the country.")

After Carter's own tax proposal was defeated in the House by a vote of 225–193, the tax bill with the Steiger capital gains tax cut amendment passed 362–49 in mid-October, three weeks before the mid-term elections. The surprising result (to conventional thinkers—not to the new supply siders) was that capital gains tax receipts immediately *went up*, and there was a 15-fold increase in capital formation in the two years immediately after the rate cut.

The passage of the tax bill blunted what had been a major effort of Republicans to make tax cuts *the* issue of the mid-term elections. The Republican Party adopted the Kemp-Roth tax cut as the official party position, and chartered a 727 airplane, dubbed the "Tax Clipper," to fly Republican leaders (including Ronald Reagan and Gerald Ford) to stump for Republican congressional candidates across the nation. Down in Carrollton, Georgia, Republican congressional candidate Newt Gingrich, making his second try for the House, was running hard on the tax cut issue, and told the *Washington Post* that the issue was "enormously effective." House Republican Leader John Rhodes predicted a "massive" Republican sweep in the election—perhaps a gain of up to 50 House seats. In fact, Rhodes said, he would be disappointed if GOP gains were only 25 to 30 seats.

Between Carter's unpopularity and the flood tide of the tax revolt in the wake of Proposition 13, Republicans should have done very well indeed. Yet Republicans gained only 12 House seats and three Senate seats for their efforts. "The ineptness of this party has almost no parallel in history," Henry Fairlie gloated in *The New Republic.* "The Democratic party is still without any real opposition."[78]

Michael Barone was more specific in his diagnosis: "There can only be one reason for the Republicans' relatively poor showing in House races: They simply do not have enough good candidates."[79] But Barone predicted that this would begin to change in the 1980s, and the shadow of the Nixon years receded. Already in 1978 the first signs could be discerned. Among the Republicans elected for the first time to the House in 1978 were Newt Gingrich and Dick Cheney. Among Democrats elected in 1978 were Congresswoman Geraldine Ferraro of New York, and, in Arkansas, 32-year-old Bill Clinton was elected to his first term as governor. *Time* magazine took note of Clinton as one of the 50 young leaders in America to watch, noting that he is "sometimes lampooned in political cartoons as a brat furiously pedaling a tricycle," and concluding that "Clinton is expected eventually to run for Congress."[80] The *Washington Post*'s David Broder, visiting Little Rock shortly after the election to size up the nation's youngest governor, thought more highly of Clinton's chances, writing in *Parade* magazine that Clinton might someday be president.

The small gains the Republicans made in Congress masked some ominous signs for the Democrats. Three prominent liberal Senators were defeated—Iowa's Dick Clark, Colorado's Floyd Haskell, and Minnesota's Wendell Anderson. Republicans were now up to 41 seats in the Senate—still far from a majority but able to sustain a filibuster.

The changing tectonics of American politics was not lost on perceptive liberals. Midway through his first term in the U.S. Senate, Pat Moynihan noticed. Having written in 1969 that Republicans lacked a cadre of intellectuals and could not expect to govern on a sustained basis, Moynihan now noted that "Of a sudden, the GOP has become a party of ideas." "Psychologists call it role reversal," Moynihan wrote in the *New York Times*. "As a Democrat, I call it terrifying. And to miss it is to miss what could be the onset of the transformation of American politics. Not by chance, but by dint of sustained and often complex argument, there is a movement to turn Republicans into Populists, a party of the People arrayed against a Democratic Party of the State." Conversely, Moynihan admitted later, "it was plain enough that the Democratic Party had nothing to offer by way of ideas about whatever it was that troubled us. But Democrats quite failed to see that the Republicans did."[81] James R. Wilson concurred, writing shortly after that "for perhaps the first time since Theodore Roosevelt, the Republican Party has become the party of change."

Across the ocean in Britain there occurred another sign of conservative insurgence. In 1975 the brash Tory politician Margaret Thatcher seized the leadership of the Conservative Party away from former Prime Minister Edward Heath. Heath had angered conservatives by promising to curb socialism, but instead saw his administration shattered by the trade unions. Thatcher's achievement in taking control of the party was seen as a rough parallel with the conservative effort to wrest control of the Republican Party in the United States.

Ronald Reagan met Thatcher in London shortly after she seized the Tory Party leadership in 1975, and Reagan told a journalist later that "We found that we were really akin with regard to our views of government and economics and government's place in people's lives and that sort of thing."[82] Reagan talked with Thatcher at greater length on a return visit to London in 1978. A friendship that would later become a collaboration began. By contrast, Carter's first encounter with Thatcher went so disastrously—Thatcher lectured Carter on foreign policy, according to Carter's aides—that Carter told his staff never again to schedule him to meet with a foreign opposition leader. For her part, Thatcher found Carter "personally ill-suited for the presidency, agonizing over big decisions and too concerned with detail. . . . [I]n leading a great nation decency and assiduousness are not enough."[83]

By the end of 1978 Thatcher was leading the incumbent Labour Party in public opinion polls, and appeared to be on the cusp of victory whenever the next general election was called. The main doubt conservatives had was whether Thatcher was too late. Many saw England's long, slow postwar decline as a harbinger of the course America was destined to follow if it continued with liberal social and economic policy. "Britain is becoming a third world country . . . an offshore industrial slum," *Economist* magazine correspondent Robert Moss wrote in 1977. "It is now impossible to govern Britain against the wishes of the man who controls the TUC [Trades Union Congress]." Moss's gloomy conclusion, which he admitted "may appear absurd" to American readers, was that "Britain has traveled more than two-thirds of the way toward becoming a fully communist society, and that it is increasingly probable that it will either complete the journey or have to endure the most shattering social and constitutional crisis the country has known since the 17th century."[84]

By the time Thatcher became Prime Minister in the spring of 1979, inflation in Britain was nearing 20 percent. Thatcher had no doubts about what to do, nor were there any doubts about the purity of her opinions. "Our aim," she said in 1978, "is not just to remove our uniquely incompetent government from office; it is to destroy the socialist fallacies—indeed the whole fallacy of socialism that the Labour Party exists to spread."[85] Conservatism had never spoken with such a confident and forceful voice. Supply-side income tax cuts and privatization of state-owned industries would form the central part of her economic agenda.

Daniel Yergin and Joseph Stanislaw recall an episode when Thatcher visited the Conservative Party's research department after she became party leader, where she found a party staffer writing a paper on how the Tory party should adopt a "middle way" between Left and Right. Thatcher erupted. "She was not interested in refurbishing Harold Macmillan," Yergin and Stanislaw recount. "Instead, she reached into her brief case and pulled out a book. It was [Friedrich] Hayek's *The Constitution of Liberty.* She held it up for all to see. 'This,' she said sternly, 'is what we believe.' She slammed it down on the table and then proceeded to deliver a monologue on the ills of the British economy."[86] Central casting could not have produced a more compatible counterpart for Ronald Reagan.

Thatcher's moment came in the winter of 1979, when several British unions went on strike demanding 20 percent wage increases. The strike idled 250,000 service and transportation workers, and threatened to halt much of the economy. It became known as Britain's "winter of discontent." Public schools were forced to close, garbage piled up in the streets, and, owing to the truckers' strike, food delivery to grocery stores slowed to a crawl. The British public was outraged; 84 percent of Britons told a Gallup Poll that labor unions had too much power. Labour Party Prime Minister James Callaghan responded weakly, summoning union leaders to 10 Downing Street to ask for "voluntary reforms." The labor commotion was the opening Thatcher needed to bring down the government. "The government has failed the nation, lost credibility, and it is time for it to go," she declared in the House of Commons. In March Thatcher's Tories carried a "No Confidence" motion in the House of Commons by a single vote, which mandated an immediate election. It was the first such defeat for a British administration in 50 years.

Thatcher's election campaign in 1979 prefigured Reagan's 1980 campaign in many ways. "Many people in Britain's political Establishment," *Newsweek* observed in words that could have been taken from the media's lexicon for Reagan, "still regard her as a neophyte, blinkered by narrow conservative views, insulated by a suburban London constituency and too inexperienced to run a government."[87] Callaghan attacked Thatcher for her belief in "simplistic solutions" and her "hardness." Just so, replied Thatcher: "What Britain needs is an iron lady." Thatcher had her own version of Reagan's "get-the-government-off-the-backs-of-the-people" message: "The proper role of government is to set free the natural energy of the people." Most importantly, Thatcher, like Reagan, directly rejected the view that Britain faced an age of limits or a path of inevitable decline. The Conservative Party platform declared: "Our country's relative decline is not inevitable." Senior Labour Party leader Neil Kinnock, who would become leader of the opposition under Thatcher, confidently asserted: "She is impetuous and accident-prone. With albatrosses in the Tory shadow Cabinet and with a vulture like Thatcher, the Tories are in trouble." Some trouble. Thatcher's Tories won a 44-seat majority in the House of Commons in the election that followed. It was Kinnock who would become widely acknowledged as an albatross for his party.

Callaghan had been Carter's favorite European leader, so it was with disappointment that he telephoned his congratulations to Thatcher upon her victory. Reagan, to the contrary, had been the very first foreign politician to call to offer congratulations; as an out-of-office politician, however, he wasn't put through to Thatcher right away. He had to wait three days until she would take his call. In one of his next radio broadcasts, Reagan expressed his jubilation: "I couldn't be happier than I am over

England's new Prime Minister. . . . I have been rooting for her to become Prime Minister since our first meeting. If anyone can remind England of the greatness it knew during those dangerous days of World War II when alone and unafraid her people fought the Battle of Britain it will be the Prime Minister the English press has already nicknamed 'Maggie.'"[88]

Reagan was not alone in seeing Thatcher's victory as a harbinger of Republican prospects in 1980. The chairman of the Republican National Committee, Bill Brock, hired the ad agency (Saatchi and Saatchi) that had produced Thatcher's television spots. If Britain would turn to a supposed "out-of-the-mainstream" conservative, then the United States could do it too. When Brock was tapped to give the Republican response to Carter's 1980 State of the Union address, he took the extraordinary step of showing two of the Thatcher commercials attacking government dominance of the economy, explaining that this was the message voters would hear from Republicans over the next year. London *Times* correspondent Geoffrey Smith offered this assessment: "The Thatcher example did more for Republicans than help them to refine their campaigning tactics. The psychological effect of her election was even more important. Brock went so far as to say that it was absolutely critical. 'We had the example of success. . . . It gave us confidence.'"[89]

It is not difficult to have confidence when the ruling party is saddled with high inflation, slow productivity growth, stagnant personal incomes, and persistent unemployment. But those were the least of Carter's troubles as his term progressed. Carter oversaw a ruin in foreign policy to match the ruin of the domestic economy. By 1980, America's worry about the prospect of war would reach it highest level since the Cuban Missile Crisis.

CHAPTER TWELVE

MALAISE

※

I F CARTER'S DOMESTIC POLICY was disastrous in its results, his foreign policy was even more so, and it was foreign policy that would prove Carter's ultimate undoing. Before he was done Carter achieved a trifecta; as Henry Kissinger would summarize it in 1980: "The Carter administration has managed the extraordinary feat of having, at one and the same time, the worst relations with our allies, the worst relations with our adversaries, and the most serious upheavals in the developing world since the end of the Second World War."[1] Carter came to be regarded as the American Neville Chamberlain, not so much for his appeasement of America's foreign critics and adversaries, but for his general incapacity to perceive and act according to the geopolitical realities of the moment. The full record shows that this judgment is not wholly fair. Carter approved—though without much enthusiasm and against resistance from his foreign policy team—several covert programs against Communist regimes. But his public rhetoric on foreign questions and his key appointments—rhetoric and personnel being two main pillars of foreign policy—were so deficient that it is understandable that he inspired such a harsh reaction.

Like his domestic policy, his foreign policy gave off contradictory signals from the start. Carter began well enough, declaring with a flourish that "human rights" would be the centerpiece of his foreign policy. His inaugural address proclaimed that "Our commitment to human rights must be absolute." This pledge cheered conservatives and liberals alike, and seemed to represent a repudiation of Kissinger-style détente that necessarily eclipsed a vocal concern for human rights in the Soviet bloc. For example, Jeane Kirkpatrick, who in due course would become one of Carter's most lacerating critics, wrote: "For having recalled Americans (and others) to historic moral imperatives and for having placed individual rights back on the international agenda, President Carter wins my applause. . . . Carter's emphasis on these themes is rewarding to people sick to death of having their motives, characters, and policies excoriated."[2]

Carter's human rights theme initially seemed to augur a return to a more robust ideological resolve vis-a-vis the Soviet bloc. In his first meeting with Soviet Ambassador Anatoly Dobrynin, Carter sternly warned that "we will not back down on the human rights issue." Carter showed he meant it when he released a letter he sent to dissident Soviet physicist Andrei Sakharov. Carter also received Vladimir Bukovsky, a prominent dissident exile, in the Oval Office—a stark contrast to Ford's refusal to meet Solzhenitsyn. The Soviets were outraged. (They were also alarmed. The KGB conducted a hurried assessment to determine whether the Soviet Union was vulnerable to an American-inspired uprising.[3])

It had been a tacit agreement of the Nixon-Kissinger détente that neither side would engage in public attacks on the internal affairs of the other, which in practice was a one-way street, since Soviet propaganda never relented in its ideological attack on "bourgeois democracy," not to mention its disinformation efforts in Third World media aimed at discrediting the United States. Even *National Review* cheered Carter: "It was exhilarating to contemplate the new Administration's straightforward criticism of Soviet treatment of nuclear physicist and political dissident Andrei Sakharov." Other signs suggested Carter was serious in his criticism of détente. For his national security adviser Carter chose Zbigniew Brzezinski of Columbia University, who brought with him a reputation as a hard-liner. During the Cuban Missile Crisis in 1962, Brzezinski had sent a telegram to Arthur Schlesinger at the White House that read: "Any further delay in bombing missile sites fails to exploit Soviet uncertainty."[4] With his thick Polish accent and heavyweight academic background, Brzezinski was intended to be Carter's answer to Kissinger. Liberals were initially dismayed at both the human rights campaign and the Brzezinski appointment. Sen. George McGovern complained that "the Carter [human rights] policy looks like a reincarnation of John Foster Dulles's attempt to bring Communism down by encouraging dissent and revolt in Eastern Europe."[5]

Before long, however, it became apparent that Carter's foreign policy was sentimental rather than hardheaded or principled, and was a combination of the fashionable view that the "bipolar" world of the Cold War should give way to a "multi-polar" worldview along with a heavy dose of liberal guilt. Jeane Kirkpatrick judged that "Carter was, *par excellence,* the kind of liberal most likely to confound revolution with idealism, change with progress, optimism with virtue." Brzezinski, on closer inspection, turned out to believe an optimistic version of Kissinger's historical determinism. Brzezinski had characterized Carter's foreign policy in 1977 as the recognition that "the world is changing under *the influence of forces no government can control.*" (Emphasis added.) Kirkpatrick noted that in practice this meant "to encourage the view that events are manifestations of deep historical forces which cannot be controlled and that the best any government can do is to serve as a 'midwife' to history, helping events move where they are already headed."[6]

The embrace of human rights and the rejection of Cold War containment turned into a rolling confessional about America's role in the world in the post-war decades. Carter quickly eased up on his complaints about human rights in the Soviet bloc (during his state visit to Poland Carter said, "Our conception of human rights is preserved in Poland"), and began using human rights as a cudgel against traditional U.S. allies. Michael Ledeen and William Lewis observed: "Implicit in the statements of Carter administration officials was the conviction that the United States had itself been the root cause of many problems of the recent past. And there was more than a hint that America would—and should—do a sort of penance for its presumed sins in Vietnam, Cuba, and other areas."[7] The veteran Democratic foreign policy expert Eugene Rostow said that "Carter was McGovernism without McGovern."[8] McGovern himself confirmed this, telling friends that, having calmed down from his first appraisal of Carter as Dulles *redux,* he regarded Carter's foreign policy appointments to be "excellent, quite close to those I would have made myself."[9]

Despite Carter's public attention to Soviet dissidents, the real orientation of human rights policy could be (and was) summarized in the phrase, "No more Pinochets" (a reference to the Chilean colonel who ousted the Marxist president Salvador Allende in 1973, supposedly with the approval and assistance of the United States), and the grand strategy of a "multi-polar" world could be (and was) reduced to the phrase, "No more Vietnams." ("There is no more South Vietnam," some realist skeptics pointed out.) Senator Henry "Scoop" Jackson complained bitterly: "For too many officials [in the Carter administration], the intensity of the struggle for human rights is inversely related to the power of the offender. . . . Thus it is that the Administration speaks more about the abuses of human rights in Chile, the Philippines, Argentina, and Guatemala, while speaking less about violations of human rights in the Soviet Union."[10] Sen. Moynihan criticized Carter more broadly for "trying to divert our attention from the central political struggle of our time—that between democracy and totalitarian communism."[11]

There was a deeper confusion with the emphasis on human rights beyond the double standard of its application. Were "human rights" the same as *civil rights*—the historic rights of individuals rooted in liberal theory and enshrined in the Declaration of Independence and the Bill of Rights—or were "human rights" to be understood more broadly to encompass "social" and "economic" rights such as a right to housing and health care? The latter understanding, which was given expression in numerous United Nations resolutions, was popular with the totalitarian socialist nations, whose propaganda machines skillfully turned human rights on its head. Socialist despots everywhere assumed the pose of standing on the moral high ground, claiming to be providing for the most important human rights, that is, economic rights to jobs, housing, and health care, while "human rights" in the Western democracies were a sham. What does freedom of the press matter to a starving man? various Third World lackeys for socialism would taunt. Indeed the new Soviet constitution of 1977 claimed that the U.S.S.R. secured the "genuine rights" of its citizens, argued openly that economic and social rights take precedence over civil rights. It is a thoroughly tendentious argument for justifying rule without the consent of the governed. And in practice the emphasis on "economic rights" provides the pretext for violating individual civil rights.

Erasing the distinction between civil rights (the negatives on government restriction of individual political freedom) and economic "rights" (which are not rights but claims or demands for government provision of material benefits) not only confuses the means with the ends of freedom, but also blurs the difference between Western democracy and totalitarian despotism, which was exactly the purpose of socialist propaganda. This was not a new line of argument from Marxists, of course, yet the Carter administration retreated before it. To the contrary, Carter's foreign policy spokespeople sometimes associated with the Marxist argument. In a speech on human rights in 1977, Secretary of State Cy Vance endorsed the view that "there is a right to the fulfillment of such vital needs as food, shelter, health care, and education. . . ." Foreign leaders could be just as muddle-headed. Former West German Chancellor Willy Brandt said: "He whose life is exposed to sheer misery can take only minor interest in civil rights." Thus the human rights theme, which began with such promise, soon became yet another manifestation of Western weakness, confusion, and lack of self-confidence.

Given Carter's many-sided pronouncements on the issues during the campaign along with his criticisms of détente, it was not easy to discern exactly which way his administration would go in foreign affairs. But there were some Carter statements that should have raised red flags. The Soviet Union, Carter said at one point during the campaign, "will continue to push for communism throughout the world and to probe for possibilities for expansion of their system, *which I think is a legitimate purpose for them.*"[12] (Emphasis added.) These were expressions of "moral equivalence" much more problematic than Kissinger's détente or the Sonnenfeldt Doctrine.

Four months into his administration, Carter made explicit his departure from the post-war foreign policy consensus. In a commencement address at Notre Dame University on May 22, Carter declared:

Being confident of our own future, we are now free of that *inordinate fear of communism* which once led us to embrace any dictator who joined us in that fear. . . .

For too many years, we've been willing to adopt the flawed and erroneous principles and tactics of our adversaries, sometimes abandoning our own values for theirs. We've fought fire with fire, never thinking that fire is better quenched with water. This approach failed, with Vietnam the best example of its intellectual and moral poverty. . . .

Our policy during this period was guided by two principles: a belief that Soviet expansion was almost inevitable but that it must be

contained, and the corresponding belief in the importance of an almost exclusive alliance among non-Communist nations on both
sides of the Atlantic. That system could not last forever unchanged.
Historical trends have weakened its foundation. The unifying threat
of conflict with the Soviet Union has become less intensive. . . .

We can no longer separate the traditional issues of war and
peace from the new global questions of justice, equity, and human
rights. (Emphasis added.)

Carter was unilaterally declaring an end to the Cold War. It would be
détente after all. *The New Republic*'s John Osborne said Carter's speech
"may be seen in time to have been the most significant presidential statement of American foreign policy since Harry Truman committed the United
States in 1948 to resisting the spread of Soviet power."[13] (The primary author of the speech, incidentally, was Anthony Lake, who later became President Clinton's national security adviser.) Pat Moynihan responded to Carter
a month later, asking in a commencement speech of his own: "What was
the evidence that our relation with our great totalitarian adversary had
changed, that the adversary had changed?" Carter's good wishes for better
relations with the Third World "must not be allowed to divert us from the
reality of the military and ideological competition with the Soviet Union
which continues and, if anything, escalates."

Carter's anti–Cold War stance was not mere rhetoric. He lost little
time changing the nation's course in concrete ways. Carter's initial foreign
policy act, taken during his first 24 hours in office, was to order the Joint
Chiefs of Staff to arrange for the withdrawal of all U.S. nuclear weapons
from South Korea. He would follow this up a few days later by announcing his intention to withdraw U.S. ground forces from South Korea as
well. Carter made these decisions without any consultation with the Pentagon, congressional leaders, the South Koreans, or any other U.S. allies,
most notably Japan, which was shocked by Carter's decisions.

Carter didn't even attempt to use the withdrawals as an enticement for
North Korea to negotiate a reduction in tensions. The decision stunned
military commanders. When the third-ranking army officer in South
Korea, General John K. Singlaub, commented that the removal of U.S.
troops would lead to war, Carter relieved Singlaub. But following bipartisan reaction against the decision on Capitol Hill, Carter had to "defer" his

decision, which was tantamount to abandoning it. Before the ink was dry on his plan to remove troops from Korea, Carter also signed an executive order granting amnesty to Vietnam-era draft evaders, which Barry Goldwater blasted as "the most disgraceful thing a president has ever done."

His defense policy closely followed his diplomacy. Among other goals, Carter wanted to reduce U.S. arms sales to other countries. He also wanted to reduce arms sales to the U.S. military. In his first month in office Carter cut an already lean defense budget by another $6 billion. He abruptly cancelled the B-1 bomber in June 1977 (so abruptly that congressional leaders had about one hour's notice, adding to his problems on Capitol Hill), and two months later he deferred the development of the "neutron bomb," a low-yield weapon designed for use in the European theater to counter the massive number of tanks the Warsaw Pact forces were deploying. He indicated his interest in scrapping the Trident nuclear submarine as well. Carter wanted to accelerate development of the stealth fighter instead of the B-1, but he was unable to disclose this secret project (at least until the political needs of the 1980 campaign made it advantageous to do so), so the political damage of these two decisions, along with the Korean pullout, was maximized. Overall, he planned to cut $57 billion from the seven-year defense-spending plan he inherited from President Ford. These reductions in America's arms development were undertaken unilaterally, without any attempt to negotiate reciprocal arms restraint from the Soviet Union.

Carter and his foreign policy team believed that the classic Cold War grand strategy of containment was no longer necessary. "The old ideological labels have lost their meaning," Carter told an incredulous audience on his first trip to Eastern Europe. Despite his reputation as a hard-liner, Brzezinski mostly agreed. Carter's other key foreign policy appointments certainly did. In one of the more peculiar utterances of Carter's ascendancy, Hamilton Jordan had told *Playboy*'s Robert Scheer during the campaign that "this government is going to be run by people you've never heard of." About foreign policy personnel, Jordan said: "If Cyrus Vance were named Secretary of State and Zbigniew Brzezinski head of National Security in the Carter administration, then I would say we failed, and I would quit. But that's not going to happen."[14] But it did happen, and Jordan didn't quit.

Vance, one of McNamara's protégés in the Pentagon during Vietnam, was named secretary of state. Vance's appointment set off the first alarm bells for conservatives in both parties. Civil rights lawyer and long-time Democratic activist Morris Abrams commented that Vance was "the closest thing to a pacifist that the U.S. has ever had as secretary of state, with the possible exception of William Jennings Bryan." Vance would tell *Time* magazine in 1978 that Carter and Soviet Premier Brezhnev held "similar dreams and aspirations about the most fundamental issues."[15] Vance's fellow cabinet member Harold Brown, who served Carter as secretary of defense, said that Vance "was persuaded that anything that involved the risk of force was a mistake," a view that eventually required Vance's resignation in 1980.

Other appointments reinforced Vance's dovishness. Carter's nomination of Theodore Sorenson to head the CIA had to be withdrawn in the face of Senate opposition. The same fate nearly met Carter's controversial pick to be chief arms control negotiator: Paul Warnke. Warnke, another denizen of the McNamara Pentagon, brought a reputation as a dovish opponent of nearly all proposed U.S. weapons systems, from ballistic missile defense to MIRV warheads. Warnke had long argued in favor of the theory that the United States and Soviet Union "aped" one another, such that U.S. "restraint" in arms would effectively end the arms race. In 1965 Warnke said that "The Soviets have decided that they have lost the quantitative race, and now they are not seeking to engage us in that contest." Subsequently the Soviets indeed sought to race ahead of the United States in every category of quantifiable strategic strength. That the Soviet Union reacted not at all to U.S. restraint failed to shake Warnke's worldview. "The chances are good," Warnke wrote in *Foreign Policy* magazine in 1975, "that highly advertised restraint on our part will be reciprocated. The Soviet Union, it may be said again, has only one superpower model to follow." From such droppings George Will concluded that Warnke's views were "almost engagingly childlike." Having scuttled the Sorenson nomination, Carter put his prestige behind Warnke, and associated himself fully with Warnke's views. The Senate confirmed Warnke by the slim margin of 58 to 40. Only one Republican Senator, John Chafee of Rhode Island, voted for Warnke. Sen. Moynihan voted against Warnke, along with Georgia Sen. Sam Nunn. The close vote was a clear signal that any new arms treaty would have a difficult time winning Senate confirmation.

Most of Carter's foreign policy appointments to the second-tier posts that *The New Republic* called "the junior varsity" were similarly dovish.

"Some among this establishment junior varsity," *The New Republic* observed, "can and almost certainly will succeed to the highest positions in a future Democratic administration, whatever their record in the next few years."[16] They had in mind such thirty-somethings as Anthony Lake, Richard Holbrooke, and Jessica Tuchman, all of whom indeed went on to senior posts in the Clinton administration in the 1990s. Still other mid-level foreign policy appointments were further to the Left, especially Patricia Derian, whom Carter picked to be assistant secretary of state for human rights. Derian had come out of the civil rights movement, had traveled little overseas and had no foreign policy credentials.

Members of the Coalition for a Democratic Majority including Ben Wattenberg and Sen. Moynihan had met with Carter and asked that he select some foreign policy appointees and ambassadors from the center and labor wing of the party—the faction that had supported Scoop Jackson against Carter in the 1976 campaign. The CDM group presented Carter with a list of 53 names of qualified people they wished Carter to consider for appointments. One of the names on the list was Georgetown University professor Jeane Kirkpatrick, whom CDM suggested would make a good ambassador to Israel. Liberals in the administration later boasted of blocking her appointment. Carter gave his assurances that he would pick appointees from all wings of the Democratic Party, but the only appointment from the CDM group was special negotiator to Micronesia. "Not even Macronesia, but Micronesia!" Moynihan complained. "A conservative governor came to town and the people he appointed regarded the ideas of the Coalition [for a Democratic Majority] as far more a threat to the republic than the ideas of the Republican National Committee."[17] Carter's pollster Pat Caddell dismissed the CDM as a significant force among Democrats; "It isn't a wing; it's a feather." "The Carter administration froze us out completely," observed Elliott Abrams, then serving as an aide to Sen. Moynihan. "That demonstrated to all of us that the Democratic party was a McGovernite party."

And then there was Andrew Young.

Carter selected fellow-Georgian Young, who was then serving as a member of the House of Representatives, to be United Nations ambassador. Young had risen to prominence with the civil rights movement in the 1960s and had become a fixture of Atlanta politics in the 1970s. Beneath Young's impressive and moderate-sounding demeanor lurked a fashionably leftist anti-American sensibility. In 1970 Young had defended the Black Panthers on an ABC TV show with the explanation that "it may take the destruction of Western civilization to allow the rest of the world to really emerge as a free and brotherly society, and if the white West is incapable of brotherhood with colored peoples, then this small body of colored peoples, black people within the white West, may be the revolutionary vanguard that God has ordained to destroy the whole thing."[18] The ABC interviewer followed up to see if Young was merely describing radical black sentiment, or associating himself with it: "Would you support the destruction of Western civilization if you were convinced that the rest of the world would thereby be liberated?" Young: "I probably would."

Young lived up to this sensibility early and often in his U.N. post. On his first trip to Africa Young disembarked from the State Department aircraft giving the "black power" clenched-fist salute, to the bewilderment of his African hosts. He said that Cuban troops in Africa could be considered a "stabilizing" influence, because they were in Africa "opposing racism" and providing "technical assistance." (Young's attitude spilled over elsewhere in the State Department, which at one point in 1978 referred to pro-Soviet guerrillas in Africa as "liberation forces." Pat Moynihan referred to this kind of rhetoric as "semantic infiltration."[19]) "Cuba is in Africa," Young clarified, "because it has a shared sense of colonial oppression and domination."[20] Young was equally candid about whom he had in mind as the colonial oppressors. He denounced Britain as a "racist" nation; Britain, Young said, "almost invented racism." (Carter made Young send a written apology to Britain's U.N. ambassador for that remark.) Richard Nixon and Gerald Ford were both racists, he told *Playboy* magazine, because "every American, black or white, is affected by racism." Would that include Abraham Lincoln? a reporter asked Young. "*Especially* Abraham Lincoln," he replied.

In 1978 Young defended the Soviet trial of dissident human rights activist Anatoly Shcharansky by asserting the moral equivalence between the United States and the U.S.S.R. The trial, Young said, was "a gesture of independence" on the part of the Soviets that should not affect détente. But then came the clincher: "After all, we also have hundreds, maybe thousands of people in our jails that I would categorize as political prisoners." Young had previously explained that the Soviet Union had "a completely different concept of human rights. For them, human rights are essentially not civil and political, but economic." Young made it clear that the Soviet conception of human rights compared favorably to human rights in the United States. "We unfortunately have been very reluctant to accept the concept of economic responsibility for all of our citizens."[21] Carl Gershman, executive director of Social Democrats USA, observed that Young seems unconcerned about the fate of freedom in the Third World "so long as the regime in question calls itself 'progressive' . . . Yet in his eagerness to demonstrate his solidarity with the new Marxist-Leninist elite of black Africa, Young finds himself not on the side of the oppressed but of the oppressors."

The State Department had to issue repeated "clarifications" (that is, repudiations) of Young's "open mouth diplomacy," but Carter defended him publicly as "the best man I have ever known in public life." But Young finally went too far when he violated explicit U.S. policy about having direct contact with the U.N. observer of the Palestine Liberation Organization (PLO). Young had argued within the Carter administration for an opening to the PLO, and for the PLO's direct participation in Middle East peace talks (as eventually happened in the 1990s). But he apparently couldn't wait on events. In the summer of 1979 Young went to a surreptitious meeting with the PLO United Nations observer at the apartment of Kuwait's U.N. ambassador to discuss a "procedural" matter related to a forthcoming U.N. vote. Young had told no one at the State Department of the meeting, but the Israelis got wind of it and complained bitterly to Washington. Young dissembled, telling the State Department that the meeting had been "inadvertent." When the truth dribbled out that the meeting had been anything but "inadvertent" and that he had misled the State Department, support for Young collapsed. He was forced to resign in September 1979.

While Young's candor and imprudence cost him his job, he undoubtedly expressed the soul of Carter's foreign policy better than anyone else in the administration. This can be most clearly seen in the way Carter approached the Panama Canal negotiations. President Carter was determined to conclude a treaty that had been under negotiations for the previous four administrations, but for very different reasons than his predecessors. Expiating American guilt was to be the basis for concluding an agreement on favorable terms to Panama. The current American ownership and control of the canal, Carter said, "exemplified those morally questionable aspects of past American foreign policy which the United

States as a nation should humbly acknowledge in its striving for higher moral ground."[22] Carter more directly said that giving back the canal would "correct an injustice" and constitute "a gracious apology." Coming as it did so soon after the nation's humiliation in Vietnam, Carter could not have deliberately calculated a justification more offensive to Americans. It didn't help that Carter had attacked President Ford on Panama during the 1976 campaign, promising that "I would never give up full control of the Panama Canal."

At the time Carter submitted the treaties (the negotiations produced two treaty instruments—one transferring legal title to Panama of the American canal zone, and a second protocol declaring the right of the United States to defend the canal's neutrality against "external" threats) to the Senate for ratification in the fall of 1977, opinion polls showed the public opposed to the treaties by more than a 2 to 1 margin. Illinois Senator Adlai Stevenson III reported that he received 5,600 letters opposing the treaties, and only five in favor. The *St. Louis-Globe Democrat* newspaper reported similar numbers: 2,289 letters against the treaties versus 29 in favor. Carter hoped for a quick and easy ratification, and revealed his naiveté once again by expressing surprise that the Senate ratification process was going to take several months. In the weeks before the treaties were formally submitted in September 1977, 40 Senators signed a resolution opposing the treaties—six more than necessary to defeat the required two-thirds vote to ratify the treaties.

Knowing that Ronald Reagan would be a formidable opponent of the treaties, Carter sent the treaties' chief negotiators Sol Linowitz and Ellsworth Bunker to meet with Reagan in New York, hoping to persuade Reagan to abridge his public criticism. Linowitz and Bunker spent 90 minutes trying to convince Reagan, who remained unmoved. Or was he? After the meeting, Reagan turned to his aides and asked, "What if they're right?" In his speech to a conservative group in New York that evening, he decided, mostly out of courtesy to the Carter emissaries, to omit any mention of the treaties. Reagan did indeed later announce his opposition to the treaties, but his rhetoric displayed a subtle shift from the campaign language of 1976, when his refrain had been "we built it, we paid for it, it's ours, and we are going to keep it!"

By early 1978 Reagan was careful to say "we can make it plain that rejection of these treaties does not mean an end to further negotiations, or to the effort to better our plans for the people of Panama." Whether this meant Reagan was willing to contemplate giving the canal to Panama under certain conditions was a moot point. (He would later embrace a muddled proposal to make the Panama Canal an internationally-owned and operated facility.) He confined his criticisms to what he regarded as the flaws in the pending treaties: There was no residual right of the United States to defend the canal, and there was no right of priority passage for U.S. ships in time of war. Reagan cited the views of retired senior military officers opposed to the treaty, which included Admiral John S. McCain, Jr., father of Senator John McCain.

A clause had been added late in the treaty talks guaranteeing "expeditious passage" to U.S. ships, but this clause had no specific meaning, Reagan complained. Above all, it rankled Reagan that the treaties called for the United States to pay Panama $80 million a year for the privilege of taking over our canal. Shouldn't the payments be the other way around? The fact that Panama was then governed by a dictator, General Omar Torrijos, who had lately become chummy with Fidel Castro, added salience to Reagan's geopolitical concerns. Torrijos's frequent anti-American broadsides (including a threat to take the canal by military force if the United States rejected the treaties) intended for domestic consumption in Panama didn't help his cause in the United States.

Elsewhere on the Right, conservative leaders seized on the Panama Canal issue as a means of clobbering Carter. It was a no-lose issue: If they defeated the treaties, they would have a scalp to hang over the mantle. If the Senate ratified the treaties, conservatives would have an issue to use against Carter and the pro-treaty senators in the next election. A direct-mail campaign by the American Conservative Union brought in $15,000 a day at its peak, as well as swelling the number of names on its donor list by tens of thousands, which funded a series of full-page newspaper ads reading "There is *no* Panama Canal. There is an *American* canal in Panama. Don't let President Carter give it away." A Republican National Committee fundraising letter bearing Reagan's signature brought in $700,000 to fund a campaign against the treaty. Reagan later complained when the RNC failed to spend the money in the manner promised, but the national party was in a tough spot since Senate Minority Leader Howard Baker had reluctantly decided to support ratification. (Baker's support was the key to the eventual ratification of the treaties.)

But conservatives were in fact far from unanimous in their opposition to the treaties. William F. Buckley Jr. and George Will both supported ratification, and debated Reagan on national television on Super Bowl Sunday in 1978. Barry Goldwater and John Wayne supported ratifying the treaties, and both spoke harshly about Reagan's opposition. One Republican who took Reagan's side against the treaties, however, was George Bush, who, with an eye to the 1980 Republican primaries, said the treaties conveyed "a perception of United States impotence."

The White House was not without its own ability to conduct a public relations campaign on behalf of the treaties. The White House mobilized its own "Committee of Americans for the Canal Treaties" and enlisted prominent political leaders, including AFL-CIO president George Meany and former President Gerald Ford, to speak publicly in favor of ratification. Along with the usual arm-twisting and favor-granting, Senators were flown to Panama to be lobbied first-hand by the Panamanians. Although opinion polls never registered a majority of the public in support of the treaties, the Senate ratified them by a one-vote margin, 68–32, on April 18, 1978. Reagan was in Japan the day the Senate ratified the treaties. Having been told in his car after breakfast that the treaties had passed, Peter Hannaford recalls, Reagan "turned the air purple" with his denunciations, but when he stepped out of his car to a greet a reporter waiting for his reaction, Reagan calmly said that the Senate vote was "a very extreme case of ignoring the sentiment of the people of our country. They were overwhelming in their disapproval."

"THE WONDER IS NOT that [Carter's] foreign initiatives sometimes misfired," Michael Barone observed, "but that some of them turned out so well."[23] The most famous of Carter's successes was the Camp David accords between Israel and Egypt in 1978. Yet even his one undeniable foreign policy triumph grew out of a near-catastrophic blunder. Henry Kissinger had developed an incremental strategy for the Middle East, believing that a lasting peace in the region could only come about through a slow, step-by-step process of confidence-building agreements, with the United States as the honest broker. Following Kissinger's guidance, Nixon and Ford had backed Israel's refusal to participate in an all-party conference at Geneva that would include both the Soviet Union and the Palestine Liberation Organization. The impatient Carter, however, thought he could get a comprehensive settlement all at once, and on October 1, 1977, Carter released a joint U.S.–Soviet statement calling for resuming the all-party peace process in Geneva. Carter had once again proceeded with no consultation with any allies (including especially Israel) or anyone in the Jewish community in the United States, including his own political adviser on Jewish affairs.

In Cairo, Egyptian President Anwar Sadat was alarmed. "I'd just spent two years throwing the Soviets out of the Middle East," Sadat reportedly said, "and now the United States is inviting them back in." Sadat decided to take matters into his own hands, and announced that he was ready to go to Jerusalem and negotiate directly with Israel. Israeli Prime Minister Menachem Begin graciously invited Sadat to address the Israeli Knesset. This ultimately led to the two weeks of hard bargaining at Camp David in September 1978, during which Carter used all of his force and persuasive skill (including convincing Sadat to keep going after he had begun packing his bags to leave halfway through) to produce exactly the kind of incremental agreement that Kissinger had foreseen. Israel agreed to withdraw from the Sinai Peninsula it had occupied since the 1967 Six-Day War.

While Carter could justly claim Camp David as a major foreign triumph, it was also in the Middle East where the greatest shipwreck of his foreign policy, and ultimately his presidency, took place: Iran. Here the full confusion and contradictions of his foreign policy were on display. "The basic problem throughout the crisis," Michael Ledeen and Bernard Lewis wrote in *Debacle: The American Failure in Iran,* "was that the President was notable for this absence. Carter never took an active role in the discussion, never gave any clear indication of the kind of solution he favored, and never put the question of Iran into the general context that would have aided the policymakers at lower levels in formulating options."[24] Most glaring was Carter's failure to mediate between the factions in the State Department and the National Security Council, who sent mixed signals to Iran through different channels of communication throughout the entire debacle. All of the hallmarks of the Vietnam debacle were present in the ruin of Iran; the debilitating effects of the political persecution of the CIA earlier in the decade also came back to haunt American policy makers.

Since the end of World War II, when President Harry Truman bluntly told the Soviet Union that Iran was off-limits to their territorial ambitions, Iran had been the West's primary strategic bastion in the Middle

East against the southern flank of the Soviet empire. Its central location between NATO member Turkey and pro-Western Pakistan made Iran the "linchpin" of the "northern tier" nations containing the Soviet Union. Over the years Iran provided a primary escape route for Soviet defectors, as well as important listening posts for the CIA to conduct electronic eavesdropping on the Soviets. In 1953 the CIA engineered a coup against a Soviet-leaning government that had taken power in Iran, thus restoring the monarchy of the Shah Reza Pahlavi. Throughout the 1960s and 1970s the United States supplied Iran with as much advanced weaponry as their oil revenues could pay for, and also provided training for Iran's army. (For a time in the 1960s, a young U.S. Army colonel named Norman Schwarzkopf ran the U.S. military assistance program in Iran.[25]) Iran was also a silent asset in the balance of power between Israel and the Arab states. Iran sold oil to Israel, and throughout his rule the Shah regularly received secret visits from Israeli leaders—a fact not lost on the Palestine Liberation Organization when the Islamic revolution began to destabilize the Shah's rule.

As a monarch the Shah was easily stereotyped in the West as an unappealing and unimaginative autocrat, but in fact he was a relatively progressive ruler compared with nearly every other regime on the Asian subcontinent. Under the Shah the literacy rate doubled, and life expectancy increased from 35 to 52. But this forced progress was a large part of his undoing. Walter Laqueur observed that "the oil boom turned out to be not a blessing but a curse."[26]

Simpleminded critics point to the aspects of "modernization" that ran counter to the fundamentalist beliefs of the Shi'ite clergy, such as opening schools and universities to women and abolishing the requirement that women wear the "chador" veil. Yet the more significant disruptions of the Iranian social fabric came from the Shah's attempts to modernize the economy through centralized means. Although the economy was awash with oil revenues, Iran was basically a backward command economy, with the Shah attempting to prop up the merchant class with subsidies. "What is going on in Iran is a transformation," the Shah proclaimed in 1974, "physical, mental, economic—on an epic scale."[27] He predicted that within the next generation Iran would take its place among the world's five mightiest powers, and he was buying arms in vast quantities from the United States toward this goal. He used the nation's surging oil revenues to subsidize public works and shore up the growing professional middle class.

The economy grew by a staggering 35 percent in 1974, and another 42 percent in 1975. Per capita income rose to nearly four times higher than next-door Turkey. Such rates of growth were clearly unsustainable. The Shah also instituted a land reform program (following the advice of some of the same American aid workers who designed the disastrous land reform program of South Vietnam), removing land from the control of the "Mullahs," the Islamic clergy, and placing it under royal control. Therein lay perhaps his largest mistaken effort at social engineering, because the Islamic clergy represented the most significant independent force in Iranian society. It was the purported "Westernization" of Iran that most offended the fundamentalist Islamic clergy. In addition to the socio-economic dislocations, the Shah's periodic lavish and self-indulgent celebrations of his rule succeeded in alienating the rising educated professional class.

To be sure, the Shah maintained a security force known as SAVAK— the Farsi language acronym for "National Security and Information Organization"—whose domestic police activities fell woefully short of Western standards of due process, to put the matter delicately. (Among other SAVAK activities that raised eyebrows was a spying program against Iranian nationals living in the United States, conducted apparently with the knowledge and tacit approval of Washington. Among the Americans who thought this worrisome was Ronald Reagan, who in early 1978 took note of a *New York* magazine article about SAVAK's American activities.) Still, on balance the Shah was not a great oppressor. He wanted to be loved rather than feared. For all the notorious excesses of SAVAK, the Shah did not permit the full force of the security organization to be brought to bear on his enemies.

There was no reason to suppose that there was any risk of instability or that the Shah's grip on the nation was less than rock solid. The Shah commanded considerable wealth along with a well-equipped army with more than 400,000 troops. So it was that President Carter went to Tehran in January 1978 and offered remarks that would become deeply embarrassing just a few months later: "Iran, because of the great leadership of the Shah, is an island of stability in one of the more troubled areas of the world." Carter also added that "The cause of human rights is one that is also shared deeply by our people and by the leaders of our two nations." The unraveling of Iran is a classic tale of historical contingency in which no one event, taken by itself, seems pivotal, but which, taken in combination, clearly point to a collapsing house of cards. This is exactly the cascade of circumstance toward which American intelligence and political judgment had proved inadequate and myopic in Vietnam and elsewhere.

There is seldom a clear starting point for a revolution, but the unraveling of the Shah's rule might be said to have begun in 1974, when French doctors diagnosed the Shah with a slow-moving form of cancer. Although it was a treatable form of cancer, it came as a heavy psychological blow to the Shah. Like most potentates, the Shah often came across as a megalomaniac, but in fact he was a deeply insecure person; a CIA profile of the Shah concluded that he had an inferiority complex. But what is most significant is that *neither American intelligence nor U.S. diplomats knew of the Shah's health condition until after the Shah left the country in 1979.* Even as the Shah began visibly to lose his grip, American diplomats failed to understand the seriousness and full extent of his withdrawal from effective rule. While the fundamental causes of any revolution are always obscure, the single most important reason why the revolutionary fervor came to fruition in Iran is easy to discern, and could be discerned while it was underway: The Shah possessed a weak character, and had neither the stomach for cracking down with the iron fist necessary to crush his opposition, nor the political skill necessary to generate a successor regime.

The Shah's aversion to violence was powerfully abetted by the Carter administration's enthusiasm for human rights. The Shah received mixed signals from the United States throughout the ordeal. Brzezinski assured the Shah that the United States would back "decisive action" fully and "without reservation," while other public and private statements from the State Department and President Carter himself emphasized the need to avoid violence and respect human rights. The Shah was throughout uncertain where he stood with the United States, and what actions the United States would support.

A fading monarch and a restive protest movement by themselves were not sufficient to bring down the Shah's regime. It required a focal point and a means of gathering momentum. Once again the chain of circumstance was impossible to foresee. In 1975, a year after the Shah's cancer diagnosis, Iran reached a settlement with Iraq over a long-running dispute involving the Kurds, whom the Shah had been supporting as a means of harassing Iraq. The treaty included a stipulation allowing for 10,000 religious pilgrims per year to travel from Iran to Iraq. This proved an immense boon to the person most determined to bring down the Shah—the Ayatollah Khomeini. Khomeini had been exiled from Iran in 1963 for having incited rioting, and had spent much of the next decade in Iraq brooding over how to foment a revolution back home. Khomeini organized thousands of the religious pilgrims who started coming through Iraq into a courier network, carrying thousands of cassette tapes back to Shi'ite mosques throughout Iran, spreading Khomeini's fundamentalist and insurrectionist views. An operation of this kind cost money, much of which came from the PLO (it is thought that Syria's Hafez Assad also provided significant support), which in turn got much of its funds from the Soviet Union.

All the while a number of other factors started to go badly for Iran. The nation was undergoing steady demographic dislocation; its urbanized population was growing by 100,000 a year by the mid-1970s, putting a strain on the ability of cities to keep up. Teheran didn't even have a sewage treatment system, for example. Inflation was accelerating, outstripping the ability to maintain subsidies for shopkeepers and merchants. Popular anger with the Shah was rising. Then on August 19, 1978, a fire of unknown origin broke out at the Rex Cinema in the port city of Abadan. Four hundred seventy-seven people died. Some of the theater's exits were suspiciously locked, giving rise to the speculation that the fire was an act of revolutionary provocation. The revolutionary clergy claimed that the fire had been the work of SAVAK, and noted that the fire brigades were slow to arrive with help. Three weeks later the government acted in a manner that lent verisimilitude to the revolutionaries' accusation. On September 5 government troops fired upon a religious rally in Jaleh Square in Tehran after the crowd of 20,000 had refused an order to disperse. The government admitted to killing 122 in what became known as the "Jaleh Square Massacre"; other estimates put the figure at more than 1,000.

There was still no recognition in Washington that the situation in Iran was becoming extreme. The CIA concluded in August of 1978 that "Iran is not in a revolutionary or even a 'pre-revolutionary' situation," while the Defense Intelligence Agency concluded in late September—*after* both the Rex Cinema fire and the Jaleh Square Massacre—that "the Shah is expected to remain actively in power over the next 10 years."[28] One reason the CIA and DIA offered such poor intelligence work is that the post-Watergate reforms to protect against the excesses of the 1960s and early 1970s made it difficult for the United States to conduct covert intelligence operations in Iran or elsewhere in the Middle East. Beside the fact that the CIA had only two analysts working full time on Iran in the late 1970s, the CIA had deliberately cut back on the covert penetration of opposition groups in Iran. Many covert CIA operatives had been purged from the agency. "U.S. intelligence capability to track the Shah's domestic opposition," Gary Sick admitted, "had been allowed to deteriorate to the vanishing point."[29]

Other nations' intelligence services were not similarly handicapped, and reached more prescient findings. Israeli intelligence had concluded as early as June 1978 that the Shah's days were numbered. The only open question, the Israelis concluded, was "how long he would last." Tel Aviv was sufficiently alarmed that it warned Jews living in Iran to make plans to leave the country. French intelligence came to the same finding as the Israelis, concluding in the Spring of 1978 that the Shah would be gone within a year. Above all, both the French and the Israelis worried about the Ayatollah Khomeini, and especially what his "clerical fascism" might do to Iran if he led a successful revolution. U.S. diplomats and intelligence officials dismissed both the Israeli and French reports as "alarmist," and never passed along these warnings to the White House.[30] The CIA, it later turned out, not only hadn't read any of Khomeini's writings, but didn't even have copies of Khomeini's writings. When the revolution started in earnest, the CIA called up the *Washington Post* to ask to see their copies of Khomeini's works. "Whoever took religion seriously?" a State Department official later asked.

In April 1978, Ronald Reagan made a quiet visit to Teheran to meet the Shah. The Shah had invited Reagan to visit on several occasions before, and as the turmoil grew Reagan decided to see firsthand what was going on. The trip was made without fanfare or publicity on Reagan's part (he usually welcomed reporters along on his foreign trips, but only Michael Deaver accompanied him to Teheran), and was appended to the end of a visit to Japan and Hong Kong that served as a "cover" for the Teheran leg of the trip. Reagan devoted a radio commentary to the visit upon his return—it was among the radio broadcasts whose handwritten draft is found in the Reagan archives.[31] Reagan made it clear that he sided with the Shah and deprecated the erosion of American support. "Iran must receive the worst press of almost any nation," Reagan said. "Where have we read of the great effort the govt. is making to upgrade the standard of living & to eliminate poverty? . . . [A]bove all we should know that Iran has been & is a staunch friend & ally of the U.S. It has a clear understanding of the *SOVIET* threat to the free world. . . . But it too worries about the U.S. and what appears to be a foreign policy based on miscalculation of Soviet intentions."

While American leaders failed to perceive the unfolding circumstances in Iran, other American acts inadvertently fueled the fires of revolution. The radicals in Iran famously declared the United States to be the "great Satan," and this was no mere piece of jingoistic rhetoric. To the populist conspiratorial mind in the Middle East the United States was thought to be pulling all the Shah's strings behind the scenes, as well as "controlling events on the ground," so to speak. As such, even a small or seemingly subtle incident could take on great significance. The oddest such episode occurred when the Shah visited President Carter at the White House in November 1977. Sixty thousand Iranian students and other nationals swarmed to Washington to protest the Shah's visit. The Iranian embassy organized other nationals into pro-Shah rallies, and so it was inevitable that the clash of both factions near the White House would get out of hand and require the firm hand of the D.C. police to put down. As President Carter and the Shah gave their welcoming remarks on the south lawn of the White House, tear gas wafted across the scene, causing the Shah to choke on his speech and Carter to wipe tears out of his eyes. At the state dinner later in the day, Carter joked: "There is only one thing I can say about the Shah—he knows how to draw a crowd."

Back in Iran the opposition movement reached a very different interpretation of events, which Carter national security assistant Gary Sick described in *All Fall Down: America's Tragic Encounter with Iran*: "When the dissidents learned of the tear gas incident on the White House lawn, they reasoned that such an event could have occurred only at the president's behest. Thus they quickly concluded that Carter had abandoned the Shah. . . ."[32] The number and intensity of protests in Iran immediately escalated. Still, as the conspiratorial mentality is usually accompanied with paranoia, the radical opposition thought that the United States must surely have some nefarious scheme in reserve to maintain the Shah in power.

In an odd bit of symmetry, the Shah believed the same thing. There was really only one serious option for the Shah to shore up his political position, and that was a firm crackdown on the opposition—probably through the declaration of martial law. Many leaders of the Iranian military expected this, and were certain that the United States would make sure such a plan succeeded. After all, had not the CIA engineered the coup in 1953 that restored the Shah to the throne? Thus the Shah remained supine, believing that the United States would somehow come to his rescue. Not until very late in the game did the Shah begin to have doubts about his American backing. By then it was too late.

Although a few advisers close to President Carter realized that a crackdown would likely be necessary, for most of the Carter foreign policy apparatus the prospect of any kind of crackdown or martial law was out of the question. To prevent such an option from even being considered, the human rights office of the State Department held up the sale of tear gas to Iran—the same tear gas that D.C. police had used in the anti-Shah protest at the White House in 1977. The State Department eventually relented on the tear gas sale, but refused to budge on the sale of rubber bullets; Iran eventually had to procure these from the British. American officials, especially national security adviser Brzezinski and the U.S. ambassador to Iran, William Sullivan, repeatedly assured the Shah that the United States backed him fully, but it became clear day by day that this backing extended little beyond private verbal cheerleading.

One reason for the tepidness and indecision of Washington was that significant factions of the administration, especially in the State Department, viewed the Shah as the problem in Iran, and not so secretly welcomed the prospect of his demise. Neither the State Department nor the intelligence community took Islamic fundamentalism seriously, while America scholars on Iran deprecated the idea that the clergy would participate directly in forming or running a government. William Miller, chief of staff to the Senate Select Committee on Intelligence, went as far as to recommend that the United States openly *support* Khomeini and the revolution, arguing that Khomeini would be a progressive force for human rights. Miller had ready access to Secretary Vance for his views.[33]

Typical of the self-delusion of American liberals was the case of Princeton University professor Richard Falk, who wrote that Khomeini's circle was "uniformly composed of moderate, progressive individuals" who shared "a notable record of concern for human rights." Falk argued that "Iran may yet provide us with a desperately-needed model of humane government for a third-world country."[34] Henry Precht, the country director for Iran in the State Department, wrote to Ambassador Sullivan in Tehran in mid-December that U.S. policy should be to find a way for the Shah to make a "graceful exit" while allowing the United States to take credit.[35] A few human rights activists in the State Department compared Khomeini to Gandhi, arguing that, like Gandhi, Khomeini would turn out to be a moral leader who would leave actual administration to a democratically elected government. "Top American officials," Michael Ledeen and William Lewis noted, "believed that Khomeini was a social democrat in priest's clothing."[36] Andrew Young even suggested that Khomeini would someday be considered "some kind of saint."

While the Shah and the United States dithered through the summer and fall, events began to accelerate. In October Khomeini decided to leave Iraq for Paris. The French had no liking for Khomeini, and considered blocking his entry into the country. The Shah, however, thought it would be to his advantage if Khomeini were further away from Iran, and told the French he had no objections to Khomeini going to Paris. It was a blunder. Whereas communications between Iraq and Iran were slow and inefficient, from Paris telephone calls and other means of communication went straight through. (It is not an accident, as the Marxists used to say, that one industry that was never disrupted during the series of strikes that paralyzed Iran was the telephone system.) "In addition," Ledeen and Lewis noted, "Khomeini discovered one of the secrets of the late twentieth century: the mass media of the bourgeois countries can easily become the tool of a revolutionary movement."[37] The media gave Khomeini's every move and utterance saturation coverage, and international broadcasts especially by the BBC found their way into Iran. Prior to his Paris exile, few Iranians even knew what Khomeini looked like, since Iranian news media were prohibited from publishing his photo.

In mid-October the most significant blow to date fell: Khomeini called for workers to go on strike in the Iranian oilfields. Within two weeks Iranian oil production was virtually shut down. Student riots followed throughout Iran. Iran's military was starting to fall apart; desertions were running between 500 and 1,000 a day. Officers were starting to be seen among the growing crowds of protestors. As Khomeini made a bid to establish himself as Iran's *de facto* ruler-in-exile, the Shah and the White House began to contemplate the extreme measures they had hitherto avoided—the declaration of martial law, followed by the establishment of a military government. In Tehran, Ambassador Sullivan reached the conclusion that the Shah would have to go, and began quietly contacting some leaders of the opposition without authorization from Washington. Meanwhile, the human rights office of the State Department sent a special emissary to Tehran to pressure Sullivan into reminding the Shah that the United States expected human rights to be upheld. Secretary of State Vance hoped that a coalition government of opposition figures could absorb Khomeini harmlessly into the mix. Undersecretary Henry Precht had argued that once the Shah was gone, moderate elements would reassert themselves and gradually establish a regime compatible with American interests.[38] Among Carter senior aides, only Brzezinski continued to argue that the fall of the Shah would have catastrophic effects. Brzezinski continued to favor a military solution—either a military government and/or a military takeover if necessary. But by January it became apparent that even this extreme option was no longer possible. The Iranian military was supine, and had not made even the most preliminary plans for seizing control.

In the midst of the deteriorating situation, the Soviet Union decided to stir the pot. The Soviet Union enjoyed a substantial presence in Iran; over 4,000 "technicians" were employed in Iran, including 1,000—some of whom were identified as KGB and GRU officers—at Iran's major steel mill. The newspaper of the Communist Tudeh Party in Iran was probably printed in the Soviet embassy in Tehran; it began to take a pro-Khomeini line in 1978.[39] Then on November 19, Leonid Brezhnev issued a warning to the United States: "It must be clear that any interference, especially military interference in the affairs of Iran—a state with directly borders on the Soviet Union—would be regarded as a matter affecting security interests. . . . The events taking place in that country constitute purely internal affairs, and the questions involved should be decided by the Iranians themselves."[40] Vance issued a typically weak response: ". . . the United States does not intend to interfere in the affairs of any other country."

In December 1978, as the Shah's ability to rule was collapsing, a reporter asked President Carter at a press conference if the United States expected the Shah to prevail. Carter replied: "I don't know. I hope so. This is something in the hands of the people of Iran. We have never had any intention and don't have any intention of trying to intercede in the internal political affairs of Iran. We primarily want an absence of bloodshed, and stability. We personally prefer that the Shah maintain a major role in the government, but that's a decision for the Iranian people to make."

Carter's poorly chosen words fell with a thud in Iran and elsewhere in the Middle East, where they were interpreted to mean that the United States was dumping the Shah. No such decision had been made, because the policy of the Carter administration throughout the entire crisis was to make no decisions but simply hope for the best. Carter even reversed the one decision intended to send a signal of American resolve: Carter quietly ordered the aircraft carrier *Constellation* to sail from the Philippines to the Persian Gulf. State Department opponents of the move leaked it to the *New York Times,* which immediately printed the story, whereupon Carter rescinded the order. But the signal to the Iranian military and opposition was clear: The Americans are tentative—it is only a matter of time before the Shah collapses for good. Almost the same day the *Constellation* story came out in late December, the Shah began making plans to leave the country.

The Shah continued to make last ditch attempts to stitch together a coalition government. But the Shah was finished. He left on January 16, 1979. Under the old constitution of Iran, the Shah was succeeded by a Regency Council headed by a new prime minister, Shapour Bakhtiar. His government would last less than a month. Bakhtiar sent word to Khomeini in Paris that he was willing to resign after meeting with Khomeini, but Khomeini stood firm: Bakhtiar was a puppet of the Shah, and must go immediately. Bakhtiar reopened Tehran's airport, paving the way for Khomeini to return in triumph to Iran on February 1, whereupon he appointed his own rival government under the leadership of Medhi Bazargan, setting up a classic power struggle. Khomeini's followers, who proved to be well organized, began taking over radio stations and military facilities. Then came the final step in securing the Islamic revolution: The army declared its neutrality in the political power struggle. The already thin support for Bakhtiar's government collapsed overnight. The military attache in the U.S. embassy in Tehran sent a terse message to Washington: "Army surrenders; Khomeini wins. Destroying all classified [documents]."[41] Khomeini wasted no time in installing a fundamentalist Islamic republic, executing homosexuals and revoking, among other secular laws, the statute granting women the right to divorce and restricting polygamy. Sixty-nine former government officials were executed in one night in March; most of Iran's senior military commanders who didn't flee the country were also put to death. Khomeini's regime executed more people in its first year in power than the Shah's SAVAK had allegedly killed in the previous 25 years.

While the collapse was under way, there was an omen of the future. On Valentine's Day the U.S. embassy was attacked by a revolutionary mob. Ambassador Sullivan and his staff were taken hostage. (On this same day, the U.S. ambassador to Afghanistan, Adolph Dubs, was murdered in Kabul.) Bakhtiar, foreign minister Ibrahim Yazdi, and some of Khomeini's forces intervened within 24 hours to end the siege. A ragtag "revolutionary guard" was then placed outside the embassy to ensure security—the foxes guarding the chicken coop. Following this episode the State Department decided to ship hundreds of boxes of sensitive material in the embassy to the United States; amazingly, they were shipped back to the embassy a few weeks later when it was decided that the embassy would return to normal operations.

How far-reaching might be the consequences of the revolution in Iran was difficult to say, but American strategists feared the worst. America's allies in the Middle East, especially Saudi Arabia, were appalled and alarmed at the outcome of the Iranian revolution and the ineffective American response. Once again the lesson drawn was that it was not necessarily advantageous to be too close to the United States. Walter Laqueur of Georgetown University warned in March 1979 that "U.S. foreign policy has written off not only Iran but a far wider area, and that the countries concerned would be therefore well advised to come to terms with the Soviet Union as best they can. . . . It may also encourage the Russians to engage in a forward policy elsewhere, as the risks involved must now appear small or non-existent."[42] Laqueur would not have to wait long to see his prediction fulfilled.

IRAN WAS NOT an isolated example of the ruin of foreign policy under the Carter administration. At the same time Iran was collapsing, Central America began to unravel, despite the initiative of the Panama Canal treaties. The focus of the trouble was Nicaragua, which, like Iran, was run by a family dynasty that Carter's State Department regarded as even more unsavory than the Shah. The president and patriarch of the current generation, Anastasio Somoza Debayle, had been educated at West Point, and ruled with the aid of a loyal National Guard. Even before Carter took office, Washington was starting to turn up its nose at Somoza's corruption and autocratic governance. Somoza and his cronies lined their pockets with millions of dollars in international relief aid that flowed into the country after a disastrous earthquake in 1972 (which meant that he merely followed the practice of the rulers of about half the membership of the United Nations General Assembly). In 1975 columnist Jack Anderson was blasting Somoza as "the world's greediest dictator," and Gerald Ford's State Department leveled strong criticism of human rights under Somoza in 1976.[43]

Nicaragua appeared to be a promising opportunity for the Carter administration's human rights policy. The Panama Canal treaties were generating goodwill for the United States in Latin America, and there was a growing moderate democratic opposition to Somoza centered around *La Presna* newspaper publisher Pedro Chamorro. Most importantly, the CIA judged, there was not much threat from the far Left. Somoza's National Guard, the CIA thought, had successfully stamped out the Marxist Sandinista guerrillas, named after Augusto Sandino, an anti-American rebel of the 1920s. In 1976 the CIA estimated that there were not more than 50 Sandinista guerrillas remaining in Nicaragua. The CIA consistently underestimated the seriousness of the Sandinistas. As late as May 1979, within two months of the Sandinistas' triumph, the CIA would still be reporting that they thought there was little chance that the Sandinistas would succeed in taking power.[44]

And so the Carter administration, declaring itself committed to the principle of non-intervention, undertook to instigate the removal of Somoza and his replacement by a genuine democratic government. What it got instead was a civil war that left 40,000 Nicaraguans dead, 100,000 homeless, and a Soviet-leaning totalitarian government in its place that became the incubus for further upheaval in the region for a decade to come. What the Nicaraguan experience showed was that Carter's human rights policy was a form of intervention. The Sandinistas would not have come to power in the absence of the Carter administration's human rights policy. As Robert Kagan observed, "With a few words and a suspension of loans, the United States had helped alter the political balance in Nicaragua in potentially revolutionary ways."[45] The

Nicaragua experience confirmed the defects of Carter's foreign policy that were apparent in its handling of Iran.

Like most Latin American nations, Nicaragua received both military and economic foreign aid from the United States, and the Carter administration decided to use aid as a lever to bolster its human rights policy. Deputy Secretary of State Warren Christopher decided to withhold aid to Nicaragua in 1977 pending an improvement in Somoza's human rights record. The Carter administration hoped to strengthen the moderate opposition and pressure Somoza into holding free elections, but the result was just the opposite: American pressure on Somoza reinvigorated the extreme Left, which recognized that American pressure provided them with a golden opportunity to step up violent guerrilla action. *New York Times'* central America reporter Alan Riding provided the Sandinistas with legitimacy and disproportionate political prominence with his coverage of their "major drive" to "topple Somoza." Riding also reported—inaccurately—that the Sandinistas had turned away from Marxism and were becoming more moderate. Once again, the State Department misjudged the political situation inside Nicaragua, and failed to foresee the consequences of its sentiment. In a hearing on the administration's aid cutoff proposal, House Appropriations Committee Chairman Clarence Long asked Undersecretary of State Lucy Benson the following question: "What would be the reaction of the State Department if this committee were to suspend all aid to Nicaragua, in view of some of the gross violations of human rights that have taken place there? What would be lost to the United States and would there be a violation of our security interests?" Benson answered: "I cannot think of a single thing."[46]

Simultaneous with events in Iran, events in Nicaragua began to spin out of control. Somoza promised that he would step down by 1981 and hold free elections, which was probably a stall for time since that date was conveniently after the next U.S. presidential election. He never got the chance. In January 1978 Pedro Chamorro was assassinated, which immediately radicalized the situation. No one knows who was behind Chamorro's killing, but it chiefly benefited the Sandinistas, as radical guerrilla doctrine would suggest, by eliminating the most formidable political figure of the center. A general strike followed, and Nicaragua's neighboring nations broke off diplomatic relations and joined the United States in pressuring for Somoza's demise.

The next major shock occurred in August, when two dozen Sandinista guerrillas captured the National Palace while the Nicaraguan Congress was in session. With the entire Congress held hostage, Somoza flinched. Rather than contemplate the bloodshed that would necessarily accompany a military attempt to end the hostage-taking, Somoza gave in to Sandinista demands for money, the release of Sandinista prisoners, the publication and broadcast of a Sandinista manifesto, and safe conduct out of Nicaragua for the guerrillas. (Most of the guerrillas went to Cuba.) Somoza's capitulation made him look weak and boosted the prestige of the Sandinistas. Many within the National Guard criticized Somoza's weakness, and Somoza, fearing a coup, jailed 85 members of the National Guard. The Sandinistas, growing in strength and flush with success, stepped up the pace and scale of their guerrilla attacks on police stations and National Guard posts throughout the country. The National Guard reacted brutally, using tanks, artillery, and aircraft to attack the Sandinistas indiscriminately, killing civilians and destroying poor neighborhoods in the process.

The Carter administration now belatedly recognized that it had a disaster on its hands. Instead of a peaceful transition to genuine democratic rule, it faced the prospect not only of violent revolution but even perhaps a regional war, as Panama's General Torrijos had threatened to bomb Nicaragua's capital city, Managua. Carter's foreign policy team didn't know what to do. The *Washington Post* took note of the precariousness of the situation in an editorial:

> [W]hat the United States is really dealing with, or so we increasingly suspect, is a revolution. It is comforting to think that the aging dictator Somoza will somehow fade away and be replaced in the scheduled 1981 elections by moderate democrats friendly to the United States. Such is the polarization and violence now building, however, that President Somoza may be forced out in an explosion well before 1981 and replaced not by centrist democrats but by elements politically and ideologically beholden to the guerrillas of the Sandinista National Liberation Front. A "second Cuba" in Central America? It is not out of the question.[47]

The prospect that Nicaragua might become a "second Cuba" derived less from the radical ideology of the Sandinistas than from the simple fact that Cuba was supplying the Sandinistas with arms. Panama, Venezuela, and Costa Rica all became willing conduits for Cuban weapons shipments, in part because of their loathing of Somoza, and in part because they understood the deeper meaning of the withdrawal of U.S. support for Somoza, namely, that it was in the self-interest of Central American nations to make their accommodations with Cuba, since the United States was no longer concerned with prohibiting Cuba's influence in the region.

Carter not only discounted Cuba's malevolent influence in Latin America, but for a time hoped to normalize U.S. relations with Castro. Latin American nations took their cue from Carter's bearings accordingly. Costa Rican president Rodrigo Carazo went as far as to remark that "It is more important for Somoza to fall than to keep out the Cubans." For his part, Castro visited several Latin American nations, repeating the boast that "Somoza will soon be in the garbage can of history."

U.S. intelligence was well-informed of the quantity of Cuban arms flowing through Panama because Panama's intelligence chief, Colonel Manuel Noriega, was on the CIA payroll. Noriega had met with Castro to help set up the arms pipeline, which included planeloads (sometimes the planes were supplied by the Panamanian air force) of .50 caliber anti-aircraft guns, AK-47 rifles, and hand-held mortars. Cuba also dispatched military advisers to Costa Rica to help manage the arms flow and advise the Sandinistas on military operations. The Carter administration resisted or downplayed evidence of Cuban influence and involvement with the Sandinistas, even to the point of directing CIA agents in Panama to pay less attention to the arms trade and trying to keep previous reports from Congress. (They leaked, naturally.)

Amidst the uncertainty within the Carter administration over what to do, a faction within the State Department came forward with the same argument that had been made about the Ayatollah Khomeini and Iran: that the United States should accept or even support a Sandinista victory, and that the United States could hope to "moderate" the Sandinistas because they weren't truly committed Marxist revolutionaries. The Sandinistas were, in the words of Assistant Secretary of State Viron Vaky, "classic *caudillo* types, searching for an ideology to sustain their search for power." Warren Christopher agreed with Vaky, but Brzezinski resisted this idealistic view, and the agony and indecision of Carter's foreign policy continued as Somoza's position steadily eroded in 1979. Somoza was determined to hang on, even though American emissaries had told him directly that he had to step aside and leave the country, and Carter had publicly stated that the United States favored a new government.

As various attempts at negotiation and mediation sputtered along unproductively, the American-led arms embargo began to have its effect on the fighting. The United States not only cut off its own military aid, but successfully pressured other nations to stop supplying arms to Nicaragua—including even forcing Israel to turn around a freighter that was nearing a Nicaraguan port. The National Guard began running short on supplies. Jeane Kirkpatrick commented bitterly that "for the second time in a decade an American ally ran out of gas and ammunition while confronting an opponent well armed by the Soviet bloc."[48]

Then in June 1979 the final public relations blow came: A National Guardsman was caught by a TV cameraman ordering ABC News correspondent Bill Stewart to kneel on the ground. Then the guardsman shot Stewart in the back of the head. Stewart's brutal televised killing caused outrage in the United States, and destroyed all of Somoza's remaining support among conservatives in Congress. The following day Secretary Vance called for Somoza's resignation. With the National Guard nearly out of arms and the Sandinistas gaining control of more cities, Somoza decided in July to leave the country. He flew to Miami on July 17, 1979.

As the Sandinistas began advancing on Managua, the National Guard disintegrated. The Sandinistas took over the government in Managua two days after Somoza's departure. Although the Carter administration was preparing to send massive amounts of American aid to Nicaragua in an effort to befriend the Sandinistas, Brzezinski understood that "the baton is being passed from the United States to Cuba." The Sandinistas did not disagree. Humberto Ortega, a member of the ruling junta and brother of the new president, Daniel Ortega, forthrightly declared that "we wanted to copy in a mechanical way the model that we knew, which was Cuba, and we identified ourselves with it. We didn't want to follow the other models."

The Cubans were happy to oblige, sending planeloads of advisers (including senior officials of Castro's secret police) to Managua within days of the Sandinistas' triumph. Within a year over 4,000 Cuban "advisers" were in place, helping to run the Nicaraguan revolution. The Palestine Liberation Organization hailed the Sandinistas (the PLO, it turned out, had helped train the Sandinistas and had supplied arms), and announced plans to open a PLO embassy in Managua. Soon Nicaragua was voting in lockstep with the Soviet Union at the United Nations.

In the United States the same confusion and double-talk that occurred over Cuba 20 years before was repeated. Carter denied publicly that Nicaragua was becoming another Cuba, even though U.S. intelligence agencies were telling Carter that the Sandinista government would soon lurch to the extreme left. It was a mistake, Carter said, "to assume or to claim that every time an evolutionary change takes place in this hemisphere it's a result of a secret, massive Cuban intervention." Deputy Secretary of State Warren Christopher testified to Congress that the Sandinista's "orientation" was "generally moderate and pluralistic." The Sandinistas were only too happy to play along with this charade since American aid was flowing to the country, so they made great public pronouncements about the inclusion of "moderates" in the government.

But before long the real course of the Sandinistas was undeniable even to the Carter administration. The "moderates" were either marginalized, driven from office, or shown to be Sandinista true-believers after all. The junta announced, among other steps, that there would be no elections before 1985 at the earliest. The most troubling portent of the situation, U.S. intelligence thought, was that Nicaragua would now agitate the guerrilla movements in El Salvador, Guatemala, and Honduras. "The Cubans," a CIA report to Carter concluded, "can also be expected in the months ahead to begin using Nicaragua to support guerrillas from countries in the northern tier of Central America."[49]

"THE FAILURE OF the Carter administration's foreign policy is now clear to everyone except its architects," Jeane Kirkpatrick wrote bitterly in the fall of 1979 in her famous *Commentary* article "Dictatorships and Double Standards." (She was not alone in this harsh judgment. Robert Tucker of Johns Hopkins University wrote in *Foreign Affairs'* annual survey of the world at roughly the same time as Kirkpatrick: "After almost three years, it is reasonably clear that the Carter Administration's foreign policy has been a failure."[50]) "The foreign policy of the Carter administration failed not for lack of good intentions," Kirkpatrick continued, "but for lack of realism about the nature of traditional versus revolutionary autocracies and the relation of each to the American national interest."[51]

Kirkpatrick's article was a sensation among political intellectuals—and also with Ronald Reagan. Several people passed the article along to Reagan. According to Kirkpatrick's own account, Reagan's principal adviser on national security issues, Richard Allen, handed Reagan a copy of the article shortly before Reagan boarded a plane in Washington to return to California. Reagan called Allen two hours later when he was changing planes in Chicago, asking Allen, "Who is he?" "Who is who?" Allen replied. "Who is this Jeane Kirkpatrick?" "Well, first, he's a she."[52] Reagan wrote to Kirkpatrick in December to praise the article. Your article, Reagan wrote, "had a great impact on me. . . . Your approach is so different from ordinary analyses of policy matters that I found myself reexamining a number of the premises and views which have governed my own thinking in recent years." If possible, Reagan closed, "I should very much like to have the opportunity to meet with you and to discuss some of the points you have raised."[53] Reagan's critics assumed his interest in Kirkpatrick was another example of the derivative nature of his ideas. In this case, as in many others, Reagan was there first. Kirkpatrick's argument, in one sentence, is that there is a qualitative and relevant distinction between totalitarian and authoritarian regimes. Kirkpatrick's article was the first time many people had thought about the matter this way. Yet in 1977, two years before Kirkpatrick's article, Reagan wrote in *Orbis* quarterly:

> President Carter has also failed to take into consideration the difference between totalitarian and authoritarian governments. . . . As a result, it has needlessly jeopardized good relations with several states which have been friendly to us and to their neighbors but whose governments have not behaved as we might wish in their internal policies.[54]

In other words, Reagan saw a kindred spirit in Kirkpatrick. She, however, was less enamored. At that moment Kirkpatrick, a lifelong loyal Democrat, hoped for her own party's revival, dismissing "this conservative Republican governor whom I have no interest in."[55] This attitude would soon change.

BEFORE 1979 WAS OUT, the bottom fell out of Carter's presidency. Khomeini's triumph in Iran turned out to be not the end, but the beginning, of America's agony in the Middle East, and became the intersection of foreign and domestic policy. Iran's cutoff of oil production in December 1978 led quickly to a 2-million-barrel-a-day reduction in the world oil supply. The U.S. share of Iran's oil exports had been 700,000 barrels a day. The collapse of Iranian oil production put the fledgling OPEC oil cartel back in business. OPEC had been having the allocation problems typical of any cartel; members were cheating on their quotas in 1978 as the world market price for oil started eroding. Iran's shortfall was all the excuse the OPEC nations needed to begin a fresh round of price hikes. OPEC announced a 14.5 percent price hike in April, but with prices on the "spot" market surging higher than the OPEC benchmark price, OPEC was able to increase its official cartel price by 50 percent before the international market stabilized over the summer.

By the end of this round of price hikes, the world price of oil had increased 1,000 percent in less than a decade. Economists estimated that the 50 percent price increase in 1979 could cost 1 million jobs in the United States, and add one percent to the inflation rate, which was already running at 13 percent in the spring. Already auto sales had slumped by 25 percent, always a harbinger of recession. This irruption of the world oil market was enough to revive the "energy crisis" in the United States, and it led directly to the summa of Carter's presidency, the infamous "malaise" speech in July.

How severe the oil disruption would be to the United States wasn't obvious at first. Total demand for oil was up only slightly from the year before, and inventories of crude oil seemed large enough to absorb a short-term shock. But Energy Secretary James Schlesinger warned in February that the looming energy shortfall was "prospectively more serious than the Arab oil embargo of 1973–74," and Carter, who never wavered in his view that changing America's energy mix was the "moral equivalent of war" swung into action. Carter asked Congress for stand-by authority to impose gasoline rationing, and gave another televised address to the nation about energy—the fourth of his presidency. Americans were paying less and less attention to Carter's pronouncements on energy; 80 million tuned in for his first energy address in 1977, but only 30 million tuned into this one, even though gas lines were spreading across the country. Carter asked individual Americans to conserve energy by cutting their driving 15 miles a week and by obeying the 55-mile-per-hour speed limit. He also sought tax credits for wood-burning stoves, promised to eliminate free parking for federal employees, and later decreed that thermostats in federal building would bet set at 78 degrees in the summer and 65 degrees in the winter.

The House rejected Carter's request for stand-by authority to impose gasoline rationing—"a complete and total repudiation of the President by his own party," Democratic Congressman Ed Markey observed—prompting Carter to say that "I was shocked and I was embarrassed for our Nation's government." House Speaker Tip O'Neill responded that "The members [of the House] don't pay any attention to him." Carter misplaced the blame. The real embarrassment of the situation was that the government was *already* rationing gasoline in the form of supply allocations to regions of the nation and to individual gas stations rather than to individuals directly. This had the practical effect of rationing gas according to who was willing to *wait* for it, rather than who was willing to *pay* for it, as markets do for all other goods. The federal allocation formulas, left over from Nixon's wage and price control regime described in chapter 6, were more than 400 pages; but even 4,000 pages could not have remedied the inherent flaws of the system. Gasoline demand was only up 3 percent from the 1978 level, but the shortfall on the world market, combined with the allocation rules that reduced supply by as much as 20 percent to some regions regardless of population and economic growth, made a gas crunch inevitable.

It was this attempt at government control of the energy marketplace that turned a temporary squeeze into a national crisis. Energy Secretary Schlesinger admitted as much, saying at the height of the crisis in July that "There would be no [gas] lines if there were no price and allocation controls." Carter recognized as much with a decision to decontrol the price of domestic oil. Decontrolling the domestic oil industry was long overdue. Domestic oil production has fallen by 11 million barrels a day since 1972; the government-mandated lower price for domestic oil had the effect of discouraging domestic exploration and production, which amounted in practice to subsidizing foreign production and increasing oil imports. But Carter mitigated the effect of this salutary decision by phasing in decontrol gradually over a two-year period, and seeking to impose a "windfall profits tax" on oil companies whose profits would soar under decontrol. Carter opposed instant decontrol of oil prices because "that would in effect be rationing by price. I am not going to do that." Even *The New Republic* savaged Carter for his gradual, halfway approach to decontrol. "Carter has stared the energy problem in the face and blinked," the journal of mainstream liberalism editorialized. "His program is a failure, and a cowardly failure at that."[56] Oil companies swore out their opposition to Carter's proposed windfall profits tax, which meant another congressional battle that Carter would likely lose.

But oil company profits were already soaring before any decontrol of prices could take effect, as they invariably do when sudden market price increases run up the inventory value of oil stocks on hand. The profits of the 25 largest American oil companies increased 74 percent in the first nine months of 1979, but this is partly because oil company profits had been *down* sharply the previous two years (during which the inflation-adjusted price of gasoline had fallen), and partly because the inventory on hand is usually booked at older prices, which typically provides a temporary boost to profit margins when prices rise quickly.[57] The subtleties of accrual accounting, let alone the notion of "replacement cost" for the next barrel of oil, are lost on the public and politicians alike, and the populist theme arose that "obscene" oil company profits proved that the oil shortage was a "conspiracy" or "hoax" of "big oil" to run up their profits even more.

Columnist Jack Anderson wrote in the *Washington Post* that there was "a conspiracy by the big oil companies to extract huge profits from the American public's belief in a shortage that was in fact a phantom." The *New York Times Magazine* and even *Reader's Digest* endorsed the conspiracy thesis. The urban legend that oil companies had tankers full of oil anchored offshore awaiting higher prices began to make the rounds. Opinion polls found that as many as two-thirds of Americans believed the oil company hoax idea, though a majority told the Gallup Poll that they opposed nationalizing the oil industry; the idea that the same people who deliver the mail would run gas stations was not attractive. The oil industry conspiracy theme was given semi-official credence when second-term Tennessee Congressman Albert Gore Jr. produced a report showing that the shortfall in the world oil market was only 80,000 barrels a day rather than 2 million.[58] (The Department of Energy shot large holes through the methodology of the Gore study.) *Business Week* magazine took a closer look at oil industry profit margins, and concluded that oil industry profits were slightly lower than the average for all manufacturing companies; large oil companies enjoyed an average profit margin of 4.6 percent, compared to 5.4 percent for all manufacturing companies. Meanwhile, Carter's new Department of Energy, whose $10 billion budget rivaled the combined profits of the entire oil industry, produced not a single barrel of oil or watt of electricity.

While price hikes and supply disruptions were rippling across the United States, there occurred another energy-related event that rattled the frayed nerves of the nation further. At 4 A.M. on an early April morning, a water coolant pump on a nuclear power plant at Three Mile Island near Harrisburg, Pennsylvania, inexplicably shut off. Normally the fail-safe systems on a reactor are supposed to compensate for the loss of coolant by shutting down the power turbines and "scramming" the reactor core by lowering the control rods that stifle atomic fission. But for some reason these steps didn't happen in a timely way, and soon alarms were going off in the control room indicating an overheating reactor and a buildup of radioactive gas inside the containment building. An automatic sump pump in the containment building then accidentally vented radioactive water outside the containment building, exposing the surrounding area to radiation. At first it wasn't clear to the power plant's operators how serious the situation was. Three Mile Island had suffered several bugs over the previous six months, but none of these indicated a threat to safety. It soon became apparent that some of the reactor's 36,000 uranium fuel rods had been damaged, that the "scram" had not been fully successful, that the reactor core was still "hot" and was continuing to build up radioactive gas pressure in the containment building. The plant operators now faced the serious problem of how to get the reactor core into "cold shutdown position." It was America's worst nuclear power mishap.

Yet to say that Three Mile Island was America's "worst" nuclear accident is not to say very much. The highest exposure to radiation of anyone near the plant was 100 millirems—about half the annual exposure a person receives from natural sources or the equivalent of two chest X rays, but only one-tenth the level the EPA considers dangerous. Radiation levels in the area had been 40 times higher after the last Chinese atomic bomb test halfway around the world a few years earlier. But the mystique and scale of nuclear power, with its imposing cooling towers, generated a wary public image that was impossible to overcome. Energy Secretary James Schlesinger tried to reassure America with the unconvincing view that Three Mile Island "underscores how safe nuclear [power] has been in the past." Pennsylvania Governor Richard Thornburgh told the public that there was no reason to panic, but that people should stay indoors with their windows shut, and that pregnant women and children under five should not go outside, which was hardly reassuring. Eventually 60,000 people were evacuated from the vicinity as a precaution.

The incident at Three Mile Island was a godsend for the growing anti-nuclear movement. By coincidence, a new Jane Fonda movie about the perils of nuclear power, *The China Syndrome,* had just opened in box offices across America, warning that a nuclear meltdown could wipe out "an area the size of Pennsylvania!" Movie-house audiences gasped at the apparent prescience of the dialogue. Suddenly all of America became familiar with the hitherto obscure Nuclear Regulatory Commission, the federal agency charged with overseeing safety at nuclear power plants. Three Mile Island spelled the end of new nuclear power facilities in the United States. The electric utility industry soon abandoned plans to build more nuclear plants. A few nuclear facilities under construction at the time were never brought into operation; other operating plants faced intense pressure to shut down. It was a blow to Carter's hopes to expand nuclear power as a means of reducing U.S. energy dependence on fossil fuels. The National Academy of Sciences issued a report pointing out that without more nuclear power, the increased emissions of carbon dioxide from fossil fuels might begin to increase world temperature. The NAS report didn't get much press, because the conventional wisdom of the time was in the opposite direction. *Newsweek* magazine reported in 1975 that scientists "are almost unanimous" that the Earth's climate faced a potentially dangerous cooling trend—perhaps even a new ice age. *Almost unanimous!*

THE FIRST LINES at gas stations started in California in the spring. The situation rapidly turned into panic buying and hoarding (the average credit card purchase during this period was only three dollars—a clear sign of hoarding), as motorists seeking to top off their half-full tanks threatened to run through monthly inventories before the month was half done. Buyers began lining up at 5 A.M. at gas stations, which began limiting the quantity of gas they sold on a daily basis so their supplies would last through the month. Many stations would stop selling gas by 10 A.M. The California shortage even affected President Carter. On a trip to California in early May, Carter's motorcade had to go 20 miles out of its way to find an open gas station. California's Governor Jerry Brown instituted an "odd-even" rationing system: Cars with license plates ending with odd numbers could buy gasoline only on odd days of the month, and vice-versa for even-numbered plates. Between price hikes and tight supplies, driving in California declined 10 percent from its level the year before.

Gas lines skipped over the heartland of the country and began to appear on the East Coast, punctuated by occasional violence that culminated in a two-day riot in Levittown, Pennsylvania, during the first week in July. The riot began, appropriately, at an intersection with a gas station on each corner. Over the July 4 holiday weekend, 90 percent of gas stations in New York City area were closed, while 80 percent of stations statewide were closed in Pennsylvania. The gas crisis began to exact a high toll on President Carter's political standing. His approval rating sank to 25 percent, lower even than President Nixon on the eve of his resignation after Watergate. Congressional leaders who had tanked Carter's requests for gas-rationing authority brazenly demanded that Carter "do something" about the mounting crisis. New York City Mayor Ed Koch accompanied a congressional delegation to a stormy White House meeting with Vice President Mondale, and told *Time* magazine that "I haven't seen a delegation this hot since the Vietnam War." A new bumper sticker started to catch on: "Carter—Kiss My Gas." (With winter fuel oil shortages looming in the Northeast, the popular bumper strip in oil-rich Texas read: "Drive Fast, Freeze a Yankee.")

Carter was equally unpopular abroad. Europe's leaders regarded the United States, with its low-mileage "gas guzzler" cars, as a profligate energy-waster whose voracious appetite for oil helped deepen the problem. Carter had pledged to the Europeans allies to cut U.S. oil imports by 5 percent to help ease the pressures on the world market, but little progress was seen in conserving oil. Carter was not well-liked by Europe's leaders (especially West German Chancellor Helmut Schmidt and French President Valery Giscard d'Estaing), so he faced harsh criticism when he went to Tokyo for the G-7 summit in June. (In a scene of hypocrisy that only government can achieve, the motorcade transporting the seven leaders and their staffs to the opening session at Tokyo's Akasaka Palace required 124 cars.) The G-7 nations tried to craft a buyers' cartel to combat

OPEC by sticking with a collective import quota. But cartel-driven import quotas in free economies are just as futile in the long run as supply cartels; the only question is which will break down fastest.

No matter what path Carter chose—including even immediate full decontrol of oil, which would have been the right policy—it was going to take time for the energy market to stabilize. Instead of waiting patiently on events and calling for perseverance by the public, Carter launched a bizarre chapter of his presidency from which he never recovered. Carter returned from the G-7 summit in Japan at the end of June to an atmosphere of heightened crisis in Washington. He announced plans to give yet another nationally televised address about the energy crisis, and alerted the networks to block out the time slot. But his administration's energy policy was in such disarray that Carter abruptly and without explanation canceled the speech with only a day's notice. Then he left town for Camp David, also without explanation.

The abruptness and silence about Carter's retreat to Camp David ignited rumors that Carter had suffered a nervous breakdown, or was involved in some secret bold stratagem to revive his sagging fortunes. Reporters noticed that most of the senior political staff to the president (but not many policy makers) were being helicoptered up to Camp David, which *Newsweek* characterized as "the nearly total disappearance of the government with no clear accounting of what it was up to."[59] The dollar took a pounding in the international exchanges, as foreign governments wondered aloud about the president's political health. The *New York Post* ran a banner headline: "WHAT ARE YOU UP TO, MR. PRESIDENT?"

What he was up to was the most remarkable exercise in presidential navel-gazing in American history. "They got up there," a White House aide told a reporter, "and they didn't know how to get out. It was chaotic, to say the least." Over the following eight days Carter invited 134 eminent Americans from various walks of life to participate in heart-to-heart conversations with Carter at Camp David. Some observers remarked on the inclusion of a Greek Orthodox archbishop, but the guest list was orthodox in another way: Carter's interlocutors were almost exclusively liberals or liberal intellectuals, including Jesse Jackson, Vernon Jordan, John Kenneth Galbraith, Clark Clifford, and numerous other labor leaders, academics, journalists, and Democratic politicians (including Arkansas's young governor Bill Clinton, who bluntly told Carter that he was not leading the nation effectively). Only four Republicans were invited.

What was most notable about the guest list, aside from its political and liberal cast, was the scarcity of expertise about energy. "The guest register," *Newsweek* observed, "invited the view that the politics of recovery preceded policy on the agenda." *The New Republic* said it looked like "a tableau from *Who's Who*." Rather than a deliberation about a new course for energy policy, the discussions were devoted to a discussion of Carter's "leadership style" and the mood of the nation. Some of these conversations lasted into the small hours of the morning, with Carter sitting on the floor cross-legged. Not content with the parade of notables to his mountain retreat, Carter organized a backyard visit with an ordinary family at the home of William Fisher in Carnegie, Pennsylvania. (Fisher, a machinist and union member, had been selected at short notice by the local Democratic Party, which didn't know about his criminal record, which included arson and assault.)

At Camp David Carter himself expressed his own deep current of pessimism about the nation's prospects, telling one group of visitors that "I think it's inevitable that there will be a lower standard of living than what everybody had always anticipated, constant growth. . . . I think there's going to have to be a reorientation of what people value in their own lives. I believe that there has to be a more equitable sharing of what we have. . . . The only trend is downward. But it's been almost impossible to get people to face up to this."

Carter's "mystifying secret summit" (as *Newsweek* called it) had the desired dramatic effect. Carter came down from Camp David on Sunday, July 15, and pre-empted *Moses—The Lawgiver* on CBS to deliver his own TV sermon before the largest audience of his presidency. The hiatus from public view had built up expectations. *The Washington Post* announced the speech with the banner headline: "Carter Seeking Oratory to Move an Entire Nation." Carter tried to be equal to the occasion. The trademark Carter smile was gone; he delivered the speech with a grim expression, flashing his eyes and gesticulating with a clenched fist for effect that looked awkward and contrived. (These physical touches had been devised and rehearsed at the advice of his top PR adviser, ad man Gerald Rafshoon.) But what he said qualifies as the most dubious piece of presidential rhetoric in American history. It deserves quotation at length:

It's clear that the true problems of our Nation are much deeper—deeper than gasoline lines or energy shortages, deeper even than inflation or recession. And I realize more than ever that as President I need your help. So, I decided to reach out and listen to the voices of America.

I invited to Camp David people from almost every segment of our society—business and labor, teachers and preachers, Governors, mayors, and private citizens. And then I left Camp David to listen to other Americans, men and women like you. It has been an extraordinary 10 days, and I want to share with you what I've heard. . . .

[A]fter listening to the American people I have been reminded again that all the legislation in the world can't fix what's wrong with America. So, I want to speak to you first tonight about a subject even more serious than energy or inflation. I want to talk to you right now about a fundamental threat to American democracy.

I do not mean our political and civil liberties. They will endure. And I do not refer to the outward strength of America, a nation that is at peace tonight everywhere in the world, with unmatched economic power and military might.

The threat is nearly invisible in ordinary ways. It is a crisis of confidence. It is a crisis that strikes at the very heart and soul and spirit of our national will. We can see this crisis in the growing doubt about the meaning of our own lives and in the loss of a unity of purpose for our Nation.

The erosion of our confidence in the future is threatening to destroy the social and the political fabric of America. The confidence that we have always had as a people is not simply some romantic dream or a proverb in a dusty book that we read just on the Fourth of July. It is the idea which founded our Nation and has guided our development as a people. Confidence in the future has supported everything else—public institutions and private enterprise, our own families, and the very Constitution of the United States. Confidence has defined our course and has served as a link between generations. We've always believed in something called progress. We've always had a faith that the days of our children would be better than our own.

Our people are losing that faith, not only in government itself but in the ability as citizens to serve as the ultimate rulers and shapers of our democracy. As a people we know our past and we are proud of it. Our progress has been part of the living history of America, even the world. We always believed that we were part of a great movement of humanity itself called democracy, involved in the search for freedom, and that belief has always strengthened us in our purpose. But just as we are losing our confidence in the future, we are also beginning to close the door on our past. . . .

In a nation that was proud of hard work, strong families, close-knit communities, and our faith in God, too many of us now tend to worship self-indulgence and consumption. Human identity is no longer defined by what one does, but by what one owns. But we've discovered that owning things and consuming things does not satisfy our longing for meaning. We've learned that piling up material goods cannot fill the emptiness of lives which have no confidence or purpose.

The symptoms of this crisis of the American spirit are all around us. For the first time in the history of our country a majority of our people believe that the next five years will be worse than the past five years. Two-thirds of our people do not even vote. The productivity of American workers is actually dropping, and the willingness of Americans to save for the future has fallen below that of all other people in the Western world.

As you know, there is a growing disrespect for government and for churches and for schools, the news media, and other institutions. This is not a message of happiness or reassurance, but it is the truth and it is a warning.

This stunning peroration about America's spiritual condition broke off halfway through the speech, however, and the speech then pivoted back to the conventional policy ideas and hortatory themes Carter had been propounding for the previous three years. In other words, there were no new real policies in the speech. However, the little personal steps Carter had been urging people to adopt took on a grandiose patriotic tone:

And I'm asking you for your good and for your Nation's security to take no unnecessary trips, to use carpools or public transportation whenever you can, to park your car one extra day per week, to obey the speed limit, and to set your thermostats to save fuel. Every act of

energy conservation like this is more than just common sense—I tell
you it is an act of patriotism. . . .

So, the solution of our energy crisis can also help us to conquer
the crisis of the spirit in our country. It can rekindle our sense of
unity, our confidence in the future, and give our Nation and all of us
individually a new sense of purpose.

Finally, Carter exhorted Americans, "Whenever you have a chance,
say something good about our country."

The first thing to notice about the speech is that Carter did not use
the word "malaise" anywhere in the speech. After the speech Carter's
pollster Pat Caddell (whose role in the speech will be discussed shortly)
used the term "malaise" in a press briefing. From then on the label stuck
(though it should be noted that Carter's notes from his Camp David
meetings do use the term "general malaise" to describe America's mood),
and ever after "malaise" is how most people recall the speech.

The public initially responded favorably, with Carter's approval rating jumping from 25 to 37 percent in the days immediately after the
speech, and 86 percent, according to one poll, agreed with Carter's central theme about the "crisis of confidence." But the critical reaction was
overwhelmingly negative. *National Review* called it "obfuscation and
Elmer Gantryism," and offered the no-nonsense reflection that "The U.S.
Government has nothing to do with spiritual crises or the meaning of
our lives. . . . The last time we looked, God was not a member of the
Carter Cabinet."[60]

The New Republic was more savage, calling the speech "pop sociology stew" filled with "servile flatteries." "Carter seems to think that
teaching us to sing 'Let a Smile Be Your Umbrella' can be a substitute for
leading us in out of the rain. Fortunately, he utterly lacks the rhetorical
skill for such a con job."[61] This represented a striking turnabout for *The
New Republic*. When Carter first declared the energy crisis to be the
"moral equivalent of war" in the spring of 1977, *The New Republic* editorialized in a vein that anticipated the Carter of July 1979: "To us, whatever contraction of affluence this country may suffer over the next few
years appears no more than a byproduct of the contraction of the spirit
we are already suffering."[62] A labor leader who had supported Carter in
1976 complained that "The fault is his, not ours, and asking us to say

something nice about America is like Gerald Ford telling us to pin on little lapel buttons and 'Whip Inflation Now.'" And naturally Carter's message rubbed Reagan the wrong way: "People who talk about an age of limits," Reagan said, "are really talking about their own limitations, not America's."

Foreign reaction was equally pungent. A high-ranking West German official was quoted in the press asking, "Is this serious, or is this just a great religious exercise for the soul?" In Britain, the *Economist* called Carter's act "amateurism," while the *Daily Mail* newspaper was bewildered: "From this side of the Atlantic, Jimmy Carter's frenzied efforts to revive his personal standing with voters before the next presidential election look more like a narcissistic crusade than a national crusade." Even Swedes found Carter's exercise odd; a Stockholm newspaper observed that "As a document of the emotional climate of the late 1970s, [Carter's] speech should be historic. It is also historic in its lack of concrete means of effecting a cure."[63]

The Swedish writer was dead on target in observing that Carter's speech was a window into the soul of the 1970s, and as such it deserves a modest defense from its critics. As we have seen, Nixon had said something similar to Carter in 1971. And the themes of "scarcity" and "limits to growth" have already been remarked upon previously. Yet there was a second element to Carter's argument about the nation's "crisis of confidence"—that the nation was in the thrall of a materialistic hedonism or narcissism. As Carter put it: "Human identity is no longer defined by what one does, but by what one owns. But we've discovered that owning things and consuming things does not satisfy our longing for meaning. We've learned that piling up material goods cannot fill the emptiness of lives which have no confidence or purpose." Odd as this may sound coming from a President of the United States—even one as publicly devout as the Southern Baptist Carter—the theme was not without resonance across the ideological spectrum.

Carter should get some credit for highlighting, however superficially, the most significant difference between the 1960s and the 1970s in the social condition of America. The individualistic or "non-conformist" hedonism that was central to the "counterculture" outlook of the 1960s ("do your own thing") was represented as the necessary challenge to the institutional and cultural forms, the moral substance, of a supposedly decadent and decayed political and social order. This is nonsense, of course: The supposed "non-conformism" of the counterculture rapidly imposed a rigid conformism of its own, which has continued with the "politically correct" successors to the counterculture.

In the 1970s, however, the political dimension behind the counter-cultural ferment of the 1960s receded from view, and we were left with a hedonism whose essential nihilism was undressed. The "consciousness-raising" of the 1960s became narrow self-absorption in the 1970s, which erupted into countless bogus therapeutic fads such as EST, TM, "rolfing," gestalt therapy, and "bioenergetics." (Many of these enthusiasms survive to this day in even more watery "new age" forms.) "Personal growth" had replaced "the revolution" and "alienation" for people who might be said to constitute "the hipoise." One of the clearest expressions of this shift could be seen in the way sixties rock music, which enjoyed a central place in the ethic of the counterculture, gave way by the late 1970s to disco music, whose primal hedonistic character was not merely undisguised, but openly celebrated.

Numerous social critics noted this none-too-subtle shift in the American character. Author Tom Wolfe famously described the self-absorption of the 1970s as "the 'Me' decade." The eminent George F. Kennan took to decrying the West for "its self-indulgent permissiveness, its pornography, its rampant materialism." The year before Carter's speech Aleksandr Solzhenitsyn caused a worldwide commotion with his Harvard commencement address, in which he attacked the materialism and spiritual emptiness of the West in terms not unlike Carter. The process of accumulation of material wealth in the West, Solzhenitsyn said, has overlooked one important psychological detail: "The constant desire to have still more things and a still better life, and the struggle to obtain them, imprints many Western faces with worry and even depression, though it is customary to conceal such feelings." First Lady Rosalynn Carter strongly criticized Solzhenitsyn's speech two weeks later, saying that Americans did not suffer from "unchecked materialism," and adding that "the people of this country are not weak, not cowardly, and not spiritually exhausted." Her remarks were considered to be the administration's semi-official response to Solzhenitsyn. But now her husband was saying much the same thing.

Carter himself is said to have been influenced by Christopher Lasch's bestselling book, *The Culture of Narcissism: American Life in an Age of*

Diminishing Expectations.[64] Lasch was prominent among New Left writers in the 1960s, but had come to regret the dissolution of the counterculture in the 1970s. The very first page of Lasch's book used both "crisis of confidence" and "malaise" to describe the American outlook. Some of Lasch's language closely tracks Carter's speech. "[T]he impending exhaustion of natural resources," Lasch wrote, "[has] produced a mood of pessimism in higher circles, which spreads through the rest of society as people lose faith in their leaders." Despite being a man of the Left, Lasch's cultural conservatism and critical appraisal of political liberalism led some conservatives to embrace his book.

Although Lasch's *Culture of Narcissism* can be read as the background text for Carter's speech (according to some accounts, it was Carter's favorite book at the time), the real motive force behind the speech was Pat Caddell, Carter's *wunderkind* pollster. It was indeed Caddell who brought Lasch's book to Carter's attention. Caddell had enjoyed a meteoric rise in the ranks of political functionaries. Caddell had broken in polling for McGovern's 1972 campaign while still a 22-year-old undergraduate at Harvard. It was Caddell, ironically, that Carter's aides approached at the 1972 Miami convention with the audacious idea that Carter should be McGovern's running mate. Caddell thought they were nuts, but four years later Caddell became Carter's principal pollster for the 1976 campaign. "Caddell," Elizabeth Drew wrote, "is an excitable young man with what many people consider a brilliant mind (some think him a genius) whose brow is often folded in worry."[65]

Since January Caddell had been pressing the "crisis of confidence" thesis on Carter, backing it up with poll data demonstrating the nation's pessimistic mood. One statistic in Caddell's poll especially alarmed Carter: For the first time since pollsters had asked the question, a majority of Americans thought that their children's lives would be worse than their own. This figure had grown from just 30 percent at the depths of the Watergate crisis five years before. "America is a nation deep in crisis," Caddell wrote to Carter in a monster 107-page memo entitled "Of Crisis and Opportunity." (Caddell's critics inside the White House dubbed it the "Apocalypse Now" memo.) "Psychological more than material," Caddell argued, "it is a crisis marked by a dwindling faith in the future." Caddell recommended that Carter undertake "consultations" with a cross-section of Americans to get his bearings—exactly the process that Carter undertook at Camp David.

Carter was hooked on the idea, but much of his staff was not. The most strenuous objection to a public embrace of Caddell's thesis came from Vice President Mondale, who was so upset with Carter's drift that he considered the extraordinary step of resigning as vice president. Mondale thought Caddell was the Rasputin of the White House, and that Carter was exhibiting catastrophic weakness. "Everything in me told me that this was wrong," Mondale said later. "I was morose about it because I thought it would destroy Carter and me with him."[66] Caddell's craziest suggestion, Mondale thought, was that President Carter should call for a constitutional convention (an idea that was discussed and finally rejected at Camp David). Mondale and other conventional political thinkers in the administration preferred a no-nonsense presidential policy speech that emphasized definite steps, not a confessional and criticism of the American mood. At one point at Camp David, Mondale bluntly told Carter that a speech based on Caddell's ideas would be "political suicide," and that he doubted he would be able to defend it. "You can't castigate the American people," Mondale told Carter, "or they will turn you off once and for all."

Even though there was a measure of truth behind Carter's speech, Mondale was correct that it was politically disastrous on several grounds. It was a poorly crafted speech because, although it had a powerful overall theme, it did not have much of an argument. The powerful current of pessimism vitiated the references to American greatness in the speech, rendering them perfunctory and unconvincing. The speech represented a drastic departure from the tradition of presidential rhetoric that places bad news within the context of America's greatness; even the melancholy of Lincoln's speeches nonetheless had an edifying character on account of his evocation of America's great principles. And finally there was the credibility problem peculiar to Carter himself. He had built up great redemptive expectations for his presidency during his 1976 campaign. Having run for office on the promise of "a government as good as the people," Carter was now saying, in effect, that the people were no good.

Whatever benefit Carter might have received from the public's tendency to rally behind the president in time of trouble was undone within the next 48 hours by Carter's capricious decision to shake up his government through the same step Nixon had employed the day after the 1972 election: Carter demanded the pro-forma resignation of his entire Cabinet along with 23 other senior White House staff. Carter accepted five of the resignations—Treasury Secretary Michael Blumenthal, Energy Secretary James Schlesinger, Transportation Secretary Brock Adams, Attorney General Griffin Bell (whose resignation had been in the works for months), and Health, Education, and Welfare Secretary Joseph Califano. Bell had wanted to leave for some time and Schlesinger was dismissed for being ineffectual. The other three were dismissed for being "disloyal," especially Califano, whose close ties to Ted Kennedy brought him under suspicion. Most troubling to Carter's political fortunes was Califano's aggressive anti-smoking campaign, which was causing Carter political heartburn in tobacco-growing states such as North Carolina. (Resisting Califano's political damage led to one of Carter's more embarrassing moments—a speech in North Carolina where he said the federal government's efforts would make cigarette smoking "even safer than it is today.") Califano got in a subtle dig at Carter's resistance to activist liberal social policy when he remarked, "It has been a deeply enjoyable experience to administer so many of the programs enacted into law under President Lyndon Johnson."

Carter thought wielding his ax would bolster the image he had tried to create in his "malaise" speech of a decisive leader setting a bold new course for the nation. The effect was just the opposite. The biggest Cabinet upheaval since 1841 (*Time* described it as "the most thoroughgoing, and puzzling, purge in the history of the U.S. presidency") sent the dollar into a new tailspin, and the price of gold shot over $300 an ounce for the first time. Califano and Adams had been well-respected in Washington, while some of the Cabinet members Carter retained (such as HUD Secretary Patricia Harris) were not. In addition to the Cabinet sackings, Carter announced he was officially elevating Hamilton Jordan to be chief of staff. In addition to the hearty dislike much of Washington had for Jordan, his elevation represented the reversal of Carter's ostentatious pledge upon taking office that he would not have a chief of staff. This was too much for Capitol Hill. Democratic Congressman Charles Wilson of Texas complained: "Good grief! They're cutting down the biggest trees and keeping the monkeys." *Time* judged that "the housecleaning . . . provoked new doubts about Carter's understanding of the Federal Government and about his own leadership ability."[67] Ken Bode wrote "It's Over For Jimmy" in *The New Republic*:

The past two weeks will be remembered as the period when President Carter packed it in, put the finishing touches on a failed presidency. . . . It's over for Jimmy Carter. He needed a new image, so he took the advice of his pollster, his ad man, and his wife and wound up immobilizing his own government, imperiling the American dollar on the international market, and looking more than ever like a crude, erratic, unstable amateur. . . . The Carter administration has simply imploded, collapsed inwardly under the weight of its own incompetence.[68]

The quick bump in Carter's polls the day after the speech proved evanescent; by the end of the week his approval rating had fallen back to the pre–malaise speech 25 percent. During the same period Carter was botching the energy situation and sacking his Cabinet, a number of personal pratfalls added to the impression of incompetence. Some observers worried whether Carter's problem was not his competence, but his state of mind. A few of these worries were spoken openly. Republican Senator Ted Stevens (one of the few Republicans who had been invited to the Camp David affair) wondered aloud on the Senate floor and again on TV: "Some of us are seriously worried that he might be approaching some kind of mental problem. He ought to take a rest." When Carter returned to Washington from a short vacation at the end of May reporters noticed that he was parting his hair on the other side of his head.

The most bizarre episode of that period concerned an incredible account of Carter fending off an attack from a ferocious . . . *rabbit*. While fishing on a pond on his Georgia farm, the story went, a frenzied "swamp rabbit" attempted to climb into Carter's boat. Carter counterattacked with his paddle, but with the intent of driving off the beast rather than striking it. Carter related the story to his press secretary Jody Powell, who made the mistake of passing the story along to Associated Press reporter Brooks Jackson. Jackson filed a "human interest" story about the episode, which the *Washington Post* ran on the front page beneath the headline, "President Attacked by Rabbit." "A 'killer rabbit' attacked President Carter on a recent trip to Plains, Georgia," Jackson's story read. "The rabbit . . . was hissing menacingly, its teeth flashing and nostrils flared, and making straight for the President." All three television networks carried the story, which seemed straight out of a Monty Python skit, on their national news broadcasts. (The *New York Times* had the sense to run the story on page 12.) Comedians had a field day: "I didn't think Carter had a paddle," Mark Russell quipped on PBS.

The story took on symbolic significance far out of proportion to its merits. Beyond the sheer incredulity of the image itself (*"killer rabbit??"*), that Carter did not strike at the rabbit with the intent to kill it was transformed into a metaphor for his weakness in office. A grainy color photo by a White House photographer of the incident existed, but Press Secretary Jody Powell refused to release it because it would have caused "the rabbit controversy" to continue. Still later in the summer Carter, an occasional jogger, decided to enter a 10-kilometer road race in suburban Maryland. He collapsed halfway through the race, a victim of the late summer heat and humidity. A photo of a faltering Carter being propped up by Secret Service agents ran on the front page of most newspapers—another unflattering symbol of weakness in the commander-in-chief.

But if domestic affairs were going poorly, Carter could take solace in thinking that foreign affairs might bring a turnaround in his fortunes. In June, Carter had at last completed the SALT II arms control treaty with the Soviet Union, and had signed the treaty at a summit with Leonid Brezhnev in Vienna. Carter's ebullience for the treaty led him to give Brezhnev a hug and kiss on the cheek, a step which startled the feeble Soviet boss and nauseated conservatives back in the United States. Carter no doubt thought the prestige of achieving a new arms treaty with the Soviet Union would provide him with a political lift sufficient to fend off the expected challenge from Ted Kennedy. Aside from the domestic political impact of a treaty, the idealistic Carter thought SALT II would ease Cold War tensions and reinvigorate détente. It had just the opposite effect: SALT II touched off the most ferocious and fundamental foreign policy debate since the beginning of the Cold War under President Truman, a debate that would persist throughout the Reagan years in the 1980s.

THE FINAL DETAILS of the SALT II treaty required a circuitous negotiating process, stemming chiefly from yet another Carter blunder early in his administration. As mentioned in chapter 9, Ford and Kissinger had reached a basic framework for a SALT II treaty at the summit meeting in Vladivostok in 1975. The core of their provisional arms deal was an agreement that each side would have the same number of inter-continental ballistic missiles

(ICBMs), which was thought to remedy a chief defect of the first SALT treaty that Nixon signed in 1972. But many important details remained to be worked through, such as whether and how to include bombers of various categories, and especially how to balance the technological differences in the forces of each side. SALT I had allowed the Soviet Union to have nearly one-third more missiles than the United States. Because the United States enjoyed superior technology—MIRVed (multiple warheads) missiles and greater accuracy—it was argued that the United States still maintained "qualitative" superiority to the Soviet Union, but the U.S. Senate attached as a condition of ratifying SALT that future arms treaties be more "equal" in the number of missiles. After hard bargaining with Kissinger in 1975, the Soviets finally agreed to an equal number of "launchers" (launchers being the more inclusive term for aircraft, submarines, and silos that could serve as platforms for delivering nuclear warheads).

Had Carter concluded SALT II swiftly in 1977, the treaty likely would have been ratified. Yet Carter's negotiators didn't get final agreement on SALT II until the spring of 1979, two years later, by which time the political climate had changed substantially. Once again the odd and contradictory nature of Carter's character generated a snafu. On the one hand, Carter had criticized Ford and Kissinger for not being tough enough with the Soviets; at the same time, Carter's pacifist sympathies led him to call for "real arms control," that is, deep *reductions* in nuclear weapons (a goal he shared, ironically, with Ronald Reagan). Yet both SALT I and the prospective Vladivostok framework for SALT II allowed the number of nuclear warheads to go up. Carter and his foreign policy team decided to try for a better deal.

Carter blundered, however, in going public with the idea rather than proposing it privately to the Soviets over the negotiating table. Carter announced his general intention to cut nuclear weapons in a speech to the United Nations. Carter followed up with a letter to Brezhnev proposing deep cuts in existing Soviet missile forces, but with little or no reduction in U.S. missile forces—the only American concession would be to slow down new weapon systems on the drawing board. Carter then announced publicly what he had in mind at a press conference: "We will be taking new proposals to the Soviet Union." But he made things worse by adding, "*We're not abandoning the agreements made. . . .*" Moreover, he signaled weakness by adding casually, "If we're disappointed—which is a possibility—then we'll try to modify our stance." The Soviets took Carter's public statements, combined with his human rights pronouncements, as a deliberate attempt to embarrass them and sour relations.

When Secretary Vance arrived in Moscow in late March to present Carter's arms cut proposals formally, the outraged Soviets reacted by canceling the scheduled negotiating sessions with Vance. Vance had been prepared to present a fallback plan based on the Ford-Kissinger framework, but the Soviets wouldn't even allow him the opportunity to offer it. Anatoly Dobrynin, the Soviet ambassador to the United States, commented bitterly that "Our leadership was offended. They felt they weren't being taken seriously. The members of the politburo were outraged."[69] Foreign Minister Andrei Gromyko called a rare press conference in Moscow blasting the United States for a "cheap and shady maneuver" designed to give the United States a "unilateral advantage" in nuclear weapons. Vance came home from Moscow early; now it was the Carter administration that was embarrassed, as arms talks were, in the words of Strobe Talbott, "degenerating into an intercontinental shouting match."[70] U.S.–Soviet relations never recovered from this shaky start by the Carter administration. Robert Gates, who served in Carter's National Security Council (and later became CIA director under President George H. Bush), wrote later that "relations between the Soviet Union and the United States were more consistently sour and antagonistic during the Carter administration than was (or would be) the case under any other President of the Cold War except Harry Truman—including Ronald Reagan."[71]

As with the early enthusiasm for Carter's emphasis on human rights, many conservatives were initially buoyant over this turn of events, thinking that Carter would indeed be tougher with the Soviet Union. Détente appeared to be in tatters, which delighted conservatives. George Will celebrated that Carter's steadiness in the face of the Soviet temper tantrum over SALT was a sign that the period of "détente drunkenness" was over. This approval dissipated instantly two months later, however, with the "inordinate fear of communism" speech, which made clear that Carter suffered a lingering détente hangover, if not a form of idealistic *delirium tremens*.

Over the next two years Carter's negotiators closed the breach (partly by apologizing for Carter's ludicrous proposal) and produced a treaty that built closely upon the framework that Kissinger and Ford had worked out in 1975 after all. The final treaty had a number of features very different from what Kissinger and Ford had envisioned, however, causing both of them to criticize (though not categorically oppose) SALT II in 1979. To be sure, the central feature of SALT II was equal numbers of "launchers" for both sides (2,400 apiece), but there were a number of what experts called "asymmetries" in the treaty. Soviet missile forces had a much larger "throw-weight" than the American missile force; that is, they had larger missiles that could carry more warheads than Americans missiles. The Soviets' largest rockets could carry up to ten warheads, while American missiles carried only three warheads. In other words, despite having an equal number of "launchers," the Soviets could deliver a larger number of nuclear warheads with just a small portion of their missile forces. At the time SALT II was signed in 1979, the Soviets had increased the number of warheads in their ICBM force to nearly 6,500, while the United States had only 2,154—a number that had not changed in nearly a decade. True equality of missile forces, SALT II critics charged, would require equal throw-weights between the two sides.

There were other problems with the 300-page treaty. The United States agreed to include its bomber forces, consisting of aging B-52s and F-111s stationed in England, within its quota of "launchers," while the Soviet Union's new generation "Backfire" bomber was not included. The Soviets assured the U.S. that even though the Backfire was nearly as large as the America's cancelled B-1 bomber, it was not an intercontinental bomber. "The Soviets have agreed to furnish specific assurances concerning the Backfire," was the Carter administration's unconvincing response to the critics. But the United States had already observed the Backfire in flight with air refueling capability, and even without aerial refueling the Backfire could fly a one-way mission against the United States and land in Cuba. This concession in SALT II was especially troubling as the United States had no serious air defense. The United States had no surface-to-air missiles, and only 309 active fighter-interceptor aircraft—"a derisory force by any estimate," commented defense analyst Edward Luttwak. The Soviets, on the other hand, took air defense seriously, with more than 2,500 fighter-interceptor aircraft and 12,000 surface-to-air missiles, vastly complicating any bombing missions by B-52s.

The U.S. trump card for these vulnerabilities was the cruise missile. These small, highly accurate missiles were the ideal deterrent weapon, because they could be deployed by a variety of mobile means: from submarines, surface ships, aircraft, and even on ordinary trucks based in Europe. Cruise missiles were an answer to the B-52s vulnerability to Soviet air defenses. That the cruise missile could be launched from American aircraft flying outside Soviet borders extended the life and credible threat of the 1950s-era B-52s. Edward Luttwak observed: "Since they are so small and versatile in deployment, CM [cruise missile] forces are inherently very stable indeed: not even the most optimistic counter-force planner could hope to target a diversified CM force distributed among ships, submarines, aircraft of various kinds, and small ground vehicles."[72] The Soviets had nothing like the cruise missile in prospect in their own arms development program.

So it was matter of dismay that the SALT II treaty included a protocol allowing long-range cruise missiles launched from heavy bombers only, and limiting the range of all other cruise missiles to 600 kilometers (less than 400 miles), effectively removing their strategic deployment on ships and submarines. The protocol was set to expire in 1985, after which the United States would theoretically be allowed to deploy long-range cruise missiles in any mode it chose. Yet the momentum of arms control (a SALT III treaty was expected by 1985) was such that it was plausible to expect that the Soviets might well demand that the cruise missile limits be made permanent. The Carter administration insisted that it would never agree to any permanent limit on cruise missiles "which were not in the interests of the U.S. and its allies," but this assurance rang hollow. Why did they agree to them in the first place if this was so? Carter was openly unenthusiastic about most major strategic weapons, from the next generation Trident ballistic missile submarine to the MX missile.

The final difficulty with the treaty concerned verification. How could we tell, without on-site inspection (which the Soviets adamantly refused to allow), whether the Soviets were cheating by adding more warheads to their heavy missiles than the treaty allowed? The Soviets' largest missiles were judged capable of carrying as many as 40 warheads, while SALT II set a limit of 10 per missile. Beyond outright cheating, there was the problem of Soviet exploitation of the ambiguities of the treaty. Whether the Soviets had violated the terms of the SALT I treaty was a subject of fierce dispute.

The SALT I treaty had included undefined language banning both sides from "substantially enlarging" the size of their missiles. This was of major concern to the United States because the Soviets' rocket arsenal featured staged missiles, which meant that converting a "light" missile into a "heavy" missile suitable for intercontinental use could be as simple as adding another booster stage to the rocket. The treaty did not define what constituted a "light" or "heavy" missile, however; the array of existing missile types on the Soviet side was taken as the frame of reference. The treaty allowed that old missiles could be scrapped and replaced with new missiles roughly the same dimension. Shortly after SALT I was signed, the Soviets began testing new missiles that were 20 to 30 percent larger than their existing "light" missiles, but with four times the payload capacity ("throw-weight" again) than the missiles they replaced. In other words, the Soviet Union exploited SALT I to increase the number and size of warheads it could deliver against the United States without going over the ceiling of "launchers" specified in the treaty. The very nightmare that American negotiators had hoped to prevent through arms control was happening right under their noses in the immediate aftermath of SALT I.

Some American officials immediately cried foul; in 1975 Ford's Defense Secretary James Schlesinger said that these new missiles "can no longer be treated as 'light' missiles," but Henry Kissinger disagreed, saying that the United States could not hold the Soviet Union to American interpretations of the treaty's ambiguous language, and hence the State Department excused the Soviet move as a "technical violation." There were numerous other troubling signs, such as the fact that the Soviets were building more missile silos than they had missiles with which to fill them; the Soviets claimed—and the United States accepted the claim—that these silos were strictly for "launch control purposes," even though they could be quickly loaded with ICBMs.

"Fool me once, shame on you," the old saying goes, "Fool me twice, shame on me." Hence the controversy over Soviet cheating under SALT I made the issue of "verification" central to the prospects of SALT II. Since there was no possibility that the Soviets would allow on-site inspections (meanwhile, the Soviets could track what the United States was up to simply by reading *Aviation Week & Space Technology*), the United States would have to verify the treaty through what it called "national technical means," that is, through spy satellites and other electronic interceptions. It was unclear, however, whether the United States could sufficiently verify the treaty through these means. The loss of a listening post on the Iranian border with the Soviet Union was a major blow to U.S. technical verification ability; perhaps, the CIA thought in another burst of obtuseness in early 1979, we could set up a similar listening post in Afghanistan. There was also lingering ambiguity about the treaty's provisions regarding the encryption of telemetry in Soviet missile tests. All of these technical difficulties led CIA director Stansfield Turner to offer the hair-splitting distinction that the CIA could "monitor," but not "verify," Soviet compliance with the treaty. Senators squirmed over this uncertainty.

THE TECHNICAL DETAILS of SALT II obscured the geopolitical realities beyond the treaty. The common sense point of view asked: So what? Why do "throw-weight," "asymmetry," and other arms control jargon matter? To the layman, the idea of "overkill" trumped all of these esoteric considerations. With each side possessing nearly 20,000 nuclear warheads, surely the capacity to "destroy" each other's cities 10 times over meant that "throw-weight" and other arcana were irrelevant, if not trivial. Carter himself promoted this understanding of the issue, declaring in his State of the Union speech in 1980 that a single U.S. missile submarine could devastate the Soviet Union, thereby implying that a single submarine was sufficient deterrence. Kissinger's famous 1975 remark also came to mind: "What in the name of God is strategic superiority? What do you do with it?"

By 1979 the out-of-office Kissinger sounded a tougher theme, implying that the popular theme of nuclear "overkill" expressed the strategic insight of a child. The central defect of SALT II was that by the early 1980s the Soviet Union would have a credible "first strike" capability, that is, a high confidence of destroying 90 percent of the U.S. land-based ICBM force with only 20 to 30 percent of their missiles. In other words, the United States found itself in the strategic position that we had entered the arms control process to avoid. The ability to destroy the accurate land-based missile force of the other side mitigated the deterrent threat of retaliation. Under this scenario, the U.S. threat to retaliate for a first strike would lack credibility, because the United States could not confidently destroy the remaining Soviet land-based missile force, and an attack on Soviet cities would entail mutual suicide, as the Soviet Union would retaliate in round three in the same fashion. The terms of art for this kind of strategic calculation were "counterforce" or "escalation dominance." This state of affairs represented, in the words of a Pentagon analyst that were later widely used by Ronald Reagan, a "window of vulnerability" for the United States.

Few analysts would say publicly that the Soviets were contemplating such a step. Churchill's famous analysis in his 1946 "Iron Curtain" speech still seemed the operative understanding: The Soviet Union did not want war, but did desire the fruits of war. On the other hand, the Soviets' extensive civil defense preparations suggested they took the idea of nuclear war seriously, and a nation spread over 10 time zones could conceivably survive a nuclear blow better than the United States or densely populated Europe. Several false nuclear launch alarms suggests how tense were the circumstances of the time. In 1979 Brzezinski was awakened one night at 3 A.M. with the news that 2,200 Soviet missiles—an all-out attack—were detected inbound on the United States. Brzezinski ordered the Strategic Air Command (SAC) to scramble U.S. bomber forces and was about to wake President Carter with the grim news when word came that it was a false alarm: Someone was running a military exercise program in the SAC computer, not unlike the plot of the 1982 film *War Games,* and forgot to make the proper notifications.

As Kissinger and other strategists explained, a massive "counterforce" advantage is useful for political ends. Eugene Rostow commented that "to the Soviets, clear nuclear superiority is the ultimate weapon of coercive diplomacy," while SALT II is "an expression of American acquiescence in the Soviet drive for overwhelming military superiority."[73] "These were flush times in the Kremlin," Robert Gates reflected later, and the superiority afforded the Soviets under SALT II "would given them the confidence to be even more assertive in their foreign policy ambitions and actions—and other countries would act on the basis of perceived Soviet superiority."[74] Kissinger concurred: "Thus [SALT II] gives the Soviets a high degree of confidence in a crisis. That confidence, in turn, may make crises more likely. . . . We could be heading into a period of maximum peril." Put simply, if something like the Cuban Missile Crisis were to repeat, it would not be the Soviet Union that had to back down.

The Carter administration's answer to the counterforce vulnerability was the development of the MX missile, a new generation ballistic missile capable of carrying 10 highly accurate MIRVed warheads. The United States planned to build and deploy 200 MX missiles by 1989. But the fundamental problem remained: 200 MX missiles could be easily annihilated with only a small portion of Soviets land-based missiles in a first strike, leaving the problem of escalation dominance unchanged. The

Carter administration needed to find a way to deploy the MX missile in a way that would make it difficult or impossible to destroy the missiles in a first strike. They proposed a mobile "racetrack" basing mode, in which the MX would be deployed on hundreds of miles of underground rails connecting 4,600 concrete shelters in Utah and Nevada. The Soviets wouldn't know where the missiles were, and wouldn't be able to target all the possible sites without using a large portion of its ICBMs. Building the underground rail basing system would have been the largest construction project in the history of mankind, requiring more concrete than the entire interstate highway system. It was a preposterous idea.

The technical controversies over the treaty's details and American rearmament took a back seat to the political debate about what the treaty implied about American resolve. The two sides of the argument quickly fell out on ideological lines, each with contrasting historical perspectives. Already in the aftermath of Vietnam's collapse, conservatives had discerned a cultural similarity between the United States in the 1970s and Britain in the 1930s. In 1977 Norman Podhoretz wrote that "I have been struck very forcibly by certain resemblances between the United States today and Great Britain the years after the first world war. . . . The parallels with England in 1937 are here, and this revival of the culture of appeasement ought to be troubling our sleep."[75] Now SALT II seemed to confirm the worst fears of conservatives about American appeasement, and the argument over SALT II and the military balance between the United States and the Soviets was very nearly identical, in form and substance, to Churchill's argument about the air power balance between Britain and Nazi Germany in the late 1930s.

Senator Henry Jackson complained, "To enter a treaty which favors the Soviets as this one does on the ground that we will be in a worse position without it, is appeasement in its purest form. . . . It is all ominously reminiscent of Great Britain in the 1930s."[76] Eugene Rostow went even further, noting that the arguments made in favor of SALT II were identical to the arguments made on behalf of the Washington Naval Treaty of 1922 that not only failed to prevent World War II, but arguably helped to bring it on.

Liberals lined up to champion SALT II on several grounds. If conservatives compared SALT II to the appeasement of the 1930s, liberals compared opposition to the treaty to the isolationism that led the United States to reject the League of Nations after World War I. Senator Frank

Church, chairman of the Senate Foreign Relations Committee and a leading Democratic liberal, said that a vote against SALT II would be "the worst setback since the Senate defeat of the Versailles treaty." Ratifying SALT II was necessary to preserve the "arms control process"—we needed SALT II so we could go on to SALT III, which would seek to limit intermediate-range missiles in Europe (of which the Soviets were deploying many, while we deployed none). Sen. George McGovern warned that "the alternative to arms control and détente is the bankruptcy and death of civilization." The devotees of the "arms control process" trotted out the insidious argument that Soviet "paranoia" justified allowing the Soviets to have an edge in nuclear deterrent capability, or that it was necessary that U.S. military power be mitigated. Hedley Bull of the Council on Foreign Relations wrote, incredibly, in *Foreign Affairs* quarterly: "It is important that some state or group of states should undertake the task of balancing the power of the U.S. For the present, this can only be the Soviet Union." And without arms control, the old refrain ran, the "arms race" would accelerate.

From Carter's point of view, without some kind of arms restraint, the Soviet Union showed every willingness to build a massive arsenal of thousands of missiles, which the United States would be required to match up to a point—a seemingly mindless exercise. The *Washington Post*'s Meg Greenfield asked, "Where are we headed for? An MX missile in every garage? An SS-18 in every dacha?" "What arms race?" Paul Nitze asked. Only the Soviets seemed to be racing, Nitze and other conservatives retorted. Carter's own defense secretary Harold Brown lent support this view with his comment that "When we build, they build. When we stop, they build." Above all, liberals sought to portray SALT II as a litmus test of whether the United States was a peace-loving nation. President Carter complained that if the United States rejected SALT II, "The world would be forced to conclude that America had chosen confrontation rather than cooperation and peace. . . . We would no longer be identified as a peace-loving nation." He also warned that a rejection of SALT II might jeopardize the NATO alliance, and, as if on cue, West Germany's foreign minister warned that without SALT II, Europe would reconsider NATO's plans to base 572 new intermediate-range American missiles, which was scheduled to take place over the next three years.

Liberals were right about one thing. The ratification debate over SALT II was shaping up to be as momentous as the debate over the Versailles treaty in 1919. Senate Majority Leader Robert Byrd pledged to Carter that the treaty would be brought up for the ratification vote before the end of the Senate session in 1979, before the 1980 election campaign began in earnest; but as Senate hearings began and summer gave way to fall the likelihood of a Senate vote, let alone ratification, grew remote. Carter knew all along that getting a two-thirds vote in the Senate would be difficult, so much so that at one point during the negotiations Carter considered making SALT II an "executive agreement" (similar to the North American Free Trade Agreement and other trade treaties) rather than a formal treaty so that it would require only a majority vote of both houses of Congress instead of a two-thirds vote in the Senate. The Senate signaled its displeasure with this trial balloon, and Carter had to abandon the idea.

As it seemed likely that the debate over SALT II would carry over into 1980 and perhaps become the central foreign policy issue of the 1980 campaign, Ronald Reagan was diligently studying up on the details of the treaty and the shape of the unfolding controversy. Reagan had expressed skepticism of, if not opposition to, arms control for a long time. President Ford, Reagan complained in 1976, "gave away too much at Vladivostok," because he didn't get equal size limits on each side's missiles. "If we are going to have a SALT II agreement, the President should order his negotiators to get *real* equality in *every* area."[77]

In the 1976 campaign Reagan had criticized SALT I because "we compromised our clear technological lead in the anti-ballistic missile system, the ABM, for the sake of a deal." Now SALT II was bargaining away the full potential of another American advantage, the cruise missile. These became familiar themes in Reagan's radio addresses and newspaper columns in the run-up to 1980. Reagan was prominent among the critics who drew a parallel with the 1930s, even going to far as to compare Carter to Neville Chamberlain. After Carter's 1979 State of the Union speech in which he hailed the upcoming SALT II treaty as a means to peace, Reagan remarked: "Heard in the background music to that speech [was] the sorry tapping of Neville Chamberlain's umbrella on the cobblestones of Munich. He, too, talked of peace in our time."[78] Reagan even worried publicly in 1979 that the Soviet Union could deliver an ultimatum to the United States "as early as next year and at least by 1981."

Reagan's reference to the parallels with the 1930s caused alarm among some of his political advisers. Reagan's toughness and clarity were his greatest strength—but also his largest political liability. Reagan's campaign strategists were sensitive to the charge that Reagan was a "warmonger." Opinion polls revealed cognitive dissonance among the public on the subject of détente and arms control. About 50 percent of Americans told pollsters that they felt America was slipping behind the Soviets militarily, but more than two-thirds expressed strong support for the arms control process, with 69 percent telling the Harris Poll that they favored "the U.S. and Russia seeking areas of agreement of cooperation." Only 42 percent said they favored a "get tough" policy.

Here the reader should pause to reflect on the precariousness of Reagan's outlook as it appeared at that time. The benefit of hindsight provided by the benign end of the Cold War has furnished Reagan and his partisans with a powerful *post hoc* vindication of the doctrine of "peace through strength." So it must be recalled that even among conservatives it was not self-evident in the late 1970s that a policy of "peace through strength" would maintain peace. To the contrary, although many conservatives drew parallels between the enthusiasm for disarmament and appeasement in the 1930s and arms control in the 1970s, some conservatives thought—though seldom openly spoke—that the U.S.–Soviet conflict must inevitably end the same way: war.

The ideological conflict between East and West in the late twentieth century was as fundamental as the conflict between Rome and Carthage or Athens and Sparta in antiquity, England and France in the seventeenth century, and France and Germany in the nineteenth and twentieth centuries. If it was inevitable that the conflict must end in open war, conservatives wanted the United States to have military superiority in order to prevail. Liberals perceived this line of thought, and recoiled in visceral horror at the possibility that Reagan the warmonger would lead the United States into war. Reagan was one of the few who didn't privately incline to the pessimistic view that war was inevitable, but it was hardly an implausible view at the time, and added considerably to the political stakes in the upcoming election.

In the summer of 1978, Reagan's principal foreign policy adviser Richard Allen sent Reagan a long memo about the political problem of Reagan's hawkish views in the summer of 1978.[79] (Allen had worked for Nixon in a similar role in 1968, but had been eclipsed by Kissinger after the election.) "We face a delicate task in creating a comprehensive political framework of foreign policy and national security policy themes for 1980. . . ." The problem, Allen bluntly told Reagan, is that "for many, you come across as a 'saber-rattler,' a 'button pusher' or as 'too willing to send in the Marines.' This false image is happily amplified by the media, which prays for you to enunciate a dream formula for them to report— one in which you suggest the first use of nuclear weapons to support reactionary and fascist dictatorships against hapless subjugated nonwhite majorities. . . . I believe that you do have certain disadvantages (to wit, a hostile press which feels you lack depth in 'complex' issues, even though the press itself may lack depth). . . ." What Reagan needed to do, Allen thought, was formulate "a political strategy that involves telling the truth without scaring the hell out of people."

Allen recommended what he called the "Strategy For Peace" theme, "which requires enormous concentration on the whole and less on specifics." This was the genesis of what became Reagan's signature theme of "peace through strength." Allen's advice was more political than substantive, and didn't offer much in the way of general language and sound bites beyond "strategy for peace." "One of your initial reactions," Allen admitted, "—if, indeed not your first one—is that I am suggesting that you become fuzzy, indefinite and 'political-sounding' on issues about which you feel strongly. *There is, to be sure, a deliberate attempt to soften the delivery of your message. . . .*" (Emphasis added.)

Other advisers agreed with Allen's concern, suggesting that Reagan tone down his rhetoric and historical analogies to the 1930s. Fred C. Ikle, who had served as head of the Arms Control and Disarmament Agency under President Nixon and was a Reagan adviser, wrote to Peter Hannaford in the spring of 1979 with the "editorial suggestion" that "analogies to the 1930s should be avoided in discussions of our foreign and defense policy addressed to the general public. I fear, to the younger generation, they may either fail to stir up the right associations or appear anachronistic. Even for expert audiences, the many differences between that era and ours tend to provoke unnecessary quibbling."[80] Allen concurred, writing to Hannaford that "In connection with Fred Ikle's suggestion concerning use of the 1930s (especially the Chamberlain line), I am in complete agreement."

Reagan was utterly confident and unmoved by the concerns of his advisers, and with his "aw-shucks" manner tried to deprecate the image that he was (as he put it in 1980) "a combination of Ebenezer Scrooge and the Mad Bomber." Hadn't Churchill been called a "warmonger" in the 1930s, and was he not vindicated? Reagan was advocating the same policy as Churchill: Peace through strength. The lesson of history seemed to be on Reagan's side. Churchill wrote that World War II was "the unnecessary war," because a policy of "peace through strength" might have prevented the war. Nobody ever got into a war because they were too strong, Reagan liked to say. Now Reagan wanted to apply this lesson in his own time.

On July 12, 1979, just a few weeks after Carter signed the SALT II treaty in Vienna, Reagan held a day-long briefing about the treaty's details at his Los Angeles campaign office, with analysis provided by William Van Cleave of USC, Fred Ikle, Richard Allen, Charles Kupperman of the Committee on the Present Danger, and Albert Wohlstetter of the University of Chicago. Van Cleave had been on Nixon's negotiating team for SALT I, and Wohlstetter was one of the leading experts on nuclear weapons and strategic doctrine, and had been a prime mover behind the pressures that led the CIA to form "Team B" in 1976. Reagan also included two hours in the schedule to hear the Carter administration's defense of SALT II from White House aide John Newhouse. More important than the briefing was a series of phone conversations Reagan had two weeks later with Senators Henry Jackson and Pat Moynihan and Lt. General Ed Rowny, who had been the Joint Chiefs of Staff observer at the SALT negotiations, but who had later resigned in opposition to the treaty. Reagan's handwritten notes on the calls are revealing: "The Senators are sending me their statements. [Reagan subsequently quoted Jackson's statements against SALT II in speeches and articles.] The talks were all good—the Senators particularly are solidly against the treaty. *Sen. Pat Moynihan flatly called the President's statements lies.*"[81] (Emphasis added.) Jackson and Moynihan were not the only Democrats with whom Reagan found common cause on SALT. Reagan had received a letter months earlier from attorney and long-time Democratic Party wise man Max Kampelman, who would likely have been Hubert Humphrey's secretary of State had Humphrey won the 1968 election, telling Reagan that "One of the great problems we face in the country now is that of SALT, and it is my impression that we may find ourselves on the same side of that debate."[82] Indeed, Kampelman would become a key member of Reagan's arms control negotiating team in the 1980s.

Three weeks after his SALT II briefing session Reagan made his much-recalled visit to NORAD (North American Aerospace Defense Command) base in Cheyenne Mountain, Colorado, where the Strategic Air Command's early warning center for missile launches is located. It is where America would get its first indication that World War III was about to begin. A Hollywood acquaintance of Reagan's, screenwriter and producer Douglas Morrow, was a friend of the current NORAD commander, Air Force General James Hill, and arranged for Reagan to meet with Hill and get a tour and briefing at NORAD. Martin Anderson, who served as point man for the policy task forces of the Reagan campaign (which will be described in the next chapter) accompanied Reagan on this trip and recollected:

> Most of the day was spent going from briefing to briefing, each one conducted by high-ranking uniformed officers in small conference rooms that looked just like other military briefing rooms except that none had windows. The briefings focused on the relative nuclear capabilities of the United States and the Soviet Union, and on our means of deterring a nuclear attack.[83]

At the end of the day, when Reagan and Anderson were shown the large radar display screen in the main control room of NORAD, someone in Reagan's party (Anderson's narrative does not say who) asked General Hill what would happen if the Soviets fired just one missile at an American city. "'Well,' the general replied carefully, 'we would pick it up right after it was launched, but by the time the officials of the city could be alerted that a nuclear bomb would hit them, there would be only ten or fifteen minutes left. That's all we can do. We can't stop it.'"

On the return flight to Los Angeles, Anderson recalls, Reagan expressed dismay at the helplessness of the United States. "We have spent all that money and have all that equipment, and there is nothing we can do to prevent a nuclear missile from hitting us." The president faced a no-win situation. "The only options he would have would be to press the button or do nothing. They're both bad. We should have some way of defending ourselves against nuclear missiles."

This episode has been misinterpreted by many to suggest that Reagan was realizing *for the first time* that the United States was without any form of ballistic missile defense, which is not true. In one of his radio broadcasts in 1978 Reagan observed that "if the Soviets push the button, there is no defense against them, no way to prevent the nuclear destruction of their targets in the United States." Reagan's critics have suggested that either he or Anderson have exaggerated or embroidered this story for dramatic effect. While it is possible to speculate about whether Reagan's trait of being affected by first-hand contact with events rendered this episode more vivid, it is no exaggeration to suggest that the NORAD visit was an important link in the chain leading to Reagan's decision to revive ballistic missile defense as a key element of America's defense posture.

Within days of the NORAD visit, Reagan had given Anderson the green light to reexamine the idea of ballistic missile defense that Nixon had abandoned with the ABM treaty. Anderson composed a memo a few days later arguing that "the idea is probably fundamentally far more appealing to the American people than the questionable satisfaction of knowing that those who initiated an attack against us were also blown away." Anderson added that "there have apparently been striking advances in missile technology during the past decade or so that would make such a system technically possible." Reagan, Anderson recalls, "embraced the principle of missile defense wholeheartedly." Top Reagan aides Richard Allen and Ed Meese were also enthusiastic.

The outline of a campaign strategy was coming into view: Missile defense would be offered as an alternative to SALT II. Reagan's resolve to make an attack on SALT II a centerpiece of his campaign was, however, overtaken by events as summer gave way to fall. As it became clear that the Senate debate would be protracted, the festering problem of Iran intruded again. The deposed Shah wanted to come to the United States.

WHEN THE SHAH left Iran in January he went first to Egypt, and then on to Morocco. In the back of his mind he harbored thoughts that the United States or the Iranian military would find a way to restore his throne, as had been done for this father in 1953. Hence he wanted to stay close to the Middle East. Once it became clear by late February that a restoration was beyond hope, the Shah wanted to come to the United States. Carter reacted angrily to the idea; "Fuck the Shah," he was reported as saying.[84] His senior foreign policy advisers were no warmer to the idea, and stalled for time. Carter worried that the Shah's entry to the United States might provoke retaliation in Iran, perhaps even the taking of hostages. Vance agreed, though Vice President Mondale argued that it reflected badly on America to turn its back on a long time ally. David Rockefeller and Henry Kissinger both pressured the administration to admit the Shah—Kissinger attacked Carter for treating the Shah "like a Flying Dutchman looking for a port of call"—and struck up the idea of having the Shah go to the Bahamas. Over the summer the Shah moved again, this time to Mexico.

The United States still did not know, even as late as September 1979, that the Shah's health was deteriorating rapidly. The United States first learned on October 18 that he had cancer—four years after it was first diagnosed. Secretary Vance changed his mind, and argued to Carter that the United States could not in good conscience refuse the Shah entrance for medical treatment. Carter was still reluctant. "Does somebody here have the answer as to what we do if the diplomats in our embassy are taken hostage?" Carter asked. When no one ventured an answer, Carter said, "I gather not. On that day we will all sit here with long, drawn, white faces and realize we've been had."[85]

The Shah was finally admitted on a tourist visa for medical treatment in New York City. He arrived on October 22. There were street protests by Iranian students in New York, and protests in Iran, but the United States had received an assurance from Iran that there would be no reprisals. But the domestic political situation in Iran was unstable; Khomeini had not succeeded in establishing firm control of the nation, and the Shah's admission to the United States began to look like an opportunity to exploit for domestic political purposes. The first sign of trouble came on October 31, when Iran sent the United States a formal note of

protest declaring that Iran "did not accept the American government's ex-
cuses for granting entry permission to the deposed Shah."

Four days later a mob of Iranian "students" stormed the U.S. embassy,
taking 67 Americans hostage. (Fourteen black hostages were released a
few weeks later in a ham-handed attempt to stir up racial animosity in the
United States) The State Department was slow to grasp the seriousness of
the matter; the operations center was not operating with its full slate of
personnel since the embassy sacking occurred over the weekend, and
there was no Iranian specialist on duty to help comprehend the situation.
But as soon as the Iranian demand, which Khomeini endorsed, that the
Shah be returned in exchange for the American hostages, it became clear
in Washington that this would not be a replay of the Valentine's Day embassy takeover, when the government intervened to end the occupation in
a few hours.

The hostage taking plunged the United States into a war-like crisis.
There were early omens that the crisis would probably drag on. The PLO,
looking for a way to ingratiate themselves with the United States, offered
to intervene—Arafat had been one of the first foreign visitors to Iran after
Khomeini's return in February—but Khomeini bluntly told Arafat to stay
out of the matter. Carter later turned to Libya's Mohammar Qaddafi for
help, asking his brother Billy—who had accepted a $200,000 dollar
"loan" from Libya that would become an embarrassment to Carter in the
summer of 1980—to intercede with the anti-American tyrant of Tripoli.
Khomeini was not impressed. Carter sent a private warning to Iran
threatening severe but unspecified consequences if the hostages were
harmed. Both Secretary Vance and Vice President Mondale opposed sending the note. Carter inexplicably decided to send former Attorney General
Ramsay Clark, of whom there has been no finer example of an advocate
of American guilt before the world (Clark had written to an Iranian official offering advice about how to seek damages for the "criminal and
wrongful acts committed by the Shah"), as an envoy to Iran, but he received the same treatment as the PLO. All U.S. attempts to make any kind
of productive diplomatic contact with Iran hit a stone wall. Even freezing
billions of dollars of Iranian assets in the United States and packing the
Shah off to Panama did nothing to alter the deadlock.

As if the United States didn't have enough to worry about with the
hostage crisis, before the end of the year the other shoe dropped. On De-

cember 13 a story in the *Washington Post* noted in passing: "Within the past several days, U.S. intelligence had picked up the movement of one or two Soviet battalions, organized and armed for combat, to the vicinity of the Afghan capital of Kabul. These 400 to 800 Soviet troops were an addition to 3,500 to 4,000 Soviet military personnel already in the country." Deputy Secretary of State Warren Christopher summoned the deputy Soviet ambassador to lodge an official U.S. protest. On December 23, an ominous headline appeared on page eight of the *Washington Post*: "U.S. Worries About Possibility of Soviet Dominance in Afghanistan." The State Department had held a briefing the day before commenting on ominous signs of increasing Soviet activity in and around Afghanistan. On that same day, Soviet "advisers" in Afghanistan persuaded two armored divisions in the Afghan army to turn over their ammunition for "inventory"—a convenient way of disarming them.

Two days later—Christmas Day—the Soviet Union invaded Afghanistan. Transport planes with crack Soviet airborne troops landed at a rate of one every 10 minutes at airfields throughout the country. There were 40,000 Soviet troops on the ground in Afghanistan in the first few days; within a few weeks the total number of troops swelled to 85,000. Soviet forces immediately invested the capital city of Kabul; a KGB team disguised as Afghan soldiers stormed the presidential palace and murdered Prime Minister Hafizullah Amin, making a hash of the Soviet claim that Amin had "invited" them into the country. Radio Kabul announced that a coup had taken place, resulting in the restoration of a previously ousted ruler, Babrak Karmal. But U.S. intelligence quickly figured out that the "Radio Kabul" transmissions were originating from a location just across the Afghan border in the Soviet Union. The Soviets were obviously orchestrating events.

The invasion was not a tactical surprise to the United States. Practical steps toward the Soviet dominance of Afghanistan (such as the construction of highways from the Soviet Union into Afghanistan) had been in train for years, and U.S. intelligence had picked up the signs of the Soviet mobilization near the Afghan border starting early December, and had been warning Carter of the possibility of greater Soviet involvement as early as July. But it was a political surprise; the United States had not expected a full-scale invasion and occupation.

Could this be the first step in a Soviet invasion of Iran, which it had long wanted to partition, or of an even wider move toward the Persian

Gulf itself, where Russia had historically wanted to establish a warm-water port? Churchill had compared the strategic position of the Soviet Union to "a giant with both nostrils pinched," since Soviet approaches to the ocean on both the Pacific and Barents Sea coast were encumbered by ice and unfriendly neighbors. Control of Afghanistan put the Soviets within 350 miles of the Arabian Gulf, and in position to preempt any American moves against Iran. American intelligence doubted the Soviets were going to follow up with an invasion of Iran, though shortly after the embassy seizure in Iran the CIA got wind of a Soviet General Staff contingency plan to occupy the northern tier of Iran, so the idea couldn't be ruled out.[86] Unrest among the Kurds, Azerbaijanis, and Baluchis would provide a pretext for "restoring order" along the Soviet border. And was it merely a coincidence that the Soviet move into Afghanistan occurred at the same moment that America's estrangement from Iran had reached a crisis? It seemed unlikely. Rather, the Afghan adventure was the "Brezhnev Doctrine" at work. Once a nation had become socialist, Brezhnev declared in the 1970s, socialist forces of the world would prevent a counterrevolution. It was the détente version of the old saying that "what's mine is mine and what's yours is negotiable." After having ruled out Soviet designs on the region, the CIA hastily re-evaluated the situation, and concluded: "The possibility that Afghanistan represents a qualitative turn in Soviet foreign policy in the region and toward the third world cannot be ruled out."[87]

Brezhnev told Carter over the hotline that the Soviets had taken this step to protect Afghanistan from outside aggression. Carter was furious for being treated as a fool—and being made to appear one as well, having hugged and kissed Brezhnev six months earlier. On New Year's Eve Carter told Frank Reynolds of ABC News that "this action of the Soviets has made a more dramatic change in my own opinion of what the Soviets' ultimate goals are than anything they've done in the previous time I've been in office," which raised questions about what Carter hitherto thought about the character of the Soviet Union. He went on to describe the invasion as "the most serious threat to world peace since World War II. . . . It is even more serious than Hungary or Czechoslovakia."

Carter now decided to take a harder line with the Soviets. He recalled the U.S. ambassador to Moscow, cancelled sales of technology, imposed an embargo on grain sales (but only on grain intended for livestock, not people, Carter hastened to point out), and decided that the United States would boycott the Moscow Olympics (36 other nations joined the U.S.-led boycott). He also approved covert aid to the Afghan resistance. In his State-of-the-Union speech to Congress in January, he announced the "Carter Doctrine": "An attempt by any outside force to gain control of the Persian Gulf region will be regarded as an assault on the vital interests of the United States of America, and such an assault will be repelled by any means necessary, including military force." True to form, Vance urged Carter not to make this declaration, but Brzezinski fought successfully to keep it in the speech. ("The Soviet invasion was a body blow to Vance," NSC aide Gary Sick wrote, "and he seemed to age visibly under the impact."[88]) The only problem with Carter's threat of war was that the United States lacked the capacity to make good its threat. Nonetheless, war fever was in the air. The Bulletin of Atomic Scientists in San Francisco moved their "doomsday clock" from nine to seven minutes to midnight—midnight being the onset of nuclear war. American public opinion quickly abandoned the neo-isolationism that was evident after the fall of Saigon five years earlier. A Harris Poll found that 75 percent of Americans would support military intervention against the Soviets in the Persian Gulf; only 18 percent were opposed.

To show he was serious, Carter acceded to the Senate's demand for 5 percent increases in defense spending over the next several years, up from the 3 percent increase he had promised our European allies. Senate Majority Leader Robert Byrd told Carter that the already dim prospects for SALT II were dead, and that Carter should shelve the treaty. This Carter did, though he did not formally withdraw it, hoping that it might yet be ratified early in his second term in 1981. Meanwhile, Carter said that the United States would abide by the terms of SALT II anyway. That the Soviets had already calculated that the chances for SALT II ratification were dim may have been a factor in their decision to invade Afghanistan. Robert Tucker observed in *Foreign Affairs:* "Given the American record of recent years, Moscow has reason to believe that once Afghanistan is reduced, we will not spurn yet another détente. Moreover, Soviet leaders have the history of 1968 to consider, when outrage in the West over the Russian invasion of Czechoslovakia soon gave way to détente in Western Europe. If Western Europe did not permit Czechoslovakia to stand in the way of détente, why should it permit Afghanistan to do so?"[89] A State Department analyst told much the same thing to the

Washington Post: "The Soviets clearly asked themselves what of value they stood to lose with the United States by going into Afghanistan and concluded the answer was: not much."[90] Carter's own dovish adviser on Soviet affairs, Marshall Shulman, predicted that the Soviets would soon launch "an old-style agitprop peace offensive."

The Soviets, perhaps thinking just as Tucker suggested, were said to be surprised at the vehemence of Carter's reaction. However, this was the first time the Soviets had invaded a country outside the Eastern Bloc. Conservative critics of Carter in the United States were also pleasantly surprised by his new toughness—at first. "Carter's more vigorous response to the invasion of Afghanistan had raised the hopes," Jeane Kirkpatrick recalled, "that he had a new realism in his assessment of the Soviet Union."[91] Kirkpatrick and much of the same group of like-minded conservative Democrats who had met with Carter in 1977 were invited back to the White House in January 1980, at the behest of Vice President Mondale. (In addition to Kirkpatrick, the group included Norman Podhoretz, Midge Decter, Ben Wattenberg, Elliott Abrams, Max Kampelman, retired Admiral Elmo Zumwalt, Austin Ranney, and Penn Kemble.) Perhaps, it was hoped, Carter would now include some of this group in his administration, having spurned them before. Austin Ranney, speaking for the group, told Carter that they were encouraged by the change in Carter's view of the Soviet Union, and hoped he would now appoint officials who were in harmony with a tougher policy.

Carter cut off Ranney: "Your analysis is not true. There has been no change in my policy. I have always held a consistent view of the Soviet Union. For the record, I did not say that I have learned more about the Soviet Union since the invasion of Afghanistan, as is alleged in the press. My policy is my policy. It has not changed, and will not change."[92] Admiral Zumwalt told Carter that existing U.S. Navy forces were incapable of defending the Persian Gulf and Indian Ocean oil routes. Carter responded with what was described as "a stare that in a less democratic society would've meant he was destined for a firing squad." Maybe, Carter went on to suggest when the topic moved on to human rights, this group could help with human rights in Uruguay. The meeting was the last straw for these "neoconservative" Democrats, despite Vice President Mondale's efforts to repair the damage. Mondale knew the meeting had been a disaster, and asked the group to stay after Carter left. It was to no avail.

Carter, Jeane Kirkpatrick told Morton Kondrake after the meeting, "threw cold water on whatever hopes we had that Iran and Afghanistan would have a broad effect on the president's foreign policy orientation."[93] Elliott Abrams was so discouraged with Carter that he wrote a memo to his boss, Sen. Moynihan, making the case that Moynihan would make a good running mate—for Ronald Reagan.[94] In subsequent months Carter's public statements began to erode the tough line he took in January. When Congress decided in May to add an additional $3.2 billion to the defense appropriation above what Carter requested, Carter complained that the defense increase "severely restrains programs for jobs, for cities, for training, for education." The increase "is more than we actually need."

Two months after the disastrous White House meeting, the White House called Kirkpatrick to ask if she would work on the Democratic platform committee. "It is too late," Kirkpatrick told the White House. "I already have a date." She had decided to meet Ronald Reagan and hear him out.

IN THE SHORT RUN both the hostage crisis and the Soviet invasion of Afghanistan provided a major political boost for Carter. Polls before the crisis showed him badly trailing Sen. Ted Kennedy among Democrats for the 1980 Democratic nomination. Kennedy suffered the bad fortune of having scheduled the formal announcement of his candidacy two days after the hostages were taken in Iran. The sudden onset of the hostage crisis provided a jump in Carter's public approval ratings, as the public rallied to their leader as Americans always do in time of crisis. Pollster George Gallup called Carter's turnabout "stunning," adding that the jump in Carter's approval rating was "the largest increase in presidential popularity recorded in the four decades of the Gallup Poll."[95] This dealt a blow to the Kennedy, who was already suffering from several self-inflicted wounds. Although Kennedy's challenge was not over and would deal Carter several setbacks over the next six months, the most formidable challenge to Carter was clearly going to come from Republicans. The two Republicans Carter's political team feared most were Sen. Howard Baker and George Bush. Their favorite opponent: Ronald Reagan. Handling the extremist 69-year-old ex-movie actor would be an easy piece of work, they thought, especially now that the issue of war and peace would be at center stage of the 1980 campaign. "The American people,"

Hamilton Jordan said, "are not going to elect a seventy-year-old, right-wing, ex-movie actor to be president." The polls supported Jordan's confidence. In mid-December, a Gallup Poll showed Carter leading Reagan by a whopping 60 to 36 percent in a head-to-head match-up. Pat Caddell was confident of Reagan's weakness. "There's so much to work with, when you look at the data you just salivate."

On November 13, ten days after the hostage crisis began, Ronald Reagan announced his candidacy for the White House in a nationally televised address in New York City. He was the clear front-runner for the Republican nomination in every poll. It appeared Carter might get his wish.

CHAPTER THIRTEEN

NOMINATION

———⇒•◦•⇐———

THE PLAUSIBILITY OF Ronald Reagan's candidacy depended on whether his character matched up with the exigencies of the moment. "Reagan," Lou Cannon wrote in 1980, "spoke to the future with the accents of the past." But did Reagan's "accents of the past" portend a campaign of nostalgia, or a campaign summoning forth the latent character of what has always been known as "American exceptionalism?"

The issue of American decline, both domestically and in the world, was going to be the clear subtext of the 1980 election. Could America's decline be reversed? Was the "American Century" over, and "American exceptionalism" along with it? What was once unthinkable—American decline—was now thought probable. "The whole country seemed slightly traumatized on the brink of the '80s," *Newsweek* opined. "[T]here was also a growing sense that the country's institutions and leaders were no longer up to managing the problems that were simply too complex to grasp."[1] *Time* magazine thought the same: "From the Arab oil boycott in 1973 onward," *Time* essayist Lance Morrow wrote in January 1980, "the decade was bathed in a cold Spenglerian apprehension that the lights were about to go out, that history's astonishing material indulgence of the U.S. was about to end."[2] The number of Americans who told the Gallup Poll that the country was on the wrong track hit a new peak of 84 percent in August 1979; 67 percent agreed with the statement that the United States was in "deep and serious trouble," and 72 percent agreed with the statement that "the U.S. is less respected in the world today than it was 10 years ago."

Gone was the economic stability and easy growth that had character-ized the rest of the post-war era. From 1948 to 1973 the economy had grown at an average rate of 2.2 percent a year. But from 1973 on, the growth rate fell by nearly half, to 1.2 percent a year.[3] Real median family income, having risen by 33 percent in the 1960s, rose only 6.5 percent in the 1970s, even though many wives and mothers had entered the work-force. After taxes, take home pay for many families fell. Inflation for the full year of 1979 came in at 13.3 percent, the highest in 33 years. The price of gold hit $800 an ounce in January 1980, almost a 20-fold in-crease from 1974, when private ownership of gold was made legal again. In 1980, prices would gallop ahead by another 12.4 percent. Mortgage rates topped 20 percent, and the median price of a home had nearly tripled, from $23,000 in 1970 to $62,200 in 1980.

Big business was in a sorry state. Capital investment, productivity growth, and profitability had all stagnated in the last half of the 1970s. Corporate profits had shrunk from 13.3 percent of national income in 1966 to 9.3 percent in 1978. Chrysler lost $1.1 billion in 1979, the largest business loss in U.S. history, requiring a government loan guaran-tee to remain in business. In 1980 Ford and GM would follow Chrysler, with Ford losing nearly $600 million, and GM losing $763 million. Two hundred thousand auto-workers had been laid off during the Carter years, with little prospect of being rehired. The big three carmakers started demanding protection from foreign competition. Their critics sug-gested that they start making better cars.

The technology boom was on the horizon; 315,000 personal comput-ers were sold in 1979, up from 172,000 the previous year. Yet its full po-tential was not evident, even to some technology leaders. IBM was readying its first desktop personal computer, but Ken Olson, the president of Digital Equipment, said in 1977 that "there is no reason for any indi-vidual to have a computer in their home." Twenty-five-year-old Bill Gates' fledgling company, Microsoft, had only 38 employees. The most popular electronic device on the market at the moment was not the computer but the new Sony "Walkman."

What people were listening to on their new Walkmans was changing as well. There was a sharp decline in record album sales in 1979, perhaps a reflection of the attenuation of popular music at the end of the disco era. But a successor to disco first appeared in 1979, when an obscure pop group named the Sugarhill Gang recorded a single entitled "Rapper's Delight," in which the lyrics were chanted rather than sung.[4] Despite the advances in the popular music art form, still no one had figured out the lyrics to "Louie, Louie," even though the Kingsmen's classic tune enjoyed a revival in the movie hit *Animal House*. On cable TV, CNN debuted, but only 20 percent of American households were hooked up to cable, and only 1.1 percent owned VCRs.

Social indicators joined economic indicators in conveying the magnitude of change over the previous decade. The crime rate rose another 50 percent during the decade, and was nearly three times higher than in 1960. More than twice as many people were murdered in the United States during the 1970s than were killed in the Vietnam War. The percentage of American households on welfare grew by 15 percent. A *New York Times* poll found that 55 percent of Americans approved of pre-marital sex, twice as many as a decade before. The divorce rate had gone from 1 in 3 marriages in 1970 to 1 in 2 marriages by 1980; the number of single-parent families increased 50 percent during the decade, and the number of unmarried couples jumped by 300 percent. In the spring of 1980 the Equal Employment Opportunity Commission issued its first sexual harassment guidelines. The U.S. Army, meanwhile, began running TV ads with the slogan, "Some of our best men are women," and the first female midshipmen graduated from Annapolis. In 1979, for the first time women outnumbered men in college enrollment.

Racial issues receded somewhat during the 1970s. In 1969 Pat Moynihan had predicted in a memo to Nixon that the decade ahead would be "a period in which Negro progress continues and racial rhetoric fades." (This was the infamous memo, leaked to the *New York Times,* in which Moynihan wrote: "The time may have come when the issue of race could benefit from a period of 'benign neglect.'") In 1977, "Black" replaced "Negro" as the federal classification for African-Americans in publications such as the *Statistical Abstract of the United States* and the Census. Just as Moynihan predicted, black progress continued apace. The number of blacks attending four-year colleges and universities doubled in the 1970s, and the proportion of the black population living in suburbs increased by a third.

After having soared in the 1960s, income growth for blacks stagnated, as it did for all Americans. One of Moynihan's less optimistic predictions from 1965 also came to pass: The black illegitimacy rate increased from 38 percent in 1970 to 55 percent in 1980. (The figure would reach 70 percent in 1994.[5]) While there were no riots and radical groups such as the Black Panthers were defunct, public sensitivity about racial matters arguably grew more acute. Howard Cosell was sacked from *Monday Night Football* for blurting out about a black Washington Redskins running back, "Look at that little monkey go!" In one sense the Cosell episode (which would be followed in the 1980s by the gaffes of a number of other sports figures, such as Jimmy "the Greek" Snyder and Al Campanis) can be taken as a sign of progress. In 15 years the nation had gone from debating blacks' right to vote and right to integrate to debating oblique transgressions of racial sensitivity, which is where the matter rests today.

THE POINT IS THIS: The character of a nation changes with time just as an individual's character changes as he matures. The only thing seemingly unchanged in the 1970s was the character of Ronald Reagan. The constancy of Reagan's views amidst the maelstrom of change in modern America is one of the marvels of his character, and also the basis of much of the criticism he received. If Reagan was going to succeed in capturing the imagination of Americans, he would have to do so by proving that, amidst the ephemera of modern life, there were immutable aspects of the American character that could provide the way out of our present discontents and show the path to a brighter future.

Although Reagan came home depressed and discouraged from his defeat in Kansas City in 1976, there was no doubt in his mind that he would run again in 1980. His experience on the campaign trail in 1976 had permanently ignited the fires of ambition. He was buoyed personally by the thousands of letters that poured in from supporters. Typical is T. G. Singlehurst of Honolulu, who wrote to Reagan: "You are the greatest leader of Americans since Lincoln." Mabel Sherry of Tamaqua, Pennsylvania, lamented that "It is almost impossible to think you did not become the nominee and our next President." Even some Ford supporters complimented Reagan. Walter and Bertha Schultz of Waconia, Minnesota, wrote to say, "We have never seen a better and more honorable losing candidate than you, Mr. Reagan, and in any other race we would have supported you."[6]

Then something startling and unprecedented occurred. When Reagan hit the campaign trail on behalf of Republican candidates in the fall of 1976, he was greeted with huge crowds and an outpouring of enthusiasm that exceeded some of his primary campaign appearances. Though Reagan was well known to the nation's political class by the fall of 1976, for much of the nation Reagan's late surge in the spring primaries—and especially his moving remarks on the closing night of the GOP convention in Kansas City—had been their first serious exposure to him. The enthusiasm went beyond just the campaign crowds turned out by Republican Party functionaries. It was typical for the entire staff of the hotel where Reagan was staying to line up to say goodbye when he checked out in the morning. Off-duty policemen would show up volunteering to serve as an escort, forming impromptu motorcades. Repeatedly people implored him: "Governor, you have to run again." Michael Deaver, who accompanied Reagan on his travels that fall, said to his colleague Peter Hannaford: "You ought to go out on the next trip. There's something remarkable going on out there."

This spontaneous outburst of enthusiasm buoyed Reagan's spirits. Even before the 1976 election was over, Reagan was making plans for 1980. He immediately resumed his newspaper column and radio commentaries (Barry Goldwater had temporarily taken over his radio commentaries during the 1976 campaign). In September 1976 Reagan hosted a meeting of his senior campaign staff at his home in Pacific Palisades, where, Lou Cannon reported, his staff expected Reagan would mark his farewell to presidential politics.[7] Instead, he laid out his political plans for 1977. "Well folks," he said, "it looks like it's time to go back to work."

Reagan seemed practically alone in his sincere belief that America's future could be just as glorious as its past. Perhaps this was a function of his age; he was too old to revise his thinking now. But if his age was a bulwark against misreading the changes taking place around him, it was also an obvious political liability. He would be 69 years old on election day in 1980, and would turn 70 two weeks after inauguration in January 1981. Reagan naturally joked about his age, usually combining a jest at his age with a political point. "I visited my doctor the other day and when he told me I was sound as a dollar I fainted dead away," he quipped on the stump. "Wage and price controls have failed since the time of the Roman Emperor Diocletian," Reagan said. "I ought to know. I'm the only one here old enough to remember." His campaign distributed a list of 40 world leaders over the age of 65 (as though reporters would be impressed by the likes of Siaka Stevens, the ruler of Sierra Leone) and 63 members of Congress over age 65. Shortly before the New Hampshire primary in February, Reagan decided the best way to neutralize the issue was to shine a spotlight on it, so he ostentatiously celebrated his 69th birthday at every campaign stop. By the fall, polls found that a majority of Americans regarded Reagan to be more vigorous than Carter—the contrast of the ruddy cowboy versus the collapsing jogger.

Reagan's "age factor" ironically propelled Reagan into being a more aggressive candidate in the run-up to 1980. Precisely because of his age, Reagan could not afford to be coy or ambiguous if he was going to run again. It was necessary that Reagan make his intentions clear early in order to keep his staff and supporters from drifting away to other potential candidates. Beyond verbal assurances, Reagan underscored his seriousness by converting his leftover campaign money (over a million dollars that under existing law he could have kept personally) into a political action committee: Citizens for Reagan, his campaign organization, which morphed into Citizens for the Republic. In addition to contributing to Republican candidates (and thereby building up chits for 1980), CFTR was used as the vehicle for promoting Reagan's issues, such as the Panama Canal treaty fight. In 1977 and 1978 Reagan made nearly 300 speaking appearances and over 500 radio broadcasts.

Beyond the organizational details, Reagan needed a fresh strategy to establish himself as the front-runner for 1980. He set out to run as the candidate of party unity, reaching out to Republican moderates, especially in the Northeast, his weakest region. In the 1978 mid-term election campaign, Reagan refused to endorse the candidacy of his former aide Jeffrey Bell, who was challenging liberal Republican Senator Clifford Case in the New Jersey primary. When Bell upset Case in the primary, Reagan took notice not so much for his victory as for the main issue Bell touted—the Kemp-Roth tax cut. (Bell lost a close election in November to Bill Bradley.) Reagan also publicly opposed a ballot initiative in California that would have banned homosexuals from being public school teachers, a controversial measure that largely disappeared beneath the shadow of Proposition 13. (The Briggs initiative, as the anti-homosexual measure was called, lost. An anti-smoking initiative Reagan opposed also lost.)

The emphasis on becoming the candidate of party unity represented a return to the strategy Reagan himself embraced in his first run for office in 1966. In fact, the 1980 presidential campaign closely paralleled his 1966 campaign for governor.

This did not mean that Reagan would self-consciously "move to the center." To the contrary, his publicly expressed opinions were as obdurate as ever. As we saw in the previous chapter, Reagan refused to back away from his vivid historical parallels with the appeasement of the 1930s, despite the urging of his advisers. In a widely quoted (and widely criticized) comment in January 1980, he compared Carter to Neville Chamberlain again. His pungent radio broadcasts, most of which he wrote himself, demonstrated that he would be no trimmer. He continued his frontal assault on liberalism. "For the average American, the message is clear. Liberalism is no longer the answer. It is the problem." But in countless ways Reagan also identified *government* as the problem; clearly in Reagan's mind *liberalism* and *government* were synonymous.

Nonetheless, Reagan's announcement speech on November 13, 1979, was noticeably moderate compared to his announcement speech in 1976. Gone were the explicit attacks on the New Deal and Great Society social programs, and his plan to cut the federal budget by $90 billion. Instead, he mused about statehood for Puerto Rico and burnished the idea for the hemispheric free-trade zone, which he called the "North American accord." There was nothing about the hostages in Iran, seized just the week before. Even the *New York Times* noted the next morning that "his words tonight appeared less dogmatic. . . . The more moderate tone apparently reflected the efforts of some of his advisers to give Mr. Reagan a more moderate image and to make him more attractive to middle-of-the-road voters."[8]

In addition to his sincere conviction and inner confidence, Reagan and his followers thought American opinion was moving steadily in their direction, and therefore that Reagan's ideas had broader appeal beyond the conservative wing of the Republican Party. Just as a majority of voters in 1966 had come to have misgivings about liberal governance in California, by the late 1970s it seemed likely that a majority of voters were ready to reject liberal governance in Washington. The major media were slow to recognize this (if they ever did). Although polls showed more Americans identifying themselves as "conservative" and fewer as "liberal," when

Newsweek offered a cover story in 1977 on "Is America Turning Right?" they described public opinion as "ambivalent" about the role of government, and furthermore singled out Massachusetts Governor Michael Dukakis and California Governor Jerry Brown as "national symbols of the pragmatic new conservatism," which was absurd.[9] James Q. Wilson was closer to the mark with his assessment that "the Reagan candidacy is a candidacy based on *issues,* issues which the candidate has developed over the better part of two decades and which now, taken as a whole, command the asset of a very large proportion of the American people."[10]

This meant Reagan could transcend the charge that he was "narrow" or too "ideological," rather than reacting defensively or by "moving to the center." In fact, as a former Democrat, Reagan found it natural to reach out to Democrats by proclaiming that his principles "speak for millions of Democrats who describe themselves in polls as 'conservative' and who find no place for themselves in a party which is firmly under the control of liberals."

Two other aspects of Reagan's interregnum between 1976 and 1980 loom larger than his political strategy. This period of Reagan's life can be seen in retrospect to have been a time of preparation to be president that was much more serious and intense than the span between leaving the governor's office in 1975 and his presidential campaign a year later. In 1975 Reagan prepared merely to be a candidate; in the late 1970s he prepared to be president. Among other political purposes of his travels during this period, Reagan sought to burnish his foreign policy credentials with several overseas trips to meet foreign political leaders. One detail of his travel plans underscores his seriousness and confidence as a political figure: As a matter of practice Reagan never informed the State Department of his travel until immediately before his departure. He didn't want the State Department to attempt to change his travel agenda or intrigue against his meetings with foreign officials.

A trip in late 1978 brought him to Berlin, where Reagan witnessed for the first time the reality of a Communist regime: He made a visit to "Checkpoint Charlie" at the Berlin Wall, and a brief foray into East Berlin. (A film crew accompanied Reagan on this trip, shooting footage for possible use in campaign TV spots.) There, Martin Anderson remembers, Reagan was shaken and angered by the spectacle of armed soldiers bullying the populace on the streets, as well as the paucity of consumer goods available for East Germans in stores and markets. Stasi, the East German secret police, tailed Reagan's party during their brief visit to East Berlin, and filed an eight-page report. Stasi clearly didn't grasp the prominence of their visitor. "The car," the Stasi report reads, "was driven by a [U.S. Army] specialist 4 in uniform. The others in the car showed their U.S. passports issued in the names of Reagan, Ronald, born February 6, 1911; Reagan, Nancy, born July 6, 1921."

Reagan departed after 45 minutes in East Berlin, the Stasi filed noted, "without incident."[11] But there were two incidents that stuck in Reagan's mind. As Reagan and his entourage were leaving the department store, two East German soldiers armed with automatic rifles stopped a man coming from the store with two small sacks of goods, demanding his internal passport. The second incident occurred the day before. While lunching high up in an office tower overlooking the Berlin Wall from the West Berlin side, Reagan's hosts recalled a recent episode in which East German border guards shot a man attempting to escape over the Wall, and left his body visible for several days as an object lesson. This was the moment, Peter Hannaford recalls, when Reagan became visibly angry, and resolved that "we must free these people." Reagan's ideological antipathy to Communism had now gained a visceral dimension beyond even his experience with Communist union infiltration in Hollywood.

Reagan visited Paris on that trip, meeting President Giscard d'Estaing. (A year later in a TV interview Reagan seemed not to know who d'Estaing was, which was taken as a sign of Reagan's supposed ignorance. It was actually a sign of his hearing loss.) He also met Mayor Jacques Chirac in the hospital, where Chirac had been confined after suffering an auto accident. Chirac was evidently confused about the identity of his important visitor from America. After Reagan returned to California, he received a thank-you note from Chirac addressed, "Dear Mr. Mayor . . ." It was during this trip that one of Reagan's less-recalled ideas was born. His conversations with Europeans about the Common Market prompted Reagan to muse, during the airplane flight home, about the idea of creating a free trade zone encompassing all of North and South America. The idea for the North American Free Trade Agreement (NAFTA) owes it origin to that moment.

During this period Reagan also intensified his interest in intellectuals and the role of ideas. One of the marketing objectives that Peter Hannaford and Michael Deaver had identified for the 1976 campaign had been "influencing intellectuals on the cogency of our issues," though this was "more to inhibit and reduce attacks than to gain adherents."[12] By the late 1970s, circumstances had changed such that more intellectuals, especially the "neoconservatives," were coming closer to harmony with Reagan's views on both foreign and domestic policy. Norman Podhoretz, still a registered Democrat in 1980 (and who had tried to convince Moynihan to challenge Carter), put the case thus:

> The irony was that the "extreme" conservative Republican Ronald Reagan had by now become closer in his thinking to John F. Kennedy than Kennedy's younger brother Teddy. Putting it even more strongly, Teddy Kennedy was running on policies that were almost the polar opposite of those on which JFK had campaigned against Nixon in 1960 (to "get the country moving again" through a tax cut, a military buildup, and a more forceful stand against Communist expansionism). Reagan's platform, by contrast, was so similar to JFK's that it might have been described (to adapt a phrase from Barry Goldwater's 1964 presidential bid) "not as a choice but an echo."[13]

Reagan and his circle recognized that this trend represented a large opportunity, not only for political arguments and campaign substance, but also for the very staffing of an administration. Peter Hannaford made sure that Reagan received a constant flow of articles from *Commentary, Policy Review,* and other journals, after which Reagan often wrote to the authors embracing their views and asking to meet. Not all of these meetings went well. Podhoretz recalls his first meeting with Reagan in New York in 1979, where Reagan seemed unaware (or at least poorly briefed) of the chief concerns of the small group of thinkers who had assembled to have dinner with him. Instead of talking about foreign policy and the Soviet Union, Reagan went on at length about efficiency gains he had achieved as governor of California, including saving file cabinet space by shifting from standard to legal-size file cabinets. Podhoretz and others at the dinner were startled. "Reagan obviously had not a clue as to what to say to this particular group, or even what subjects to talk about," Podhoretz recalled. "Rather than being reassured, most of us left wondering whether he had any brains at all." Podhoretz had to convince himself that it "could not possibly be the case" that Reagan was as vacuous as he seemed on this occasion, and eventually he settled upon the view that Reagan was much more of a conventional politician that either his supporters or detractors recognize.

An alternative explanation, borne out by numerous other encounters with intellectuals, is that Reagan's self-confidence was such that he was comfortable and relaxed with people he knew to be his intellectual superiors and felt no need to compete with or impress such people. A similar dinner party in July of 1978 at the home of George Shultz in California went swimmingly for Reagan. Shultz, according to Martin Anderson, had never been a fan of Reagan, and had supported Ford in 1976. Shultz's dinner party included, among others, Ford's economic adviser Alan Greenspan as well as Milton Friedman and William Simon. Shultz was impressed with Reagan, and began commenting favorably upon Reagan's candidacy. Shultz wrote later of the occasion: "He was questioned, argued and agreed with, lectured and listened to. . . . I had been trying to decide whether he had real views or canned statements. I could see that his views were real and ran deep."[14]

A more deliberate format for harnessing intellectual talent came into view before the formal campaign began. As early as 1978 Martin Anderson began to tout the benefit of organized issue task forces. "They provide an opportunity for you to become acquainted with literally hundreds of the country's top experts in problem areas that will be crucial to a Reagan administration," Anderson wrote to Reagan. "In the event you should become President, these experts will become an extremely valuable source of talented manpower to staff key positions in the government." Anderson added that "virtually all the media will be impressed with the wealth of talent that you will be able to assemble (some of them may even be stunned)."[15] By election day, Reagan had signed up 461 top experts to 48 different task forces—23 for domestic policy issues and 25 for foreign policy. The media mostly ignored this talent pool, with a few notable exceptions. "Reagan is expanding his network of advisers beyond a tight core of right-wingers to include experienced, often learned heavyweights," Morton Kondracke wrote in *The New Republic*. "By election day Reagan is likely to have a plausible, not-at-all scary position on most every issue, and a set of advisers who will convey confidence that Reagan can run the government competently and responsibly."[16]

Heading into 1980 Reagan was the clear front runner for the GOP nomination in all the polls. Even with this impressive organization and forward momentum, doubts about Reagan's candidacy were massive in both parties and in the news media. *The New Republic* characterized Reagan as an "ex-movie actor, darling of the rabid right, . . . an international innocent, and an economic extremist," while their reporter covering the campaign beat, Morton Kondracke, referred to Reagan as "that wrinkled old two-time loser, that joke of an ex-movie actor."[17] John Osborne, the longtime White House correspondent for *The New Republic,* was even more caustic: "Ronald Reagan is an ignoramus, a conscious and persistent falsifier of fact, a deceiver of the electorate and, one suspects, of himself."[18] Author Robert Coles called the prospect of Reagan winning the GOP nomination "preposterous," while James Conaway wrote in the *Atlantic Monthly* that, among the news media, the idea of Reagan as president "was more than the press could bear." He is, *Atlantic Monthly* editor Robert Manning wrote, nothing more than "a Casting Office Goldwater. . . . there's little more to the fellow than meets the eye." The *Washington Post*'s Richard Harwood spoke openly of what was on the mind of the media: "Was he too ignorant or too dumb for the presidency?"[19]

Time magazine judged that Reagan was "the propounder of unqualified conservative answers to the most fearsomely complex problems." George Ball returned from Europe to report that "the thought of Ronald Reagan as president terrifies them."[20] Elizabeth Drew wrote in *The New Yorker* that "it was assumed that he was too old, too blunder-prone, simply too improbable. . . . [I]f Reagan is the Republican nominee, the election of a Democrat is certain."[21] Even after Reagan locked up the GOP nomination, *The New Republic* was incredulous: "It is still hard to believe that Ronald Reagan may actually be elected president of the U.S."[22] The press corps was appalled that Reagan's favorite reading was supposedly *Reader's Digest* (ignoring the fact that he also read *National Review* devotedly). Reagan was asked frequently on the campaign trail what book he had read lately, to which he usually replied that he had been too busy campaigning to read any books. How about your favorite book, then? The Bible, Reagan would answer, to the dismay of the press corps, who prefer their politicians to make up something about Gibbon or Kierkegaard because it makes better copy.

The gulf between Reagan and the media went well beyond the divergence of opinion between a mostly liberal media and a conservative candidate. The most familiar complaint about Reagan by journalists covering his campaign was that he was "inaccessible," which is not to be confused with "unavailable." As Elizabeth Drew put it, "Reagan is at once a very familiar figure and a remote one, accessible and at the same time inaccessible," while James Conaway observed that "Reagan's 'niceness,' so apparent in public, is impenetrable in private." Although Reagan's campaign, like all serious campaigns, limited the candidate's exposure to the media, Reagan engaged in a steady stream of one-on-one interviews throughout the course of the campaign. Yet reporters were exasperated because he gave them the same answers in interviews that he gave to public audiences on the stump. "Talking to Reagan can be like grappling with a wet cake of soap," Drew complained. "He follows much the same script that he does onstage, and many of his answers slide away."

Reagan's straightforwardness and consistency, an unappreciated aspect of his self-discipline, reinforced the media image that he was a shallow simpleton. Yet this phenomenon may teach more about the mentality of the media that it does about Reagan. Reporters were hoping then as biographers do now to find the "authentic" or private Reagan that was hidden from public view, which made it difficult for them to take Reagan at his own terms, to comprehend that the authentic Reagan was right in front of them the whole time. The root of the problem is perhaps best captured by an aphorism of Alfred North Whitehead, who wrote that there are two kinds of people in the world, the simpleminded and the muddleheaded. It might be said that Reagan was indeed simpleminded, while journalists are muddleheaded.

The self-aggrandizement of journalism that began in the 1960s and accelerated with Vietnam and Watergate had transformed journalism from a mere craft or trade into a prestige "profession." Starting in the 1970s, more journalists became celebrities in their own right, with reputations rivaling the public figures they covered. This was made most explicit with the rise of the so-called "new journalism," where the journalist himself became part of the story. Many of the most critical articles about Reagan were written from a first-person point of view, where the atmosphere and texture of the journalist's experience in encountering Reagan was as large a part of the story as what Reagan had to say about the issues. Such an approach would have been unflattering to Harry Truman (the only modern president without a college degree), let alone to the taciturn Calvin Coolidge.

Once again, Reagan was on to this at some instinctual level. He began a speech to a media luncheon by asking, "Do I get a cigarette and a blindfold?" In sterner moments, Reagan would counterattack the media for "journalistic incest," where "one person reads another person's story and then it is accepted as gospel." Reagan's campaign knew this would be one of their largest problems. Richard Wirthlin noted in an early campaign memo: "We can expect Ronald Reagan to be pictured as a simplistic and untried lightweight (dumb), a person who consciously misuses facts to overblow his own record (deceptive) and, if president, one who would be too anxious to engage our country in a nuclear holocaust (dangerous)."[23]

To be fair to the media critics, however, it must be noted that Reagan did frequently misstate facts, making him fair game for heightened media scrutiny. He confused Pakistan with Afghanistan. He displayed deep confusion about farm subsidies in Iowa. His claims about the cost of government services at the Department of Health and Human Services were off by an order of magnitude. He wrongly asserted that Vietnam veterans weren't receiving benefits under the GI Bill. He claimed that the Occupational Safety and Health Administration (OSHA) had 144 regulations on ladders, when it had only two. *The Nation* magazine predictably hit Reagan: "What is troubling in the case of Reagan is not simply that he is a Presidential candidate and ought to be more careful but that his facts and statistics are an inextricable part of his programs, indeed his world view."[24] But even Reagan's allies at *National Review* were troubled. In an editorial entitled "Get It Right, Ron," *National Review* pointed out that media scrutiny of every factual claim "will be like swimming in a piranha pool with a bloody nose. . . . [T]herefore, it's important, when he makes a statement, to *get it right*."[25] (Emphasis in original.) Pollsters started asking the public about Reagan's "shoot-from-the-lip" problem. In early spring the Harris Poll found that by a margin of 68 to 27 percent, the public agreed with the statement that Reagan "seems to make too many off-the-cuff remarks which he then has trouble explaining or has to apologize for."

As has been pointed out previously in this narrative, Reagan's factual lapses were always subordinate to a larger political point about which he was usually on firmer ground. So what if OSHA had only two regulations for ladders? The private sector cost of OSHA regulations for the decade of the 1970s was estimated to be $25 billion; the broader point that regulation was diverting significant resources in an unproductive way was undoubtedly correct. OSHA, and the new kind of government it represented, stuck in the craw of small business people across the country. Even Carter fundamentally agreed with this, telling one of his first cabinet meetings in 1977: "If I were an employer, I'd like for all my employees to be safe. But with the mention of OSHA there kind of rises something up in me to resist it and not cooperate with it."[26] *The Nation* was ironically correct: It was Reagan's "world view," not his facts, that counted most for many voters. Reagan was seldom more compelling than when he attacked government regulation, and he had an endless supply of one-liners, such as: "Sometimes giving a bureaucrat a new rule is like handing a pyromaniac a lighted match in a haymow."

Yet the accumulation of factual errors and the intense media criticism it engendered fueled widespread apprehension about Reagan not just within the media, but within the GOP itself. The memory of George Romney's foot-in-mouth self-destruction in 1967 was on everyone's mind. So as the campaign began in earnest in late 1979 Reagan faced a crowded field of fellow Republicans who were positioning themselves to pick up the GOP standard if and when Reagan fatally stumbled. The field of declared candidates included Senators Howard Baker and Bob Dole; Congressmen Phil Crane of Indiana and John Anderson of Illinois; former Texas Governor (and former Democrat) John Connally; and former everything George H.W. Bush. Liberal Republican Senator Lowell Weicker of Connecticut briefly entered the field and withdrew when he recognized that his popularity had to be measured in decimal fractions. General Alexander Haig, having retired as NATO commander, also considered making a run, but thought better of the idea and became a corporate CEO instead.

Crane, Dole, and Connally were running as hard-core conservatives. Crane had supported Reagan in 1976, but said he thought Reagan was too old now. Dole advertised himself as "a younger Ronald Reagan with experience." Connally played to his strength as a tough-talking Texan, and was especially popular with corporate executives, from whom he raised a substantial campaign war chest. (As of the end of 1979, Connally had raised nearly $2 million more than Reagan.) Baker and Bush were running as moderate conservatives, with few explicit differences from Reagan on the issues, but with supposedly wider appeal to independents. Anderson was the lone liberal Republican in the race, and he would provide the most unexpected twist to the entire campaign.

But the most important factor in the race at the outset was the non-candidacy of Gerald Ford, whose poll numbers rivaled Reagan's within the GOP. "I firmly believe," pollster Richard Wirthlin wrote to Reagan in July of 1979, "that there are only two ways your nomination could be endangered: if we give it away ourselves, over our own internal mistakes, or if Gerald Ford, for whatever reasons, should decide to marshal his political strength directly against us."[27] Ford thought about entering the race, and met several times with his inner circle from his White House days (including former chief of staff Dick Cheney). Lacking the advantages of incumbency, Ford recognized that he would face a hard and divisive fight against Reagan. Many of his former operatives—and many of his financial backers—had already moved to other candidates, particularly George Bush. The GOP might well turn to him, however, if the convention was deadlocked, or if Reagan faltered. The best strategy for Ford was not to run, but to be "available." With Ford out of the race, Baker and Connally were regarded as Reagan's most formidable challengers—Baker for his prestige as ranking member of the televised Senate Watergate hearings in 1973, and Connally because of his fundraising prowess. By December 1979, however, Wirthlin discerned that the most serious challenge to Reagan might well come from Bush, even though Bush was polling in the low single digits and nearly half of Republicans polled professed to having little knowledge of Bush. "[S]hould he [Bush] grab the early headlines by a win in Iowa," Wirthlin wrote shortly before Christmas, "he could fast become, through favorable and massive media exposure, a rather and perhaps the only formidable opponent."[28]

Bush announced his candidacy six months before Reagan, on May 1, 1979. Early polls found him with 2 percent support among Republican voters. Although half of Republican voters knew little about Bush, his tenure as chairman of the Republican National Committee in 1973–74 provided him with extensive contacts within the party apparatus in nearly every state. This advantage he worked assiduously; in 1979 Bush was on the road a total of 328 days, visiting 42 states and logging 246,000 miles in the air. Barbara Bush kept a campaign schedule of her own that was nearly as arduous. Like Jimmy Carter in 1976, whose campaign Bush carefully studied, no crowd was too small or too humble. Bush even spoke at a $6-a-plate fundraiser for a county Republican committee in Clanton, Alabama, which was co-sponsored by the Possum Growers and Breeders of America. "He spent enough time in Iowa to qualify as a registered voter," Richard Brookhiser observed. Bush's hard work paid off. Before the first contest in Iowa in January, he had garnered more newspaper endorsements than Reagan. He made a public spectacle of jogging three miles a day as a subtle reminder of Reagan's age, and for those who were slow to pick up the point, he made a refrain out of his fitness to serve two terms in the White House.

Even with his extensive party connections, Bush's chances seemed remote. He was, as observers pointed out frequently, a two-time loser in statewide races in Texas. What would make him more compelling in a national race? Bush's chief selling point was his extensive government experience—CIA director, U.N. ambassador, envoy to China, member of Congress. Hence his slogan, which was a direct slap at Carter and an indirect slap at Reagan: "A President we won't have to train." Bush would drop into his stump appearances phrases such as "the last time I saw Mao" to underscore his experience. Most of the time Bush sounded every bit as conservative as Reagan, agreeing with Reagan about the Panama Canal treaties, attacking the prospect of "socialized medicine," denouncing the "Marxist-Leninist takeover" of Nicaragua, and promising to fire "McGovern-type regulators" if he got to the Oval Office. *National Review* observed that "he differs little from Reagan, to the point, indeed, where he is being called the Tweed Reagan," while John Anderson charged that Bush was merely "Ronald Reagan in Brooks Brothers suits."[29]

But Bush differed significantly from Reagan on some of the hot-button social issues. Bush favored the moribund Equal Rights Amendment, and he opposed a constitutional amendment banning abortion. He did oppose federal funding for abortion, and thought abortion should be left up to the states to legislate—the same position McGovern took in 1972. His most important difference with Reagan, however, was over tax cuts. Bush opposed the Kemp-Roth plan, which Reagan embraced, to cut income tax rates across the board by 30 percent, famously calling the "supply side" logic of tax cuts "voodoo economics" and predicting it would cause a 30 percent inflation rate. He favored tinkering with the tax code for specific purposes, such as "stimulating production." Bush's memorable attack on "voodoo economics" was as close as he came to a harsh attack on Reagan. For the most part he conducted himself in the gentlemanly manner that fit his image, refraining from attacking Reagan directly. The worst he would do was to call some of Reagan's positions "unreasonable" and some of his promises "phony," which *Newsweek* observed were "fighting words in Bush's pacific vocabulary."

Yet beyond Bush's relatively small differences from Reagan on the issues was a large difference in pedigree, style, and edge. With his New England patrician roots and his education at Andover and Yale, Bush was an unconvincing Texan. He exuded less populist appeal than Alistair Cooke, even though he drank beer (favorite brand: Miller High-Life) and listened to country music (favorite artists: Dolly Parton and Crystal Gayle). Bush's mild manner mitigated his conservatism, and his tone was decidedly moderate. "The symphony of outrage sounded by Ronald Reagan on welfare fraud," Joseph Kraft observed, "finds no echo in the music of George Bush."[30] In a foreshadowing of the theme his son George W. would campaign with in the election of 2000, Bush professed that "I am a conservative, but I have compassion." There were doubts about Bush's toughness that would dog him for the rest of his political career—the "wimp factor." "Even those who like and admire him," Joseph Kraft wrote, "wonder whether he has the steeliness—the weight—to be an effective president." There seemed to be a thinness to Bush's extensive resume. "The more he records every step of his career," Henry Fairlie wrote, "the less sign there is of any progression."[31] If the Republicans really want a patrician for their nominee, Fairlie argued, why not just get the real article—Elliott Richardson—instead.

Most of this criticism was unfair. It was borne of the fact that Bush didn't fit comfortably into either the camp of the ideological conservatives, nor did he fit into the maw of the moderate or liberal Establishment. To the contrary, for someone of his elite background Bush was utterly unaffected by the crisis of conscience that had overtaken most Establishment figures in the aftermath of Vietnam and Watergate. In this regard he had the same innocence and sincerity as Reagan. About Vietnam, for example,

Bush expressed many of the same sentiments as Reagan. "I never got caught up in the immorality of our role in Vietnam," Bush said on the stump. "We were not immoral in our purpose. I'm sick and tired of apologizing for the United States."[32] Somehow, Joseph Kraft observed, Bush escaped the class suicide that had demolished the self-confidence of the Eastern Establishment: "Far from being a common type, he is the remnant of a dwindling band. Virtually alone in the old governing class, he has survived the upheavals of the last two decades."

This made Bush a man without a clear home in his own party. The most vocal fever swamps on the Right distrusted him deeply. Bush belonged to the Trilateral Commission (though he had quietly resigned from the Commission at the start of the campaign), the bogeyman of the conspiratorial Right, which tarred Bush as a Rockefeller "country club" Republican. The fact that so many of Ford's inner circle had gravitated to Bush didn't help. William Loeb of New Hampshire's *Manchester Union-Leader* newspaper had it in for Bush, calling him "a spoon-fed little rich kid," and "an incompetent liberal masquerading as a conservative."[33] All of these aspects combined to produce a class divide among Republican voters. A Reagan campaign aide remarked that "We have the Schlitz drinkers; Bush has the sherry drinkers."

Such was the shape of the race in the weeks before the first contest in Iowa in January.

"THERE ARE TWO problems in politics," Reagan campaign manager John Sears told a reporter in January. "One is being ahead, and the other is being behind." With his commanding lead in the polls, Reagan's political strategists worried that he had only one direction to go in Iowa—down. Reagan himself observed that for a front-runner, "the death watch begins early." Most polls showed Reagan's support in Iowa at 50 percent or better, with his nearest rival, Howard Baker, in the mid-teens. Reagan was so far above the other candidates that it seemed to make more sense to conduct a "Rose Garden"–style campaign almost as though he were the White House incumbent. "It wouldn't do any good to have him going to coffees and shaking hands," Sears told a reporter. "People will get the idea he's an ordinary man, like the rest of us."[34] Sears added, "We're not going to sit on our lead and kill the clock." But that is exactly what Sears tried to do.

Sears thought that the downside risks in Iowa would be minimized if Reagan ran a low-key campaign. Reagan would probably win in Iowa anyway, and if he didn't win convincingly, his absence from active campaigning would reduce media attention to the contest. These overconfident calculations were disastrous. Reagan limited himself to only eight campaign stops in Iowa—pollster Richard Wirthlin called them "cameo appearances"—for a grand total of just 49 hours. The week before the caucus found Reagan campaigning in New York and Connecticut. One Reagan campaign staffer admitted that "almost every precinct chairman I talked to wondered if we were serious about Iowa. . . . We just seemed to lie dead in the water, trying to hold our position."[35] The Reagan campaign wasn't even running many TV spots.

Bush, on the other hand, spent 27 days campaigning in Iowa in the three months before the caucuses, and had an organization in place in all 99 Iowa counties. (Bush also refused Secret Service protection in Iowa, making it easier for him to press the flesh.) Bush's Iowa campaign was much more intense than Reagan's. Bush's campaign sent out a "caucus kit" to every person who had been identified as a Bush voter, giving them the location of their caucus (almost 700 caucuses were held in private homes) and each Bush supporter was contacted at least four times by caucus day. Even Reagan's Iowa campaign chairman, Pete McPherson, admitted that Bush was out-hustling everyone: "Of the first 25,000 people who go to the caucuses, Bush will have probably shaken hands with every last one." "BUSH BUILDS IMPRESSIVE IOWA SUPPORT," declared a headline in the *Des Moines Register.* Howard Baker, meanwhile, had no on-the-ground organization, and was relying solely on $100,000 worth of television ads.

Yet it was Baker whom Reagan's campaign figured to be Reagan's most potent rival in the early primaries, so much so that Reagan's campaign gave Bush a boost in a straw poll in November 1979 in Maine. Reagan was weak in Maine, so his supporters decided to throw their votes to Bush as a way of keeping Baker from getting an expected and publicity-generating win. But now Bush had an "upset" win to hold up, and the cooperation between Reagan and Bush set off speculation of some kind of deal. "If you're the betting type," a *National Review* reporter wrote in January before the Iowa caucuses, "you might want to consider a modest wager on a Reagan-Bush ticket."[36]

The Maine straw vote gambit was a minor tactical error compared to Reagan's refusal to participate in a debate on January 7 sponsored by the *Des Moines Register*. Reagan knew that he would be the target of attacks from most of the other candidates, so he ducked the debate, citing the "11th Commandment" ("Thou shalt not speak ill of another Republican"), giving the weak excuse that the debate would be "divisive." But his absence from the debate emboldened the other six candidates to criticize him all the more fulsomely. The most noted broadside came from John Anderson, who zeroed in on Reagan's supply-side economic plan: "How do you balance the budget, cut taxes, and increase defense spending at the same time? It's very simple. You do it with mirrors." Bush, sitting at the end in a dark suit, got generally poor reviews. But the main object of criticism was the candidate who wasn't on the stage. The media was withering in its censure of Reagan's absence. "Reagan doesn't care enough to campaign here" was the tone of media coverage, with NBC's Roger Mudd going as far as to say that Iowans should vote against Reagan because of his insulting non-campaign.

Post-debate surveys showed that 58 percent of Iowa voters had watched, suggesting huge interest in the candidates and the election to come. The surveys also showed Reagan's support plummeting. He dropped 24 points in the *Des Moines Register* poll, from 50 percent in November to 26 percent a week before the caucus. Baker came in second, at 18 percent, and Bush third, at 17 percent. The conventional wisdom was that Reagan would still win, but that Bush's superior organization would propel him into second place.

Bush's campaign strategists estimated that 35,000 Republicans would turn out for the caucuses on January 21, based on the fact that GOP caucus turnout in 1976 had been 22,000. The Reagan campaign had made a similar calculation, believing that 20,000 votes would win first place. The Bush campaign sought to turn out 15,000 voters pledged to him, and was stunned when it became evident early on caucus night that turnout would be sharply higher than expected. Before the night was over, 115,000 Republicans would express themselves in the caucus meeting rooms. This big turnout augured a Reagan victory, yet when all the votes were counted Bush had surged to a narrow victory, 31.6 percent to Reagan's 29.5 percent. Baker was a distant third at 15.2 percent. Bush ended up garnering

35,000 votes, though the Bush campaign did not know where they all came from. One county GOP executive told *Time* magazine: "Reagan was thumbing his nose at Iowa. Iowa has done the same thing to him."

Even though Reagan's margin of defeat was only 2,182 votes (less than one vote per precinct), it was a devastating blow. The media started writing Reagan's political obituary. The morning after the caucuses NBC's Tom Pettit declared on the *Today Show* that "Ronald Reagan is dead." Reagan had gone to see a movie (*Kramer vs. Kramer*) in Los Angeles the night of the caucus and looked, in the words of author Frank van der Linden, "like a man who had been knocked down by a car but was too stunned to realize what had happened to him."[37] His friend and campaign chairman Sen. Paul Laxalt was blunt: "You were sitting on your ass in Iowa."[38] A jubilant Bush declared that he now had "Big Mo," for big momentum, and the phrase was splashed across the covers of the weekly news magazines. A new Harris poll showed Bush ahead of Reagan in the East by 34 to 24 percent, and surging in New Hampshire, scene of the next primary five weeks later. Some polls even showed Bush pulling ahead in the Granite State by as much as 9 percent. Contributions to Bush's campaign soared. Reagan's supporters were both panicked and furious. A grim Reagan said to Ed Meese, "There are going to be some changes made."

AT THIS POINT it is necessary to fix our gaze on a figure who has appeared previously, Reagan's chief campaign strategist, 39-year-old John P. Sears III—not only for what it adds to the story, but also for what it tells us of Reagan's strengths and weaknesses as a leader and decision-maker. Sears, in the words of *Washington Post* reporter Nicholas Lemann, was "widely assumed to be Reagan's Svengali." On the surface Reagan and Sears were an odd couple—Reagan the sincere, gregarious ideologue, Sears the quiet, brooding Machiavelli with uncertain or dubious ideological convictions. Conservatives widely and noisily distrusted Sears (among other causes for suspicion, Sears had been chairman of "Students for Kennedy" at Notre Dame University in 1960), but had grudging respect for his abilities. "Sears was the most brilliant political strategist I've ever known," said Jeffrey Bell.[39] Martin Anderson, who was one of Sears' casualties in campaign infighting, concurs: "If it had not been for John Sears, Ronald Reagan would never have been president of the United States. He was the guy who got it going."[40] Reagan himself was irritated with the pervasive idea that Sears was pulling his strings. "There's all this talk that he is 'moderating' me," Reagan complained to *Time* magazine before the Iowa caucuses. "*I'm* the candidate and *I* decide what I think the issues are and what my position is."[41] What was the basis for this unlikely pairing?

It was Sears' political insight that attracted Reagan. Sears had been an associate in Nixon's New York law firm the mid-1960s, and so highly did Nixon regard Sears' abilities that Nixon chose Sears, at the age of 27, to be the chief conventional delegate hunter for Nixon's 1968 campaign. But after Nixon won, Sears was edged aside in the administration, reportedly by Attorney General John Mitchell, for siding with the liberal faction in the administration over the direction of policy. Sears floated around the periphery in Washington for the next few years, becoming a chain smoker and, by some accounts, an alcoholic (he became a teetotaler after the 1976 campaign), keeping in touch with Nixon on matters of political strategy. The most tantalizing rumor about Sears, advanced by former Nixon insider Leonard Garment in a book published in 2000, is that Sears was "Deep Throat," the secret source for Bob Woodward and Carl Bernstein's reporting on Watergate.[42] (Sears denies the story, and has threatened a libel action against Garment.)

Reagan and Sears first met in the spring of 1974 when Reagan was pondering a presidential campaign in 1976. According to separate accounts of these discussions by Lou Cannon and Jules Witcover, Reagan's circle of advisors discussed a scenario that assumed Nixon would survive Watergate and serve out his full second term. Reagan wouldn't have to contemplate challenging an incumbent president of his own party (Ford). Sears assertively disagreed. Nixon will be gone in six months, Sears predicted. Moreover, he added, "Jerry Ford can't cut the mustard. He's not perceived as a leader. He can't lead the Congress or the country."[43] Ford was ripe to be taken in challenge.

Reagan was impressed with Sears' insight, and Reagan's willingness to embrace someone of Sears' contrary temperament and uncertain ideological commitment is yet another example of Reagan's practical side, although this should not have come as a shock to his followers. Hadn't he done much the same thing with Stuart Spencer, a Rockefeller man, back in 1966? Conversely, Sears was said to be impressed with Reagan's willingness to listen to others, to change his mind in the presence of new facts. Above all, Sears came to see that, for whatever ideological differences they might have, Reagan possessed a steady character. "Ronald Reagan wants to be president badly," Sears said in 1979. "But the refreshing thing is that if he doesn't get it, it won't destroy him." Sears' friends were even more surprised than conservatives when he signed up with Reagan for the 1976 race. It appeared like pure opportunism on Sears' part. He had no prospects with Ford. Reagan was going to be the only game in town in 1976.

The mystery over the Reagan-Sears match deepened when Sears signed on early with Reagan for the 1980 campaign. "There had subsequently grown between them," Murray Kempton observed, "a bond as unmistakable and as mysterious as one that might, in the best of cases, tie trainer to horse to trainer."[44] Conservatives, some of them within Reagan's long-time inner circle, were still in a rage against Sears for his success in persuading Reagan to pick Richard Schweiker as his running mate before the convention in 1976, and feared that Sears at the helm meant that Reagan was going to try to become a moderate. To be sure, Sears was quietly wooing moderates and a number of key Ford supporters from the 1976 campaign to Reagan's camp, with considerable success. Sears' most significant recruit was Drew Lewis, the Pennsylvanian who had held the convention delegation in line for Ford in 1976 after the Schweiker gambit.

Sears may have thought himself smarter than his candidate, and certainly he could condescend to Reagan as much as anyone in the media. Sears sometimes described Reagan in terms indistinguishable from Reagan's liberal critics, telling Hedrick Smith of the *New York Times,* for example, that "There's a generation gap between what Reagan thinks he knows about the world and the reality. His is a kind of 1952 world. He sees the world in black and white terms."[45] Perhaps this hauteur was reinforced by Reagan's near total delegation of authority to Sears. Reagan's trust and confidence in Sears would lead to Sears' undoing, because Sears' largest personal weakness was his secretiveness combined with a desire for complete control, which did not match up well with Reagan's style or the style of his old circle. "John didn't want anyone near the governor that he couldn't control," one Reagan insider told *Newsweek.*

Even though Reagan and the campaign were based in Los Angeles, Sears insisted on setting up a Washington office, where he was based, thus creating a rival power center in the campaign (as well as a management headache). Political campaigns are always the scene of ambition and behind-the-scenes faction and conflict, but Sears became the locus of more than the usual share of campaign intrigue in part because of his own furtive nature, and in part because Reagan's hands-off style of management allowed intramural divisions to fester. One-by-one Sears moved to oust several of Reagan's long-time California insiders, starting with Lyn Nofziger. "He apparently believed that the old people around Reagan were a danger to his ability to control the campaign, so he set out to get us," Nofziger said later.[46] Nofziger, who had been Reagan's press secretary during Reagan's governorship, was shunted aside as campaign press secretary in favor of a Sears' man, James Lake, in August 1979. Martin Anderson was next, abruptly announcing that he was returning to his academic position at the Hoover Institution in mid-November, shortly after Reagan announced his candidacy.

Sears trained his sights next on Mike Deaver, which was the beginning of Sears' undoing. If Deaver was on the hit list, Ed Meese couldn't be far behind. In addition to their longstanding connection with Reagan in Sacramento, Deaver and Meese represented the two parts of Reagan's political soul—the crowd-wowing showman and the serious conservative statesman. Deaver was a pure public relations man, and might be regarded as the producer of Reagan's public image, seeking to make the most of Reagan's star quality on the stump. "I always thought my role was to fill up the space around [Reagan]," he later described himself.[47] Deaver started out as the number two man in the campaign behind Sears on the organizational chart, but because of his longstanding relationship with Reagan he was Sears' *de facto* co-equal. Meese, a lawyer and Reagan's chief of staff in Sacramento, was Reagan's ideological soul-mate and alter ego, and was responsible for the substance of the campaign. This meant he was in charge of research and briefing Reagan on the issues, both of which tasks Sears thought Meese was doing poorly. Sears had his own issues team in the Washington office that he preferred to use (which was part of the reason for Anderson's departure).

The irony of Deaver's departure was that Deaver was instrumental in convincing Reagan after the 1976 loss that Sears should be brought back to head the 1980 campaign. "Deaver convinced Reagan that he could not win without John Sears," Nofziger reflected.[48] Many conservatives around Reagan never wanted to hear Sears' name again. It had become an article of conservative folklore that Reagan had only begun to surge in 1976 after Sears had been pushed aside in favor of a more aggressive strategy in the North Carolina primary. As the next campaign began in earnest in the fall of 1979, Deaver and others began to have second thoughts about Sears' dominance in the campaign, his penchant for keeping Reagan under wraps, and his own hogging of the media limelight.

Things came to a head on November 26, 1979, when the Reagans asked Sears and Deaver to their home in hopes of resolving the conflicts among them. Sears and his associates Charles Black and James Lake laid out their complaints about Deaver's supposed financial mismanagement of the campaign to Reagan. They wanted Deaver out. Incensed and disgusted, Deaver quit on the spot. "You need to put somebody in charge," Deaver recalls saying to Reagan, "and if these gentlemen have you convinced that I am ripping you off, after all these years, then I'm out. I'm leaving." (Lou Cannon's account of the episode has Nancy Reagan telling Ron that he had to make a choice between Deaver and the Sears camp. According to Cannon, Deaver intervened: "No, governor, you don't have to make that choice. I'll resign.")

A stunned Reagan followed Deaver to the front door of the house, imploring him not to go. Reagan, ever the optimist and averse to staff conflict, hoped to work it out. "This is not what I want," Reagan said. But Deaver was adamant, and Reagan lacked the forcefulness to stop Deaver from leaving or to impose a compromise on his warring campaign staff. To the contrary, as columnist Murray Kempton observed, Reagan held the door.

Reagan returned angry to his living room, telling Sears and his colleagues, "The biggest man here just left the room. He was willing to compromise and you bastards weren't." He later told Nancy: "They'll be in here again and next time they'll be after Ed Meese. And goddamnit, I'm not going to let that happen."[49] With the ouster of Deaver, the infighting could no longer be kept under wraps. "SHIFTS ON REAGAN STAFF STRENGTHEN ROLE OF CAMPAIGN CHIEF, was the *New York Times* headline in early December. An anonymous Reagan staffer told *Times* reporter Hedrick Smith: "There's a new Ronald Reagan who wants the presidency so bad that he's willing to dump old friends."[50] Cynical reporters compared the hasty changes to the Reagan press kit staff descriptions to the new editions of Soviet encyclopedias that were issued whenever a Soviet leader had fallen from favor.

Reagan, according to Lou Cannon, "never talked warmly to Sears again."[51] Reagan began complaining of Sears that "I look him in the eye, and he looks me in the tie." He also said that he was not enjoying the campaign: "Every morning I wake up with a knot in my stomach." It was at this time, Cannon believes, that Reagan "began to realize that he did not know what was going on in his own campaign." At some point in the weeks between the Iowa caucuses and the New Hampshire primary, Reagan reached an uncharacteristic decision: Sears would have to go. This was the inevitable direction of Reagan's thought when he said to Ed Meese after Iowa, "There are going to be some changes made."

SEARS WAS UNFAZED by Bush's upset win in Iowa. Although keeping Reagan under wraps in Iowa was clearly a mistake, Sears understood the salient fact that should have been obvious to Reagan's rivals: Reagan had run very strong in Iowa *without campaigning*. In the upset of the moment, however, no one recognized this, including Reagan. As Lou Cannon had observed, Reagan had a useable temper, and was "invariably impressive when aroused." He was fuming about Iowa, and agreed with the editorial judgment of the *Manchester Union-Leader,* which said that Reagan's problem was that he had been "Searscumcised." He was also haunted by his narrow loss in New Hampshire in 1976, and knew that if he lost there again, he would be finished.

It might be said, to borrow the old Bible verse, that it was at this moment that "the iron entered into his soul." The five weeks between the Iowa caucus and the New Hampshire primary made Ronald Reagan president. Now it was time to let Reagan do what he did best—campaign. But beyond mere retail campaigning, Reagan displayed in some of his toughest moments in New Hampshire a depth that convinced many skeptical observers that he was fit to be president. *National Review* observed at the time: "Reagan cannot be 'packaged.' When he campaigns as, of all people, Ronald Reagan, he is formidable. . . . A Reagan campaign manager needs only two words of advice for the candidate: Be thyself."[52] A famous slogan was born (though it did not yet become public currency): "Let Reagan be Reagan." Reagan put the campaign's gas pedal to the floor, doubling his New Hampshire schedule. In the words of Jack Germond and Jules Witcover, Reagan began "campaigning with a vigor that belied his sixty-nine years."[53] Among other steps, he dumped his ad agency and turned to Philadelphia ad-man Elliott Curson, who had produced Jeff Bell's TV spots in the 1978 New Jersey Senate race that touted tax cuts. Now Reagan would run full-throttle on the tax cut plan. And he decided he would need to meet his competition head-to-head in debates.

Now it was Bush's turn to make campaign mistakes. The first was claiming the mantle of front-runner with his braggadocio about "Big Mo." "We beat all the big shot candidates in Iowa," Bush celebrated. "Now we'll beat 'em all in New Hampshire!" By claiming front-runner status, Bush made himself the target of the other candidates, especially Howard Baker, more than Reagan. The strategy of every other campaign depended on becoming the alternative to Reagan, and hoping to set up a one-on-one contest with Reagan in the later primaries. Now Bush was in the way. While Baker and the rest of the field began training their fire on Bush, Bush failed to distinguish himself from Reagan in a compelling way. Did Bush really think he was going to best Reagan in a personality contest? "We answered the question, 'George Who?'" James Baker reflected later, "but we failed to answer the question, 'George What?'"

At first Bush's prospects looked good, especially after Reagan got caught in a flap over an ethnic joke he told reporters on the campaign bus. The joke Reagan told: "How do you tell a Polish guy at a cockfight? He brings a duck. How do you tell the Italian guy? He bets on the duck. How do you know the Mafia is there? The duck wins." Fairly tame as ethnic humor goes—the kind of joke that seemed straight out of a booth at the Brown Derby in the Hollywood of the 1950s—and certainly more tame than the kind of jokes candidates habitually told reporters in previous years. But these were new times, and even tame ethnic jokes were now off limits. Wirthlin's next poll in New Hampshire found Bush had pulled ahead of Reagan by 13 points; a *Boston Globe* poll had Bush up by nine points with a week to go before the primary. A University of New Hampshire poll put Bush four points ahead.

The turning point for Reagan was the first all-candidate debate in Manchester, New Hampshire, on February 20, six days before the primary. Reagan got generally poor reviews from the media, who said he looked stiff and hesitant. He made an apology for the ethnic joke, and offered the lame excuse that he had told the joke as an example of unacceptable humor, ending with the promise that "from now on, I'm going to look over my shoulder and then I'm only going to tell stories about Irishmen, because I'm Irish." He closed the debate with his boilerplate homily about his "vision for America," but Reagan delivered it well and it was new to many New Hampshire voters who had never seen a sustained Reagan performance on TV. Bush, meanwhile, "looked tinny" in the debate, in the words of Meg Greenfield. According to Wirthlin's post-debate polls, more than a third of New Hampshire Republicans had watched, and twice as many viewers thought Reagan rather than Bush had won. Suddenly Reagan was moving up fast in the polls, and began to open a lead over Bush with five days to go.

But it took one more decisive episode to turn a narrow Reagan win into a blowout that virtually ended the nomination contest: the Nashua debate three nights later. It was at this event that Reagan spontaneously delivered one of his most famous lines: "I am *paying* for this microphone, Mr. Green."

A series of quirks, reversals, and Bush blunders delivered that sterling moment to Reagan. Reagan's campaign had decided that it would be useful for Reagan to have a one-on-one debate with Bush. The Bush campaign was eager to oblige. For Reagan it offered the chance to isolate his most serious rival; for Bush it provided the chance to be seen as Reagan's equal and above the rest of the GOP field. The Nashua *Telegraph* newspaper jumped at the chance to sponsor a head-to-head debate, delighted with an opportunity to upstage its noisy rival, the *Union-Leader*. There was one problem with the newspaper's sponsorship: It might be illegal under the still-evolving post-Watergate campaign finance laws. Bob Dole threatened a lawsuit claiming that sponsoring a debate for just two of the candidates constituted an illegal "in-kind corporate contribution" to those two campaigns. The election law allowed an exception for legitimate "news events," but the Federal Election Commission hadn't issued rules and regulations yet. (The FEC later issued rules that would have permitted the proposed debate.) The *Telegraph* decided to withdraw its sponsorship rather than face a lawsuit. The Reagan campaign, wanting to go ahead with the debate, asked Bush's campaign to split to cost of the event. Bush declined, so the Reagan campaign decided to pay the full $3,500 tab. This was Bush's first mistake in the affair; had he split the cost, he would have been entitled to a legitimate share of control over the event.

This set up a peculiar state of affairs under which the *Telegraph* was the "sponsoring" organization and would set the format and ground rules for the debate. But the Reagan campaign, operating under the maxim that "he who pays the piper calls the tune," began to have second thoughts about the arrangement. Since Reagan was paying for the event, *he* would receive the blame, instead of the *Telegraph*, for excluding the other candidates. Flying back to New Hampshire from a quick fundraising trip to Atlanta, Reagan said to his aides, "Maybe we ought to include those other guys."

Sears was also having second thoughts about the one-on-one debate. Since Reagan had done so well in the all-candidate debate, why not stick with what works? The Reagan campaign contacted the other candidates and invited them to turn up. John Connally had already left New Hampshire, but Anderson, Baker, Dole, and Crane agreed to show up. Both Bush and the *Telegraph,* however, resisted. Both wanted to stick with the one-on-one debate. Reporters began getting wind of the fracas, and made plans to show up for what might turn out to be a climactic moment in the campaign.

A crowd of 2,400 people packed the Nashua High School gymnasium on Saturday night. By now nearly everyone had heard the rumor that all the candidates would appear. Twice Reagan's people attempted to persuade Bush to agree to opening up the debate to the other candidates. First John Sears spoke with James Baker. Baker refused, telling Sears that it was up to the *Telegraph* to decide. Then New Hampshire Senator Gordon Humphrey spoke directly to Bush, but Bush reacted angrily, refusing even to meet with the other four candidates who were present in another room with Reagan. This was Bush's second mistake, as it added to the anger of the excluded four.

There was now less than a minute before the debate was scheduled to begin. What was Reagan going to do? At first Reagan threatened to hold out with the other four candidates, and walk out of the debate if they were excluded. Sen. Humphrey told Reagan, "If you do that, you'll lose New Hampshire." "Well," Reagan said, "I have to go out there and explain to those people what's happened." Then Nancy Reagan intervened: "No, you should all go out."

Bush had already sat down on one end of the long table on the gymnasium stage, and pretended the other candidates did not exist as they filed on stage with Reagan. The *Telegraph*'s publisher, Herman Pouliot, attempted to brush off the four other candidates standing awkwardly on the stage behind a seated Reagan as he introduced the debate. From the boisterous crowd came shouts of "bring them chairs!" "In the rear are four other candidates who have not been invited by the Nashua *Telegraph* but I will introduce them to you just so you will know who they are," Pouliot said. "At the end of the debate we will allow these four people to make statements." Then Pouliot turned over the microphone to *Telegraph* editor Jon Breen, who attempted to begin the debate by calling on Jim Dickinson of the *Washington Star* to ask the first question.

A fuming Reagan interrupted before Dickinson could begin his question. Reagan wanted to explain what was happening, and make a last appeal to include the other four candidates, who were still standing on the stage. Breen moved quickly to cut off Reagan: "Would the sound man please turn Mr. Reagan's mike off for the moment. Will you turn that microphone off, please?"

Reagan never had a better cue in all his days in the movies, and exploded with the famous line, "I am *paying* for this microphone, Mr. Green!" Reagan got Breen's name wrong—another sign of his incipient hearing loss. Breen was also unaware that his command to turn off Reagan's microphone was not going to be obeyed, because the sound technician had been hired by the Reagan campaign. It may have been an act; we'll never know. Most recollections of the episode portray Reagan as hesitant and angry, but press secretary James Lake said that Reagan winked at him right before going on stage. And Reagan critics who were attuned to all possible Hollywood echoes recalled a similar line from a 1948 Spencer Tracy–Katherine Hepburn movie, *State-of-the-Union*. ("Don't you shut me off!" Tracy glowers at the movie's climax. "I'm paying for this broadcast.") As Jack Germond and Jules Witcover noted, it was "a rare moment in a political campaign—an instant of genuine drama that no media consultant could have plotted."[54]

Whether acting or not, a red-faced Reagan started to rise out of his chair as if to walk off the stage as the crowd erupted. But he thought better of the idea, settled back in his chair, and took command, explaining to the audience:

> Ladies and gentlemen, I feel that there is some explanation due to you and this is why I asked these gentlemen to come out here, and I realize that some effort has been made to embarrass them. I accepted the invitation for what was to be a two-man debate. As controversy arose over whether it should be or not, it was the paper that was sponsoring it, I even read in the paper where Mr. Breen said it was up more or less up to the candidates, but then it developed that the Federal Election Commission said that the paper could not finance this debate because that would be an illegal corporation contribution to the campaign.
>
> I then volunteered to pick up the tab from our campaign funds and pay for this debate. Having done so and feeling I thus was technically the sponsor of the program, and sponsors have certain rights, I then issued an invitation and told the paper, and we have been talking to them all day, issued the invitation for all of the candidates who are still here. John Connally happens to be absent. These gentlemen were here and accepted that we make this a debate of including all of the candidates because I . . . and the newspaper since I've been here this evening refused to meet with me personally about this matter. So I asked that at least these gentlemen come out here for me to us willing to debate.
>
> I was perfectly willing to say that if we could not all debate that then I would not debate, and yet there are people that tell me that it would be unfair to all of you if we didn't continue with the debate but I want you to know the circumstances and I want you to know why these gentlemen are not included in this debate.

Reagan had placed the onus on Bush for the dispute. Bush responded weakly: "I just want to set the record straight. I have been invited here as a guest of the Nashua newspaper. I will play by their rules. They are free to make any rules they want on it. I am their guest and I am very glad to be here. Thank you very much." Breen then attempted to back up Bush. It was too late to change the rules, Breen said. Then he added to the confusion by claiming that the *Telegraph* was "technically" the sponsor of the debate, implying that Reagan had no rights in the matter even though his campaign was paying for it. Bush remained stiff and sullen throughout the entire tableau, not even acknowledging the presence of the other Republican candidates on the stage.

At this point the other four candidates shuffled off the stage to a press conference where they denounced Bush, and the two-man debate went forward. But it was an anticlimax, and no one much paid attention to the substance of it, though Reagan was judged the winner. Bush got horrible reviews, even from his own campaign. The *Manchester Union-Leader* summed it up with the observation that Bush "looked like a small boy who had been dropped off at the wrong birthday party." Reagan's poll numbers shot up overnight by 16 points. "The thing just exploded," Wirthlin said.

With Reagan's "I am paying for this microphone" line being rerun countless times on television, Bush committed his final blunder—the same blunder that Reagan had made in New Hampshire four years earlier. He went home to Houston the morning after the Nashua debate. Former Governor Hugh Gregg, who as chairman of Reagan's 1976 New Hampshire campaign had told Reagan to leave the state so as to get out of the way of the get-out-the-vote effort, was the chairman of Bush's campaign this time around, and gave Bush the same bad advice. Reagan wasn't going to make the same mistake twice; he stayed in New Hampshire campaigning down to the wire. TV viewers saw Reagan in an overcoat continuing to stump the state, but saw Bush out jogging in sunny Houston.

Reagan had another reason for remaining in New Hampshire through primary day. He had one more crucial task to complete. While Reagan was reversing his fortunes with hard campaigning in New Hampshire, the wheels of the John Sears saga continued to turn behind the scenes. Accounts and recollections of events behind the scenes were murky and contradictory even at the time, and have not become clearer in the two decades since. The most complete account, in Jack Germond and Jules Witcover's campaign chronicle *Blue Smoke and Mirrors,* has Sears claiming to have overheard Ed Meese on the phone telling Reagan's personal aide David Fischer that Sears, James Lake, and Charles Black would soon be cashiered from the campaign. Meese denies this account, but admits talking about "adjustments" that would be made after New Hampshire. Regardless of the actual circumstances, Sears was smart enough to know that his stature in the campaign had weakened because of the Iowa result, and set about to recoup his standing and authority with yet another attempt at reorganizing the campaign.

Sears first suggested to Nancy Reagan that the campaign bring in William Clark, who had been Reagan's chief of staff in Sacramento, to be chief of staff on the campaign. As Germond and Witcover commented on this episode: "The use of Nancy Reagan as a broker in such a situation told a great deal about her role in her husband's campaign. Even at the tensest moments, she had maintained a friendly, easy relationship with Sears, Black, and Lake, as well as with Ed Meese."[55] But the implication of Sears' idea was clear: install another layer between Reagan and Meese, and prepare the way for Meese to join Deaver, Nofziger, and Anderson on the sidelines.

But Clark, who was then a justice on the California Supreme Court, didn't want to step down to join the campaign, which is something that Sears surely should have known or ascertained beforehand. The entire gambit appears to have been a trial balloon for Sears to judge whether he could get away with it. On February 15, eleven days before the New Hampshire primary, Sears returned to the idea with a new name—William Casey, a New York investment banker and head of the Securities and Exchange Commission under President Nixon. Casey was an important Reagan supporter, and as a member of the campaign's finance committee had helped raise campaign cash. Casey had come up to New Hampshire to help out, and Reagan may have already had Casey in mind for an important campaign role—perhaps even taking over. But now Sears demanded that Casey be put in charge of issues management for the campaign. Sears threatened to quit unless he got his way—the third time he had presented Reagan with an ultimatum.

The moment Reagan had predicted two months before had now arrived. "I know what you're doing," Reagan said. "You're after Ed [Meese]!" As Germond and Witcover's narrative describes the scene: "At one point [Reagan] leaped out of his chair, his face flaming red, and raged at Sears in strong enough terms that it crossed Lake's mind that the candidate was about to punch the campaign manager."[56] The meeting ended without resolution, but on the Sunday before the primary—the day after Reagan's triumph at the Nashua debate—Reagan said to Casey and Meese: "This is an intolerable situation. It can't go on any longer. I've decided to make a change." Reagan decided to dismiss Sears on Tuesday, the day of the New Hampshire primary, so as to be too late to make news before the vote.

Sears, Black, and Lake were caught unaware when Reagan summoned them on short notice to a meeting in his suite at the Holiday Inn in Manchester at 2 P.M. on primary day. Reagan handed Sears a press release: "Ronald Reagan today announced that William J. Casey has been named executive vice chairman and campaign director of his presidential campaign, replacing John Sears who has resigned to return to his law practice." Note both the active, personal voice, "*Ronald Reagan* today announced," and the possessive, "*his* presidential campaign." For too long it had seemed as if Reagan was the mere prop for Sears' campaign. As one campaign staff member told *Newsweek,* "I think he finally got tired of Sears telling him what to do." Black and Lake "resigned," too. "I'm not surprised," was Sears' bland reaction.

It was a bombshell, surprising reporters and stunning the political world. By 9 P.M. that night, however, the Sears' firing was already receding beneath a bigger breaking story—Reagan's blowout win in the New Hampshire primary. It wasn't even close. Reagan swamped Bush by more than two to one, 50 to 23 percent, with Howard Baker coming in a distant third with 13 percent. John Anderson was the only other candidate to break into double digits with 10 percent of the vote; John Connally and Phil Crane got 2 percent each, and Bob Dole began looking for a graceful way to exit the contest after getting only 1 percent. As was the case in Iowa, Republican turnout was higher than expected. "Congratulations, sir," Bush said to Reagan in his concession phone call, "You beat the hell out of us." Bush's "Big Mo" had turned into "No Mo."

Reagan accomplished two major steps in New Hampshire. He broke the back of his party rivals with his large margin of victory, virtually assuring himself the nomination, and he broke the back of campaign discord by dismissing Sears. Herbert Asquith once told a young Winston Churchill that the first essential for a chief executive is the ability to be "a good butcher." Reagan was never any good at it. (Neither was Churchill, incidentally.) "Firing anyone was a painful ordeal for Reagan," Meese observed. He was abysmal at firing people as governor. "It evoked the traumatic memory from his boyhood when he had seen his own father lose his job—on Christmas Eve."[57] Firing Sears showed for the first time to Reagan's many skeptics the kind of ruthlessness that is necessary for a president. Several months later, Rowland Evans and Robert Novak noted the significance of this step: "From the moment the autocratic John Sears was sacked as campaign manager February 26, Reagan has functioned on his own as major-party candidates seldom do."

But now Reagan had a new problem. He was not only out of money, but had already spent two-thirds of the amount allowed under the federal campaign finance laws. If spending kept going at its present pace, the campaign would hit the federal spending limit by April, with half of the primaries still ahead. Though Bush was damaged in New Hampshire, he still had ample campaign funds and a strong organization. Casey's first act upon taking over for Sears was to fire nearly half the campaign's 310 paid staff members. The traveling party of 17 was cut down, required to double-up in hotel rooms, and fly coach. The budget for TV ads was slashed. Meanwhile, even as dozens of staff were cut from the campaign, Mike Deaver, Lyn Nofziger, and Martin Anderson were back.

If Reagan faced money trouble, Bush and the rest of the field faced a new problem of their own. Gerald Ford was having second thoughts, and started making noises about jumping into the race to stop Reagan. Three days after Reagan's New Hampshire blowout Ford said publicly that "there is growing sentiment that Governor Reagan cannot win the election" because he is "too conservative," which generated newspaper headlines: "FORD: REAGAN CAN'T MAKE IT." "The most important point is that the polls reflect that I would be the most electable Republican candidate against the Democratic nominee," Ford repeated over and over again. Ford told Barbara Walters in a TV interview that chances he would enter the race were "50–50." Reagan responded with his typical jauntiness: "He should pack his long johns and come out here on the primary trail."

Reagan's money woes were one factor on Ford's mind. If Reagan ran out of money, Ford thought he might be even able to beat Reagan in the June California primary. There was never a realistic chance of this, and Ford would have had to sweep all the other remaining primaries, most of them in states where Reagan had beaten Ford in 1976. This is the kind of fanciful enthusiasm that politicians get in their head when surrounded by loyalists. But Ford was also still bitter at Reagan for the 1976 challenge, which Ford thought cost him the election, and he itched for vindication, both against Reagan and Carter. Ford began a series of meetings with old supporters and even met with Reagan's dismissed campaign strategist John Sears.

It took three weeks for Ford to come to his senses and publicly put an end to his prospective candidacy with the statement that "I am not a candidate; I will not be a candidate." Ford's brain trust met in Washington in mid-March to go over the primary schedule and the delegate numbers. It was clear that it would require a miracle to win. During this time Reagan had beaten Bush in three more primaries, by margins of 2 to 1 in Florida, 3 to 1 in Alabama, and 6 to 1 in Georgia. Ford's tentative support from several state governors collapsed, as it became clear that he could only play the spoiler.

Ford's flirtation devastated whatever chance Bush had for remaining viable against Reagan. What little oxygen remained for the Bush campaign was being sucked out from the left by the quirky candidacy of John Anderson. Bush had led Reagan in the polls in Illinois even after New Hampshire, but his lead vanished between Reagan's hearty campaigning and the Anderson frenzy. In nearly every presidential election there is a surprise candidate who captivates the imagination of the press corps and the chattering class. In 1968 it was Gene McCarthy; in 1976 it was Jerry Brown; in 1984, Gary Hart, and in 2000, John McCain. In 1980, it was Anderson, most of whose career had been characterized by mainstream Republican conservatism; against food stamps, against federal transit subsidies, for Goldwater in 1964, and a zero rating from the Americans for Democratic Action. As a young congressman in the early 1960s Anderson three times sponsored a Constitutional amendment to recognize "the authority and law of Jesus Christ, savior and ruler of nations." But now Anderson saw an opening on the left, endorsing the ERA, abortion on demand, the SALT II treaty, and recanting his earlier support for the Vietnam War. He quickly became a celebrated figure. Bush hoped to recover some of his "Big Mo" by winning the Massachusetts primary. He did, narrowly, but Anderson's close second-place finish dominated the media spin, scrambling Bush's efforts. (And once all the write-in votes were tallied several days later, it appeared that Anderson had overtaken Bush and won Massachusetts after all.) And Anderson drained enough votes away from Bush in Vermont to hand the state to Reagan.

Soon the usual suspects—Paul Newman, Kurt Vonnegut, Gore Vidal, Gloria Steinem, Stewart Mott, Norman Lear—were giddy over Anderson. "Doonesbury" cartoonist Gary Trudeau positively swooned, devoting weeks of his comic strip to boosting Anderson's candidacy. The media began singing his praises as a "maverick." Richard Reeves wrote that "If there were a press caucus, Anderson would be the front runner. . . . He is a giant among pygmies." George Will offered the commonsense observation that "Anderson is the pin-up of columnists not famous for wishing the Republican Party well. . . . Anderson has a rendezvous with the wrong convention." Anderson understood this, and began employing the old formula of calling for a "new coalition," openly seeking crossover votes from Democrats. Over $1 million in campaign contributions came in over a three-week period—more than Anderson had raised in the entire previous year. He was embraced by everyone—everyone except Republican primary voters. Anderson should have returned to reality after Reagan clobbered him in his home state of Illinois in mid-March (48.4 to 36.7 percent) and two weeks later in "progressive" Wisconsin. (These two Reagan wins also drove a stake through the heart of the Bush campaign.) Instead Anderson announced in May, just a few days before Bush dropped out, that he would run in November as an independent, which set off a fatuous round of media speculation about his chances of winning and wishful thinking about "the first real three-way race since 1912." At one point the rumor that Walter Cronkite would agree to be Anderson's running mate was taken seriously. The first polls showed Anderson with support approaching 30 percent, which is what spring polls often show of independent candidacies that, like spring flowers wilting in the summer heat, usually shrink down to single digits by November.

Trendy liberals and the chattering class created the Anderson starburst only because of what was happening on the Democratic side. The candidacy of Ted Kennedy, keenly anticipated since his last brother's death 12 years before, was imploding.

FOR MORE THAN a decade it seemed that fate would eventually bring about a decisive right-left clash between Ronald Reagan and Ted Kennedy. Each was the most articulate and charismatic representative of their ideological creeds, and each inspired fanatical devotion among a vocal segment of party regulars. Some conservatives dreaded the matchup, assuming that "the Kennedy Mystique" would win out. In the fall of 1979, before Kennedy formally announced, *National Review* observed: "A sense of resignation before the inevitable Kennedy victory has become peculiarly widespread. . . . In one way or another, these days, you hear the sentiment expressed that since Kennedy is going to win anyway, why not let Ronald Reagan go ahead and have the race for which he has worked so long."[58] The polls bore out this judgment. A Gallup Poll found Kennedy beating Reagan 61 to 33 percent in a hypothetical pairing, a bigger margin than Carter's lead over Reagan in the same poll.

Kennedy privately informed Carter in September 1979 that he was going to run. In the aftermath of Carter's dreadful "crisis of confidence" speech, a parade of Democratic politicians trouped through Kennedy's office begging him to save the party by taking out Carter, which removed whatever doubts or reservations Kennedy may have had about running. (Among Kennedy's supporters were Pat Moynihan and Scoop Jackson, both of whom described themselves as "comprehensively" disillusioned with Carter.) At that point, polls showed Kennedy leading Carter among Democrats by as much as 38 points in one poll. The biggest strategic concern of Kennedy's advisers was how and when they would approach Carter to ask him to bow out.

Carter had shrewdly agreed to attend the dedication of the John F. Kennedy Library in Boston in late October, which caused Ted Kennedy to delay the public launch of his campaign. By the time Kennedy was ready for his formal announcement in early November, the hostages had been seized in Iran, which changed the political landscape overnight. World events Kennedy could not control, but an event that he could have controlled a month before dealt a blow from which he never recovered. On October 12, Roger Mudd of CBS News sat down with Kennedy at his Senate office to tape the second half of an interview to be broadcast several weeks before Kennedy formally became a candidate. Mudd previously interviewed Kennedy at the family home in Hyannis Port, where Mudd politely asked a number of personal questions about Kennedy and his family, and broached the subject of Chappaquiddick with kid gloves. Kennedy stonewalled and deflected Mudd's attempts to get a new explanation of the lingering imponderables of that infamous incident, and Mudd finally gave up. In this second interview Mudd tried again to broach the subject of Chappaquiddick, and once again Kennedy merely referred Mudd to the inquest report. Frustrated, Mudd changed the sub-ject: "Why do you want to be president?"

This is the sort of question that candidates have down cold. Kennedy flubbed it, rambling incoherently for 256 words, beginning with "Well, I'm—were I to—to make an announcement and—to run, the reasons that I would run is because I have a great belief in this country. . . ." He ended worse than he began: "And I would basically feel that—that it's impera-tive for this country to either move forward, that it can't stand still, or otherwise it moves back." CBS originally planned to broadcast the inter-view on November 7, having been told off-the-record by Kennedy's people that Kennedy would not announce his candidacy until December. But then Kennedy decided to announce on November 7. CBS hurriedly moved up the broadcast to Sunday, November 4 (the same day the Iran-ian hostage crisis began), but it was going to be up against the network premier of *Jaws* on ABC. Even before the Sunday night broadcast, rumors began circulating among media circles that it would be "a major media event." CBS gave an advance screening to a few journalists hoping for some publicity, and a handful of transcripts leaked. Although the Mudd interview got predictably low viewership (even Carter's press secretary Jody Powell watched *Jaws* instead), the effect was devastating. The chat-tering classes were aghast: *How could it be that Ted Kennedy is even worse without a script than Ronald Reagan?*

Kennedy never fully recovered from his Mudd-bath. Suddenly any verbal mistake on the stump was fodder for TV news. Two networks ran segments on his stumbles, such as saying "fam farmily" in Iowa. Verbal miscues were the least of his troubles, though. Kennedy's judgment had always been in question because of Chappaquiddick; a poll in January 1980 found that 55 percent believed that Kennedy handled Chappaquid-dick "improperly," and a *People* magazine survey reported that Ameri-cans regarded Kennedy as less trustworthy than Nixon by a two-to-one margin. As he began campaigning in earnest, questions about his judg-ment grew. Kennedy displayed a tin ear for the public sentiment of the moment and the general anti-liberal current of opinion that was driving the issues of the election. For the energy crisis he proposed federal gaso-line rationing. His solution for inflation and unemployment was wage and price controls and a massive federal spending program to pump up demand. This old-fashioned Keynesian elixir landed with a thud.

Kennedy's missteps on the hostage crisis deepened public doubt about his judgment more than any other issue. He turned on the ailing Shah at a delicate moment in the unfolding crisis. Carter was hoping the Shah would "voluntarily" leave the country (which he later did). Reagan called for giving the Shah permanent asylum in the United States if the Shah wished to remain. But Kennedy disagreed, attacking the Shah in terms hardly different from what was heard out of Tehran. Khomeini claimed that the Shah had killed 350,000 people and had fled the country with $35 billion. In early December 1979, one month into the crisis, Kennedy said: "The Shah had the reins of power and ran one of the most violent regimes in the history of mankind. . . . How can we justify . . . accepting that individual because he would like to come here with his umpteen billions of dollars that he's stolen from Iran?" These remarks were taken out of context; Kennedy repeatedly supported Carter's handling of the crisis, but as a veteran politician he should have known that the media would highlight any words that represented a conflict with the commander-in-chief. The reaction was savage. In a rare moment of bipartisan concord, the chairmen of the Republican and Democratic National Committees issued a joint statement disapproving Kennedy's remarks. The *New York Post* blasted "TEDDY: THE TOAST OF TEHRAN" on its front page, but the broadsheets were scarcely less stinging. The *Washington Post* ran a photo of a smiling Kennedy shaking hands with the Shah on a visit to Tehran in 1975 along with a tisk-tisking editorial that concluded, "It wasn't right, it wasn't responsible, and it wasn't smart."[59]

It was that last sentence that became the whispered subtext about Kennedy. *"He's not as smart or as good as his brothers."* Kennedy's poll numbers were dropping by 1 percent a day, and liberals started jumping ship. The *Boston Globe*'s Ellen Goodman wrote: "I feel embarrassed. I want to change the channel. His voice is strained, his timing is off. . . . Everything is wrong."[60] Jimmy Breslin was equally dismissive, writing in the *New York Daily News* of a Kennedy TV appearance: "I found him to be annoying, wanting, and disturbing . . . insincere . . . maddening and unacceptable." Garry Wills observed the spectacle of Teddy's descent and proclaimed "the end of the entire Kennedy time in our national life." Carter surged ahead of Kennedy in the polls overnight, and won by large margins in both Iowa (59 to 31 percent) and New Hampshire (49 to 38 percent). By the end of March Kennedy had lost five more primaries to Carter (including Illinois), and polls showed that he would lose to Reagan, at a time when Reagan still trailed Carter. Kennedy wasn't even winning a majority of Roman Catholic voters. Now the talk was of when and how Kennedy would bow out gracefully.

But for the collapse of Kennedy's candidacy, John Anderson would have been an asterisk in the chronicles of the 1980 election. Anderson gave liberals a safety value to avoid having to confront the implications of Kennedy's failure. It was thought that the breakdown of the Kennedy candidacy was the fault of the messenger and not the message. To be sure, Kennedy's doubtful character and incompetence on the campaign trail lent credence to this idea, but in fact the failure of his campaign demonstrated the declining allure of pure Kennedy-style liberalism. This political fact was further obscured by Kennedy's revival in the late primaries, which came about as a result of Carter's decline more than Kennedy's cunning.

The glow of patriotic fervor over the Iranian hostage crisis began to ebb in the spring as Carter appeared ineffectual in making progress. Carter's public approval rating, sky-high in November and December, was steadily sliding. But he was hanging on to his lead over Kennedy among Democrats, and polls showed him leading Kennedy in New York by as much as 27 points shortly before the New York primary on March 25. Kennedy's campaign was running low on cash, and his staff began preparing a speech to announce Kennedy's withdrawal from the race. But then one of Carter's most boneheaded blunders caught up with him.

On Saturday, March 2, the United Nations Security Council called a vote on a resolution condemning new Israeli settlements on the West Bank, the Gaza strip, *and Jerusalem*—in other words, the resolution denied Israeli sovereignty over Jerusalem. Anti-Israel resolutions were a perennial at the U.N. in those years. The United States, torn between the desire to prod Israel to restrain new West Bank settlements and our longstanding general support for Israel, had abstained on previous similar resolutions. This time Vance persuaded Carter that the time had come for the United States to signal its displeasure with Israel by voting in favor of the resolution. The resolution passed unanimously, and all hell broke loose. An angry Robert Strauss, Carter's campaign chairman, told Carter, "Either this vote is reversed or you can kiss New York goodbye."[61] Invoking a parliamentary technicality, the United States managed to get a revote on the resolution the next day, and changed its vote from "yes" to "abstain."

Carter attempted to explain the "mistake" by claiming that the inclusion of settlements in Jerusalem was supposed to have been struck from the resolution, and said that the U.S. vote resulted from a "failure of communication." This story might be true, although it strains credulity. Copies of the resolution with the Jerusalem language had been circulating at the State Department and the National Security Council well before the vote, making a clear instruction to U.N. Ambassador Donald McHenry an uncomplicated task. Whatever the truth of the matter, the administration was either politically or diplomatically incompetent. Vance didn't help matters by defending the original yes vote to the Senate Foreign Relations Committee four days before the New York primary. Jewish voters, who had never been enthusiastic about the Southern Baptist president anyway, were outraged. Jewish communities in New York and Connecticut voted for Kennedy by margins of four or five to one over Carter, and Kennedy racked up his first primary wins (excepting his home state of Massachusetts), beating Carter by 16 points in New York and 18 points in Connecticut. Kennedy finally had something to cheer about; his concession and withdrawal speeches were thrown away. No one paid close attention to the exit polls, which revealed that a large proportion of the vote was anti-Carter rather than pro-Kennedy. Four out of 10 Kennedy voters in New York said they would not vote for him in November if he won the nomination.

The depth of anti-Carter sentiment expressed in the New York vote alarmed the White House. Carter and his strategists knew they were losing momentum and, though the delegate numbers still favored Carter, could still lose their grip on the nomination. In other words, what the New York primary proved was that when Jimmy Carter was the issue, Jimmy Carter lost. Something needed to be done to stop Carter's hemorrhaging and Kennedy's newfound momentum. Kennedy finally began campaigning with the vigor and effectiveness that had always been expected. During this phase of the contest Kennedy hit hard on Carter's weak leadership, in exactly the same terms Reagan was using. In his best booming oratory, Kennedy said, "I reject the counsel of the voices, no matter how high in government, that talk about a *malaaaaaise* of the spirit."

The next primary showdown was a week later in Wisconsin—liberal territory. Kennedy territory. In the dark hours of the morning before the polls opened, word came from Tehran that Iranian President Abolhassan

Bani-Sadr was arranging for the Revolutionary Council to vote out an order requiring the "students" to turn over the hostages to the "government." (Quotation marks are helpful here in reminding that "students" and "government" could not be taken at face value in that affair. Both were more accurately described as complementary factions of a mob.) Bani-Sadr's move was seen as a first step in gaining the release of the hostages, though on what timetable it was impossible to say. Carter decided to call a live press conference to announce the news, at 7:13 A.M. eastern time. As voters awoke in the midwest to head to the polls (Kansas was holding its primary on the same day as Wisconsin), they saw Carter on the morning news announcing that a "positive development" was underway in the hostage crisis. This "positive step" meant that the United States would not have to impose additional sanctions against Iran. Although Carter didn't directly say that the end of the crisis was at hand, he implied that the end game was near. A reporter asked, "Well, do you know when they'll be actually released, I mean, brought home?" Carter: "I presume that we will know more about that as the circumstances develop. *We do not know the exact time schedule at this moment.*" (Emphasis added.)

It was April 1—April Fool's Day—and there were many candidates for the biggest fool of the day, starting with Carter. Even the ostensible transfer of the hostages from the "students" to the "government" hardly represented a breakthrough, so Carter's exploitation of the moment bred deep cynicism that would come back to haunt him in the fall. Carter was made to look an even bigger fool when it soon became evident that Bani-Sadr couldn't deliver on his promise of a Revolutionary Council measure to transfer control of the hostages. Maybe sometime in the summer we'll take this up again, came the latest word out of Tehran. But Carter's morning announcement on April 1 may have been enough to sway some voters in Wisconsin and Kansas, where Carter beat Kennedy. Pat Caddell thought the announcement affected a significant number of voters; Carter's other political advisers scurried to deny it, sensing political disaster when Iran reversed course. A week after this dramatic breakthrough announcement, Carter reluctantly imposed additional sanctions on Iran and finally broke diplomatic relations after it became clear that he had been had. Then two weeks later Kennedy beat Carter again in Pennsylvania—the state where Carter had made his breakthrough in 1976—and in Michigan.

Once again Carter's presidency seemed to be falling apart. For the first time polls showed Reagan pulling ahead of Carter. Whether Carter deliberately and cynically exploited the hostage crisis for his political benefit on the morning of the Wisconsin primary, there is no doubt that it had been helpful to him *at first* to allow the hostage crisis to become the dominant factor in American politics. Elevating the crisis and saying he would not leave the White House until the crisis was resolved provided a convenient excuse to avoid meeting Kennedy on the campaign trail or in debate, which Carter had previously agreed to do. But as the crisis dragged on, it became a rapidly depreciating asset, and finally a liability. Carter needed a "long bomb" to reverse his fortunes. He was about to attempt one. It blew up in his face.

AT 5 P.M. EASTERN TIME on Thursday, April 24, three days after the Pennsylvania primary, press secretary Jody Powell announced the daily "lid" on White House news, meaning that there would be no more presidential news that day and reporters could go home. No one knew that Carter was in the midst of the most agonizing moment of his presidency. The next morning the nation awoke to learn that an aborted hostage rescue mission had turned into a catastrophe, with eight American servicemen killed in an aircraft collision deep inside Iran. Beyond the blow this delivered to Carter and his presidency, the episode seemed to sum up the deterioration of American military capability, the result of the debilitating bureaucratization of the armed forces over the previous two decades. How did it happen?

Within days of the hostage-taking in November Carter ordered the Joint Chiefs of Staff to begin exploring options and making a plan for a military rescue. Recollections of the Israeli's successful hostage rescue raid at Entebbe, Uganda, in 1976 (led by a young army officer named Ehud Barak) came immediately to mind, but the more difficult circumstances of the Iranian situation seemed to rule out a similar effort. Among other difficulties, the Pentagon didn't have a planning process for hostage rescue missions, so everything had to be devised from scratch. Even if a tactical plan for overcoming the "students" at the embassy compound could be devised, Tehran was hundreds of miles inland, beyond the round-trip range of American helicopters.

The sheer difficulty and improbability of a rescue assault are what encouraged the Pentagon to believe a surprise raid could be done. A plan was beginning to take shape within three weeks of the hostages' seizure. A number of factors looked favorable. The United States supposedly had an intelligence agent inside the embassy compound, an Iranian cook who regularly relayed information to other U.S. agents in Tehran about the number and disposition of guards on the scene. By the spring, the number of armed guards had dropped to about 20—a number that could be easily overcome by highly trained American special forces.

But how to get forces in, and back out with the hostages, remained the crux of the problem. From the start the plan violated the basic military maxims of simplicity and quick entry and exit. The Pentagon planners settled on a three-day, three-stage plan that involved flying a 120-man commando force on eight heavy lift RH-53D "Sea Stallion" helicopters at night to a location outside of Tehran. This would require refueling the helicopters at some point. This involved the first and ultimately the most fateful decision. The natural choice for such a mission would be Air Force pilots, who were trained for long-range flights using terrain-following radar (TFR) and forward-looking infrared systems (FLIR) on RH-53D helicopters, which made precise night-time flying possible. But it was decided to use Marine pilots, typically only trained for short-range helicopter missions, instead. The Marine pilots would fly with night-vision goggles and navigate by dead-reckoning and old-fashioned compass headings. Although the Pentagon never admitted it, the decision to use Marine instead of Air Force pilots seems to have been the result of inter-service rivalry. As the initial plan began to take shape, every branch of the service had a clear role—except the Marines. But because Navy helicopters were not equipped for, nor Marine pilots trained for, aerial refueling, the plan required a ground refueling stop somewhere deep inside Iran where American fuel tanker planes and helicopters could rendezvous.

Planners selected a site 265 miles southeast of Tehran, and 500 miles inland from the Persian Gulf, near the middle of the Dasht-e-Kavir desert. It was code-named "Watchband," but would become better known by its designation in the operational plan, "Desert 1." One story, since disputed, held the CIA built a landing site at this location a few years before (supposedly as a possible escape route for the Shah), and it appeared to be the only suitable location for American C-130 tanker planes to land, even though the site was close to a well-traveled highway.

According to the plan, after refueling, the eight helicopters would fly on under cover of darkness to a second hideout near Tehran, "Desert 2," where the commando force would hide out until the next night. Then they were to proceed on several Mercedes trucks, acquired by an advance team that had slipped into Iran weeks before from Turkey and Pakistan, to the embassy. Planners thought the force could be in-and-out with the hostages in less than an hour, whereupon five helicopters would come from their hiding places to collect the hostages and the rescue force. The United States was prepared to call in massive air cover if needed. The last part of the plan called for 80 Army Rangers to capture an Iranian airfield southwest of Tehran, where the helicopters would rendezvous with three C-141 airplanes that would take the hostages, the rescue force, and the advance team out of the country. Green Beret Col. Charles Beckwith would lead the mission. Beckwith was known as "Chargin' Charlie"; at the rendezvous at Desert 1 he greeted the arriving helicopters with, "Welcome to World War III."

It was an audacious and complicated plan, requiring precise timing and allowing little margin for anything to go wrong. The plan had to be conceived, rehearsed, and launched with maximum secrecy and diversion, chiefly to keep the Soviet Union from observing it with their spy satellites and tipping off Iran. This concern for secrecy led the planners to compartmentalize every phase of preparation, such that each of the military units involved in the plan had its own commander and never rehearsed together. (Despite this security, the mission was nearly blown when pilots training in Arizona blabbed about the mission to impress women they met in a local bar.) Some of the unit commanders met for the first time at Desert 1 in Iran. Although the planners thought that taking the embassy would be the easiest part of the plan, estimating that only one or two hostages might be killed. (There is controversy about these estimates, with reports that the CIA thought half or more would be killed.)

Contrary to widespread accounts, President Carter did not hobble the plan with any restrictions as to the amount or kind of force used. Carter did caution that he did not wish to see "wanton killing," but he understood the score. The stories, popular in the media in the weeks after the mission, that the assault force was going to use some kind of "sleeping gas" to avoid killing Iranians are false; the commando team fully intended to use deadly force. Still, the plan seemed to face long odds; some planners in the Pentagon rated the chance of success as one in four, while some independent military experts put the chances of success as low as 1 in 25. Secretary of State Vance opposed the plan entirely, telling Carter that he would resign after the operation whether it succeeded or not. Vance warned Vice President Mondale: "I'll guarantee you something will go wrong. It never works the way they say it's going to work. There's a good chance disaster could occur here."[62]

Vance didn't have to wait long after the launch of the mission to be proven correct. Eight helicopters lifted off from the aircraft carrier *Nimitz* in the Persian Gulf just after nightfall on April 24, while six C-130 tanker planes took off from Masirah Island near Oman several hundred miles to the southwest. The helicopters would only have a little more than an hour to refuel at Desert 1 if they were going to reach the Desert 2 hideout before sunrise. Two hours into the flight, a warning light flashed in helicopter #6 indicating a crack in a main rotor blade. The pilot landed to inspect the rotor, and found no visible crack. Not knowing that the RH-53D had a history of false warning lights for rotor cracks, the pilot decided to abandon helicopter #6 and continue to Desert 1 on another helicopter.

Three hours into the flight, the seven remaining helicopters flew into a large dust cloud (the Iranians called these "haboobs") and became disoriented. American meteorologists knew that dust clouds were a common occurrence in the Iranian deserts at this time of year, but the pilots *were not briefed about the possibility of dust clouds,* nor had the crews trained to fly through dust clouds in the rehearsals for the mission. (The Pentagon had recommended that the mission be launched before the end of March, in part because it knew of the April dust storms, and in part because the longer nighttime hours left more margin for error in the refueling step.) Taken by surprise—one pilot said, "It was like flying in a darkened milk bowl"—the helicopters lost formation and began drifting apart. Because the mission was being conducted under strict radio silence, the helicopters could not communicate with one another. As the helicopters floundered in the dust, a second helicopter developed mechanical trouble. The navigational system on helicopter #5 failed, and the pilot, lost in the dust, decided to turn around and head back to the *Nimitz*. Helicopter #5 had nearly reached the end of the dust cloud; had he known, the pilot said later, he would have pressed on.

The six remaining helicopters straggled into Desert 1 far behind schedule, the last helicopter arriving 85 minutes late. The second leg of the flight to Desert 2 would now take until after daybreak, seriously increasing the risk of the mission. The pilots were shaken by the flight conditions; some expressed reluctance to continue on to Tehran. But there were more immediate problems. There was no central command post; many of the pilots and officers did not know who was in command. The airplane engines were left running during the entire time at Desert 1 so as to eliminate the risk that an engine might fail to restart, which made the site dusty and noisy. A busload of Iranians drove through the landing site and had to be detained. (If the mission had gone forward, these 44 Iranians would have been taken out of the country on a C-130 to avoid compromising the mission, raising the specter that the United States would now have hostages of its own.) A second pair of Iranians escaped from the area after their gasoline tanker truck was shot at and blown up.

Then a new mechanical problem was discovered. Helicopter #2 had experienced a hydraulic pump failure and had lost its hydraulic fluid. There were no spare parts; helicopter #2 could not go on. The moment of decision had arrived. Knowing that helicopters are prone to breakdowns on long missions, planners had assumed that one or more would be lost to the mission. The plan required *five* helicopters for the final stage of the mission in Tehran, but called for six working helicopters reaching Desert 2. In addition to having one spare copter, six were needed to get all of the personnel and their weapons to Desert 2. The Air Force commander on the scene, Col. James Kyle, asked Col. Beckwith: "Charlie, would you consider taking five and going ahead?" Beckwith thought for a moment and replied: "There's just no way." It was now 2 A.M. local time in the desert.

Beckwith and Kyle relayed the news to the task force commander in Cairo, who immediately passed it along to Washington. Within minutes Defense Secretary Harold Brown, Brzezinski, and Carter were conferring on the decision. Carter reluctantly agreed with the decision to abort. The abort scenario was never rehearsed, so confusion at Desert 1 deepened as the entire process of loading helicopters with equipment for the Tehran leg of the mission was reversed. Catastrophe struck 45 minutes later when helicopter #3, lifting away from a C-130 tanker to make room for another helicopter to take on fuel, suddenly pitched to the side, its main rotor blade slicing into the airplane behind the cockpit. Both the helicopter and the tanker exploded, killing the five-man crew on the plane and three Marines on the helicopter.

In the panic that followed a last set of blunders was committed. Col. Kyle decided to abandon Desert 1 as fast as possible. Even though plans called for the helicopters to be destroyed in the event they were inoperable, they were left intact at Desert 1—with copies of the complete classified plan for the mission which Iran subsequently recovered from the scene. (Included in the plans was a map of Tehran showing the Ayatollah Khomeini's residence. Perhaps the commandoes were contemplating taking a hostage of their own?) Iran hastily scattered the hostages from the embassy to several locations in Tehran to make another rescue attempt impossible. It took almost two months for the American advance team in Tehran to make their escape.

Operation Eagle Claw, the rescue mission's official code name, joined the Son Tay P.O.W. raid and the *Mayaguez* rescue mission as the third major military fiasco of its kind in the last decade. Was this another symptom of "the Vietnam Syndrome," of a corrupted command structure that was incompetent at warfare? Could Eagle Claw have worked if planners had used more helicopters or experienced better luck? Skeptics outnumber believers by a wide margin. "The planning and execution were too incompetent to believe," an Israeli officer told *Newsweek*. Military analyst Richard A. Gabriel argued that the hostage rescue mission "was an operation so poorly planned and executed that failure was almost guaranteed."[63] It may not be fair to extend the failure of the rescue mission into a metaphor of declining American prowess, but the perception was undeniable. American elites as well as its allies believed that the declining confidence in America's military was indissolubly linked to the increasing timidity of U.S. foreign policy. More than a bigger defense budget would be needed to fix this problem.

Beyond the tactical second-guessing, the political fallout was swift and severe. *The New Republic* dubbed it "The Jimmy Carter Desert Classic," saying the failed mission was yet another example of Carter's "incompetence." Reagan refrained from criticizing the mission (in general Reagan tried to avoid commenting on the hostage crisis, though now and then he would attack Carter's foreign policy weakness as the reason the hostages were taken in the first place). Carter's own reaction was vintage doublespeak: He called the failed mission "an incomplete success," and, because he defined it as a "humanitarian mission," he would persist in his proud boast of being "the first American president in 50 years who has never sent troops into combat," and that no American soldiers had died "in combat" during his administration.

More inscrutable were Carter's subsequent political comments. He was going to have to emerge from his self-imposed Rose Garden internment to campaign if he was going to beat off Kennedy, let alone face Reagan in the fall. In a press conference five days after the rescue mission, Carter justified his newfound willingness to travel by saying that "a lot of the responsibilities that have been on my shoulders in the past few months have now been *alleviated to some degree.* . . . None of these challenges are completely removed, but I believe they are *manageable enough* now for me to leave the White House for a limited travel schedule, including some campaigning if I choose to do so. . . ." (Emphasis added.) In the wake of the failed rescue mission, the Iranian hostage crisis could hardly have been said to be more "manageable," nor were the nation's economic problems "alleviated."

KENNEDY SURGED LATE in the spring, winning five of the last eight primaries held on June 3. But it was too late. Carter had accumulated enough delegates to assure himself of winning renomination. Kennedy ended up winning only 10 of the 34 Democratic primaries, and five of the 25 caucuses. But he refused to drop out of the race, as several leading Democrats (including Moynihan) called for an "open convention," holding on to the slim hope that Carter might yet be forced to step aside. On the Republican side, Bush managed to win the Pennsylvania and Michigan primaries in April, but it wasn't enough to revive his campaign. Reagan ended up winning 29 of 33 primaries, garnering 60 percent of all votes cast in Republican primaries. Saying "I know how to count," Bush dropped out on May 26. Right after the Pennsylvania primary reporters spotted Bush wearing gold cuff links bearing the vice-presidential seal (they were a gift from Nelson Rockefeller), prompting the obvious query: Would you settle for the number two spot? "No way," Bush said.

Several things were noteworthy about the 1980 primary season. Republican turnout was up sharply in the early primaries before the contest was decided in Reagan's favor. GOP turnout increased 32 percent over 1976 in Massachusetts, 46 percent in Illinois, and 52 percent in Wisconsin. Second, Reagan ran far ahead of his polls in several primaries, suggesting a large hidden pro-Reagan vote. In Florida, pre-primary polls showed Reagan with 42 percent of the vote; he got 57 percent. In Georgia, polls had Reagan at 40 percent; he got 73. In Alabama, polls had him at 39; he got 70. In Illinois, polls had him at 36 (against 34 for Anderson); he got 48. Reagan was also drawing a large number of independent and crossover Democratic votes, as he had in 1976. Yet few people recognized the emergence of what would become known as "Reagan Democrats." *Washington Post* political reporter Bill Peterson wrote in April that "Reagan's support among conservative blue-collar Democrats has been one of the most under-reported phenomena of the 1980 presidential race."

With the nomination locked up early, the Reagan campaign was becalmed in the late spring and early summer. "Politics is like show business," Reagan remarked to Stu Spencer in 1966. "You have a hell of an opening, you coast for a while, you have a hell of a closing."[64] Reagan may have coasted fine on the screen, but he always got into trouble when he coasted in politics, as the Iowa experience showed. During the lull between the last primaries and the Republican national convention in Detroit six weeks later, Republican Party leaders developed a case of the jitters. "MANY IN GOP CHARGE REAGAN CAMPAIGN IS FALLING INTO DISARRAY, LOSING SUPPORT," read a *Wall Street Journal* headline in mid-June.

An aborted attempt to oust Republican National Committee chairman Bill Brock made Reagan look indecisive and his supporters petulant. Reagan's campaign chairman Sen. Paul Laxalt was behind the move to oust Brock, as conservatives wanted to cement total control of party machinery. Reagan only put an end to the effort after a one-on-one meeting with Brock. Complaints resurfaced about disorganization among Reagan's senior campaign staff. An offhand remark about repealing the minimum wage and a meeting between Reagan and the Egyptian ambassador during which Reagan reportedly indicated his willingness to negotiate with the Palestinian Liberation Organization revived concern about Reagan's "gaffability." Rowland Evans and Robert Novak wrote in a June newspaper column: "He is far from being ready to take on Jimmy Carter and his resourceful Georgia politicians."

The most fateful aspect of the pre-convention weeks concerned the selection of Reagan's running mate. Early in the spring, as soon as the nomination appeared secure, Reagan asked his senior campaign aides to begin the process of winnowing down a list of potential running mates. The first list included nearly 20 people, including two women, Ambassador Anne Armstrong and Sen. Nancy Landon Kassebaum, and some of the predictable names such as Bush, Sen. Howard Baker, Rep. Jack Kemp, Sen. Richard Lugar, and a few governors. Also on the list were former cabinet members William Simon and Donald Rumsfeld. The two women were on the list for symbolic political reasons. The most ideological and temperamentally compatible pick—Jack Kemp—was ruled out because it was judged that Reagan needed a more senior and established running mate to balance out his own lack of Washington experience. Pairing an ex-NFL quarterback with an ex-actor was thought to be too vulnerable to criticism about a lack of gravitas. Besides, although Kemp was by then well known in political circles, he had almost no name ID in polls of the general public. Reagan's personal first choice was Sen. Paul Laxalt, but it was recognized that, coming from Nevada, a state with only three electoral votes that Reagan was bound to carry anyway, Laxalt didn't help the ticket, and might have some downside risk because his home state's gambling industry reputation.

As in 1976, Reagan's deliberations about his running mate showed that he wanted to win more than he wanted to make points for ideological purity. The conventional wisdom of political scientists and historians is that running mates matter little except in helping to deliver their home state. With Reagan's candidacy this started to change. Reagan eschewed a "cattle call" in which prospective running mates would trudge through a media gauntlet to meet with Reagan. Instead, Richard Wirthlin quietly conducted an extensive poll to see which prospective running mates would help the ticket with swing voters. Three names emerged: Baker, Bush, and Gerald Ford. Reagan had reservations about all three. (Bush actually received the most support in an open-ended question that asked who Reagan should pick as his running mate. Bush got 20 percent to Ford's 13 percent.) Baker had supported the Panama Canal treaty, which earned him considerable enmity among conservatives. Besides, Reagan's circle believed that Baker would be more useful as Senate Republican leader. "There's a lot of resistance to Bush," a Reagan campaign staffer told *Newsweek*. "And it begins with Ronald Reagan."

Reagan had a poor impression of Bush from the campaign, especially the famous clash in the New Hampshire debate in Nashua. "It imprinted with Reagan that Bush was a wimp," an unnamed campaign aide told Jack Germond and Jules Witcover.[65] Reagan himself said of Bush that "He just melts under pressure."[66] "If he can't stand up to that kind of pressure, how could he stand up to the pressure of being President?" Reagan remarked to an aide. Reagan's advisers argued the contrary case for Bush. "You can't ignore the strength he showed in some key primaries," Reagan was told. Stu Spencer was favorable to Bush, but perhaps the most important Bush-backer among the Reaganites was Ed Meese. Reagan bridled at their importunings, however, leading Spencer to reflect later, "There was no way he was going to pick Bush."

Whatever Reagan's lingering feelings about Ford from the 1976 campaign were, his hesitations about Bush caused him to consider the Ford idea with an open mind. Ford as a running mate was a bad idea from the start, and, despite the polls showing Ford boosting the ticket, might well have dragged the ticket down on election day. Meese acknowledged that "if Reagan brought back a former president, it would look as if Reagan didn't feel he could do the job himself. . . . Some of the people from the East apparently were not sure that this guy from California could do the job."[67] A number of Republican leaders who backed the idea may well have thought this privately. Whatever the motivations, the Ford nimbus was alight, and it was destined to play out to the last possible moment.

In late May *U.S. News and World Report* published a squib in its "Washington Whispers" section: "Discount trial balloons floated by backers of Ronald Reagan, suggesting that Gerald Ford as a running mate would virtually ensure a Republican victory in November. It's largely a symbolic effort to restore party unity—and furthermore, Ford's friends say the former President would turn the bid down flat."[68] There was more to the story than this. As rumors intensified in the weeks before the convention, one frequently reported story held that Reagan would submit three names to the convention and allow the delegates to select his running mate. This was a gambit, the story went, to hold public interest in what would otherwise be a dull convention without any drama or news. More likely it was part of a maneuver to cajole Ford into becoming Reagan's running mate, perhaps by the anachronistic device of a convention "draft." The idea of Ford joining the ticket was first mooted early in the spring when Bryce Harlow wrote to Ford suggesting that Ford could assure Reagan's victory by agreeing to join the ticket. Harlow urged Ford to trust Reagan and not demand any formal concessions from Reagan about Ford's potential role in a Reagan White House. Other intermediaries broached the subject with Ford, but he rebuffed all entreaties, sometimes with an emphatic "Hell no."

Reagan met with Ford for an hour and a half on June 5 at Ford's Rancho Mirage home near Palm Springs, formally burying the hatchet from the 1976 campaign. Ford is said to have warmed to Reagan during this meeting—"no one in politics forgives a grudge as easily as Jerry Ford," Lou Cannon observed—but turned away Reagan's query about his willingness to join the ticket, which was duly passed along to the media immediately after the meeting ended. Reagan didn't give up on the idea, however, and intrigue over the matter only grew as the convention approached a month later. Reagan came to the convention in mid-July with the intention of trying again to convince Ford to be his running mate. A series of back-channel efforts were set in motion to persuade Ford to accept. Thus began a five-day sequence of events that came close to attempting to reinterpret Article II of the Constitution in the midst of political campaign.

On Friday, July 11, two days before the GOP delegates assembled in Detroit, Reagan campaign manager William Casey called John Marsh, one of Ford's closest assistants during his presidency, and asked to meet when he arrived in Detroit. Marsh suspected what Casey had on his mind, and his suspicions were confirmed when the following day William Timmons, a former Ford aide now working for Reagan, implored Marsh to persuade Ford to accept the vice presidency. Marsh said, not for the first time, that Ford was not interested. But now Timmons and other Reaganites upped the ante: Ford would be assured of important functions in a Reagan White House if he was vice president, perhaps including the budget process and defense policy. This wrinkle made it difficult for Ford's emissaries to shut down the idea. Now events accelerated, and like the proverbial traffic accident at a four-way corner, recollections differ widely as to the sequence of events, the content of conversations, and the key turning points. As best as can be pieced together from the numerous and conflicting accounts, the episode unfolded as follows:

Sunday, July 13, 1980
Ford tells Barbara Walters at noon that "under no circumstances would I be the candidate for the vice presidency." This seems to close to door. Ford even tells his pollster Robert Teeter that he is thinking of going home after his speech to the convention Monday night in order to avoid facing a groundswell of enthusiasm from the convention delegates to join the ticket. But later in the afternoon, Ford asks Alan Greenspan if he would be willing to serve as an intermediary with the Reagan campaign about the possibility of becoming the running mate. Ford is leaving the door ajar. Reagan's staff is burning up the phone lines with calculations of their own, and hatches a plan.

Monday, July 14
Reagan arrives in Detroit, and plans to drop by to wish Ford a happy birthday, and ask Ford once again to join the ticket. If Ford accepts, Reagan plans to appear at a big reception for the convention delegates with the surprise announcement. Peter Hannaford had drafted remarks for Reagan, and entrusts the only copy of the remarks to convention floor manager William Timmons. Hannaford's draft would have Reagan saying:

> For the past several weeks, I have carefully reviewed the qualifications of many men and women in public and private life each of whom is a great credit to this nation and each of whom possesses talent, experience and excellent qualities. But, there is one person more than any other I want as my running mate. He is a man uniquely qualified in terms of experience; a man of ability, compassion, and commitment. That man is Gerald Ford. . . .
>
> I talked with former President Ford just this evening and I told him that I wanted to talk with you about this. We have discussed the subject of the vice presidency in the past and he has expressed to me his very understandable reasons for not seeking the position. . . .
>
> I am convinced that Gerald Ford would respond to a direct call from his party to return to public service, and I am asking you to make that call tonight. . . .[69]

The preparation of remarks for Reagan shows how far their thinking had gone on the idea, and how far they were prepared to go to bring pressure on Ford if Ford indicated the slightest willingness. Reagan, accompanied by Nancy, calls on Ford and his wife Betty in the afternoon. Reagan presents Ford with a gift: an antique Indian peace pipe—another symbol of Reagan's desire to lay their old feud to rest. "Almost immediately," Ford recalled, "he says that he and Nancy have concluded that if I were to be on the ticket as vice president, it would be more certain that we could beat Jimmy Carter."[70] (All of the contemporary accounts mistakenly place Reagan's first solicitation of Ford at a one-on-one meeting they had the following day.) Ford balks but does not refuse, calling for aides for both men to discuss what formal role Ford would have in a Reagan White House. Ford picks Greenspan, Henry Kissinger, and Robert Barrett, another adviser from his own administration, to represent him. Reagan selects Casey, Meese, and Wirthlin. Ford reportedly tells Reagan that he should choose Bush instead. Reagan's remarks imploring the delegates to draft Ford are not given.

Later that night Ford makes a prime-time speech to the convention that has the effect of rekindling hopes that he might be willing to join the ticket after all. "Some call me an elder statesman," Ford tells the delegates in the climax of his speech. "I don't know. I don't mind telling you that I am not ready to quit yet. . . . Elder statesmen are supposed to sit quietly and smile wisely from the sidelines. I've never been much for sitting. I've never spent much time on the sidelines. . . . This country means too much for me to comfortably park on the bench. *So, when this convention fields the team for Governor Reagan, count me in!*" (Emphasis added.) To Reagan and his senior advisers, these words seem like an indication that Ford is favorable to the idea of joining the ticket. Reagan decides to redouble his efforts to get Ford. "I must say," Reagan told Germond and Witcover after the election, "we all got swept up with the idea."[71]

Tuesday, July 15

At mid-morning Reagan turns up the pressure on Ford by asking a group of visiting House and Senate members what they think of Ford as a potential veep. (Among the group visiting Reagan are Sen. Strom Thurmond, Sen. John Tower, Rep. Bob Michel, and Delaware Gov. Pete DuPont.) Reagan is undoubtedly hoping to create a "buzz" that will sweep Ford along. The key moment arrives in the afternoon, when Reagan meets privately with Ford for over an hour. Reagan presses Ford directly, and offers various enticements to gain his assent. "I know you've made it plain already that you didn't want anything of this kind," Reagan tells Ford, "but I'm asking, will you please reconsider?" Reagan suggests that Ford could serve as a member of the Cabinet, perhaps as Secretary of Defense. Ford rejects that idea outright, and tells Reagan that he thinks the whole scheme is unworkable. *But he doesn't say no.* Instead, Ford offers the first troublesome sign that the price for his acceptance will be too steep for Reagan to pay.

Ford recalls telling Reagan, "If I'm going to be on the ticket, I want some impact as to who you are going to have in your Cabinet. I would strongly recommend that you have Henry Kissinger, so that you have some continuity in foreign policy."[72] But Kissinger was anathema to Reagan and his key supporters; "continuity" in foreign policy is exactly what Reagan is against. (Reagan will later instruct his floor whips to tell delegates not to boo Kissinger when he speaks at the convention that night.) Reagan reacts politely but negatively to this suggestion. When word leaks out that Ford has tried to impress Kissinger on Reagan, speculation begins that Kissinger and other Ford retinues are behind the scheme as a way to get back in power. Kissinger will later disavow any interest in returning to office, and deny that Ford had brought up his name with Reagan.

Backroom discussions intensify. Casey talks with Kissinger, asking Kissinger to intercede with Ford. Kissinger is enthusiastic about the idea of Ford joining Reagan's ticket (so is Greenspan, it turns out). Late Tuesday night Kissinger talks alone with Ford for 45 minutes, imploring Ford to accept Reagan's invitation. Ford resists. "Henry, it won't work."

Wednesday, July 16
This is D-Day for what is starting to be called "the dream ticket." Reagan is running out of time, and gently presses Ford for a decision. Reagan will speak to Ford four times during the day in person and by phone, and all four times Ford will refuse to say yes or no. The day begins with Ford appearing on NBC's *Today* show, giving another public signal that he might be willing to be vice president. Ford is asked if his pride would be hurt by serving as number two. "Honestly, if I thought the situation would work, if all the other questions could be resolved, the problem of pride would not bother me in any way." At midmorning, Ford meets with GOP party chairman Bill Brock and several members of the House and Senate. They urge Ford to work out an agreement with Reagan to run. Ford again ex-

presses skepticism, but again *does not say no*. Ford gives the okay for Kissinger, Greenspan, Barrett, and Marsh to continue discussions with Reagan's people.

Ford insists that if he is to be vice president there must be "meaningful participation by me in the major decision areas." There now begins 12 hours of discussions between the Reagan and Ford camps about the details of a possible arrangement for Ford. It is not accurate to think of these contacts as "negotiations." Greenspan, in fact, is at the convention as a member of *Reagan's* stable of advisers. Reagan's people begin to offer specifics, even putting down a page and half of "talking points" about Ford's formal role in a Reagan White House. The Reagan team's "talking points" suggest Ford overseeing the National Security Council, the Office of Management and Budget, and the Council of Economic Advisers. Does this mean that Ford would be a "super chief of staff" or a de facto "deputy president"? Kissinger presses the practical questions of this sketchy arrangement: "What does 'major input' mean? Will he have his own staff? Can he stop something? Can he send a paper back?" As the unprecedented character of what is being proposed begins to sink in, it starts to occur to a few of the Reaganites that they are close to bargaining away the presidency.

To keep up appearances Reagan lunches with potential running mates Kemp, Bush, and Simon. But despite the best efforts to keep the matter under wraps, it is impossible to stop the news of a possible Reagan-Ford ticket from leaking out to convention delegates and the media. Reagan and Ford's teams are bogged down as the seriousness of the issue becomes more clear. Meese tells Reagan that a deal with Ford is unlikely. Reagan replies that he is ready to select Bush if the Ford discussions end. At midafternoon a group of senior Republicans including Baker, Brock, and Bob Dole begin shuttling between Ford and Reagan's hotel suites urging them to make a deal. (Ford's suite is one floor above Reagan's in the same hotel.) At 3 P.M., Kissinger, Marsh, and Greenspan meet with Ford and go over the difficulties with the idea. Ford is pessimistic. Kissinger telephones Casey, saying, "Bill, I think it is 'no'." But some of Ford's people are still eager to keep trying. Robert Barrett says, "Today may be the most important one in the campaign. We may win or lose it today."

At 5 P.M., Ford goes down to see Reagan in person. Sensing that the details of a deal are irresolvable in the short time left, Ford suggests the only other step that would make him comfortable as vice president:

Greenspan as Secretary of the Treasury, and Kissinger as Secretary of State. These were not conditions for accepting, Ford stresses, but soundings to see if he and Reagan were truly a compatible team. Since these were not formal demands, it is easy for Reagan to demur.

As Reagan and Ford's teams toil away, the turning point of the story unfolds. At 7 P.M. Ford honors a previous commitment to appear live on CBS with Walter Cronkite. Kissinger and Greenspan both urge Ford to postpone the appearance, but Ford overrules them. By this time, rumors of the "dream ticket" are "flying at the speed of light," in the words of NBC's John Chancellor. Cronkite's colleague Dan Rather has gotten some of the details of the meetings between the Reagan and Ford teams, and reports this on camera just before Ford goes on. Cronkite asks Ford whether he would accept a draft from the convention. His answer is still "no," Ford says, but again he leaves the door ajar, adding:

> I would not go to Washington . . . and be a figurehead vice president. If I go to Washington—and I'm not saying that I'm accepting—I have to go there with the belief that I will play a meaningful role across the board in the basic and the crucial and the important decisions that have to be made in a four-year period. . . . I have to have responsible assurances. . . .

Cronkite now offers the famous phrase that crystallizes the problem with the whole idea: *"It's got to be something like a co-presidency?"* Ford answers hastily: *"That's something Governor Reagan really ought to consider."* (Emphasis added.)

Reagan, watching from his suite, sits up in his chair and reacts with mock innocence: "Is that Jerry Ford? Can you believe it? Did you hear what he said about a co-presidency?" Reagan is later described by aides present as "aghast" and "perturbed" at Ford's remarks. "No way," Martin Anderson recalls Reagan saying. "No co-presidency. If he wants to be vice president, fine."

"I knew that such a thing could not work," Reagan will later tell Germond and Witcover. "And this was probably the first time I began to wonder if all of us in our belief in the dream ticket, if we had thought beyond the election."[73] But at this point Reagan is still willing to go the extra mile to get Ford. At 9 P.M. Reagan calls Ford and tells him that he needs a decision. Ford tells Reagan that he still has reservations and would like to sleep on it. Reagan says no; "I have to have a decision within an hour." Nancy Reagan calls Betty Ford a few minutes later, expressing her hopes that a deal can still be made.

At this point the convention hall is buzzing over the "dream ticket," and the rumor that Reagan and Ford are on their way to the convention to announce the deal. The competitive instincts of the TV networks fuel the rumors. At 10:10 P.M. eastern time, Cronkite goes on the air to proclaim the deal consummated: "CBS News has learned that there is a definite plan for Ronald Reagan and the former President of the United States, Gerald Ford, who will be selected as his running mate, an unparalleled, unprecedented situation in American politics . . . to appear together in this platform for Ronald Reagan to announce that Ford will run with him."[74] In fact the possibility of the "dream ticket" is in its terminal phase. At 10:30 Ford decides to tell Reagan that the answer is "no." He goes down to Reagan's suite and meets privately with Reagan to put an end to the idea. Reagan is relieved; he has already come to the conclusion that the deal won't work. Minutes after Ford leaves the room, Reagan says, "Now, where the hell's George Bush." At about 11:40 P.M. Reagan calls Bush. Bush is expecting that Reagan will tell him that he has selected Ford, and is jubilant to be offered the second spot on the ticket.

There remains one more task to bring the episode to a conclusion. Reagan knows that he needs to put an immediate halt to the "dream ticket" talk on the convention floor. If delegates go to bed that night thinking Ford is the running mate, there will be a huge letdown Thursday when the news is otherwise. As Reagan is en route to the convention hall, Reagan's aides decide to leak the news so that the delegates won't be shocked by Reagan's announcement. Chris Wallace of NBC News gets the first tip and goes on the air with the story; this is the first that anyone in the convention hall learns that the "dream ticket" is just that—a dream. It is unprecedented for a candidate to appear before a convention prior to the delegates' formal nomination vote and acceptance speech. Reagan begins by acknowledging the unprecedented nature of his appearance, adding:

> But in watching at the hotel the television and seeing the rumors
> that were going around and the gossip that was taking place here, I
> felt that it was necessary to break the tradition. . . . It is true that a

number of Republican leaders, people in our party, officeholders, felt, as I am sure many others have felt, that a proper ticket would have included the former President of the United States, Gerald Ford. We have gone over this and over this and over this, and he and I have come to the conclusion, and he believes deeply, that he can be of more value as the former president campaigning his heart out, which he has pledged to do, and not as a member of ticket.

Reagan ends by telling the delegates that "I am recommending to this convention that tomorrow when the session reconvenes that George Bush be nominated." With a dizzying swiftness, the "dream ticket" vanishes into the mists.

NOT UNTIL THE FRENZY subsided in the days that followed was it recognized how precipitous was the Ford adventure. Even if Ford had unconditionally agreed to be the vice president, protocol alone would have made it an awkward arrangement. "How would he be addressed?" one wit pointed out; "Mr. President Vice President, or Mr. Vice President President?" Any kind of formal power-sharing arrangement would have been even worse. Murray Kempton wrote caustically of the possibilities of the more formal arrangement that had been discussed: "Visions arose of Henry Kissinger as Secretary of the Vice President's State and Donald Rumsfeld as Secretary for the Defense of the Vice President and daily press briefings where Lyn Nofziger would lay down the President's policy and Ron Nessen would announce the Vice President's reservations." *National Review* put the problem more succinctly: "The continuous undertow of past habits and loyalties would have pulled [Reagan's] administration apart."[75]

Kissinger and others close to the discussions said later that given more time, a suitable arrangement could have been worked out. This is more than doubtful. "To try to do something that is inherently impossible," political philosopher Michael Oakeshott wrote, "is always a corrupting enterprise." Oakeshott's axiom aptly applies to the idea of dividing or qualifying the unitary power of a constitutional chief executive in a republican form of government. It was only the pressure of time that propelled the discussions as far as they went. At some point it occurred to Reagan's people that they were not just trying to redefine or enhance the vice presidency on the fly; they were bargaining away the indivisible power of the chief executive. A Reagan aide told *The New Republic:* "All Reagan would have had left was the Bureau of Indian Affairs." *Newsweek* had a clear-eyed view: "It was a 'dream ticket' that threatened a political morass and a constitutional nightmare."[76]

Media coverage of the "dream ticket" story was almost universally critical of Reagan. David Broder called it a "fiasco," adding that Reagan "did enough damage to himself to make Mr. Carter seem smart to have left Mr. Reagan onstage alone." Elizabeth Drew wrote that "The whole thing suggests a picture of Reagan passively, without much thought, dealing out his Presidency. . . . It is a picture of some chaos." Even the *Wall Street Journal* expressed dismay, writing that "The episode struck a disquieting note about Mr. Reagan's staffing and decision-making ability. . . . The spectacle was scarcely reassuring."

Yet it should be noted in fairness to Reagan that it was *Ford* who strung out the affair with his refusal to say flatly yes or no, and that the most significant factor in derailing any possible arrangement was Ford's refusal to trust Reagan to arrive at a cooperative structure *after* the election. Reagan's motives in putting up with Ford's indecision are easy to understand: He wanted to win. Ford's motives and thought process are more obscure. To be sure, the idea of a former president serving as an active vice president is inherently awkward and demeaning, and Ford seemed to be well within his rights to "explore" a fitting way to make such a situation more palatable politically and personally. Yet Ford also expressed remarkable befuddlement about the nature of the problem, opening the way for a more dubious interpretation of his motives. Most revealing were comments Ford made to *Newsweek*'s editors Wednesday afternoon when discussions were at a fever pitch, saying that perhaps what would emerge was something akin to the relationship between a prime minister and a president or head of state in a European parliamentary system; in Ford's words, "a format where you have a head of state and a head of government." But the "head of state" in European parliamentary government is a leftover of the ancient hereditary monarchies, which the American republican scheme, with its unitary executive and strictly separated powers between the branches of government, explicitly rejects. It makes no constitutional sense, let alone common sense.

If Ford meant this with any degree of literalness, he was effectively proposing to replace Reagan as the president; Reagan would give the speeches, and Ford would run the government. Was Ford really holding out for a grand deal that would involve the *de facto* reversal of their places on the ticket? Some observers suspected that by holding out and holding out, events might have arrived at the point on the last day of the convention where Reagan had no choice but to accede to Ford's requirements. Such a Machiavellian interpretation doesn't fit the persona of Ford we know from all other experience. Ford's expressed reluctance was surely sincere (several people close to Ford said that he was never close to accepting any deal), and his confusion about the nature of executive power can be attributed to having spent so much of his career in Congress during the years it steadily encroached on the prerogatives of the executive branch. This was one of Reagan's chief complaints about Ford in 1976. The "dream ticket" episode suggests that he had a point.

HAD FORD BEEN selected as the running mate, it might have overshadowed several important aspects of the Republican convention. For one thing, the thoroughly Reaganite platform would have led to embarrassing questions about Ford's public disagreements with it. As it was, Bush's infamous "voodoo economics" comment had to be squared with Reagan's tax cut plan; Ed Meese came up with the quip that Bush underwent an exorcism at the convention. The GOP platform opposed the Equal Rights Amendment (which Ford criticized when he arrived at the convention) and called for the Human Life Amendment to ban abortion (which Ford also disputed).

The media mostly fixed on these hot-button social issues, and missed the deeper story. Party platforms are a relic of nineteenth-century–style political pamphleteering, and as such are not much read any more, even by the media who supposedly pay attention to detail. This is unfortunate, as platforms are useful guides to the temper and character of parties, and comparing them side-by-side provides the kind of debate that seldom takes place in modern election campaigns. The platforms of the two parties in 1980 made explicit their fundamental division between their philosophies of government. Harvey Mansfield summarized this opposition to a conflict between *opportunity* and *entitlement*.[77] By 1980, Republicans emphasized opportunity, while Democrats emphasized entitlement. Republicans stressed individualism, liberty, and the capacity of the private sector; the Democrats, egalitarianism, redistribution, and the capacity of the public sector. The Democratic platform alternated between boasts of programs whose budgets they had expanded, and pledges to institute new spending programs for a long laundry list of unmet needs.

The Democratic platform, for example, read: "The Democratic Party has long stood for an active, responsive, vigorous government. . . . In all of our economic programs, the one overriding principle must be *fairness*. . . . We must continue to improve the targeting of federal programs in order to maximize their benefit to those most in need. We must begin to think of federal expenditures as capital investments. . . ." The Republican platform argued: "[Democrats] believe that every time new problems arise beyond the power of men and women as individuals to solve, it becomes the duty of government to solve them, as if there were never any alternative. . . . Government should foster in our society a climate of maximum individual liberty and freedom of choice. Properly informed, our people as individuals or acting through instruments of popular consultation can make the right decisions affecting personal or general welfare, free of pervasive and heavy-handed intrusion by the central government into the decision-making process."

This basic divide can be seen throughout specific issue areas. Regarding the family, the Democratic platform said: "The Democratic Party supports efforts to make federal programs more sensitive to the needs of the family, in all its diverse forms." In this sentence one not only sees the programmatic bias of liberalism, but also the tacit acceptance of "lifestyle liberalism" that "the family" is any arbitrary conglomeration of consenting adults. The GOP platform emphasized the opposite: "We seek to restore the family, the neighborhood, the community, and the workplace as vital alternatives in our national life to ever-expanding federal power. . . . Unlike the Democrats, we do not advocate new federal bureaucracies with ominous power to shape a national family order."

The Republican platform was predictably harsh in its attack on government regulation. The platform contained 17 references to regulation, all of them critical, while the Democratic platform contained only five, most of which were equivocal or in favor of extending regulation. The Democrats: "We will adopt regulatory requirements to meet the needs of smaller firms, *where such action will not interfere with the objectives of the regulation*." (Emphasis added.) The GOP questioned the very legitimacy of regulation itself: "The emergence of policies and programs which will revitalize the free enterprise system and reverse the trend toward regulation is essential. . . . Regulation restricts personal choices, tends to undermine America's democratic public institutions, and threatens to destroy the private, competitive free market economy it was originally designed to protect."

Beyond the conservative platform, however, the Republican convention evinced a deliberate strategy to appeal to non-traditional constituencies, especially working-class voters and minorities. Ben Hooks, president of the National Association for the Advancement of Colored People, spoke to the convention. (The Republican platform also approvingly cited the NAACP's criticism of Carter's energy policy.) The most audacious feat of political jujitsu was Reagan's direct appeal to union members. As a former head of an AFL-CIO affiliated union (the Screen Actors Guild), Reagan's slogan was "Elect a former union president, President." Reagan even picked up the endorsements of a few unions, including the Professional Air Traffic Controllers Organization (PATCO), which would become an ironic fact a year later when President Reagan fired striking air traffic controllers and dismembered their union.

Reagan's greatest act of political larceny, however, occurred in his convention speech, where he concluded:

> The time is now to redeem promises once made to the American people by another candidate, in another time and another place. He said, ". . . For three long years I have been going up and down this country preaching that government—federal, state, and local—costs too much. I shall not stop that preaching. As an immediate program of action, we must abolish useless offices. We must eliminate unnecessary functions of government. . . . I propose to you, my friends, and through you that government of all kinds, big and little, be made solvent and that the example be set by the President of the United States and his cabinet."
>
> So said Franklin Delano Roosevelt in is acceptance speech to the Democratic National Convention in July 1932.

It was a neat trick, at once associating himself with the greatest Democratic hero of the twentieth century, and using that hero's words against the desuetude of the contemporary Democratic Party. This drove liberals out of their mind. Arkansas Gov. Bill Clinton complained: "Everyone can quote him, but his words out of context mean nothing."

Forgetting the ancient axiom of Aeschylus—"Those whom the gods would destroy they first make mad"—liberals reached into the back of their file drawers and dusted off the Goldwater playbook from 1964. Columnist Richard Reeves wrote that the Republican convention gave off "a whiff of moral fascism," while Henry Fairlie wrote in the *Washington Post* that "The Reaganites on the floor were exactly those who in Germany gave the Nazis their main strength and who in France collaborated with them and sustained Vichy." Fairlie was just warming up; adding that Reagan's constituency was "narrow minded, book banning, truth censoring, mean spirited; ungenerous, envious, intolerant, afraid; chicken, bullying; trivially moral, falsely patriotic, family cheapening, flag cheapening, God cheapening; the common man, shallow, small, sanctimonious."[78] One imagines that Fairlie's thesaurus could have outlasted the *Post's* printing press. House Speaker Tip O'Neill warned that "John Birchers control the Republican Party." (Ironically, the only member of the John Birch Society then serving in Congress was a Democrat: Georgia Rep. Larry McDonald.) *The New Republic* gasped: "American reaction—racial, and social and economic—has invested its energies, its hopes, and its ample dollars in Reagan's candidacy."[79] This was a mere preview of what would come in the fall campaign.

Carter, meanwhile, had a poor convention a month after the Republicans. Kennedy dominated the writing of the platform, skewing it far to the left of what Carter wanted. Kennedy's rousing speech to the convention—"The dream will never die!"—assured that Carter's acceptance speech would be an anti-climax. (Kennedy's speech, Germond and Witcover wrote, "seemed to touch every liberal nerve and revive every liberal memory on the floor.") Then in his acceptance speech, Carter committed a horrendous blooper. In a litany of Democratic worthies from the past, Carter came to Hubert Humphrey's place on the list. Out of his mouth came: "Hubert Horatio *Hornblower*—er, Humphrey!" It became the most memorable excerpt from his speech, and was exceeded as a low moment only by the closing tableau of the convention, when Carter literally chased Kennedy around the stage hoping to get him in the traditional linked-arms victory clasp.

Despite this near-disastrous convention, Carter received a substantial "bounce." Pre-convention polls found Reagan leading Carter by as much as 20 points. In early August Carter's approval rating fell to a new low of 21 percent—lower than Truman at his worst point, lower even than Nixon on the eve of his resignation. A Reagan landslide appeared probable. Yet three weeks later, on Labor Day, the traditional beginning of the fall campaign, polls suddenly had the race within the margin of error—a statistical dead heat. A series of mistakes on the campaign trail had derailed Reagan's momentum; he experienced perhaps the worst first 10 days of campaigning of any modern candidate. Journalists began writing of the "gloomy" atmosphere inside Reagan's campaign. The *Washington Post*'s Robert Kaiser wrote at the end of August that "All that can be said with confidence now is that Reagan squandered the initiative and revived the one issue that probably can hurt him most—his own plausibility as a president—during the opening days of the campaign season."[80] *U.S. News and World Report* wondered in a headline, "HAS REAGAN DROPPED THE BALL?" A Reagan aide told the *Wall Street Journal*, "I have this terrible feeling we're about to snatch defeat right from the jaws of victory."

The GOP establishment worried that its worst fears about Reagan were coming true. Could he recover?

CHAPTER FOURTEEN

REAGAN'S MOMENT

W E NOW ARRIVE at the point of the story where every reader
knows the outcome. But as historian John Lukacs has written:
"The actuality of history (as indeed the actual life of a man) must be considered together with its potentialities."[1] Among the plausible counterfactual potentialities of 1980 worth pondering is that a more "conventional"
Republican candidate might have run away with the election. On the
merits, the election contest should never have been close. Yet Reagan's
eventual victory was far from the likely outcome it seems today. Reagan
had to overcome a series of mistakes and major doubts among swing voters about his fitness for office. He overcame these difficulties through his
unparalleled skill at defining the terms of political discourse in a compelling way. Reagan made the election of 1980 his moment by shaping
the electorate around a new set of issues, and he solidified a new coalition
that was first hinted in the Nixon victory of 1972. He brought the Republican Party to the cusp of realignment, the consummation of which did
not occur for more than another decade. Reagan's good humor and light
touch made it look easy. It was not easy. Three key turning points in the
fall of 1980 made Reagan the 40th President of the United States, each of
which will be discussed in due course.

Political scientists typically regard an election with an incumbent
president on the ballot as a referendum on the president's performance in
office. The quantitative models further suggest that a poor economy

dooms an incumbent, and Carter had the worst economy since Herbert Hoover. The closeness of the 1980 contest throughout the fall shows Reagan's vulnerabilities as a national candidate. The principal task for Reagan at the outset of the fall campaign was to cement his plausibility to be president and make Carter the central issue of the election. Instead, he succeeded in making himself as much the main issue as Carter. It was as if the Democrats had nominated the flamboyant and controversial Huey Long instead of Franklin Roosevelt against the hapless Hoover in 1932, a selection that would have assured a close and perhaps losing campaign.

Reagan's problems stemmed from his greatest personal strength: his candor and his fearlessness about saying what he really thought. On August 16, just two days after the conclusion of the Democratic convention, Reagan remarked at a news conference that he believed the United States should have "an official government relationship" with Taiwan, which implied reversing not only U.S. policy toward China but repealing the Taiwan Relations Act that Congress had enacted in 1979. Bush was on his way to Beijing for a visit that was intended to burnish the foreign policy stature of the ticket. Instead, the trip was a fiasco. Beijing took public offense at Reagan's remarks; Reagan had to carefully back down 10 days later after Bush returned. (At first Reagan stubbornly refused to recant. Bush had to enlist the help of Ed Meese to convince Reagan.[2]) The episode raised legitimate questions about Reagan's capacity for foreign diplomacy.

Reagan quickly overshadowed his Taiwan gaffe with another provocative statement bearing on the conduct of foreign affairs. On August 18, two days after his initial Taiwan remarks, Reagan went to Chicago to receive the endorsement of the Veterans of Foreign Wars—the first time in the 81-year history of the VFW that it had endorsed a presidential candidate. Before a sympathetic audience seemed the ideal opportunity to outline his "peace through strength" views. Reagan's foreign policy team had developed a measured speech that struck a careful balance between Reagan's sincerely expressed desire for peace and his principle of military strength. But Reagan decided himself to add the most noteworthy passage to the speech:

> For too long, we have lived with the "Vietnam Syndrome." Much of
> that syndrome has been created by the North Vietnamese aggressors
> who now threaten the peaceful people of Thailand. Over and over

they told us for ten years that we were the aggressors bent on imperialistic conquest. They had a battle plan. It was to win on the city streets of America and in our news media what they could not win on the field of battle. As the years dragged on, we were told that peace would come if we would simply stop interfering.

It is time we recognized that ours was, in truth, a noble cause. A small country newly freed from colonial rule sought our help in establishing self-rule and the means of self-defense against a totalitarian neighbor bent on conquest. We dishonor the memory of 50,000 young Americans who died in that cause when we give way to feelings of guilt as if we were doing something shameful. . . .

There is a lesson for all of us in Vietnam; if a war does come, we must have the means and the determination to prevail or we will not have what it takes to secure the peace. And while we are at it, let us tell those who fought in that war that we will never again ask young men to fight and possibly die in a war our government is afraid to let them win. (Emphasis added.)

Once again Reagan could be said to have been ahead of his time. Fifteen or 20 years later the statement that America's effort in Vietnam was a "noble cause" might have found broad acceptance or approval, but in 1980 that phrase was, in Germond and Witcover's assessment, "viewed as an attempt to open up national wounds that had scarcely healed."[3] At that time, it is useful to recall, popular perceptions of Vietnam were still highly antipathetic: Think merely of the movies such as *Coming Home, The Deer Hunter,* and *Apocalypse Now,* all of which partook of the left-liberal demonology about the war. Reagan was once again flying directly in the face of the conventional wisdom without apology or equivocation.

It is somewhat surprising that the media fixed on the phrase "noble cause" as the most objectionable part of the passage, given Reagan's explicit attacks on the antiwar movement and the media. The passage obliterated the main points Reagan wanted to get across; instead of something like "Reagan Outlines Peace Through Strength," the headline in the *Chicago Tribune,* which was echoed in newspapers and TV coverage throughout the nation, was "REAGAN DEFENDS VIET WAR." NBC News led with the story in its nightly newscast. "Ronald Reagan said today," John Chancellor began, "that the Vietnam War was a noble cause in which the United States tried to help a small country newly freed from colonial rule against a totalitarian neighbor bent on conquest." Tom Shales, the *Washington Post*'s television critic, thought that NBC "was giving the clear impression that Reagan's remark was wildly insensitive (so insensitive as to make it the top news story of the day) and that he didn't quite know what he was saying. It cast doubt on his fitness as a leader, if not, by implication, on his sanity."[4] Perhaps prompted by the media frowns, Wirthlin's polls revealed that a majority of Americans re- acted negatively to Reagan's comments. Although Reagan had long made "No more Vietnams" a slogan, many people wondered whether someone who thought the original Vietnam was a good idea might get the country into another one.

It took only four days for Reagan to transgress conventional wisdom again. On August 22 Reagan went to Dallas to appear before the Reli- gious Roundtable's National Affairs Briefing, a gathering of 15,000 evan- gelicals. Appearing before this officially non-partisan but increasingly conservative and politicized group, Reagan deftly said, "I know you can't endorse me. But I want you to know that I endorse you." This was all done with a wink and a nod; the Rev. Jerry Falwell was pointedly saying, yes, "the Moral Majority is non-partisan, which is why I tell people to vote for the Reagan of their choice." Falwell and other conservative evan- gelicals boasted of plans to get four million Christian voters to the polls on election day. (The Rev. Pat Robertson, curiously, wasn't yet marching with this parade; Robertson told *Newsweek* that "active partisan poli- tics" is the wrong path for evangelicals.) But Reagan sat uncomfortably on the dais while one preacher argued that America should be run by God-fearing Christians, and another assailed the "perverts, radicals, left- ists, communists, liberals, and humanists" who run the country. The worst moment came when Southern Baptist Rev. Bailey Smith said that "God Almighty does not hear the prayer of the Jew."

Reagan naturally disavowed any association with this kind of narrow sectarianism, but he managed to get off another gaffe at the post-conference press availability. A reporter asked Reagan if he shared the evangelicals' rejection of Darwin's theory of evolution and demand that creationism be taught in public schools. This is the kind of question a politician should duck on the grounds that it has no relevance for the would-be oc- cupant of the White House. At the very least, Reagan could have repaired to his oft-expressed view that we should get God back in the classroom by allowing school prayer, a position that was highly popular according to polls. Not Reagan. He wanted to answer straightforwardly. "I think that recent discoveries down through the years pointed [out] great flaws in it," Reagan said; "creationist theory" should be taught side-by-side with evolution.

Four days later, Reagan struck again. On August 27, Reagan said in a speech in Ohio that the economy was in a "severe depression." Alan Greenspan, traveling with the campaign, had to admit that this was an overstatement. The media once again pounced on Reagan's imprecision. "Depression is the wrong term," NBC's John Chancellor huffed; "Reagan was again forced to explain himself." Reagan's gaffe parade was all the excuse the media needed to recycle Reagan's old questionable or controversial statements into thumb-sucking "news analysis" articles. "For connoisseurs of skeletons in the closet," Robert Kaiser wrote in the *Washington Post,* "candidate Reagan has left literally thousands of closets to search through."

Enlightened opinion thought Reagan's most troglodyte remark was his 1976 comment that "Fascism was really the basis for the New Deal." Ted Kennedy had attacked this remark in his speech to the Democratic convention, and in September the media took up the issue, again chiefly in "news analysis" articles. Reagan was not about to backpedal; to the contrary, he stoutly defended his comment. In late August Reagan told reporters: "Anyone who wants to look at the writings of the Brain Trust of the New Deal will find that President Roosevelt's advisers admired the fascist system. . . . They thought that private ownership with government management and control *a la* the Italian system was the way to go, and that has been evident in all their writings." This was, Reagan added, "long before fascism became a dirty word in the lexicon of the liberals." The *Washington Post,* among others, was agog: "Several historians of the New Deal period questioned by the *Washington Post* said they had no idea what Reagan was referring to."[5]

Once again Reagan deserves a modest defense. To be sure, such a comment was politically imprudent, and is also dissonant with Reagan's favorable evocation of Roosevelt's legacy at other moments in his campaign (especially before labor union and Democratic audiences). To most people fascism means storm troopers, dictators with funny uniforms, and persecution of minorities. Reagan meant it in the precise sense of political economy: public control of private resources. Even so, the comment was out of proportion with the improvisational character of New Deal political economy, and is not explicit in the writings of New Deal authors (which is why most historians, as opposed to economists or political philosophers, will miss it). But is Reagan's view wholly outlandish? The economic coordination functions of the National Recovery Administration partook of Reagan's definition of fascism; that the Supreme Court ruled so many of these forms of economic planning to be unconstitutional—in cases that still stand as precedent today—should suggest that Reagan's view, while unconventional, was not entirely insensible.

Where did Reagan get it? The most likely source was a book well known to Reagan, F. A. Hayek's *The Road to Serfdom*. There Hayek noted: "Indeed, there is scarcely a leaf out of Hitler's book which somebody or other in England and America has not recommended us to take and use for our own purposes. . . . In 1934 the newly established National Planning Board devoted a good deal of attention to the example of planning provided by these four countries: Germany, Italy, Russia, and Japan."[6] With Reagan's phenomenal memory and vivid imagination, this may have been the only reference Reagan needed to stimulate the remark. (Reagan was not the only major political figure Hayek influenced. *The Road to Serfdom* also inspired one of Winston Churchill's most controversial post-war speeches in 1945.)

A more challenging question about Reagan's mistakes needs to be entertained. Aside from the unquestionable error about Taiwan, were these Reaganisms really "gaffes"? While such comments flew in the face of well-established opinion, is there not a sense in which these gaffes were a source of *reassurance* to some constituencies? The comment on creation and evolution is worth refracting through this prism. There are few subjects that excite more passion among evangelical and fundamentalist Christians than the rejection of evolution. And the current "intelligent design" movement among scientists, although a distinct minority position, shows that the controversy is not settled.[7] To evangelical Christians, Reagan's remark shouted: *He's one of us.* This was politically significant because evangelical Christians who had supported the born-again Carter in 1976 felt betrayed by his administration. The last straw came when the IRS threatened to deny the tax-exempt status of Christian private schools in 1980.

Reagan's other bloopers, especially the "noble cause" of Vietnam, were the kind of thing that caused ideological conservatives to stand up on their chairs and say, "damn right!" Lyn Nofziger admitted as much to the *London Times:* "The conservative Reagan constituency—and that's not small—got worried when moderates like Bill Casey and Anne Armstrong and George Bush took the leading roles in the campaign. They wondered where Reagan was going. They liked those remarks about Vietnam [and] evolution. It was like revaccinating the Reagan constituency."[8]

Between the comments themselves and the media criticism they evoked, long-suffering conservatives were whipped to an intensity level that topped the Goldwater phenomenon of 1964. It is doubtful that there was any deliberate political calculation involved in Reagan's remarks. This was "Reagan being Reagan." It also showed Reagan as his versatile best. He neatly found a way to turn his "depression" remark to his advantage. On Labor Day Reagan drew cheers when he said: "A recession is when your neighbor loses his job. A depression is when you lose your job. And recovery is when Jimmy Carter loses his!" Reagan himself came up with the line.

Reagan's campaign staff, however, was concerned that they could not go on letting Reagan be Reagan. James Baker, who came over from the Bush team after the convention, warned Reagan that he had to be more careful. Reagan himself was said to have developed a case of the jitters, and he became noticeably edgy and defensive with reporters. When a reporter asked Reagan whether his message was being overshadowed by his controversial throw-away remarks, Reagan bristled: "Well, that's because you fellas every once in a while are more interested in finding something sensational than in printing the facts." On September 4, Stuart Spencer joined the Reagan campaign plane in an effort to settle Reagan down. The concern was not limited to the campaign staff alone. *National Review* had to send out an all-clear signal to jittery conservatives: "It's time to stop worrying about Ronald Reagan. . . . His mind has an unfashionable and even home-made quality, he knows a lot more than people expect him to know, and he will win or lose as Ronald Reagan."[9]

REAGAN'S COLORFUL GAFFES were not his most significant problem, however. He also had substantive problems to work out if he was going to be taken seriously as a potential president. The most significant problem facing the Reagan campaign was that it had not fully worked out its economic plan, and the economy was Carter's largest vulnerability, overshadowing even the hostage crisis and the Soviets in Afghanistan. The economy started to free-fall in the spring of 1980. In April and May 1.7 million Americans lost their jobs. The unemployment rate jolted upward from 6.2 percent in March to 7.8 percent in May, the sharpest two-month rise in 32 years. Auto sales slumped to their slowest pace since 1963. Gross Domestic Product (GDP) dropped at an annual rate of 9.6 percent in the second quarter. Inflation was still running close to 18 percent, and the prime rate jumped to 20 percent in April—a rate that violated the usury laws in some states. Scenes reminiscent of the Great Depression started showing up on the evening news; in Baltimore, 26,000 people lined up for 77 job openings in the local Social Security Administration office. Reagan had a vivid image of his own: "We talk about unemployment lines. If all the unemployed today were in a single line allowing two feet for each of them, that line would reach from New York City to Los Angeles."

The stagflation of 1980—high inflation and high unemployment—represented a crisis in economic theory. Conservative economists had been warning for more than a decade that this moment would come. It was called "the death of the Phillips' Curve," after the theorem of British economist A. W. Phillips that there was a direct, linear tradeoff between inflation and unemployment. The Phillips' Curve was the chief instrument of Keynesian-style "fine-tuning" in the 1960s, under which unemployment could be reduced by deliberately increasing inflation, and, conversely, inflation reduced by tolerating a (temporary) bout of higher unemployment. The "rational expectations" school of economists warned starting in the 1960s that sooner or later people would adjust their expectations for higher inflation, and the Phillips' Curve tradeoff would collapse. By the late 1970s, Americans understood that accepting inflation to counter unemployment meant reducing their real income. Workers were demanding automatic cost-of-living increases, and most government entitlement programs, such as Social Security, had automatic cost-of-living provisions. Inflation was becoming embedded in the very structure of the economy while having no effect on unemployment. In fact, as inflation became increasingly difficult to unwind, it would become the engine of recession and higher unemployment, rather than its cure.

A faltering economy is always the great liability of the incumbent party, but in 1980 the economic climate proved to be problematic for *both* parties. Whichever party could figure out an effective new policy to solve the problem in a politically acceptable way would determine the shape of debate over political economy for the next generation, just as Roosevelt's embrace of Keynesian stimulus ideology ruled political economy for a generation after the Great Depression. "By 1980," Herbert Stein wrote, "the country was ready for a more radical turn of economic policy to the right than had been seen since 1896—possibly ever."[10] It was an article of faith especially for Democratic politicians to proclaim that they would never use unemployment to reduce inflation. Austerity was always the Republican remedy, sometimes called "deep root-canal" or "castor oil" economics. Reagan himself strongly endorsed this view in 1976: "Several economists—hardheaded ones who aren't afraid to draw unpopular conclusions from logic and history—have said that higher unemployment is the necessary evil we must face if we are going to stop inflation. . . . We have to be able to accept that unemployment is going to rise before we can get over the disease of inflation. To pretend it isn't going to rise is like trying to ignore the fever by breaking the thermometer." But now it was Carter embracing the castor oil remedy. Carter proposed spending cuts to balance the federal budget. (He also quietly considered wage and price controls, but found this would require an act of Congress, so he had to abandon the idea.) Congressional Democrats balked, and Kennedy flayed Carter alive, calling him a Republican. *Time* magazine observed, "While no one would ever admit it publicly, [Carter's] policies seemed designed to produce a recession deliberately."[11]

It was at this moment that the two parties completed trading places. Carter attacked Reagan's plan for a tax rate cut with traditional *Republican* arguments, that is, a tax cut would swell the budget deficit and increase inflation. This was the same argument Barry Goldwater had made against the Kennedy tax cut in the early 1960s. Now Carter sounded more like Goldwater than Reagan. "I will not consider a reduction in taxes," Carter said in March, "until I am convinced that the 1981 budget will be balanced." He pledged to veto any tax cut that reached his desk: "I reject the easy promise that massive tax cuts and arbitrary roll-backs of government programs are the answer. Such facile, quick fixes should be recognized as political double-talk and ideological nonsense."

Reagan upped the ante, calling for Congress to enact the first 10 percent of the Kemp-Roth 30 percent income tax rate reduction *right away*, as a down payment on the plan. Republicans in Congress threatened to attach the tax cut to every piece of legislation they could, putting pressure on Democrats to cast votes against a politically popular idea. Carter tried to stand his ground, repeatedly calling the "Reagan-Kemp-Roth plan perhaps the most inflationary piece of legislation ever to be seriously considered by the U.S. Congress." The deteriorating economy and nervous Democrats compelled Carter to relent in his categorical opposition to tax reduction. By June, Carter's top economic adviser Charles Schultze was sounding retreat: "Obviously we are going to have a tax cut. The real question is when." Carter finally put forward his alternative to Reagan's plan, which defined the fault-line between the two parties over tax cuts for the next 20 years. "We need *targeted* tax cuts that encourage economic growth," Carter argued.

The Republican platform attacked Carter with what sounded like the old-time Democratic religion: "The Democratic Congress and the Carter Administration are espousing programs that candidate Carter in 1976 said were inhumane: using recession, unemployment, high interest rates, and high taxes to fight inflation. The Democrats are now trying to stop inflation with a recession, a bankrupt policy which is throwing millions of Americans out of work. . . . We specifically reject the Carter doctrine that inflation can be reduced only by throwing people out of work." *Time* magazine noted this "weird role reversal: the Republican candidate assailing a Democratic President for fighting inflation by inducing unemployment; the President countering by accusing the Republican of proposing inflation to combat recession." But Reagan's tax cut plan was not without its own political liabilities. Inside the Reagan campaign a debate was underway about the fine points and weaknesses of Reagan's economic prescription. Press accounts at the time portrayed a split among Reagan's advisers, between old-line conservative economists such as Milton Friedman, Alan Greenspan, George Shultz, and William Simon, and the "supply-siders" such as Jack Kemp, Paul Craig Roberts, Arthur Laffer, and Martin Anderson. Both *Business Week* and the *Village Voice* ran frothy articles about the "division" among Reagan's economic advisers. The familiar journalistic device—the unnamed campaign insider—was trotted out to predict that "the battle for the heart and mind of Ronald Reagan is on."

This is not true. Reagan's camp was unanimous in its support for the tax cut, and the enthusiasm for it originated with Reagan himself. Milton Friedman always said that he was for cutting any tax, any time, for any reason. The debate within Reagan's camp concerned how the tax cut was to be understood theoretically, and how it would be articulated on the stump. What distinguished a so-called "supply-side" tax cut from old-fashioned Keynesian "pump-priming" to stimulate demand? Since conservatives had always attacked Keynesian pump-priming for their budget deficits and inflationary effects, they had some explaining to do as to how Reagan's proposed tax cut would not be inflationary. Herbert Stein summed up the political problem Reagan faced: "A tax cut that would greatly increase the deficit was not acceptable to the Republicans or salable to the country."[12] Indeed, campaign chairman William Casey complained to Martin Anderson as the economic plan was being developed: "Damn it Marty, we can't have the governor propose a deficit of $50 billion a year. The press will kill us."[13]

Supply-siders, led by Laffer, Kemp, and the flamboyant Jude Wanniski, argued that a cut in marginal income tax rates differed from Keynesian pump-priming tax cuts because the Keynesians merely aimed to stimulate demand by putting more cash in circulation (though of course it was more fun to stimulate demand with government spending rather than reduced taxes), while high income tax rates reduced incentives to produce. This is why the supply-siders were careful to make a distinction between a tax cut and a tax *rate* cut. To many conservative economists such as Herbert Stein this was a distinction without a difference. Nonetheless, Kemp employed an easy-to-digest rationale that captured a larger mood: Tax something and you get less of it; subsidize something and you get more of it. In the United States, Kemp's mantra held, we tax thrift, investment, and production, and we subsidize poverty, unemployment, and welfare dependency.

No one in Reagan's camp disagreed with this basic logic as a *political* matter. However, there were serious doubts about the innovative claim that tax cuts would stimulate so much new production on the "supply side" of the economy that *they would pay for themselves.* Alan Greenspan remarked, "I'm for cutting taxes, but not for Laffer's reasons. I don't know anyone who seriously believes his argument." George Stigler didn't. Stigler, another "Chicago School" economist headed for a rendezvous with the Nobel Prize who advised Reagan, dismissed supply-side economics out of hand. "Laffer is no longer a very serious scholar," Stigler said in 1978. "He is playing the role of a propagandist, and as such he is performing some service. But I would not base a $125 billion tax cut on his work."

Other conservative or Republican-leaning economists were more scornful. Former Fed chairman Arthur Burns said: "One listens with a sense of dismay to those candidates who promise to cure inflation by massive cuts in taxes."[14] Herbert Stein derisively called it "the economics of joy." Many corporate leaders were leery of supply-side theory, and although the *Wall Street Journal* was enthusiastic about supply-side economics, many other senior business executives and publications were not. A leading Wall Street economist at Kidder, Peabody wrote that "the continued advocacy of massive tax cuts is bound to create an image of fiscal irresponsibility on the part of Mr. Reagan." *Business Week* charged that the tax cut plan was based on "flaky arithmetic," and that "it would be a completely irresponsible way to approach the federal budget problem, and it would generate an inflation that would destroy the value of the currency."[15] Carter and Mondale delighted in quoting this exemplar of the business establishment on the campaign trail. *Business Week* did understand the political virtue of tax cuts, however, noting in 1980, "For a Republican Party that has been in danger of becoming an increasingly ineffectual minority, Reagan's embrace of the new supply-side economics gives the GOP an opportunity to offer a politics of hope."

The problem with supply-side economics was not the theory but the arithmetic. Economic growth would need to be phenomenal in order for the lost revenue to be recouped. Greenspan estimated that only about 20 percent of the lost revenue would be made up by higher economic growth. Other estimates were higher, however; the Chase Econometrics model projected that 41 percent of the tax cut would be recovered the first year, rising to 72 percent by the seventh year.[16] But other economic models, such as DRI, projected Kemp-Roth would produce $100 billion deficits by 1983. The true believers, especially Kemp, Laffer, and Wanniski, thought either that the tax base would be so enlarged (perhaps by causing the underground economy to surface) that the entire revenue loss would be more than made up (an implausible scenario in the short run, even with the most generous assumptions), or that the transcendent importance of the tax-cut philosophy overrode the objections of the green-eye-shade number-crunchers.

Reagan sympathized with the true believers about the transcendent importance of the tax cuts, and the misperception was firmly planted that Reagan believed that tax cuts would raise revenues. He listened to the skeptics who thought the numbers might not add up. "There is a tendency for some supply-side advocates to overpromise," Ed Meese admitted. Reagan's tax cut would reduce taxes by $130 billion over the first three years (and more than $500 billion over five years), which would entail a huge budget deficit. Reagan kept postponing a major speech on economic policy until this problem could be resolved.

In thinking through these weaknesses in his economic themes, Reagan's advisers stumbled across some overlooked revenue projections from the Congressional Budget Office (CBO). Under the present tax structure, revenues were growing faster than spending. Even though the CBO forecast a budget deficit for 1981 and 1982, by 1983 the CBO expected a budget *surplus* of $37 billion, rising to $175 billion by 1985. The Senate Budget Committee in August produced an even more optimistic projection. The combined projected surplus for 1983, 1984, and 1985 came to more than $300 billion. Suddenly there was ample room for Reagan's tax cut. These projections assumed, however, three important things: a growing economy, an 8.7 percent inflation rate, and modest federal spending growth—none of which could be confidently assumed beyond a year or two. Martin Anderson reflected later that such long-range economic forecasting was as unrealistic as predicting the score of the Super Bowl for the next five years. When the federal budget deficit subsequently ballooned during Reagan's presidency, critics charged that Reagan's plan had been a deception—"smoke and mirrors"—from the beginning. This is incorrect; the plan was wholly sincere and plausible based on what was expected at the time.

But even if the forecasts were rock-solid, the tax cut would still mean larger deficits—over $100 billion in 1981 and 1982—in the short run. How could Reagan possibly propose a larger budget deficit than Jimmy Carter? Several of Reagan's advisers tried to convince him to stretch out his tax cut from three years to five, but Reagan firmly said no. Some other way of harmonizing the tax cut with the imperative of a balanced budget had to be found. William Simon and other advisers wanted a plan that would have dollar-for-dollar spending reductions to match the tax cut. Reagan understood the futility of trying to cut spending before cutting taxes: It had never worked in the past. Reversing the order—putting tax cuts *before* budget cuts—had become a practical imperative of conservative principle. But it was politically necessary to have some kind of spending reduction in prospect.

Reagan still remembered the predicament of the 1976 campaign, where the specific target list of programs to be cut in order to achieve a $90 billion reduction in federal spending hobbled the momentum of his campaign. He was determined not to fall into that trap again. Rather than target specific programs for cuts, Reagan's advisers came up with a plan that emphasized a lower rate of growth in federal spending and unspecified savings from reducing "waste, fraud, and mismanagement" in federal programs. Greenspan and Kevin Hopkins (Anderson's research assistant) worked the numbers, outlining a fiscal scenario under which the projected deficits for 1981 and 1982 were only $27 billion rather than $100 billion. By 1985, the new plan expected a surplus of $121 billion, and this included Reagan's planned increase in defense spending. Reagan went public with the plan in a speech on September 9 in Chicago. The *Washington Post* wrote that "the new computations provided what Reagan's economic plan most lacked before—a reasonably credible accounting of how he can cut taxes, increase defense spending and balance the budget all at once." *Newsweek* came up with a new label for this unprecedented approach: "Reaganomics."

It took the Reagan campaign an uncommonly long time to develop its plan in detail. Reagan's September 9 speech did not end the controversy over his tax cut, but by transforming it into a duel between technical economic forecasts, which always glazes over the eyes of the public, Reagan regained the upper hand politically. It changed the subject back to the issue of the size and scope of government and Washington's role in causing inflation and unemployment. In hindsight it can be seen as the first of the three key turning points in Reagan's campaign.

IF THE ECONOMY were the sole focus of the election, Reagan would win handily. Although Reagan regained the offense on the economy, he was still on the defensive about foreign policy. What the Carter campaign called "the Tolstoy issue"—war and peace—was Reagan's single greatest vulnerability. One of Wirthlin's polls late in the summer found that 44 percent of voters considered Reagan "dangerous," or agreed with the statement that "He is most likely to get us into an unnecessary war."[17] On the other hand, polls also showed that voters considered Reagan to be a stronger leader than Carter. A Yankelovich, Skelly and White poll in mid-September found that voters by a 59–28 margin favored Reagan over Carter for "keeping our defenses strong" and by 57–25 for "standing up to the Russians." But the survey also found that by a margin of 50–29 voters thought Carter less likely to overreact in a crisis, and by a 41–16 margin voters trusted Carter more than Reagan to keep the nation out of war.[18]

These mixed findings show ambivalence in the mind of voters, that the issue of how best to conduct America's global responsibilities was up for grabs. Both campaigns had ample poll data on this problem, and it clearly informed their strategies. Carter's main hope rested in being able to tag Reagan as a threat to peace; Reagan had to reassure voters of his equanimity. Reagan seemed to have the tougher job, given his hawkish reputation and long record of belligerent statements over the years, such as turning North Vietnam into a parking lot. Yet a closer look at the cognitive dissonance of voters on the question of war and peace suggests Reagan had an advantage. A majority of voters claimed to want a tougher line against the Soviet Union and increased defense spending. In increasing the defense budget already, Carter was playing on Reagan's home turf. The twofold task for Reagan, then, was to convey his own sincere desire for peace, and convince voters of the logic of his "peace through strength" outlook. Carter would counter with the charge that Reagan would re-ignite the "arms race," and would increase the risk of war.

We have already seen that Reagan's first attempt to gain control of this issue backfired with his "noble cause" comment about Vietnam. In subsequent speeches he managed to get back "on message." Reagan alternated between self-deprecation and sincere protestations to blunt the charge that he was a warmonger. "Sorry I'm late," Reagan told an audience in New York. "I've been too busy making nuclear war and cutting Social Security." And in his most earnest countenance Reagan made an eloquent plea about his pacific *bona fides,* which reached its crescendo in his late-October debate with Carter: "I have seen four wars in my lifetime. I'm a father of sons; I have a grandson. I don't ever want to see another generation of young Americans bleed their lives into sandy beachheads in the Pacific, or rice paddies and jungles in Asia or the muddy battlefields of Europe." This or some variation became a part of Reagan's standard stump speech.

While Reagan was trying to be soothing in his rhetoric about peace, he did not equivocate on his long-stated view of the Soviet Union or the need for the United States to engage in a significant military build-up. He did not make the slightest concession to the conventional wisdom about the "arms race." To the contrary, Reagan embraced the prospect. "We're already in an arms race," said Reagan in one of his most widely repeated remarks, "but only the Soviets are racing." He also employed another of his effective acts of political larceny—quoting John F. Kennedy that America should be "first, period" in force of arms. "'Only we can prevent war by preparing for it,'" Reagan further quoted JFK. But most significantly, Reagan displayed an insight into why he thought the United States could win an arms race: "I think there's every indication and every reason to believe that the Soviet Union cannot increase its production of arms. . . . I think the Soviet Union is probably near the very limit of its military output. They've diverted so much to the military that they can't provide for the consumer needs. . . ." Although several of Reagan's advisers believed this, it was not the accepted view of American intelligence agencies.

A decade later we would learn that Reagan was right. In an interview with the Associated Press in September, Reagan said that a Soviet arms negotiator "will be far more inclined to negotiate in good faith if he knows that the United States is engaged in building up its military. . . . The one card that's been missing in these negotiations has been the possibility of an arms race." (This was not a new theme for Reagan. In March he had told the *National Journal:* "They know that if we turned our full industrial might into an arms race, they cannot keep pace with us. Why haven't we played that card? Why haven't we said to them when we're sitting at the SALT table, 'Gentlemen, the only alternative to you being willing to meet us half way on these things is an arms race'? And maybe we wouldn't have to have the arms race because that's the last thing they want us to do.") The media didn't treat Reagan's view kindly. The *New York Times* ran a front page headline: "REAGAN CALLS ARMS RACE ESSENTIAL TO AVOID A SURRENDER OR DEFEAT."

The furor over the "arms race" issue overlooked a more significant part of Reagan's defense view. His defense plan also called for the revival of ballistic missile defense, and by implication the repudiation of the McNamara-Nixon "MAD" strategy. A little-noted section of the Republican platform said: "We will seek increased funding to guarantee American superiority in this critical area and to enable us to deal with possible breakthroughs in anti-missile defense, anti-satellite killers, directed energy systems, and the military and civilian exploitation of space."

Although Reagan called for an arms buildup and for scraping the already lifeless SALT II treaty, he made a point of pledging that "As president, I will immediately open negotiations on a SALT III treaty. My goal is to begin arms reductions. My energies will be directed at reducing destructive nuclear weaponry in the world."

Here a striking similarity between Carter and Reagan should be noted. Both Carter and Reagan described their goal to be a *reduction* in nuclear weapons, and not merely the *regulation* of their increasing numbers, which is all the arms control process and SALT treaties promised to accomplish. Both Reagan and Carter can be seen as sincere sentimentalists, and their contrasting approaches to achieving the same goal represented the widely divergent views of human nature and superpower relations that mark left and right in our time. To a degree almost unsurpassed in American elections, the voters in 1980 were treated to a contrast of fundamental moral premises.

Carter was a representative *par excellence* of the Kantian moral view that the purity of intentions should be the guide to moral reasoning and the benchmark of policy. Under such a view, there is no conflict that cannot be understood and resolved by good-faith reasoning and negotiation. As was discussed in chapter 12, Carter's desire to achieve an arms control treaty that reduced the number of nuclear weapons caused him to embark on a new course in negotiations with the Soviet Union—negotiations that went nowhere. Whether the Soviet Union might be negotiating in bad faith is inconceivable to such an outlook; even if they were, it would only be a matter of time until they "come around" under the coaxing of patient American negotiation.

Reagan's view, following JFK and Churchill, that war is best prevented by preparing to win was anathema to liberal opinion by 1980. Liberals thought that Reagan's axiom of "peace through strength," and his idea that the path to arms reduction was to build up first, was not simply incorrect in its practical reasoning but also *immoral. New York Times* columnist Flora Lewis, for example, attacked Reagan's proposal for an arms buildup not simply because it increased the risk of war, but for its "moral degradation."[19] Carter relished the attack: "If the American people get the idea, which is mistaken, that a nuclear arms race on our side is going to cause the Soviets to quit building nuclear weapons on their side, they are silly." (Carter felt sufficiently vulnerable on this point, however, that he told the American Legion that "if an unlimited nuclear arms race should be forced upon us, we will compete successfully.")

So as with economics, Reagan had a strong message that commanded the assent of a large number of voters. But would voters buy the messenger?

WITH THE ARRIVAL of the traditional start of the fall campaign on Labor Day, the election contest settled down for the usual daily thrust and parry, charge and counter charge. Although Reagan promised his aides to "stick to the script," he continued making gaffes. In early October Reagan suggested at a campaign stop in Ohio—coal country—that Mount St. Helens in Washington, which had erupted violently the previous May, was responsible for more air pollution than industry. "I'm not a scientist, and I don't know the figures," Reagan said, "but I have a suspicion that one little mountain out there in these last several months released more sulfur dioxide into the atmosphere of the world than has been released in the last ten years of auto driving or things of that kind." Reagan wasn't even close to being right, and the media delighted in ridiculing this remark. He went on to add to his previous remarks about trees causing pollution with the statement that "growing and decaying vegetation in this land are responsible for 93 percent of the oxides of nitrogen." Reagan is partly correct about this point, though in typical Reagan fashion, his anecdotes were partly garbled and out of proportion to the whole story.

His most serious gaffe, however, occurred on September 1. Carter was opening his fall campaign that day in Tuscumbia, Alabama, while Reagan was appearing at the Michigan State Fair outside Detroit. A woman wearing a Carter mask walked near the stage, heckling Reagan. Reagan usually responded deftly to hecklers, but this time he misfired. "I thought you were in Alabama today," Reagan said, addressing the woman as though she were Carter. "You know, I kind of like the contrast, though. I'm happy to be here, where you're dealing at first hand with the economic problems that have been committed, and he's opening his campaign down in the city that gave birth to and is the parent body of the Ku Klux Klan." A gasp went up from the crowd, and Reagan immediately regretted the remark. For one thing, he had his facts wrong again; Tuscumbia was not the founding city of the Klan. Someone in his campaign entourage had mentioned before the event that Tuscumbia was a "center" of Klan activity (in fact on the day of Carter's appearance 40 robed Klansmen paraded through town), and Reagan filed it away in his mind. It was another instance of where Reagan's near-photographic memory reproduced a mental picture that looked more like cubist painting than a Polaroid. Reagan later telephoned an apology to the mayor of Tuscumbia.

The damage was done, however. Carter reacted with righteous indignation: "Anybody who resorts to slurs and innuendoes against a whole region of the country based on a false statement, a false premise, is not doing the South or our nation a good service." It was especially embarrassing for Reagan because the largest Klan chapter in the nation, based in New Orleans, publicly endorsed Reagan shortly after the GOP convention. The Republican platform, the KKK said, "reads as if it were written by a Klansman." Reagan promptly repudiated the endorsement: "I have no tolerance whatsoever for what the Klan represents. Indeed I resent them using my name."

This sideshow over the Klan led Carter into a series of gaffes of his own, which became the second key turning point of the fall campaign. In a play book that has become depressingly familiar in national elections since 1980, Democrats attempted to play the race card against Reagan. Carter's campaign was probably hoping to goad Reagan into some kind of undignified outburst, knowing from their opposition research that this was the one charge about which Reagan was most sensitive, and recalling how Reagan blew a gasket in his first campaign in 1966 when he was called a racist. Reagan's impolitic remark about the Klan in September was probably a reaction to criticism he received over the Klan endorsement. Maybe, Carter's tacticians probably thought, he could be goaded into more missteps.

But is not clear who baited whom in the end. Right after the Republican convention Reagan appeared in Philadelphia, Mississippi, near where civil rights activists Michael Schwerner, Andrew Goodman, and James Chaney were murdered in 1964. In the course of his remarks, Reagan said:

What we have to do is bring back the recognition that the people of this country can solve its problems. I still believe the answer to any problem lies with the people. *I believe in state's rights* and I believe in people doing as much as they can for themselves at the community level and at the private level. I believe we have distorted the balance of our government today by giving powers that were never intended to be given in the Constitution to that federal establishment. (Emphasis added.)

To be sure, it is difficult to imagine that Reagan was oblivious to the historical baggage of the phrase "states' rights" in Mississippi, and it cannot be ruled out that he was conscious of the problematic implication of his choice of words, just as Jimmy Carter was not presumed innocent of his use of "ethnic purity" in 1976. But Reagan was clearly reiterating his well-known opinion against centralized government power, similar to his 1976 pledge to return control of many social programs to the states. "Most of those at the rally," the *New York Times* generously reported, "apparently regarded the statement as having been made in that context."

And as a Westerner Reagan had fully associated himself with the "Sagebrush Rebellion," for whom "states' rights" meant wresting control of land from Washington. This was far from an outlandish or minority view, and Reagan's speech received unexceptional news coverage the next day. The same day Reagan made his "states' rights" remark, the National Governors Association issued what the Associated Press described as "a militant call for reduced federal involvement in state and local affairs." Arizona Governor Bruce Babbitt, while affirming his liberal and Democratic credentials, nonetheless wrote in the *New York Times* that "It is time to take hard look at 'states' rights'—and responsibilities—and to sort out the respective functions of the federal government and the states."[20]

To liberals, however, employing the phrase "states' rights" in any context is to waive the bloody shirt of racism and segregation. Little time was wasted in accusing Reagan not simply of pandering to old-fashioned segregationist sentiment in the South, but of actively sympathizing with it. Patricia Harris, Carter's secretary of Health and Human Services, told a steelworkers' union conference in early August: "I will not attempt to explain why the KKK found the Republican candidate and the Republican platform compatible with the philosophy and guiding principles of that notorious organization." But, she added, when Reagan speaks before black audiences (Reagan was scheduled to speak to the National Urban League in New York and meet with Jesse Jackson in Chicago), many blacks "will see the specter of a white sheet behind him."

Andrew Young went even further, saying that Reagan's remarks seemed "like a code word to me that it's going to be all right to kill niggers when he's President." Coretta Scott King managed to top Young: "I am scared that if Ronald Reagan gets into office, we are going to see more of the Ku Klux Klan and a resurgence of the Nazi Party." Maryland Congressman Parren Mitchell, a leader of the Congressional Black Caucus, said that "Reagan represents a distinct danger to black Americans." Garry Wills wrote in *Esquire:* "Reagan croons, in love accents, his permission to indulge a functional hatred of poor people and blacks."[21] (Reagan, it should be noted, received the endorsement of several black leaders who were fed up with Carter, including the Rev. Ralph David Abernathy, King's successor as head of the Southern Christian Leadership Council, and the Rev. Hosea Williams, another prominent cleric from the civil rights movement.)

It is one thing for campaign surrogates to engage in the lowest hyperbole in the service of firing up constituency groups. The candidates themselves, especially incumbent presidents, usually find a way of staying above the fray. Right after the Democratic convention in August, Richard Reeves, who had detected the "whiff of moral fascism" at the Republican convention, offered a prescient observation: "The Carter campaign is as mean-spirited as any you'll see in American politics. Where this meanness comes from is obvious to anyone who has watched Carter's rise to the Presidency and the attempts to keep him there—it comes from the top, from Jimmy Carter."[22] Carter was about to prove Reeves correct by joining in the chorus of race-baiting himself. Speaking at Martin Luther King's Ebenezer Baptist Church in Atlanta on September 15, Carter said: "You've seen in this campaign the *stirrings of hate* and *the rebirth of code words like 'states' rights'* in a speech in Mississippi, in a campaign reference to the Ku Klux Klan relating to the South. . . . Obviously the Ku Klux Klan is an obnoxious blight on the American scene and anyone who injected it into the campaign made a serious mistake. . . Hatred has no place in this country." (Emphasis added.)

Carter and the Democrats had said they would try to rerun the Goldwater playbook, and perhaps believed that the media would amplify their caricature of Reagan in much the same way they did for Johnson in 1964. They were wrong. The media was harsh on Carter for his indulgence of race-baiting. *The New Republic:* "President Carter has made a grave moral error in trying to portray Ronald Reagan as a racist." Carter's statements "are frightful distortions, bordering on outright lies."[23] *Boston Globe* columnist Curtis Wilkie wrote: "Just as surely as the werewolf grows long fangs and facial hair on a full moon, the darker side of President Carter emerges in election years." The Associated Press sent out a wire story noting that it was Carter's followers (Harris, et al.), not Reagan, who first "injected" the Klan into the campaign. *Washington Post* reporter Richard Harwood wrote that "There is nothing in Reagan's record to support the charge that he was 'racist.'" The editorial page of the *Post* was savage:

> Mr. Carter has abandoned all dignity in his round-the-clock attack on Mr. Reagan's character and standing, jumping (in a most sancti-monious tone of voice) for "offenses" similar to many Mr. Carter himself has committed, and, most recently, concluding from all this that Mr. Reagan is a "racist" and a purveyor of "hatred." This de-scription doesn't fit Mr. Reagan. What it fits, or more precisely, fits into, is Jimmy Carter's miserable record of personally savaging polit-ical opponents (Hubert Humphrey, Edward Kennedy) whenever the going got rough. . . . Jimmy Carter, as before, seems to have few lim-its beyond which he will not go in the abuse of opponents and recon-struction of history.[24]

The "meanness" issue, first spotted by Carter's own staff in the 1976 campaign, now took on major importance in the campaign. He immedi-ately backed down, claiming that he was not saying or implying that Rea-gan was a racist: "I am not blaming Governor Reagan," Carter said to the amazement of reporters. "That's exactly the point. The press seems to be obsessed with this issue. I am not blaming Governor Reagan. . . . I do not indulge in attacking personally the integrity of my opponents and I hope that I never shall."

But he did, several times. At first Carter repaired to the warmonger theme, telling a Los Angeles audience that the election "will determine what kind of life you and your families have, whether this nation will make progress or go backward, and *whether we have peace or war.*" (Emphasis added.) Carter may have thought his comment was merely raising the "war and peace" issue in stark terms that would focus voters' minds on Reagan's views, but it backfired. Media stories dwelled on the harshness of Carter's charge—the "meanness" issue again. Reagan began reacting with an air of wounded innocence that played perfectly, especially on television news, to the "meanness" story line. "I think to accuse that anyone would deliberately want a war is beneath decency," Reagan said. The media started asking Carter directly about "the meanness issue." Carter had to back down again, telling the *Detroit News*, "I'm not accusing Reagan of wanting a war."

A week later in Chicago Carter let fly again with his most self-destructive comment of the campaign. Appearing in a backyard setting on October 6, Carter said: "You'll determine whether or not this America will be unified or, if I lose the election, *whether Americans might be separated, black from white, Jew from Christian, North from South, rural from urban.*" (Emphasis added.) Reporters in the press pool couldn't believe it, and the comment was the lead sound bite on all the network news broadcasts that night, along with Reagan's sorrowful response: "I just have to say this. I can't be angry. I'm saddened that anyone, particularly someone who has held that position, could intimate such a thing. I'm not asking for an apology from him. I know who I have to account to for my actions. But I think he owes the country an apology." Carter tried lamely the next day to wiggle out again, telling Barbara Walters: "I don't intend to apologize for that statement, except to say that I did not insinuate and do not claim that Governor Reagan would deliberately try to set one American against another." The network news spin was devastating to Carter. NBC's Chris Wallace said Carter's comment "showed Mr. Carter as mean and unpresidential, Reagan as caring and mature." ABC's Sam Donaldson said, "Carter campaign officials are deeply worried tonight that the President's re-election is slipping away."

The Reagan campaign thought so, too. Richard Wirthlin later said that "[Carter] came close to handing us the election that night." Carter had squandered his largest remaining asset with voters, the view that he is a decent and honorable person. Three days later in a "town meeting" (Carter's favorite format) at the Grand Ole Opry in Nashville, a high school student from Winston-Salem, North Carolina, named David Mangum made it to the microphone to ask Carter a question. He delivered a roundhouse: "Sir, why is it that if you are the right man for the job, that you and your staff have to lower yourself to the extent of slinging mud and making slanderous statements with [sic] your rival, Ronald Reagan?" The audience erupted in applause. Carter could be forgiven for thinking life is unfair, because Reagan had made a number of gamy statements about Carter that attracted little criticism. At one appearance Reagan said that Carter was "the greatest deceiver ever to occupy the White House." (Greater than Nixon?) On *60 Minutes* Reagan said: "I think very definitely the Soviet Union is going to throw a few bones to Mr. Carter during this coming campaign in order to help him continue as president."

The media was not, however, laying off Reagan. CBS News ran a controversial story about "the real Ronald Reagan," assaying some of his frothier statements from the past and his current, more moderate positions. Reagan was fair game for such a story, but CBS overdid it by superimposing a large white "X" over Reagan's face after each item. (Walter Cronkite later apologized for the graphical element of the story.) Print media reports followed this genre. An October 18 story by *Washington Post* reporter Robert Kaiser frankly admitted that "the media coverage of Reagan has turned negative," and the *Washington Post*'s TV critic Tom Shales, who thought Reagan was being treated unfairly, observed what conservatives have long believed: "It's hard not to entertain at least the possibility that Reagan is getting less than a fair shake because one finds more atheists in foxholes than conservative Republicans in network news."[25]

Carter's attacks, despite the damage they were inflicting on himself, also appeared to be taking their toll on Reagan. Wirthlin was stunned when the campaign's daily tracking polls showed Reagan's slim lead slipping away. "For five or six days, from October 4 to about October 9 or 10, our support collapsed." On October 14 Wirthlin's polls found Carter ahead by two points. Other public polls were reporting the same thing; a CBS/*New York Times* poll gave Carter a one-point edge, while a Gallup Poll put Carter ahead by three. Most worrisome was the finding that the number of voters who thought Reagan "does not understand the complicated problems a president has to deal with" was rising. Equally alarming to both campaigns was the high number of undecided voters. In 1976, only 6 percent of voters described themselves as "undecided" in mid-October, but now 20 percent of voters were undecided. This suggested that a large proportion of independent and swing voters were unhappy with Carter but uncomfortable with Reagan. "For the first time," Democratic pollster Peter Hart said in mid-October, "I feel the election may be starting to elude Ronald Reagan's grasp."[26]

Adding to the anxiety of the Reagan campaign was the fear of an "October surprise" with the Iranian hostages. If Carter could contrive to bring the hostages home on election eve, it would probably swing the close context. The memory of Carter's announcement about "progress" in the hostage crisis the morning of the Wisconsin primary was in the back of everyone's mind. (Some poll data suggested that the public remembered this, too, and might react cynically to another hostage ploy close to election day.) On October 15 the *Washington Post* reported that a breakthrough in the hostage crisis might come in the next two weeks, and on October 19 columnist Joseph Kraft wrote that "The Carter Administration has embarked on an all-out effort to win release of the American hostages. . . . The present scheme bears all the marks of a mad electoral maneuver."[27] Washington was thick with rumors that a deal was all but done. Jack Anderson produced a breathless column asserting that Carter was preparing an election-eve invasion of Iran, but the *Post* refused to print the piece. Anderson's tissue-thin pieces had already long been relegated to the comics page anyway.

It may be fair to say that the Reagan campaign was paranoid about this possibility, given the elaborate precautions they took to anticipate and counter such an event. The campaign prepared contingency radio and TV ads, and lined up Kissinger and Ford to hit the TV talk shows to respond to any Carter moves. The Reagan campaign even had its own intelligence operation. Even though the Reagan campaign received regular State Department and National Security Council briefings (a routine courtesy for presidential candidates), the Reagan campaign had its own network of people watching Air Force bases hoping for any glimpse of preparations that would signal an imminent move to bring the hostages home. (All of this fed into wild speculation years later that the Reagan campaign, specifically Bush and Bill Casey, had intervened with the Iranians to derail a deal to release the hostages before the election. Repeated investigations have failed to substantiate this story.)

The erratic polls and the fear of an "October surprise" led Reagan to decide that he had to shake up the race. His first step was a promise to name a woman to the Supreme Court, which dominated the news cycle for a day or two. But the most significant decision, and the third key turning point of the election campaign, came on October 18: Reagan agreed to debate Carter one-on-one. The debate was scheduled for Tuesday, October 28—exactly one week before election day—in Cleveland. Until this point the prospect of a Reagan-Carter debate had been a shadow boxing sideshow between the two camps. Carter was eager to debate Reagan one-on-one, thinking he could easily dispose of this Hollywood lightweight, though several of his senior advisers disagreed with him. Pat Caddell warned Carter in a prescient memo that "the risks outweigh the possible advantages. . . . There is a 75 percent chance that Carter will 'lose' the debate even if he 'wins' on points."[28] The Reagan campaign was privately against a debate, believing that as the front-runner a debate posed more risks than rewards. Reagan's campaign insisted in their debate negotiations that third-party candidate John Anderson, who was steadily sinking in the polls, had to be included, which was an effective dealbreaker and political stalling tactic. Carter's campaign flatly refused to allow Anderson's inclusion, arguing that it was unfair of Carter to have to debate two Republicans. (The real reason was that Anderson was drawing more votes from Carter than Reagan, and any help for Anderson damaged Carter's chances.) Reagan debated Anderson in September, hoping to bring pressure on Carter for a three-way debate, but it had little effect.

The 10-day hiatus between the announcement of the debate and the debate itself had the effect of freezing the dynamic of the contest in place until debate day. No debate had ever been held this late in the campaign. Reagan actually would have preferred to have the debate the Monday night before the election, betting everything on one roll of the dice. The focus of the two campaigns shifted to preparation for what was shaping up to be the make-or-break moment. Carter and his closest aides retreated to Camp David for rehearsal, and Reagan repaired to a rented house in the Virginia countryside outside Washington for the same purpose. Political scientist Samuel Popkin served as Reagan's stand-in at Carter's Camp David debate rehearsals; out in the Virginia countryside, 33-year-old Congressman David Stockman of Michigan served as Carter's stand-in, while George Will and Jeane Kirkpatrick played the role of the media panel asking questions. Reagan professed to be startled at how well Stockman portrayed Carter in their mock debates. "After Stockman," Reagan said, "Carter was easy." Perhaps that's because Stockman was privy to Carter's debate briefing book.

The day of the actual debate, October 28, Stockman kept an appointment to speak to an Optimist Club luncheon back in his Michigan congressional district. There Stockman regaled the lunch audience with tales of his work helping Reagan to prepare for the debate—remarks that were reported in a local newspaper, the *Elkhart Truth*, based in the nearby Indiana town of Elkhart. In a news story printed the next day, *after* the debate had taken place, *Elkhart Truth* reporter Dee Bourdon's story had a tantalizing detail buried in the middle of the article, which was printed on page 15 of the paper. Stockman, the story said, had used a "pilfered copy of the briefing book Carter was going to use. . . . Stockman outlined the 'white lies' Carter was going to center on in the debate. Apparently the Reagan camp's 'pilfered' goods were correct, as several times both candidates said almost word for word what Stockman predicted."

The story never went beyond the pages of the *Elkhart Truth* until 1983, when Laurence Barrett's book about Reagan, *Gambling with History,* repeated the story, touching off a full-scale scandal excursion in Washington that predictably became known as "Debategate." It could never be determined how up to 700 pages of Carter's preliminary debate materials found their way to the Reagan campaign. (The papers were similar but not identical to the final briefing book Carter used in his rehearsals at Camp David.) A receptionist later told the FBI that a "clean cut young man" brought a large stack of documents into Reagan campaign headquarters in Arlington, Virginia, in mid-October. Speculation eventually turned to a Democratic political consultant named Paul Corbin, whose connections with Ted Kennedy were thought to have been a motive to betray Carter. Corbin received a $1,500 payment from the Reagan campaign for "research" work three days before the debate; the check was issued by Bill Casey. But there was no record of Corbin ever having been to the White House or the Carter campaign offices, so the mystery remained unsolved. Whatever their provenance, the Carter materials were a considerable embarrassment when they turned up in David Gergen's White House files in 1983. (Gergen had been on Reagan's debate preparation team.)

The "whodunnit" aspect of this subplot to the campaign story overshadows a more basic question: Was there anything in the Carter debate papers that the political professionals in the Reagan camp could not already have anticipated? This late in a presidential contest, the strengths and weaknesses and strategies of both sides are fairly transparent. Both sides knew what they needed to do in the debate, and how they would try to do it. Indeed, neither candidate said much in the debate that they had not said previously. This may be why Stockman so casually disclosed the story in his Optimist Club lunch. Stockman received the papers the day before the first mock-debate with Reagan; it is hard to see how he could have discerned from *700 pages* of material what Carter's specific debate strategy and tactics would be, and thereby provide a decisive edge to Reagan that was otherwise unattainable. Stockman later said, "The only person I can imagine this stuff was useful to was the guy who had to digest in one day the entire sorry history of the Carter administration."

Another telling contrast between the two campaigns, reflecting the style of their candidates, also emerges from this episode: While Carter's campaign produced nearly 1,000 pages of debate preparation material, which was contained in four notebooks, Reagan had a single debate briefing book. It was only 71 pages. Carter's debate strategy was to convey his mastery of the job and the facts, and he crammed in the same dutiful, paperwork-heavy fashion that he chose to govern. Reagan resisted the efforts of his advisers to get him to memorize intricate arguments and voluminous facts, believing, Lou Cannon reported, "that the viewing public was more apt to remember a deft phrase than a technical argument." During a review of a mock debate, Reagan said to his team, "I was about ready to say, 'There you go again.' I may save it for the debate."[29] Nothing in Carter's briefing book could have suggested the use of that line. Meanwhile, up at Camp David, Carter mentioned during his debate rehearsals that he was thinking about mentioning the concern of his 12-year-old daughter Amy about world peace. Carter's advisers thought it a bad idea and warned him against it.

ONE HUNDRED MILLION PEOPLE—the largest political audience in American history, rivaled in size only by the Super Bowl—tuned in for the debate on October 28. In the days leading up to the debate, Pat Caddell's tracking polls showed undecided voters breaking for Carter. Caddell's polls actually found Carter ahead of Reagan by two points, though Wirthlin's polls had Reagan with a small but consistent lead. For the media, it might as well have been the Super Bowl. Walter Cronkite introduced the debate by saying, "It's not inconceivable that the election could turn on what happens in the next 90 minutes." Carter won the coin toss, and opted to let Reagan answer the first question, which turned out to be about war and peace. Carter's strategists believed that Reagan might be nervous and stumble out of the starting gate. Reagan was a little halting and hesitant, but got out a pre-planned answer emphasizing that "our first priority must be world peace," and including his refrain about having seen four wars in his lifetime and not wishing to see another. Lou Cannon quipped that "Reagan mentioned 'peace' so often it sounded like he had invented the word." Reagan soon settled into a relaxed rhythm for the rest of the debate, accomplishing his most important objective: He reassured viewers that he was not a "mad bomber."

Carter, on the other hand, appeared stiff and uptight throughout. *Washington Post* columnist Mary McGrory wrote: "Carter seemed stricken with nerves, so tense that he looked affronted when Reagan bounded over to shake hands before the hostilities began." Carter hit Reagan hard on Reagan's "out of the mainstream" views, and six times used the adjective "disturbing" to describe Reagan's policies. Conversely, Carter kept saying "Oval Office" as though he thought viewers might have forgotten that he was president. Reagan parried effectively, though a strict scoring of the debate would have awarded Carter points for consistently putting Reagan on the defensive.

The public, of course, does not judge presidential debates by careful scoring of points and counter-points. The demeanor and bearing of the candidates counts as much, if not more, than the substance of the debate. The relaxed and confident Reagan showed some of his quickness and instinct for the cut and thrust of debate, especially during the argument over his economic plan. Carter repeated his charge that it would be inflationary. Reagan answered with a rhetorical question that focused viewers on his broader philosophical point about government: "I would like to ask the President why it is inflationary to let the people keep more of their money and spend it the way they like, and it isn't inflationary to let him take that money and spend it the way he wants?" Reagan also hoisted Carter by his own petard. In 1976, Carter had blasted Ford with the "misery index," the combination of inflation and unemployment. In 1976, Carter's "misery index" was 12.5, and Carter had said "that no man with that size misery index had a right to seek reelection to the presidency." Today, Reagan observed, the misery index is over 20.

Carter never did loosen up. One of Carter's own aides observed that in the TV cutaway shots showing Carter while Reagan was speaking, "Jimmy looked like he was about to slug him." Carter's one attempt at humanizing himself was a disaster. About two-thirds of the way through the debate, at the close of several questions about foreign policy and arms control, Carter said: "I had a discussion with my daughter Amy the other day, before I came here, to ask her what the most important issue was. She said she thought nuclear weaponry, and the control of nuclear arms." Reagan's line about having sons and a grandson had gone over fine, but Carter's line, delivered in a rapid-fire staccato burst, landed with a thud, and became a source of ridicule against Carter over the next week. Republican groups were quick with a bumper sticker: "Ask Amy, She Knows."

Carter then unwittingly set up one of the most famous lines of Reagan's career. "Governor Reagan," Carter charged, "began his political career campaigning around this nation against Medicare," and now Reagan was opposing any steps toward national health insurance. The camera swung to Reagan for his reply. Reagan nodded his head at Carter, and said with a slight smile: *There you go again.* Reagan's formal answer that followed didn't really matter. *There you go again* seemed to sum up both Reagan's easy-going character and the overreach of Carter's relentless attacks on Reagan's supposed extremism. It may well stand the test of time as the most memorable line of any presidential debate. (The *Washington Post* transcript of the debate curiously omitted "There you go again.")

But Reagan saved his toughest blow at Carter for the end. In his closing comment, Reagan said:

> Next Tuesday all of you will go to the polls, will stand there in the polling place and make a decision. I think when you make that decision, it might be well if you ask yourself, are you better off than you were four years ago? Is it easier for you to go and buy things in the stores than it was four years ago? Is there more or less unemployment in the country than there was four years ago? Is America as respected throughout the world as it was? Do you feel your security is safe, that we're as strong as we were four years ago? And if you answer all those questions 'yes," why then, I think you choice is very

obvious as to whom you will vote for. If you don't agree, if you don't think that his course that we've been on for the last four years is what you would like to see us follow for the next four, then I could suggest another choice that you have.

David Gergen had suggested these lines to Reagan, and it was a devastating closer. Reagan, who had answered the first question, got in the last word.

Carter's camp believed they won hands-down. "We won, we won," Hamilton Jordan said immediately after the TV lights went down. So did much of the media, if only slightly. Hedrick Smith's lead in the *New York Times* news story the next day said that "The Presidential debate produced no knockout blow, no disastrous gaffe and no immediate, undisputed victor," though Smith gave the edge to Carter further down in the story. "If anyone gains politically from the Tuesday night matchup," Morton Kondracke wrote in *The New Republic*, "it will be Carter. . . . [B]y every measure except aw-shucks niceness, Carter was the clearly superior performer."[30]

The viewing public didn't think so. Wirthlin conducted an overnight poll of 500 voters that found Reagan the winner by a two-to-one margin. Other polls by Lou Harris and the Associated Press found a similar result. The most controversial spin on the debate came from ABC News, who promoted a call-in phone poll after the debate on *Nightline*. Bell Labs, which facilitated the phone poll, expressed "shock" when over 600,000 people phoned in over the next hour, at a cost of 50 cents per call. The tabulation found Reagan the winner, again by a two-to-one margin. This self-selected phone-in "poll" was utterly unscientific and drew heavy criticism that it was no more accurate than the *Literary Digest* telephone poll in 1936 that predicted Alf Landon would defeat Franklin Roosevelt. Nevertheless, the poll took on a life of its own and received wide news coverage. (And Bell Labs made $300,000 on the deal.) "Whatever the poll's shortcomings," the *New York Times* suggested, "a margin that wide probably reflected something of substance about the debate's impact."[31]

The *Times* was right, though it didn't become clear until 48 hours before election day. Wirthlin's tracking polls, based on more than 10,500 phone calls in the week after the debate, detected Reagan's numbers moving up steadily, but public polls continued to find the race still to be within the margin of error—too close to call. Gallup reported the Sunday before the election: "Never in the forty-five year history of presidential election surveys has the Gallup Poll found such volatility and uncertainty." Pat Caddell's daily tracking poll on Sunday found Reagan and Carter dead even, as did the *New York Times*/CBS poll. Caddell told Elizabeth Drew Sunday night, "I just wish we hadn't debated."

More important than the polls on the national popular vote split were the state-by-state readings, which found Reagan with a solid lead in the all-important contest for electoral votes. Reagan felt confident and had a bounce in his step during the last week of campaigning. When a heckler in Michigan taunted Reagan with "Bonzo, Bonzo"—a reference to Reagan's ignominious movie role in the forgettable *Bedtime for Bonzo*—Reagan's face lit up as he thumped the heckler: "You better watch out. Bonzo grew up to be King Kong." The Reagan campaign had carefully conserved its advertising budget, and outspent Carter on media over the last week by a three-to-two margin.

Carter, meanwhile, entered a fresh agony over the Iranian hostages. Late Saturday, November 1, Iran announced four conditions for releasing the hostages, the most crucial of which was unfreezing billions of dollars of Iranian assets held in the United States. This, Carter's team immediately recognized, it might not legally be able to accomplish, at least not in 48 hours. This was, at best, just a start, and not an end, to negotiations that might succeed. Nonetheless, Carter canceled his campaign events on Sunday and flew back to the White House in haste. The Reagan campaign feared that the "October surprise" was about to be sprung 48 hours before voters headed to the polls. Reagan held his tongue, telling reporters on a campaign stop in Ohio that "this is too delicate a situation." Henry Kissinger was less reticent, telling ABC News that the Ayatollah Khomeini is trying to manipulate the election. There were lots of street-smart reasons for thinking the Iranians might well do such a thing. One joke making the rounds went: "What's flat as a pancake and glows in the dark? Iran after Reagan becomes president."

Reagan's camp needn't have worried. Wirthlin had polled extensively for this contingency, and found that nearly half the voters would be skeptical of any last-minute hostage release deal, believing that Carter would manipulate the situation for political purposes. Carter came on television shortly after 6 P.M. eastern time Sunday night (interrupting the NFL football games on the networks), with a carefully worded announcement reminiscent of his statement the morning of the Wisconsin primary. Iran hadn't formally transmitted its demands, but Carter said "they appear to offer a positive basis" for achieving a deal. "Let me assure you," Carter added, "that my decisions on this crucial matter will not be affected by the calendar." It was clear, though, that no deal was imminent. It was, coincidentally, the one-year anniversary of the beginning of the hostage crisis. On Monday night, Walter Cronkite signed off the CBS Evening News, as he had for the past year, with the modification of his signature closing: "And that's the way it is, Monday, November 3rd, 1980, the 366th day of captivity for the American hostages in Iran."

The hostage crisis, which had revived Carter's political fortunes a year ago, had now become prominent among the factors that crushed him. In the last 48 hours both Wirthlin and Caddell discerned a huge move toward Reagan in their tracking polls. Both arrived at the same conclusion—Reagan could win by 10 points or more, and score an electoral landslide. The public polls—Gallup, CBS, and others—were behind the curve, mostly because they had stopped surveying over the weekend, before the last-minute hostage drama. The media was still reporting that the election would be a squeaker.

There was movement in the polls down the ticket as well, which is the last important element to the election story that deserves exposition. In 1972, as we have seen, Nixon ran for reelection largely detached from the Republican Party, and Carter had run as *de facto* independent in 1976. Many political scientists found this unremarkable, given the slow decline of political parties and party identity in the wake of the expansion of modern bureaucratic government. With increasing numbers of voters eschewing partisanship, it makes sense for national candidates to de-emphasize solidarity with their party. Reagan's 1980 campaign was therefore exceptional for being the most party-oriented campaign in decades. In 1978 Republicans had experimented with $1 million for "generic" ads boosting the Republican Party rather than a specific local candidate. The intent was to appeal to voters to change their voting habits rather than appeal simply on the basis of a specific personality. The GOP's disappointing gains in the House in 1978 seemed to suggest the strategy was ineffective.

In 1980 Republicans were determined to try again to connect the nation's discontent not only with the occupant of the White House, but with the ruling party of Congress as well. In other words, they wanted to "nationalize" the election, which many political scientists thought was next to impossible in the era of weakened party identification. In August the Harris Poll released the startling finding that for the first time in several decades, a majority of voters intended to vote for Republican candidates for Congress. The GOP decided to devote $8 million to generic ads with the simple tag line: "Vote Republican. For a change."

Reagan played an important part of this strategy when he joined with 285 Republican House and Senate candidates on the steps of the capitol in Washington on September 15. Reagan and the GOP "governing team," as they called themselves, pledged to enact a five-point economic and defense platform if elected in November. The idea originated with an obscure Republican strategist, but it attracted the enthusiastic backing of freshman Republican Congressman Newt Gingrich, who said, "If we play it safe for the next month and a half, we'll pick up 25 seats. If we're courageous, we could win 60 to 90." Gingrich urged Republicans to adopt a stance of confrontation in the House to dramatize the differences between the two parties. The GOP House leadership was not much taken with his suggestions, but it did set the precedent for Gingrich's 1994 "Contract With America" that made him Speaker of the House.

As the tidal wave for Reagan was unseen before election day, neither was the undertow that would reshape Congress. David Broder wrote a few weeks before the election, "There is no evidence of a dramatic upsurge in Republican strength or massive turnover in Congress." Republicans needed to pick up 10 seats to reach a majority in the Senate. The most optimistic forecast thought the GOP could gain seven; the consensus of forecasts predicted a gain of between four and six. *Congressional Quarterly* predicted that Republicans would only pickup about 15 seats in the House. *The New Republic* concluded in late September: "There is no great tidal wave sweeping down threatening to engulf the Democratic Congress." And a week before the election, the same *New Republic* writer (Morton Kondracke) said "it seems more likely by the day that Ronald Reagan is not going to execute a massive electoral sweep. In fact, the movement of the presidential campaign suggests a Carter victory."[32]

Kondracke, a fine reporter, was nonetheless representative of media prognostications in 1980.

WASHINGTON WAS RAINY and cool on election day. An omen of how the election would unfold occurred early in the day when John White, chairman of the Democratic National Committee, couldn't get a lunch reservation at one of his favorite restaurants. No one in Carter's entourage, which had criss-crossed the country in a last-minute mad-dash campaign effort, had much of an appetite. Caddell had seen "the bottom fall out" of Carter's poll numbers. He relayed the news to Jody Powell, who told Carter the bad news in the middle of the night on board Air Force One en route from the West Coast.

At 2 P.M. eastern time the first exit poll results began coming in to news organizations, and the TV networks, having expected a close race, faced the dilemma of what to do with the stunning results. Prior to 1980, no news organization had ever "called" a state solely on exit poll results alone. They typically waited until a few early vote counts, which were becoming more widely computerized and faster to report with each election, offered confirmation of the exit poll models. But by 1980 exit poll techniques were thought reliable enough to dispense with waiting for actual hard vote counts except in very close elections (such as the 2000 election). The exit polls correctly showed that this was not going to be a close contest.

NBC News decided it would be aggressive in "calling" states and getting out ahead of the other networks on the story. Anchor John Chancellor tipped their hand when he opened the network's broadcast at 7 P.M. eastern time: "According to an NBC-AP poll, Ronald Reagan appears headed for a substantial victory." *This, even though the polls were still open in 44 states.* Polls in four states closed at 7 P.M. eastern time: Indiana (actually at 6 P.M.), Virginia, Mississippi, and Georgia. In two other states, Florida and Alabama, polls closed in the eastern time zones; polls in the western parts of those states would remain open for another hour. NBC couldn't wait: They projected the winner in all six states. Reagan won five of the six; Carter carried only his home state of Georgia. NBC was half an hour ahead of the other two networks in calling a state.

At 7:30 P.M. the polls closed in Ohio, a key Midwest state with 25 electoral votes. NBC called the state for Reagan 40 seconds later. At

8 P.M., polls closed in 13 more states. Within two minutes and 40 seconds, NBC had called 12 of the 13—all went for Reagan. Included in this batch were the key industrial and upper Midwest states of Michigan, Illinois, and Missouri, along with Pennsylvania and New Jersey in the Northeast. Reagan's electoral vote total was already at 261, just nine short of assuring victory. At 8:15 P.M., two hours and 45 minutes before the polls closed on the West Coast, NBC made it "official," flashing on the screen "REAGAN WINS." By this time NBC had projected the results in 20 states; ABC, following the more cautious method of making projections, had called only 10 states; CBS had called only four. At the time NBC projected that Reagan would be the 40th President of the United States, less than 4 percent of the national vote total had been officially tabulated.

At about the time NBC was calling the election for Reagan, Jimmy Carter was on the phone to Reagan conceding. It was only a little after 5 P.M. in Los Angeles, where Reagan was observing election night, and he was not expecting Carter to phone so early. In fact, Nancy Reagan had to get him out of the shower to take Carter's call. Carter knew all day that he was going to lose big, so the early phone call to Reagan was not extraordinary. But what Carter did next was. Shortly after 9:30 eastern time, an hour and a half before the polls closed on the West Coast, Carter came out in the ballroom of the Washington Sheraton Hotel to make his formal public concession. House Speaker Tip O'Neill was livid. It was Carter's final insult to his Democratic colleagues in Congress, because there were still several close House and Senate contests on the West Coast, and Carter's concession would discourage last-minute Democratic voters from turning out. O'Neill may have been right, though it is hard to blame Carter alone, with NBC calling the election before the country had finished voting. Democrats lost an incumbent Senator (Warren Magnuson) in Washington; and two veteran House members out West, including the powerful chairman of the House Way and Means Committee, Al Ullman of Oregon, lost razor-close races. "One wonders if the President entertained the idea of conceding even before the polls opened," *The Nation* wrote; "it might have rescued a few of the more worthy Democrats who the President brought down with him."[33]

By the end of the night Reagan won 44 states, for an electoral vote landslide of 489 to 49 for Carter. Reagan won 50.8 percent of the total popular vote to Carter's 41 percent. Reagan rolled up huge majorities among Protestants, which accounted for his strong showing in the South, but he also received 45 percent of the Catholic vote and an astounding 35 percent of the Jewish vote, which helped him carry New York. John Anderson ended up receiving 6.6 percent of the vote nationally, but he probably tipped several close states to Reagan, including New York. Reagan's margin over Carter in New York was 2.7 percent; Anderson got 7.5 percent in New York.

Exit polls showed that the economy was the overriding issue for most voters, and Reagan had a clear advantage over Carter on this score. But Reagan carried the day on the issue of war and peace as well. The *New York Times*/CBS exit poll asked voters whether they agreed or disagreed with the statement, "We should be more forceful in our dealings with the Soviet Union even if it increases the risk of war." Fifty-four percent agreed with this statement, and Reagan won two-thirds of their votes. Perhaps the most revealing finding of the exit polls is that Carter only did well with one group of voters, those who agreed with the statement, "Today, regardless of who holds the office, no President can be very effective in solving our nation's problems." In other words, Carter won the votes of pessimists.

Reagan didn't come out to claim victory until three hours after Carter's concession—after all the polls were closed. As the evening wore on the second half of the story became equally prominent. Democratic Senators, especially liberals, were being mowed down at nearly every turn. Birch Bayh lost in Indiana to Congressman Dan Quayle; John Culver lost in Iowa; Richard Morgan in North Carolina; Frank Church in Idaho; John Durkin in New Hampshire; Gaylord Nelson in Wisconsin. The biggest shocker was George McGovern, who lost in South Dakota. At his concession, a bitter McGovern promised to found a new organization to combat the influence of right-wing extremism. (McGovern later said he knew his reelection was lost when two elderly women in a grocery store told him they would vote against him because he is too liberal, and then paid for their groceries with food stamps.) Only California's Alan Cranston among liberal senators on the ballot in 1980 had an easy reelection. Colorado's Gary Hart held on to his seat by a narrow margin. There was one ironic dark spot for Republicans; out in Arizona, Barry Goldwater was locked in a tight contest to hold on to his Senate seat. (Several days would pass before all the absentee ballots were tallied in Arizona; Goldwater hung on—barely.)

When the dust settled Republicans had picked up 12 Senate seats, and their first majority in the Senate in 26 years. On the House side, Republicans were also picking off 27 incumbent Democrats, and won another six open seats, giving the GOP a net gain of 33 seats. The Democrats would still enjoy a comfortable 243–192 majority in the next Congress, but their feeling of invincibility was shattered. "For the first time," a veteran Democratic congressman told political scientist Norm Ornstein, "we can *really* see the possibility of losing *our* majority in 1982." They had good reason to be worried. Republican House candidates actually received a majority of the votes cast on a nationwide basis. And by appealing to conservative Southern Democrats in the House, Republicans would enjoy an *ideological* working majority right away.

The GOP also gained seven governorships and 300 seats in state legislatures. One of the ousted Democratic governors was Arkansas's 34-year-old Bill Clinton. Clinton had defied the political trend of the time. While most other governors were cutting taxes in the aftermath of the tax revolt in 1978, Clinton had raised taxes by $47 million, and Arkansas voters were not happy about it. TV commentators on election night thought that Clinton's brilliant young political career was finished.

Conservatives were understandably triumphant. The moment they had waited on for a generation had arrived. The long-suffering American Right was about to enter the political Promised Land. The conservative weekly *Human Events* ran a banner headline in 64-point type: "AT LAST!" Liberals and people on the far Left alternated between denial and panic. *The Nation* magazine went into overdrive: "Prepare for the worst. The signs are clear as they could be that we are about to have a Government that will hide a regressive and repressive domestic policy behind an aggressive and adventurous foreign policy."[34] Sociologist Alan Wolfe wrote: "[T]he United States has embarked on a course so deeply reactionary, so negative and mean-spirited, so chauvinistic and self-deceptive that our times may soon rival the McCarthy era."[35] Many liberals blamed Carter for their defeat as a way of deflecting searching questions about the decadence of liberalism. Carter Cabinet exile Joseph Califano told a gathering of Democratic leaders that assembled in Washington to sort through the rubble that "Jimmy Carter was the most incompetent Democratic President in history." Jerry Brown was more honest and circumspect: "Let's not fool ourselves. We are at the end of an era in this party and this country."[36] Massachusetts Sen. Paul Tsongas agreed: "Basically, the New Deal died yesterday." We lost, Moynihan said, because the voters perceived, not incorrectly, that Democrats believe that "government should be strong and America should be weak."

An electoral sweep of this magnitude and breadth immediately prompted talk of whether 1980 was a genuine "realigning" election like 1860 or 1932. Pat Moynihan reflected ruefully: "Even Herbert Hoover got more electoral votes than President Carter. We have to ask what happened and why. There was no stock market crash, no Vietnam War."

"For the first time in a generation," David Broder wrote a few days after the election, "it is sensible to ask whether we might be entering a new political era—an era of Republican dominance. . . . [Y]ou had to be dense to miss a flat-out repudiation of basic economic, diplomatic, and social policies of the reigning Democratic liberalism."[37] Political scientists Thomas Mann and Norm Ornstein wrote that "The 1980 election provided as clear and distinct a message of general policy direction as any election since 1964."[38]

A closer look at the numbers shows a more ambiguous picture and explains why declarations of realignment turned out to be more than a decade premature. The Republican Senate blow-out was accomplished by the thinnest of margins; a shift of only 50,000 votes would have changed the result in *seven* Senate races the GOP won. Many of the Republican gains were in small states. Democrats outpolled Republicans in all 34 Senate races by 3 million votes, winning by large margins (1.6 million votes in California, for example) in the larger states. The Republicans won the close ones.

Although 1980 might not turn out to be a classic "realignment" election, it was nonetheless a "critical" election for the simple reason that Ronald Reagan proved an ideological conservative could win the presidency. And if it could be done once, it could be done again. He had now to prove whether an ideological conservative could govern. Could he succeed in rolling back the regulatory apparatus of the federal government? Balance the budget while cutting taxes and hiking defense spending? Skeptics were legion, especially among liberals in denial about the magnitude of their defeat. Sen. Gary Hart said, "I give the Reagan Administration about 18 to 24 months to prove that it doesn't have any answers either." Gov. Jerry Brown said that Reagan's economic plan was "doomed to failure." Alan Wolfe predicted in *The Nation* that "Ronald Reagan will slide America deeper into its decline. . . . Reagan will be hoisted by the same petard that blew away Carter."[39] Political scientist Curtis Gans wrote that "there is nothing in the Republican outlook on either the American economy or foreign affairs that suggests the party can successfully govern for any long period of time."[40]

Beyond the pressing policy issues of the campaign lay a more fundamental challenge. The basic mien of modern conservatism had been best expressed in the famous slogan of the first issue of *National Review* in 1955: "It stands athwart history, yelling Stop, at a time when no one is inclined to do so, or to have much patience with those who so urge it."[41] In other words, conservatism stands in opposition to many of the basic premises of modernity, which form the foundation of the modern welfare state. It is one thing to articulate these doubts and attack incumbent liberalism. It is another thing to work a reformation on deeply rooted philosophical and moral sentiments through politics alone. Would Reagan be equal to this historic challenge?

By 1980 the world was on the cusp of recognizing the transition to what it calls the "post-modern age." In practical terms this first came to sight as the "post-industrial" information and professional service economy that exploded in the 1980s. Yet there is an intellectual or cognitive side to "post-modernism" that is more important. While much of what passes for "post-modernism" these days is extremely radical, the postmodern viewpoint is characterized by nothing so much as its rejection of the idea of progress based on reason—the quintessential *liberal* idea from the Enlightenment. Taking the long view, contemporary conservatism has in many ways become the inheritor of the best of the classical liberal tradition, which is one reason why so many old liberal intellectuals have become self-identified conservatives in recent decades. In smashing the monopoly of liberalism in 1980, Reagan exposed the fractured and increasingly hollow character of what passes for liberalism in the late twentieth century, and prepared the ground of political debate on which American politics is still being conducted today. That is what makes the closing decades of the twentieth century the "Age of Reagan." Like the post–New Deal era—the "Age of Roosevelt"—the Age of Reagan may prove equally durable.

At the close of 1980, however, none of this was evident or foreseeable. The persistent doubts about Reagan among many people across the political spectrum prompted the thought that Reagan's election was a fluke, the political version of a 1938 movie in which Reagan appeared, titled *Accidents Will Happen.* (Several other old Reagan film titles symbolically appealed to liberals, including *Dark Victory, That Bad Man, Desperate Journey, Night unto Night,* and *Storm Warning.* Conservatives could point to other Reagan roles such as *Going Places, It's a Great Feeling,* and *The Winning Team.*) But the question on the minds of most people came not from any of Reagan's film titles, but from the title of Reagan's much-referenced 1965 autobiography: *Where's the Rest of Me?*

The world was about to find out.

NOTES

———➤●◄———

PROLOGUE

1. *Time*, 31 December 1999, p. 47.
2. Jules Witcover and Richard M. Cohen, "Where's the Rest of Ronald Reagan?" *Esquire*, March 1976, p. 92.
3. Anne Edwards, *Early Reagan: The Rise to Power* (New York: William Morrow, 1987), p. 486.
4. Garry Wills, *Reagan's America* (New York: Doubleday, 1987), chapter 9.
5. John P. Roche, "The Passing of the Class of 1941," *National Review*, 19 October 1984, p. 26.
6. *Newsweek,* 2 November 1970, p. 29.
7. Lou Cannon, *Reagan* (New York: G. P. Putnam's Sons, 1982), p. 196.
8. Charles D. Hobbs, "How Ronald Reagan Governed California," *National Review*, 17 January 1975, p. 29.
9. Richard Harwood, ed., *The Pursuit of the Presidency 1980* (New York: Putnam, 1980), pp. 333–334.
10. *National Review,* 14 November 1980, p. 1369.
11. Vermont Royster, "On Appraisals of the Presidents," *Wall Street Journal,* 10 July 1987.
12. Thomas Byrne Edsall and Mary D. Edsall, *Chain Reaction: The Impact of Race, Rights, and Taxes on American Politics* (New York: W. W. Norton, 1991), p. 174.
13. George Nash, "The Historical Roots of Contemporary American Conservatism," *Modern Age*, Summer/Fall 1982, p. 299.
14. John Kenneth Galbraith, "An Agenda for American Liberals," *Commentary*, June 1966, p. 29.
15. Ibid.
16. Henry Fairlie, "Johnson and the Intellectuals," *Commentary*, October 1965, p. 49.
17. Daniel Patrick Moynihan, *A Dangerous Place* (Boston: Little, Brown, 1978), p. 24.
18. Ronald Radosh, *Divided They Fell: The Demise of the Democratic Party, 1964–1996* (New York: The Free Press, 1996), p. 161.

19. Shelby Steele, "A New Front in the Culture War," *Wall Street Journal*, 2 August 2000, p. A22.

20. James Q. Wilson, "A Guide to Reagan Country: The Political Culture of Southern California," *Commentary*, May 1967, p. 45.

21. Daniel Patrick Moynihan, "The President and the Negro," *Commentary*, February 1967, p. 35.

22. James Q. Wilson, "Reagan and the Republican Revival," *Commentary*, October 1980.

23. Lord Charnwood, *Abraham Lincoln* (New York: Henry Holt & Co, 1917), p. 2.

24. Godfrey Hodgson, *The Gentleman from New York: Daniel Patrick Moynihan* (Boston: Houghton Mifflin, 2000), p. 20.

25. *Time*, 5 April 1976, p. 18.

26. Daniel Patrick Moynihan, *Maximum Feasible Misunderstanding: Community Action and the War on Poverty* (New York: The Free Press, 1969), p. xii; Moynihan, *Coping: Essays on the Practice of Government* (New York: Random House, 1973), p. 15.

27. Daniel Patrick Moynihan, *The Politics of a Guaranteed Income: The Nixon Administration and the Family Assistance Plan* (New York: Random House, 1974), p. 131.

CHAPTER 1

1. Samuel Lubell, *The Future of American Politics*, third edition (New York: Harper & Row, 1965), p. vii.

2. Michael Barone, *Our Country: The Shaping of America from Roosevelt to Reagan* (New York: The Free Press, 1990), p. 388.

3. Daniel Patrick Moynihan, *Maximum Feasible Misunderstanding: Community Action and the War on Poverty* (New York: The Free Press, 1969), p. 148.

4. Henry Fairlie, "Johnson and the Intellectuals," *Commentary*, October 1965, p. 49.

5. James T. Patterson, *Grand Expectations: The United States, 1945–1974* (New York: Oxford University Press, 1996), p. 527.

6. Matusow, Allen J. *The Unraveling of America: A History of Liberalism in the 1960s* (New York: Harper & Row, 1984), p. 132.

7. *Time*, 5 January 1968, p. 14.

8. Patterson, p. 583.

9. Matusow, p. 56.

10. Robert Trumbull, "Homosexuals Proud of Deviancy, Medical Academy Study Finds," *New York Times*, 19 May 1964, p. 1.

11. Daniel Patrick Moynihan, *Coping: Essays on the Practice of Government* (New York: Random House, 1973), p. 8.

12. John Kenneth Galbraith, "An Agenda for American Liberals," *Commentary*, June 1966, p. 29.

13. Lyndon Johnson, *The Vantage Point: Perspectives on the Presidency, 1963–1969* (New York: Holt, Reinhart and Winston, 1971), pp. 73–74.
14. Nicholas Lemann, "The Unfinished War," *Atlantic Monthly*, December 1988.
15. Matusow, p. 121.
16. Irving Bernstein, *Guns or Butter: The Presidency of Lyndon Johnson* (New York: Oxford University Press, 1996), p. 97.
17. Cited in Gareth Davies, *From Opportunity to Entitlement: The Transformation and Decline of Great Society Liberalism* (Lawrence: University Press of Kansas, 1996), p. 36.
18. Cited in Bernstein, *Guns or Butter*, p. 106.
19. Michael Beschloss, *Taking Charge: The Johnson White House Tapes, 1963–1964* (New York: Simon & Schuster, 1997), pp. 185–186.
20. Cited in Bernstein, p. 100.
21. Christopher Jencks, "Johnson vs. Poverty," *The New Republic*, 28 March 1964, p. 16.
22. Matusow, p. 239.
23. Daniel Patrick Moynihan, *Maximum Feasible Misunderstanding: Community Action and the War on Poverty* (New York: The Free Press, 1969), p. 99.
24. Ibid., pp. 87, 82.
25. Ibid., p. xvii.
26. Cited in Davies, p. 38.
27. Ibid., p. 44.
28. Ibid., p. 41.
29. Matusow, p. 123.
30. Moynihan, *Maximum Feasible Misunderstanding*, p. 170.
31. Walter Miller, in Daniel Patrick Moynihan, ed., *On Understanding Poverty: Perspectives from the Social Sciences* (New York: Basic Books, 1968), p. 270.
32. Daniel Patrick Moynihan, "The Professors and the Poor," *Commentary*, August 1968, pp. 27, 26.
33. Cited in Charles Murray, *Losing Ground: American Social Policy, 1950–1980* (New York: Basic Books, 1984), p. 25.
34. Moynihan, "The Professionalization of Reform," *The Public Interest*, 1965.
35. Robert Dallek. *Flawed Giant: Lyndon Johnson and His Times, 1961–1973* (New York: Oxford University Press, 1998), p. 330.
36. Cited in Davies, p. 36.
37. James Tobin, "Tax Cut Harvest," *The New Republic*, 7 March 1964, p. 14.
38. Gunnar Myrdal, "The War on Poverty," *The New Republic*, 8 February 1964, p. 16.
39. *The New Republic*, 14 March 1964, p. 3.
40. *New York Times*, 27 December 1964, p. E–8.
41. Davies, p. 48.

42. Adam Walinsky, "Keeping the Poor in Their Place," *The New Republic*, 4 July 1964, p. 18.

43. Matusow, p. 217.

44. Clare Booth Luce, "Extremism in Defense of the Democratic Party," *National Review*, 25 August 1964, pp. 719–720.

45. Todd Gitlin, *The Sixties: Years of Hope, Days of Rage* (New York: Bantam Books, 1987), p. 136.

46. Stephan and Abigail Thernstrom, *America in Black and White: One Nation, Indivisible* (New York: Simon & Schuster, 1997), p. 141.

47. Ibid., p. 140.

48. Ibid., p. 147.

49. Richard Epstein, *Forbidden Grounds: The Case Against Employment Discrimination Laws* (Cambridge: Harvard University Press, 1992), pp. 186–188.

50. Cited in Russell Nieli, ed., *Racial Preference and Racial Justice: the New Affirmative Action Controversy* (Washington, D.C.: Ethics and Public Policy Center, 1991), p. 40.

51. *Katzenbach v. McClung*, 379 U.S. 241 (1964).

52. F. Clifton White, *Suite 3505: The Story of the Draft Goldwater Movement* (New Rochelle, New York: Arlington House, 1967), p. 403.

53. *Newsweek*, 3 August 1964, p. 17.

54. Lee Edwards, *Goldwater: The Man Who Made a Revolution* (Washington, D.C.: Regnery, 1995), p. 243.

55. Cited in *National Review*, 20 September 1966, p. 918.

56. Edward Banfield, *The Unheavenly City Revisited* (Boston: Little, Brown, 1974), p. 220.

57. *Newsweek*, 3 August 1964, p. 17.

58. Robert A. Caro, *The Power Broker: Robert Moses and the Fall of New York* (New York: Alfred A. Knopf, 1974), pp. 318–319.

59. Beschloss, p. 462.

60. Jim and Sybil Stockdale, *In Love and War* (New York: Harper & Row, 1984), pp. 3–36.

61. Cline cited in Lloyd C. Gardner, *Pay Any Price: Lyndon Johnson and the Wars for Vietnam* (Chicago: Ivan Dee, 1995), pp. 137–138.

62. Cited in *National Review*, 22 September 1964, p. 799.

63. Beschloss, p. 503.

64. Gardner, p. 87.

65. Beschloss, p. 504.

66. Barry Goldwater with Jack Casserly, *Goldwater* (New York: Doubleday, 1988), pp. 192–193. Goldwater gives a similar account of this meeting in his 1979 memoirs, *With No Apologies* (New York: William Morrow, 1979), pp. 192–193. Though Goldwater places this meeting *after* the Gulf of Tonkin incident in both of

his memoirs, the White House press release about the meeting places the meeting in late July.

67. John P. Roche, *Sentenced to Life: Reflections on Politics, Education, and Law* (New York: Macmillan, 1974), p. 68.

68. For more background on the role of American weakness in the outcome of the Cuban Missile Crisis, see Donald Kagan, *On the Origin of War* (New York: Doubleday, 1995), pp. 437–548.

69. Jeffrey Record, *The Wrong War: Why We Lost in Vietnam* (Annapolis, Maryland: Naval Institute Press, 1998), p. 51.

70. H. R. McMaster, *Dereliction of Duty: Lyndon Johnson, Robert McNamara, the Joint Chiefs of Staff, and the Lies that Led to Vietnam* (New York: HarperCollins, 1997), p. 30.

71. Cyrus Vance, Oral History Transcript, LBJ Library, 9 March 1970, section 3, p. 11.

72. CIA report cited in Larry Berman, *Planning a Tragedy: The Americanization of the War in Vietnam* (New York: Norton, 1982), p. 24.

73. Roger Hilsman memo cited in John P. Roche, *Sentenced to Life* (New York: Macmillan, 1974), pp. 96–97.

74. *National Review*, 1 December 1964, p. 1080.

75. Berman, p. 35.

76. Richard Nixon, *The Memoirs of Richard Nixon* (New York: Simon & Schuster, 1978), p. 257.

77. Cited in Gardner, p. 102.

78. Ibid., p. 124.

79. McMaster, p. 132.

80. Roche, p. 74.

CHAPTER 2

1. Taylor Branch, "The Year the GOP Went South," *Washington Monthly*, March 1988, p. 35.

2. Darrell M. West, *Air Wars: Television Advertising in Election Campaigns, 1952–1992* (Washington, D.C.: CQ Press, 1993).

3. Lee Edwards, *Goldwater: The Man Who Made a Revolution* (Washington, D.C.: Regnery, 1995), p. 314.

4. Robert Lekachman, "The Postponed Argument," *The New Leader*, 23 November 1964, p. 6.

5. Ibid. p. 7.

6. Hans J. Morgenthau, "Goldwater—The Romantic Regression," *Commentary*, September 1964.

7. Quoted in Alan Brinkley, *Liberalism and Its Discontents* (Cambridge: Harvard University Press, 1998), p. 279.

8. David Danzig, "Conservatism After Goldwater," *Commentary*, March 1965.

9. Richard Rovere, "The Conservative Mindlessness," *Commentary*, March 1965.

10. Seymour Martin Lipset, "Waiting for the Pendulum," *The New Leader*, 7 December 1964.

11. *Time*, 24 July 1964, p. 19.

12. F. Clifton White, *Suite 3505: The Story of the Draft Goldwater Movement* (New Rochelle, New York: Arlington House, 1967), p. 224.

13. Daniel Patrick Moynihan, *Coping: Essays on the Practice of Government* (New York: Random House, 1973), p. 15; *The Politics of a Guaranteed Income*, pp. 76, 131.

14. Quoted in *National Review*, 7 September 1965, p. 755.

15. Paul Samuelson, *Economics*, 13th edition (New York: McGraw-Hill, 1980), p. 837.

16. *The New Yorker*, September 3, 1984.

17. *Facts on File*, 12 March 1964, p. 86.

18. Nathan Glazer, "What Happened at Berkeley," *Commentary*, February 1965, p. 40.

19. David Lance Goines, *The Free Speech Movement: Coming of Age in the 1960s* (Berkeley: Ten Speed Press, 1993), p. 150.

20. Lipset, "Out of the Alcoves," *The Wilson Quarterly*, Winter 1999, p. 89.

21. John Searle, "The Faculty Resolution," in Michael Miller and Susan Gilmore, eds., *Revolution at Berkeley* (New York: Dial Press, 1965), p. 98.

22. Searle, p. 102.

23. Todd Gitlin, *The Sixties: Years of Hope, Days of Rage* (New York: Bantam Books, 1987), pp. 90, 183.

24. John A. Andrew, III, *The Other Side of the Sixties: Young Americans for Freedom and the Rise of Conservative Politics* (New Brunswick: Rutgers University Press, 1997), p. 83.

25. Cited in Terry H. Anderson, *The Movement and the Sixties: Protest in America from Greensboro to Wounded Knee* (New York: Oxford University Press, 1995), p. 39.

26. Paul Goodman, "Thoughts on Berkeley," *New York Review of Books*, 14 January 1965, p. 24.

27. Goldwater cited in John A. Andrew III, *The Other Side of the Sixties*, p. 82.

28. Speech to the Commonwealth Club, San Francisco, 13 June 1969.

29. Norman Podhoretz, *Breaking Ranks: A Political Memoir* (New York: Harper & Row, 1979), p. 208.

CHAPTER 3

1. Irving Howe, "New Styles in 'Leftism'," *Dissent*, Summer 1965, p. 297.

2. Cited in Paul Berman, *A Tale of Two Utopias* (New York: Norton, 1996), p. 46.

3. Tom Kahn, "The Problem of the New Left," *Commentary*, July 1966, p. 30.

4. Norman Podhoretz, *Breaking Ranks: A Political Memoir* (New York: Harper & Row: 1979), p. 200.

5. Quoted in Clark Clifford, *Counsel to the President: A Memoir* (New York: Random House, 1991), p. 417.

6. "Last Chance in Vietnam," *Dissent*, Summer 1964, p. 276. Schlesinger cited in Tom Wells, *The War Within: America's Battle Over Vietnam* (Berkeley, California: University of California Press, 1994), p. 32.

7. Wells, p. 26.

8. LeMay cited in H. R. McMaster, *Dereliction of Duty: Lyndon Johnson, Robert McNamara, the Joint Chiefs of Staff, and the Lies That Led to Vietnam* (New York: HarperCollins, 1997), p. 20.

9. *National Review*, 21 July 1972, p. 778.

10. Pentagon Papers, p. 336.

11. Larry Berman, *Planning a Tragedy: The Americanization of the War in Vietnam* (New York: W. W. Norton, 1982), p. 42.

12. McMaster, pp. 221–222.

13. Berman, p. 43.

14. Cited in McMaster, p. 187.

15. Cited in Berman, p. 45.

16. Jeffrey Record, *The Wrong War: Why We Lost in Vietnam* (Annapolis, Maryland: Naval Institute Press, 1998), p. 102.

17. Berman, p. 53.

18. James L. Greenfield, et al., *The Pentagon Papers* (Chicago: Quadrangle Books, 1971), p. 442.

19. Palmer cited in James J. Wirtz. *The Tet Offensive: Intelligence Failure in War* (Ithaca, New York: Cornell University Press, 1991), p. 28.

20. McMaster, p. 221.

21. Pentagon Papers, p. 395.

22. Cited in Mark Clodfelter, *The Limits of Air Power: The American Bombing of North Vietnam* (New York: Free Press, 1989), p. 138.

23. McMaster, p. 265.

24. Record, p. 109.

25. Berman, p. 58.

26. Berman, p. 51.

27. Clodfelter, p. 138.

28. Pentagon Papers, p. 449.

29. Berman, p. 72.

30. Robert Dallek, *Flawed Giant: Lyndon Johnson and His Times, 1961–1973* (New York: Oxford University Press, 1998), pp. 253–254.

31. Pentagon Papers, p. 443.

32. Berman, p. 57.
33. William Manchester, *The Glory and the Dream* (Boston: Little, Brown, 1973), p. 1286.
34. McMaster, p. 291.
35. John P. Roche, "The Demise of Liberal Internationalism," *National Review*, 3 May 1985, p. 32.
36. Dallek, p. 249.
37. McMaster, p. 308.
38. Mike Mansfield cited in Gareth Davies, *From Opportunity to Entitlement: The Transformation and Decline of Great Society Liberalism* (Lawrence: University Press of Kansas, 1996), p. 77.
39. Daniel Patrick Moynihan, "The President and the Negro," *Commentary*, February 1967, p. 39.
40. Todd Gitlin, *The Sixties: Years of Hope, Days of Rage* (New York: Bantam Books, 1987), p. 247.
41. Daniel Patrick Moynihan, *Maximum Feasible Misunderstanding: Community Action and the War on Poverty* (New York: The Free Press, 1969), p. 87.
42. Daniel Patrick Moynihan, "The Professors and the Poor," *Commentary*, August 1968, p. 28.
43. Moynihan, *Maximum Feasible Misunderstanding*, p. 100.
44. Ibid., p. 133.
45. Dallek, p. 331.
46. Ibid., p. 331.
47. Allen J. Matusow, *The Unraveling of America: A History of Liberalism in the 1960s* (New York: Harper & Row, 1984), p. 270.
48. Lee Rainwater and William L. Yancey, *The Moynihan Report and the Politics of Controversy* (Cambridge: MIT Press, 1967), pp. 427–428.
49. Stephan and Abigail Thernstrom, *America in Black and White: One Nation, Indivisible* (New York: Simon & Schuster, 1997), p. 172.
50. Davies, p. 83.
51. Bayard Rustin, "From Protest to Politics: The Future of the Civil Rights Movement," *Commentary*, February 1965, p. 27.
52. Rainwater and Yancey, *The Moynihan Report and the Politics of Controversy*.
53. "Interview with a Policeman Assigned to the Watts Area," *National Review*, 7 September 1965, p. 774.
54. Most of this account is from Jerry Cohen and William S. Murphy, *Burn, Baby, Burn* (New York: Dutton, 1966).
55. *National Review*, 8 August 1967, p. 837.
56. Dallek, p. 223.
57. Cohen and Murphy, pp. 83–84.

58. David O. Sears and John B. McConahay, "Riot Participation," in Nathan Cohen, editor, *The Los Angeles Riots: A Socio-Psychological Study* (New York: Praeger, 1970), pp. 259–260

59. *National Review*, 29 November 1966, p. 1199.

60. Tom Bray, "Reading America the Riot Act," *Policy Review*, Winter 1988, p. 34.

61. T. M. Tomlinson and David O. Sears, "Negro Attitudes Toward the Riot," in Nathan Cohen, ed., *The Los Angeles Riots: A Socio-Psychological Study* (New York: Praeger, 1970), pp. 288–296.

62. Fred Siegel, *The Future Once Happened Here: New York, D.C., L.A., and the Fate of America's Big Cities* (New York: The Free Press, 1997), p. 13.

63. *National Review*, 23 April 1968, p. 379.

64. Gerald Horne, *Fire This Time: The Watts Uprising and the 1960s* (Charlottesville: University of Virginia Press, 1995), p. 183.

65. *National Review*, 8 August 1967, p. 874.

66. *National Review*, 6 September 1966, p. 978.

67. Davies, p. 79.

68. Ibid., p. 96.

69. Moynihan, "The President and the Negro," pp. 40, 42.

70. Rainwater and Yancey, p. 248.

71. Davies, p. 96.

72. Ibid., p. 97.

73. Rainwater and Yancey, p. 261.

74. Thernstrom, p. 175.

75. Moynihan, "The President and the Negro," p. 44.

76. Michael L. Gillette, *Launching the War on Poverty: An Oral History* (New York: Twayne, 1996), p. 102.

77. Anne Edwards, *Early Reagan: The Rise to Power* (New York: William Morrow, 1987), p. 488.

78. Lee Edwards, *Ronald Reagan: A Political Biography* (Houston: Nordland Publishing, 1981), p. 75.

79. Rowland Evans and Robert Novak, *The Reagan Revolution* (New York: Dutton, 1981), p. 30.

80. Matthew Dallek, *The Right Moment: Ronald Reagan's First Victory and the Decisive Turning Point in American Politics* (New York: The Free Press, 2000), p. 175.

81. Bob Colacello, *Vanity Fair*, July 1998, p. 135.

82. Totten J. Anderson and Eugene C. Lee, "The 1966 Election in California," *Western Political Quarterly*, June 1967, p. 543.

83. Lee Edwards, *Ronald Reagan: A Political Biography* (Houston: Nordland Publishing, 1981), p. 89.

84. *National Review*, 5 October 1965, p. 892.

85. David Broder and Stephen Hess, *The Republican Establishment: The Present and Future of the GOP* (New York: Harper & Row, 1967), p. 268.
86. Peter Hannaford, ed., *Recollections of Reagan: A Portrait of Ronald Reagan* (New York: William Morrow, 1997), p. 35.
87. *New York Times*, 30 January 1966, p. 34.
88. *National Review*, 28 June 1966, p. 613.
89. William E. Pemberton, *Exit with Honor: The Life and Presidency of Ronald Reagan* (Armonk, New York: M. E. Sharpe, 1997), p. 69.
90. Anderson and Lee, pp. 545–546.
91. *National Review*, 23 August 1966, p. 818.

CHAPTER 4

1. John P. Roche, *Sentenced to Life* (New York: Macmillan, 1974) , p.110.
2. Larry Berman, *Lyndon Johnson's War* (New York: W. W. Norton, 1989), p. 19.
3. Guenter Lewy, *America in Vietnam* (New York: Oxford University Press, 1978), p. 73.
4. Berman, p. 21.
5. Jeffrey Record, *The Wrong War: Why We Lost in Vietnam* (Annapolis, Maryland: Naval Institute Press, 1998), p. 80.
6. Berman, p. 37.
7. Lewy, p. 59.
8. Berman, p. 43.
9. David Farber, *The Age of Great Dreams: America in the 1960s* (New York: Hill and Wang, 1994), p. 147; Farber, ed., *The Sixties: From Memory to History* (Chapel Hill, North Carolina: University of North Carolina Press, 1994). p. 93.
10. Lewy, p. 59.
11. Ibid., p. 104.
12. Record, *The Wrong War*, p. xi.
13. Lewy, p. 93.
14. Ibid., p. 105.
15. Farber, ed., *The Sixties*, p. 102.
16. Roche, *Sentenced*, p. 110.
17. Pentagon Papers, p. 523.
18. Paul Seabury and Angelo Codevilla, *War: Ends and Means* (New York: Basic Books, 1989), p. 100.
19. Pentagon Papers, p. 502.
20. Mark Clodfelter, *The Limits of Air Power: The American Bombing of North Vietnam* (New York: Free Press, 1989) p. 136.
21. Pentagon Papers, pp. 506–507.
22. Berman, p. 52.
23. "Poll Finds More Back Escalation," *New York Times*, 17 May 1967, p. 12.

24. Berman, p. 121.
25. "Gallup Finds 1 of 4 Backs A-Bomb Use," *New York Times*, 15 May 1967, p. 16.
26. *U.S. News*, 20 November 1967, p. 44.
27. Roche, *Sentenced to Life*, p. 118.
28. John P. Roche, "The Demise of Liberal Internationalism," *National Review*, 3 May 1985, p. 26.
29. Berman, p. 84.
30. Ibid., p. 16.
31. Colin Powell, with Joseph E. Persico, *My American Journey* (New York: Random House, 1995), p. 145.
32. *National Review*, 1967 edition, p. 594.
33. Record, p. 165.
34. Berman, p. 36.
35. Pentagon Papers, p. 555.
36. Berman, pp. 50–51.
37. Berman, p. 112.
38. *New York Times*, 9 May 1967, p. 24.
39. Charles Murray, *Losing Ground: American Social Policy, 1950–1980* (New York: Basic Books, 1984), p. 166; Richard K. Caputo, *Welfare and Freedom American Style II: The Role of the Federal Government, 1941-1980* (Lanham, MD: University Press of America, 1994), p. 342.
40. Daniel Patrick Moynihan, "The Professors and the Poor," *Commentary*, August 1968, p. 26.
41. Murray, p. 182.
42. Cited in Fred Siegel, *The Future Once Happened Here: New York, D.C., L.A., and the Fate of America's Big Cities* (New York: The Free Press, 1997), p. 54.
43. Siegel, p. 54.
44. Moynihan, *Losing Ground*, p. 47.
45. Richard Cloward and Frances Fox Piven, "A Strategy to End Poverty," *The Nation*, 2 May 1966, p. 510.
46. Gareth Davies, *From Opportunity to Entitlement: The Transformation and Decline of Great Society Liberalism* (Lawrence: University Press of Kansas, 1996), p. 124.
47. "Clark Says Crime Rise Is Small," *New York Times*, 19 May 1967, p. 8.
48. Paul G. Cassell, *Handcuffing the Cops: Miranda's Harmful Effects on Law Enforcement* (Dallas: National Center for Policy Analysis, 1998), p. 3.
49. *The Challenge of Crime in a Free Society*, President's Commission on Law Enforcement and the Administration of Justice, February 1967.
50. Murray, p. 117.
51. Daniel Patrick Moynihan, *Politics of a Guaranteed Income: The Nixon Administration and the Family Assistance Plan* (New York: Random House, 1974), p. 155.
52. Roche, *Sentenced to Life*, p. 43.

53. David Horowitz, *Radical Son* (New York: The Free Press, 1997), pp. 86, 107.

54. John Patrick Diggins, *Rise and Fall of the American Left* (Orlando: Harcourt, Brace, Jovanovich, 1973), p. 237.

55. Saul Landau, "Cuba: The Present Reality," *New Left Review*, No. 9 (1961), pp. 15, 18.

56. Todd Gitlin, *The Sixties: Years of Hope, Days of Rage* (New York: Bantam Books, 1987), p. 263.

57. Gitlin, p. 274.

58. Cited in Gitlin, p. 273.

59. From Alexander Bloom and Wini Breines, eds, *Takin' It to the Streets: A Sixties Reader* (Oxford University Press, 1995), pp. 127, 131.

60. Tom Wells, *The War Within: America's Battle Over Vietnam* (Berkeley, California: University of California Press, 1994), pp. 125–126.

61. Aaron Wildavsky, *Revolt Against the Masses, and Other Essays on Politics and Public Policy* (New York: Basic Books, 1971), p. 44.

62. David Farber, ed. *The Sixties: From Memory to History* (Chapel Hill, North Carolina: University of North Carolina Press, 1994), p. 215.

63. John F. Lulves, Jr., "Is There a Student Conservatism?" *National Review*, 31 May 1966, p. 530.

64. David Farber, *The Age of Great Dreams: America in the 1960s* (New York: Hill and Wang, 1994), pp. 150, 159.

65. Julius Lester, "Notes of a Journey," in John H. Bunzel, ed., *Political Passages: Journeys of Change, 1968–1988* (New York: The Free Press, 1988), p. 73.

66. Godfrey Hodgson, *America in Our Time: From World War II to Nixon—What Happened and Why* (New York: Random House, 1976), p. 221.

67. Tom Milstein, "A Perspective on the Panthers," *Commentary*, September 1970, p.35.

68. Ibid., p. 37.

69. Theodore White, *Making of the President 1972* (New York: Atheneum, 1973), p. 45.

70. *New York Times*, 28 May 1966, p. 1.

71. David Lewis, *King: A Biography* (University of Illinois Press, 1970), p. 322.

72. Lewis, p. 324.

73. Stephen Oates, *Let the Trumpet Sound: The Life and Times of Martin Luther King* (New York: Harper & Row, 1982), p. 390.

74. Ibid., p. 391.

75. *New York Times,* 8 July 1966, p. 1.

76. *National Review*, 12 December 1968, p. 1288.

77. *National Review*, 25 July 1967, p. 822.

78. Bayard Rustin, "Black Power' and Coalition Politics," *Commentary*, September 1966, p. 40.

79. Allen J. Matusow, *The Unraveling of America: A History of Liberalism in the 1960s* (New York: Harper & Row, 1984), p. 375.

80. Daniel Patrick Moynihan, "The President and the Negro," *Commentary*, January 1967, p. 42.

81. Edward Banfield, *The Unheavenly City Revisited* (Boston: Little, Brown, 1974), p. 221.

82. Jane Brody, "Black Power Linked to Sex Conflicts," *New York Times*, 13 May 1967, p. 1.

83. *National Review*, 5 September 1967, p. 944.

84. Tom Wolfe, *Radical Chic and Mau-Mauing the Flak-Catchers* (New York: Farrar, Straus and Giroux, 1970), pp. 79–80.

85. Ronald Radosh, *Divided They Fell: The Demise of the Democratic Party, 1964–1996* (New York: The Free Press, 1996), p. 41.

86. Jeffrey L. Hodes, "New Left in Disarray," *The New Leader*, 11 September 1967, pp. 6–8.

87. Radosh, pp. 48–49.

88. *Time*, 4 August 1967, p. 17.

89. *Time*, 21 July 1967, p. 16.

90. Joseph A. Califano, Jr., *The Triumph & Tragedy of Lyndon Johnson* (New York: Simon & Schuster, 1991), p. 219.

91. Daniel Patrick Moynihan, *A Dangerous Place* (Boston: Little, Brown, 1978), p. 4.

92. Tom Bray, "Reading America the Riot Act," *Policy Review*, Winter 1988, p. 34.

93. Siegel, *The Future Once Happened Here*, p. 3.

94. Banfield, p. 228.

95. Bray, p. 33.

96. *National Review*, 23 August 1966, p. 820.

97. *National Review*, 13 August 1968, p. 790.

98. Banfield, pp. 225–226.

99. *The Public Interest*, Summer 1973, p. 6.

100. "The Politics of Stability," *The New Leader*, 9 October 1967, p. 6.

101. *Time*, 6 January 1996, p. 23.

102. Joan Didion, *Slouching Toward Bethlehem* (New York: Farrar, Straus and Giroux, 1968), pp. 121–122.

103. Quoted in J. P. Diggins, *The Rise and Fall of the American Left* (New York: Norton, 1992), p. 242.

104. Daniel Patrick Moynihan, "Nirvana Now," *Coping: Essays on the Practice of Government* (New York: Random House, 1973), p. 125.

105. Ibid., p. 120.

106. Will Herberg, "Who Are the Hippies?" *National Review*, 8 August 1967, p. 845.

107. Hunter S. Thompson, *Fear and Loathing in Las Vegas* (New York: Random House, 1972), p. 68.

108. Horowitz, *Radical Son*, p. 176; Allen J. Matusow, *The Unraveling of America: A History of Liberalism in the 1960s* (New York: Harper & Row, 1984) p. 300.

109. *Time*, 7 July 1967, p. 21

110. *National Review*, 8 August 1967, p. 872.

111. *Newsweek*, 9 May 1966, p. 62.

112. *Time*, 7 July 1967, p. 22.

113. *Time*, 7 April 1967, p. 78.

114. *Time,* 9 May 1966, p. 60.

115. Michael Medved, *Hollywood Versus America* (New York: HarperCollins, 1992) p. 282.

116. Peter Biskind, *Easy Riders, Raging Bulls: How the Sex-Drugs-and-Rock 'N' Roll Generation Saved Hollywood* (New York: Simon & Schuster, 1998), p. 15.

117. Biskind, pp. 39, 40.

118. Biskind, p. 48.

119. *New York Times*, 9 January 1968.

120. Medved, p. 282.

121. "The Politics of Stability," *The New Leader*, 9 October 1967; Moynihan, *Coping*, p. 22.

122. Edward Shills, "Totalitarians and Antinomians," in John Bunzel, ed., *Political Passages* (New York: Free Press, 1988), p. 31.

123. Andrew Kopkind, "Waiting for Lefty," *New York Review of Books*, 1 June 1967, p. 3.

124. John P. Roche, "The Second Coming of R.F.K.," *National Review*, 22 July 1988, p. 34.

125. Michael Knox Beran, *The Last Patrician: Bobby Kennedy and the End of American Aristocracy* (New York: St. Martin's Press, 1998), pp. 103, 106.

126. Gladwin Hill, "Reagan Derides Kennedy Stands," *New York Times*, 21 May 1968, p. 28.

127. Beran, p. 105.

128. Richard P. Nathan, *The Plot That Failed: Nixon and the Administrative Presidency* (New York: Wiley, 1975), p. 15; *New York Times*, 28 March 1968.

129. Beran, p. 259.

130. Quotes from Jack Newfield, *Robert Kennedy: A Memoir* (New York: Putnam, 1969), pp. 97–98.

131. Douglas Schoen, *Pat: A Biography of Daniel Patrick Moynihan* (New York: Harper & Row, 1979), p. 141.

132. Newfield, p. 103.

133. White, p. 158–159.

134. *Newsweek*, 22 May 1967, p. 27.

135. Lou Cannon, *Ronnie and Jesse: A Political Odyssey* (Garden City, New York: Doubleday, 1969), p. 135.

136. Cannon, *Ronnie and Jesse*, p. 153.

137. Julius Duscha, "Not Great, Not Brilliant, But a Good Show," *New York Times Magazine*, 10 December 1967, p. 128.

138. *Time*, 11 August 1967, p. 17.

139. Cannon, *Ronnie and Jesse*, p. 182.

140. Statement, 11 March 1976, Deaver-Hannaford Papers, Hoover Institution, Box 13.

141. Cannon, *Ronnie and Jesse*, p. 140.

142. *Newsweek*, 22 May 1967, p. 30

143. Duscha, p. 29.

144. Wicker, "Reagan's Role in '68," *New York Times*, 8 July 1966, p. 13.

145. *Time*, 14 April 1967, p. 31.

146. "What About Ronald Reagan," *CBS Reports*, transcript, 12 December 1967, p. 18.

147. Lou Cannon, *Reagan* (New York: G. P. Putnam's Sons, 1982), p. 159.

148. Cited in Cannon, *Reagan*, p. 158.

149. *U.S. News and World Report*, 24 July 1967, p. 53.

150. *National Review*, 21 March 1967, p. 285.

151. *Time*, 20 October 1967, p. 18.

152. *National Review*, 26 December 1967, p. 1415.

153. "Town Meeting of the World" transcript, Ronald Reagan Collection, Press Unit, Box 59, Hoover Institution.

154. Beran, p. 150.

155. *Newsweek*, 29 May 1967, pp. 30–31.

156. Jules Witcover and Richard M. Cohen, "Where's the Rest of Ronald Reagan?" *Esquire*, March 1976, p.153.

157. Andrew Gilder, "Reviving Republican Liberalism," *The New Leader*, 24 October 1966, p. 5.

158. *New York Times*, 10 December 1967.

CHAPTER 5

1. *Time*, 5 January 1968.

2. John Kenneth Galbraith, "An Agenda . . .", *Commentary*, June 1966, p. 30.

3. *U.S. News and World Report*, 23 October 1967, p. 34.

4. Lewis Chester, Godfrey Hodgson, and Bruce Page. *An American Melodrama: The Presidential Campaign of 1968* (New York: The Viking Press, 1969), p. 183.

5. *National Review*, 12 December 1967, p. 1382.

6. *The New Leader*, 25 September 1967, p. 3.

7. Jonathan Aitken, *Nixon: A Life* (Washington, D.C.: Regnery, 1993), p. 307.

8. Ibid., p. 309.

9. Ibid., p. 330.

10. *U.S. News*, 8 January 1968, p. 21.

11. James J. Wirtz, *The Tet Offensive: Intelligence Failure in War* (Ithaca, New York: Cornell University Press, 1991), p. 74.

12. Larry Berman, *Lyndon Johnson's War* (New York: W. W. Norton, 1989), p. 181.

13. *Time*, 2 February 1968, p. 11.

14. "Defector Confirms Suspicions Moscow Plotted Pueblo Seizure," *Combat* (a *National Review* publication) Vol. 1, No. 21 (1 July 1969), p. 2.

15. Guenter Lewy, *America in Vietnam* (New York: Oxford University Press, 1978), p. 434.

16. William McGurn, "Vietnam Through a Lens Darkly," *Wall Street Journal*, 27 April 2000, p. A26.

17. Peter Braestrup, *Big Story: How the American Press and Television Reported and Interpreted the Crisis of Tet 1968 in Vietnam and Washington* (Boulder, Colorado: Westview, 1977), p. 508.

18. Ibid., p. 92.

19. Robert Elegant, "How To Lose a War," *Encounter*, August 1981, p. 73.

20. Cited in Berman, p. 151.

21. Colin Powell, with Joseph E. Persico, *My American Journey* (New York: Random House, 1995), p. 123.

22. Charles Kaiser, *1968 in America: Music, Politics, Chaos, Counterculture, and the Shaping of a Generation* (New York: Grove Press, 1988), p. 77.

23. Braestrup, p. 493.

24. Ibid., p. 509.

25. William Westmoreland, *A Soldier Reports* (New York: Doubleday, 1976), p. 352.

26. Ibid., p. 355.

27. Lewy, p. 160.

28. Jeffrey Record, *The Wrong War: Why We Lost in Vietnam* (Annapolis, Maryland: Naval Institute Press, 1998), p. 97.

29. Kaiser, p. 103.

30. Braestrup, p. 506.

31. Kaiser, p. 88.

32. Douglas Schoen, *Pat*, p.168.

33. Robert M. Collins, "The Economic Crisis of 1968 and the Waning of the 'American Century,'" *American Historical Review*, April 1996, p. 396.

34. Matusow, *The Unraveling of America*, p. 166.

35. David Halberstam, *The Best and the Brightest* (New York: Random House, 1969), p. 610.

36. *U.S. News and World Report*, 30 October 1967, p. 52.

37. Collins, p. 403.

38. *Economic Report of the President*, February 1968, p. 119.

39. *National Review*, 26 March 1968, p. 274.

40. Collins, p. 415.

41. Ibid., p. 417.

42. Joseph A. Califano, Jr., *The Triumph & Tragedy of Lyndon Johnson* (New York: Simon & Schuster, 1991), p. 260.

43. George Berkeley, "The Myth of War Profiteering," *The New Republic*, 20 December 1969, p. 15.

44. Jules Witcover, *Marathon: The Pursuit of the Presidency, 1972–1976* (New York: Viking, 1977), p. 160.

45. *National Review*, 23 April 1968, p. 376.

46. Ibid.

47. Witcover, pp. 165–166.

48. Robert Friedman, *Up Against the Ivy Wall: A History of the Crisis at Columbia* (New York: Atheneum, 1969), p. 25.

49. Friedman, *Up Against the Ivy Wall*, p. 294.

50. Kaiser, p. 154.

51. Friedman, *Up Against the Ivy Wall*, p. 287.

52. Diana Trilling, "On the Steps of Low Library: Liberalism and the Revolution of the Young," *Commentary*, August 1968, p. 49.

53. Friedman, *Up Against the Ivy Wall*, p. 290.

54. *U.S. News and World Report*, 11 September 1967, p. 38.

55. *National Review*, 1967 volume, p. 640.

56. Cannon, *Ronnie and Jesse*, p. 264.

57. Chester, *An American Melodrama*, p. 438.

58. Richard Nixon, *The Memoirs of Richard Nixon* (New York: Simon & Schuster, 1978), p. 309.

59. Chester, *An American Melodrama*, p. 437.

60. Ibid., p. 466.

61. Cannon, *Reagan*, pp. 164–165.

62. Chester, *An American Melodrama*, p. 493.

63. William F. Buckley, Jr., "On the Right" Column, 22 October 1968.

64. Chester, *An American Melodrama*, p. 402.

65. William F. Buckley Jr., *The Governor Listeth* (New York: G.P. Putnam's Sons, 1969), pp. 79–80.

66. Ibid., pp. 88–89.

67. Todd Gitlin, *The Sixties: Years of Hope, Days of Rage* (New York: Bantam Books, 1987), p. 311.

68. Terry H. Anderson, *The Movement and the Sixties: Protest in America from Greensboro to Wounded Knee* (New York: Oxford University Press, 1995), p. 201.

69. *The New Leader*, 25 March 1968, p. 4.

70. Aitken, p. 350.

71. *National Review*, 27 February 1968, p. 208.

72. Chester, *An American Melodrama*, p. 406.
73. Ronald Radosh, *Divided They Fell: The Demise of the Democratic Party, 1964–1996* (New York: The Free Press, 1996), p. 121.
74. Cited in *National Review*, 24 September 1968, p. 959.
75. David Farber, *Chicago '68* (Chicago: University of Chicago Press, 1988), p. 39.
76. Ibid., p. 94.
77. Gitlin, p. 289.
78. Farber, *Chicago '68*, p. 255.
79. Tom Wells, *The War Within: America's Battle Over Vietnam* (Berkeley, California: University of California Press, 1994), p. 283.
80. Anderson, p. 225.
81. Matusow, p. 423; Farber, *Chicago '68*, p. 206.
82. Radosh, p. 126.
83. Ibid., p. 139.
84. Ibid., p. 137.
85. *National Review*, 28 April 1972, pp. 450–451.
86. McGinniss, *The Selling of the President* (New York: Trident Press, 1969), p. 138.
87. Cannon, *Ronnie and Jesse*, p. 261.
88. Witcover, p. 489.
89. Chester, *An American Melodrama*, p. 231.

CHAPTER 6

1. *The Haldeman Diaries* (New York: G. P. Putnam, 1994), pp. 23–24.
2. Henry Kissinger, *Years of Renewal* (New York: Simon & Schuster, 1999), pp. 43, 44.
3. Milton Friedman and Rose Friedman, *Two Lucky People: Memoirs* (Chicago: University of Chicago Press, 1998), pp. 375, 387.
4. Kissinger, *Years of Renewal*, p. 43.
5. White, *Making of the President 1972*, p. 351.
6. Jonathan Aitken, *Nixon: A Life* (Washington, D.C.: Regnery, 1993), p. 371.
7. Paul Johnson, "In Praise of Richard Nixon," *Commentary*, October 1988, p. 52.
8. Daniel Patrick Moynihan, *Coping: Essays on the Practice of Government* (New York: Random House, 1973), p. 35; *Politics of a Guaranteed Income*, p. 67.
9. Michael Barone, *Our Country: The Shaping of America from Roosevelt to Reagan* (New York: The Free Press, 1990), p. 463.
10. Cited in James Reichley, *Conservatives in an Age of Change* (Washington, D.C.: Brookings Institution, 1981), p. 229.
11. White, *Making of the President 1972*, p. 78.
12. Robert Blake, *Disraeli* (New York: St. Martin's Press, 1967), p. 759.
13. Rowland Evans, Jr. and Robert Novak, *Nixon in the White House: The Frustration of Power* (New York: Random House, 1971), p. 213.

14. White, *The Making of the President 1968*, p. 170.
15. Herbert Stein, *Presidential Economics* (New York: Simon & Schuster, 1984), p. 139.
16. Daniel Patrick Moynihan, *The Politics of a Guaranteed Income: The Nixon Administration and the Family Assistance Plan* (New York: Random House, 1974), p. 159.
17. Daniel Patrick Moynihan, *A Dangerous Place* (Boston: Little, Brown, 1978), p. 6.
18. Gareth Davies, *From Opportunity to Entitlement: The Transformation and Decline of Great Society Liberalism* (Lawrence: University Press of Kansas, 1996), p. 217.
19. Richard Nixon, *Public Papers*, I (1969), p. 695.
20. Richard Nixon, *RN: The Memoirs of Richard Nixon* (New York: Simon & Schuster, 1978), p. 424.
21. Evans and Novak, p. 224.
22. Vincent J. Burke and Vee Burke, *Nixon's Good Deed: Welfare Reform* (Columbia University Press, 1974), p. 1.
23. *U.S. News and World Report*, 5 May 1969, p. 32.
24. Moynihan, *Politics*, pp. 81–82.
25. *U.S. News and World Report*, 3 February 1969, p. 54.
26. Moynihan, *Politics*, p. 131.
27. *National Review*, 29 September 1978, p. 1196.
28. Moynihan, *Politics*, p. 201.
29. John Osborne, "The Welfare Story—Plot and Subplot," *The New Republic*, 8 November 1969, p. 17.
30. Richard P. Nathan, *The Plot That Failed: Nixon and the Administrative Presidency* (New York: Wiley, 1975), p. 18.
31. Nixon, *Memoirs*, p. 427.
32. Davies, p. 225.
33. Burke and Burke, p. 162.
34. Hobbs, "How Ronald Reagan Governed California," *National Review*, 17 January 1975, pp. 37–38.
35. Transcript, "The Advocates," PBS Television, 1 December 1970, p. 11.
36. *National Review*, 19 December 1975, p. 1469.
37. Benson to Reagan, 1 May 1970 (Correspondence Unit, Federal Issues/1970, Box 725, Reagan Papers, Hoover Institution).
38. Reagan to Nixon, 29 April 1970 (Correspondence Unit, Federal Issues/1970, Box 725, Reagan Papers, Hoover Institution).
39. Bush to Reagan, 11 June 1970 (Correspondence Unit, Federal Issues/1970, Box 725, Reagan Papers, Hoover Institution).
40. William E. Pemberton, *Exit with Honor: The Life and Presidency of Ronald Reagan* (Armonk, New York: M. E. Sharpe, 1997), p. 79.
41. Ibid., p. 79.

42. Lou Cannon, *Reagan* (New York: G. P. Putnam's Sons, 1982), p. 181.
43. Bill Boyarski, *Ronald Reagan: His Life and Rise to the Presidency* (Random House, 1981), p.136.
44. Ibid., p. 138.
45. *New York Times*, 6 February 1969, p. 19.
46. Testimony to the Senate Public Works Committee, 5 February 1969.
47. Ross MacDonald and Robert Easton, "Thou Shalt Not Abuse the Earth," *New York Times Magazine*, 12 October 1969.
48. *Time*, 13 June 1969, p. 21.
49. Dale Straughan, ed., *Biological and Oceanographical Survey of the Santa Barbara Channel Oil Spill 1969–1970, Volume 1, Biology and Bacteriology* (Alan Hancock Foundation, University of Southern California, 1971), p. 417.
50. *Newsweek*, 24 February 1969, p. 37.
51. MacDonald and Easton.
52. R. Robert Lichter and Stanley Rothman, *Environmental Cancer—A Political Disease?* (New Haven: Yale University Press, 1999), p. 9.
53. Peter N. Carroll, *It Seemed Like Nothing Happened: America in the 1970s* (New York: Holt, Rinehart and Winston, 1982), p. 125.
54. James Ridgeway, *The Politics of Ecology* (New York: Dutton, 1970), p. 13.
55. *Time*, 4 May 1970, p. 16.
56. Nicholas King, "Do We Want Environment?" *National Review*, 2 June 1970, pp. 557–558.
57. Ronald Reagan, "Our Environmental Crisis," *Nation's Business*, February 1970, p. 25.
58. Pemberton, pp. 78–79.
59. Lee Edwards, *Ronald Reagan: A Political Biography* (Houston: Nordland Publishing, 1981), p. 172.
60. Norman Podhoretz, "Reflections on Earth Day," *Commentary*, June 1970, p. 26.
61. *Time*, 3 August 1970, p. 42.
62. *The New Republic*, 7 March 1999, pp. 8–9.
63. Amitai Etzioni, "The Wrong Top Priority," *Science*, 22 May 1970.
64. *Time*, 3 August 1970, p. 42.
65. Cited in Christopher Foreman, Jr., *The Promise and Peril of Environmental Justice* (Washington, D.C.: Brookings Institution, 1998), p. 15.
66. Joan Hoff, *Nixon Reconsidered* (New York: Basic Books, 1994), p. 23.
67. *National Review*, 3 August 1973, pp. 818–819.
68. Stein, *Presidential Economics*, p. 190.
69. James Reichley, *Conservatives in an Age of Change* (Washington, D.C.: Brookings Institution, 1981), p. 206.
70. *Time*, 9 August 1971, p. 15.
71. Reichley, p. 215.

72. Henry Kissinger, *The White House Years* (Boston: Little, Brown, 1979), p. 951.

73. Stein, p. 162.

74. Evans and Novak, *Nixon in the White House*, p. 372.

75. Allen J. Matusow, *Nixon's Economy: Booms, Busts, Dollars & Votes* (Lawrence: University Press of Kansas, 1998), p. 115.

76. *Time*, 30 August 1971, p. 34.

77. *Newsweek*, 30 August 1971, p. 22.

78. Stein, p. 180.

79. *Newsweek*, 30 August 1971, p. 9.

80. *National Review*, 31 December 1971, p. 1452.

81. Nixon, *Memoirs*, p. 521.

82. Matusow, *Nixon's Economy*, p. 266.

83. Adam Ulam, *Expansion and Coexistence: Soviet Foreign Policy 1917–1973* (New York: Praeger, 1974), p. 695.

84. Hearings before the Subcommittee on Priorities and Economy in Government, Joint Economic Committee, Part 2, 24 May–15 June 1976, p. 68.

85. Kissinger, *White House Years*, pp. 65, 120.

86. Ibid., p. 191.

87. William F. Buckley Jr., *Inveighing We Will Go* (New York: G.P. Putnam's Sons, 1972), p. 19.

88. *National Review*, 2 March 1979, p. 290.

89. James C. Thomson, Jr., "Nixon to China: Time to Talk," *Atlantic Monthly*, February 1969, p. 71.

90. Richard Nixon, "Asia After Vietnam," *Foreign Affairs*, October 1967.

91. Aitken, p. 425; James Mann, *About Face: A History of America's Curious Relationship with China, From Nixon to Clinton* (New York: Alfred A. Knopf, 1999), p. 19.

92. Kissinger, *White House Years*, p. 177.

93. Mann, p. 20.

94. Kissinger, *White House Years*, pp. 745, 746.

95. *Time*, 3 January 1972, p.15.

96. Nguyen Tien Hung and Jerrold Schecter, *The Palace File* (New York: Harper & Row, 1986), p. 10.

97. Kissinger, *White House Years*, p. 766.

98. Mann, p. 38.

99. William F. Buckley, "Nixon's Long March to China," *Inveighing We Will Go* (New York: G. P. Putnam's Sons, 1972), p. 89.

100. Ibid., pp. 95, 96.

101. "A Hard Look at Nixon's Performance," *Human Events*, 17 July 1971, p. 1.

102. 24 November 1972, p. 1287.

103. *National Review*, 9 June 1972, p. 616.

104. *Time*, 3 January 1972.

CHAPTER 7

1. Henry Kissinger, *Years of Renewal* (New York: Simon & Schuster, 1999), p. 30.
2. Ibid., p. 34.
3. Ibid., p. 55.
4. *Newsweek*, 2 November 1970, p. 28.
5. Daniel Patrick Moynihan, "Peace: Some Thoughts on the 1960's and 1970's," *The Public Interest*, Summer 1973, p. 5.
6. Ben Wattenberg, *The Real America: A Challenge to the Chaos of Failure and Guilt* (New York: Doubleday, 1974), p. 258.
7. Ibid., p. 19.
8. Edmund Stillman, "America After Vietnam," *Commentary*, October 1971, p. 47.
9. Wattenberg, p. 14.
10. Ibid., pp. 15, 16.
11. *Facts on File*, 1969, pp. 466, 472.
12. See Jonathan Aitken, *Nixon: A Life* (Washington, D.C.: Regnery, 1993), p. 352.
13. Cited in Lewis Sorley, *A Better War: The Unexamined Victories and Final Tragedy of America's Last Years in Vietnam* (Orlando: Harcourt, Brace, 1999), p. 107.
14. Ibid., p. 17.
15. Shoup, "The New American Militarism," *The Atlantic*, April 1969, p. 51.
16. Guenter Lewy, *America in Vietnam* (New York: Oxford University Press, 1978), p. 195.
17. Richard A. Gabriel, *Military Incompetence: Why the American Military Doesn't Win* (New York: Hill & Wang, 1985), pp. 35–60.
18. Stanley I. Kutler, *The Wars of Watergate: The Last Crisis of Richard Nixon* (New York: W. W. Norton, 1990). p. 499.
19. *National Review*, 29 September 1972, p. 1054.
20. Lewy, pp. 322–324.
21. Ibid., p. 325.
22. Ibid., pp. 451, 304.
23. Hannah Arendt, *Crises of the Republic* (New York: Harcourt, Brace, 1972), p. 4.
24. Tom Wells, *The War Within: America's Battle Over Vietnam* (Berkeley, California: University of California Press, 1994), p. 299.
25. Stephen Young, "How North Vietnam Won the War," *Wall Street Journal*, 3 August 1995.
26. Lewy, p. 335.
27. Cited in Norman Podhoretz, *Why We Were in Vietnam* (New York: Simon & Schuster, 1982), p. 91.
28. Joseph Epstein, "Intellectuals—Public and Otherwise," *Commentary*, May 2000, p. 49.
29. Lewy, pp. 334–342.

30. Peter N. Carroll, *It Seemed Like Nothing Happened: America in the 1970s* (New York: Holt, Rinehart and Winston, 1982), p. 96.

31. Paul Berman, *A Tale of Two Utopias: The Political Journey of the Generation of 1968* (New York: W. W. Norton, 1996), p. 88.

32. Todd Gitlin, *The Sixties: Years of Hope, Days of Rage* (New York: Bantam Books, 1987), p. 345.

33. John Searle, "A Foolproof Scenario for Student Revolts," *New York Times Magazine*, 29 December 1968, p. 4.

34. *Time*, 9 May 1969, p. 10.

35. "Thunder Left and Right," *The Washington Star*, 14 June 1969.

36. *U.S. News and World Report*, 19 May 1969, p. 34.

37. *Time*, 27 April 1970, p. 21.

38. Norman Podhoretz, "The New Hypocracies," *Commentary*, December 1970, p. 5.

39. Citizens for Reagan Papers, Box 50, accession number: 81141-211.03/215.04, Hoover Institution, Stanford University.

40. Diana Furchtgott-Roth and Christina Stolba, *Women's Figures: An Illustrated Guide to Economic Progress of Women in America* (Washington, D.C.: American Enterprise Institute, 1999), p. xvii.

41. Sylvia Ann Hewlett, *A Lesser Life: The Myth of Women's Liberation in America* (New York: William Morrow, 1986), p. 211.

42. Paul Berman, *A Tale of Two Utopias*, p. 149.

43. Peter Biskind, *Easy Riders, Raging Bulls: How the Sex-Drugs-and-Rock 'N' Roll Generation Saved Hollywood* (Simon & Schuster, 1998), p. 75.

44. Mason Wiley and Damien Bona, *Inside Oscar* (New York: Ballantine Books, 1987), p. 431.

45. Alex McNeil, *Total Television* (New York: Penguin, 1996), p. 26.

46. Carroll, p. 62.

47. Stephan and Abigail Thernstrom, *America in Black and White: One Nation, Indivisible* (New York: Simon & Schuster, 1997), p. 289.

48. *Time*, 27 April 1970, p. 19.

49. George Will, *Newsweek*, 27 September 1999, p. 76.

50. *Newsweek*, 25 August 1969, p. 88.

51. *Time*, 29 August 1969, pp. 32–33.

52. Maurice Isserman and Michael Kazin, *America Divided: The Civil War of the 1960s* (New York: Oxford University Press, 2000), p. 161.

53. Andrew Kopkind, "Coming of Age in Aquarius: Woodstock Bash," *Hard Times*, 25 August–1 September 1969.

54. Philip P. Ardery, Jr., "Upon a Time in Woodstock," *National Review*, 9 September 1969.

55. William F. Buckley, Jr., ed. *Odyssey of a Friend: Whittaker Chambers Letters to William F. Buckley, Jr., 1954–1961* (New York: G. P. Putnam's Sons, 1969), p. 285.

56. Speech before the Independent Colleges of Southern California, 23 May 1969.

57. Testimony before Subcommittee on Education of the Committee on Education and Labor of the U.S. House of Representatives, Washington, D.C., 19 March 1969.

58. John Searle, "A Foolproof Scenario for Student Revolts," *New York Times Magazine*, 29 December 1968, p. 15.

59. *Time*, 31 May 1971, p. 15.

60. Peter G. Bourne, *Jimmy Carter* (New York: Scribner, 1997), p. 201.

61. Cited in Kenneth E. Morris, *Jimmy Carter: American Moralist* (University of Georgia Press, 1996), p. 189.

62. *Newsweek*, 2 November 1970, p. 31.

63. *Newsweek*, 20 December 1971, p. 29.

CHAPTER 8

1. Henry Kissinger, *Years of Renewal* (New York: Simon & Schuster, 1999), p. 60.

2. Theodore White, *Making of the President 1972* (New York: Atheneum, 1973), pp. 250, 390.

3. Stanley I. Kutler, *The Wars of Watergate: The Last Crisis of Richard Nixon* (New York: W. W. Norton, 1990), p. 190.

4. Joan Hoff, *Nixon Reconsidered.* (New York: Basic Books, 1994), p. 311.

5. A. James Reichley, "The Time Bomb Inside the Democratic Party," *Fortune*, February 1972, p. 126.

6. *National Review*, 9 February 1972, p. 76.

7. White, p. 99.

8. *National Review*, 3 March 1972, p. 190.

9. *National Review*, 1 September 1972, p. 928.

10. White, p. 103.

11. Joseph Kraft, "The Muskie Problem," *The Atlantic Monthly*, June 1971, p. 6.

12. *National Review*, 18 February 1972, p. 147.

13. George McGovern, *Grassroots* (New York: Random House, 1977), p. 41.

14. *Time*, 26 June 1972, p. 17.

15. *National Review*, 28 April 1972, p. 451; Kraft, p. 8.

16. *National Review*, 26 October 1973, p. 1150.

17. White, p. 56.

18. *National Review*, 31 March 1972, p. 310.

19. Ibid., p. 318.

20. White, p. 152.

21. *Time*, 26 June 1972, p. 18.

22. Michael Barone, *Our Country: The Shaping of America from Roosevelt to Reagan* (New York: The Free Press, 1990), p. 503.

23. "Vietnam Napalm Victim Named UNECSO Envoy," *Washington Times*, 11 November 1997, p. A–7.

24. White, p. 314.

25. *National Review*, 18 August 1972, p. 876.

26. Richard Nixon, *The Memoirs of Richard Nixon* (New York: Simon & Schuster, 1978) p. 591.

27. White, p. 313.

28. Henry Kissinger, *The White House Years* (Boston: Little, Brown, 1979), p. 1200.

29. *National Review*, 26 May 1972, p. 567.

30. *National Review*, 9 June 1972, p. 627.

31. *Time*, 26 June 1972, p. 19.

32. *National Review*, 31 July 1972, p. 784.

33. *Time*, 24 July 1972, p. 25.

34. Michael Oakeshott, "On Being Conservative," *Rationalism in Politics and Other Essays* (Indianapolis: Liberty Fund, 1991 [originally published, 1962]), p. 436.

35. *National Review*, 27 October 1972, p. 1179.

36. *National Review*, 4 August 1972, p. 824.

37. Penn Kemble and Josh Muravchik, "The New Politics and the Democrats," *Commentary*, December 1972, p. 83.

38. *National Review*, 4 August 1972, p. 824; Lewis Feuer, *National Review*, 27 October 1972, p. 1178.

39. White, p. 213.

40. Ben Wattenberg, *The Real America: A Challenge to the Chaos of Failure and Guilt* (New York: Doubleday, 1974), p. 22.

41. Feuer, p. 1179.

42. Ronald Radosh, *Divided They Fell: The Demise of the Democratic Party, 1964–1996* (New York: The Free Press, 1996), p. 184.

43. Kemble and Muravchik, p. 84.

44. White, p. 240.

45. Kutler, p. 195.

46. A. James Reichley, "The McGovern Wave Is No Passing Ripple," *Fortune*, September 1972, p. 116.

47. *Time*, 26 June 1972, p. 19.

48. *National Review*, 19 January 1973, p. 70.

49. White, p. 291.

50. Ibid., p. 321.

51. *National Review*, 1 September 1972, p. 928.

52. *National Review*, 24 November 1972, p. 1284.

53. David Maraniss, *First in His Class: The Biography of Bill Clinton* (New York: Simon & Schuster, 1995), pp. 280–284.

54. Norman Podhoretz, "What the Voters Saw," *Commentary*, January 1973, p. 6.

55. *National Review*, 24 November 1972, p. 1287.

56. Henry Kissinger, *Years of Upheaval* (Boston: Little, Brown, 1982), p. 1209.

57. White, p. 61.

58. Ibid., p. 402.

59. Ibid., p. 475.

60. Richard P. Nathan, *The Plot That Failed: Nixon and the Administrative Presidency* (New York: Wiley, 1975), p. vii.

61. Nixon, *Memoirs*, p. 717.

62. Nathan, p. 83.

63. Nathan, p. 69.

64. *Commentary*, February 1974, p. 77.

65. *National Review*, 16 February 1973, p. 192.

66. Cited in Nathan, p. 87.

67. Nixon, *Memoirs*, p. 768.

68. Ibid., p. 761.

69. Ibid., p. 761.

70. Kutler, p. 135.

71. Kissinger, *White House Years*, pp. 1393, 1375.

72. Nixon, *Memoirs*, p. 732.

73. Ibid., p. 731.

74. Martin F. Herz, *The Prestige Press and the Christmas Bombing, 1972* (Washington, D.C.: Ethics and Public Policy Center, 1980), p. 29.

75. Guenter Lewy, *America in Vietnam* (New York: Oxford University Press, 1978), p. 413.

76. Herz, p. 58.

77. Lewy, p. 414.

78. Cited in Earl H. Tilford, *Setup: What the Air Force Did in Vietnam and Why* (Alabama: Air University Press, 1991), p. 290.

79. James B. Stockdale, *A Vietnam Experience: Ten Years of Reflection* (Palo Alto: Hoover Institution, 1984), pp. 146–147

80. Nixon, *Memoirs*, p. 770.

81. Norman Podhoretz, "Making the World Safe for Communism," *Commentary*, April 1976, p. 34.

82. U.S. Congress, Senate Conference Committee, *Conference Report to Accompany S. 1541* (12 June 1974) S. Rept. 93–924, p. 49.

83. Margaret N. Davis, "The Congressional Budget Mess," in Gordon S. Jones and John A. Marini, eds., *The Imperial Congress: Crisis in the Separation of Powers* (New York: Pharos Books, 1988) pp. 161–162.

84. Kutler, p. 236.

85. Hoff, p. 301.

86. Kutler, p. 137.

87. See Jonathan Aitken, *Nixon: A Life* (Washington, D.C.: Regnery, 1993), p. 541.

88. Nixon, *Memoirs*, p. 764.

89. *National Review*, 31 January 1975, p. 78.

90. *National Review*, 18 July 1975, p. 748.

91. Jones and Marini, p. 207.

92. Lee Edwards, *Ronald Reagan: A Political Biography* (Houston: Nordland Publishing, 1981), p. 161.

93. *Baltimore Sun*, 16 November 1975.

94. Lou Cannon, *Reagan* (New York: G. P. Putnam's Sons, 1982), p. 191.

95. Deaver-Hannaford Papers, Hoover Institution, Box 1.

96. "Building a National Organization," memo, Deaver-Hannaford Papers, Hoover Institution, Box 1.

97. Reagan, "Reflections on the Failure of Proposition #1," *National Review*, 7 December 1973, p. 1358.

CHAPTER 9

1. John Robert Greene, *The Presidency of Gerald R. Ford* (Lawrence: University Press of Kansas, 1995), p. 30.

2. Jules Witcover, *Marathon: The Pursuit of the Presidency, 1972–1976* (New York: Viking, 1977), p. 504; Herbert S. Parmet, *George Bush: The Life of a Lone-Star Yankee* (New York: Scribner, 1997), p. 168.

3. Parmet, p. 172.

4. Greene, pp. 30–31.

5. Parmet, p. 168.

6. William Safire, "On Closing Hurley's Bar," *New York Times*, 16 October 1975.

7. Lou Cannon, *Reagan* (New York: G. P. Putnam's Sons, 1982), p. 193.

8. Henry Kissinger, *Years of Renewal* (New York: Simon & Schuster, 1999), p. 25.

9. George F. Will, *The Pursuit of Happiness and Other Sobering Thoughts* (New York: Harper & Row, 1978), p. 165.

10. Kissinger, *Years of Renewal*, p. 464.

11. See Guenter Lewy, *America in Vietnam* (New York: Oxford University Press, 1978), p. 221.

12. Ibid., pp. 202–203.

13. Ibid., p. 208.

14. Ibid., p. 210.

15. *National Review*, 25 April 1975, p.428.

16. Kissinger, *Years of Renewal*, p. 531.

17. *U.S. News and World Report*, 19 April 1999, p. 44.

18. *National Review*, 20 June 1975, p.653.

19. Kissinger, *Years of Renewal*, p. 546.

20. Ibid., p. 515.

21. *New York Times*, 13 March 1975 [cf. *National Review*, 11 April 1975, p. 383.]

22. Peter Rodman, "Sideswipe: Kissinger, Shawcross, and the Responsibility for Cambodia," *The American Spectator*, March 1981, p. 15.

23. Jean-Louis Margolin, "Cambodia: The County of Disconcerting Crimes," *The Black Book of Communism: Crimes, Terror, Repression* (Harvard University Press, 1999), p. 611.

24. Ibid., pp. 588–591.

25. Margolin, "Vietnam and Laos: The Impasse of War Communism," *Black Book*, p. 572.

26. Shawcross, "Shrugging Off Genocide," *The Times* [London], 16 December 1994.

27. Stephanie Groueff, "The Nation as Concentration Camp," *National Review*, 2 September 1977, p. 990.

28. Margolin, *Black Book*, p. 624.

29. Jim Wallis, "Compassion, Not Politics, for Refugees," *Sojourners*, September 1979.

30. Charles Horner, "Who Won Vietnam?" *Commentary*, May 1994, pp. 40–43.

31. *National Review*, 25 May 1975, p. 541.

32. Daniel Patrick Moynihan, *A Dangerous Place* (Boston: Little, Brown, 1978), pp. 298–299.

33. "The Fading of America," *The Economist*, 5 April 1975, p. 12.

34. *National Review*, 11 April 1975, p. 374.

35. Daniel Patrick Moynihan, "The American Experiment," *The Public Interest*, Fall 1975, pp. 5, 6.

36. Kissinger, *Years of Renewal*, pp. 831, 832.

37. Richard A. Gabriel, *Military Incompetence: Why the American Military Doesn't Win* (New York: Hill and Wang, 1985), pp. 61–83.

38. Henry Kissinger, *Diplomacy* (New York: Simon & Schuster, 1994), p. 766.

39. "Soviet Navy Plans Better Than U.S., Zumwalt Says," *Washington Post*, 28 July 1975, p. A1.

40. *Newsweek*, 7 February 1977, p. 36.

41. Moynihan, *Dangerous Place*, p. 56.

42. R. Emmett Tyrrell Jr., *Public Nuisances* (New York: Basic Books, 1979), p. 237.

43. Moynihan, *Years of Renewal*, p. 842.

44. *National Review*, 21 November 1975, p. 1274.

45. Anne Hessing Cahn, *Killing Détente: The Right Attacks the CIA* (University Park, Pennsylvania: Pennsylvania State University Press, 1998), p. 162.

46. Angelo Codevilla, *Informing Statecraft: Intelligence for a New Century* (New York: Free Press, 1992), p. 223.

47. Ibid., pp. 223–224.
48. Cahn, p. 129.
49. Codevilla, p. 222.
50. Cahn, p. 136.
51. Richard Pipes, "Team B: The Reality Behind the Myth," *Commentary*, October 1986, p. 34.
52. Cahn, p. 161.
53. Henry Kissinger, *The Troubled Partnership: A Reappraisal of the Atlantic Alliance* (New York: McGraw-Hill, 1965), p. 198.
54. William Shawcross, *Sideshow: Kissinger, Nixon, and the Destruction of Cambodia* (New York: Simon & Schuster, 1979), p. 308.
55. G. Warren Nutter, *Kissinger's Grand Design* (Washington, D.C.: American Enterprise Institute, 1975), p. 12.
56. Norman Podhoretz, "Making the World Safe for Communism," *Commentary*, April 1976, p. 35.
57. Kissinger, *Diplomacy*, p. 746.
58. Peter Drucker, *Adventures of a Bystander* (New York: Harper & Row, 1978), p. 154.
59. Marvin Kalb and Bernard Kalb, *Kissinger* (Boston: Little, Brown, 1974), p. 195; James and Diane Dornan, "The Works of Henry A. Kissinger," *Political Science Reviewer* 5 (Fall 1975), p. 115.
60. George Will, *National Review*, 31 January 1975, p. 95.
61. Thomas Noer, "Henry Kissinger's Philosophy of History" *Modern Age* 19 (Spring 1975), p. 185.
62. Henry Kissinger, *The White House Years* (Boston: Little, Brown, 1979), p. 192.
63. Luigi Barzini, *The Europeans* (New York: Simon & Schuster, 1983), p. 223.
64. *The Necessity for Choice: Prospects for American Foreign Policy* (New York; Harper & Brothers, 1961), pp. 356–357.
65. Walter Isaacson, *Kissinger* (New York: Simon & Schuster, 1992), p. 697.
66. Elmo R. Zumwalt, Jr., *On Watch: A Memoir* (New York: Quadrangle, 1976), pp. 317–319.
67. Robert G. Kaufman, *Henry M. Jackson: A Life in Politics* (Seattle: University of Washington Press, 2000), p. 252.
68. William Barrett, *The Truants: Adventures Among the Intellectuals* (New York: Doubleday, 1982), p. 190.
69. *National Review*, 6 February 1976, p. 69.
70. Bernard-Henri Levy, *Barbarism with a Human Face* (New York: Harper & Row, 1979), pp. 153, 158.
71. *National Review*, 29 August 1975, p. 935.
72. George Will, syndicated column, 13 December 1976.
73. Kissinger, *Years of Renewal*, pp. 108–109.

74. *National Review*, 2 April 1976, p. 311.
75. Daniel Patrick Moynihan, "Was Woodrow Wilson Right? Morality and American Foreign Policy," *Commentary*, May 1974, pp. 29, 30–31.
76. Moynihan, *Dangerous Place*, p. 316.
77. Ibid., pp. 322–323.
78. Harry V. Jaffa, *How To Think About the American Revolution: A Bicentennial Cerebration* (Durham: Carolina Academic Press, 1978), p. 1.
79. Daniel Bell, "The End of American Exceptionalism," *The Public Interest*, Fall 1975, p. 197.

CHAPTER 10

1. Jules Witcover, *Marathon: The Pursuit of the Presidency, 1972–1976* (New York: Viking, 1977), p. 70.
2. Lou Cannon, *Reagan* (New York: G. P. Putnam's Sons, 1982), p. 197.
3. Witcover, *Marathon*, p. 90.
4. *The New Republic*, 3 January 1976, p. 10.
5. Barry Farrell, "The Candidate from Disneyland," *Harper's*, February 1976, p. 9.
6. "Taking Reagan Seriously," *Chicago Daily News*, 21 November 1975.
7. J. J. Kilpatrick, "The Goldwater and Reagan Campaigns: A Difference?" *National Review*, 19 December 1975, p. 1467.
8. Peter Hannaford memo to Reagan, 6 November 1976, Deaver-Hannaford Papers, Hoover Institution, Box 3.
9. *Pravda*, 11 April 1976.
10. Cannon, *Reagan*, p. 202.
11. Jeffrey Hart, "White House Report," *National Review*, 19 March 1976, pp. 265–266.
12. *National Review*, 6 February 1976, p. 74.
13. Hart, *National Review*, 19 March 1976, p. 266.
14. Ibid., p. 267.
15. Witcover, *Marathon*, p. 100.
16. *The New Republic*, 24 January 1976, p. 6.
17. *National Review*, 2 April 1976, p. 320.
18. Witcover, *Marathon*, pp. 97–98.
19. Ibid., p. 387.
20. Cabinet Issue Memo, Box 15, Citizens for Reagan Papers, Hoover Institution, Stanford University.
21. Witcover, *Marathon*, pp. 401–403.
22. *Time*, 17 May 1976, p. 16.
23. Martin Anderson, *Revolution: The Reagan Legacy* (Orlando: Harcourt, Brace Jovanovich, 1988), p. 43.
24. Lou Cannon, *Reagan* (New York: G. P. Putnam's Sons, 1982), pp. 217, 218.

25. *Time*, 17 May 1976, p. 19.

26. Witcover, *Marathon*, p. 482.

27. Albert Hunt, "When a Convention Mattered," *Wall Street Journal*, 27 July 2000, p. A23.

28. Witcover, *Marathon*, p. 456.

29. *National Review*, 17 September 1976, p. 1000.

30. Anderson, *Revolution*, p. 67.

31. *Newsweek*, 30 August 1976, p. 45.

32. Winston Churchill, *Thoughts and Adventures* (London: Thornton Butterworth, 1932), p. 15.

33. *National Review*, 17 September 1976, pp. 992–993.

34. John Coyne, Jr., "Endings and Beginnings in Illinois," *National Review*, 16 April 1976, pp. 410–411.

CHAPTER 11

1. Jules Witcover, *Marathon: The Pursuit of the Presidency 1972–1976* (New York: Viking, 1977), p. 194.

2. Nathan Miller, *Star-Spangled Men: America's Ten Worst Presidents* (New York: Touchstone, 1998), p. 25.

3. Christopher Matthews, *Hardball* (New York: Summit Books, 1988), p. 60.

4. Witcover, p. 195.

5. Ibid., pp. 118, 13.

6. Peter G. Bourne, *Jimmy Carter* (New York: Scribner, 1997), p. 251.

7. *Newsweek*, 25 October 1976, p. 68.

8. Howard Norton and Bob Strosser, *The Miracle of Jimmy Carter* (Plainfield, New Jersey: Logos Books, 1976), p. 9.

9. Bourne, p. 305.

10. Norton and Strosser, p. 57.

11. Martin Anderson, *Revolution: The Reagan Legacy* (Orlando: Harcourt, Brace Jovanovich, 1988), p. 93.

12. Garry Wills, *Lead Time: A Journalist's Education* (New York: Penguin Books, 1984), pp. 255, 257.

13. Witcover, p. 211.

14. Norton and Strosser, p. 93.

15. Steven Brill, "Jimmy Carter's Pathetic Lies," *Harper's*, March 1976, p. 84.

16. Richard Harwood, ed., *The Pursuit of the Presidency 1980* (New York: Putnam, 1980), p. 202.

17. Norton and Strosser, pp. 58–59.

18. Patrick Anderson, *Electing Jimmy Carter: The Campaign of 1976* (Baton Rouge: Louisiana State University Press, 1994), p. 14.

19. Ibid., p. 162.

20. Witcover, p. 225.

21. Ibid., p. 336.

22. Bourne, p. 279.

23. Witcover, p. 207.

24. Patrick Anderson, p. 164.

25. Norton and Strosser, p. 106.

26. *National Review*, 16 April 1976, p. 391.

27. *The New Republic*, 6 March 1976, p. 4.

28. *Newsweek*, 30 August 1976, p. 27.

29. Witcover, p. 306.

30. Reg Murphy, "The New Jimmy Carter," *The New Republic*, 14 January 1976, p. 15.

31. Matthews, *Hardball*, p. 60.

32. Brill, p. 79.

33. *National Review*, 15 October 1976, p. 1098.

34. Kenneth E. Morris, *Jimmy Carter: American Moralist* (University of Georgia Press, 1996), p. 245.

35. Ibid., p. 247.

36. *National Review*, 1 October 1976, p. 1040.

37. John Coyne, "Niceguyin' His Way to the White House," *National Review*, 14 May 1976, p. 504.

38. Walter Dean Burnham, "Jimmy Carter and the Democratic Crisis," *The New Republic*, 3 July 1976, p. 17.

39. Patrick Anderson, p. 65.

40. *National Review*, 1 October 1976, p. 1046.

41. *The New Republic*, 24 July 1976, p. 11.

42. *National Review*, 29 October 1976, p. 1159.

43. *Atlantic Monthly*, July 1976, p. 34.

44. *The New Republic*, 23 October 1976, p. 5.

45. *The New Republic*, 31 July 1976, p. 6.

46. Witcover, p. 524.

47. John Robert Greene, *The Presidency of Gerald R. Ford* (Lawrence: University Press of Kansas, 1995), p. 183.

48. *Time*, 23 August 1976, p. 10.

49. *National Review*, 26 November 1976, p. 1277.

50. Thomas P ("Tip") O'Neill, *Man of the House* (New York: Random House, 1987), pp. 310–311.

51. Charles O Jones, *The Trusteeship Presidency: Jimmy Carter and the United States Congress* (Baton Rouge: Louisiana State University Press, 1988), p. 1.

52. Robert G. Kaufman, *Henry M. Jackson: A Life in Politics* (Seattle: University of Washington Press, 2000), p. 342.

53. Charles Jones, *The Trusteeship Presidency*, p. 149.
54. Robert Shogan, *Promises to Keep* (New York: Thomas Y. Crowell, 1977), pp. 282–283.
55. Bourne, p. 416–417.
56. Burton I. Kaufman, *The Presidency of James Earl Carter, Jr.* (University Press of Kansas, 1993), pp. 53–54.
57. *The New Republic*, 23 December and 30 December 1978, p. 2.
58. *National Review*, 27 May 1977, p. 588.
59. Jones, p. 154.
60. Morris, p. 245.
61. Bourne, p. 421.
62. James Fallows, "The Passionless Presidency," *The Atlantic Monthly*, March 1979, p. 38.
63. Jones, p. 16.
64. *Time*, 26 April 1976.
65. Bourne, p. 417.
66. Margaret Thatcher, *The Downing Street Years* (New York: HarperCollins, 1993), p. 69.
67. *National Review*, 30 September 1977, p. 1096.
68. *National Review*, 24 October 1975, p. 1160.
69. *National Review*, 28 April 1978, p. 510.
70. *National Review*, 26 May 1978, p. 637.
71. Bourne, p. 431.
72. "Carter Shaped Energy Plan with Disregard for Politics," *New York Times*, 24 April 1977.
73. *National Review*, 6 January 1978, p. 11.
74. "Friedman's Currency," *The New Republic*, 6 November 1976, pp. 8–9.
75. *The New Republic*, 10 July 1971, p. 5.
76. Godfrey Hodgson, *The World Turned Right Side Up: A History of the Conservative Ascendancy in America* (New York: Houghton Mifflin, 1996), p. 206.
77. Martin Anderson, *Revolution*, p. 147.
78. Henry Fairlie, "Dank Victory," *The New Republic*, 18 November 1978, p. 17.
79. Michael Barone, "Nixon's Gift to the GOP," *The New Republic*, 16 December 1978, p. 13.
80. *Time*, 6 August 1979, p. 38.
81. Daniel Patrick Moynihan, *Miles to Go: A Personal History of Social Policy* (Cambridge: Harvard University Press, 1996), pp. 9–10.
82. Geoffrey Smith, *Reagan and Thatcher* (New York: Norton, 1991), p. 1.
83. Thatcher, *Downing Street Years*, p. 69.
84. Robert Moss, "Anglocommunism," *Commentary*, February 1977, pp. 27, 28, 29.
85. *Human Events*, 16 September 1978.

86. Daniel Yergin and Joseph Stanislaw, *The Commanding Heights: The Battle Between Government and the Marketplace That Is Remaking the Modern World* (New York: Simon & Schuster, 1998), p. 107.

87. *Newsweek*, 9 April 1979, p. 52.

88. Smith, *Reagan and Thatcher*, pp. 18–19.

89. Ibid., p. 21.

CHAPTER 12

1. Cited in Nathan Miller, *Star-Spangled Men: America's Ten Worst Presidents* (New York: Touchstone, 1998), p. 23.

2. Jeane Kirkpatrick, *Dictatorships and Double Standards: Rationalism and Reason in Politics* (New York: Simon & Schuster, 1982), pp. 92, 91.

3. Michael Ledeen and Bernard Lewis, *Debacle: The American Failure in Iran* (New York: Alfred A. Knopf, 1981), p. 71.

4. Fallows, "The Passionless Presidency," *Atlantic Monthly*, June 1979, p. 76.

5. *Harper's*, October, 1977, p. 34.

6. Kirkpatrick, *Dictatorships and Double Standards*, pp. 45, 37.

7. Ledeen and Lewis, p. 67.

8. Burton I. Kaufman, *The Presidency of James Earl Carter, Jr.* (Lawrence: University Press of Kansas, 1993), p. 365.

9. Robert Shogan, *Promises to Keep* (New York: Thomas Y. Crowell, 1977), p. 217.

10. Kaufman, pp. 370–371.

11. Godfrey Hodgson, *The Gentleman from New York: Daniel Patrick Moynihan* (Boston: Houghton Mifflin, 2000), p. 295.

12. Norton and Slosser, p. 77.

13. *The New Republic*, 4 June 1977, p. 8.

14. Peter G. Bourne, *Jimmy Carter* (New York: Scribner, 1997), p. 366.

15. *Time*, 4 April 1978, p. 20

16. "The Junior Varsity," *The New Republic*, 19 February 1977, p. 12.

17. Jay Winik, *On the Brink* (New York: Simon & Schuster, 1996), p. 84.

18. *National Review*, 18 February 1977, p. 194.

19. Daniel Patrick Moynihan, "Further Thoughts on Words and Foreign Policy," *Policy Review*, Spring, 1979, p. 53.

20. Carl Gershman, "The World According to Andrew Young," *Commentary*, August 1978, p. 19.

21. Gershman, pp. 28–29.

22. Bourne, p. 382.

23. Michael Barone, *Our Country: The Shaping of America from Roosevelt to Reagan* (New York: The Free Press, 1990), p. 569.

24. Ledeen and Lewis, p. 158.

25. Ibid., p. 36.

26. Walter Laqueur, "Why the Shah Fell," *Commentary*, March 1979, p. 49.

27. Tom Bethell, *The Noblest Triumph: Property and Prosperity Through the Ages* (New York: St. Martin's Press, 1998), p. 218.

28. Ledeen and Lewis, p. 124.

29. Gary Sick, *All Fall Down: America's Tragic Encounter with Iran* (New York: Penguin Books, 1986), p. 193.

30. Ledeen and Lewis, p. 126; Sick, p. 43.

31. Kiron K. Skinner, Annelise Anderson, and Martin Anderson: *Reagan in His Own Hand* (New York: Free Press, 2001), pp. 113–114.

32. Sick, p. 36.

33. Ledeen and Lewis, pp. 144–145.

34. Sick, p. 195.

35. Ibid., p. 142.

36. Ledeen and Lewis, p. 233.

37. Ibid., p. 149.

38. Sick, p. 219.

39. Robert Moss, "Who's Meddling in Iran?" *The New Republic*, 2 December 1978, p. 16.

40. Ledeen and Lewis, p. 163.

41. Sick, p. 183.

42. Walter Laqueur, "Why the Shah Fell," *Commentary*, March 1979, p. 55.

43. Robert Kagan, *A Twilight Struggle: American Power and Nicaragua, 1977–1990* (New York: The Free Press, 1996), p. 31.

44. Robert Gates, *From the Shadows* (New York: Simon & Schuster, 1996), p. 126.

45. Kagan, p. 52.

46. Ibid., p. 736.

47. *Washington Post*, 3 August 1978, p. A–22.

48. Jeane Kirkpatrick, p. 74.

49. Gates, p. 128.

50. Robert W. Tucker, "America in Decline: The Foreign Policy of 'Maturity,'" *Foreign Affairs*, Winter 1980, p. 468.

51. Kirkpatrick, "Dictatorships and Double Standards," *Commentary*, November 1979.

52. Strober and Strober, *Reagan: The Man and His Presidency: An Oral History* (Boston: Houghton-Mifflin, 1998), p. 42.

53. Deaver-Hannaford Papers, Hoover Institution, Box 3.

54. Ronald Regan, "The Canal of Opportunity: A New Relationship with Latin America," *Orbis*, Fall 1997, p. 560.

55. Winik, *On The Brink*, p. 106.

56. *The New Republic*, 4 August 1979, p. 8.

57. Bruce Chapman, "The Gas Lines of '79," *The Public Interest*, Summer, 1980, pp. 40–49.

58. *Newsweek*, 12 March 1979, p. 68.

59. *Newsweek*, 16 July 1979, p. 21.

60. *National Review*, 3 August 1979, p. 954.

61. *The New Republic*, 4 August 1979, p. 6.

62. *The New Republic*, 21 May 1977, p. 5.

63. *Time*, 30 July 1979, p. 23.

64. Christopher Lasch, *The Culture of Narcissism: American Life in an Age of Diminishing Expectations* (New York: W. W. Norton, 1978).

65. *The New Yorker*, 27 August 1979, p. 45.

66. Bourne, p. 442.

67. *Time*, 30 July 1979, p. 11.

68. *The New Republic*, 4 August 1979, p. 15.

69. Bourne, p. 389.

70. Strobe Talbott, *Endgame: The Inside Story of SALT II* (New York: Harper & Row, 1979), p. 75.

71. Gates, p. 178–179.

72. Edward Luttwak, "Ten Questions About SALT II," *Commentary*, August 1979, p. 28.

73. Eugene Rostow, "The Case Against SALT II," *Commentary*, February 1979, p. 30.

74. Gates, p. 108.

75. Norman Podhoretz, "The Culture of Appeasement," *Harper's*, October 1977, pp. 29, 32.

76. Talbott, *Endgame*, p. 5.

77. Reagan speech, 10 February 1976, Deaver-Hannaford Paper, Box 16, Hoover Archives, Stanford University.

78. *National Review*, 16 March 1979, p. 334.

79. Allen memo to Gov. Reagan, 25 August 1978, Deaver-Hannaford Papers, Box 3, Hoover Institution, Stanford University.

80. Ikle letter to Hannaford, 8 March 1979, Deaver-Hannaford Papers, Box 2, Hoover Institution, Stanford University.

81. Memo, Hannaford to Reagan, 26 July 1979, Deaver-Hannaford Papers, Box 3, Hoover Institution, Stanford University.

82. Kampelman to Reagan, 8 December 1978, Deaver-Hannaford Papers, Box 2, Hoover Institution.

83. Martin Anderson, *Revolution: The Reagan Legacy* (Palo Alto: Hoover Press, 1990), p. 81.

84. Morris, p. 276.

85. Bourne, p. 455.

86. Gates, p. 130.

87. Ibid., p. 148.

88. Sick, p. 343.

89. Tucker, p. 483.

90. *Washington Post,* 30 December 1979, p. A–1.

91. Robert G. Kaufman, *Henry M. Jackson: A Life in Politics* (University of Washington Press, 2000), p. 397.

92. Winik, *On the Brink,* p. 100; Author interview with Ben Wattenberg, 29 September 2000.

93. *TNR,* August 2 and 9, 1980, p. 11.

94. Hodgson, p.291.

95. Nelson Polsby, "The Democratic Nomination," in Austin Ranney, ed., *The American Elections of 1980,* (Washington, D.C.: American Enterprise Institute, 1981), p. 45.

CHAPTER 13

1. *Newsweek,* 19 November 1979, pp. 89, 96.

2. *Time,* 7 January 1980, p. 38.

3. Edward F. Dennison, *Accounting for Slower Economic Growth: The United States in the 1970s* (Washington, D.C.: Brookings Institution, 1979), p. 15.

4. Terry Teachout, "Bad Rap," *National Review,* 22 February 1999, p. 14.

5. Stephan and Abigail Thernstrom, *America in Black and White: One Nation, Indivisible* (New York: Simon & Schuster, 1997), pp. 192, 240.

6. Citizens for Reagan Archives, Box 7, Hoover Institution, Stanford University.

7. Lou Cannon, *Reagan: A Political Odyssey* (Garden City, New York: Doubleday, 1969), p. 229.

8. *New York Times,* 14 November 1979, p. A25.

9. *Newsweek,* 7 November 1977, p. 34.

10. James Q. Wilson, "Reagan and the Republican Revival," *Commentary,* October 1980, p. 25.

11. John O, Koehler, *Stasi: The Untold Story of the East German Secret Police* (Boulder, Colorado: Westview Press, 1999), p. 145.

12. Memo, "Communications Strategy for 1975," Deaver-Hannaford Papers, Box 1, Hoover Institution, Stanford University.

13. Norman Podhoretz, "The Riddle of Ronald Reagan" *The Weekly Standard,* 9 November 1998, p. 23.

14. George P. Shultz, *Turmoil and Triumph: Diplomacy, Power, and the Victory of the American Ideal* (New York: Charles Scribner's Sons, 1993), p. 8.

15. Deaver-Hannaford Papers, Box 1, Hoover Institution, Stanford University.

16. *The New Republic,* 5 April 1980, p. 9.

17. *The New Republic,* 5 March 1998, p. 5; 1 December 1979, p. 16.

18. *The New Republic,* 14 June 1980, p. 10.

19. Richard Harwood, ed., *The Pursuit of the Presidency 1980* (New York: Putnam, 1980) p. 290.

20. Austin Ranney, ed., *The American Elections of 1980* (Washington, D.C.: American Enterprise Institute, 1981), p. 63.
21. Drew, *The New Yorker,* 24 March 1980, p. 49.
22. *The New Republic,* 16 August 1980, p. 5.
23. Ranney, p. 143.
24. "Reagan's Goofs," *The Nation,* 26 April 1980, p. 484.
25. *National Review,* 2 May 1980, p. 515.
26. Robert Shogan, *Promises to Keep* (New York: Thomas Y. Crowell, 1977), p. 183.
27. Wirthlin memo to Reagan, 19 July 1979, Deaver-Hannaford Papers, Box 11, Hoover Institution, Stanford University.
28. Jack W Germond and Jules Witcover, *Blue Smoke & Mirrors: How Reagan Won & Carter Lost the Election of 1980* (New York: Viking, 1981), p. 116.
29. *National Review,* 22 February 1980, p. 197.
30. *The New Republic,* 16 February 1980, p. 17.
31. Ibid., p. 18.
32. *Time,* 4 February 1980, p. 26.
33. Herbert S. Parmet, *George Bush: The Life of a Lone-Star Yankee* (New York: Scribner, 1997), p. 226.
34. Harwood, p. 123.
35. *National Review,* 7 March 1980, p. 262
36. *National Review,* 25 January 1980, p. 74.
37. Frank van der Linden, *The Real Reagan* (New York: William Morrow, 1981), p. 172.
38. Lou Cannon, *Reagan* (New York: G. P. Putnam's Sons, 1982), p. 249.
39. Bell, *Weekly Standard,* 5 February 2001, p. 21.
40. Strober and Strober, *Reagan: The Man and His Presidency: An Oral History* (Boston: Houghton-Mifflin, 1998), p. 15.
41. *Time,* 21 January 1980, p. 31.
42. Leonard Garment, *In Search of Deep Throat* (New York: Basic Books, 2000).
43. Jules Witcover, *Marathon: The Pursuit of the Presidency 1972–1976* (New York: Viking, 1977), p. 66.
44. Murray Kempton, *Rebellions, Perversities, and Main Events* (New York: Times Books, 1994), p. 527.
45. *New York Times Magazine,* 16 November 1980.
46. Strober and Strober, p. 15.
47. Ibid., p. 83.
48. Ibid., p. 15.
49. Germond and Witcover, p. 133.
50. *NewYork Times,* 4 December 1979, p. B19.
51. Cannon, *Reagan,* p. 239.
52. *National Review,* 21 March 1980, p. 329.

53. Germond and Witcover, *Blue Smoke,* p. 123.

54. Ibid., p. 129.

55. Ibid., p. 135.

56. Ibid., p. 136.

57. Edwin Meese, III. *With Reagan: The Inside Story* (Washington, D.C.: Regnery, 1992), p. 7.

58. *National Review,* 26 October 1979, p. 1343.

59. *Washington Post,* 4 December 1979, p. A20.

60. Peter Collier and David Horowitz, *The Kennedys: An American Drama* (New York: Simon & Schuster, 1984), p. 550.

61. Peter G. Bourne, *Jimmy Carter* (New York: Scribner, 1997), p. 459.

62. Ibid., p. 460.

63. Richard A. Gabriel, *Military Incompetence: Why the American Military Doesn't Win* (New York: Hill and Wang, 1985), p. 86.

64. Elizabeth Drew, *Portrait of an Election: The 1980 Presidential Campaign* (New York: Simon & Schuster, 1981), p. 263.

65. Germond and Witcover, *Blue Smoke,* p. 169.

66. Cannon, *Reagan,* p. 263.

67. Strober and Strober, p. 22.

68. *U.S. News and World Report,* 26 May 1980, p. 16.

69. Deaver-Hannaford Papers, Box 12, Hoover Institution.

70. Strober and Strober, p. 21.

71. Germond and Witcover, *Blue Smoke,* p. 173.

72. Strober and Strober, p. 22.

73. Ibid., p. 183.

74. William C. Adams, ed., *Television Coverage of the 1980 Presidential Campaign* (Norwood, New Jersey: ABLEX Publishing, 1983), p. 82.

75. *National Review,* 8 August 1980, p. 942.

76. *Newsweek,* 28 July 1980, p. 23.

77. Harvey C. Mansfield, Jr., *America's Constitutional Soul* (Baltimore: Johns Hopkins University Press, 1991).

78. *National Review,* 22 August 1980, p. 1023.

79. *The New Republic,* 16 August 1980, p. 5.

80. *Washington Post,* 28 August 1980, p. A3.

CHAPTER 14

1. John Lukacs, *The Duel* (New York: Tichnor & Fields, 1990), p. 186.

2. James Mann, *About Face: A History of America's Curious Relationship with China, From Nixon to Clinton* (New York: Alfred A. Knopf, 1999), p. 118.

3. Jack W Germond and Jules Witcover, *Blue Smoke & Mirrors: How Reagan Won & Carter Lost the Election of 1980* (New York: Viking, 1981), p. 214.

4. Tom Shales, "The Harassment of Ronald Reagan," *Washington Post*, 31 October 1980, p. C1.

5. Robert Kaiser, "Those Old Reaganisms May Be Brought Back to Haunt Him," *Washington Post*, 2 September 1980, p. A2.

6. F. A. Hayek, *The Road to Serfdom* (Chicago: University of Chicago Press, 1944), p. 184.

7. William A. Dembski, *Intelligent Design: The Bridge Between Science and Technology* (Downers Grove, Illinois: InterVarsity Press, 1999).

8. *New York Times*, 22 September 1980, p. A27.

9. *National Review*, 19 September 1980, p. 1120.

10. Herbert Stein, *Presidential Economics* (New York: Simon & Schuster, 1984), p. 261.

11. *Time*, 16 June 1980, p. 64.

12. Stein, p. 239.

13. Martin Anderson, *Revolution: The Reagan Legacy* (Palo Alto: Hoover Press, 1990), p. 122.

14. *The New Republic*, 20 September 1980, p. 3.

15. *Business Week*, 7 August 1978, p. 94.

16. Robert L. Bartley, *The Seven Fat Years and How To Do It Again* (New York: The Free Press, 1992), p. 74.

17. Elizabeth Drew, *Portrait of an Election: The 1980 Presidential Campaign* (New York: Simon & Schuster, 1981), p. 313.

18. *National Journal*, 11 October 1980, p. 1688.

19. *New York Times*, 27 June 1980, p. A31.

20. *New York Times*, 9 September 1980, p. A19.

21. *National Review*, 22 August 1980, p. 1041.

22. *National Review*, 5 September 1980, p. 1057.

23. *The New Republic*, 27 September 1980, p. 7.

24. *Washington Post*, 18 September 1980, p. A18.

25. *Washington Post*, 31 October 1980, p. C1.

26. Austin Ranney, ed., *The American Elections of 1980*, p. 165.

27. Richard Harwood, ed., *The Pursuit of the Presidency 1980* (New York: Putnam, 1980), p. 300.

28. Drew, *Portrait*, pp. 410–411.

29. Lou Cannon, *Ronnie and Jesse: A Political Odyssey* (Garden City, New York: Doubleday, 1969), p. 297.

30. *The New Republic*, 8 November 1980, p. 7.

31. *New York Times*, 30 October 1980, p. C26.

32. *The New Republic*, 25 October 1980, p. 9.

33. *The Nation*, 15 November 1980, p. 497.

34. *The Nation*, 3–10 January 1981, p. 3.

35. *The Nation*, 31 January 1981, p. 109.
36. *New York Times*, 26 November 1980, p. B4.
37. *Washington Post*, 19 November 1980.
38. Ranney, p. 300.
39. *The Nation,* 22 November 1980, p. 534.
40. *The Nation*, 13 December 1980, p. 632.
41. *National Review,* 19 November 1955, p. 5.

BIBLIOGRAPHY

———◦———

BOOKS

Adams, William C., ed. *Television Coverage of the 1980 Presidential Campaign*. Norwood, New Jersey: ABLEX Publishing, 1983.

Aitken, Jonathan. *Nixon: A Life*. Washington, D.C.: Regnery, 1993.

Anderson, Martin. *Revolution: The Reagan Legacy*. Orlando: Harcourt, Brace Jovanovich, 1988.

Anderson, Patrick. *Electing Jimmy Carter: The Campaign of 1976*. Baton Rouge: Louisiana State University Press, 1994.

Anderson, Terry H. *The Movement and the Sixties: Protest in America from Greensboro to Wounded Knee*. New York: Oxford University Press, 1995.

Andrew, John A., III. *Lyndon Johnson and the Great Society*. Chicago: Ivan R. Dee, 1998.

_____. *The Other Side of the Sixties: Young Americans for Freedom and the Rise of Conservative Politics*. New Brunswick: Rutgers University Press, 1997.

Arendt, Hannah. *Crises of the Republic*. New York: Harcourt, Brace, 1972.

Banfield, Edward. *The Unheavenly City Revisited*. Boston: Little, Brown, 1974.

Barone, Michael. *Our Country: The Shaping of America from Roosevelt to Reagan*. New York: The Free Press, 1990.

Barrett, William. *The Truants: Adventures Among the Intellectuals*. New York: Doubleday, 1982.

Bartley, Robert L. *The Seven Fat Years and How To Do It Again*. New York: The Free Press, 1992.

Barzini, Luigi. *The Europeans*. New York: Simon & Schuster, 1983.

Beckwith, Charlie A., and Knox, Donald. *Delta Force*. San Diego: Harcourt, Brace, Jovanovich, 1983.

Bell, Jeffrey. *Populism and Elitism: Politics in the Age of Equality.* Washington, D.C.: Regnery, 1992.

Belz, Herman. *Equality Transformed: A Quarter-Century of Affirmative Action.* New Brunswick, New Jersey: Transaction Publishers, 1991.

Beran, Michael Knox. *The Last Patrician: Bobby Kennedy and the End of American Aristocracy.* New York: St. Martin's Press, 1998.

Berman, Larry. *Lyndon Johnson's War.* New York: W. W. Norton, 1989.

_____. *Planning a Tragedy: The Americanization of the War in Vietnam.* New York: W. W. Norton, 1982.

Berman, Paul. *A Tale of Two Utopias: The Political Journey of the Generation of 1968.* New York: W. W. Norton, 1996.

Bernstein, Irving. *Guns or Butter: The Presidency of Lyndon Johnson.* New York: Oxford University Press, 1996.

Beschloss, Michael R. *Taking Charge: The Johnson White House Tapes, 1963–1964.* New York: Simon & Schuster, 1997.

Bethell, Tom. *The Noblest Triumph: Property and Prosperity Through the Ages.* New York: St. Martin's Press, 1998.

Biskind, Peter. *Easy Riders, Raging Bulls: How the Sex-Drugs-and-Rock 'N' Roll Generation Saved Hollywood.* New York: Simon & Schuster, 1998.

Blake, Robert. *Disraeli.* New York: St. Martin's Press, 1967.

Bloom, Alexander, and Wini Breines, eds. *Takin' It to the Streets: A Sixties Reader.* New York: Oxford University Press, 1995.

Bourne, Peter G. *Jimmy Carter.* New York: Scribner, 1997.

Boyarski, Bill. *Ronald Reagan: His Life and Rise to the Presidency.* New York: Random House, 1981.

Bradley, Robert L., Jr. *The Mirage of Oil Protection.* Lanham. Maryland: University Press of America, 1989.

Braestrup, Peter. *Big Story: How the American Press and Television Reported and Interpreted the Crisis of Tet 1968 in Vietnam and Washington.* Boulder, Colorado: Westview, 1977.

Brinkley, Alan. *Liberalism and Its Discontents.* Cambridge: Harvard University Press, 1998.

Broder, David, and Stephen Hess. *The Republican Establishment: The Present and Future of the GOP.* New York: Harper & Row, 1967.

Brookes, Warren. *The Economy in Mind.* New York: Universe Books, 1982.

Buckley, William F., Jr. *A Hymnal: The Controversial Arts*. New York: G. P. Putnam's Sons, 1978.

_____. *Inveighing We Will Go*. New York: G. P. Putnam's Sons, 1972.

_____. *The Governor Listeth*. New York: G.P. Putnam's Sons, 1969.

_____, ed. *Odyssey of a Friend: Whittaker Chambers Letters to William F. Buckley, Jr. 1954–1961*. New York: G. P. Putnam's Sons, 1969.

Bunzel, John H., ed. *Political Passages: Journeys of Change, 1968–1988*. New York: The Free Press, 1988.

Burke, Vincent J. and Vee Burke. *Nixon's Good Deed: Welfare Reform*. New York: Columbia University Press, 1974.

Burr, William, ed. *The Kissinger Transcripts: The Top-Secret Talks with Beijing and Moscow*. New York: The New Press, 1999.

Cahn, Anne Hessing. *Killing Détente: The Right Attacks the CIA*. University Park: Pennsylvania State University Press, 1998.

Califano, Joseph A., Jr. *The Triumph & Tragedy of Lyndon Johnson*. New York: Simon & Schuster, 1991.

Cannon, Lou. *President Reagan: The Role of a Lifetime*. New York: Simon & Schuster, 1991.

_____. *Reagan*. New York: G. P. Putnam's Sons, 1982.

_____. *Ronnie and Jesse: A Political Odyssey*. Garden City, New York: Doubleday, 1969.

Caputo, Richard K. *Welfare and Freedom American Style II: The Role of the Federal Government, 1941-1980*. Lanham, MD: University Press of America, 1994.

Caro, Robert A. *The Power Broker: Robert Moses and the Fall of New York*. New York: Alfred A. Knopf, 1974.

Carroll, Peter N. *It Seemed Like Nothing Happened: America in the 1970s*. New York: Holt, Rinehart and Winston, 1982.

Cassell, Paul G. *Handcuffing the Cops: Miranda's Harmful Effects on Law Enforcement*. Dallas: National Center for Policy Analysis, 1998.

Charnwood, Lord. *Abraham Lincoln*. New York: Henry Holt & Co., 1917.

Chester, Lewis, Godfrey Hodgson, and Bruce Page. *An American Melodrama: The Presidential Campaign of 1968*. New York: The Viking Press, 1969.

Churchill, Winston. *Marlborough: His Life and Times*. London: George G. Harrap & Co., 1933.

_____. *Thoughts and Adventures*. London: Thornton Butterworth, 1932.

Clifford, Clark. *Counsel to the President: A Memoir.* New York: Random House, 1991.

Clodfelter, Mark. *The Limits of Air Power: The American Bombing of North Vietnam.* New York: The Free Press, 1989.

Codevilla, Angelo. *The Character of Nations: How Politics Makes and Breaks Prosperity, Family, and Civility.* New York: Basic Books, 1997.

_____. *Informing Statecraft: Intelligence for a New Century.* New York: The Free Press, 1992.

_____. *While Others Build: A Commonsense Approach to the Strategic Defense Initiative.* New York: The Free Press, 1988.

Cohen, Elliot A., and John Gooch. *Military Misfortune: An Anatomy of Failure in War.* New York: The Free Press, 1990.

Cohen, Jerry, and William S. Murphy. *Burn, Baby, Burn.* New York: Dutton, 1966.

Cohen, Nathan, ed. *The Los Angeles Riots: A Socio-Psychological Study.* New York: Praeger, 1970.

Collier, Peter, and David Horowitz. *The Kennedys: An American Drama.* New York: Simon & Schuster, 1984.

Colodny, Len, and Robert Gettlin. *Silent Coup: The Removal of a President.* New York: St. Martin's Press, 1991.

Dallek, Matthew. *The Right Moment: Ronald Reagan's First Victory and the Decisive Turning Point in American Politics.* New York: The Free Press, 2000.

Dallek, Robert. *Flawed Giant: Lyndon Johnson and His Times, 1961–1973.* New York: Oxford University Press, 1998.

Davies, Gareth. *From Opportunity to Entitlement: The Transformation and Decline of Great Society Liberalism.* Lawrence: University Press of Kansas, 1996.

Dembski, William A. *Intelligent Design: The Bridge Between Science and Technology.* Downers Grove, Illinois: InterVarsity Press, 1999.

Denison, Edward F. *Accounting for Slower Economic Growth: The United States in the 1970s.* Washington, D.C.: The Brookings Institution, 1979.

Didion, Joan. *Slouching Toward Bethlehem.* New York: Farrar, Straus and Giroux, 1968.

Diggins, John Patrick. *The Rise and Fall of the American Left.* Orlando: Harcourt, Brace, Jovanovich, 1973.

Drew, Elizabeth. *Portrait of an Election: The 1980 Presidential Campaign.* New York: Simon & Schuster, 1981.

Drucker, Peter. *Adventures of a Bystander.* New York: Harper & Row, 1978.

Dugger, Ronnie. *On Reagan: The Man and His Presidency*. New York: McGraw-Hill, 1983.

Edsall, Thomas Byrne and Mary D. *Chain Reaction: The Impact of Race, Rights, and Taxes on American Politics*. New York: W. W. Norton, 1991.

Edwards, Anne. *Early Reagan: The Rise to Power*. New York: William Morrow, 1987.

Edwards, Lee. *Goldwater: The Man Who Made a Revolution*. Washington, D.C.: Regnery, 1995.

_____. *Ronald Reagan: A Political Biography*. Houston: Nordland Publishing, 1981.

Epstein, Richard. *Forbidden Grounds: The Case Against Employment Discrimination Laws*. Cambridge: Harvard University Press, 1992.

Evans, Rowland, Jr., and Robert Novak. *Nixon in the White House: The Frustration of Power*. New York: Random House, 1971.

_____. *The Reagan Revolution*. New York: Dutton, 1981.

Farber, David. *The Age of Great Dreams: America in the 1960s*. New York: Hill and Wang, 1994.

_____. *Chicago '68*. Chicago: University of Chicago Press, 1988.

Farber, David, ed. *The Sixties: From Memory to History*. Chapel Hill, North Carolina: University of North Carolina Press, 1994.

Friedman, Milton, and Rose Friedman. *Two Lucky People: Memoirs*. Chicago: University of Chicago Press, 1998.

Friedman, Robert, ed. *Up Against the Ivy Wall: A History of the Columbia Crisis*. New York: Atheneum, 1969.

Furchtgott-Roth, Diana, and Christina Stolba. *Women's Figures: An Illustrated Guide to Economic Progress of Women in America*. Washington, D.C.: American Enterprise Institute, 1999.

Gabriel, Richard A. *Military Incompetence: Why the American Military Doesn't Win*. New York: Hill and Wang, 1985.

Galbraith, John Kenneth. *The Affluent Society*. Boston: Houghton-Mifflin, 1958.

Gardner, Lloyd C. *Pay Any Price: Lyndon Johnson and the Wars for Vietnam*. Chicago: Ivan Dee, 1995.

Garment, Leonard. *In Search of Deep Throat*. New York: Basic Books, 2000.

Gates, Robert M. *From the Shadows: The Ultimate Insider's Story of Five Presidents and How They Won the Cold War*. New York: Simon & Schuster, 1996.

Germond, Jack W., and Jules Witcover. *Blue Smoke & Mirrors: How Reagan Won & Carter Lost the Election of 1980*. New York: Viking, 1981.

Gillette, Michael L., ed. *Launching the War on Poverty: An Oral History.* New York: Twayne, 1996.

Gillon, Steven M. *The Democrats' Dilemma: Walter Mondale and the Liberal Legacy.* New York: Columbia University Press, 1992.

Ginzberg, Eli, and Robert M. Solow, eds. *The Great Society: Lessons for the Future.* New York: Basic Books, 1974.

Gitlin, Todd. *The Sixties: Years of Hope, Days of Rage.* New York: Bantam Books, 1987.

Goines, David Lance. *The Free Speech Movement: Coming of Age in the 1960s.* Berkeley, California: Ten Speed Press, 1993.

Goldwater, Barry. *With No Apologies.* New York: William Morrow, 1979.

Goldwater, Barry, with Jack Casserly. *Goldwater.* New York: Doubleday, 1988.

Greene, John Robert. *The Presidency of Gerald R. Ford.* Lawrence: University Press of Kansas, 1995.

Greenfield, James L., et al. *The Pentagon Papers.* Chicago: Quadrangle Books, 1971.

Halberstam, David. *The Best and the Brightest.* New York: Random House, 1969.

Haldeman, H. R. *The Haldeman Diaries.* New York: G. P. Putnam, 1994.

Hannaford, Peter, ed. *Recollections of Reagan: A Portrait of Ronald Reagan.* New York: William Morrow, 1997.

Harwood, Richard, ed. *The Pursuit of the Presidency 1980.* New York: Putnam, 1980.

Hayek, F. A. *The Road to Serfdom.* Chicago: University of Chicago Press, 1944.

Herz, Martin F. *The Prestige Press and the Christmas Bombing, 1972: Images and Reality in Vietnam.* Washington D.C.: Ethics and Public Policy Center, 1980.

Hewlett, Sylvia Ann. *A Lesser Life: The Myth of Women's Liberation in America.* New York: William Morrow, 1986.

Hodgson, Godfrey. *America in Our Time: From World War II to Nixon—What Happened and Why.* New York: Random House, 1976.

_____. *The Gentleman from New York: Daniel Patrick Moynihan.* Boston: Houghton Mifflin, 2000.

_____. *The World Turned Right Side Up: A History of the Conservative Ascendancy in America.* New York: Houghton Mifflin, 1996.

Hoff, Joan. *Nixon Reconsidered.* New York: Basic Books, 1994.

Horne, Gerald. *Fire This Time: The Watts Uprising and the 1960s.* Charlottesville, Virginia: University of Virginia Press, 1995.

Horowitz, David. *Radical Son.* New York: The Free Press, 1997.

Hung, Ngyuen Tien, and Jerrold Schecter. *The Palace File.* New York: Harper & Row, 1986.

Isaacson, Walter. *Kissinger: A Biography.* New York: Simon & Schuster, 1992.

Isserman, Maurice, and Michael Kazin. *America Divided: The Civil War of the 1960s.* New York: Oxford University Press, 2000.

Jaffa, Harry V. *How To Think About the American Revolution: A Bicentennial Cerebration.* Durham, North Carolina: Carolina Academic Press, 1978.

Johnson, Lyndon. *The Vantage Point: Perspectives on the Presidency, 1963-1969.* New York: Holt, Reinhart and Winston, 1971.

Jones, Charles O. *The Trusteeship Presidency: Jimmy Carter and the United States Congress.* Baton Rouge: Louisiana State University Press, 1988.

Jones, Gordon S. and John Marini, eds. *The Imperial Congress: Crisis in the Separation of Powers.* New York: Pharos Books, 1988.

Kagan, Donald. *On the Origins of War.* New York: Doubleday, 1995.

Kagan, Robert. *A Twilight Struggle: American Power and Nicaragua, 1977–1990.* New York: The Free Press, 1996.

Kaiser, Charles. *1968 in America: Music, Politics, Chaos, Counterculture, and the Shaping of a Generation.* New York: Grove Press, 1988.

Kalb, Marvin, and Bernard Kalb. *Kissinger.* Boston: Little, Brown, 1974.

Karnow, Stanley. *Vietnam: A History.* New York: Viking, 1983.

Katzmann, Robert A., ed. *Daniel Patrick Moynihan: The Intellectual in Public Life.* Baltimore: Johns Hopkins University Press, 1998.

Kaufman, Burton I. *The Presidency of James Earl Carter.* Lawrence: University Press of Kansas, 1993.

Kaufman, Robert G. *Henry M. Jackson: A Life in Politics.* Seattle: University of Washington Press, 2000.

Kempton, Murray. *Rebellions, Perversities, and Main Events.* New York: Times Books, 1994.

Kirkpatrick, Jeane. *Dictatorships and Double Standards: Rationalism and Reason in Politics.* New York: Simon & Schuster, 1982.

Kissinger, Henry. *Diplomacy.* New York: Simon & Schuster, 1994.

_____. *The Necessity for Choice: Prospects for American Foreign Policy.* New York; Harper & Brothers, 1961.

_____. *The Troubled Partnership: A Reappraisal of the Atlantic Alliance.* New York: McGraw-Hill, 1965.

_____. *The White House Years.* Boston: Little, Brown, 1979.

_____. *Years of Renewal.* New York: Simon & Schuster, 1999.

_____. *Years of Upheaval.* Boston: Little, Brown, 1982.

Koehler, John O. *Stasi: The Untold Story of the East German Secret Police.* Boulder, Colorado: Westview Press, 1999.

Kutler, Stanley I. *The Wars of Watergate: The Last Crisis of Richard Nixon.* New York: W. W. Norton, 1990.

Kutler, Stanley I., ed. *Encyclopedia of the Vietnam War.* New York: Macmillan, 1996.

Kyle, James H. *The Guts to Try: The Untold Story of the Iran Hostage Rescue Mission by the On-Scene Commander.* New York: Orion Books, 1990.

Lasch, Christopher. *The Culture of Narcissism: American Life in an Age of Diminishing Expectations.* New York: W. W. Norton, 1978.

Ledeen, Michael, and William Lewis. *Debacle: The American Failure in Iran.* New York: Alfred A. Knopf, 1981.

Levy, Bernard-Henri. *Barbarism with a Human Face.* New York: Harper & Row, 1979.

Lewis, David. *King: A Biography.* Urbana, Illinois: University of Illinois Press, 1970.

Lewy, Guenter. *America in Vietnam.* New York: Oxford University Press, 1978.

Lichter, R. Robert, and Rothman, Stanley. *Environmental Cancer—A Political Disease?* New Haven: Yale University Press, 1999.

Lubell, Samuel. *The Future of American Politics.* New York: Harper & Row, 1965.

Lukacs, John. *The Duel.* New York: Tichnor & Fields, 1990.

Manchester, William. *The Glory and the Dream: A Narrative History of America, 1932–1972.* Boston: Little, Brown, 1973.

Mann, James. *About Face: A History of America's Curious Relationship with China, From Nixon to Clinton.* New York: Alfred A. Knopf, 1999.

Mann, Robert. *The Walls of Jericho: Lyndon Johnson, Hubert Humphrey, Richard Russell, and the Struggle for Civil Rights.* San Diego: Harcourt, Brace & Company, 1996.

Mansfield, Harvey C., Jr. *America's Constitutional Soul.* Baltimore: Johns Hopkins University Press, 1991.

Maraniss, David. *First in His Class: The Biography of Bill Clinton.* New York: Simon & Schuster, 1995.

Margolin, Jean-Louis, ed. *The Black Book of Communism: Crimes, Terror, Repression.* Cambridge: Harvard University Press, 1999.

Matthews, Christopher. *Hardball.* New York: Summit Books, 1988.

Matusow, Allen J. *Nixon's Economy: Booms, Busts, Dollars & Votes*. Lawrence: University Press of Kansas, 1998.

_____. *The Unraveling of America: A History of Liberalism in the 1960s*. New York: Harper & Row, 1984.

McGinniss, Joe. *The Selling of the President*. New York: Trident Press, 1969.

McGovern, George. *Grassroots*. New York: Random House, 1977.

McMaster, H. R. *Dereliction of Duty: Lyndon Johnson, Robert McNamara, the Joint Chiefs of Staff, and the Lies That Led to Vietnam*. New York: HarperCollins, 1997.

McNeil, Alex. *Total Television*. New York: Penguin, 1996.

Medved, Michael. *Hollywood vs. America*. New York: HarperCollins, 1992.

Meese, Edwin, III. *With Reagan: The Inside Story*. Washington, D.C.: Regnery, 1992.

Miller, James. *Democracy Is in the Streets: From Port Huron to the Siege of Chicago*. New York: Simon & Schuster, 1987.

Miller, Nathan. *Star-Spangled Men: America's Ten Worst Presidents*. New York: Simon & Schuster, 1998.

Miller, Nathan, and Susan Gilmore, eds. *Revolution at Berkeley*. New York: Dial Press, 1965.

Morris, Kenneth E. *Jimmy Carter: American Moralist*. Athens, Georgia: University of Georgia Press, 1996.

Moynihan, Daniel Patrick. *Coping: Essays on the Practice of Government*. New York: Random House, 1973.

_____. *A Dangerous Place*. Boston: Little, Brown, 1978.

_____. *Maximum Feasible Misunderstanding: Community Action and the War on Poverty*. New York: The Free Press, 1969.

_____. *Miles to Go: A Personal History of Social Policy*. Cambridge: Harvard University Press, 1996.

_____. *The Politics of a Guaranteed Income: The Nixon Administration and the Family Assistance Plan*. New York: Random House, 1974.

Moynihan, Daniel Patrick, ed. *On Understanding Poverty: Perspectives from the Social Sciences*. New York: Basic Books, 1968.

Murray, Charles. *Losing Ground: American Social Policy, 1950–1980*. New York: Basic Books, 1984.

Nathan, Richard P. *The Plot That Failed: Nixon and the Administrative Presidency*. New York: John Wiley & Sons, 1975.

Newfield, Jack. *Robert Kennedy: A Memoir*. New York: Putnam, 1969.

Nieli, Russell, ed. *Racial Preference and Racial Justice: the New Affirmative Action Controversy.* Washington, D.C.: Ethics and Public Policy Center, 1991.

Nixon, Richard. *The Memoirs of Richard Nixon.* New York: Simon & Schuster, 1978.

Norton, Howard, and Bob Strosser. *The Miracle of Jimmy Carter.* Plainfield, New Jersey: Logos Books, 1976.

Nutter, G. Warren. *Kissinger's Grand Design.* Washington, D.C.: American Enterprise Institute, 1975.

Oakeshott, Michael. *Rationalism in Politics and Other Essays.* Indianapolis: Liberty Fund, 1991. [Originally published, 1962.]

Oates, Stephen. *Let the Trumpet Sound: The Life and Times of Martin Luther King.* New York: Harper & Row, 1982.

O'Neill, Thomas P ("Tip"). *Man of the House.* New York: Random House, 1987.

Parmet, Herbert S. *George Bush: The Life of a Lone-Star Yankee.* New York: Scribner, 1997.

Patterson, James T. *Grand Expectations: The United States, 1945–1974.* New York: Oxford University Press, 1996.

Pemberton, William E. *Exit with Honor: The Life and Presidency of Ronald Reagan.* Armonk, New York: M. E. Sharpe, 1997.

Podhoretz, Norman. *The Bloody Crossroads: Where Literature and Politics Meet.* New York: Simon and Schuster, 1986.

_____. *Breaking Ranks: A Political Memoir.* New York: Harper & Row, 1979.

_____. *Why We Were in Vietnam.* New York: Simon & Schuster, 1982.

Powell, Colin, with Joseph E. Persico. *My American Journey.* New York: Random House, 1995.

Public Papers of the Presidents: Jimmy Carter 1977–1981. Washington, D.C.: Government Printing Office.

Public Papers of the Presidents: Gerald R. Ford 1974–1977. Washington, D.C.: Government Printing Office.

Public Papers of the Presidents: Richard M. Nixon 1969–1974. Washington, D.C.: Government Printing Office.

Radosh, Ronald. *Divided They Fell: The Demise of the Democratic Party, 1964–1996.* New York: The Free Press, 1996.

Rainwater, Lee, and William L. Yancey. *The Moynihan Report and the Politics of Controversy.* Cambridge, Massachusetts: MIT Press, 1967.

Ranney, Austin, ed. *The American Elections of 1980*. Washington, D.C.: American Enterprise Institute, 1981.

Record, Jeffrey. *The Wrong War: Why We Lost in Vietnam*. Annapolis, Maryland: Naval Institute Press, 1998.

Reichley, James. *Conservatives in an Age of Change*. Washington, D.C.: Brookings Institution, 1981.

Ridgeway, James. *The Politics of Ecology*. New York: Dutton, 1970.

Roche, John P. *Sentenced to Life*. New York: Macmillan, 1974.

Rood, Harold W. *Kingdoms of the Blind: How the Great Democracies Have Resumed the Follies That So Nearly Cost Them Their Life*. Durham, North Carolina: Carolina Academic Press, 1980.

Safire, William. *Before the Fall: An Inside View of the Pre-Watergate White House*. New York: Doubleday, 1975.

_____. *Safire's Washington*. New York: Times Books, 1980.

Scammell, Michael. *Solzhenitsyn: A Biography*. New York: W. W. Norton, 1984.

Schoen, Douglas. *Pat: A Biography of Daniel Patrick Moynihan*. New York: Harper & Row, 1979.

Seabury, Paul, and Angelo Codevilla. *War: Ends and Means*. New York: Basic Books, 1989.

Shawcross, William. *Sideshow: Kissinger, Nixon, and the Destruction of Cambodia*. New York: Simon & Schuster, 1979.

Shogan, Robert. *Promises to Keep*. New York: Thomas Y. Crowell, 1977.

Shultz, George P. *Turmoil and Triumph: Diplomacy, Power, and the Victory of the American Ideal*. New York: Charles Scribner's Sons, 1993.

Sick, Gary. *All Fall Down: America's Tragic Encounter with Iran*. New York: Penguin Books, 1986.

Siegel, Fred. *The Future Once Happened Here: New York, D.C., L.A., and the Fate of America's Big Cities*. New York: The Free Press, 1997.

Skinner, Kiron K., Annelise Anderson, and Martin Anderson. *Reagan in His Own Hand*. New York: The Free Press, 2001.

Smith, Geoffrey. *Reagan and Thatcher*. New York: W. W. Norton, 1991.

Sorley, Lewis. *A Better War: The Unexamined Victories and Final Tragedy of America's Last Years in Vietnam*. New York: Harcourt, Brace & Company, 1999.

Stein, Herbert. *Presidential Economics*. New York: Simon & Schuster, 1984.

Stockdale, James B. *A Vietnam Experience: Ten Years of Reflection*. Palo Alto: Hoover Institution, 1984.

Stockdale, Jim and Sybil. *In Love and War.* New York: Harper & Row, 1984.

Straughan, Dale, ed. *Biological and Oceanographical Survey of the Santa Barbara Channel Oil Spill 1969–1970, Volume 1, Biology and Bacteriology.* Los Angeles: Alan Hancock Foundation, University of Southern California, 1971.

Strober, Deborah Hart and Gerald S. *Reagan, The Man and His Presidency: The Oral History of an Era.* Boston: Houghton-Mifflin, 1998.

Summers, Harry G., Jr. *On Strategy: A Critical Analysis of the Vietnam War.* Novato, California: Presidio Press, 1982.

Talbott, Strobe. *Endgame: The Inside Story of SALT II.* New York: Harper & Row, 1979.

Thatcher, Margaret. *The Downing Street Years.* New York: HarperCollins, 1993.

Thernstrom, Stephan and Abigail Thernstrom. *America in Black and White: One Nation, Indivisible.* New York: Simon & Schuster, 1997.

Thompson, Hunter S. *Fear and Loathing in Las Vegas.* New York: Random House, 1972.

Tilford, Earl H. *Setup: What the Air Force Did in Vietnam and Why.* Alabama: Air University Press, 1991.

Timberg, Robert. *The Nightingale's Song.* New York: Simon & Schuster, 1995.

Tyrrell, R. Emmett Jr. *Public Nuisances.* New York: Basic Books, 1979.

Ulam, Adam. *Expansion and Coexistence: Soviet Foreign Policy 1917–1973.* New York: Praeger, 1974.

van der Linden, Frank. *The Real Reagan.* New York: William Morrow, 1981.

Wallop, Malcolm, and Angelo Codevilla. *The Arms Control Delusion: How Twenty-Five Years of Arms Control Has Made the World Less Safe.* San Francisco: Institute for Contemporary Studies, 1987.

Wattenberg, Ben J. *In Search of the Real America: A Challenge to the Chaos of Failure and Guilt.* New York: Doubleday, 1976.

Wells, Tom. *The War Within: America's Battle Over Vietnam.* Berkeley, California: University of California Press, 1994.

West, Darrell M. *Air Wars: Television Advertising in Election Campaigns, 1952–1992.* Washington, D.C.: CQ Press, 1993.

Westmoreland, William. *A Soldier Reports.* New York: Doubleday, 1976.

White, F. Clifton. *Suite 3505: The Story of the Draft Goldwater Movement.* New Rochelle, New York: Arlington House, 1967.

White, Theodore. *The Making of the President, 1964.* New York: Atheneum, 1965.

———. *The Making of the President, 1968.* New York: Atheneum, 1969.

_____. *The Making of the President, 1972.* New York: Atheneum, 1973.

Wildavsky, Aaron. *Revolt Against the Masses, and Other Essays on Politics and Public Policy.* New York: Basic Books, 1971.

Wiley, Mason, and Damien Bona. *Inside Oscar.* New York: Ballantine Books, 1987.

Will, George F. *The Pursuit of Happiness and Other Sobering Thoughts.* New York: Harper & Row, 1978.

Wills, Garry. *Lead Time: A Journalist's Education.* New York: Doubleday, 1983.

_____. *Reagan's America.* New York: Doubleday, 1987.

Winik, Jay. *On The Brink.* New York: Simon & Schuster, 1996.

Wirtz, James J. *The Tet Offensive: Intelligence Failure in War.* Ithaca, New York: Cornell University Press, 1991.

Witcover, Jules. *Marathon: The Pursuit of the Presidency, 1972–1976.* New York: Viking, 1977.

_____. *The Year the Dream Died: Revisiting 1968 in America.* New York: Warner Books, 1997.

Wolfe, Tom. *Radical Chic and Mau-Mauing the Flak-Catchers.* New York: Farrar, Straus and Giroux, 1970.

Yergin, Daniel, and Joseph Stanislaw. *The Commanding Heights: The Battle Between Government and the Marketplace That Is Remaking the Modern World.* New York: Simon & Schuster, 1998.

Zumwalt, Elmo R., Jr. *On Watch: A Memoir.* New York: Quadrangle, 1976.

NEWSPAPERS AND PERIODICALS

American Historical Review

The American Spectator

The Atlantic Monthly

Commentary

Dissent

The Economist

Encounter

Esquire

Facts on File

Foreign Affairs

Fortune

Grand Strategy: Countercurrents

Harper's

Human Events

The Los Angeles Times

Modern Age

The New Leader

The Nation

The National Journal

National Review

The New Left Review

The New Republic

The New York Review of Books

The New York Times

The New Yorker   *U.S. News and World Report*

Newsweek   *Vanity Fair*

Orbis   *The Wall Street Journal*

Policy Review   *The Washington Monthly*

The Public Interest   *The Washington Post*

Reason   *The Washington Times*

The Spectator   *The Western Political Quarterly*

Time   *The Wilson Quarterly*

ARCHIVAL SOURCES

Ronald Reagan Gubernatorial Papers, Hoover Institution, Stanford University

Citizens for Reagan Papers, Hoover Institution, Stanford University

Deaver-Hannaford Papers, Hoover Institution, Stanford University

ACKNOWLEDGMENTS

A LONG LIST of people deserve thanks for their help and encouragement in making this book happen, but the list must begin with Adam Meyerson, vice president of educational affairs at the Heritage Foundation in Washington. Adam first encouraged me to write about Reagan in the pages of *Policy Review* while I was still a green graduate student in the mid-1980s. More than a decade later, Adam invited me to spend a "sabbatical" year as a Bradley Fellow at Heritage, where the first six chapters of the book took shape.

Ed Meese and Peter Hannaford both kindly granted access to the Reagan papers from his pre–White House career that were, until their recent transfer to the Reagan Presidential Library at Simi Valley, housed at the Hoover Institution at Stanford. Both were gracious with their time and thoughts about my project. The Reagan papers at Hoover fill nearly 4,000 boxes; without the guidance of archivist Carol Leadenham, I'd still be lost in the stacks.

The insights of many individuals influenced the thinking and course of this narrative, including most especially Hadley Arkes, Michael Glennon, Harry V. Jaffa, Charles Kesler, John Marini, Daniel Oliver, Harold Rood, Peter Schramm, Michael Uhlmann, Tom Silver, Ben Wattenberg, Thomas G. West, and the late John Adams Wettergreen. Christopher DeMuth of the American Enterprise Institute was helpful in more ways than he knows.

To K.L. Billingsley I owe special thanks for invaluable help with numerous cultural references and interpretations, especially regarding the 1960s, and for bucking me up, usually during a long bike ride, when my spirits were flagging. My nephew, Jared Hayward, cheerfully tracked down obscure references and trivia, which I hope relieved the tedium of high school life.

At Prima Publishing, Steven Martin was more than just an editor; he was a "champion" of this project in the medieval sense of the term. I am sure I gave him and his colleagues more than a few Maalox moments as this book grew in scope and fell behind schedule. Steven's enthusiasm and support for this book has been warmly embraced by his successor, David Richardson, and project editor Andrew Vallas.

This project would have been impossible without the support of the irrepressible leader of the Pacific Research Institute, Sally Pipes, who graciously adjusted my duties and work schedule so that I could concentrate on writing. This, in turn, would not have been possible without the Sarah Scaife Foundation, the Lynde and Harry Bradley Foundation, the D & D Foundation, and other supporters who have provided funds for my work at PRI.

My wife Allison had to put up with the usual bloody-mindedness of a writer on far too many Saturday mornings, Sunday afternoons, and much of the rest of the week. Yet in the middle of writing this book, about the time chapter 5 was finished, a daughter, Winston Margaret, arrived, which should offer some evidence that I occasionally put my keyboard aside.

INDEX